Gender and the Politics of

by the same editors

Gender Under Scrutiny
New inquiries in education
Edited by Gaby Weiner and Madeleine Arnot

Gender and the Politics of Schooling

**Edited by Madeleine Arnot and Gaby Weiner
at The Open University**

London
UNWIN HYMAN
Boston   Sydney   Wellington
in association with
The Open University

© The Open University 1987

Published by the Academic Division of
Unwin Hyman Ltd
15/17 Broadwick Street, London W1V 1FP, UK

Unwin Hyman Inc.,
8 Winchester Place, Winchester, Mass. 01890, USA

Allen & Unwin (Australia) Ltd,
8 Napier Street, North Sydney, NSW 2060, Australia

Allen & Unwin (New Zealand) Ltd
in association with the Port Nicholson Press Ltd,
Compusales Building, 75 Ghuznee Street, Wellington 1, New Zealand

First published in 1987
Second edition 1989

ISBN 0 04 445642 5

Printed in Great Britain by
Richard Clay Ltd, Bungay, Suffolk

Preface

This collection of readings has been designed to complement the Open University Master's degree option *Gender and Education*.* The volume has been designed to help students appreciate the major theories and frameworks in the study of gender and education and their implications for state policy. The articles selected also provide a context in which to interpret research on gender and education, the different lines of inquiry and research methodologies discussed in the other reader for this course, *Gender Under Scrutiny: New inquiries in education*, edited by G. Weiner and M. Arnot (also published by Hutchinson).

As the reader forms only part of the course (which also consists of a written study guide and cassette material discussing the issues raised in the reader articles), it cannot claim to offer a comprehensive account of perspectives on gender and education. The selection of articles has been designed to highlight specific problems and to develop students' critical understanding. Opinions expressed within articles are therefore not necessarily those of course writers nor of the university. However, the editors believe that the selection focuses on major issues in the field and will be useful to anyone with an interest in gender and education.

*Further information about the course associated with this book may be obtained by writing to: Higher Degrees Office, PO Box, 49, The Open University, Milton Keynes MK7 6AD.

Contents

Acknowledgements

The editors and publisher would like to thank the copyright holders below for their kind permission to reproduce the following material. Every effort has been made to obtain permission from the relevant copyright holders but where no reply was received we have assumed that there was no objection to our using the material.

The American Sociological Association and S. Kessler, D. Ashenden, B. Connell and G. Dowsett for pp. 223–36, reproduced from *Sociology of Education*, **58**, 1985, pp. 34–45 and 47–8.

Associated Book Publishers (UK) Ltd and V. Amos and P. Parma for pp. 211–22, from A. McRobbie and T. McCabe (eds.), *Feminism for Girls: an adventure story*, Routledge and Kegan Paul plc, 1981, pp. 129–48.

Associated Book Publishers (UK) Ltd and E. M. Byrne for pp. 23–34, from *Women and Education*, Tavistock Publications, 1978, pp. 14–15, 18–26 and 30–9.

British Educational Research Association for pp. 122–6 by H. Goldstein from *Research Intelligence*, **23**, 1986, pp. 2–4.

Carfax and Alison Kelly for pp. 127–39 from *British Journal of Sociology of Education*, **6** no. 2, 1985, pp. 133–46 and 151–4.

Centre for Contemporary Cultural Studies, Birmingham for pp. 64–75 by H. V. Carby, from *The Empire Strikes Back: race and racism in '70s Britain*, Hutchinson, 1982.

Discourse for pp. 76–91 by S. Middleton, from *Discourse*, **5** no. 1, 1984, pp. 43–62.

Falmer Press Ltd and T. Grafton for pp. 108–21 by T. Grafton, H. Miller, L. Smith, M. Vegoda and R. Whitfield, from M. Hammersley and H. Hargreaves (eds.), *Curriculum Practice: some sociological case studies*, Falmer Press, 1983, pp. 151–69.

Heinemann Educational Books Ltd for pp. 95–107 by B. G. Licht and C. S. Dweck, from M. Malland (ed.), *Sex Differentiation and Schooling*, Heinemann, 1983, pp. 72–84 and 93–7.

Open University Press for 237–50, by C. Wallace, from S. Walker and L. Barton (eds.), *Youth, Unemployment and Schooling*, Open University Press, 1986.

Pergamon Press for pp. 143–54 by D. Spender, from D. Spender (ed.), *Men's Studies Modified*, Pergamon, 1981, pp. 155–73.

Pergamon Press for pp. 155–65 by K. Clarricoates, from *Women's Studies International Quarterly*, **1**, 1978, pp. 353–64.

Pergamon Press for pp. 290–306 by A. Wickham, from R. Dale (ed.), *Education Training and Employment: towards a new vocationalism*, Pergamon Press, 1985.

June Purvis for pp. 253–75 from *Westminster Studies in Education*, **4**, 1981, pp. 45–71.

Routledge and Kegan Paul and Linda Valli for pp. 189–210 from *Becoming Clerical Workers*, Routledge and Kegan Paul, 1986, pp. 137–82.

Society for Education in Film and Television Ltd and Valerie Walkerdine for pp. 166–74 from *Screen Education*, **38**, 1981, pp. 14–23.

University of Chicago Press for pp. 371–84 from D. L. Kirp, M. G. Yudof and M. Strong Franks, *Gender Justice*, University of Chicago Press, 1986, pp. 124–39 and 227–30.

Unwin Hyman Ltd for pp. 35–49 from H. Eisenstein *Contemporary Feminist Thought*, Unwin Paperbacks, 1984, pp. 5–22, 25–6.

Verso for pp. 50–63 from M. Barrett, *Women's Oppression Today: problems in Marxist feminist analysis*, Verso.

Introduction

In the selection of articles and extracts chosen for this volume we have attempted to give an indication of recent theoretical and empirical research and policy developments in the area of gender and education. We have also tried to illustrate how gender relations have shaped different levels of education and different educational experiences.

Current interest in gender and education originates from a number of social, political and economic features affecting education policy since the Second World War. However, there were important antecedents, for instance, in the energetic feminist campaigns concerning female education in the second half of the nineteenth century and the fights over equal pay in the inter-war years. The 1944 Education Act, however, was particularly significant as it provided the first formal recognition of equality of opportunity as a legitimate educational goal – children were to be encouraged to fulfil their intellectual and social potential according to the classifications of intellectual ability laid down by educational psychologists. Psychological testing was the means by which pupils could be identified according to their intellectual potential, and so be helped to surmount disadvantages of home and class.

By the 1960s, however, the possibility of individual self-improvement through education was challenged by social scientists. According to them, education had failed to achieve greater social equality, particularly in terms of social class. Similarly, ideas about educational autonomy and the political neutrality of state schooling were reassessed by academics, and by teachers who were clearly aware of the unequal economic and cultural outcomes of their work in schools. The importance of these challenges was revealed in the reduced influence of psychological and mental testing in moves towards comprehensive schools.

A decade later different lines of thinking had emerged. First, a number of critiques of education were published (see, for example, Bowles and Gintis (1976), Dale *et al*, (1981)),* which showed that education legitimates and reproduces class relations. In contrast to perceptions of education as central and essential to social reform, the new critics pointed to the close ties between education, the requirements of corporate capitalism and dominant class interests. By the 1980s, this analysis had broadened to focus, not merely on the formal structures of schooling but on, for example, the influences of the 'hidden' curriculum and the implicit messages in texts, class cultures within education, and the relationship between education and the state. The political struggles over, and within, education were also foci of analysis and criticism.

*Full references quoted in the text are contained in the References sections at the end of chapters.

Following charges of excessive functionalism and pessimism contained in these critiques, attempts were made to try and look 'inside' the processes of schooling – to find out 'how' as well as 'why' schooling reproduces class relations. Youth cultural studies provided a core element in this account of educational experience. Studies were made of how individuals 'lived' within educational structures and how they made sense of the ideological messages transmitted through education.

However, these analyses of schooling were characterized by their concentration on male educational experiences. Schools had been investigated in terms of the preparation of male pupils for male occupational and vocational destinations. Access to higher education, social mobility, class conflict and school counter-cultures were discussed predominantly in terms of white, male, working-class youth, as the group most subject to class control and educational disadvantage.

The second line of thought emerged from the turbulence brought about by the women's liberation movement on both sides of the Atlantic, and by the black Civil Rights Movement, particularly in the United States. Both these movements were critical not only of the social injustices perpetrated by the structural inequalities of western capitalism, but of the academic 'left' for its failure to place the experience of women or black people on the political agenda. The expansion of education and the increase in employment opportunities in the 1960s provided some women with the material conditions to fight for greater participation in the economy and in public life. In the UK the successful passage of the Sex Discrimination Act (1975) and the Race Relations Act (1976) gave added impetus to those who wished to remove some of the more formal obstacles to social inequality. In the educational world, the legislation, particularly the education sections of the Sex Discrimination Act, legitimated efforts to secure a broader and more challenging education for girls and women.

Education, as well as other social institutions such as the welfare state and the family, were criticized by feminists for maintaining patriarchal relations and 'white' dominance. Teachers and academics sought to uncover the schooling processes which nurtured gender and 'race' inequalities, and were critical of previous 'weak' equal opportunities policies in education (such as the reorganization of comprehensive schools and progressivism) which focused on individual achievement and learning to the detriment of structural inequalities. They also utilized the conceptual tools of the women's liberation movement such as consciousness-raising and establishing support networks in order to construct alternative feminist models of education.

As a consequence of these developments, a variety of feminist educational critiques emerged – located within different theoretical traditions. Each looked at the 'problem' of female education in different ways and took different routes in researching and theorizing the structures and processes of schooling, choosing distinctive topics and methodologies for research. Some researchers felt comfortable within one tradition, others consciously tried to break down the boundaries between traditions. But many also were confused about how to bring together the wealth of information available and to use it to formulate coherent educational policies. Some even felt it divisive to describe work on gender as belonging to discrete traditions and perspectives. They felt that the ultimate aim of all work on gender, namely greater equality for women, was too important to be analysed as containing theoretical (and perhaps damaging) divisions (Whyld, 1983).

Nevertheless it seems to us that educational research and practice within gender and education have taken different perspectives in addressing the problem of sex inequality. These have been described as liberal feminist, radical feminist, Marxist or socialist feminist, and black feminist perspectives (Acker, 1987).

As we have already noted, the ideas generated by those concerned with equality of educational opportunity in the 1960s and early 1970s failed to address issues concerning sex inequality. Liberal feminists were the first to focus on the considerable divergence between the educational routes taken by girls and boys, particularly evident in the choices of subject areas at secondary level. They exposed these patterns of gender differentiation (or sex differences) and their consequences for male and female training, access to higher education and to the professions, and to work opportunities. The attention of educational policy-makers was drawn to the continuation of male and female occupational patterns within a sex-segregated labour market, which placed women at a distinct disadvantage compared with men.

Perhaps the most controversial of the critiques of schooling generated by feminists has been that concerning male and female relations in education and, in particular, the dominance of male interests. This critique has generated a great deal of interest among teachers, both in the UK and elsewhere, and has also been the focus of considerable media attention. Radical feminism, which operated outside the 'liberal' traditions of equality of opportunity, the main path of educational reform in the UK, reshaped the political agenda to include the power relations between men and women, and how these are legitimated and reproduced through schooling.

The development of women's studies courses also provided an incentive to evaluate the processes of female education, its history and the current educational experiences of girls and women. Attention focused on the *gendered* 'hidden' curriculum and the shaping of educational knowledge by the world views and interests of men. The dominance and control of education by men, particularly in terms of curriculum content and classroom interaction, was also of major concern.

While radical feminists debated concepts of patriarchy and patriarchal education, Marxist feminists directed their attention to existing 'left' accounts of education, criticizing their failure to address gender relations within class relations. Class theory, concepts of work and production, and the importance of the family, were all reconsidered in the light of women's experiences under capitalism. How could the relationship between education and the economy be reformulated to incorporate gender relations?

While liberal, radical and Marxist theories of gender and education concentrated on identifying and changing differential patterns of female education, they did not, to any extent, explore the impact of 'race' on gender relations. As black feminists demonstrated, each perspective had framed the 'problem' of sex inequality around the concerns of white (and often middle-class) women. Discussions of girls' underachievement, for instance, did not consider the different achievements of middle- and working-class girls except in observations about their relative positions in option and examination patterns. Little attention was paid to the routing of black pupils into CSE and non-examination streams, and the experiences of black female students in further or higher education was largely ignored.

Radical feminists were challenged for their perceived overemphasis on sexuality and male/female power relations without consideration of how these were shaped by the dynamics of white power. Marxist feminists were also criticized for their lack of understanding of, and reference to, the history of imperialism and colonialism in their analyses of women's oppression. It was clear that gender relations within the education system could not be understood without reference to 'race' and class.

These critiques, taken together, represented a powerful challenge to accepted policy and practice within the education system and argued, at the very least, for a reconceptualization of categories, theories, and explanations used in educational analysis. The dynamic tensions between the four perspectives are clearly difficult to represent accurately in one reader. Each perspective has generated its own momentum and corpus of work, and has become more sophisticated in its analysis.

In this selection of readings we have tried to capture some of the flavour of these debates. For the first section, we have chosen a number of different theoretical pieces drawn from the area of women's studies, which exemplify the stance taken by each perspective. The chapters by Byrne, Barrett, Eisenstein and Carby indicate the different ways in which the problem of inequality between the sexes has been conceptualized. Byrne discusses equality and equality of opportunity, concepts of underachievement and the existence of aggregated inequality. Eisenstein, in contrast, focuses on the concept of patriarchy and debates about public and private life, both characteristic of radical feminism.

The framework presented by Barrett addresses theories of social reproduction – theories in which the role of education is defined as that of reproducing class relations. The problem for Marxist theorists has been how to merge explanations of class and gender in education. In contrast Carby argues that there are considerable limitations to both reproduction and patriarchal analyses. For her the key issue is whether such explanations throw light on the experiences of black women and the continued racism in society. Middleton, in her summary of feminist and education paradigms which completes Part One, shows how this range of feminist perspectives provides a basis for a sociology of women's education.

The key concepts for liberal theorists have been those of *access* and *choice* for individuals within education and society, whereas for radical feminists, a far more important dimension has been that of *power*. In Parts Two and Three in this volume these concepts are analysed by different authors. In Part Two, explanations of gender differentiation in education are located in individual achievement orientations (see Chapter 6 by Licht and Dweck). Grafton *et al.*, in contrast, search for explanations of differential patterns of subject take-up by exploring the processes of choice, i.e. the various factors which impinge on girls and boys as they make their way through option choice procedures at 13+.

Other elements have been identified by those focusing on equality of opportunity, namely the removal of obstacles to individual female achievement. Goldstein identifies educational assessment – a neglected area for researchers of gender – as problematic. He discusses the use of separate sex norms in intelligence testing for selection at 11+, considering the possibilities of 'gender fair' examinations and the desirability of equality of educational outcomes. Finally Kelly delves into the intricacies of classroom life. Her research into science lessons indicates the ways in which science is constructed and experienced as 'male'. Her analysis suggests that the explanations of curriculum differentiation and choice will have to address not merely the formal aspects of schooling but also the informal world of classroom life and the under-currents of male and female power relations.

Part Three contains examples of research and conceptual explorations of those concerned primarily with male and female power relations in education. The concept of male power is critical to what Dale Spender defines as the patriarchal paradigm of education. Here male control of education (and educational research) has shaped both the nature of knowledge promulgated in schools, colleges and universities, and the concerns of educationists and policy-makers. Spender's perspective on male dominance in education is given credibility by the research, reported in this volume, conducted by Walkerdine in the nursery sector, by Clarricoates in the primary school, and by Lees at secondary level. In these different schooling environments, the dominance of boys in terms of teacher attention or over female pupils or teachers, is revealed as a major factor shaping schooling experience.

We chose to include the Clarricoates article, although already well known, in this reader because it so clearly illustrates the factors involved in radical feminist perceptions of the 'hidden' curriculum. She recognizes that the often taken-for-granted aspects of schooling, such as the formal school structure, can be understood as key aspects of the maintenance of male culture in education – *institutional sexism* might be an apt description. Walkerdine's portrayal of the dynamics between young male and female pupils and their female teacher provides a sophisticated and complex analysis of how power struggles are played out in the classroom, and the forms of resistance utilized by the girls themselves. Her contention that the 'progressive' ideology of a 'child-centred' teaching and learning environment condones, and exacerbates, the male dominance of education, provides an open challenge to primary school educators and teacher trainers.

Language has been a key feature in debates about gender and education. Spender's *Man Made Language* (1980) set the agenda for research into how language is used in schools, and there has been considerable interest in the language used in school texts and male dominance of classroom discussion. Lees, however, approaches the topic from a different stance, and considers how sexual labels constructed by adolescent and older boys are imposed on girls, and how they then come to be used by the girls themselves. She shows that the use of male defined categories such as 'slags' and 'drags' as a means of framing relationships between young men and women has particular implications for the girls – in terms of the construction of their sexual identities and their feelings of confidence about, and orientation towards, educational achievement.

Part Four of this volume focuses on the issues concerning gender and education developed in the context of class and race relations. We have drawn together black feminist and Marxist perspectives since both emphasize the impact of *structures* and *ideologies* on educational experiences and practices. For both, the economic and political context of schooling has shaped its internal structures and its outcomes. The focus of Valli, for instance, on the social reproduction of capitalism is reflected in the discussion by Amos and Parmar of the economic requirements for immigrant workers and the impact of imperialism on the lives of black people in Britain. However, there are also considerable differences between Marxist and black feminist perspectives, as can be seen in *Gender under Scrutiny*, the 'sister' book to this volume (Weiner and Arnot, 1987). Here, there are distinctive black critiques of gender theories, accounts of black female educational experiences, and the evaluation of educational texts and classroom dynamics from black feminist points of view.

Valli's research into office education in the United States raises a number of issues of particular relevance to those involved in work experience or vocational courses in schools, or in the Youth Training Scheme (YTS). Here exchange, authority and gender relations are seen as factors simultaneously shaping the schooling experiences of female students. Valli indicates possible areas of female resistance, as do Amos and Parmar in Chapter 15 – however, in the latter black girls' responses to education are interpreted in relation to their experiences of racism *and* sexism. The impact of 'race' on gender relations – for example, through myths surrounding arranged marriages, black female sexuality and black family life – give an indication of some of the means by which race and gender come together in the lives of black schoolgirls in Britain. Such analyses suggest that theories of gender and education will not be complete without recognition of how 'white racism', as well as sexism, shapes the lives of white and black girls.

The last two chapters in this section, by Kessler *et al.* and Wallace, illustrate the directions in which social reproduction theory has moved in the mid 1980s. Kessler *et al.* indicate shifts away from simple theories of gender reproduction to concepts of hegemonic masculinity, analyses which consider the class basis of different versions of masculinity and how well pupils respond to those versions, given their families and class cultures. Their analysis of case studies stresses the different *gender regimes* found in working-class and ruling-class schools and the contradictions which occur.

Wallace, in contrast, develops social reproduction theory by addressing the problems of youth unemployment, and the consequences of this for theories which have adjudged the role of education solely in terms of the reproduction of work relations. Wallace's interviews with older pupils, young workers and the young unemployed suggest that the reproduction of the *domestic* cycle is critically important to young men and women in how it shapes their response to the realities of unemployment.

These chapters show that each perspective has developed its own distinctive corpus of research and theory. Yet there are areas of agreement; for example, Kelly's research on classroom dynamics has much in common with the work of Clarricoates and Walkerdine in their portrayal of the male domination of classroom life. Similarly, Walkerdine focuses on reproduction theory developed by Marxists in her description of pupils actively negotiating their own gender and classroom identities. We hope that the articles we have chosen for these sections give an indication of the richness and diversity of theoretical and empirical work on gender and education.

In the remaining two parts of this volume we have concentrated upon the historical development of education provision and policy, and in particular, on the political struggles within and for education. Feminist historians of education have shown that throughout the development of state education, there has been a commitment (often explicit) to the principle of maintaining gender differentiation (and until recently sex-segregation, particularly in secondary education). It is impossible within the space of this book to cover the entire history of educational provision. We have therefore selected three 'case-studies' which illuminate some of the gendered dimensions of education and training provision. Purvis's overview of female education in the nineteenth century provides a glimpse of the impact of social class ideology on the education of girls and women, and how the curriculum came to be differentiated to cater for two different class ideals of femininity. Oram, on the other hand, provides a history of the more recent struggles of women teachers in the 1920s, when they fought against the imposition of the marriage bar and for equal pay. Oram's account raises similar questions to those of Wickham (on training), concerning the extent of discrimination against women in education, training and employment. In the case of training, Wickham shows that training policy did not so much consciously discriminate against women; rather it rendered their interests as marginal or invisible.

By the 1980s, feminist ideas and debates began to form a major, and largely underappreciated, influence on school life and educational policy. Some local education authorities began taking an active part in promoting gender equality, and a variety of school-based projects was initiated, principally by teachers. In the final section of this volume we consider aspects of this growth of interest in 'sex-equality' activities and policy. Here the issue is not one of distinguishing between liberal, radical, Marxist, or black feminist perspectives, since in practice many of these distinctions overlap. Alliances have, in fact, been forged between practitioners and policy-makers holding different views, in the hope of making greater gains through a show of unity. None the less differences between 'equal opportunity', 'anti-sexist' and 'anti-racist' approaches can be discerned in initiatives at central and local levels.

The first chapter in Part Six, by Arnot, considers whether central government, in particular the EOC, DES, and MSC have made serious commitments to promoting sex equality. She investigates recent policy statements and campaigns, and concludes that the impact of central government on gender issues in education has been limited through lack of real political will. Arnot shows that a number of strategies have been adopted to challenge sex discrimination and inequality in education. Interestingly these strategies have differed from actions taken to eliminate race discrimination and racial inequality from education. Williams, in Chapter 22, analyses the ways in which the 'problems' of black and female students have been differently constructed, and how solutions have been attempted, especially through anti-sexist and anti-racist LEA policies.

In creating policies to promote sex equality in education, it has been assumed, both by central and local government, that teachers should act as agents of change. Yet, curiously, little has been written about the part teachers themselves have played in establishing gender initiatives and promoting change within schools and colleges. In their review of such initiatives, Weiner and Arnot suggest that feminist teachers have shown a profound depth of commitment to making schools better places for the pupils they teach, and constituted a reform movement which is a worthy successor to earlier feminist campaigns.

The first three chapters in this section illustrate the renewed interest in policy on gender in the 1980s, showing how progress has been made from the formulation of explanations about the extent of sex differences in education, to the development of strategies for change and policy implementation. While there is optimism for the future, there have also been criticisms of equality initiatives, and the beginnings of a backlash against calls for more concerted central government action and intervention. The extract from *Gender Justice* by Kirp *et al.* (1986) is representative of the backlash in the United States in terms of its reassertion of freedom of choice as a principle, and its celebration of the 'private' sphere, independent from state intervention. Such a backlash should be placed in the context of the emergence of a new 'Moral Right' political movement in the UK, and renewed support for traditional family patterns (David, 1983).

We have tried, in this volume, to provide some structure to the range of theoretical, research and policy developments within gender and education, and to open up and strengthen discussions about the relative successes and failures of the different strategies adopted. What is interesting is not whether the perspectives and approaches identified are mutually exclusive in real terms, but what the key problems have been for those concerned about gender and education, and how they have framed their investigations and explanations: how important are the differences in opinion of central and local policy-makers, and of teachers, in their perceptions of the most challenging and urgent issues confronting feminists in education today.

References

Acker, S., 'What feminists want from education', in Hartnett, A. and Naish M. (eds), *Education and Society Today*, Barcombe, Falmer Press, 1986.

Bowles, S. and Gintis, H., *Schooling in Capitalist America*, London, Routledge and Kegan Paul, 1976.

Dale, R., Esland, G., Fergusson, R., and MacDonald, M. (eds), *Education and the State*; vol. 1, *Schooling and the National Interest*; vol. 2, *Politics, Patriarchy and Practice*, Barcombe, Falmer Press, 1981.

David, M., 'Sex, education and social policy; a new moral economy?', in Walker, S. and Barton, L. (eds), *Gender, Class and Education*, Barcombe, Falmer Press, 1983.

Kirp, D. L., Yudof, M. G. and Strong Franks, M., *Gender Justice*, Chicago, University of Chicago Press, 1986.

Spender, D., *Man Made Language*, London, Routledge and Kegan Paul, 1980.

Weiner, G. and Arnot, M. (eds), *Gender Under Scrutiny: new inquiries in education*, London, Hutchinson, 1987.

Whyld, J. (ed), *Sexism in Secondary Education*, London, Harper and Row, 1983.

Part One

Conceptualizing Gender

1 Education for equality

Eileen M. Byrne

Education has long been one of the most decisive of our life-chances, the key to equal opportunity and the ladder to advancement, since men first learned that literacy and communication in the hands of a few meant power, government, and the control of the many. Without education, and especially without *equal* educational experiences or skills and qualifications, men and women alike of certain classes and social groups have over the years been condemned to inferior lives in their personal development, in their choice of work, as citizens, and in their power to influence government, leadership, and the national decisions which affect their local lives.

But it is a double-edged tool. Before the coming of state education in the late nineteenth century, the careful rationing of education by an élite, with its comfortable sop to Cerberus by way of charity schools and Sunday schools for the children of the poor, was unquestionably the major cause of under-achievement in every civic and working sense, of the main body of the people, until they were given a more real educational choice and opportunity in this century. But the sophistication of a multidisciplinary state education has brought with it a new discrimination. The more simplistic differentiation by social class was a hallmark of the Taunton Commission in 1868 (secondary education until 18-plus for the sons of gentlemen and the upper professions; a more commercially based and practical education until 16 for the sons of the mercantile classes; and 'very good reading, writing and arithmetic' until 13-plus for the artisans). No one will now admit to overt class differentiation in education objectives (although hidden indirect distinctions can still be found). Yet we justify gross differentiation of curricula as between the sexes, and between rural and urban children, and between the intellectually gifted and the average, based on assumptions of hypothetical normative homogeneity as unthought and unresearched as the original class differentiation used to justify different educational objectives by social status and not by diagnosed needs.

It has been widely believed that the coming of state education brought equality of educational opportunity. In an otherwise admirably argued book, for example, a leading woman educationalist, Dame Katherine Ollerenshaw, suggested as far back as 1961 that: 'It might be said that women have largely won the battle for equal educational opportunity with men . . . this is largely true . . .'[1]* (1961, p. 14). I believe Dame Kathleen might review that assumption now. I *question* it for the

Source: Extracted from Byrne, E. M., *Women and Education*, London, Tavistock Publications, 1978, pp. 14–15, 18–26 and 30–9.
*Superior figures refer to the Notes and references at the end of chapters.

65 per cent of less able girls in school; and for working-class women. Success has, as always, come to the middle-class girl in the grammar school (or academic stream in comprehensive schools) who has crept through the net to university or polytechnic. It has come in only parsimonious measure to the girl workers denied day release; to the middle-ability girl offered a less solid curricular 'option' than her brother; to the women denied further education and retraining because they are married and therefore 'kept' – as if education's only purpose were to provide bread and a roof over one's head.

I am more especially concerned with education for the twentieth and twenty-first centuries, and with the missing girl apprentices and women supervisors and technicans of a scientific and technological age, than with the intellectual minority of girls whose élite wings have helped them to fly up T. H. Huxley's ladder from the gutter to the university, despite the many missing rungs on the way. My deepest concern is with girls whose alternative to staying at home for forty years is not the professions – not even the skilled bench, the high wage packet bringing financial independence, the industrial training which gives her job security, responsibility, and mobility. It is low pay, canteen cleaning, helping with school meals, the typewriter, the unskilled labour market, short-term employment. The cause: a different, often inferior education planned perhaps with no conscious ill-intent by the men who represent 97 per cent of the government of education, but which nevertheless gives no foundation for a later career in either work or government.

Theories are of course still advanced that the opportunities are there, and if any under-achieving group – girls, the working classes, rural children – does not take advantage of them, it is because they do not wish to, are too lazy, or do not need the same chances of development; and by rationalization it is argued that a different, often inferior, education is therefore right.

Span and limitations

It is of course impossible to discuss the education of women without looking at education for girls and boys as a whole, and at the differences that we have fashioned for them in our schools, or the different preconceived adult roles tailored for them by an unreflecting society, working on reflex and not on reason. It is, above all, the naive acceptance by our sophisticated western society that the superficiality of plenty has meant the achievement of equality in education, that makes a review of the respective opportunities and achievements of women and men especially timely. Implicit in the argument underlying this chapter is an expectation that society must and will change but that it is unlikely to do so unless forced by a certain amount of ruthless logic and by social and political pressure to rethink the balance of economic adult roles of women and men. Change is a cyclical process. Teachers are reluctant to alter courses seen as 'relevant' to local outlets for less able leavers until employers change their expectations. Employers and local communities cannot change if their yearly injection of school leavers remains immutably the same in character and type.

In the continuing controversy about inequality in its wider sense, indeed, the education service has at least paid Jencks and Jensen the compliment earned by

Tawney some fifty years earlier. It has acknowledged, for example, the seriousness of their arguments at the most minimal level of recognition, by conducting a public, thoughtful, and informed debate which draws on widely known, if conflicting, data and research for its reasoning. The analogous question of inequality of educational opportunity for girls and women, and of deliberate and discriminating differentiation of curricula for girls and for boys, has evoked, however, no such similar public reaction or debate. It is not yet 'respectable', in academe or government.

There are two or three fundamental principles whose definition (rightly or wrongly as readers may perceive them) underlies the whole review of the educational rights of girls. One is the *defined* purpose of education. The second is the antithesis of inequality and of discrimination. The third is the principle that 'equal means the same' − not the specious 'equivalent'.

Equal means the same

The recognition of this aspect of the key role of education received formal accolade in 1967 when the United Nations passed one of its most far-reaching resolutions:

All appropriate measures shall be taken to ensure to girls and women, married or unmarried, equal rights with men in education at all levels, and in particular

(a) equal conditions of access to and study in educational institutions of all types, including universities and vocational, technical and professional schools;

(b) the *same choice of curricula, the same examinations*, teaching staff *with qualifications of the same standard*, and school premises and equipment *of the same quality, whether the institutions are coeducational or not*;

(c) equal opportunities to benefit from scholarships and other study grants;

(d) equal opportunies for access to programmes of continuing education, including adult literacy programmes, and

(e) access to educational information to help in ensuring the health and well-being of families.[2]

The rejection of this principle by educational planners, and their addiction to the highly questionable principle of equivalence, underlies the whole curricular debate about housecraft versus handicraft, physics or biology, separation for physical education, educating boys for work and girls for domestic life, motherhood and part-time work. It is central to the equality debate. It must now be faced by government and community alike, both of whom have evaded it so far by refusing to agree on any defined educational objectives at all. We are the only European country to reject responsibility for common, national educational objectives; and in doing so, we endorse and perpetuate inequalities of all kinds. The most serious of these is the *aggregation of inequality* from which girls and women suffer worse than their brothers. There is considerable research evidence that social class and intelligence are more decisive single factors of advantage or disadvantage than sex alone. Given however that there is a range of factors, the 'compound interest of inequality' becomes apparent. I suggest that there are five major indices of potential inequality which, where two or more are aggregated, create a cumulative cycle of underachievement which can only be overcome by positive, affirmative, interventionist programmes aimed at increasing resources, counteracting cultural and social barriers, and adding to the skills and experience. The five factors are:

1 sex
2 lower social class
3 lower range of intelligence
4 residence in certain regions with a history of under-achievement
5 residence in rural areas.

This is emerging as a European pattern. France, Germany, and Italy all have problems of differential under-achievement as between regions. Rural, relative under-achievement is evident in Ireland and Italy, and is unquestionably a factor in the United Kingdom. Girls who are less able, northern, of lower social class, and rural are quadruply disadvantaged.

For what are we educating girls?

It has always seemed to me that one major setback in achieving a balanced and full secondary education for girls, geared to a career for economic independence and a choice of external and internal roles in family and community, is the consistent and unaccountable refusal of the education service to define agreed *national* minimum objectives.

The traditionally insoluble debate about the aims of education, which has filled publishers' bookshelves over the years, enables us comfortably to evade answering questions like, why do some groups of children (girls, rural children, immigrants, those in the north) appear so consistently to under-achieve?

Further, because monitoring is also impossible against unknown and undefined factors, well-worn placebos like 'examinations don't mean one is educated' or 'you can't measure education', become the traditional defensive reflex against demands for accountability for the different actual standards of achievement and expectation of different groups and classes of children in our care. In this case, it is the girls who still lack the physics, maths, and technical studies that would lead to recruitment to further education, industrial training, a break into the world of men's work and skilled wages, instead of the unskilled assembly line. Qualifications do matter. One major cause of failure to acquire equal pay is in my view the unequal training and therefore lesser skills of women, which prevent them from doing really comparable work. One is reminded of the recommendation of Lloyd George's Committee of the War Cabinet on Women in Industry nearly seventy years ago that

Good training is the factor which comes next to good health in increasing the value of women in industry. The removal of all educational disabilities of women and the provision of equal facilities for technical training and apprenticeships is urged (HM Government, 1919, p. 170).[3]

The committee said equally bluntly that

The prejudice of male workers must share the responsibility with the prejudice of employers for the fact that the training of women is deficient. . . . Technical dexterity is certainly attained by women to a degree not inferior to men (p. 170).

It does not follow that achievement of equal qualifications will necessarily and alone achieve equal promotion and advancement; but it does follow that failure to reach the same level of qualification as men will actively debar women from access to advanced training programmes, recruitment, and advancement. Graduates may choose to drop out of managerial roles and become clerks; but clerks cannot choose to become managers unless they are trained and qualified for leadership roles.

Whether or not the leadership of the education service is allowed to continue to evade clearer definitions of the purposes of educating both boys and girls, which underlie their organization of education (and their discriminatory allocation of resources to achieve their allegedly unknown objectives), I am suggesting a number of perfectly definable objectives which, in my view, the education service must accept if we are to survive economically and individually into the twenty-first century. They all have clear implications for the establishment of some form of national basic secondary curriculum up to the age of 16 common to both sexes (which does not, however, necessarily imply control of *how* subjects are taught, of what curricular content should be included, nor of what precise educational media and books to use). I am outlining some of the objectives below because the whole argument of this chapter is set against the assumption that these are desirable, acceptable, necessary, and attainable. If these objectives are rejected, girls will continue to be educated for a home-based domestic role or for short-term, lower-paid employment; and if they are accepted for both sexes, there can be no justification whatever for allowing the imposition of a different curriculum for each sex. I propose in fact to nail a flag to the mast, and indeed several pennants as well, on this question of objectives. The purpose of education is perfectly definable. Objectives are measurable. Educational achievements are measurable both at personal and at school and college levels. *Input* (that is resources of staff, money, buildings, equipment) is measurable against specific educational purposes – for example, the achievement of literacy; of the five GCE/CSE passes in basic subjects which are the key to entry to nine-tenths of all further education courses above craft level; of a sound scientific base for later retraining. *Output* (that is pupils' and students' educational achievements) is also measurable – the success rate or the take-up of examinations; pupils can or cannot read, spell and add; they do or do not go on to further and higher education, skilled employment, or unskilled work; they can or cannot reason from evidence observed. Finally our consistent deliberate refusal actually to monitor the direct relationship of discriminatory practices of resource allocation, both to educational achievement and to success of defined objectives, is one major and direct cause of continuing and worsening inequality between the sexes, and between social classes.

Let me therefore first define what I consider to be the objectives of educating young people – girls and boys strictly alike. *Personal fulfilment* and individual excellence have always been accepted in theory as the first and principal aim of education, and the present government of education, mostly trained over twenty-five years ago, are quite likely to quote Sir Percy Nunn's still relevant seminal work of the 1920s on educational principles: 'The primary aim of all educational effort should be to help boys and girls to achieve the highest degree of individual development of which they are capable' (Nunn, 1945, preface).

But as long as girls' schools remain deficient in comparable facilities for teaching maths, science, and the background to technology, and boys' schools lack any teaching in the homecrafts and parenthood; as long as boys are denied activities like ballet education because they are 'unmasculine', or equivalent facilities for music, drama, and cultural subjects; as long, in fact, as the curriculum remains stereotyped into girls' subjects and boys' subjects for which different practical investment is made, then personal fulfilment will remain an unattainable goal for many of both sexes.

Yet even the influential government-sponsored Central Advisory Council reinforced an ideology of a 'different but equal' education which can owe nothing to education for individuality. The Crowther Report put the (regrettable) seal of its approval on the pressure to educate boys for a career and girls for a different 'relevance', which I personally reject as educationally unacceptable: 'It is true that there is a broad distinction between boys' and girls' interests which is *rightly* reflected in curriculum planning' (Crowther Committee 1959, para. 170, my italics).[4]

The committee found it *'natural'* that the strength of the vocational test of relevance (i.e. to future work) should be more frequent in boys than in girls, 'for a good many of whom wage earning is likely to seem a more temporary preoccupation' (1959, para. 172). The committee, however, did recommend that the tendency to regard physics and maths as masculine empires, and biology and literature as feminine, should be corrected, not accepted or indeed accentuated by the tendency for certain subject areas to be taught by men or women only and thus become sex-linked.

Second only to this in my view is the need to educate both sexes for the best job or *career* of which we are capable – which 86 per cent of the boys *and 88 per cent of the girls* and 89 per cent of their parents rated as a major school objective in the Schools Council's survey of nearly 5000 pupils in 1968. (The *teachers*, however, rated this very lowly – only 28 per cent of heads and 47 per cent of teachers thought this important.) Production of the country's skilled manpower (womanpower) is also essentially a task of education and training, however much the academic may shy away from it. There are many factors for change that make a healthy scepticism about many of the current attitudes towards the education of girls gain momentum. Our bland refusal to take on manpower planning below the prestigious level of nuclear physicists and tame economists at Westminister leaves us regularly bereft of enough gas fitters; of electricians to repair our deficient old domestic systems; of plumbers to deal with burst pipes and pouring overflows; all of the service industries in fact. Where are the extra medical technicians to man all the kidney machines, service the thalidomide aids, provide electronic back-up for brain and heart surgery, and keep Queen Mary's, Roehampton, and Stoke Mandeville Hospitals at peak working? How do we find the missing dental auxiliaries; or maintenance technicians for all those washing machines and freezers? What could be more suitable for girl school-leavers as well as for the retrained lost generations of mature women who are too far along their current road to take on a completely new full career, than to retrain for part-time technical work in the service industries in their own locality with regular 'topping up' retraining courses at the local college of further education?

The employment field is constantly changing. Education for later retraining in this century of mobility, recession, technological development, and consumer demand is of growing importance – and implies clearly a common measurable minimum secondary base – back to common core. Education for full participation in government is a social and economic need which has so far been recognized for boys but side-stepped for girls – despite their generally higher exercise of social responsibility. Education for leisure comes back to personal fulfilment and can no longer legitimately be interpreted as merely flower-arranging and cake-icing for women and car maintenance or basketball for men. Education for parenthood, for community welfare, education in personal relationships, is in my view equally needed for both sexes. Neither boys nor girls should continue to accept that the pastoral role is a feminine prerogative, or that it is unmasculine to enter the caring professions or to show gentleness and thought in family relationships. Mopping up broken hearts or mending broken emotions is a two-fold responsibility of both sexes. So is mopping up the mess left by inadequate governmental actions over the years. Poverty, bad housing, deprivation, social breakdown, mental illness, handicap, rehabilitation after crime – women predominate in the remedial professions which stitch together parts of society that largely male governments have allowed to fall apart because of their universal preoccupation with war and aggression, and giving priority to the space race over social reconstruction on this earth.

Inequality or discrimination?

The antithesis is important if we are to understand the social dimensions of educational planning. Inequality is generally inherited, environmental, and passive, rarely accurately recognized by those who suffer it, while discrimination is active and clearly characterized by those who practise it. Put another way, the former is a state; the latter an action. To confuse the two dimensions in educational debate is to mingle concepts springing from different sets of causes – like Rousseau's natural and his moral and political inequality. Inequality in education has its roots in social history, which records the stereotyping of expected adult roles for men and women and the translation of these into different curricula. The most pervasive inherited unexamined assumption is the alleged inferiority of women, somewhat starkly stated here:

As women therefore, the first thing of importance is to be content to be inferior to men – inferior in mental power, in the same proportion that you are inferior in bodily strength . . . woman's strength is in her influence (Mrs Ellis, 1842).[5]

Inequality itself is two-dimensional, innate on the one hand, and conditioned by outside factors (like human decision on what different groups of people should have and how they should receive it) on the other. The key question is, which kinds of actual inequalities between the sexes are in fact caused by allegedly innate qualities, and which by social conditioning? Dahrendorf makes one kind of distinction:

Four types of inequality emerge . . . in relation to the individual there are (a) *natural differences of kind* in features, character and interests, and (b) *natural differences of fact* in intelligence, talent and strength (leaving open the question of whether such differences do in fact exist). Correspondingly, in relation to society (and in the language of contemporary sociology) there are (c) *social differentiation* of positions essentially equal in rank and (d) *social stratification* based on reputation and wealth and expressed in a rank order of social status. (Dahrendorf, 1974, p. 119).[6]

In Dahrendorf's terms, his distinction of differences in kind or in fact may be illustrated by the now keenly debated issue of whether girls are or are not born with innately inferior spatial ability; or whether their poorer actual performance in problem arithmetic, mechanical relationships in mathematics and the physical sciences is due to developmental and social conditioning, and an attitude pre-set by their (mainly women) teachers at primary school that they are unlikely to do well. His rank differentiation and stratification are in my view also interestingly illustrated by the heightened hierarchy of descending academic respectability of the different sectors of education. It would be true to say that public prestige, as distinct from the real value to student and community, gives a rank of descending perceived value to university teaching, grammar school education, advanced further education in polytechnics, other secondary education, primary education, non-advanced further education, day release, and adult education, in that order. That is not only the priority order in which we allocate our resources, but how the value of the education in each sector is presented to boys and girls and to their parents, both by the education service itself and by the perceived public image. Not only are the costs per head heavily weighted towards the academic, the intellectual, and the older pupil or student, but the salary differentials reflect this rank order as well.

This in turn indirectly affects girls' opportunities within those perceived priorities. For not only do girls tend to opt for the 'Cinderella' kinds of education, but when they later train as teachers and lecturers they are to be found in far greater numbers in the less well paid sectors (primary, non-advanced further education, lower secondary).

Tackled another way, Rousseau's two kinds of inequality anong the human species,

One which I call natural or physical because it is established by nature and consists in a difference of age, health, bodily strength and the qualities of the mind and the soul, and another, which may be called moral or social inequality, because it depends on a kind of convention, and is established, or at least authorised, by the 'consent of men' (*Dissertation on the Origins of Inequality*).

both illustrate quite sharply to me the different views on the causes of sex inequalities. Which are caused by alleged differences in natural endowment? Which by moral and social convention, by the consent of the men who dominate the government of education?

It is difficult to say how far the ways in which we organize fourth year options, advise girls about their careers, assess them for discretionary student awards, and plan their housecraft-based curriculum, are a matter of instinctive tradition, prejudice, or conscious priority for boys, which is an indirect form of discrimination. Only by continued analysis and question does a pattern emerge. For example, the greater investment in boys than in girls is not recognized as an active, consciously chauvinistic policy. But is is a disturbing decisive fact with complex causes. In this particular context, there is a useful distinction to be drawn between the words *discriminal* and *discriminatory* to describe educational practices. The former, dating from 1842, means simply 'of the nature of a distinction or division', and is not yet a loaded word: discriminatory has, however, come to have an adverse and a pejorative meaning, a conscious will to penalize a particular group by giving them deliberately unequal rights and resources. I suggest that discriminal accurately describes those educational practices that aim to distinguish different needs and remedies on firm evidence of innate physical or developmental differences, which (in the view of the educator) can only be dealt with by different means.

I can find no respect in which the concept of discriminal practices can be validly justified on educational, as distinct from social, grounds on an assumption that girls have any (relevant) difference in starting point. Yet we have in fact planned consciously separate curricular routes (housecraft; handicraft; pre-apprenticeship courses versus typing) for the two sexes; a practice now open to legal challenge under the Sex Discrimination Act, 1975. Because, unlike inequality, discrimination is active rather than passive, its negative characteristic is that it is more often used to deny full opportunity, equal quality and quantity of resources (housing, salary, access to education, social freedom, political enfranchisement), and social esteem to the particular group whom prejudice has classified as a section apart. Its positive quality is that it can only be evident where those who control policy and resources have decided to fix limiting criteria in their rules, practices, and policy decisions which will achieve their deliberately different objectives for the different groups of people for whom they are responsible. Discrimination, once identified, can therefore be attacked at the active source, in the practices of a single, finally accountable group – the employers, the head teachers, or governors, the committees that authorize rules and practices.

Causal relationships

What is implicit in much that is touched upon here is the strength of the network of causal relationships which are imperfectly understood but which riddle our organizational and curricular practices and which are the principal causes of under-achievement. In looking at the education and training of all young people, but especially of girls, those causal relationships are crucial, between the most ordinary school practices and attitudes, organization and limits, achievements and innovations on the one hand, and girls' later lifetime earnings, mobility of employment, ability to follow further and higher education, the achievement of a good educational base for retraining, on the other.

Girls are often discouraged from mathematical work in their primary years. They therefore dislike it in the secondary years. They therefore drop it at 'O' and 'A' level in far greater numbers than boys. There are therefore fewer women mathematics graduates. As a result, fewer women are employed in industry in posts needing mathematical ability. Very few women accordingly teach maths in polytechnics. As a result, there are frequently no women candidates for relevant top posts in the technical sector.

Women have equally not yet achieved equal pay in hard cash because they are less well qualified than men in factories and industry generally, and have been debarred often from industrial training schemes geared to 'men's' work. This is because fewer girls stay on to take technician and craft training. This in turn is directly due to the secondary schools' obsession with freedom of choice for 13- and 14-year-old pupils, thus allowing (and encouraging) girls to drop physics, to 'opt' for typing and mothercraft, and to settle for CSE in arts subjects. The imbalance between the subjects studied by girls at 18-plus and 16-plus is bred at 13-plus and in the primary school. It is one major negative determinant of lower later pay.

I have of course somewhat over-simplified the argument in order to sharpen the causal relationships and will reinstate their interrelated complexities later. Many other factors like the married woman's dual role, the attitude of women and men to responsibility, reorganization fever, all have a part to play. But they do not cloud the central causal relationship. If subjects have not been studied at school and college, if attitudes have not been formed earlier, the complete removal of all the social stereotypes and repressions will still not qualify under-qualified women retrospectively to play a role for which they have neither the education nor training.

Underlying all of these themes, and inextricably interwoven with the related but distinct influences of innate or conditioned inequality and subtle or overt discrimination, are the less tangible factors of prejudice, role-conditioning, the whole area of sex-role stereotyping, the influence of inherited assumptions from the (male) leadership of the past and what might bw called the 'euthenics' of inequality. That is, the restrictive influence of the practical factors, like the structural sexism of the organization of the school or college, or the methods, formulae, and administrative framework by which resources are allocated differently to different groups for allegedly different needs; the whole translation of theory into practice, in fact.

The headteacher or principal who timetables boys into the one physics laboratory and girls into a converted classroom for biology, is planning on prejudice, not reason, whether he recognizes it or not. The (woman) infant teacher who tells 7-year-old Bobby that 'big boys don't cry' and 8-year-old Jenifer that 'little girls mustn't be bossy' is reacting from inherited prejudice in her attitude to her pupils as sex-groups, and not as individuals. Such influence is inseparable from the question of under-achievement and under-expectation, and a young adolescent of either sex needs above-average poise, self-confidence, motivation, and a good and secure education to overcome its deadening impact.

Prejudice comes from the Latin *praejudicium*, a precedent or judgement based on previous decisions (but not necessarily on evidence). Its present leading characteristic is of judgements and attitudes formed precipitately without reference to logic, to facts, or to evidence; an emotional and unfavourable reaction based on unsupported thoughts. First thoughts or impressions become prejudices when they are not reversible if exposed to new knowledge or first-hand experience. Moreover, stereotypes are essential for the maintenance of prejudice, usually developing from frequently asserted statements or images which are the production of past ideas handed on unexamined. A shrewd comment from one of the earliest and most radical protagonists of women's equality, John Stuart Mill, on the unshakeable tenor of deeply held convictions, has an uncomfortably familiar ring today:

The difficulty is that which exists in all cases in which there is a mass of feeling to be contended against. So long as an opinion is strongly rooted in the feelings, it gains rather than loses stability by having a preponderating weight of argument against it (J. S. Mill, 1974, p. 219).[7]

One more general point should be understood however. One of the most familiar (and in my view dangerous) characteristics of prejudice is what Allport (1954)[8] describes as 'the device of admitting exceptions'. By excluding a few favoured cases as allegedly untypical, the negative rubric is kept intact for all other cases, as an unsupported generalization. It means in practice that to use the pioneer groups, the one woman director of an institute of education, the minority of women heads of mixed large comprehensive schools, as illustrative examples to encourage the generation following, arouses the immediate response, 'But they are hardly typical'. Every minority woman has met the bland assumption, sooner or later, that she is unusually off-beat, articulate, gifted, divergent, lucky, determined, and totally uncharacteristic of the 'normal' woman. This is worrying in the context of the negative, but irrelevant, image sometimes presented to adolescent girls by careers teachers, of the allegedly 'untypical' minority women ahead of them. Who knows what is typical until a majority have actually tried and achieved it? And yet to talk of majorities is also double-edged, because few boys or girls want to be regarded as deviant, as 'unmasculine' or 'unfeminine' and divergence carries subconscious psychological strains of implicit guilt at acting 'out of character'. If a norm is based on, say, 64 per cent, as many as 36 per cent are therefore divergent. Why should they carry a label of untypicality? Or be forced into the majority mould?

One effective counter to prejudice (*pace* John Stuart Mill) may well be, first, so to educate the majority of people in objective realization of the real facts that they recognize that the inherited or acquired assumptions on which mindless reactions are based are unfounded. The clarity with which we expose the illogicality of under-investment in girls when the country needs more skilled labour and more economic productivity will not shake the deeply hostile; but it will almost certainly help to mobilize the more receptive and adaptable, to call the bluff and to monitor what we actually do in schools and colleges to give (and to encourage) real freedom of curricular choice and of aspiration.

Notes and references

1 Ollerenshaw, K., *Education for Girls*, London, Faber and Faber, 1961.
2 Resolution no. 2263 adopted by The General Assembly of the United Nations, 7 November 1967, under Article 9, the 'Declaration on the Elimination of Discrimination against Women'.
3 HM Government, *War Cabinet Report on Women in Industry*, Cmnd 135, London, HMSO, 1919.

4 Crowther Committee, *15 to 18*, London, HMSO for DES, 1959.

5 Ellis, Mrs, *The Daughters of England*, London, Fisher and Son and Co, 1842.

6 Dahrendorf, R., 'The nature and types of social inequality', in Beteille, J. (ed.), *Social Inequality*, Harmondsworth, Penguin, 1974.

7 Mill, John Stuart, *The Subjection of Women* (1974) London, Everyman, 1869.

8 Allport, G. W., *The Nature of Prejudice*, Reading, Mass., Addison-Wesley, 1954.

2 Patriarchy and the universal oppression of women: feminist debates

Hester Eisenstein

In 1970, when Kate Millett published her now classic work, *Sexual Politics*,[1] she used a word which has become part of the standard vocabulary of feminist writing, although in recent years its meaning and even its legitimacy as a concept have come in for considerable criticism. To refer to the fact that, in many parts of the world (and, some would argue, everywhere), men exert control over women, Millett spoke of 'patriarchy', literally, from the Greek, the rule of the father.[2]

The word 'patriarchy' might at first glance seem an inappropriate term to characterize the situation of women in the modern world, at least in western industralized countries. But users of the term argued that, despite many differences of detail distinguishing the lives of women in the west from those of their sisters both in the developed socialist countries and in the underdeveloped Third World, the fundamental fact of male domination over women could be discerned in all societies. The term 'patriarchy' was therefore justified by this fact, that of the 'universal' oppression of women by men. As Adrienne Rich wrote,

Patriarchy is the power of the fathers: a familial-social, ideological, political system in which men – by force, direct pressure, or through ritual, tradition, law, and language, customs, etiquette, education, and the division of labor, determine what part women shall or shall not play, and in which the female is everywhere subsumed under the male. . . . Under patriarchy, I may live in *purdah* or drive a truck; . . . I may serve my husband his early-morning coffee within the clay walls of a Berber village or march in an academic procession; whatever my status or situation, my derived economic class, or my sexual preference, I live under the power of the fathers, and I have access only to so much of privilege or influence as the patriarchy is willing to accede to me, and only for so long as I will pay the price for male approval.[3]

Or, in Kate Millett's more succinct formulation:

Our society, like all other historical civilizations, is a patriarchy. The fact is evident at once if one recalls that the military, industry, technology, universities, science, political office, and finance – in short, every avenue of power within the society, including the coercive force of the police, is entirely in male hands.[4]

Given the constraints of religious belief and social custom, it might seem clear, at least to western eyes, how the oppression of women could be perpetuated in more traditional societies. But, Millett asked, how was it possible for patriarchy to continue in a world in which women had education, access to financial resources and extensive civil and political rights, and were not visibly subject to forms of

Source: Extracted from Eisenstein, H., *Contemporary Feminist Thought*, London, Unwin Paperbacks, 1984, pp. 5–22, 25–6.

direct coercion?[5] The answer, she suggested, lay in psychology. The social control of women in a 'free' society such as the United States was not carried out through a rigid, authoritarian system of force. Rather, it took place by means of the engineering of consent among women themselves. Instead of being openly coerced into accepting their secondary status, women were conditioned into embracing it by the process of sex-role stereotyping. From early childhood, women were trained to accept a system which divided society into male and female spheres, with appropriate roles for each, and which allocated public power exclusively to the male sphere.[6]

How could such a division be accepted by women? What were the elements of the system of sex-role socialization and how did they operate? Millett's view of the subordination of western women was historical and dialectical. She traced the history of the first wave of feminism, from the campaign for women's rights arising from the movement for the abolition of slavery to the winning of suffrage for women in the United States in 1920. She then documented how, in the years since women won the vote, a vast counter-offensive had been launched against them, using the weapons of psychology, literature, and culture, broadly defined. All of these were used to convince women, against at least the evidence of recent history, that they were not in fact the equals of men.

The villains of Millett's piece were many, including notably Sigmund Freud, and psychoanalytic thought as it had developed following him. Like Betty Friedan, Millett accused Freud of helping to organize a counter-revolution against the emancipation of women.[7] The theory of 'penis envy' was devised, she argued, to stigmatize women who sought to escape the confines of socially correct 'feminine' behaviour.

The theory of penis envy shifts the blame of her suffering to the female for daring to aspire to a biologically impossible state. Any hankering for a less humiliating and circumscribed existence is immediately ascribed to unnatural and unrealistic deviation from her genetic identity and therefore her fate. A woman who resists 'femininity', e.g. feminine temperament, status, and role, is thought to court neurosis, for femininity is her fate as 'anatomy is destiny' (p. 189).

In addition to Freud himself, Millett blamed the academics in social psychology who had helped to create what was essentially an ideology of sex roles. This was a set of rigid role prescriptions that served to keep women from deviating from the behaviour expected of them, for fear of being thought abnormal, or undesirable, or finally, mad. Sex roles, and sex-role stereotyping, were, then, the means by which an entire society kept women subject to the rules of the patriarchy.

In her analysis, Millett drew upon the language and concepts of sociology and social psychology. In particular, she relied on the work of Robert Stoller, John Money, and others on 'core gender identity'. In this work, Stoller and other researchers into the psychology of gender convincingly demonstrated that biological sex and social gender were separable concepts, from a developmental point of view. Biologically, the sex of a normal baby was obvious from anatomical details at birth. Psychologically, however, the acquisition of a sense of one's own sexual identity as male or female, as a 'boy' or 'girl', could be dated fairly precisely at the age of around 18 months. That is, it could be shown to be acquired culturally. Further, research showed that this sense of gender – this 'cognitive sense of gendered self', as Nancy Chodorow has called it[8] – was acquired independently of, and in exceptional cases in opposition to, the anatomical 'facts'.

The sense of one's gender, in short, was arrived at in response to the environment of the family, to the interaction between parents and child. It was produced psychologically and socially, rather than physiologically, in an automatic response triggered by mechanical or physical means. Conceptually, then, it was possible to make a distinction between sex and gender. Sex meant the biological sex of a child – was it born anatomically a male or a female member of the human species? Gender was the culturally and socially shaped cluster of expectations, attributes, and behaviours assigned to that category of human being by the society into which the child was born.

The significance of the distinction between sex and gender depended, in part, on the prior knowledge that expectations of behaviour and even character formation for men and women varied widely from culture to culture. In this, feminist theory built on the work of Margaret Mead and other anthropological researchers in the 1920s and 1930s. In *Sex and Temperament in Three Primitive Societies* (1935), Mead had sought to demonstrate that, in other societies around the world, the attributes assigned to and expected of males and females differed widely from those of western culture. There were cultures, for example, in which men were expected to be, and were, peace-loving, while women were expected to be, and were, warlike. Cross-cultural research of this kind built up evidence for the argument that gender behaviour was a social artifact.[9] The attributes that western societies considered normal and natural for women and men, respectively, were in fact, created by means of social pressures, in short, by what psychologists called 'conditioning'.

What, then, was the cluster of attributes that had been assigned to women in contemporary western culture? What was considered to be 'normal' for the gender 'female' as opposed to the gender 'male'? How did these attributes contribute to the continuation of patriarchy? Millett took her evidence on these questions from the work of social psychologists, who for years had been busy setting forth a catalogue of normal gender behaviour. Millett demonstrated that for female, 'normal' meant passive, while for male, it meant active. Men had instrumental traits: they were tenacious, aggressive, curious, ambitious, responsible, original, and competitive. Women had expressive traits: they were affectionate, obedient, responsive to sympathy and approval, cheerful, kind, and friendly.[10] Social pressure kept women conforming to the expressive role expected of them, a role that dictated conformity and obedience, while men occupied the instrumental role of rationality and power.

In arguing that sex could be separated, at least conceptually, from gender, and that expectations for sex roles, or more accurately, gender roles radically differentiated men from women, Millett implied that it was above all the psychology of women that kept them subject to the rule of patriarchy. She itemized a number of realms and modes within which patriarchy operated. Besides the categories of ideological, biological, sociological, class, economic, and educational, she included a category 'force', under which she listed rape, hostility, and ridicule. But in the wake of the 'counter-revolution' against the first 'sexual revolution' from 1830 to 1930, patriarchy in modern times was upheld chiefly by attitudes, more than by political and/or economic structures. In her words,

It must be clearly understood that the arena of sexual revolution is within human consciousness even more pre-eminently than it is within human institutions. So deeply embedded is patriarchy that the character structure it creates in both sexes is perhaps even more a habit of mind and a way of life than a political system (Millet, 1971, p. 63).

What accounted for the strength and the persistence of the system of male domination in the modern era? What were the elements in the system of sex roles that kept women in their place? Another account based on social roles was that offered by Elizabeth Janeway, in *Man's World, Woman's Place*.[11] Eschewing the word 'patriarchy' Janeway spoke instead of 'social mythology'. She traced the origins and the persistence of the notion that 'woman's place is in the home', by way of exploring the discrepancy of power between the sexes, or, as she put it, the 'subordination of woman to man' (Janeway, 1971, p. 51).

The social mythology outlined by Janeway rested on a set of beliefs about roles. She traced the historical development of the idea that women belonged in the domestic sphere, pointing out that the 'home' of the adage was a relatively modern invention, dating approximately from the eighteenth century as was the nuclear family, to which women were assigned as their major duty. From these fairly recent historical developments emerged the concept of the woman's 'role', which, Janeway pointed out, had no direct counterpart to any man's role. Thus the role of mother, homemaker (or housewife or houseworker), and wife was said to define what a woman was in ways that were directly related to her being female. No such strictures related to men, who were more likely to be defined by what they did in the public world of work than by what sex they were.[12]

Janeway argued that the strength of sex-role differentiation derived in part from male propaganda. Ideas about women's place appeared with alarming frequency in all the venues that served to make ideology public, from scientific journals to the popular media, including especially women's magazines. But these ideas were also internalized by women, and perpetuated by them in large measure. The 'psychology' of women was not entirely invented and imposed by men. Were there, then, elements in the social mythology that women found useful, helpful, or even compelling? Janeway argued that many women had, in fact, 'bought in' to the mythology, on the ground that it held certain rewards for them. In her view, these women, in accepting their subordinate place in the modern world, had essentially made a secret bargain with men: they had agreed to exchange 'private power in return for public submission. That is the regular, orthodox bargain by which men rule the world and allow women to rule in their own place' (January, 1971, p. 56). The power exerted by women in the domestic sphere over the lives of their children and in the sexual arena of the marriage bed was, emotionally, enough of an inducement to some women to keep them from exerting any kind of claim upon the realms of other kinds of power – intellectual, economic, political – available in the public sphere.

To recapitulate, then: in the feminist analysis set forth by Millett and Janeway, the meaning of 'sex roles' became transformed. What had been presented by (male) social scientists as 'value-free' description now encapsulated a critique.[13] In conventional sociological terms, 'sex role' was a social role dictated by the biological sex of the actor. In the hands of feminists, 'sex role' became a role assigned to the actor because of the gender-associated behaviour linked by society (more or less arbitrarily) with that biological sex. To feminists like Millett or Janeway, sex roles – that is, roles assigned because of biological sex – were a form of oppression, keeping women restricted and limited in their scope.

The oppression of women rested upon more than the establishment of sex roles. Kate Millett argued that a major pillar of patriarchy was what she called 'sexual politics'. This was the system of interpersonal power by means of which individual men dominated individual women. Conventionally, she said, politics had been defined by political scientists as the arena of public power, that is, chiefly electoral politics. Academic analysis concentrated on the issue of how the pie of political power was divided among those holding or seeking public office, and those seeking to influence them. Millett introduced a different, expanded definition of politics, one that incorporated a notion of the political nature of the relationships between men and women. Like the relationships of men to one another in political life, this was also a relationship of domination and subordination, in the Hegelian sense. But it was expressed in and through the medium of sexual relationships, conventionally referred to as connections of love, rather than power. Much of *Sexual Politics* was devoted to a devastating analysis and deconstruction of the erotic descriptions in four major male writers: D. H. Lawrence, Henry Miller, Norman Mailer, and Jean Genet. Millett wanted to expose the crude expression of power relationships, of the intention to dominate, in the vision of modern sexuality as set forth in these 'modern classics'.[14]

'The personal is the political' was an important slogan of the second wave of the women's movement. Coined by Carol Hanisch, it had many layers of meaning.[15] In Millett's analysis, the chief of these meanings was the sense in which sexual relationships between men and women, at the most intimate and personal level, embodied a political dimension. The domination of one woman by her husband or lover, through the 'conquest' enacted repeatedly in the sexual act between them, was part of the social control of all women by all men exerted under patriarchy. Thus the class of women, the group of all women, in a given society, was kept subordinate to the class of men, the group of all men in that society, by a variety of means: economic, psychological, legal, and ideological. But this control was ultimately exerted at the private, personal level, in the bedroom.

In Millett's view, however, the political aspect of sexual intercourse was not limited to heterosexual couplings. That the relation of power had no necessary connection to the players being male and female was the burden of Millett's analysis of the writing of Jean Genet. The same dynamic of conquest – of winner and loser, dominant and subordinate – could be seen to be operating in the sexual relations between man and man, in a homosexual relationship where all parties were reduced to relative powerlessness: in prison. This, she argued, was a 'pure' case, which, in the absence of 'real' women, created 'pseudo' women out of the men who assumed the passive role, the role of the conquered or dominated partner. This was, in a sense, the exception that proved the rules: relations of sexuality were used as relations of power, and the balance of power lay with men.[16]

Shulamith Firestone took the analysis one step further. She examined the phenomenon of 'love', which she called 'the pivot of women's oppression'.[17] Firestone argued that the concept of love was a kind of ideological cover-up or disguise of the relations of power that prevailed in heterosexual relationships. In this sense, the emotion of love, as experienced by men and women alike, served to disguise the actual political meaning of sex by putting it within the context of a confusing and misleading set of expectations.

A man must idealize one woman over the rest in order to justify his descent to a lower caste. . . . This idealization process acts to artificially equalize the two parties. . . . *Thus 'falling in love' is no more than the process of alteration of male vision through idealization, mystification, glorification – that renders void the woman's class inferiority*[18].

The subordination of women under patriarchy in the western industrial countries, then, was a complex matter. As Millett and others pointed out, the rule of men was not enforced by means of visible coercion, but rather through the continued reproduction of an ideology that reinforced a separation between male and female roles, and then created or sustained a set of beliefs about the roles thus created. Among these beliefs was the most cherished of ideas, namely, that of physical and emotional love between men and women. Sexual love was revealed as a crucial part of the ideological structure that perpetuated male power over women, with their full participation. For women, to fall in love with men was no metaphor, but an action that each time it was repeated reinforced their subordination, both individually and collectively.

The public/domestic dichotomy and the universal oppression of women

What were the underpinnings of patriarchy? Was the cultural, sociological, and psychological analysis of the oppression of women sufficient to explain it? Or was there another layer of reality that needed examination, as well? Theorists of the second wave looked for evidence that the basis of patriarchy lay in material conditions. But on this point, there was considerable variation in the interpretation of the term material, and in the degree of significance accorded to material factors.

Marxism, of course, claimed the title deeds to materialism as a scientific theory of society. But Shulamith Firestone disputed this claim on behalf of feminism. In *The Dialectic of Sex*, she announced that she was launching a new materialist theory of history, that would go beyond and complete the theoretical work of Marx and Engels. She recalled that in setting forth the theory of historical materialism, Marx and Engels had intended to supersede what they called derisively 'utopian socialism', which moralized ineffectually about social inequities. 'Scientific socialism', in contrast, would be able to analyse the sources of injustice, predict and guide revolutionary change, and eventually institute genuine social justice. In their theory, said Firestone, they had correctly focused upon economic class and the class struggle as the motor of history. But they had paid inadequate attention to sex, or what Firestone termed 'sex class'.[19] She proposed to remedy this omission by developing 'a materialist view of history based on sex itself' (Firestone, 1970, p. 5), which could lead to the true and final revolution in which women would seize control of the means of reproduction. In this 'expanded' definition of historical materialism, the basic division in society, and the motor of history, was not economic class but sex class. Firestone 'rephrased' Engels' definition from *Socialism, Utopian and Scientific*, to read:

Historical materialism is that view of the course of history which seeks the ultimate cause and the great moving power of all historic events in the dialectic of sex: the division of society into two distinct biological classes for procreative reproduction, and the struggles of these classes with one another; in the changes in the modes of marriage, reproduction and childcare . . .; in the connected development of other physically-differentiated classes (castes); and in the first division of labor based on sex which developed into the (economic-cultural) class system (Firestone, 1970, p. 12).

In *The Origin of the Family, Private Property and the State*, Engels had propounded the original insight that the first division of labour was that between men and women, and the first expropriation of labour that of women by men, in the reproduction of the human species. This truth had since been allowed to disappear from the centre of Marxist theory, where, in Firestone's view, it properly belonged.

Firestone held that the historical basis of patriarchy was indeed 'material'. Marx and Engels had defined 'materialism' to signify a relation to the economic development of society, via changes in the modes of production and exchange, with the resulting creation of classes and of class struggle. Thus, in the broad sense, 'materialist' designated a relation to economic conditions. In Firestone's version, however, the 'material' basis of history was the physical realities of female and male biology, along with those political and cultural structures erected to ensure that biology would remain determinative of the social order. She argued that the fundamental inequality between men and women could be traced, not to the differences between them, but to the reproductive functions of these differences.

Unlike economic class, sex class sprang directly from a biological reality: men and women were created different, and not equally privileged. Although, as de Beauvoir points out, this difference of itself did not necessitate the development of a class system – the domination of one group by another – the reproductive *functions* of these differences did. The biological family is an inherently unequal power distribution (Firestone, 1970, p. 8).

The power difference between men and women, then, was embodied in what Firestone called the 'biological family'. This contained the following four 'funda-mental – if not immutable' elements: **1** the physical dependency of women upon men for survival, because of the debilitating effects of childbirth (at least, before the availability of birth control – although Firestone included here 'menstruation, menopause, and "female ills" ' as well); **2** the long period of dependency of human infants; **3** the psychological effects of this 'mother/child interdependency'; and **4** the division of labour between the sexes, based on the 'natural repro-ductive difference' between them (Firestone, 1970, pp. 8–9). The feminist revol-ution would come about, therefore, only by means of the final dissolution of the 'biological' family, through the creation of conditions whereby 'genital differences between human beings would no longer matter culturally' (Firestone, 1970, p. 11). That is, the physical realities of reproduction and childcare would be overcome, through establishing the option of 'artificial reproduction', and the socialization of childcare (that is, sharing the work among all members of the society). Only with the abolition of women's physical and psychological responsibility for the reproduction of the species could women's liberation be accomplished.

It is relevant to note that the claim of the Firestone theory to a materialist base rested, as the account has indicated, on the physical realities of reproductive biology. But Firestone argued that it was the psychological effects that were at the root of the social ills she diagnosed.

Unless revolution uproots the basic social organization, the biological family – the vinculum through which the psychology of power can always be smuggled – the tapeworm of exploitation can never be annihilated. We shall need a sexual revolution much larger than – inclusive of – a socialist one to truly eradicate all class systems (Firestone, 1970, p. 12).

Ultimately, then, the materialism of this theory depended upon an implicit notion of causality that apparently differed considerably from the materalism of Marx and Engels. Firestone did not make clear what was the dialectical relation between the physical or biological, on the one hand, and the psychological or social, on the other. How did the one in some sense produce the other? Firestone did not use the term reproduction in its full Marxist sense, to refer not only to biological reproduction, but also to the daily maintenance of the labour force, and to social reproduction, that is, the perpetuation of social systems. Her focus was upon the reproduction of the species in the narrow sense, that is, on child-rearing.[20] In Firestone's view, to change society, was it sufficient to change biology? The details of her feminist revolution – sexual, social, biological – remained vague. But one point was clear: for women to be liberated, motherhood and the family in their current forms would have to be abolished.

In *Woman's Estate*, Juliet Mitchell rejected the claim of Firestone to have created a new historical materialism.[21] While she agreed that her 'invigorating book' (1973, p. 87) contained a materialist theory, it was in Mitchell's view neither historical nor dialectical.

To say that sex dualism was the first oppression and that it underlies all oppression may be true, but it is a general, non-specific truth, it is simplistic materialism, no more. After all we can say there has always been a master class and a servant class, but it does matter *how* these function. . . there have always been classes, as there have always been sexes, how do these operate within any given, specific society? Without such knowledge (historical materialism) we have not the means of overcoming them (Mitchell, 1973, p. 90).

Mitchell criticized Firestone, and radical feminism generally, for not speaking of women's oppression in a historically specific way. In order to account for the situation of women, and the changes in this situation over time, Mitchell argued, an adequate account must be given of the elements that made women's situation unique. Among the oppressed social groups of the world, what distinguished women, 'half of the human species', was that women had historically inhabited two worlds, and had been subject to oppression in both: the world of production, that is, the labour market; and the world of reproduction, that is, the family. While Mitchell cited biological reproduction, that is, childbearing, as one of the elements in the oppression of women, she argued that this was only one of four 'structures' that an analysis would need to take into account. These were: production, that is, women's role in economic production; reproduction of children; sexuality, and its regulation and control (since historically this meant the regulation and control of *women's* sexuality, predominantly); and the socialization of children (Firestone, 1973, p. 120). Women's oppression depended on a number of elements created by her situation of straddling two worlds, home and work, and of being caught in the contradictions produced by both. As Mitchell remarked, 'Women's position in society is in the home – and outside it, in production' (Firestone, 1973, p. 173). The analysis, then, of the oppression of women could not focus only upon biology and reproduction. It must examine, too, the economic and psychological realities that stemmed from women's place in the labour force, in production, and her place in the family, in the reproduction of children, and (via their socialization) of culture and ideology.

In practical terms, this meant an examination of women's participation in the labour force, the use of women as a reserve army of labour, the kinds of work women did or did not get paid to do, and the historical changes in what was considered 'women's work'. Mitchell argued that one needed to examine these changes in the western, capitalist economies, and in the socialist, post-revolutionary economies as well, to see what changes had or had not been made in the position of women as participants in production. Similarly, one needed a history of reproduction: what was the impact of contraception, 'an innovation of world-historic importance'? (Mitchell, 1973, p. 108). What about the ideology of parenthood, the 'social cult of maternity', in which the woman's activity of bearing and raising children came to be seen as a replacement for work, and the child became 'an object created by the mother, in the same way as a commodity is created by a worker'? (Mitchell, 1973, p. 109). Similarly, for sexuality, whose history, said Mitchell, had been virtually ignored by socialists, and distorted by liberal 'ideologues'. She called for cross-cultural accounts that would explore the relationship between degrees of sexual freedom, on the one hand, and variations in the position and dignity of women, on the other. And finally, like Firestone, Millett, and Janeway, Mitchell emphasized the importance of demystifying the ideologies governing the socialization of children: the notion of instrumental versus expressive roles assigned to male and female parents, respectively; and the obsession with correct child-rearing (always the responsibility of the mother).

Mitchell wrote that socialist countries had assumed, rather simplistically, that the liberation of women would flow automatically from their inclusion as full members of the work-force. Thus the experiments of Russia and China had failed to free women, because they had concentrated only upon the element of production, while they had systematically inhibited or prevented changes in the other three areas. But in bourgeois capitalist countries, she argued, radical feminists were stressing only the structures relative to women's 'private', domestic experience. Only a 'transformation of *all* the structures into which [women] are integrated, and all the contradictions' coalescing and exploding – 'a *unité de rupture'* – would bring about the 'authentic liberation of women' (Mitchell, 1973, pp. 121–2).

What Mitchell was pointing to was the complexity of the relationship between women and economic production, and the importance of the changes in the historic relations between the two over time. Whatever their disagreements, Mitchell and Firestone agreed on one point, and that was the relation of women's oppression to the ideological association of women with the private sphere. (I am using the word 'ideological' here to mean insistence upon an idea, whether or not it accords with the reality.) In this, they seconded the analysis of Elizabeth Janeway, who had argued that the fact that 'woman's place' was adjudged to be in the home, and only in the home, was a key element in the social mythology that helped to keep women relatively powerless. Janeway traced the history of the family, following Philippe Ariès and others, to show that the very concepts of the 'home', the domestic 'hearth', and the nuclear family, as 'woman's sphere', were all fairly recent historical developments. The role of women in the process of the production of goods, which had been substantial in the pre-industrial period, had been drastically reduced with the advent of industrialization, which moved most areas of production out of the home into the factories. Even after this development, early factory work in England and the United States was largely carried out by women and children. But gradually, as a result of many historical forces the importance of women's role in the paid labour force had been reduced. Women's economic contributions, in the majority, were limited to home rather than workplace, after marriage, from the mid-nineteenth century onward. The trend only began to be reversed during the Second World War; accelerating in the 1950s, this reversal was doubtless one of the major factors in the revival of the feminist movement in the 1960s.[22]

In the meantime, the association of women with the private sphere and of men with the public had hardened into a truism and an ideology. Men had become associated with what was public: the workplace, politics, religion in its institutional forms, intellectual and cultural life, and in general terms, the exercise of power and authority; women, with what was private: the home, children, domestic life, sexuality (or its repression). The split between public and private, or domestic, appeared, then, as a major, even universal characteristic of how men and women, maleness and femaleness, were viewed.

In the connection of women to the 'private' or 'domestic' sphere, the most obvious element was, of course, their reproductive function. Not just the fact that women bore children, but their apparently 'natural' association with children in rearing them, appeared to be the factor that connected women to the domestic realm. This was the view set forth in an influential essay by the anthropologist Michelle Rosaldo. Rosaldo offered the hypothesis that the assignment of women to the domestic sphere and of men to the public one was characteristic of all societies. This was the thread that linked all known human societies, from the most primitive to the most complex, and that underlay the universal oppression of women, despite the variety of forms that this took worldwide.[23]

Rosaldo proposed that, despite all of the variations that could be observed cross-culturally in the roles assigned to the sexes, all cultures distinguished between male and female, and assigned appropriate behaviours and tasks to each.

Further, she observed that in all cases, no matter what form the sexual division of labour took, the tasks and roles assigned to men were given greater significance and importance. 'Male, as opposed to female, activities,' she wrote, 'are always recognized as predominantly important, and cultural systems give authority and value to the roles and activities of men. . . . An asymmetry in the cultural evaluation of male and female, in the importance assigned to women and men, appears to be universal' (p. 19).

Rosaldo distinguished between authority, and power and influence, using the definitions first proposed by Max Weber. Women were not without certain forms of power, she argued, and in some societies were able to exert a good deal of influence in social decision making. But even in the most apparently egalitarian of societies, authority, the source of legitimacy in the exercise of power, lay with men. Rosaldo traced this authority to the importance granted male activities, as opposed to female activities, in a given society. 'Men,' she wrote, 'are the locus of cultural value' (p. 20).

What was the basis of this assignment of 'cultural value' to men? For Rosaldo, it lay in the differentiation between the 'domestic' and 'public' spheres. This, in turn, stemmed from women's activities and responsibilities in child-rearing. Rosaldo offered the following definitions of 'domestic' and 'public':

'Domestic' . . . refers to those minimal institutions and modes of activity that are organized immediately around one or more mothers and their children; 'public' refers to activities, institutions, and forms of association that link, rank, organize, or subsume particular mother–child groups (p. 23).

Rosaldo rejected the view, based on Engels, that the relegation of women to the domestic sphere was a relatively recent historical phenomenon, growing out of the development of industrial capitalism, which had pushed women out of the area of 'social production'. She held, instead, that 'a domestic/public asymmetry is general in economic forms of human organization as in other forms. Advanced and capitalistic societies, although they are extreme in this regard, are not unique' (p. 35).

Part of the basis of male authority, for Rosaldo, was the ability of men to maintain distance from the domestic sphere. She proposed a direct relationship between the degree of the subordination of women in a given society, and the degree to which the realms of public and domestic were separated. Drawing on the example of the Philippine society of the Ilongots, whom she had studied, she pointed out that where men were more closely involved in domestic life, the distance between men and women, and the degree of authority that men exerted over women, appeared to diminish. 'Societies that do not elaborate the opposition of male and female,' she suggested,

and place positive value on the conjugal relationship and the involvement of both men and women in the home seem to be most egalitarian in terms of sex roles. When a man is involved in domestic labour, in child care and cooking, he cannot establish an aura of authority and distance. And when public decisions are made in the household, women may have a legitimate public role (p. 39).

A parallel interpretation was advanced by Sherry Ortner.[24] Unlike Firestone, she located women's oppression in culture rather than in biology. But, with

Simone de Beauvoir, she saw the relegation of women to the private sphere as arising out of an interpretation of biology: the association of women with nature, and of men with culture, civilization, and the control of nature (including, therefore, of women).

In Ortner's interpretation, in all cultures, world wide, women were 'considered inferior to men'. Although this devaluation of women took different forms, it was indisputably universal. 'I would flatly assert,' she wrote, 'that we find women subordinated to men in every known society. The search for a genuinely egalitarian, let alone matriarchal culture, has proved fruitless' (Ortner, 1974, p. 70). If the subordination of women was universal, so, too, then must be the cause of this subordination. Ortner argued that one element characterizing every known society was the process by which human consciousness created what anthropologists term 'culture'. In this process, Ortner said, every society recognized a distinction between 'culture' and 'nature' (although as she noted both of these terms referred to 'conceptual categories' rather than aspects of 'reality'). Culture, as expressed in ritual, was an expression of the need to regulate and control, 'rather than passively move with and be moved by the givens of natural existence'. In other words, Ortner argued, 'We may . . . broadly equate culture with the notion of human consciousness (i.e. systems of thought and technology), by means of which humanity attempts to assert control over nature' (Ortner, 1974, p. 72). In the distinction between 'culture' and 'nature', then, 'culture' was seen not only as separate from, but as superior to, 'nature', because of its ability to control and transform the natural environment.

Ortner concluded that women were seen to be closer to nature than men, and intermediary between nature and culture, while men were the controllers and manipulators of culture itself. Until this set of associations could be disassembled, the universal subordination of women would continue. While none of these associations of women with nature was 'true', taken together they constituted a '(sadly) efficient feedback system', in which 'various aspects of woman's situation (physical, social, psychological) contribute to her being seen as closer to nature, while the view of her as closer to nature is in turn embodied in institutional forms that reproduce her situation' (Ortner, 1974, p. 87). Both institutions and cultural assumptions would have to be transformed, in order for 'both men and women . . . [to] be equally involved in projects of creativity and transcendence' (Ortner, 1974, p.87).

Juliet Mitchell had underlined the importance of cross-cultural studies, and had emphasized the need to look at all aspects of women's experience – in production as well as reproduction – in order to arrive at a correct interpretation of woman's estate. It is noteworthy that in seeking the causes of the 'universal' oppression of women, both Rosaldo and Ortner gave short shrift to the Marxist conception of the sexual division of labour – a focus of much work by socialist feminist writers – in favour of an examination of the cultural and symbolic significance of reproduction and the domestic sphere. In so doing, they lent some of the authority of anthropological theory to the hypothesis of Firestone, namely, that women's connection to biological reproduction was the root cause of their oppression.

Whatever the interpretation – whether one saw the association of women with the domestic sphere as universal and defining of their situation in all cultures like Ortner, Rosaldo, and Firestone, or whether one saw this association as having developed in a historically specific moment like Janeway and Mitchell – it was clear that an analysis of the oppression of women must take account of more than one level of reality. The biological realities of women's lives – specifically, their reproductive capacities – interacted with the psychological and the cultural, that is, the meanings attributed to them. Similarly, the economic roles performed by women interacted with the ideological accounts of these roles. Whether one talked about production and reproduction, or public and private realms, the perpetuation of male power over women was a complex phenomenon. It seemed as though the analysis of the origins of women's oppression presented a kind of chicken-and-egg dilemma. In the dialectic between biology and culture, which came first?

Notes and references

1 Millett, Kate, *Sexual Politics*, reprint edn, New York, Avon Books, 1971.

2 The term was not, of course, invented by feminists, although it was used by feminist writers such as Virginia Woolf before the 'second wave', as Veronica Beechey has noted; see Beechey, 'On patriarchy', *Feminist Review*, no. 3, 1979 pp. 66–82. For other discussions of the use of the word by feminists, see Barrett, *Women's Oppression Today*, Verso, 1980, pp. 10–19, and Eisenstein, Z., *The Radical Future of Liberal Feminism*, New York, Longman, 1981, pp. 18–30.

3 Rich, Adrienne, *Of Woman Born: Motherhood as Experience and Institution*, New York, W. W. Norton, 1976, pp. 57–8. The universalism of patriarchy has become a major focus of feminist debate.

4 Millett, *Sexual Politics*, New York, Avon Books, 1971, p. 25. Hereafter page numbers to this and other books are cited in the text.

5 While Millett mentioned rape in passing, the emphasis on it and wife battering as forms of male coercion emerged later.

6 Millett, *Sexual Politics*, pp. 26 ff.

7 See Friedan, *Feminine Mystique*, New York, Dell Publishing, 1963, pp. 95 ff. Millett's other villains include literary figures such as D. H. Lawrence, Henry Miller, and Norman Mailer. I refer the reader to the literary and historical analysis that makes up the bulk of her text, which is too rich and complex for summary here.

8 Chodorow, 'Gender, relation, and difference in psychoanalytic perspectives', in *Future of Difference*, Eisenstein and Jardine (eds), pp. 3–19, p. 12.

9 In insisting on the cultural origins of sex differences Millett and others built not only on the work of Margaret Mead, but on that of the preceding, now largely obscure, generation of feminist researchers, as Rosalind Rosenberg has shown; see *Beyond Separate Spheres: Intellectual Roots of Modern Feminism*, New Haven, Yale University Press, 1982, passim. See also Rosaldo, Michelle Z., 'Woman, culture, and society: A theoretical overview', in *Woman, Culture, and Society*, Rosaldo and Louise Lamphere (eds), Stanford, Stanford University Press, 1974, p. 18; and Kessler, Suzanne J., and McKenna, Wendy, *Gender: An Ethnomethodological Approach*, New York, John Wiley & Sons, 1978, pp. 23–4, citing Mead and Millett. The controversy over Derek Freeman's critique of Mead's work in Samoa (*Margaret Mead and Samoa: The Making and Unmaking of An Anthropological Myth*, Cambridge, Mass.; Harvard University Press and Canberra; Australian National University Press, 1983) does not invalidate the broader conclusions of her writings; see Murphy, Robert F., Alland, Jr, Alexander, and Skinner, Elliott P., 'An abortive attack on *Coming of age*, letter to the *New York Times*, 6 February 1983.

10 From table drawn up by Orville G. Brim, Jr., using the work of Talcott Parsons, R. F. Bales, and others as a theoretical basis; see Millett, *Sexual Politics*, pp. 228–30. This point was expanded upon by feminist psychologists later on.

11 Janeway, Elizabeth, *Man's World, Woman's Place: A Study in Social Mythology*, New York, Dell Publishing Co., 1971.

12 After more than a decade of the women's movement, this split has reappeared as one experienced internally by working mothers. See Ehrensaft, Diane, 'When women and men mother', *Socialist Review*, no. 49 (January–February 1980), p. 55; 'within her own psyche the sharing mother has a hard time integrating a work indentity with being a mother: "When you go out to work, the job is something you *do*. But the work of a housewife and mother is not just something you do, it's something you *are*."

13 On Parsons, see also Beechey, Veronica, 'Women and Production: a critical analysis of some sociological theories of women's work', in *Feminism and Materialism*, Kuhn and Wolpe (eds), pp. 158ff. An honourable exception in the sex roles literature was Mirra Komarovsky, whose writing dissented from the conventional wisdom. See Komarovsky, 'Functional analysis of sex roles', *American Sociological Review*, **15**, no. 4, August 1950; pp. 508–15, cited by Millett; 'Cultural contradictions and sex roles', *American Journal of Sociology*, **52**, 1946; pp. 184–9; and Komarovsky, *Women in the Modern World: Their Education and Their Dilemmas*, Boston, Little Brown, 1953.

14 Millett, *Sexual Politics*, pp. 1–22, 237–361.

15 Hanisch, Carol, 'The personal is political', in *The Radical Therapist*, Jerome Agel (ed.) New York, Ballantine Books, 1971, pp. 152–7; reprinted from *Notes from the Second Year: Women's Liberation, Major Writings of the Radical Feminists*, Shulamith Firestone and Anne Koedt (eds), New York, Radical Feminists, 1970.

16 Hanisch, 'The personal is political' pp. 336 ff.

17 Firestone, Shulamith, *The Dialectic of Sex: The Case for Feminist Revolution* New York, Bantam Books, 1970, p. 126.

18 Firestone, *The Dialectic of Sex.*, pp. 131–2.

19 Firestone, *The Dialectic of Sex*, pp. 1–12.

20 See Beneria, Lourdes, and Sen, Gita, 'Accumulation, reproduction and women's role in economic development: Boserup revisited', *Signs* **7**, no. 2, 1981, p. 290, n. 32; on the ambiguities in the use of the term 'reproduction', see Edholm, Felicity; Harris, Olivia, and Young, Kate, 'Conceptualizing women', *Critique of Anthropology* **3**, nos. 9–10, 1977, pp. 101–30. Obviously the link between economic base and cultural and social superstructure in Marxist theory is also a much vexed question. But Firestone's materialism seemed to gloss over the transition from biology to culture much too glibly. For an account of the debate among socialist feminists over Firestone's biological materialism, see Barrett, *Women's Oppression*, pp. 11 ff, and Vogel, Lise, 'Marxism and feminism: unhappy marriage, trial separation, or something else?' *Women and Revolution*, Sargent (ed.), Boston, South End Press, 1981, pp. 206 ff.

21 Mitchell, Juliet, *Woman's Estate*, reprint edn, New York, Vintage Books, 1973.

22 See Milkman, Ruth, 'Organizing the sexual division of labour: historical perspectives on "women's work" and the American labour movement', *Socialist Review*, no. 49, January–February 1980, p. 100; 'while the proportion of adult women in the paid labour force had grown from 18 per cent in 1890 to 26 per cent in 1940, it skyrocketed to 35 per cent in 1955 and then to over 50 per cent today'. For the European developments, see McBride, Theresa, 'The long road home: women's work and industralization', in *Becoming Visible: Women in European History*, Renate Bridenthal and Claudia Koonz (eds), Boston, Houghton Mifflin, 1977, pp. 280–95. The combination of protective legislation and exclusion from male-dominated trade unions in the reduction of women in the paid work-force has been a focus of discussion among feminist scholars as an instance of the

collaboration between capitalism and patriarchy; on this point see Hartmann, Heidi, 'Capitalism, patriarchy, and job sergregation by sex', in *Women and the Workplace: The Implications of Occupational Segregation*, Martha Blaxall and Barbara Reagan (eds), Chicago, University of Chicago Press, 1976, pp. 137–69.

23 Rosaldo, 'A theoretical overview', pp. 17–42.

24 Ortner, Sherry, 'Is female to male as nature is to culture?' in *Woman, Culture and Society*, Rosaldo and Lamphere (eds), pp. 67–87.

25 For an alternative interpretation by an anthropologist see Sacks, Karen, 'Engels revisited: women, the organization of production, and private property', in *Women, Culture and Society*, Rosaldo and Lamphere (eds), pp. 207–22. For an account of the development of socialist feminist theory on the 'mode of reproduction' and the sexual division of labour, see Vogel, L. 'Marxism and feminism', in *Women and Revolution*, Sargent, L. (ed.), Boston South End Press 1981, pp. 195–217.

3   Gender and class: Marxist feminist perspectives on education

Michèle Barrett

Sociological and Marxist accounts of the educational system have, until recently, focused on the question of class to the exclusion of any systematic consideration of gender. The dominant tradition in Britain has sought to document empirically the ways in which educational opportunity, and hence social mobility, has depended upon social class. The progressive character of this work should not be overlooked, since it has provided successive Labour governments in this country with evidence and arguments on which to base their programme of reforms, notably in the democratization of secondary education. Yet this tradition of work is vulnerable to criticism on two major grounds. First, it offers no analysis of the role of the educational system in the creation of a sharply sex-segregated labour force. This question is not addressed theoretically and, indeed, it is hard to see how it could be, given that many of the now classic studies in this field are, literally, studies of the education of boys.[1] A parallel case may be made on the question of racial division. Second, from a Marxist point of view, such studies operate within a descriptive sociological framework of ideas about stratification and, as AnnMarie Wolpe has argued,[2] cannot provide a satisfactory explanation of the processes involved.

Feminist response to this problem has taken three forms. There has been an important drive towards describing and analysing the processes and elements in the educational system that have been neglected in previous work. This research has been extremely valuable and I shall discuss it later in this chapter. Second, some feminists have argued that approaches such as the one developed by Michael F. D. Young (known in the profession as the 'new' sociology of education) provide, through their emphasis on the social and political definition of legitimate knowledge, useful insights into the problem of a male-defined curriculum. The third response, which I consider to be the most important in the context of developing a Marxist feminist theoretical perspective, has been the attempt to consider systematically the place of gender in an analysis of the educational system as a principal agent in the reproduction of capitalism. These arguments have not only been dominated by the influence of Louis Althusser, but have historically been constructed as a debate with the analysis of education provided in his 'Ideology and ideological state apparatuses'.[3]

In the first section I discuss attempts by Marxist feminists to explore the educational system from the point of view of an Althusserian conception of social reproduction. The most serious difficulty with this approach is the problem of

Source: Extracted from Barrett, M., *Women's Oppression Today: problems in Marxist feminist analysis*, London, Verso, 1980.

transposing on to the divisions of gender a theoretical framework conceived and elaborated in terms of class relations. Feminists attempting this analysis are brought back necessarily to the 'sex and class' debate, which needs to be resolved in one way or another for us to move on. For this reason the second section of the chapter is centred on a detailed consideration of the different ways in which this question has been addressed, and some conclusions are suggested. In the light of these the third and final section of the chapter explores some specific aspects of the contemporary British educational system and its relation to the division of labour.

I

Althusser's main points as regards education may be summarized as follows. Capitalist production ultimately depends on the continued reproduction not only of the means (such as raw materials, buildings, machinery) and forces (such as labour power) but also the relations of production (dominance and subordinacy). Labour power must be reproduced in a form where differentiation exists according to definitions of 'skill' and this provision is met through ideological processes. In Althusser's view, consideration of these problems requires a reformulation of the Marxist theory of the state.

He argues that some apparatuses of the state function primarily by repression (the army, the police), others primarily by ideology (the educational system, the family, the law, the political system, trade union institutions, communications and cultural institutions). In contemporary capitalism, the dominant ideological state apparatus is the educational system (Althusser here suggests, but does not explore, the possibility that the 'School–Family couple' is dominant). Schools take children and drill them in the ruling ideology. Around the age of 16 a huge mass are ejected, as workers or peasants; others continue to become the petty bourgeoisie; others proceed further to emerge as agents of exploitation, agents of repression or professional ideologists. Each group is provided with the ideology to suit its role, yet the mechanisms whereby this occurs are disguised by the apparently neutral character of the school.

These theses, and the debate surrounding them, have been enormously influential; in particular, Althusser has placed the question of the *reproduction* of the relations of production firmly on the agenda of Marxist concerns. It is not difficult to see that posing the analysis in terms of relations of production and the division of labour provides a more hospitable ground for the insertion of feminist questions about gender than do analyses which pose the problem strictly in terms of the labour–capital contradiction and conventional Marxist definitions of social classes. The concepts of 'dominance' and 'subordinacy' are flexible ones; they may perhaps provide a useful framework for the analysis of women's subordination in capitalism.

I want now to examine, in the context of this general concern with education as a dominant agent of capitalist reproduction, attempts to develop a Marxist feminist perspective on the processes by which a gender-divided work-force is trained and reproduced. Such attempts are indebted to the theoretical groundwork undertaken by AnnMarie Wolpe and it is necessary to consider her arguments in some detail. Wolpe's article 'Education: the road to dependency', published in 1977, has been particularly influential in Britain.[4] It begins with a concise statement of how we should understand the educational system in relation to the sexual division of labour. She argues that there is a division of labour within the family whereby women (through their domestic labour) reproduce not only the future generation of labour power, but also current members of the employed labour force. This division within the family is paralleled by the sexual division of labour in employment, where women habitually occupy the 'secondary' sector of the labour market with its characteristic features of low pay, little training and ease of dispensability. These two systems are closely linked, and the educational system 'functions to satisfy the requirements' of both. The dominance of men and the dependence of women, both within and outside the family, are here posed mainly in terms of the ideological system by which they are secured. Wolpe argues that 'the educational system is a key means of the production and reproduction of the ideological structure' and that it embodies the dominant ideology in its organization.[5] Within the system two processes can be isolated: basic training in the skills and qualifications appropriate to the concrete division of labour, and the transmission of ideologies. Wolpe concentrates her subsequent discussion on the latter, documenting from empirical research the ways in which the curriculum, school organization, the teachers as agents, and state policy reports all contribute to the reproduction of the ideology of women's role. She concludes that change will not be secured by, for instance, changing the curriculum: 'the education system is too closely linked with the division of labour in society, as are the ideologies which legitimate this structure'.[6]

Wolpe's formulation here is in many ways very useful. She rightly insists on the relations between the educational system and the division of labour, and she rightly examines the ideological processes by which a gender-differentiated workforce is produced and sustained. This analysis is a creative and stimulating attempt to apply the perspective developed in (the first part of) Althusser's essay to the question of gender. It remains the case, however, that this line of argument poses important theoretical questions which need to be resolved. These can be summarized as (a) the 'problem' of functionalism, (b) the conceptualization of the state and its relation to ideology, and (c) the question of gender and class.

In the summary given above Wolpe's argument appears to be functionalist to a high degree. The educational system is posed as an instrument by which an existing division of labour is somewhat mechanistically reproduced. Even the particular constituent elements identified (occupationally related skills and the transmission of ideologies) are reminiscent of the 'functions' of the educational system ('allocation' and 'socialization') identified by the functionalist sociologist Talcott Parsons.[7] Several points can be made here. First, programmatic theoretical statements frequently give rise to this problem: what the reader gains from concise, lucid statements is inevitably counterbalanced by over-simplification. In the discussion which follows (her) theoretical introduction, Wolpe examines in some detail the precise processes through which the ideology of gender is constructed. Second, she has in her subsequent work developed an alternative (non-functionalist) approach to these questions and it perhaps tells us more about the readership than about the author that the most functionalist formulation is invariably seized on as having, apparently, the greater explanatory value.

In 'Education and the sexual division of labour', Wolpe argues that the specificity of the educational system is defined by a process of struggle and is not directly functional for production. The educational system is hence ascribed a 'relative autonomy' in relation to the capitalist mode of production; it is presented as an agency of 'mediation' between pupils and their allocation to places in the division of labour. Wolpe points to a series of contradictions within official British educational discourse and she emphasizes that the educational system is the product of historical struggle. 'At any one time', she argues, 'there is ... a necessary disjunction between the "requirements" of the economy and the range of skills the educational system can produce.'[8] These points are important qualifications of Wolpe's earlier position. The reproduction of technically and ideologically equipped agents becomes dependent upon the outcome of struggle, and the allocation of these agents to places in the division of labour is a *mediated* rather than a direct process.

In these respects Wolpe's later arguments are not unlike those put forward by Bourdieu and Passeron in their analysis of *Reproduction in Education, Society and Culture*. A central point of this recondite text on the subject of pedagogic mystification is that the educational system makes a 'relatively autonomous' contribution to the reproduction of class relations and that its operations should not be reduced mechanistically to the expression of class interests.[9] Bourdieu and Passeron argue that the ideology of democracy insists that class privilege be legitimated by certification from an apparently neutral educational system. Legitimation *by* the school rests on social recognition of the legitimacy and neutrality *of* the school. The relative autonomy of the educational system resides in its ability to conceal the truth of its functions and mask its relationship to the class structure.

There is not space here to go into these arguments in detail. They are relevant, however, to the question of gender division in the educational and training processes of capitalism in that the position taken on these general theoretical issues will affect the analysis produced. My own view is that the attempt to move away from a functionalist perspective on education is somewhat misplaced. Education systems are generically, in capitalism, instruments of state policy in a sense that is simply not true of, say, systems of cultural production. We should not let a general hostility to 'functionalist' forms of explanation blind us to the fact that some institutions of capitalism are the product of explicit state policy and that therefore *any* account of them must inevitably be a 'functionalist' one. I am not convinced that the argument of Bourdieu and Passeron, that the strength of the school's legitimating power lies in social recognition of its neutrality and legitimacy, could ever establish the autonomy of the school in the way they imply. A distinction should be made between the ideology and *appearance* of autonomy (which will have important effects) and the analytic ascription of autonomy. In this case, I would argue, the legitimating force of the school could be achieved through successful social representation of its autonomy and neutrality; we do not need to assume from this that it *is* therefore autonomous. Nor am I convinced by AnnMarie Wolpe's argument that there is a 'necessary disjunction' between the requirements of the economy and the skills the educational system can provide. A disjunction there may be but I am unclear as to why it should be necessary. It is more fruitful, surely, to approach this disjunction by asking why the state fails in its intentions with regard to the training of the labour force, rather than by attempting to establish theoretically the relative autonomy of the educational system. We can then ask, as Richard Johnson does in his discussion of the expansion of schooling in the nineteenth century, why state policy on education may have 'effects . . . which were not those that were intended'.[10] Undoubtedly the answer will be framed in terms of struggle, the 'obstinacy' of the working class and the inefficiency or failure of the state in securing its ends.

I am arguing, therefore, that analysis of gender division in education would benefit from the analytic separation of two elements: the relationship of the educational system to the state (where a functionalist argument is inevitable), and the relationship of gender division to the state (where a functionalist argument would be much more contentious). Feminist use of Althusser's work must, therefore, depend upon a resolution of the question of the relationship of women and of men to the class structure.

II

In order to discuss this question it is necessary to outline schematically the alternative ways of posing the relation between gender and class which are currently on offer.

1 First there is the view that gender is not a separable element of class relations, but is completely absorbed within them. This perspective depends upon seeing the family, rather than the individual, as the basic unit of which classes are composed: it aggregates the members of the family into an internally unified entity which can then be located in the class structure. This assumption has undoubtedly characterized sociological approaches to stratification, the class position of all members of a family being allocated on the basis of the occupation of the (normally male) head of household. It has, quite rightly, been criticized by numerous recent feminist studies.[11] Feminists have argued that this assumption rules out of court some important considerations: conflict of interest within the family, women's own occupational position, the extent to which women's employment is related to their work in the household, for example. These critiques, although principally directed towards sociological analysis of class, are in fact equally applicable to Marx's own work. Marx defines class with reference to relationship to ownership of the means of production. As Geoffrey Kay explains in his clear presentation of Marx's theory of the working class, the proletariat is defined by its complete dependence on the wage.[12] Yet it is evident that for Marx the typical wage-labourer is male. In his discussion of the introduction of machinery, Marx refers to 'women and children' as 'that mighty substitute for labour and labourers'. He states that 'the value of labour power was determined, not only by the labour-time necessary to maintain the individual adult labourer, but also by that necessary to maintain his family'.[13] Furthermore, Marx goes on to argue that capital's expansion into the employment of women and children had the consequences of usurping the labour necessary in the home, of depreciating the value of labour power and raising the degree of exploitation. It is currently a matter of dispute as to whether Marx is correct in this argument,[14] and I shall discuss below some alternative formulations offered within the broader Marxist tradition. In so far as Marx's own position occupies a privileged and influential role within Marxist thought as a whole, it is important to emphasize the inadequacy of his assumptions on this question. In regarding both women and children simply as 'substitutes' for the male labourer, Marx is clearly guilty of the naturalistic aggregation of individuals into the family unit which feminists have criticized in sociological theory.

2 In radical opposition to this perspective, various arguments have been put forward to the effect that gender division constitutes a system of oppression which is utterly independent of class division. Such arguments are commonly posed in terms of the concept of patriarchy. My reservations there are applicable here. Perhaps the strongest formulation of this position is that which argues that gender division is analytically prior to class division, as in Firestone's conception of struggle between men and women as the prime motor of history or in Millett's view that 'women tend to transcend the usual class stratifications in patriarchy'. These claims, although politically significant for feminism, are difficult to substantiate and have been convincingly criticized.[15] A more plausible argument has been developed in the view that patriarchy can be seen as independent of class structure but as operating through analogous mechanisms. Different formulations are possible here. One involves posing patriarchy and capitalism as two identifiably separate structures, historically coexisting in particular societies. This, as I understand it, is the sense in which the term 'capitalist patriarchy' has been used (particularly in the United States) to describe contemporary societies such as are found in western Europe and the USA.[16] A second formulation would be constituted by posing a 'domestic mode of production', with its own mechanisms of exploitation, which may be held to coexist alongside a capitalist mode of production.[17] Third, the analogy with social class can be extended to the point of arguing that women do in fact constitute, themselves, an indentifiable social class.[18] These formulations are not necessarily, in this work, mutually exclusive and some writers draw on more than one of them in their analysis.[19] All of them, in my view, are difficult to reconcile with a Marxist analysis, and I should stress that this comment applies to the self-consciously 'Marxist feminist' analyses of 'capitalist patriarchy' just as it does to the non-Marxist arguments put forward by some feminists.

The reasons for this difficulty are complex. I am not suggesting that Marxism is a rigid explanatory framework which cannot be modified, and I shall discuss below some possible avenues for a more satisfactory reconceptualization of a Marxist theory of class and gender. I am simply suggesting here that there is no unproblematic way in which Marxist categories of class can be juxtaposed with, or transposed on to, feminist categories of gender. To do so would be to strip from Marxism precisely its ability to analyse the mechanisms underlying the appearance of social reality, reducing it to a set of descriptive, empirical categories.

This danger is particularly acute in the argument that women can be said to constitute a social class. In purely descriptive terms it is plausible to argue that certain categories of women, most obviously full-time housewives, occupy a unique occupational role which we might want to designate as a social class. In terms of a sociological definition of class, based on occupational status, this would be acceptable. Marxist categories of class, however, are not descriptive of occupation in this way; they operate according to specified *relations* within a mode of production.

I want now to consider the attempts made from a Marxist feminist position to reconcile theoretically the arguments about gender division and class structure. One way of approaching this is to argue that the oppression of women differs significantly from class to class. Engels stressed this point, asserting that the proletarian home in which both husband and wife were engaged in wage-labour was in broad material terms an egalitarian one. Certainly he argued that the situation of the bourgeois wife, where upkeep was provided in return for the production of legitimate heirs, was tantamount to prostitution. This was the basis of his view that the entrance of all women into social production was the precondition for their emancipation. Although Engels' work has been extensively criticized by Marxist feminists, his central insistence on the material factors distinguishing proletarian from bourgeois women has been influential. McDonough and Harrison, for instance, argue that 'patriarchal' control of woman's procreative capacity and sexuality takes different forms for different social classes. For the bourgeoisie this arises from the requirement to produce legitimate heirs, for the proletariat, with the need to reproduce efficiently the next generation of labour-power.

It is not, in fact, adequate to address the question of class and gender by posing a unity of interest between capitalists and men, since the capitalist class is composed of both men and women. This problem is to some extent avoided by the argument that gender division, and hence women's oppression, is historically constituted as outside the labour/capital relation with which a Marxist analysis of capitalist society is fundamentally concerned. Much of the discussion of the sexual division of labour is directed, ultimately, at the question of women and class. For if women's position in the relations of production in capitalism could be established then clarification of their class position would follow. Lucy Bland and her co-authors have argued that women's subordination cannot be understood through the categories of capital alone. They argue that 'outside' these economic relations, and historically prior to their emergence, lie the patriarchal relations between men and women which capital has 'taken over' or 'colonized'.[20]

The most obvious drawback of these arguments is that they run the risk of characterizing Marxism simply as a method for identifying the essential component parts of the capitalist class structure, and stripping it of any ability to explain these in concrete rather than abstract terms. The argument leads to the conclusion that Marxist theory can specify the 'places' which need to be filled, but that feminist theory must be invoked to explain who fills them.[21] This problem of 'dualism', as Veronica Beechey has argued, also arises in attempts to bring Marxist analysis to bear on the question of capitalist *production*, and feminist analysis to bear on the question of the *reproduction* of these relations of production.[22]

Many of the difficulties encountered in considering the position of women in the class structure are related to a general confusion in contemporary Marxist analysis of class. The terms in which Marx himself posed the issue, as an increasing polarization between those who owned the means of production and those who depended for their subsistence on the sale of their labour power, have been to some extent overtaken by subsequent developments of capitalist production in the twentieth century. The economy has increasingly had to be analysed not only in terms of capitalist production but also in terms of state production and domestic production, and the implications of this for a Marxist analysis of class structure are as yet far from clear. The twentieth century has seen the exponential expansion of 'service' or 'non-productive' industries, in relation to manufacturing industry. The distinction between 'mental' and 'manual' labour was useful to Marx as an element of an account of the processes whereby the wage labourer was degraded and alienated in the division of labour which emerged in the course of capital accumulation; it is now a rather different object of Marxist analysis. As Braverman has convincingly argued, the degradation of work in the twentieth century has stripped the 'mental' labourer of the illusions of control previously suggested by this definition.[23] In so far as the expansion of wage labour among women has been primarily located in the clerical and service sectors, analysis of women's position in the class structure has encountered many of these general difficulties.[24]

We can see that none of the existing formulations of the class and gender relation is entirely satisfactory, although this situation reflects a general difficulty with the contemporary Marxist theory of class as well as a particular difficulty in dealing with the class positions of women.

It is important to stress here the importance of an historical approach to the question of gender and class. Consideration of the effect of the transition to capitalism on the sexual division of labour is essential. It is clear that on the one hand the wage relation characteristic of capitalism, and the accompanying separation of home and workplace, have historically made a substantial contribution to the formation of the present sexual division of labour in which women's position is located principally in relation to responsibility for domestic labour and financial dependence on a male wage-earner. On the other hand, some elements of this sexual division undoubtedly existed prior to the development of capitalism.[25] In addition to this historically prior sexual division of labour, upon which capitalism has built a more rigidly segregated division, we can isolate many points of struggle in which the eventual outcome is not pre-given in terms of requirements of capital. The classic case in point here is the protective legislation on women's working conditions passed in the mid nineteenth century. Although interpretations of this vary,[26] I would argue that this represented a material defeat of the interests of working women and, furthermore, a defeat that is not simply explicable in terms of a proposed logic of capitalist development. It involved an assumption, shared by the labour movement among others, that the relegation of women to domesticity and childcare was natural and desirable. In this respect the eventual outcome was a product of an ideology of gender division that was incorporated into the capitalist division of labour rather than spontaneously generated by it. If this argument is correct, it would suggest that although we may usefully argue that gender division has been built into the capitalist division of labour and is an important element of capitalist relations of production, it is more difficult to argue that gender division *necessarily* occupies a particular place in the class structure of capitalism. It has not, at least as yet, been demonstrated that the sexual division of labour forms not simply a *historically constituted* but a *logically pre-given* element of the class structure that would *automatically* be reproduced by the reproduction of this class structure.

III

This lengthy discussion of gender and class has been necessary in order to re-consider the question of whether an Althusserian approach to the reproduction of capitalism can provide an analysis of the reproduction of gender division in capitalism. I suggested that our ability to integrate gender and class would have implications for the validity of this analysis. If it were true that the sexual division of labour was so functional for capitalism that reproduction of the latter depended upon reproduction of the former, the Althusserian approach would prove relatively unproblematic. If, however, it is seen as more autonomous then we would encounter serious difficulties, and my view is that this is in fact the case. Hence the *substance* of Althusser's argument would need to be modified in profound ways for it to be of use to feminists. Nor am I convinced that the *method* which seeks to understand education and training processes in terms of the reproduction of relations of dominance and subordinacy can be transposed on to the question of gender. To do this would be to argue that just as the capitalist class is reproduced in a relationship of total dominance over the working class, so men are reproduced as totally dominant over women. Without denying the general pattern of male dominance, we can still see particular drawbacks in this argument. It would be difficult to argue, for instance, that the qualifications and skills imparted to a girl at a major independent school would in any sense 'equip' her for a place in the division of labour that was subordinate to that of a working-class boy who left school at the minimum age with no formal qualifications.

The notion that women have a *dual* relationship to the class structure is perti-nent here. The education and training that a woman receives by virtue of her class background provide a highly significant contribution to the position she will occupy in the labour force. Yet it is equally clear that the relationship she has to the class structure by virtue of her wage labour (or her ownership of the means of production) will be substantially influenced by the mediation of this direct relationship through dependence on men and responsibility for domestic labour and childcare. For working-class women this may result in simultaneous direct exploitation by capital via their own wage-labour and indirect exploitation via vicarious dependence on the wage of a male breadwinner. For bourgeois women this may result in simultaneous ownership of, yet lack of control over, capital.

The dual character of women's class positions can be seen in the processes of educating and training a work-force which is divided by both class and gender. In the discussion that follows I shall concentrate on the aspects of these systems which reproduce gender division and a mediated relationship to the wage, and am to some extent taking as read the importance of the educational system in the processes by which class differentiation is secured.

It is clear that within the culture of the school, as outside it, there exist processes by which femininity and masculinity are defined and constructed. I have already mentioned the growing concern with the rigidly stereotyped imagery of gender presented to children in the books used in schools. Anna Davin, in her fascinating account of the parallel imagery used in late nineteenth-century school-books,[27] rightly points to the difficulty of assessing the impact of these stereotypes on the reader, but it is nevertheless likely that they do have some effect on the children who are daily exposed to them. There is considerable continuity between the ideal of conformity to domesticity expressed for girls in such books and the findings of recent studies on the behaviour of girls and boys in the classroom. Elena Belotti, for instance, has described the ways in which the assumption that girls should perform domestic services for boys is acted out in the classroom at a very early age in the various tasks of clearing up and so on that little girls are enjoined to perform.[28]

Similarly, Rosemary Deem has pointed to the various studies of classroom interaction which have suggested that girls are encouraged to be more conformist in school than boys.[29] AnnMarie Wolpe's observation of girls in a secondary school led to a description of various incidents where adolescent girls were implicitly and even explicitly 'coached' by their teachers into appropriately feminine behaviour, and she comments that social relations in the school situation were more overtly sexualized than she had anticipated.[30] As many writers have noted, children are in school for much of the period when they are maturing sexually, becoming aware of the importance of sexual relationships, and learning the definitions of adult masculinity and femininity. The perceptions of self consolidated in this period tend to reflect the perceptions of teachers, which in turn frequently reflect the ideology of gender in society at large. Michelle Stanworth has uncovered, in observation of a further education college, some of the ways in which male teachers tended to marginalize or simply ignore the female students and the extent to which this contributed to the passive and self-deprecating perceptions the girls had of themselves.[31]

It seems reasonable to suppose that these processes, although taking place within the educational system, are not necessarily constructed by and for that system but are essentially located in the general ideology of gender in the society of which educational institutions are part. If we consider, however, the structure and organization of the school system we can see that in fundamental ways it has incorporated a division between the sexes to a degree that is inexplicable in any strictly educational terms.

Gender is a salient organizing category in the educational system. In some respects it constitutes an apparently arbitrary division which relates solely to administrative convenience: children have to be marshalled in some way, so why not into boys and girls? During roll-call, when children are sent out for milk or in to dinners,[32] the distinction between boys and girls presents itself as an obvious organizational aid. Yet this arbitrary appearance is deceptive, since these administrative classifications are symptomatic of significant gender divisions engrained in the structure of the institutions themselves. This can be seen by considering the sexual division of labour in schools from the point of view of its similarity with the sexual division of labour in the family. In many schools at the secondary level there is a headmaster, with whom executive and disciplinary powers reside, and a senior mistress, whose role is conceived of as primarily 'pastoral'. Indeed it is virtually a requirement in British coeducational schools that the second most senior staff member be of the opposite sex from the head. Similarly, pastoral and welfare work is in general more readily assigned to female members of staff, often on the assumption that they will prove more conscientious in their 'care'. This pattern clearly mirrors the norm of the nuclear family, and is refracted in many other aspects of school structure.

The teaching profession is divided by gender in several ways, and these, I would argue, are closely connected with the sexual division of labour generally. The profession is divided hierarchically by gender: as you move to more senior posts the proportion of women falls.

The profession is also divided by subject area. I shall discuss below the processes by which boys and girls are 'channelled' into different subjects, principally in secondary and tertiary education, and it is clear that the existing segregation by subject of the teaching staff may have something to do with this. Much of the pattern of subject-stereotyping by sex, which results in girls going into arts and social science subjects and boys into science and technology, is established very firmly in terms of the teaching staff. Indeed, most institutions reproduce the contemporary sexual division of labour in the staffing of both academic and non-academic posts. In most British universities, colleges and polytechnics, for instance, the principal, senior staff and technical and portering staff are male, with female employees located in junior teaching and research positions and in secretarial, catering and cleaning work.

It has been suggested in the past that the extension of coeducational schooling would have advantages over sex-segregated education in this respect. But research on this question indicates that the reverse may be true: girls in single-sex schools are more likely than girls in coeducational schools to pursue further and higher education generally, and in particular, are more likely to take advanced courses in science subjects.[33] The only explanation for this is that the processes of stereotyping are more marked in schools where the divisions between girls and boys are daily confronted and the pupils are constantly exposed to differentiation by gender.

There is now a considerable amount of data relating to the processes of subject 'channelling' in the educational system, and I shall simply mention some basic points here. First, we have to contend with the tradition in British schools that girls should take subjects related to their future domestic role: needlework, cookery, domestic science and 'housecraft', and that boys should take woodwork, metalwork and technical drawing. Under the Sex Discrimination Act, 1975, it is now illegal to ban either sex from such classes, but legal action in such cases has not been very successful.

The question of 'legitimate knowledge' has been taken up vigorously in both Marxist and feminist work. The notion underlying many of these analyses is frequently the view articulated by Marx that the knowledge validated by a particular society is not neutral but is constructed in the interests of the dominant class. Feminist critiques of legitimate knowledge have addressed the problem at various levels. It has been easy to point to instances where the curriculum, for example in school courses, blatantly incorporates sexist assumptions. The sexual division of labour is built into the context and objectives of the curriculum; many feminists have commented on the assumptions explicit in the various home economics and housecraft courses that girls have been encouraged to take.[34] Feminists have argued also that sexism is not only a part of the school curriculum but a salient factor in the theory and methods employed by specific academic disciplines. In sociology feminists have suggested that the sub-divisions within the discipline, and the weight attached to industrial sociology compared with the sociology of the family, for instance, reflect the absence of any systematic consideration of gender.[35] Feminist anthropologists have likewise commented on an 'androcentric' bias in the subject.[36] In the area of literary studies feminists have argued that the establishment of 'the canon' of reputedly excellent writers is equally dominated by male prejudice.

At a more general level it is also important to point to the alleged congruence between rationality, knowledge and masculinity. This is obviously somewhat intangible but it is possible to discern a general ideological polarization between the logical, scientific, rational, technological, numerate and 'masculine', and the literate, sensitive, insightful, unfalsifiable and 'feminine'. Such a polarity is encouraged by a situation where it is precisely in the arts and 'qualitative' subjects that women are most frequently found, whereas in the scientific and technological subjects they are most notably absent. It is at least arguable that the cultural imagery of gender in our society has been incorporated into the very framework in which we receive and assess all forms of knowledge.

The latter part of this chapter has concentrated on aspects of the educational system that relate to the reproduction of a work-force divided by gender. I have to a large extent assumed the processes by which the system reproduces class division, and I am not convinced that these two processes can in any unproblematic way be integrated. It is clear, however, that the educational system does function to reproduce both of these fundamental divisions in the work-force, and that the relation between class and gender must be examined further. I have suggested that one useful way of posing the complex relation would be to argue that, as Jean Gardiner has put it,[37] women have a dual relationship to the class structure. This duality consists in a direct relation of exploitation by capital in so far as the majority of women are wage labourers, and an indirect one in so far as many women depend upon the mediated wage of a male breadwinner.

Notes and references

1 See, for example, Brian Jackson and Dennis Marsden's *Education and the Working Class*, Harmondsworth, 1972, or David Hargreaves's *Social Relations in a Secondary School*, London, 1966.

2 Wolpe, AnnMarie, 'Education and the sexual division of labour', in Kuhn, A. and Wolpe, A. M. (eds), *Feminism and Materialism*, London, 1978.

3 In *Lenin and Philosophy and Other Essays*, pp. 123–73.

4 Published in *Some Processes in Sexist Education*, by AnnMarie Wolpe, London, Women's Research and Resources Centre, 1977.

5 Wolpe, *Some Processes* . . . pp. 2–3.

6 Wolpe, *Some Processes* . . . p. 18.

7 Talcott Parsons, 'The school class as a social system', in *Harvard Educational Review*, **29**, 1959, pp. 297–318.

8 'Education and the sexual division of labour', p. 314.

9 Bourdieu, Pierre, and Passerson, Jean-Claude, *Reproduction in Education, Society and Culture*, trans. R. Nice, London, 1977.

10 Johnson, Richard, 'Notes on the schooling of the English working class, 1780–1850', in Dale, R. *et al.* (eds), *Schooling and Capitalism*, London, 1976.

11 See, for example, Acker, J., 'Women and social stratification: a case of intellectual sexism', *American Journal of Sociology*, **78**, no. 4, 1973.

12 Kay, Geoffrey, *The Economic Theory of the Working Class*, London, 1979.

13 *Capital*, vol. 1, London 1980, p. 395.

14 See Barrett Michèle, and McIntosh, Mary, 'The "family wage": some problems for socialists and feminists', *Capital and Class*, no. 11, 1980.

15 Middleton, C., 'Sexual inequality and stratification theory', in Parkin, F. (ed.), *The Social Analysis of Class Structure*, London, 1974.

16 See the collection edited by Eisenstein, Z., *Capitalist Patriarchy and the Case for Socialist Feminism*, New York, 1978.

17 See Harrison, J., 'The political economy of housework', *Bulletin of the Conference of Socialist Economists*, winter 1973.

18 See (for a sociological treatment of this argument) Morgan, D. H. J., *Social Theory and the Family*, London, 1975 (chapter 5, 'Women as a social class').

19 Some of the difficulties encountered here are discussed by Maxine Molyneux in 'Beyond the domestic labour debate', *New Left Review*, no. 116, 1979.

20 Bland, Lucy, Brunsdon, Charlotte, Hobson Dorothy, and Winship, Janice, 'Women "inside and outside" the relations of production', in Women's Studies Group, Centre for Contemporary Cultural Studies, *Women Take Issue*, London, 1978.

21 I am indebted to Anne Phillips for this succinct way of expressing the problem.

22 'On patriarchy', *Feminist Review*, no. 3, 1979.

23 Braverman, Harry, *Labour and Monopoly Capital*, New York, 1974; see especially chapter 15.

24 See West, Jackie, 'Women, sex, and class', in Kuhn, A. and Wolpe, A. M. (eds.), *Feminism and Materalism*, London, 1978.

25 See Middleton, Christopher, 'The sexual division of labour in feudal England', *New Left Review*, nos. 113–114, 1979.

26 See Humphries, Jane, 'Class struggle and the persistence of the working class family', *Cambridge Journal of Economics*, **1**, no. 3, 1977; Barrett and McIntosh, 'The family wage'; and Taylor, Barbara, 'Socialism, feminism and sexual antagonism in the London tailoring trade in the early 1830s', *Feminist Studies*, **5**, no. 1, 1979.

27 Davin, Anna, ' "Mind that you do as you are told": reading books for Board School Girls, 1870–1902', *Feminist Review*, no. 3, 1979.

28 Belotti, Elena G., *Little Girls*, London, 1975.

29 Deem, Rosemary, *Women and Schooling*, London, 1978, pp. 39–40.

30 Wolpe, AnnMarie, *Some Processes in Sexist Education*, p. 36.

31 Stanworth, Michelle, *Gender and Schooling*, London, 1983.

32 The effect of current public expenditure cuts may make these particular exercises redundant.

33 See Shaw, Jenny, 'Finishing school: some implications of sex-segregated education',

in Leonard Barker D , and Allen, S. (eds), *Sexual Divisions and Society*, London, 1976; and Byrne, p. 135.

34 See Wolpe, AnnMarie, 'The official ideology of education for girls', and Deem, Rosemary, *Women and Schooling*, p. 45.

35 See Oakley, Ann, *The Sociology of Housework*, London, 1974 (chapter 1).

36 See Molyneux, Maxine, 'Androcentrism in Marxist Anthropology', in *Critique of Anthropology*, no. 9/10, 1977.

37 Gardiner, Jean, 'Women in the labour process and class structure', Hunt, A. (ed.), *Class and class structure*, London, 1977.

4   Black feminism and the boundaries of sisterhood

Hazel V. Carby

*I'm leaving evidence. And you got to leave evidence too. And your children got to leave evidence. . . .
They burned all the documents. . . . We got to burn out what they put in our minds, like you burn out
a wound. Except we got to keep what we need to bear witness. That scar that's left to bear witness.
We got to keep it as visible as our blood.*[1]

The black women's critique of *his*tory has not only involved us in coming to terms
with 'absences'; we have also been outraged by the ways in which it has made
us visible, when it has chosen to see us. *His*tory has constructed our sexuality
and our femininity as deviating from those qualities with which white women, as
the prize objects of the western world, have been endowed. We have also been
defined in less than human terms.[2] Our continuing struggle with *his*tory began
with its 'discovery' of us. However, this chapter will be concerned with herstory
rather than *his*tory. We wish to address questions to the feminist theories which
have been developed during the last decade; a decade in which black women
have been fighting, in the streets, in the schools, through the courts, inside and
outside the wage relation. The significance of these struggles ought to inform the
writing of the herstory of women in Britain. It is fundamental to the development
of a feminist theory and practice that is meaningful for black women. We cannot
hope to reconstitute ourselves in all our absences, or to rectify the ill-conceived
presences that invade herstory from *his*tory, but we do wish to bear witness to
our own herstories. The connections between these and the herstories of white
women will be made and remade in struggle. Black women have come from
Africa, Asia and the Caribbean and we cannot do justice to all their herstories
in a single chapter. Neither can we represent the voices of all black women in
Britain, our herstories are too numerous and too varied. What we will do is to
offer ways in which the 'triple' oppression of gender, race and class can be
understood, in their specificity, and also as they determine the lives of black
women.

  Much contemporary debate has posed the question of the relation between race
and gender, in terms which attempt to parallel race and gender divisions. It can
be argued that as processes, racism and sexism are similar. Ideologically for
example, they both construct common sense through reference to 'natural' and
'biological' differences. It has also been argued that the categories of race and
gender are both socially constructed and that, therefore, they have little internal
coherence as concepts. Furthermore, it is possible to parallel racialized and

Source: Extracted from Carby, H., 'White women listen! Black feminism and the boundaries of
sisterhood' in Centre for Contemporary Cultural Studies, *The Empire Strikes Back: race and racism
in '70s, Britain*, London, Hutchinson, 1982.

gendered divisions in the sense that the possibilities of amelioration through legislation appear to be equally ineffectual in both cases. Michèle Barrett, however, has pointed out that it is not possible to argue for parallels because as soon as historical analysis is made, it becomes obvious that the institutions which have to be analysed are different, as are the forms of analysis needed.[3] We would agree that the construction of such parallels is fruitless and often proves to be little more than a mere academic exercise; but there are other reasons for our dismissal of these kinds of debate. The experience of black women does not enter the parameters of parallelism. The fact that black women are subject to the *simultaneous* oppression of patriarchy, class and 'race' is the prime reason for not employing parallels that render their position and experience not only marginal but also invisible.

In arguing that most contemporary feminist theory does not begin to adequately account for the experience of black women we also have to acknowledge that it is not a simple question of their absence, consequently the task is not one of rendering their visibility. On the contrary we will have to argue that the process of accounting for their historical and contemporary position does, in itself, challenge the use of some of the central categories and assumptions of recent mainstream feminist thought. We can point to no single source for our oppression. When white feminists emphasize patriarchy alone, we want to redefine the term and make it a more complex concept. Racism ensures that black men do not have the same relations to patriarchal/capitalist hierarchies as white men. In the words of the Combahee River Collective:

We believe that sexual politics under patriarchy is as pervasive in Black women's lives as are the politics of class and race. We also often find it difficult to separate race from class from sex oppression because in our lives they are most often experienced simultaneously. We know that there is such a thing as racial–sexual oppression which is neither solely racial nor solely sexual e.g. the history of rape of Black women by white men as a weapon of political repression.

Although we are feminists and lesbians, we feel solidarity with progressive Black men and do not advocate the fractionlisation that white women who are separatists demand. Our situation as Black people necessitates that we have solidarity around the face of race, which white women of course do not need to have with white men, unless it is their negative solidarity as racial oppressors. We struggle together with Black men against racism, while we also struggle with Black men about sexism.[4]

It is only in the writings by black feminists that we can find attempts to theorize the interconnection of class, gender and race as it occurs in our lives and it has only been in the autonomous organizations of black women that we have been able to express and act upon the experiences consequent upon these determinants. Many black women had been alienated by the non-recognition of their lives, experiences and herstories in the WLM. Black feminists have been, and are still, demanding that the existence of racism must be acknowledged as a structuring feature of our relationships with white women. Both white feminist theory and practice have to recognize that white women stand in a power relation as oppressors of black women. This compromises any feminist theory and practice founded on the notion of simple equality.

Three concepts which are central to feminist theory become problematic in

their application to black women's lives: 'the family', 'patriarchy' and 'reproduction'. When used they are placed in a context of the herstory of white
(frequently middle-class) women and become contradictory when applied to the
lives and experiences of black women. In a recent comprehensive survey of
contemporary feminist theory, *Women's Oppression Today*, Michèle Barrett sees the
contemporary family (effectively the family under capitalism) as the source of
oppression of women:

It is difficult to argue that the present structure of the family–household is anything
other than oppressive for women. Feminists have consistently, and rightly, seen the
family as a central site of women's oppression in contemporary society. The reasons for
this lie both in the material structure of the household, by which women are by and
large financially dependent on men, and in the ideology of the family, through which
women are confined to a primary concern with domesticity and motherhood. This
situation underwrites the disadvantages women experience at work, and lies at the root
of the exploitation of female sexuality endemic in our society. The concept of
'dependence' is perhaps, the link between the material organisation of the household,
and the ideology of femininity: an assumption of women's dependence on men structures
both of these areas.[5]

The immediate problem for black feminists is whether this framework can be
applied at all to analyse our herstory of oppression and struggle. We would not
wish to deny that the family can be a source of oppression for us but we also
wish to examine how the black family has functioned as a prime source of
resistance to oppression. We need to recognize that during slavery, periods of
colonialism and under the present authoritarian state, the black family has been
a site of political and cultural resistance to racism. Furthermore, we cannot
easily separate the two forms of oppression because racist theory and practice is
frequently gender-specific. Ideologies of black female sexuality do not stem
primarily from the black family. The way the gender of black women is
constructed differs from constructions of white femininity because it is also subject
to racism. Black feminists have been explaining this since the last century when
Sojourner Truth pointed to the ways in which 'womanhood' was denied the black
woman.

That man over there says women need to be helped into carriages, and lifted over ditches,
and to have the best place everywhere. Nobody ever helps me into carriages, and lifted
over ditches, or over mud-puddles, or gives me any best place! And aint I a woman?
Look at me! Look at my arm! I have ploughed, and planted, and gathered into barns,
and no man could head me! And aint I a woman? I could work as much and eat as
much as a man – when I could get it – and bear the lash as well! And aint I a woman?
I have borne thirteen children, and seen most all sold off to slavery, and when I cried
with my mother's grief, none but Jesus heard me! And aint I a woman?[6]

In another examination of common sense Errol Lawrence indicated the racist
nature of ideologies of black female sexuality.[7] Black women are constantly challenging these ideologies in their day-to-day struggles. Asian girls in schools, for
example, are fighting back to destroy the racist mythology of their femininity. As
Pratibha Parmar has pointed out, careers officers do not offer them the same
interviews and job opportunities as white girls. This is because they believe that

Asian girls will be forced into marriage immediately after leaving school. The common-sense logic of this racism dictates that a career for Asian girls is thought to be a waste of time. But the struggle in schools is not just against the racism of the careers service:

'Yes, and then there are some racist students who are always picking on us. Recently, we had a fight in our school between us and some white girls. We really showed them we were not going to stand for their rubbish.'

Sangeeta and Wahida's statements reflect a growing confidence and awareness amongst young Asian girls about themselves and their situations in a climate of increased racist attacks on black people generally.

Many Asian girls strongly resent being stereotyped as weak, passive, quiet girls, who would not dare lift a finger in their own defence. They want to challenge the idea people have of them as girls 'who do not want to stand out or cause trouble but to tip-toe about hoping nobody will notice them'.[8]

The use of the concept of 'dependency' is also a problem for black feminists. It has been argued that this concept provides the link between the 'material organis-ation of the household, and the ideology of femininity'. How then can we account for situations in which black women may be heads of households, or where, because of an economic system which structures high black male unemployment, they are not financially dependent upon a black man? This condition exists in both colonial and metropolitan situations. Ideologies of black female domesticity and motherhood have been constructed, through their employment (or chattel position) as domestics and surrogate mothers to white families rather than in relation to their own families. West Indian women still migrate to the United States and Canada as domestics and in Britain are seen to be suitable as office cleaners, National Health Service domestics, etc. In colonial situations Asian women have frequently been forced into prostitution to sexually service the white male invaders, whether in the form of armies of occupation or employees and guests of multinational corporations. How then, in view of all this, can it be argued that black male dominance exists in the same forms as white male domi-nance? Systems of slavery, colonialism, imperialism, have systmatically denied positions in the white male hierarchy to black men and have used specific forms of terror to oppress them.

Black family structures have been seen as pathological by the state and are in the process of being constructed as pathological within white feminist theory. Here, ironically, the western nuclear family structure and related ideologies of 'romantic love' formed under capitalism, are seen as more 'progressive' than black family structures. An unquestioned common-sense racism constructs Asian girls and women as having absolutely no freedom, whereas English girls are thought to be in a more 'liberated' society and culture. However, one Asian schoolgirl points out:

Where is the freedom in going to a disco, frightened in case no boy fancies you, or no one asks you to dance, or your friends are walked home with boys and you have to walk home in the dark alone?[9]

The media's 'horror stories' about Asian girls and arranged marriages bear very little relation to their experience. The 'feminist' version of this ideology presents

Asian women as being in need of liberation, not in terms of their own herstory and needs, but *into* the 'progressive' social mores and customs of the metropolitan West. The actual struggles that Asian women are involved in are ignored in favour of applying theories from the point of view of a more 'advanced', more 'progressive' outsider observer. In fact it is very easy for this ideology to be taken up and used by the state in furtherance of their racist and sexist practices. The way in which the issue of arranged marriages has been used by the government to legitimate increased restrictions on immigration from the sub-continent is one example of this process.

Too often concepts of historical progress are invoked by the left and feminists alike, to create a sliding scale of 'civilized liberties'. When barbarous sexual practices are to be described the 'Third World' is placed on display and compared to the 'First World' which is seen as more 'enlightened' or 'progressive'. The metropolitan centres of the west define the questions to be asked of other social systems and, at the same time, provide the measure against which all 'foreign' practices are gauged. In a peculiar combination of Marxism and feminism, capitalism becomes the vehicle for reforms which allow for progress towards the emancipation of women. The 'Third World', on the other hand, is viewed as retaining pre-capitalist forms expressed at the cultural level by traditions which are more oppressive to women. For example, in an article comparing socialist societies, Maxine Molyneux falls straight into this trap of 'Third Worldism' as 'backwardness'.

A second major problem facing Third World post-revolutionary states is the weight of conservative ideologies and practices; this is often subsumed in official literature under the categories of 'traditionalism' or 'feudal residues'. The impact and nature of 'traditionalism' is subject to considerable variation between countries but where it retains any force it may constitute an obstacle to economic and social development which has to be overcome in the formation of a new society. In some societies customary practices tend to bear especially heavily on women. Institutions such as polygyny, the brideprice, child marriages, seclusion, and forms of mutilation such as footbinding or female 'circumcision' are woven into the very fabric of pre-capitalist societies. They often survive in Third World countries long after they have been made illegal and despite the overall changes that have occurred.[10]

Maxine Molyneux sees 'systems of inheritance and arranged marriages' as being one of the central ways 'by which forms of pre-capitalist property and social relations are maintained'.

One immediate problem with this approach is that it is extraordinarily general. The level of generality applied to the 'Third World' would be dismissed as too vague to be informative if applied to western industralized nations. However, Molyneux implies that since 'Third World' women are outside of capitalist relations of production, entering capitalist relations is, necessarily, an emancipating move.

There can be little doubt that on balance the position of women within imperialist, i.e. advanced capitalist societies is, for all its limitations, more advanced than in the less developed capitalist and non-capitalist societies. In this sense the changes brought by imperialism to Third World societies may, in some circumstances, have been historically progressive.[11]

At this point we wish to indicate that the use of such theories reinforces the view that when black women enter Britain they are moving into a more liberated or enlightened or emancipated society than the one from which they have come. Nancy Foner saw the embodiment of West Indian women's increased freedom and liberation in Britain in the fact that they learned to drive cars![12] Different herstories, different struggles of black women against systems that oppress them are buried beneath Eurocentric conceptions of their position. Black family structures are seen as being produced by less advanced economic systems and their extended kinship networks are assumed to be more oppressive to women. The model of the white nuclear family, which rarely applies to black women's situation, is the measure by which they are pathologized and stands as a more progressive structure to the one in which they live.

It can be seen from this brief discussion of the use of the concept 'the family' that the terms 'patriarchy' and 'reproduction' also become more complex in their application. It bears repetition that black men have not held the same patriarchal positions of power that the white males have established. Michèle Barrett argues that the term patriarchy has lost all analytic or explanatory power and has been reduced to a synonym for male dominance. She tries therefore to limit its use to a specific type of male dominance that could be located historically.

I would not . . . want to argue that the concept of patriarchy should be jettisoned. I would favour retaining it for use in contexts where male domination is expressed through the power of the father over women and over younger men. . . . Hence I would argue for a more precise and specific use of the concept of patriarchy, rather than one which expands it to cover all expressions of male domination and thereby attempts to construe a descriptive term as a systematic explanatory theory.[13]

Barrett is not thinking of capitalist social organization. But if we try to apply this more 'classic' and limited definition of patriarchy to the slave systems of the Americas and the Caribbean, we find that even this refined use of the concept cannot adequately account for the fact that both slaves and manumitted males did not have this type of patriarchal power. Alternatively, if we take patriarchy and apply it to various colonial situations it is equally unsatisfactory because it is unable to explain why black males have not enjoyed the benefits of white patriarchy. There are very obvious power structures in both colonial and slave social formations and they are predominantly patriarchal. However, the historically specific forms of racism force us to modify or alter the application of the term 'patriarchy' to black men. Black women have been dominated 'patriarchally' in different ways by men of different 'colours'.

In questioning the application of the concepts of 'the family' and 'patriarchy' we also need to problematize the use of the concept of 'reproduction'. In using this concept in relation to the domestic labour of black women we find that in spite of its apparent simplicity it must be dismantled. What does the concept of reproduction mean in a situation where black women have done domestic labour outside of their own homes in the servicing of white families? In this example they lie outside of the industrial wage relation but in a situation where they are providing for the reproduction of black labour in their own domestic sphere, simultaneously ensuring the reproduction of white labour power in the 'white' household. The concept, in fact, is unable to explain exactly what the relations are that need to be revealed. What needs to be understood is, first, precisely *how* the black woman's role in a rural, industrial or domestic labour force affects the construction of ideologies of black female sexuality which are different from, and often constructed in opposition to, white female sexuality; and second, how this role relates to the black woman's struggle for control over her own sexuality.[14]

If we examine the recent herstory of women in post-war Britain we can see the ways in which the inclusion of black women creates problems for hasty generalization. In pointing to the contradiction between 'home-making as a career' and the campaign to recruit women into the labour force during post-war reconstruction, Elizabeth Wilson fails to perceive migration of black women to Britain as the solution to these contradictory needs. The Economic Survey for 1947 is cited as an example of the ways in which women were seen to form 'the only large reserve of labour left'; yet, as we know, there was a rather large pool of labour in the colonies that had been mobilized previously to fight in the Second World War. The industries that the survey listed as in dire need of labour included those that were filled by both male and female black workers, though Elizabeth Wilson does not differentiate them.

The survey gave a list of the industries and services where labour was most urgently required. The boot and shoe industry, clothing, textiles, iron and steel, all required female workers, as did hospitals, domestic service, transport, and the women's land army. There was also a shortage of shorthand typists, and a dire shortage of nurses and midwives.[15]

This tells us nothing about why black women were recruited more heavily into some of these areas than others; perhaps we are given a clue when the author goes on to point out that women were welcomed into the labour force in a 'circumscribed way',

as temporary workers at a period of crisis, as part-time workers, and as not disturbing the traditional division of labour in industry along sex lines – the Survey reflected the view which was still dominant, that married women would not naturally wish to work.[16]

Not all black women were subject to this process: Afro-Caribbean women, for example, were encouraged and chose to come to Britain precisely to work. Ideologically they were seen as 'naturally' suitable for the lowest paid, most menial jobs. Elizabeth Wilson goes on to explain that 'work and marriage were still understood as alternatives . . . two kinds of women . . . a wife and a mother or a single career woman'. Yet black women bridged this division. They were viewed simultaneously as workers and as wives and mothers. Elizabeth Wilson stresses that the post-war debate over the entry of women into the labour force occurred within the parameters of the question of possible effects on family life. She argues that 'wives and mothers were granted entry into paid work only so long as this did not harm the family'. Yet women from Britain's reserve army of labour in the colonies were recruited into the labour force far beyond any such considerations. Rather than a concern to protect or preserve the black family in Britain, the state reproduced common-sense notions of its inherent pathology: black women were seen to fail as mothers precisely because of their position as workers.

One important struggle, rooted in these different ideological mechanisms, which determine racially differentiated representations of gender, has been the black woman's battle to gain control over her own sexuality in the face of racist experimentation with the contraceptive Depo-Provera and enforced sterilizations.[17]

It is not just our herstory before we came to Britain that has been ignored by white feminists, our experiences and struggles here have also been ignored. These struggles and experiences, because they have been structured by racism, have been different to those of white women. Black feminists decry the non-recognition of the specificities of black women's sexuality and femininity, both in the ways these are constructed and also as they are addressed through practices which oppress black women in a gender-specific but none the less racist way.

This non-recognition is typified by a very interesting article on women in Third World manufacturing by Diane Elson and Ruth Pearson. In analysing the employment of Third World women in world market factories they quote from an investment brochure designed to attract foreign firms:

The manual dexterity of the oriental female is famous the world over. Her hands are small and she works fast with extreme care. Who, therefore, could be better qualified by *nature and inheritance* to contribute to the efficiency of a bench-assembly production line than the oriental girl?[18] (original emphasis)

The authors, however, analyse only the naturalization of gender and ignore the specificity signalled by the inclusion of the adjective 'oriental', as if it didn't matter. The fact that the sexuality of the 'oriental' woman is being differentiated, is not commented upon and remains implicit rather than explicit as in the following remarks.

It is in the context of the subordination of women as a gender that we must analyse the supposed docility, subservience and consequent suitability for tedious, monotonous work of young women in the Third World.[19]

In concentrating an analysis upon gender only, Elson and Pearson do not see the relation between the situation they are examining in the periphery and the women who have migrated to the metropole. This last description is part of the common-sense racism that we have described as being applied to Asian women in Britain to channel them into 'tedious, monotonous work'. Elson and Pearson discuss this ascription of docility and passivity and compare it to Frantz Fanon's analysis of colonized people, without putting together the ways in which the women who are their objects of study have been oppressed not by gender subordination alone but also by colonization. The 'oriental' sexuality referred to in the advertising brochure is one of many constructions of exotic sexual dexterity promised to western male tourists to South East Asia. This ideology of 'Eastern promise' links the material practice of the move from the bench – making micro-chips – to the bed, in which multinational corporate executives are serviced by prostitutes. This transition is described by Elson and Pearson but not understood as a process which illustrates an example of racially demarcated patriarchal power.

If a woman loses her job in a world market factory after she has re-shaped her life on the basis of a wage income, the only way she may have of surviving is by selling her body. There are reports from South Korea, for instance, that many former electronics workers have no alternative but to become prostitutes. . . . A growing market for such services is provided by the way in which the tourist industry has developed, especially in South East Asia.[20]

The photographs accompanying the article are of anonymous black women. This anonymity and the tendency to generalize into meaninglessness, the oppression of an amorphous category called 'Third World women', are symptomatic of the ways in which the specificity of our experiences and oppression are subsumed under inapplicable concepts and theories. Black feminists in the US have complained of the ignorance, in the white women's movement, of black women's lives.

The force that allows white feminist authors to make no reference to racial identity in their books about 'women' that are in actuality about white women, is the same one that would compel any author writing exclusively on black women to refer explicitly to their racial identity. That force is racism. . . . It is the dominant race that can make it seem that their experience is representative.[21]

In Britain too it is as if we don't exist.

There is a growing body of black feminist criticism of white feminist theory and practice, for its incipient racism and lack of relevance to black women's lives.[22] The dialogues that have been attempted[23] have concentrated more upon visible, empirical differences that affect black and white women's lives than upon developing a feminist theoretical approach that would enable a feminist understanding of the basis of these differences. The accusation that racism in the women's movement acted so as to exclude the participation of black women, has led to an explosion of debate in the USA.

from a black female perspective, if white women are denying the existence of black women, writing 'feminist' scholarship as if black women are not a part of the collective group American women, or discriminating against black women, then it matters less that North America was colonised by white patriarchal *men* who institutionalised a racially imperialist social order, than that white women who purport to be feminists support and actively perpetuate anti-black racism.[24]

What little reaction there has been in Britain has been more akin to lighting a damp squib, than an explosion. US black feminist criticism has no more been listened to than indigenous black feminist criticism. Yet, Bell Hooks' powerful critique has considerable relevance to British feminists. White women in the British WLM are extraordinarily reluctant to see themselves in the situations of being oppressors, as they feel that this will be at the expense of concentrating upon being oppressed. Consequently the involvement of British women in imperialism and colonialism is repressed and the benefits that they – as whites – gained from the oppression of black people ignored. Forms of imperialism are simply identified as aspects of an all embracing patriarchy rather than as sets of social relations in which white women hold positions of power by virtue of their 'race'.

Had feminists chosen to make explicit comparisons between . . . the status of black women and white women, it would have been more than obvious that the two groups do not share an identical oppression. It would have been obvious that similarities between the status of women under patriarchy and that of any slave or colonized person do not necessarily exist in a society that is both racially and sexually imperialistic. In such a society, the woman who is seen as inferior because of her sex can also be seen as superior because of her race, even in relationship to men of another race.[25]

The benefits of a white skin did not just apply to a handful of cotton, tea or sugar plantation mistresses; all women in Britain benefited – in varying degrees – from the economic exploitation of the colonies. The pro-imperialist attitudes of many nineteenth- and early twentieth-century feminists and suffragists have yet to be acknowledged for their racist implications. However, apart from this herstorical work, the exploration of contemporary racism within the white feminist movement in Britain has yet to begin.

Feminist theory in Britain is almost wholly Eurocentric and, when it is not ignoring the experience of black women 'at home', it is trundling 'Third World women' on to the stage only to perform as victims of 'barbarous', 'primitive' practices in 'barbarous', 'primitive' societies.

It should be noted that much feminist work suffers from the assumption that it is only through the development of a western-style industrial capitalism and the resultant entry of women into waged labour that the potential for the liberation of women can increase. For example, foot-binding, clitoridectomy, female 'circumcision' and other forms of mutilation of the female body have been described as 'feudal residues', existing in economically 'backward' or 'underdeveloped' nations (i.e. not the industralized west). Arranged marriages, polygamy and these forms of mutilation are linked in reductionist ways to a lack of technological development.

However, theories of 'feudal residues' or of 'traditionalism' cannot explain the appearance of female 'circumcision' and clitoridectomy in the United States at the same moment as the growth and expansion of industrial capital. Between the establishment of industrial capitalism and the transformation to monopoly capitalism, the United States, under the influence of English biological science, saw the control of medical practice shift from the hands of women into the hands of men. This is normally regarded as a 'progressive' technological advance, though this newly established medical science was founded on the control and manipulation of the female body. This was the period in which links were formed between hysteria and hysterectomy in the rationalization of the 'psychology of the ovary'.

In the second half of the [nineteenth] century . . . fumbling experiments with the female interior gave way to the more decisive technique of surgery – aimed increasingly at the control of female personality disorders. . . . The last clitoridectomy we know of in the United States was performed in 1948 on a child of five, as a cure for masturbation.

The most common form of surgical intervention in the female personality was ovariotomy, removal of the ovaries – or 'female castration'. In 1906 a leading gynecological surgeon estimated that there were 150,000 women in the United States who had lost their ovaries under the knife. Some doctors boasted that they had removed from fifteen hundred to two thousands ovaries apiece . . . it should not be imagined that poor women spared the gynecologist's exotic catalog of tortures simply because they couldn't pay. The pioneering work in gynecological surgery had been performed by Marion Sims on black female slaves he kept for the sole purpose of surgical experimentation. He operated on one of them thirty times in four years.[26]

These operations are hardly rituals left over from a pre-capitalist mode of production. On the contrary, they have to be seen as part of the 'technological' advance in what is now commonly regarded as the most 'advanced' capitalist economy in the world. Both in the USA and in Britain, black women still have a 'role' – as in the use of Depo-Provera on them – in medical experimentation. Outside of the metropoles, black women are at the mercy of the multinational drug companies, whose quest for profit is second only to the cause of 'advancing' western science and medical knowledge.

The herstory of black women is interwoven with that of white women but this does not mean that they are the same story. Nor do we need white feminists to write our herstory for us, we can and are doing that for ourselves. However, when they write their herstory and call it the story of women but ignore our lives and deny their relation to us, that is the moment in which they are acting within the relations of racism and writing *his*tory.

Notes and references

1 Jones, Gayle, *Corregidora*, Random House, 1975, pp. 14, 72.

2 Jordan, Winthrop, *White Over Black*, Penguin, 1969, pp. 238, 495, 500.

3 My thanks to Michèle Barrett who, in a talk given at the Social Science Research Council's Unit on Ethnic Relations, helped to clarify many of these attempted parallels.

4 Combahee River Collective, 'A black feminist statement', in Moraga and Anzaldúa (eds), *This Bridge Called My Back: Writings by Radical Women of Colour*, Persephone Press, 1981, p. 213.

5 Barrett, Michèle, *Women's Oppression Today*, Verso, 1980, p. 214.

6 Loewenberg J., and Bogin, R. (eds), *Black Women in Nineteenth Century American Life*, Pennsylvania State University Press, 1978, p. 235.

7 Lawrence, Errol, 'Just plain common sense: the "roots" of racism', in Centre for Contemporary Cultural Studies, *The Empire Strikes Back*, Hutchinson, 1982.

8 Parmar, Pratibha, and Mirza, Nadira, 'Growing angry, growing strong', *Spare Rib*, no. 111, October 1981.

9 Parmar and Mirza, 'Growing angry, growing strong'.

10 Molyneux, Maxine, 'Socialist societies old and new: progress towards women's emancipation?', *Feminist Review*, no. 8, summer 1981, p. 3.

11 Molyneux, 'Socialist societies old and new', p. 4.

12 Foner, Nancy, *Jamaica Farewell*, Routledge and Kegan Paul, 1979. She also argues that:

> In rural Jamaica, most women do not smoke cigarettes; in London, many of the women I interviewed smoked, and when I commented on this they noted that such behaviour would not have been approved in Jamaica. Thus in England there is an enlargement of the women's world (pp. 69–70).

13 Michèle Barrett.

14 See *The Empire Strikes Back*, chapter 7 for an elaboration of this point.

15 Wilson, Elizabeth, *Only Halfway to Paradise: Women in Postwar Britain 1945–1968*, Tavistock, 1980, pp. 43–4.

16 Wilson, *Only Halfway to Paradise*.

17 OWAAD, *Fowaad*, no. 2, 1979.

18 Elson, Diane, and Pearson, Ruth, 'Nimble fingers make cheap workers: an analysis of women's employment in Third World export manufacturing', *Feminist Review*, no. 7, spring 1981, p. 93.

19 Elson and Pearson, 'Nimble fingers make cheap workers', p. 95.

20 Elson and Pearson, 'Nimble fingers make cheap workers'.

21 Hooks, Bell, *Ain't I a Woman*, South End Press, 1981, p. 138.

22 Much of this critical work has been written in America but is applicable to the WLM in Britain. Apart from the books cited in this chapter, interested readers should look out for essays and articles by Gloria Joseph, Audre Lourde, Barbara Smith and Gloria Watkins that represent a range of black feminist thought. In Britain, the very existence of the feminist Organisation of Women of Asian and African Descent (OWAAD) is a concrete expression of black feminists critical distance from 'white' feminism. See also Amos, Valerie and Parmar, Pratibha, 'Resistances and responses: black girls in Britain', in McRobbie, A. and McCabe, T. (eds), *Feminism For Girls: An Adventure Story*, Routledge and Kegan Paul, 1982, (extract in Chapter 15 this volume) who criticize the WLM for its irrelevance to the lives of black girls in Britain.

23 See Joseph, Gloria, and Lewis, Jill, *Common Differences: Conflicts in Black and White Feminist Perspectives*, Anchor, 1981, for an attempt at a dialogue that shows just how difficult it is to maintain.

24 Hooks, Bell, pp. 123–4.

25 Hooks, Bell, p. 141.

26 Erenreich, Barbara, and English, Dierdre, *For Her Own Good*, Doubleday Anchor, 1979.

5   The sociology of women's education as a field of academic study

Sue Middleton

The sociology of women's education may usefully be seen as consisting of three major discourses; liberal (or 'equal rights') feminism, radical feminism, and socialist feminism. Liberal feminism is the discourse of feminists seeking equality with men within capitalist hierarchies; it is the discourse of government, the rhetoric feminists use to influence policy-makers in public bodies. Radical feminism is primarily a method of generating understanding through consciousness-raising (McKinnon, 1982); it has emerged from the radical movements of the 1960s (see Freeman, 1973; Mitchell, 1973), and has been heavily influenced by the phenomenological perspectives in educational theory and sociology. Socialist feminism has emerged from both a dissatisfaction with radical feminism's emphasis on description rather than explanation and a recognition that Marxism did not adequately explain the specific nature of women's oppression under capitalist patriarchy. I shall outline the distinctive features of each of these three perspectives, indicate some major critiques each has contributed to the sociology of education.

Liberal feminism

As a social theory which developed with the breakdown of the feudal system, the rise of the bourgeoisie and the onset of commodity production, liberalism is the legitimating ideology of capitalist free enterprise, emphasizing the rights of the individual to own property and to accumulate wealth. No longer determined by birth, one's position in the social hierarchy is seen as resulting from 'merit' and hard work. Liberal feminists demand the extension of the liberal ideology to women.

Early advocates of liberal feminism, e.g. Mary Wollstonecraft (1792) and John Stuart Mill (1869), argued that the power to reason was humanity's highest achievement and women, like men, must have the right to the fullest cultivation of this faculty through education. Access to education and the attainment of the franchise were major focuses of the 'first wave' of feminism (Banks, 1982; Bunkle, 1980). These early liberal feminists did not challenge the capitalist social formation, but demanded legal, or formal (O'Neill, 1977), equality of opportunity within it.

Contemporary liberal feminists of the 'second wave' take a slightly more radical perspective (Eisenstein, 1981), arguing that mere formal equality is insufficient

Source: Extracted from Middleton, S., 'The sociology of women's education as a field of academic study', *Discourse*, **5** no. 1, 1984, pp. 43–62.

and that without actual, or 'substantive' (O'Neill, 1977) equality, a society cannot claim to have true equality of opportunity. Within contemporary liberal feminist rhetoric, women and girls are seen as disadvantaged by their socialization in that they are conditioned for passivity and subservience (Broverman *et al.*, 1972; Hoffman, 1972; Horner, 1972). For the liberal feminist, true equality of opportunity can be brought about only through the elimination of sex-role stereotypes; this can be achieved through education which changes the attitudes of pupils, teachers, parents and employers. The ideology of femininity termed by Betty Friedan the 'feminine mystique' (Friedan, 1963), is seen as having psychological origins. The liberal feminist perspective questions neither the historical/material basis of these 'stereotypes' nor the hierarchies of capitalist meritocracy. All it seeks, as Bunkle puts it, is 'a slice of the capitalist action without changing its structure. All women's rights wants, and all it will get, is a change in the genitalia of the people at the top' (Bunkle, 1979, part one, p. 27).

Liberal feminist research in the sociology of education falls within what has been termed the 'Normative Paradigm' (Wilson, 1970; Lawton, 1975). Research in this tradition shares at least some of the following three characteristics. First, it adopts as suitable for the social sciences a positivist (usually quantitative) methodology modelled on the natural sciences. Second, it rests on functionalist assumptions about human nature and society: although the explicit sexism of functionalism's 'founding fathers' has been rigorously criticized by feminist sociologists (e.g. Eichler, 1980; Friedan, 1963; Lengermann *et al.*, 1978; Oakley, 1974; Schwendinger and Schwendinger, 1971), liberal feminist research leaves the basic functionalist framework intact in its acceptance of current social structures and its implicitly behaviourist (Wilson, 1970) theory of socialization – women and girls are victims of their stereotyped conditioning for social inferiority. The third characteristic of liberal feminist research in the sociology of education is its theme of inequality, the dominant theme of educational sociology in the 1960s (Young and Whitty, 1977), when researchers had focused on the 'failure' rates of working-class children and children from ethnic minorities. Early liberal feminist sociologists of education adopted this framework with its rhetoric of cultural deprivation, disadvantage, and compensatory education.

The central concerns of this early sociology of women's education have been summarized by Wolpe, who observes that

The literature has primarily chronicled the inequalities within the school itself, and has then set out to account for the divergences in the level of educational attainment of girls as compared to boys and, thereby, to explain their inescapable failure to achieve equality with boys in the higher reaches of the educational system (Wolpe, 1978, p. 291).

In what is probably the most comprehensive contemporary statement of a liberal feminist perspective on women and education, Eileen Byrne views this situation of inequality as a result of 'the stereotyping of expected roles for men and women and the translation of these into curricula. The most pervasive inherited unexamined assumption is the alleged inferiority of women.' Byrne sees a causal link between

the most ordinary school practices and attitudes, organisation and limits, achievements and innovations on the one hand, and girls' later lifetime earnings, mobility of employment, ability to follow further and higher education, the achievement of a good educational base for retraining on the other (Byrne, 1978, p. 34).

Liberal feminist sociologists have investigated the nature of discriminatory career structures (Department of Education, 1982) and practices within schools (Abigail, 1983). The political aims of liberal feminism are the removal of discriminatory practices and policies and the active encouragement of women into management positions and fields of employment non-traditional to their sex ('Girls can do anything'). Much liberal feminist educational research is undertaken to provide information, evidence of inequalities within the education system, to decision-making authorities, and to press for programmes of affirmative action.[1] These measures may, of course, be desirable for feminists of all persuasions – no doubt many socialist and radical feminists also wish to see more women in senior and non-traditional occupations (see Eisenstein, 1981); liberal feminists, however, see a more equitable distribution of the sexes in the current social formation as an end in itself.

Feminists of more radical persuasions have criticized the assumptions on which the liberal paradigm rests. From a radical feminist standpoint, Fenwick notes that

the findings of the Teacher Career and Promotion Study are reported largely within a male framework. The taken-for-granted is the existing hierarchical promotion structure and the data are oriented towards testing how well women and men match up to the 'model career' and investigating the reasons for any deviations . . . the hierarchical nature of the promotion system is not challenged by the research (Fenwick, 1983, pp. 14–15).

Wolpe suggests, from a Marxist position, that educational sociologists abandon the liberal/functionalist framework, since it

can merely give a description of an unequal system of material and status rewards which is said to attach to occupations, but it does not in any way tell us how that system of inequality is itself produced. . . . That is to say, since it does not deal with the conditions of existence of the inequality, it can only concern itself with a redistribution of actors while retaining an unequal system (Wolpe, 1978, p. 307).

For Wolpe and other socialist feminists, such descriptions must be accounted for by a coherent materialist theory of capitalist patriarchy.

Another major focus of criticism of liberal feminist sociology of education is that its explanations rest on psychological assumptions that 'women will cease to underachieve when they discard their attitudes' (Wolpe, 1978, p. 305). Radical critics have commented that in their efforts to measure 'sex-role stereotypes', positivist researchers have failed to account for the 'stereotypes' themselves as cultural constructions. For example, with respect to Maori society, Rose Pere (1983) has shown that at least for the Tuhoe and Ngati Kahungunu tribes (of which she is a member), the passive 'feminine' stereotype of ideal womanhood portrayed in sex-role research did not exist before the coming of the pakeha (European) – she sees it as an import of the missionaries. Margrit Eichler argues that the 'stereotypes' are, in fact, the constructions of the scientists who measure them and suggests that the use of positivist devices such as sex-role stereotyping scales (see Broverman *et al.*, 1972) may be counterproductive in leading, ironically, to the 'reification of sex role stereotypes. The stereotype takes on a life of its own, becomes normative, and empirical reality has been stood on its head' (Eichler, 1980, p. 64). She comments that 'As the scales become widely used and penetrate the media, the sex-role stereotypes that underlie them are enhanced by an aura of scientific credibility. . . . The stereotypes have been reinforced by science' (Eichler, 1980, p. 64).

Despite these major criticisms, it is still essential for feminists to learn to use liberal discourse as a means of influencing policy-makers. The position of women and girls within capitalist hierarchies has improved little and the vehemence of the current right-wing backlash makes it all the more imperative that educationists continue to pressure for the removal of discriminatory practices and the encouragement of women into decision-making positions where they can influence policy.

Radical perspectives

The radical perspectives on women have in common the belief that women are an oppressed (as distinct from the liberal 'disadvantaged') group, and that this oppression is structural – for women's liberation a social revolution is necessary. There are, however, major debates within the radical strands of feminist thought between classical Marxists, radical feminists and socialist feminists. I shall sketch the major differences between these positions, then indicate the contributions of radical feminism and socialist feminism to the sociology of women's education.[2]

A major source of the classical Marxist position on women (Jaggar and Struhl, 1978; Sayers, 1982) is Engels' treatise *The Origin of the Family, Private Property and the State* (1891; 1940 edition). Writing at the same time as Mill, Engels attacked the assumption that women had always been dominated by men. The basis of women's oppression, he argued, lay in the institution of private property. While his liberal contemporaries were arguing for the extension to women of the right to own property, and to protection in law of that right, Engels argued that human (including women's) liberation could only come about when the institution of private property itself was abolished. According to Engels, male-dominance (patriarchy) had come about when men began to accumulate wealth through the domestication of animals. Wishing to ensure that this wealth was passed to their own children, men instituted monogamous marriage to ensure paternity. The liberation of women could be brought about with the entry of women into the paid work-force where, in solidarity with men, they would bring about the socialist revolution. Patriarchy, then, is a product of the capitalist class structure. Contemporary exponents of the classical Marxist position on women have concentrated on women as workers and raised questions concerning the role of domestic labour in the creation of surplus value (see discussions in Foreman, 1977; Guettel, 1974; Hartman, 1981; Novitz, 1982).

In contrast, radical feminists argue that patriarchy is the root cause of women's oppression and that capitalism is a product of patriarchy (Firestone, 1979). As Delmar points out,

It is this approach which marks radical feminism off decisively from Marxism. Revolutions in the sphere of reproduction rather than those in the sphere of production are given primacy; explanations of systems of domination and submission are given by personal and psychological attributes – physical strength and the wish for power (Delmar, 1979, p. 8).

Firestone sees woman's oppression as grounded in her capacity for biological reproduction – other radical feminists have not supported her demand for the technologization of childbearing (e.g. Rich, 1977), but agree that western culture has been split into 'masculine' and 'feminine' modes. For Firestone, 'the aesthetic is the cultural creation of that half of the psychological spectrum that has been assigned to the female, whereas the technological response is the cultural magnific-ation of the male half' (Firestone, 1979, p. 166). Radical feminism as research seeks to describe the experience of 'femininity' under patriarchy; to make visible the 'androcentricity' of the male-dominated academic disciplines, to rediscover lost works by women of the past, and to construct knowledge which expresses the female predicament. Women's oppression is a product of male power.

Socialist feminists are critical of both the classical Marxist and radical feminist positions, and seek to develop an analysis which will both describe and explain the complex interrelationships between capitalism and patriarchy. Engels' thesis is criticized for its failure to explain the original division of labour between men and women – why were the 'herds' a male responsibility? (Foreman, 1977; Sayers, 1982). It is also argued that Engels did not explain the specific nature of women's oppression as *women*; the housewife, for example, serves both the capitalist and her husband:

Patriarchal relations, far from being atavistic leftovers, being rapidly outmoded by capitalism, as the early Marxists suggested, have survived and thrived alongside it.
And since capital and private property do not cause the oppression of women as *women*, their end alone will not result in the end of women's oppression (Hartmann, 1981, p. 5).

While accepting radical feminism's *descriptions* of the psychology, the experience, of oppression as a woman under contemporary patriarchy (e.g. de Beauvoir's notion of 'alterity'), socialist feminists reject its *explanations*, e.g. Firestone's biological materialism is seen as ahistorical in that

it projects male and female characteristics as they appear in the present back into all of history. Radical feminist analysis has greatest strength in its insights into the present.
Its greatest weakness is a focus on the psychological which blinds it to history (Hartmann, 1981, p. 14).

The socialist feminist seeks to understand 'femininity' and 'masculinity' as constructs of capitalism: 'If we examine the characteristics of men as radical feminists describe them – competitive, rationalistic, dominating – they are much like our description of the dominant values of capitalist society' (Hartmann, 1982, 28). The socialist feminist sociology of education seeks to describe and account for the role of schooling in the reproduction of class and gender and to develop an educational praxis, a radical pedagogy.

Radical feminism and the interpretive paradigm
The 'interpretive paradigm' in the sociology of education (Wilson, 1970; Lawton, 1975; Giroux, 1982) is based on a phenomenological view of knowledge as socially

constructed (Berger and Luckmann, 1971) and is concerned with describing the processes of its construction. Rejecting the uncritical acceptance by previous functionalist researchers of the schools' definitions of 'success' and 'failure', researchers in the 'new' sociology of education (Bates, 1978) made problematic what the functionalists had taken for granted; in the words of Michael Young (1971b, p. 2), 'what counts as educational knowledge, and how it is made available, become objects of enquiry'. Within the new perspective, sociologists of education focused on both overt and covert dimensions of school curricula. While sociologists of the curriculum studied the selection and organization of 'school knowledge' (e.g. Bernstein, 1971; Bourdieu, 1971), classroom interaction researchers focused on the social construction of pupil identities in the process of school and classroom interaction (e.g. Nash, 1973; Hargreaves, 1972). 'Knowledge' came to include the everyday, or common-sense, as well as the 'academic'. The culture of the school and its knowledge codes came to be seen as a reflection of that of the white middle class; the rhetoric of 'cultural deprivation' was replaced by the discourse of cultural relativism (Keddie, 1973). The school, not the child, was responsible for 'failure'.

Research in this paradigm has been criticised from a feminist perspective by Sandra Acker (1981), who noted that in Britain, few of the 'new' sociologists had addressed the issue of the *male* bias of school knowledge, and in this they showed themselves blind to the relativism of their own perspectives:

Male researchers clearly have greater access to boys' schools than do women, thus our sociology of schools is about boys' schools and our sociology of youth cultures about boys' youth cultures. Consciousness is just as important. First, one's membership in or identification with a social group shapes one's conception of the problematic. Many of us study aspects of our autobiographies partially diguised as a 'detached' choice of an interesting problem (Acker, 1981, p. 96).

The questions raised within the radical feminist problematic mirror the central concerns of sociology of education within the 'interpretive paradigm' in that the focus of both is on exposing the cultural biases of knowledge and on describing the world from 'within' a particular cultural perspective. Commenting on the work of phenomenologists, Maxine Greene observes that

it is interesting that Berger and Luckmann talk of a 'reality interpreted by *men*', because the constructs normally used for mapping and interpreting the common-sense world are largely those defined by males. It seems evident that, whenever they were developed, the dominant modes of ordering and categorizing experiences of private as well as public life have been functions of largely male perspectives – because in Western culture, males have been the dominant group, the ones in power (Greene, 1978, p. 214).

Radical feminist educational researchers have studied the school as a site for the reproduction of patriarchy; sexist language as control of the 'power of naming' (Spender, 1980), the patriarchal biases of academic subjects (Spender (ed.), 1981b), the social construction of femininity in the process of classroom interaction (Clarricoates, 1978; 1980), the nature of patriarchal power in the academic professions (Bernard, 1973; Spender, 1981b). Feminist historians are writing the history of education (Marks, 1976; Stock, 1978; Tennant, 1977) from a woman's perspective.

Radical feminism is the least clearly articulated of the theoretical perspectives on women and education, its focus being primarily descriptive rather than explanatory. Patriarchy, or male power, is seen as the determinant of women's subordination, but, apart from biologically determinist theories such as Firestone's, the reasons for male dominance remain under-theorized within this perspective. The strength of the position is in its descriptive powers. Radical feminist 'knowledge' is grounded in the *experience* of being oppressed as a woman in a patriarchal society. Through sharing this experience, women come to see what was once seen as a 'personal problem' as a product of oppression, as shared with other women, and as changeable through political action; this process of generating theory from experience is known as consciousness-raising – in feminist terms, 'the personal is political'.

'School knowledge' (both the overt and covert dimensions of curricula) as an artifact of male dominance is seen as oppressive to women. Feminist scholars, therefore, seek to construct new knowledge which is authentic for women – to rediscover and disseminate lost works by women scholars and to organize courses run by women for women (women's studies). Dale Spender expresses the radical feminist position clearly when she observes that

While males control education there is no direct means for women to pass on their understandings. What women know frequently dies with them, until feminists periodically rediscover them and their writing and attempt to reconstruct women's heritage and tradition. Each generation of women forges understandings about subordination, within their own lifetime and from the circumstances of their own lives, but because these meanings do not become the general currency of the culture they are not passed on to the next generation with the result that neither women nor men know about the women who have gone before (Spender, 1983b, p. 18).

Spender herself has restored to contemporary literature the works and deeds of many forgotten women (Spender, 1983a; 1983c).

The radical feminist method of generating theory through consciousness-raising, of seeking to describe and understand the experiences of women under patriarchy, is compatible with the methodologies of the 'interpretive paradigm'. While some radical feminists seek to develop a totally separatist scholarship untainted by 'male' theoretical constructs (Rich, 1976), many feminist sociologists have indicated the compatibility of the 'interpretive' perspectives with a feminist approach to social science, e.g. phenomenology (Green, 1978; Lengermann *et al.*, 1979; Oakley, 1974); ethnomethodology (Stanley and Wise, 1983); symbolic interactionism (Lengermann *et al.*, 1979) and life history analysis (Barrington and Grey, 1981; Middleton, 1983a; Novitz, 1982).

The sociological critiques of the radical feminist perspective in the sociology of education are similar to those made of the 'interpretive paradigm' in general, in that both fail to account adequately for the social realities they describe. Commenting on the phenomenological framework, Sharp and Green note that it

does not enable us to pose the question of why it is that certain institutionalised meanings emerge from practice rather than others or the extent to which the channelling of interpreted meanings is socially structured and related to other significant aspects of social structure (Sharp and Green, 1975, p. 24).

Seeking to develop a theory which will account for, as well as describe the effects of patriarchy, feminist sociologists are increasingly incorporating Marxian analysis into their theorizing; in the sociology of women's education, as in 'mainstream' (male-stream?) sociology of education, the socialist frameworks have become the dominant paradigm.

Socialist feminist perspectives

The major focuses of socialist feminist educational research have been described by Madeleine Arnot (formerly Madeleine MacDonald) (1981, p. 109) as first,

the analysis of the historical and contemporary nature of state ideology and provision of women's education, and . . . second . . . the analysis of the relationship between female education and the 'dual' location of women in the family and the waged labour process.

Examples of studies on the first of these topics are AnnMarie Wolpe's (1976) study of the 'official ideology' of British schooling for girls and Helen Cook's (1983) thesis on the provision of childcare in New Zealand: examples of the second are works by Rosemary Deem (1978), Miriam David (1978), Madeleine MacDonald/Arnot, and Angela McRobbie (1978a; 1978b).

As the dominant paradigm, the socialist feminist framework contains within it a wide variety of positions, to which it is impossible to do justice in a chapter of this scope. Madeleine MacDonald (1980b) has made a useful distinction between theories of social reproduction and theories of cultural reproduction within the socialist feminist sociology of education. Within the first category she includes the structuralist perspectives of Althusser and Bowles and Gintis, both theorists having been substantially critiqued by feminist scholars. In the second category, I shall include studies in the cultural studies perspective, particularly the feminist criticisms of Paul Willis. I shall then indicate some of the major directions being taken by contemporary socialist feminist educational sociologists.

In *Schooling in Capitalist America*, Bowles and Gintis studied the form of the hidden curriculum of the school, which they saw as corresponding structurally to the social relations of capitalist production: 'Specifically, the relationships of authority and control between administrators and teachers, teachers and students, students and students, and students and their work replicate the hierarchical division of labour which dominates the workplace' (Bowles and Gintis, 1976, p. 12). Although Bowles and Gintis recognize some reflection of the sexual division of labour in the social relations of the school, they see this not as a product of the school itself, but as a product of the family; for them, '. . . the family's impact on the reproduction of the sexual division of labour . . . is distinctly greater than that of the education system' (Bowles and Gintis, 1977, p. 143). However, they see the social patterns of the family as differing substantially from those of the workplace in that 'The close personal and emotional relationships of family life are remote from the impersonal bureaucracy of the wage-labour system. Indeed, the family is often esteemed as a refuge from the alienation and psychic poverty of work life' (Bowles and Gintis, 1977, p. 144).

Miriam David comments that their analysis is contradictory and inconsistent in that

they do not provide an understanding of how schools provide different experiences for boys and girls. . . . Yet they argue that the experience of schooling prepares children for the experience of the labour force. The family, on the other hand, cannot achieve this because its ideology is counter to that experience. Given that there is a sexual division of labour in the economy . . . this division has to be reproduced (David, 1978, p. 167).

Because they ignore the school curriculum, and do not see the school as in the business of reproducing gender relations, their analysis is gender-blind, resting on the assumption that 'within the differential forms of schooling catering for different sectors of the wage labour force, both sexes experience on the whole similar conditioning' (MacDonald, 1980b, 17). According to Wolpe 'Their failure to account for the position of women is quite clear. In the final analysis all they do is to ascribe to women a particular position which is determined by their sex' (Wolpe, 1978, p. 301).

Similar criticisms have been made by socialist feminists of Althusser's essay, 'Ideology and ideological state apparatuses' (David, 1978; MacDonald, 1980b), although these and other feminist writers (e.g. Deem, 1978) have found his framework useful. Regarding the school as an Ideological State Apparatus (ISA), Althusser saw its function as reproducing

rules of respect for the sociotechnical division of labour and ultimately the rules of the order established by class domination . . . the reproduction of labour power requires not only a reproduction of its skills, but also, at the same time, a reproduction of its submission to the rules of the established order . . . (Althusser, 1971, p. 132).

While Deem (1978, p. 2) argues that Althusser's analysis applies equally to the reproduction of class and gender relations, MacDonald disagrees, commenting that 'Althusser concentrates upon class domination with no mention of the ways in which patriarchal ideology is transmitted in the school, mediating and contextualising the ruling ideology of class domination within the structures of sexual oppression' (MacDonald, 1980b, p. 19). Like that of Bowles and Gintis, Althusser's analysis is gender-blind. However, observing that his paper is entitled 'Notes towards an investigation', Miriam David finds that in framing the family–education couple as the dominant ISA, Althusser provided a model which is useful for the socialist feminist who can develop it further: '. . . several issues remain unexplored. In particular, the family is presented as a homogeneous entity and is not subject to rigorous analysis. The sexual divisions within the family are not identified' (David, 1978, p. 161). David asserts that, as a site of class struggle, the 'family–education couple' may be more contradictory than Althusser asserts, since

his framework does not pose adequately the nature and form of the link between the family and education. It asserts that parents trust the teachers to instil appropriate values into their children. Parents are not differentiated into mothers and fathers who also have different posts and positions within the socio-economic system, which, moreover, have to be sustained (David, 1978, p. 165).

The socialist feminist sociology of education needs a critical theory of the family (see Poster, 1978). Madeleine Arnot (MacDonald, 1979/80) is drawing on the works of Bourdieu in this enterprise. The insights of radical psychoanalysts (see Burniston *et al.*, 1978; Mitchell, 1974) and socialist psychotherapists such as R.

D. Laing (Laing, 1970; 1976, Collier, 1976) have much to offer researchers in understanding the 'family–education couple' as sites for both the reproduction of class and gender and the struggle for liberation. The incorporation of a critical theory of the family would help rectify the under-emphasis on the forms of oppression specific to women in much Marxist-inspired educational sociology; as Arnot has commented,

In treating these factors as 'secondary', such critiques often attribute to the sexual division of labour a minor role in the formation of social inequalities and identities. Sexual oppression (when not wholly neglected) tends to be subsumed into the broader context of economic exploitation, thus avoiding the need to explain how particular forms of patriarchal relations operate within specific modes of production (Arnot, 1981, p. 142).

Rejecting the determinism of structuralist accounts, many socialist sociologists of education have turned to ethnography[3] to explain 'how subjectivity is actually constituted in schools' (Giroux, 1982, p. 18). Strongly influenced by Gramsci's notion of hegemony, such researchers attempt to describe and account for the cultural practices of groups of oppressed pupils; despite their overt resistance to the authority of the school, 'anti-school' subcultures accept their position as unskilled labour. In this perspective, culture is viewed as

a number of different instances in which power is used unequally to produce different meanings and practices which in the final analysis reproduces a particular kind of society that functions in the interests of a dominant class. Thus it is more appropriate to speak of cultures rather than culture (Giroux, 1982, p. 27).

As Paul Willis puts it (1977, p. 171),

we need to understand how structures become sources of meaning and determinants on behaviour in the cultural milieu *at its own level*. Just because there are structural and economic determinants it does not mean that people will unproblematically obey them.

Willis's study of an 'anti-school' male subculture is of considerable value to the socialist feminist, as he regards patriarchy as a central organizing principle of capitalism. The 'lads' regard women as inferior:

Their most nuanced and complex attitudes are reserved for the opposite sex. There is a traditional conflict in their view of women: they are both sexual objects and domestic comforters. In essence, this means that while women must be sexually attractive, they cannot be sexually experienced (Willis, 1977, p. 43).

The 'lads' identify two 'ideal types' of woman: the girlfriend (or 'missus', modelled on the mother) and the 'easy lay'. The 'lads' identity as manual workers is reinforced by their sense of masculine superiority; inverting the expressed values of the school, they regard 'mental work' as 'sissy' or effeminate. Willis affirms the centrality of patriarchy in the reproduction of capitalist social relations; for,

If the currency of femininity were revalued then that of mental work would have to be too. A member of the counter school culture can only believe in the effeminacy of white collar and office work so long as wives, girlfriends and mothers are regarded as restricted, inferior and incapable of certain things (Willis, 1977, p. 149).

Willis argues the need 'for a dialectical and connected notion of a determinate capitalist patriarchy which transforms and fixes the whole social totality' (Willis, 1977, p. 155). In this, his quest is compatible with that of those socialist feminists who seek to analyse the material base of patriarchy (e.g. Eisenstein, 1982; Hartmann, 1981), although he is critical of the dualism of feminists such as Mitchell (1973; 1974), who regard patriarchy as an ideological phenomenon (Willis, 1977, p. 155).

Feminist critics of cultural studies have commented on its male bias in that if girls are visible at all, '. . . it is through men's eyes as "birds", "scrubbers" or "hangers on" ' (Llewellyn, 1980, p. 42). Angela McRobbie suggests that feminist sociologists of education should 'combine a clear commitment to the analysis of girls' culture with a direct engagement with youth culture as it is constructed in sociological and cultural studies' (McRobbie, 1980, p. 37). She accuses Willis of failing to

integrate these observations on masculinity and patriarchal culture into the context of the working class family. The family is the obverse face of hard, working-class culture, the softer sphere in which fathers, sons and boyfriends expect to be, and are, emotionally serviced. It is this link between the lads' hard outer image and their private experiences – relations with parents, siblings and girlfriends – that still needs to be explored (McRobbie, 1980, p. 41).

Feminist research on working-class girls has shown that their forms of 'resistance' to the authority of the school involve their saturation in the ideology of love and romance (McRobbie, 1978a), a precocious exaggeration of the 'feminine stereotype'. The 'bedroom subculture' of teenage girls (so much more restricted physically than boys) is permeated by the romanticism of capitalist mass media – the ideology of feminine domesticity is daily constructed on the radio (Hobson, 1980), records (Frith and McRobbie, 1978), and through teenage 'love' magazines (McRobbie, 1978a). 'Resistance' is a sham, merely entrenching more deeply these girls' low social class position.

Exploration of the 'family–school couple' is becoming a major focus of the sociology of women's education (David, 1978, 1980; MacDonald, 1979/80; McRobbie, 1980). Approaches such as oral history, or life-history analysis (Novitz, 1982; Middleton, 1983a) have much to offer the sociologist in the analysis of the relationship between the 'cultural capital' transmitted in the family and patterns of school 'success'. If, as Althusser argued, the 'family–school couple' is the dominant site of cultural reproduction, the socialist sociology of women's education must become less 'education bound' (Ahier, 1977, p. 61) and focus on how family and school together reproduce ideologies of class and gender and mediate the contradictions of the wider society.

Conclusion

In this chapter I have attempted to construct a typology of the major theoretical perspectives which underlie research in the sociology of women's education and the thrust of the major critiques which have been made of these perspectives. Like all typologies, it runs the risks of incompleteness and oversimplification.

However, it is offered as a starting point for debates and as material which may be useful as a guide for students new to the field.

Notes

1 The question of how great a degree of 'affirmative action' is consistent with liberal ideology is a matter of continual debate not only in feminist circles, but also within employing bodies such as government departments and universities. A useful philosophical exploration of some of the issues can be found in Vetterling–Braggin (ed.) *Part Four: Equal Opportunity and Preferential Hiring*, 1977.

2 The major focuses of contemporary classical Marxist feminist sociology have been on women as waged and unwaged workers; although feminist sociologists of education draw substantially on Marxist insights (such as the concept of women as a 'reserve army' of labour and the school as reproducing the ideologies of gender which maintain the capitalist social formation) their analysis is primarily socialist feminist in that women's oppression is seen as to some extent independent of capitalism – capitalism's overthrow alone will not liberate women.

3 Although ethnography has been popular with both radical feminist and socialist feminist researchers, there is a difference in emphasis between the two perspectives. While radical feminist ethnographers, like their phenomenological counterparts in 'mainstream' sociology, may leave their analysis at the descriptive level, or account for it by reference to some vague concept of 'patriarchy', socialist ethnographies focus on the interconnections between lived cultures and their determinant structural forces. In the words of Paul Willis (1978, p. 193) in such an analysis society is viewed not as 'a series of disconnected individuals living out their own particular lives but as a structured whole within which individuals and groups live under differing degrees of domination, expressing *and reproducing* in different degrees through symbolic patterns and cultural practices a sense of *positionality* within and perhaps resistance to the hidden, misunderstood or unseen overarching structures which limit their field of choices and help to constitute them in the first place'. (Willis's emphases)

References

Acker, S., 'No-woman's-land: British sociology of education, 1960–1979', *Sociological Review*, **29**, no. 1, 1981, pp. 77–104.

Ahier, J. 'Philosophers, sociologists and knowledge in education', in M. F. D. Young *et al.* (eds), *Society, State and Schooling*, Ringmer, The Falmer Press, 1977.

Althusser, L., 'Ideology and ideological state apparatusses', in *Lenin and Philosophy*, London, Monthly Review Press, 1971, pp. 127–86.

Arnot, M., 'Culture and political economy: dual perspectives in the sociology of women's education', *Educational Analysis*, **3**, no. 1, 1981, pp. 97–116.

Arnot, M., 'Male hegemony, social class and women's education', *Journal of Education*, **164**, 1, 1982, pp. 64–89.

Banks, O., *Faces of Feminism*, Oxford, Martin Robinson, 1981.

Barrington, R. and Grey, A., *The Smith Women*, Reed, 1981.

Barton, L. *et al.*, (eds), *Schooling, Ideology and the Curriculum*, Barcombe, The Falmer Press, 1980.

Bates, R., 'The new sociology of education: directions for theory and research', *New Zealand Journal of Education Studies*, **13**, no. 1, 1978, pp. 3–22.

Berger, P. and Luckmann, T., *The Social Construction of Reality*, Harmondsworth, Penguin, 1971.

Bernard, J., 'My four revolutions: an autobiographical history of the A.S.A.', in J. Huber (ed.), *Changing Women in a Changing Society*, University of Chicago Press, 1973.

Bernstein, B., 'On the classification and framing of educational knowledge', in M. F. D. Young (ed.), *Knowledge and Control*, London, Collier-Macmillan, 1971, pp. 47–69.

Bourdieu, P. 'Intellectual field and creative project', in M. F. D. Young (ed.), *Knowledge and Control*, 1971.

Bowles, D. and Gintis, S., *Schooling in Capitalist America*, New York, Basic Books, 1976.

Boverman, I. K., *et al.*, 'Sex-role stereotypes: a current appraisal', *Journal of Social Issues*, **28**, no. 2, 1972, pp. 59–78.

Bunkle, P., 'A history of the women's movement', in five consecutive issues of *Broadsheet*, September 1979, pp. 24–8; October 1979, pp. 26–8; November 1979, pp. 26–8, December 1979, pp. 28–32, January/February 1980, pp. 30–5.

Bunkle, P., 'The origins of the women's movement in New Zealand: The Women's Christian Temperance Union 1885–1895', P. Bunkle and B. Hughes (eds.), *Women in New Zealand Society*, Auckland, Allen Unwin, 1980.

Burniston, S., *et al.*, 'Psychoanalysis and the cultural acquisition of sexuality and subjectivity', in Women's Studies Group, *Women Take Issue*, London, Hutchinson, 1978, pp. 109–31.

Byrne, E., *Women and Education*, London, Tavistock, 1978.

Clarricoates, K., 'Dinosaurs in the classroom: a re-examination of some aspects of the "hidden curriculum" in primary schools', *Women's Studies International Quarterly*, **1**, no. 4, 1978, pp. 353–64.

Clarricoates, K., 'The importance of being Ernest . . . Emma . . . Tom . . . Jane. The perception and organisation of gender conformity and gender deviation in primary schools', in R. Deem (ed.), *Women and Schooling*, pp. 26–41.

Collier, A., *R. D. Laing: The Philosophy and Politics of Psychotherapy*, New York, Pantheon, 1977.

Cook, H., *The Politics of Child Care: An Analysis of Growth and Constraint*, M A Thesis, Victoria University of Wellington, 1983.

David, M., 'The family–education couple: towards an analysis of the William Tyndale Dispute', in G. Littlejohn *et al.*, *Power and the State*, London, Croom Helm, 1978, pp. 159–95.

David M., *The State, the Family and Education*, London, Routledge & Kegan Paul, 1980.

de Beauvoir, S., *The Second Sex*, Harmondsworth, Penguin, 1959; 1971 edition.

Deem, R. (ed.), *Schooling for Women's Work*, London, Routledge & Kegan Paul, 1980.

Deem, R., *Women and Schooling*, London, Routledge & Kegan Paul, 1978.

Delmar, R., 'Introduction' to S. Firestone, *The Dialectics of Sex*, London, The Women's Press, 1979, pp. 1–10.

Eichler, M., *The Double Standard: a Feminist Critique of Feminist Social Science*, London, Croom Helm, 1980.

Eisenstein, Z., *The Radical Future of Liberal Feminism*, New York, Longman, 1981.

Eisenstein, Z., 'The sexual politics of the New Right – understanding the "crisis of liberalism" for the 1980s', in N. Keohane *et al.*, *Feminist Theory*, Chicago, Harvester, 1982.

Engels, F., *The Origin of the Family, Private Property and the State*, Sydney, Current Books, 1940 edition, 1891.

Fenwick, P., 'Feminist research and research on women: the response of the state', paper presented to the sixth conference of the New Zealand Women's Studies Association, Christchurch, August 1983.

Firestone, S., *The Dialectics of Sex*, London, The Women's Press, 1979.

Foreman, A., *Femininity as Alienation: Women and the Family in Marxism and Psychoanalysis*, London, Pluto, 1977.

Freeman, J., 'The origins of the Women's Liberation Movement', in J. Huber (ed.), *Changing Women in a Changing Society*, University of Chicago Press, 1973.

Friedan, B., *The Feminine Mystique*, Harmondsworth, Penguin, 1963.

Frith, S. and McRobbie, A., 'Rock and sexuality', *Screen Education*, **29**, winter 1978, pp. 97–109.

Giroux, H., *Critical Theory and Educational Practice*, Victoria, Deakin University Press, 1983a.

Gramsci, A., *Selections from the Prison Notebooks*, Q. Hoare and L. Smith, (eds), London, Lawrence and Wishart, 1971.

Greene, M., *Landscapes of Learning*, New York, Teachers College Press, 1978.

Guettel, C., *Marxism and Feminism*, Toronto, Canadian Women's Educational Press, 1974.

Hall, S., (ed.), *Culture, Media, Language*, Hutchinson for Centre for Contemporary Cultural Studies, 1980.

Hargreaves, D., *Interpersonal Relations and Education*, London, Routledge & Kegan Paul, 1972.

Hartmann, H. C., 'The unhappy marriage of Marxism and feminism: towards a more progressive union', L. Sargent (ed.), *Women and Revolution*, Boston, South End, 1981.

Hobson, D., 'Housewives and the mass media', in S. Hall (ed.), *Culture, Media, Language*, 1980, pp. 105–14.

Hoffman, L. W., 'Early childhood experiences and women's achievement motives', *Journal of Social Issues*, **28** no. 2, 1972, pp. 129–55.

Horner, M., 'Towards an understanding of achievement – related conflicts in women', *Journal of Social Issues*, **28**, no. 2, 1972, pp. 157–75.

Huber, J. (ed.), *Changing Women in a Changing Society*, University of Chicago Press, 1973.

Jaggar, A. and Struhl, P., *Feminist Frameworks*, New York, McGraw Hill, 1978.

Keddie, N., *Tinker Tailor: The Myth of Cultural Deprivation*, Harmondsworth, Penguin, 1973.

Keohane, N. *et al.* (ed.), *Feminist Theory: a Critique of Ideology*, Chicago, Harvester, 1982.

Kuhn, A. and Wolpe, A. M. (eds), *Feminism and Materialism*, London, Routledge & Kegan Paul, 1978.

Kuhn, T. S., *The Structure of Scientific Revolutions*, University of Chicago Press, 1962.

Laing, R. D., *Sanity, Madness and the Family*, Harmondsworth, Penguin, 1970.

Laing, R. D., *The Politics of the Family*, Harmondsworth, Penguin, 1971.

Lawton, D., *Class, Culture and the Curriculum*, London, Routledge & Kegan Paul, 1975.

Lengermann, P. M., *et al.*, 'Sociological theory in teaching sex roles: Marxism, functionalism and phenomenology', *Women's Studies International Quarterly*, **1**, 1978, pp. 275–385.

Llewellyn, M., 'Studying girls at school: the implications of confusion', in R. Deem (ed.), *Schooling for Women's Work*, London, Routledge & Kegan Paul, 1980.

MacDonald, M., 'Cultural reproduction: The Pedagogy of Sexuality', *Screen Education*, Autumn/Winter, 1979/80, pp. 141–53.

MacDonald, M., 'Schooling and the reproduction of class and gender', in L. Barton *et al.*, (eds), *Schooling, Ideology and the Curriculum*, Boscombe, Falmer Press, 1980a.

MacDonald, M., 'Sociocultural reproduction and women's education', R. Deem (ed.), *Schooling for Women's Work*, London, Routledge & Kegan Paul, 1980b.

MacKinnon, C. A., 'Feminism, Marxism, method and the state: agenda for theory', N. Keohane *et al.*, pp. 1–30.

McRobbie, A., *Jackie: an Ideology of Adolescent Femininity*, CCCS Stencilled Occasional Paper, no. 53 Birmingham Centre for Contemporary Cultural Studies, 1978a.

McRobbie, A., 'Settling accounts with subcultures: a feminist critique', *Screen Education*, no. 34, 1980, pp. 37–49.

Marks, P. 'Femininity in the classroom: an account of changing attitudes', in A. Oakley and J. Mitchell (eds), *The Rights and Wrongs of Women*, Harmondsworth, Penguin, 1976.

Marx, K., *Capital*, vol. 1, 1867, Harmondsworth, Penguin (1976 edition).

Middleton, S., 'On being a feminist educationalist doing research on being a feminist educationist. . . . Reflections on life history analysis as feminist research methodology', Conference Paper, Australian Association for Research in Education, Canberra, November 1983.

Mill, J. S., *On Liberty, Representative Government, the Subjection of Women: Three Essays*, London, Oxford University Press, 1948 edition, 1869.

Mitchell, Juliet, *Psychoanalysis and Feminism*, New York, Pantheon, 1974.

Mitchell, Juliet, *Women's Estate*, Harmondsworth, Penguin, 1973.

Nash, R., *Classroom Observed*, London, Routledge & Kegan Paul, 1973.

Novitz, R., 'Feminism', in P. Spoonley *et al.* (eds), *New Zealand*, Palmerston North, Dunmore, pp. 293–323.

Oakley, A., *The Sociology of Housework*, London, Martin Robinson, 1974.

O'Brien, M., 'Feminist theory and dialectical logic', in N. Keohane *et al.*, *Feminist Theory*, Chicago, Harvester, pp. 59–112.

O'Neill, O., 'How do we know when opportunities are equal?', in M. Vetterling–Braggin (ed.), *Feminism and Philosophy*, Totowa, Littlefield Adams, 1977, pp. 177–89.

Pere, R., 'Ako: concepts and learning in the Maori tradition', Department of Sociology, University of Waikato, 1983.

Poster, M., *Critical Theory of the Family*, New York, Pluto, 1978.

Rich, A., *Of Woman Born*, New York, Bantam, 1977.

Rich, A., 'Towards a woman-centred university', *On Lies, Secrets, Silence: Selected Prose*, New York, Norton, 1979, pp. 125–55.

Sayers, J., *Biological Politics*, London, Tavistock, 1982.

Schwendinger, J. and Schwendinger, H., 'Sociology's founding fathers: Sexist to a man', *Journal of Marriage and the Family*, November 1971 pp. 359–74.

Sharp, R. and Green, A., *Education and Social Control*, London, Routledge & Kegan Paul, 1975.

Smith, A., 'The family, school and sex-roles', in G. Robinson and R. O'Rourke, *Schools in New Zealand Society*, Auckland, Longman Paul, 1980.

Smith, D., 'Women's perspective as a radical critique of sociology', *Sociological Inquiry*, **44**, 1, 1974, pp. 7–13.

Spender, D., *Man Made Language*, London, Routledge & Kegan Paul, 1980.

Spender, D., 'Education: the patriarchal paradigm and the response to feminism', in D. Spender (ed.), *Men's Studies Modified*, Pergammon, 1981a.

Spender, D. (ed.), *Men's Studies Modified: the Impact of Feminism on the Academic Disciplines*, Oxford, Pergammon, 1981b.

Spender, D., (ed.), *Feminist Theorists*, London, The Women's Press, 1983a.

Spender, D., *Invisible Woman: The Schooling Scandal*, London, Writers and Readers Cooperative, 1983b.

Spender, D., *There's Always been a Woman's Movement this Century*, London, Routledge & Kegan Paul, 1983c.

Spoonley, P., *et al.* (eds), *New Zealand: Sociological Perspectives*, Palmerston North, Dunmore, 1982.

Stanley, L. and Wise, S., *Breaking Out: Feminist Consciousness and Feminist Research*, London, Routledge & Kegan Paul, 1983.

Stock, P., *Better Than Rubies: A History of Women's Education*, New York, Capricorn, 1978.

Tennant, M., 'Natural directions: the New Zealand movement for sexual differentiation in the twentieth century', *New Zealand Journal of Educational Studies*, **12**, no. 2, 1979, pp. 142–53.

Willis, P., *Learning to Labour*, Westmead, Saxon House, 1977.

Willis, P., *Profane Culture*, London, Routledge & Kegan Paul, 1978.

Wilson, T., 'Normative and interpretative paradigms in sociology', in J. Douglas, (ed.) *Understanding Everyday Life*, Chicago, Aldine, 1970, pp. 57–79.

Wollstonecraft, M., *A Vindication of the Rights of Women*, Harmondsworth, Penguin, 1972 (1975 edition).

Wolpe, A. M., 'Education and the sexual division of labour', in A. Kuhn and A. M. Wolpe, (eds), *Feminism and Materialism*, pp. 290–328.

Wolpe, A. M., 'The official ideology of education for girls', in M. Flude and J. Ahier (eds), *Educability, Schools and Ideology*, London, Croom Helm, 1976.

Women's Studies Group, *Women Take Issue*, Centre for Contemporary Cultural Studies, London, Hutchinson, 1978.

Young, M. F. D., 'An approach to the study of curricula as socially organised knowledge', in M. Young (ed.), *Knowledge and Control*, London, Collier-Macmillan, 1971a, pp. 19–46.

Young, M. F. D., *Knowledge and Control*, London, Collier-Macmillan, 1971b.

Part Two

Equality of Opportunity: Defining the Issues

6 Sex differences in achievement orientations

Barbara G. Licht and Carol S. Dweck

A large body of recent literature has examined children's beliefs about their performance in situations of intellectual achievement. One of the most intriguing findings is that girls, relative to boys, have less confidence in their ability to succeed in challenging intellectual tasks. This pattern emerges during the pre-school and early school years despite the fact that girls consistently perform as well as, if not better than, boys during these years across a variety of achievement domains. Girls' lower level of confidence is of great interest not only because it seems unrealistic, but because it appears to have a detrimental effect in the long run on girls' intellectual accomplishments. In this chapter we examine children's achievement-related beliefs which seem to affect their intellectual performance; the nature and origins of sex differences in these beliefs; and the ways in which an understanding of these variables can help us explain some known patterns of sex differences in achievement that emerge in the later school years.

Sex differences in achievement-related beliefs and behaviours

A number of studies have examined how children view the causes of the difficulties[1] they experience in achievement situations (i.e., causal attributions for failures). It has been found that children's causal attributions are among the best predictors of how they will perform in the face of failure. When confronted with difficulty, children who attribute their failures to variable or controllable factors (in particular, insufficient effort) are more likely than other children to maintain high expectations for future successes (Diener and Dweck, 1980; McMahan, 1973; Nicholls, 1975; Weiner et al., 1971; Weiner et al., 1976; Jackaway, 1975). They are more likely to respond with increased effort and, consequently, they may be prompted to show higher levels of problem-solving as a result of confronting failure (Diener and Dweck, 1978, 1980; Dweck, 1975; Dweck and Bush, 1976; Dweck and Reppucci, 1973; Weiner, 1972, 1974; Weiner et al., 1971; Licht and Dweck, 1982). In contrast, children who attribute their failures to factors that are stable and beyond their control (particularly insufficient ability) tend, in the face of difficulty, to lower their expectations for future successes; and they are less likely than other children to increase their efforts in order to meet such challenges. In fact, they may respond with a deterioration of effort and performance so

Source: Extracted from Licht, B. G. and Dweck, C. S., 'Sex differences in achievement orientations', in Marland, M. (ed.) *Sex Differentiation and Schooling*, London, Heinemann, 1983, pp. 72–84 and 93–7.

marked that they are unable to solve virtually the same problems they had solved with ease prior to confronting difficulty. These children have been called 'learned helpless' since their causal attributions imply that the termination of failure is beyond their control (see Dweck and Reppucci, 1973; Seligman and Maier, 1967). The term 'helpless' in this context, however, does not imply that these children are actually facing an uncontrollable failure, but rather that they appear to believe they are.

Several investigators have tried to alter the way that helpless children respond to failure by altering their causal attributions for failure. They have directly taught children to attribute their failures to insufficient effort in order to determine whether the children would then maintain or even increase their efforts when confronted with difficulty. The success of these procedures (Andrews and Debus, 1978; Chapin and Dyck, 1976; Dweck, 1975; Fowler and Peterson, 1981; Schunk, 1982) is important, not only because of its clinical/educational implications, but also because it demonstrates that children's beliefs about their achievements are more than just predictors or reflections of their achievement behaviours – they can actually be among the *causes*.

As suggested as the outset, girls are more likely than boys to show the helpless pattern of achievement-related beliefs and behaviours. Girls are more likely than boys to attribute their failures to ability, while boys are more likely to view their difficulties as stemming from insufficient effort (Dweck and Bush, 1976; Dweck and Reppucci, 1973; Nicholls, 1975; Licht and Shapiro, 1982; Nicholls, 1978a). Boys are also more likely than girls to blame the evaluator (for example, the teacher's unfairness or fussiness) for their difficulties (Dweck and Bush, 1976; Licht and Shapiro, 1982). While this attribution may result in lower expectations and efforts in the current situation (as long as that teacher or evaluator is in charge), it still allows a boy to maintain confidence in his intellectual abilities. Thus, when the evaluator is no longer present, the child should respond with renewed hope of success (Dweck, Goetz and Strauss, 1980).

While girls are more likely than boys to use ability as an explanation for failure, they are less likely than boys to use ability as an explanation for their successes. They show instead a stronger tendency than boys to view their successes as due to factors such as luck, which imply some uncertainty about their ability to succeed in the future – particularly if the tasks are expected to become more difficult (Nicholls, 1975, 1976b; Licht and Shapiro, 1982; Nicholls, 1978a).

Consistent sex differences also emerge when investigators ask children to indicate how well they expect to do on novel achievement tasks that the children are about to undertake. In this setting, girls tend to underestimate their chances for success – given their level of past achievements and given the performances that they subsequently display. In contrast, the expectations of boys are inclined to be overestimates (Crandall, 1969; Montanelli and Hill, 1969; Parsons *et al.*, 1976; Jackaway, 1975; see also Lenney, 1977 and Maccoby and Jacklin, 1974 for reviews). This sex difference can also be found when children are asked to predict future academic performances (Battle, 1966; Crandall, 1969; Dweck *et al.*, 1980; Heller and Parsons, 1981; Parsons *et al.*, 1982), despite girls' history of superior grades during elementary school (Dweck *et al.*, 1980; McCandless *et al.*, 1972; see also Maccoby and Jacklin, 1974 for review).

Not only do girls hold lower expectations of success for themselves when they enter a new situation than do boys, but girls' expectancies are also more likely to deteriorate when encountering difficulty or heightened evaluative pressure (Dweck, Goetz and Strauss, 1980; Dweck and Gilliard, 1975; Nicholls, 1975); and girls' expectations are less likely to recover again even when the situation changes substantially. Dweck *et al.* (1980) found that after encountering failure (which lowered the expectations of both sexes), a change in the evaluator resulted in a greater recovery of expectations for boys than for girls (predicted on the basis of boys' greater tendency to blame the evaluator); and a change in both the task and the evaluator resulted in a return of boys' expectations to their pre-failure levels. Girls, however, failed to show such a complete recovery. As the authors suggested, it may be that when girls blame their ability for their failures, the ability that they condemn is not specific to any one task. Rather they may be blaming a more general ability which would lead them to view a failure on a particular task as an indication that they will encounter difficulty across a variety of achievement situations.

It is not only the case that girls and boys may provide different explanations and draw different implications from their successes and failures, but there is also some data to suggest that the sexes may differ in how they evaluate their performance in the first place. Parsons *et al.* (1976), for example, report a study where girls rated their performance on a concept identification task more poorly than boys did, despite the fact that the girls had actually performed better.[2]

In view of these sex differences in children's achievement-related beliefs, it is not surprising to find sex differences in the tasks children seek and in how they respond to the challenges they confront in intellectual achievement situations. Boys are more likely than girls to choose difficult tasks over easy ones both in the laboratory and in a naturalistic free-play setting (Butterfield, 1965; Crandall and Rabson, 1960; Molnar and Weisz, 1981; Nicholls, 1978b; Veroff, 1969); and once they have chosen to begin a difficult task, they are more likely than girls to persist until it is successfully completed (Molnar and Weisz, 1981). Girls, in contrast, are more likely to avoid those situations that hold the threat of failure. Furthermore, in situations where children do not have the option of choosing the tasks they wish to work on, boys are more likely to meet difficult tasks and evaluative pressures with an escalation of effort, while girls sometimes show lower achievement efforts in difficult and evaluative situations than in situations where success is more assured (Dweck and Bush, 1976; Dweck and Gilliard, 1975; Harter, 1975; Nicholls, 1975).[3]

While girls' response to failure and evaluative pressure may seem unreasonable given the evidence of their ability (high grades, etc.), it is quite consonant with their causal attributions. However, given the evidence of girls' actual ability, it is reasonable to ask how they come to attribute failures to low ability.

The origins of sex differences in children's achievement-related beliefs and behaviours

As suggested earlier, sex differences among children in the confidence with which they approach challenging situations of intellectual achievement is particularly intriguing since it emerges at an age when girls and boys do not seem to differ in terms of their relevant reinforcement histories. If anything, girls should come to expect greater academic achievements, since in the primary years they receive consistently higher grades. A number of explanations have been offered to account for this apparent irrationality.

It has been suggested that the sex difference in children's confidence may not be 'real' at all, and that it may reflect no more than the attempts of both sexes to present themselves in a socially desirable light (Hill and Sarason, 1966; Sarason *et al.*, 1960; see also Crandall, 1969, and Lenney, 1977, for discussion). That is, girls may be responding in a way that makes them appear modest because modesty is in line with society's stereotype of what females should be. Boys, in turn, may be responding in a highly confident manner because self-confidence is consistent with society's masculine stereotype (see Bem, 1974, for description of stereotypes).

While there may be some truth in this argument, it cannot adequately account for the large body of research that demonstrates girls' lesser confidence in their intellectual abilities. First, as Lenney (1977) points out, in several studies, assessments of expectations and other achievement-related beliefs were solicited with procedures that provided anonymity to the respondents. Thus, there should have been little motivation for those subjects to present themselves in a socially desirable fashion (that is, in accordance with sex-role stereotypes). Crandall (1969) also examined the plausibility of the social desirability hypothesis. She reasoned that if socially desirable responding were an important influence in these studies, then children who were most strongly motivated to present themselves in a socially desirable light should also be the most likely to state expectations in the manner that was 'appropriate' for their own sex. She found, however, no relationship within either sex between the tendency to present oneself in a socially desirable light and the degree to which one responded in a sex-appropriate manner. Thus, the sex differences outlined above appear to be quite 'real'.

Many of those who accept girls' lower level of confidence as a 'real' phenomenon also invoke sex-role stereotyping explanations. It has been proposed, for example, that the parents of girls generally reinforce dependency and insecurity while parents generally reinforce their sons for being independent and self-confident (Hoffman, 1972). However, there has been little positive support for such differential treatment of young boys and girls (see Maccoby and Jacklin, 1974 for review). Furthermore, even if this differential upbringing does occur to some degree, it cannot fully account for the particular pattern of sex differences that occurs. Specifically, Dweck and Bush (1976) found that the sex difference in helplessness varied as a function of who was evaluating the children's performances. Girls showed the helpless pattern of attributions and performance primarily when the evaluator was an adult female. In fact, when the evaluator was perceived to be a peer – particularly one of the same sex – the pattern of sex differences was actually reversed. That is, boys showed greater helplessness than girls. If boys were generally socialized to be confident about certain abilities and girls were generally socialized to be insecure about theirs, girls should have responded more helplessly than boys regardless of who was providing the evaluation. That this was clearly not the case suggests instead that if one wishes to understand why girls respond in a 'helpless' fashion to situations of intellectual achievement with adult female evaluators, the most fruitful approach would be to examine the kinds of interactions children have had in that very situation. In the elementary school years, most evaluations for intellectual performances are given by the teacher, who in most cases will be female.

It has been suggested that the differential expectations that teachers hold for boys and girls may have an impact on their differential levels of confidence (Fox, 1976a). While research supports the view that teachers' expectations can have an impact on children's performances (see Brophy and Good, 1974, for review), it has not been demonstrated that elementary-school teachers hold lower expectations for girls. In fact, in the elementary school years, teachers often hold girls in higher esteem. They rate girls more highly than boys on almost every conceivable dimension, including their effectiveness as learners (Coopersmith, 1967; Digman, 1963; Stevenson *et al.*, 1968). Furthermore, children of both sexes accurately perceive the teachers' more favourable view of girls (Dweck and Goetz, 1977). It is unlikely therefore that elementary-school teachers foster lower levels of confidence in girls by directly communicating lower expectations for them. Further support for this argument is provided by a study reported in Parsons *et al.* (1976) where children were asked to give their expectations of their future performances on a series of tasks as well as their perceptions of how other people – their teacher, parents, and best friend – would expect them to perform. There were no differences between girls and boys in their perceptions of what significant others would expect from them. Girls and boys differed markedly, however, in how their own expectations corresponded to their perceptions of what others would expect. For boys there was a very strong correspondence between these two sets of expectations. For girls, their own expectations were related only to the expectations they felt their teachers would hold for them, and even here this relationship was considerably weaker for girls than it was for boys (for boys, $r = \cdot90$; for girls $r = \cdot53$). It is clear that, at least in the elementary school years, girls and boys do not develop different expectations because they believe that significant others have different expectations of them. Rather, girls and boys appear to differ in how they interpret or incorporate the expectations that others may have for them.[4]

Another explanation for the sex differences described above was proposed by Crandall (1969). In view of the fact that girls do not receive more negative evaluations of their abilities, she suggested that girls were more *sensitive* to the negative feedback they did receive, while boys were more sensitive to the positive. Indeed the attributions children make for their successes and failures (at least when it is delivered by adult female evaluators) are clearly in line with this. As discussed above, girls are inclined to see their failures as indicative of their abilities; therefore, it is their failures that will be viewed as predictive of future outcomes. Since girls are less likely to view their successes as predictive of future performances, they should pay less attention to their successes than to their failures. For boys, the situation is reversed – it is their successes that are viewed as informative.

In order to examine some of the factors that might lead girls to see their failures as indicative of ability and boys to view their successes as indicative of theirs, Dweck *et al.* (1978) examined teacher–student interactions in fourth- and fifth-grade classrooms. The observers coded every instance of evaluative feedback in terms of the sex of the child receiving the feedback, whether the feedback was positive or negative, and to what the feedback referred. Feedback could either refer to the child's schoolwork or to the child's conduct (for example, 'get back to your seat'; 'you're sitting so nicely and quietly'). Work-related feedback was further categorized into feedback that referred to the intellectual quality of the child's work (for example, 'your answer is wrong'; 'your ideas are good') versus feedback that referred to non-intellectual aspects of the child's work (for example, 'you didn't skip lines'; 'your paper was neat').

Several aspects of the teachers' evaluations were expected to affect the way in which children would interpret this feedback; and the Dweck *et al.* (1978) investigation examined whether the evaluations given to boys versus girls differed along these dimensions. It was predicted that the overall positive or negative quality of the teacher–student interaction would affect the child's interpretation of negative evaluations. That is, if a teacher were generally critical of certain children, these children might, over time, come to attribute their low marks to the teacher's overall negative attitude toward them rather than to the actual quality of their work (see Enzle *et al.*, 1975; Kelley, 1971). It was also expected that children would be less likely to view negative evaluations (for example, a low grade) as indications of intellectual inadequacies if the negative feedback they received in class referred largely to non-intellectual aspects of their school work (Cairns, 1970; Eisenberger *et al.*, 1974; Warren and Cairns, 1972). In contrast, a negative evaluation would more readily be viewed as an indication of low ability if in the past the criticisms received referred exclusively to the intellectual quality of the child's work. Finally, children's causal attributions should be affected by any explicit attributions that the teachers made for the children's failures.

Parallel predictions could be made regarding how children come to interpret success feedback. If a teacher has been generally positive toward certain children and has in the past praised them for non-intellectual matters, then a high grade may be attributed to factors that do not reflect on the children's intellectual competence (for example, favourable attitude of the teacher, one's neatness). In contrast, when a child receives a positive evaluation from a teacher who has in the past been generally negative and who has given little praise for non-intellectual matters, the positive evaluation is more likely to be viewed as a reflection of the intellectual quality of the child's work.

Thus, boys' tendency to discount their failures as indications of their abilities and girls' tendency to discount their successes would be understandable if first, teachers were generally more negative towards boys (see also Brophy and Good, 1974); second, a substantial proportion of the criticisms directed toward boys, but not toward girls, referred to conduct and non-intellectual aspects of their work; and third, the teacher explicitly attributed boys' failures to factors other than ability (for example, lack of effort). This is indeed what was found. While the amount of positive and negative feedback that was directed at the *intellectual* quality of the children's work was virtually equivalent for the two sexes, there were striking differences in the receipt of negative feedback for non-intellectual matters. Boys received far more criticism than girls for their conduct and for the non-intellectual aspects of their work. In fact, of all the negative feedback boys received in the classroom, nearly two-thirds was directed at non-intellectual matters. Even if one looks only at the feedback directed towards the children's work, nearly half (45 per cent) of the work-related criticism boys received referred to aspects of their performance that could not reflect on their intellect (for example, neatness). The girls, however, received relatively little criticism for non-intellectual matters. Thus, the proportion of all negative evaluation that was related to the intellectual quality of their work was extremely high (nearly 90 per cent). Further, while teachers only infrequently made explicit attributions for children's failures, they were eight times more likely to attribute a boy's failure to insufficient effort than they were a girl's. The sex differences in the positive evaluations that the teachers gave were also in the predicted direction, although the results were not as striking as they were for the negative evaluations.

Thus it appears that when boys receive a negative evaluation, their history of classroom feedback can provide many plausible and readily available interpretations other than insufficient ability. They can more easily than girls see a negative evaluation as a reflection of the teachers' overall attitude toward them, or they can view it as a reflection of the non-intellectual aspects of their school work. Finally, even if boys view a negative evaluation as resulting from inadequacies in the intellectual quality of their work, the teachers' explicit attributions make it more likely that they will attribute their errors to a lack of motivation.

One may wonder at this point whether this differential treatment of boys and girls in the classroom actually causes the interpretations that boys and girls give for their successes and failures. It is important to note that the issue here is not whether the behaviour of girls and boys warrants this differential treatment, but whether such feedback will influence the interpretations they give to subsequent evaluations. To investigate this, Dweck *et al.* (1978) simulated the two reinforcement histories characteristic of what happened to girls and boys in the classroom. Children performed on a task which could be evaluated both in terms of the intellectual quality of their performance (correctness of the solution) as well as its non-intellectual aspects (for example, how neatly they printed their answers); and the task was arranged so that all children would succeed on some trials and fail on others.

Children in one group (half of whom were males and half females) were given a reinforcement history similar to what boys receive in the classroom. That is, the negative feedback given by the evaluator referred sometimes to the intellectual quality of their work and sometimes to non-intellectual aspects. Children in another group (also half male and half female) were given a reinforcement history more characteristic of what girls girls experience in the classroom. That is, the evaluator's criticisms referred exclusively to the incorrectness of the child's solution. The children then all performed on a second task on which they received failure feedback that did not have a clearly specified referent, and the children were asked to give an explanation for the negative evaluation they received. In accordance with prediction, children gave the attribution more characteristic of boys. Most of them attributed their negative evaluation to insufficient effort. In contrast, children of both sexes who received the feedback girls receive in the classroom overwhelmingly attributed their negative evaluation to their abilities. This research clearly demonstrates that the differential treatment of boys and girls that Dweck *et al.* (1978) observed in the classroom can indeed have an impact on the subsequent interpretations that children make for the outcomes they experience in achievement situations.

There is an interesting irony in how girls come to develop the pattern of achievement-related beliefs that seems to hinder them when they confront intellectual challenges. They seem to develop this maladaptive pattern as a consequence of their *more* favoured treatment by teachers – for example, less criticism and fewer complaints about their not trying hard enough. While this differential treatment may reflect, in part, differential responses to boys and girls for the same behaviours, it also appears to be the case that the behaviour of the two sexes warrants such differential treatment (Serbin *et al.*, 1973; Etaugh and Harlow, 1973). That is, it is likely that girls actually are neater, better behaved, and more likely to work hard in order to do well and please the teacher. In other words, it appears to be girls' greater compliance to the demands of elementary school that results in their more favoured treatment by teachers, which in turn contributes to girls' failure to develop the achievement orientations necessary to succeed later on in the really challenging areas. It is also likely that girls' greater compliance to the demands of elementary school will affect their achievement orientations in more direct ways as well. When a child generally does try hard to do well and please the teacher, not only should the teacher be less inclined to attribute the child's difficulties to insufficient effort, but independent of any teacher feedback, the child herself/himself should be less inclined to attribute difficulties to insufficient effort. Unfortunately, this should result in a greater inclination to attribute one's difficulties to insufficient ability – even when the most realistic and adaptive attribution in a given situation may be that a little more effort than usual and/or an alteration of strategies was needed.

There is further irony in the logical implications that follow from the Dweck *et al.* (1978) investigation. One might reason that in order to help girls develop more adaptive achievement orientations, one should give girls the classroom feedback that boys typically receive. However, to do so would mean criticizing girls in areas (for example, neatness, conduct, effort) where criticisms may be wholly unwarranted.

Implications of sex differences in achievement orientations for performance in specific academic areas

At first glance, the picture we have painted for girls appears rather grim; and one might predict that girls would come to expect certain doom in any situation of intellectual achievement, and that they would avoid them all. Yet we know this is not the case. As we have proposed elsewhere (Dweck and Licht, 1980), academic tasks vary in the degree to which they possess the characteristics that are most debilitating to girls. Indeed, certain academic tasks and certain academic areas in general may possess characteristics that are compatible with girls' achievement orientations and that should facilitate their performance. Similarly, boys' achievement orientations may make them well-suited for certain academic pursuits, but ill-suited for other academic areas.[5]

As an example of how this analysis may help explain commonly observed achievement differences between the sexes, we have argued (Dweck and Licht, 1980) that mathematics appears to be an area that in general possesses the characteristics that fit best with boys' achievement orientations, while the verbal areas seem to possess those qualitites that fit best with the achievement orientations of girls. In other words, we proposed that an analysis of sex differences in achievement-orientations may help explain their differential choice of mathematical versus verbal areas and their differential performance in these areas.

The performance differences to which we refer are among the best-documented sex differences reported in the literature. In verbal areas, females perform as well as or better than males throughout the school years (Anastasi, 1958; Maccoby, 1966; Maccoby and Jacklin, 1974; Donlon *et al.*, 1976). While girls' mathematical achievement is equivalent to that of boys' during most of the elementary school years, girls begin to fall behind around the start of junior high; and the male–female discrepancy in mathematics becomes more pronounced over the years (Fennema and Sherman, 1977; Flanagan *et al.*, 1964; Fox, 1976b; Hilton and Berglund, 1974; Maccoby and Jacklin, 1974; Donlon *et al.*, 1976; Ekstrom *et al.*, 1976).

It is important to note that some of the most recent data we have collected also show some sex differences in mathematics achievement. This is despite society's changing views of mathematics as a male 'domain' (Sherman and Fennema, 1977; Farley, 1969). This is not to suggest that sex-role stereotyping explanations of sex differences in achievement (for example, girls perceive mathematics as a male domain and lower their expectations of success as a result) are not important. Nor for that matter do we wish to discount the possible contribution of biological factors. However, our analysis is intended to demonstrate that there are other critical factors that must be considered in attempting to explain sex differences in mathematics versus verbal achievement. These factors are children's achievement orientations that arise in the early elementary school years and may render girls and boys most willing or best able to cope with the demands of different kinds of intellectual pursuits. It is later, at the end of elementary school or beginning of junior high, that the mathematical and verbal areas become noticeably discrepant in terms of those characteristics that would favour the achievement orientations of one sex over the other.

Notes

1 The terms 'difficulty', 'failure', 'obstacles', 'challenges' are frequently used interchangeably in this chapter. They generally refer to difficulties of the magnitude that children frequently encounter in school (for example, a series of difficult problems). These terms are not meant to imply a *major* academic setback (for example, failing a subject or grade level).

2 It is worthwhile to underscore an issue that, while suggested at several earlier points, could easily get lost. That is, girls do not demonstrate lower levels of confidence in their abilities to succeed on all tasks in all achievement situations. Rather, as others (Crandall, 1969; Dweck *et al.*, 1980; Dweck and Licht, 1980; Lenney, 1977; Parsons *et al.*, in press) have noted, the characteristic pattern of sex differences is most likely to emerge when there is some uncertainty of success. The expectations of both sexes are more in line with 'reality' when the tasks are highly familiar and/or perceived as easy;

when children have received unambiguous feedback reflecting on the likelihood that they will succeed or fail; and when children are prompted to attend carefully to the relevant data from their past performance or feedback. The confidence of the two sexes diverges, however, when the tasks are novel and/or difficult – in other words, when children are confronted with challenges.

3 It should be noted that it is not *all* girls who show the helpless pattern of beliefs and behaviours nor is it the case that *all* boys are mastery-oriented. Within each sex, one is bound to find almost the entire range of helpless and mastery-oriented patterns. Nevertheless, sex differences in these patterns do emerge in a large number of studies; and they can be of sufficient magnitude to cause concern. An understanding of the mechanisms that underline sex differences in achievement-orientations will undoubtedly help us explain individual differences within each sex.

4 The expectations that parents hold for the intellectual accomplishments of their daughters also fall short of accounting for the lower confidence of girls. Parents, like teachers, do not appear to develop differential expectations for the two sexes until adolescence (see Maccoby and Jacklin, 1974, for review) – long after girls begin to doubt their own abilities. It may be the beliefs that children hold concerning their own abilities that shape the expectations parents develop for their children.

5 This is not intended as justification for the status quo (that is, sex segregation into 'sex-appropriate' fields), but rather as a potential explanation for the status quo and why it is so difficult to modify. Our intention is to provide a refined analysis that will allow us to predict more precisely when debilitation versus facilitation will occur for each sex. This can then serve as the basis for appropriate interventions designed to alleviate debilitation.

References

Anastasi, A., *Differential Psychology* (3rd edn), New York, Macmillan, 1958.

Andrews, G. R., and Debus, R. L., 'Persistence and the causal perception of failure: modifying cognitive attributions', *Journal of Educational Psychology*, **70**, 1978, pp. 154–66.

Battle C. S., 'Motivational determinants of academic competence', *Journal of Personality and Social Psychology*, **4**, 1966, pp. 634–42.

Bem, S. L., 'The measurement of psychological androgyny', *Journal of Consulting and Clinical Psychology*, **42**, 1974, pp. 155–62.

Brophy, J. E., and Good, T. L., *Teacher-Student Relationships*, New York, Holt, 1974.

Butterfield, E. C., 'The role of competence motivation in interrupted task recall and repetition choice', *Journal of Experimental Child Psychology*, **2**, 1965, pp. 354–70.

Cairns, R. B., 'Meaning and attention as determinants of social reinforcer effectiveness', *Child Development*, **41**, 1970, pp. 106–82.

Chapin, M. and Dyck, D. G., 'Persistence in children's reading behaviour as a function of N length and attribution retraining', *Journal of Abnormal Psychology*, **85**, 1976, pp. 511–15.

Coopersmith, S., *The Antecedents of Self-esteem*, San Francisco, Freeman.

Crandall, V. C., 'Sex differences in expectancy of intellectual and academic reinforcement', in C. P. Smith (ed.), *Achievement-related Motives in Children*, New York, Russell Sage Foundation, 1969.

Crandall, V. C., and Rabson, A., 'Children's repetition choices in an intellectual achievement situation following success and failure', *Journal of Genetic Psychology*, **97**, 1960, pp. 161–8.

Diener, C. I. and Dweck, C. S., 'An analysis of learned helplessness: continuous changes in performance, strategy and achievement cognitions following failure', *Journal of Personality and Social Psychology*, **36**, 1978, pp. 451–62.

Diener, C. I. and Dweck, C. S., 'An analysis of learned helplessness: II. The processing of success', *Journal of Personality and Social Psychology*, **39**, 1980, pp. 940–52.

Digman, J. M. 'Principal dimensions of child personality as inferred from teachers' judgments'. *Child Development*, **34**, 1963, pp. 43–60.

Donlon, T., Ekstrom, R. and Lockheed, M., 'Comparing the sexes on achievement items of varying content', paper presented at the meeting of the American Psychological Association, Washington, DC, September 1976.

Dweck, C. S. 'The role of expectations and attributions in the alleviation of learned helplessness', *Journal of Personality and Social Psychology*, **31**, 1975, pp. 674–85.

Dweck, C. S. and Bush, E. S., 'Sex differences in learned helplessness: I. Differential debilitation with peer and adult evaluators', *Developmental Psychology*, **12**, 1976, pp. 147–56.

Dweck, C. S., Davidson, W., Nelson, S. and Enna, B., 'Sex differences in learned helplessness: II. The contingencies of evaluative feedback in the classroom, and III. An experimental analysis', *Developmental Psychology*, **14**, 1978, pp. 268–76.

Dweck, C. S. and Gilliard. D., 'Expectancy statements as determinants of reactions to failure: sex differences in persistence and expectancy change', *Journal of Personality and Social Psychology*, **32**, 1975, pp. 1077–84.

Dweck, C. S., Goetz, T. E. and Strauss, N. L., 'Sex differences in learned helplessness: IV. An experimental and naturalistic study of failure generalization and its mediators', *Journal of Personality and Social Psychology*, **38**, 1980 pp. 441–52.

Dweck, C. S. and Licht, B. G., 'Learned helplessness and intellectual achievement', in J. Garber and M. Seligman (eds), *Human Helplessness: Theory and Application*, New York, Academic Press, 1980.

Dweck, C. S. and Reppucci, N. D., 'Learned helplessness and reinforcement responsibility in children', *Journal of Personality and Social Psychology*, **25**, 1973 pp. 109–16.

Eisenberger, R., Kaplan, R. M. and Singer, R. D., 'Decremental and nondecremental effects of noncontingent social approval', *Journal of Personality and Social Psychology*, **30**, 1974, pp. 716–2.

Ekstrom, R., Donlon, T. and Lockheed, M., 'The effect of sex-biased content in achievement test performance', paper presented at the meeting of the American Educational Research Association, San Francisco, California, 21 April 1976.

Enzle, M. E., Hansen, R. D. and Lowe, C. A., 'Causal attributions in the mixed-motive game: effects of facilitory and inhibitory environmental forces', *Journal of Personality and Social Psychology*, **31**, 1975, pp. 50–4.

Etaugh, C. and Harlow, H., 'School attitudes and performance of elementary school children as related to teacher's sex and behaviour', paper presented at the meeting of the Society for Research in Child Development, Philadelphia, March 1973.

Farley, S. M. C., 'A study of the mathematical interests, attitude and achievement of tenth and eleventh grade students' (Doctoral dissertation, University of Michigan, 1968), *Dissertation Abstracts International*, **29**, 1969, 3039 (University Microfilms No. 69–2312).

Fennema, E. and Sherman, J., 'Sex-related differences in mathematics achievement, spacial visualization and affective factors', *American Educational Research Journal*, **14**, 1977, pp. 51–71.

Flanagan, J., Davis, F., Dailey, J., Shaycoft, M., Orr, D., Goldberg, I and Neyman, C., *The American High-school Student*, Pittsburgh, University of Pittsburgh, 1964.

Fowler, J. W. and Peterson, P. L., 'Increasing reading persistence and altering attributional style of learned helpless children', *Journal of Educational Psychology*, **73**, 1981, pp. 251–60.

Fox, L., 'The effects of sex-role socialization on mathematical participation and achievement', paper prepared for Education and Work Group, Career Awareness Division of National Institute of Education, December 1976.

Harter, S., 'Mastery motivation and need for approval in older children and their relationship to social desirability response tendencies', *Developmental Psychology*, **11**, 1975, pp. 186–96.

Heller, K. A. and Parsons, J. E., 'Sex differences in teachers' evaluative feedback and students' expectancies for success in mathematics', *Child Development*, **52**, 1981, pp. 1015–19.

Hill, K. T. and Sarason, S. B., 'The relation of test anxiety and defensiveness to test and school performance over the elementary school years: a further longitudinal study' *Monographs of the Society for Research in Child Development* serial no. 104, **31**, 1966, (whole no. 2).

Hilton, T. and Berglund, G. 'Sex differences in mathematics achievement a longitudinal study', *Journal of Education Research*, **67**, 1974, pp. 23–7.

Hoffman, L. W., 'Early childhood experiences and women's achievement motives', *Journal of Social Issues*, **28**, 1972 pp. 129–55.

Jackaway, R., 'Achievement attributions and the low expectation cycle in females', paper presented at convention of American Psychological Association, Chicago, 1975.

Kelley, H. H., *Attribution in Social Interaction*, Morristown, NJ, General Learning Press, 1971.

Lenney, E., 'Women's self-confidence in achievement settings', *Psychological Bulletin*, **84**, 1977 pp. 1–13.

Licht, B. G. and Dweck, C. S., 'Determinants of academic achievement: the interaction of children's achievement orientations with skill area', *Developmental Psychology*, 1984.

Licht, B. G. and Shapiro, S. H., 'Sex differences in attributions among high achievers', paper presented at the meeting of the American Psychological Association, Washington, DC, 1982.

Maccoby, E. E., *The Development of Sex Differences*, Stanford, California, Stanford University Press, 1966.

Maccoby, E. E. and Jacklin. C. N., *The Psychology of Sex Differences*, Stanford, California, Stanford University Press, 1974.

McCandless, B., Roberts, A. and Starnes, T., 'Teachers' marks, achievement test scores, and aptitude relations with respect to social class, race, and sex', *Journal of Educational Psychology*, **63**, 1972, pp. 153–9.

McMahan, I. D., 'Relationships between causal attributions and expectancy of success', *Journal of Personality and Social Psychology*, **28**, 1973, pp. 108–14.

Molnar, J. M. and Weisz, J. R., 'The pursuit of mastery by preschool boys and girls: an observational study', *Child Development*, **52**, 1981, pp. 724–7.

Montanelli, D. S. and Hill, K. T., 'Children's achievement expectations and performance as a function of two consecutive reinforcement experiences, sex of subject, and sex of experimenter', *Journal of Personality and Social Psychology*, **13**, 1969, pp. 115–28.

Nicholls, J. G., 'Causal attributions and other achievement-related cognitions: effects of task outcome, attainment value, and sex', *Journal of Personality and Social Psychology*, **31**, 1975, pp. 379–89.

Nicholls, J. G., 'Effort is virtuous, but it's better to have ability', *Journal of Research in Personality*, **10**, 1976, pp. 306–15.

Nicholls, J. G., 'When a scale measures more than its name denotes: the case of the Test

Anxiety Scale for Children', *Journal of Consulting and Clinical Psychology*, **44**, 1976, pp. 976–85.

Nicholls, J. G., 'Sex differences in achievement behaviour and causal attributions for success and failure in New Zealand children', paper presented at meeting of the American Educational Research Association, Toronto, 1978.

Nicholls, J. G., 'The development of the concepts of effort and ability, perception of academic attainment and the understanding that difficult tasks require more ability', *Child Development*, **49**, 1978 pp. 800–14.

Parsons, J. E., Adler, T. F., Futterman, R., Goff, S. B., Kaczala, C. M., Meece, J. L. and Midgley, C., 'Expectancies, values, and academic behaviours', in J. T. Spence (ed.), *Perspectives on Achievement and Achievement Motivation*, San Francisco, Freeman, 1984.

Parsons, J. E., Kaczala, C. M. and Meece, J. L., 'Socialization of achievement attitudes and beliefs: classroom influences', *Child Development*, **53**, 1982, pp. 322–39.

Parsons, J. E., Ruble, D. N., Hodges, K. L. and Small, I., 'Cognitive-developmental factors in emerging sex differences in achievement-related expectancies', *Journal of Social Issues*, **32**, 1976, pp. 47–61.

Sarason, S. B., Davidson, K. S., Lighthall, F. F., Waite, R. R. and Ruebush, B. K., *Anxiety in Elementary School Children: A Report of Research*, New York, Wiley, 1960.

Schunk, D. H., 'Effects of effort attributional feedback on children's perceived self-efficacy and achievement', *Journal of Educational Psychology*, **74**, 1982, pp. 548–56.

Seligman, M. E. P. and Maier, S. F., 'Failure to escape traumatic shock', *Journal of Experimental Psychology*, **74**, 1967, pp. 1–9.

Serbin, L. A., O'Leary, K. D., Kent, R. N. and Tonick, I. J., 'A comparison of teacher response to the pre-academic and problem behaviour of boys and girls', *Child Development*, **44**, 1973, pp. 796–804.

Sherman, J. and Fennema, E., 'The study of mathematics by high school girls and boys: related variables', *American Educational Research Journal*, **14**, 1977, pp. 159–68.

Sohn, D., 'Affect-generating powers of effort and ability self attributions of academic success and failure', *Journal of Educational Psychology*, **69**, 1977 pp. 500–5.

Stevenson, H. W., Hale, G. A., Klein, R. E. and Miller, L. K., 'Interrelations and correlates in children's learning and problem solving', *Monographs of the Society of Research in Child Development*, **33** (7, serial no. 123), 1968.

Veroff, J., 'Social comparison and the development of achievement motivation', in C. P. Smith (ed.), *Achievement-related motives in children*, New York, Russell Sage, 1969.

Warren, V. L. and Cairns, R. B., 'Social reinforcement satiation: An outcome of frequency or ambiguity?', *Journal of Experimental Child Psychology*, **13**, 1972, pp. 249–60.

Weiner, B., *Theories of Motivation*, Chicago, Markham, 1972.

Weiner, B., *Achievement Motivation and Attribution Theory*, Morristown, NJ, General Learning Press, 1974.

Weiner, B., Freize, I., Kukla, A., Reed, L., Rest, S. and Rosenbaum, R., *Perceiving the Causes of Success and Failure*, New York, General Learning Press, 1971.

Weiner, B., Nierenberg, R. and Goldstein, M., 'Social learning (locus of control) versus attributional (causal stability) interpretations of expectancy of success', *Journal of Personality*, **44**, 1976, pp. 52–68.

Weiner, B., Russell, D. and Lerman, D., 'The cognition-emotion process in achievement-related contexts', *Journal of Personality and Social Psychology*, **37**, pp. 1211–20.

7 Gender and curriculum choice

Teresa Grafton, Henry Miller, Lesley Smith, Martin Vegoda and Richard Whitfield

We are trying to build a cage around the children rather than putting the children into the cage.

This is a statement made by a deputy headteacher in a mixed comprehensive school about the process of curriculum construction and choice there. She was describing a situation which she saw as catering to the perceived needs and interests of pupils as opposed to imposing a rigid curriculum upon everyone. However, there is a paradox here, indicated by the metaphor of the cage. The constraints imposed by traditional assumptions, for example, concerning the nature of male and female social roles, may be just as real in a situation of open choice as they are in the context of a curriculum without choice.

This chapter attempts to illustrate the relationship between gender and curriculum choice by focusing upon the processes involved within a curriculum which includes a subject centrally concerned with childcare and the parental, specifically the maternal, role amongst the options available. Subjects such as this constitute the thinnest point in the ice for any claim that schools are offering a genuinely open and equal curriculum to girls and boys.

Curriculum options focusing on parenthood skills have grown out of home economics departments and been staffed for the most part by teachers (invariably women) with a background in domestic craft subjects. They occur as examination subjects in the curriculum for fourth- and fifth-year pupils. They have childcare, child development, parental roles and family life as core themes and are becoming increasingly more academic, although primarily they attract pupils in the low to middle ability range. Such subjects may involve pupils in playground activities outside the school; other practical work is also undertaken in cookery, needlework, toy making as well as the physical aspects of childcare. The theoretical component of these subjects may include human biology and child development, contraception and family planning as well as discussion of responsibility and commitment in relationships.

When Cox (1976) surveyed secondary schools in three counties he found that the curriculum of 51 per cent of schools contained subjects which aimed to educate pupils in aspects of parenthood and family life; these had developed during the previous five years. Of the twenty-six teachers involved in such courses who were selected by Cox for interview, the majority were doing so in the belief that they would influence the educational and personal development of the next generation.

Source: Extracted from Grafton, T., Miller, H., Smith, L., Vegoda, M, and Whitfield, R., 'Gender and curriculum choice: a case study' in Hammersley, M. and Hargreaves, A. (eds), *Curriculum Practice: some sociological case studies*, Barcombe, Falmer Press, 1983, pp. 151–69.

The reasons given for starting courses in the schools surveyed by Cox were to break the cycle of deprivation or to provide education relevant to pupils' lives, both currently and in the future.

One of the major influences on the development of these courses was the influential work of Bowlby (1951, 1953) on child development, with its emphasis on the significance of early childcare and on the primary caring role of the mother. This became linked to the notion that maternal deprivation in childhood constituted a significant factor in relation to malfunction in adult life. This was an important concept in the 1970s when Sir Keith Joseph, discussing the consequences of inadequate or insufficient parental care, only partly attributable to external considerations such as poor housing and low income, suggested that intergenerational cycles of deprivation underlay persistent social problems and breakdown of the family. Following Joseph's initiative, consultation between government departments focused attention upon preparation for parenthood as a preventive measure. In 1974 the DHSS published two booklets entitled *Preparation for Parenthood* and *Dimensions of Parenthood*, which included discussion of the role of the school curriculum in the area of personal life, a theme taken up in successive government Green and White Papers and committee reports (for example, DES, 1977; DES, 1979; DHSS, 1978).

Concern about the impact on interpersonal relationships and family structure of an increased incidence of divorce, maternal depression, illegitimacy, latchkey children, non-accidental injury and delinquency, was a further influence on the development of parenthood-related subjects in the school curriculum. Pilling and Kellmer Pringle (1978) and Whitfield (1980) are among those who have written of apparent threats to the stability of family structures and to the security offered to young children. Education about parenthood in the curriculum, therefore, can be seen as arising out of concern for the quality of life that pupils will experience in relationships, as parents and in their social roles outside school. In addition, from the 1960s onwards education with a specific emphasis upon preparation for parenthood began to be viewed by many teachers as one way of avoiding what they saw as a transference of inadequate parent behaviour from one generation to another.

In the last twenty years there has been a mushrooming of subjects with an external examination in the areas of childcare and development and parentcraft, both at CSE and GCE 'O' level. The vast majority of pupils who take these subjects are girls. We suggest, as does Scott (1980, pp. 106–7), that the existence in the school curriculum of subjects like these, specifically at examination level, constitutes a 'natural choice' for girls who 'select them voluntarily and opt out of the traditional boys' subjects'. This is likely to have significant consequences for future roles. Scott sees the school as playing a key part in relegating girls and women to a 'unique place in the family and a specific place in the workforce' (p. 100) for it furnishes women (and also men) with the requisite range of appropriate skills as well as the relevant level of consciousness. In her view, educational assumptions made about women are that: the main priority in girls' lives (particularly low ability girls) is to marry and raise a family; paid work will play a nonessential part in their adult lives; they will enter paid work only in limited fields; and the work they perform in the labour force is not important to society and only necessary to women as 'pin money'. In its emphasis on the link between girls and the roles of wife and mother, the presence of an option in childcare reduces the possibility of girls being offered and selecting the same curriculum as boys. The teaching of preparation for parenthood through such an option can thus be seen as facilitating the movement of girls and boys into traditional roles within the family and labour market.

The subject choice process

Ball (1981, p. 122) describes the process of subject choice as a 'crucial point in the school careers of pupils. Decisions made at this point by them, and their teachers and parents, clearly have implications for their future lives which reach far beyond the limits of schooling'. Ball and Woods (1979) have provided detailed analyses of the subject choice process. They note how the orientations of pupils and parents to the selection of curriculum options tends to vary by social class. In addition, they document the ways in which teachers channel the choices pupils make, cooling out or re-routing those who select courses which are judged to be 'inappropriate' for them. However, neither Ball nor Woods pays much attention to the way in which gender shapes the choices pupils make and teachers' conceptions of what courses are 'appropriate' to particular pupils. This issue is the focus of our paper. We look at two basic questions: *who* takes a subject dealing with preparation for parenthood and *why*?

The data on which our analysis is based come from a case study which took place in 1980 in a coeducational comprehensive school in south-west England. Its catchment area, though predominantly well-to-do and middle-class, included working-class districts containing a good deal of public housing and very few amenities. These districts were a distance from the school, on the edge of its catchment area. In the course of the research we carried out a detailed investigation of the fourth-year intake for a two-year family and child option.

Pupils made a choice of subjects at two points in their school career; at the end of the third year and then in the fifth year for those staying on into the sixth form. When pupils arrived in the school they were placed in one of three ability bands. Streaming by ability, therefore, began in the first year. This was done on the basis of a primary school assessment consisting of a verbal reasoning test score and recommendations made by headteachers and, in some cases, class teachers.

While curriculum differentiation by ability only began in the third year, it occurred on the basis of sex from the beginning. Girls took two craft subjects, cookery and needlework, while boys took metalwork and woodwork. Some flexibility was technically possible although the practical facilities were said to limit numbers and in practice very few boys and girls took 'atypical' subjects. In one teacher's opinion, the extent to which this might occur depended upon the awareness of pupils or parents that there was any choice in the matter; however, in any such case special applications would have been required.

In February of the third year a lengthy process of option choice began, involving consultation at varying levels between school, parents and pupils. As well as English and maths and various other compulsory subjects (such as games and

RE), pupils studied five subjects chosen from an options scheme composed of seven 'lines', selecting one subject from each line:

Fourth-year Options 1980/81: The Choices

All pupils will take English (which includes Language for *all* pupils and Literature for those wishing and able to take this to 'O' level or CSE) and Mathematics in 'ability' sets. Choices must, however, be made between the alternatives listed below, one subject being chosen from each 'line'.

LINE 1 English

LINE 2 Mathematics

LINE 3 Biology ('O' and CSE), French ('O' and CSE), History ('O' and CSE), Religious Education ('O'/CSE), Citizenship (CSE), Rural Science (CSE)

LINE 4 Chemistry ('O' and CSE), French ('O' and CSE), Geography ('O' and CSE and possibly non-exam), German ('O')

LINE 5 Physics (Nuffield 'O' and CSE), Geography ('O' and CSE), History ('O' and CSE), Physical Science (CSE), Human Biology (CSE)

LINE 6 Biology ('O'/CSE), Woodwork ('O' and CSE), Metalwork ('O' and CSE), Cookery ('O' and CSE), Needlework ('O'/CSE), Art ('O'/CSE), Music ('O'/CSE), Commercial Skills (RSA/CSE)

LINE 7 Physics (Traditional 'O'), Chemistry (Nuffield 'O'), Technical Drawing ('O' and CSE), Motor Mech. (non-exam), Art ('O'), Cookery ('O'), Typing (CSE), Family and Child ('O' and CSE), Commerce ('O'/CSE)

Note: Periods for Games, PE, General Studies including RE, Careers, Education in Personal Relationships, etc., will be provided outside the options scheme.

On lines 3 to 7 subjects were arranged with the intention of allowing sufficient choice for as wide a variety of pupil needs as possible. Some subjects were available in more than one line, for example, geography, French, history, chemistry, art and biology, whereas others such as family and child and the practical subjects occurred only once. Therefore, needlework and commercial skills competed with woodwork and metalwork on line 6 and none of these subjects could be picked up from another line. On line 7 family and child, typing and commerce competed with motor mechanics and technical drawing; again, none of these occurred elsewhere. Cookery was available on two lines, 6 and 7, along with all the other craft subjects. It is interesting to note that line 7 also contained the more academic subjects of physics (traditional 'O') and chemistry (Nuffield 'O'). While these subjects were available on other lines they were not the same syllabi; physics (Nuffield 'O' and CSE) was available on line 5 and chemistry ('O' and CSE) on line 4. The significance of this lies in the fact that the Nuffield syllabus tended to be taken by the most able children.

Subjects were setted where possible to cater for a range of abilities. Each line contained an option geared to those pupils for whom it was felt that 'an external examination would be unsuitable'. Such options were citizenship, geography, physical science, human biology, art, motor mechanics, typing and family and child.

Course outlines were provided for third-year tutors in order that they could advise pupils and parents appropriately. Information was given as to which band – top, middle or lower – the subject would be likely to suit. Also pupils were advised that in the case of competition for a particular subject, the school's decision would be based upon its suitability in relation to a pupil's ability or intended career. The tutor was asked to consider the pupil's need for a broad general education; paradoxically this appeared to be waived in the case of 'high fliers' who might be directed towards more academic subjects. As one teacher at the school put it:

We like them all, as far as possible, to do some sort of creative subject, but there are one or two who will miss out on that because, for instance, they choose three sciences; because we do make it possible for our better children to do three sciences, and if you've got a humanity and you've got a language, you haven't really got any scope then for the creative subjects perhaps.

Finally, certain subjects, for example, woodwork, metalwork, cookery, technical drawing and family and child, were described as open to both sexes. However, tutor's guidelines requested 'prior discussion' in the case of boys who wanted to take the family and child option, while girls who wanted to take woodwork or metalwork had to 'show a sincere desire' to do so. (Perhaps not surprisingly, few boys and girls took up options traditionally associated with the other sex.) Needlework was described in the guidelines as being taken by girls only. It has already been noted that cookery and needlework were for the most part mandatory for girls in the first three years, as were woodwork and metalwork for boys.

Family and child was also offered as a one-year subject in the sixth form, where the system of curriculum choice operated in a similar way to the third year. Considerable help or direction was offered to pupils at this stage, including the involvement of the school's careers department. It was in the sixth form that a small number of boys opted to take the course.

For pupils at this school the structure of the curriculum had the following implications with reference to the third-year options scheme:

1 the gender differentiation of craft subjects taken in earlier years had a pre-empting effect on later choice;
2 academic children taking a number of science subjects would be guided away from family and child or practical subjects;
3 the juxtaposition between science subjects and family and child could also be seen as making the choice of science by girls less likely than it might otherwise have been;
4 the grouping of subjects made it less likely that boys and girls would choose a subject which was untypical; if they wished to do motor mechanics or technical drawing, for example, as well as family and child, the structure would not have allowed it.

The next section of this paper considers the nature of the choice process as it was experienced by a group of third-year pupils about to undertake the family and child option.

The characteristics of the pupils

Twenty-eight pupils from the 1980 fourth-year family and child intake (out of a total of thirty-one) were interviewed in small groups of four or five. All were girls aged between 14 and 15. Virtually no boys took the course in the fourth and fifth years, with the exception of a very few from a remedial group who took part until they left at Easter. Of the twenty-eight girls, some were taking the 'O' level examination whereas others were to be entered for the CSE. Most would be doing one or other of the examinations and some would be double-entered. Pass rates for the subject in this school were good. The intake was initially divided into two classes or 'sets' for teaching purposes, according to teachers' assessment of the girls' ability. The ratio between the two sets was 13:15 (GCE 'O' level: CSE). Practical lessons were taught as mixed ability in the fourth year, whereas theory lessons were setted. There was flexibility in the setting, and girls might be moved up and down in the course of the year.

The course taken by each group was identical in most respects, and they were timetabled in parallel. Our discussions with pupils took place on the occasion of the first meeting of the class in September 1980. The girls were still together and had not been informed about their allocation to a particular set, although we were aware of who was going where. We were able to gather a certain amount of background information about the girls. All were white, reflecting the ethnic compsition of the school as a whole. The family and child intake also reflected the nature of the school's catchment area, with a relatively small proportion (less than 25 per cent) coming from the working-class fringe. It was interesting to note, however, that when the twenty-eight were divided into the two ability based groupings around 50 per cent of the lower set came from this area as opposed to only 13 per cent of the higher group. Teachers also distinguished between pupils from the different areas, noting, for example, that most of the school's problems tended to be located in the fringe. These problems were defined by one teacher as comprising: '. . . "behaviour", low achievement, involvement with the police outside the school, emanating, as these things nearly always do, from family difficulties, separation, ineptitude on the part of the parents'.

As far as family background was concerned the picture that emerged was as follows. All but five of the girls were living with both parents. Eleven girls were living in families which contained more than two children and most did a fair amount of babysitting. Girls tended to know more about their mothers' educational background than their fathers', suggesting that mothers may consti-tute a more important reference in relation to their daughters' own plans. As far as parental occupations were concerned, most parents were currently in some form of paid employment – nineteen out of twenty-seven mothers; twenty-one out of twenty-six fathers. Most of the jobs listed were manual or routine non-manual (most of them relating to mothers), while three of the girls came from farming families.

Ability and aspirations

In relation to their stated aspirations for the future, nineteen out of the twenty-eight were planning to leave school as soon as possible. Only three intended to go into the sixth form; these were all higher set girls. Most girls' immediate intentions focused on leaving school and not on further or higher education. However, their ideas about future jobs suggested that they might need some further education or training. Table 7.1 contains the girls' ideas about what they wanted to do on leaving school.

There was a lack of precision on this issue, though it should be remembered that these girls were only 14. Some girls gave more than one occupation as an alternative. The three who intended to stay on longest at school were thinking of careers with the police, secretarial work, nursing or work with children. There was a general vagueness typified by phrases like 'something to do with children' or 'work with horses or animals'. The girl who wanted to be a beautician was one of the few currently aiming at a particular career singlemindedly and knowing something definite about what it entailed.

Table 7.1 *Girls' aspirations regarding post-school activities*

Areas mentioned	Frequency
Looking after/working with children	10
Working with animals	4
Catering (various aspects)	4
Secretarial/office work	3
Nursing	3
Policewoman/mounted policewoman	2
Something to do with needlework/art	2
Modelling	1
Beautician	1
Working with people	1
Total	31

These future career plans, when related to the reasons which the girls gave for their choice of family and child as an option, suggested that their choices did have a vocational aspect. Relatively few of the girls gave the probability that they would become parents themselves one day as the prime reason for undertaking the course. The most popular reason advanced was that they 'liked children'. However, when we asked the girls why they thought others in the group had chosen the subject, its utility in relation to future parenthood was often cited, for example: 'I think it's something everybody ought to know – how to look after children before you have them.' It was also very obvious that most of the girls had a great deal of experience already of looking after younger children, not only in their own families but also in those belonging to friends and neighbours. Curriculum subjects like this one would, therefore, appear to fit caring roles already adopted by many girls outside school.

There were virtually no differences between girls in the higher and lower ability groups in the matter of their future plans; yet in the options choices of the intake as a whole considerable differences could be seen between the subject profiles characteristic of the two ability sets (see Table 7.2).

How choices were made

As has already been explained, the sequence of subject choice took place throughout most of the third year and involved all senior staff, third-year tutors, careers and subject teachers, as well as pupils and their parents. In his study of

Table 7.2 *Options choices of higher and lower ability sets*

Lines	Higher ability set	Lower ability set
1	Maths	Maths
2	English	English
3	Biology	* Citizenship or rural science
4	French	* Geography
5	History	* Human biology
6	Cookery or commercial skills	* Needlework or art
7	* Family and child	* Family and child

* these subjects could be taken without pupils taking an exam.

the subject choice process in a secondary modern school, Woods describes the relative roles of the three main parties concerned – that is, the school, parents and pupils themselves. These also seemed to be the main parties to the process of subject choice in the school we studied, though the influence on pupils of the experience of others who had taken the course previously, particularly sisters or friends, was also important, contradicting a finding of the recent Schools Council study of fourth-year options (Bardell, 1982).

Of all those potentially involved in the choice process a significant amount of influence would, not surprisingly, appear to have come from parents, particularly mothers:

My parents did it. They chose which ones would be best for me, for my career. I want to be a chef and I need certain qualifications.

I want to be a policewoman and my dad helped me. He said which subjects would be best.

Mum says it is useful to know how to look after children; she said it's something good to have if you can get it.

I just really want to do it and my mum wanted me to.

However, at least two girls had chosen the family and child option despite parental advice to the contrary:

She [mother] said 'I don't see why you want to take it. If you ever need anything when you're older and you've got a family, you can ask me, so I don't see why you don't take needlework or something like that.' But I thought needlework – there's a lot of dressmaking. So I thought I can use these two lessons, they're something more interesting than needlework that will help me in my older life.

(This girl wanted to 'work with people' or do 'something with art'.) Another girl said: 'My friends who had taken it before had said it is a nice course to take so I thought "Well better than motor mechanics". My dad wanted me to take that.' Parental involvement was quoted more frequently by girls in the upper rather than lower ability set. Girls in the latter group tended to stress their own part in the matter: 'Well, my mum and dad just let me make up my own mind.' For the most part, tutors were not mentioned at all and, when questioned, pupils tended to deny they had been a major source of influence. In view of the emphasis placed upon the role of third-year tutors in the sequence of events as outlined by the school, their low profile is of interest. Here is one account of the process of interaction between home and school which shows the system operating 'by the book':

I talked to my mum and my auntie and my tutor. My tutor discussed it with me. . . . She asked me how I was doing and then she got the ones she didn't think I'd get very far in. She got the teachers to say if they thought I was good enough. She got the reports back and gave them to me and sent a little letter to my mum and my mum said it was all right.

In relation to the role played by third-year tutors and by the school generally, we also asked the girls what information they had been given about the course at the time they were thinking about what to do. A group of pupils, all of whom had been allocated to the lower set for teaching purposes, were particularly emphatic that they had been given little or no previous information about the subject by teachers or tutors. On the other hand, another girl said that her 'old' tutor who also taught family and child used to bring in slides 'showing how accidents were caused in the home and prevention to stop them'. She would also answer any questions they had.

To summarize this account of how choices appear to have been made by these pupils, we noted with interest the primacy given to the opinions of parents, sisters and others with first-hand experience of the subject in question as opposed to official school-based advisers. We are, however, unable to assess the extent to which this may be an accurate reflection of what really took place.

Reasons and expectations

Discussion with the girls helped to indicate some of the relevant factors which lay behind their selection of subjects. A consistent theme was the way future job aspirations influenced choice. Many girls also said they chose those subjects they liked best or were best at. Occasionally someone suggested she had not had an entirely free hand; for example, one girl seemed to think she had had to take geography on line 4, and another said of line 7: 'You either get typing or family and child', in spite of the fact that there were other choices she could have made. In general, however, responses to the question as to how the choice of options was made centred on the twin notions of utility and feasibility. One girl, when asked whether it was difficult or easy to make the decisions, said: 'It's easy if you know what you want, definitely know what jobs you want to do and what qualifications you've got to have.'

Reasons frequently given for choosing the family and child option were:

Because I like children
I (might) want to work with children
I thought it would be useful/interesting
It will help me when I have children of my own
There was nothing else I could/wanted to do.

The order of these statements reflects the relative significance of each, with the first two often presented together. The emphasis was on the vocational motive. Relatively few of the girls gave the probability that they would become parents themselves one day as the *prime* reason for undertaking the course. One example, from the only girl in her discussion group who made this point, was:

Well I don't really know. It's just something I think all mums should know, either learn it at school or go somewhere before they have a baby, how to look after children. I just thought it would be helpful if anyone got into difficulties when they're older.

Other reasons presented included:

Just for fun
I didn't want to do typing
I wanted to be with my friends
I chose childcare because it's a different subject to before. . . .

The fact that there are some distinct differences between this and other subjects in the curriculum emerged strongly in the course of discussion with pupils about their expectations of it. Most expected themes like learning about babies and children; food, diet and cooking; making clothes and toys; looking after a home; visiting playgroups and dealing with problems. Comments ranged from the very vague: 'I don't know . . . I suppose it'll be about children. I don't know' to:

I think it will be about coping with the problems that you come across with them. The way they feel and think about things. You know, things they want to do and why they want to do them. Just really how to cope with their problems when they ask for anything. If they get into tantrums and that, learning what to do in that situation.

One or two girls mentioned the things they had heard others say about the course – especially its more sensational aspects: 'Well, when you're pregnant the things that go wrong, miscarriages and things like that. The things that make you miscarry. I think that puts you off.' When asked whether they did not also hear about the things that 'go right', one response was: 'Yes, but you tend to take more notice of the things that go wrong,' though 'Things like that just happen don't they. It's best to know about them.' Another girl, asked what she expected the course to be about, said:

Well the safety in the home thing and that. My sister took it and she's got a baby now . . . she was too young to have a baby really so she missed half the course through the baby. She didn't know that much, but she knew quite a bit.

The bit that she did take was, according to her sister, useful.

A number of the girls talked of the playgroup visits. This was a popular aspect of the course:

Well, it's different, isn't it, nicer . . . you're with them [children] as well. It's sort of different learning about them and you'll be with them, you can learn something real.

You get to see babies and handicapped children and you get to handle them as well.

Well my sister did it before and she enjoyed it because she went down to a playgroup just down the road from us and she helped and she made clothes for the children and she did cooking and she enjoyed it, so I thought well I'll take it as well.

My friend said she didn't like the first part because it was just writing and things like that but the second part was good because you went on trips and got about.

Again the impression given was that the subject was considered to be 'different':

'I spoke to a girl in the 5th year who's doing it at the moment and she says you don't read from books, you learn from actual experience.'

This positive emphasis on the practical aspects of the family and child course and its relevance to 'real' things like children's day-to-day needs, presented a contrast to more negative attitudes towards school in general expressed particularly by some of the lower ability girls: 'You can't do nothing in school. It's boring – you're not allowed to do nothing'; 'It's like being in jail or something.'

Some indication of the way this subject was seen by the girls is also reflected in the following dialogue which occurred in a discussion group whose members had all been allocated to the higher ability teaching set: 'Some of the people skive'; 'They just want to doss around'; 'Some of them do, not all of them.' and

If you want to actually get the 'O' level then you are going to have to work but it's a subject where people can mess about if they don't want to take the 'O' level.

It is interesting that for some pupils family and child appeared to have been chosen as an additional subject over and above the more 'academic' subjects which they saw themselves requiring for career purposes. These girls expected to experience this subject differently from the others they were taking. For example, one girl, when asked if she wished she could enjoy the other subjects in the way she expected to enjoy family and child, said:

Well, I don't know, I like work, I like to be pushed but I like to have a muck about sometimes . . . some people can't cope with it. They take the academic subjects and work for them and take this as a rest period. You don't get proper homework do you or anything like that?

Another girl said she regarded it:

as an easy subject – because I don't know what everybody else thinks but I find maths very difficult. I much prefer to do something quite easy and interesting for a relaxing afternoon or morning or whenever we have it. But you can't take that attitude in other subjects because you have to sit down and learn, but this is a subject I'd find easier to learn than maths or something like that.

The general view of the girls was that compared with subjects like maths, English and science, the school considered family and child 'a lower subject, an easier subject to take, and that the lower classes take it, the ones that aren't quite as bright as the top group'. Their own attitudes varied. Some did not agree with this view: 'You don't need to speak proper English, like posh or anything', and 'I do think that family and child care is more important . . . because it does help you later on, maybe the other things do but that is more important in a way.'

However, the majority accepted the conventional status hierarchy of subjects, aware of the vocational implications of the relative status of these subjects in the curriculum:

Well, maths and English are most important – you need that for any job you want don't you?

If you're going for a job it's not really what they're asking for. They want the science and the academic subjects. They don't really consider this as one.

Well, if you go into a job, like you wanted to be an accountant and they said 'what 'O' levels or 'A' levels have you got?' and then you said family and child – they wouldn't take much notice of that. But if you went into nursing and said you'd got family and child care they'd take notice of that and probably put you on the children's ward.

Girls' subjects, boys' subjects

At this school the very few boys who took this subject were either in a remedial stream and not expected to take an examination, or they were taking it as a one-year extra 'O' level in the sixth form. The number of boys involved was very small. We were interested to know why boys did not choose this option. It was obvious that pupils had very definite notions about which subjects were taken by girls as opposed to boys. For example, during a general discussion about options available to them, one of the girls commented: 'They're the boys' ones, the metalwork and the woodwork.'

When it came to discussing boys' attitudes towards the family and child option, one girl said simply: 'It's not for boys, is it?', and when asked why not, said: 'Well I don't know, ask the boys.' We did ask a group of boys who were part of a small mixed group of pupils who had taken the subject as a one-year 'O' level in the sixth form for their opinions on this issue. The boys, while enjoying it, were aware of peer group reactions to their choice:

It's always been thought of as a girls' subject and it's very risky, so to speak, I mean. I wouldn't have done it if it hadn't been for . . . whatever you say you get a lot of. . . .

Yes, people sort of laugh. When I was queuing for the exam people said 'what are you doing?' and when I said family and child they laughed.

The second boy went on to say that he would not have done the course if others of his friends had not been doing it as well. A similar theme was expressed by two of the girls in the group. According to one, 'I think boys think it's sissyish or babyish looking after children. They think it's girls' work or women's work.' The other said:

Well, I think it's that as well really because if a boy said to his friend, 'I'm taking the child care course' I think he'd get a lot of teasing. I think half of it is because of that. I also think that I don't think it really interests them. I've never found a boy that really likes getting hold of his little brothers and sisters. You know, I do think they think it's for the women to do all that.

The way both groups of pupils saw the parental division of labour was, on the whole, very traditional. There was some acknowledgement that boys might in time become fathers and need to know something about bringing up a family, although it seemed to be assumed by both sexes that a man would only be called upon for this if his wife died, went into hospital, or left home for whatever reason. Otherwise he would be occupied outside the home earning the wherewithal to support his wife and family. So why did these boys decide to take this subject as part of their sixth form programme? Unlike the girls, no mention was made of any occupational motive associated with the decision. One boy who had taken science 'A' levels and already had a place at university commented that the fact that he had taken family and child gave him something to talk about in interviews.

In general these boys gave the impression of filling in time, having already gained the more marketable qualifications. In this respect there were some similarities between them and the higher ability girls.

Conclusion

The differences between girls and boys in the choice of options are clearly closely related to sexual divisions in the home and the labour market. Despite the efforts of the women's movement and some legal reform, women remain disadvantaged in the home and in the work-force (Deem, 1978). While the dynamics of gender relations are different within the family and the labour market, they are nevertheless interrelated. The traditional definition of women within the family, as housewives and mothers with prime responsibility for child-rearing, means that most women, whatever the realities of the situation, are seen as transient or second earners. Thus it is usual for them to be paid less than men. This not only finds its expression in the fact that they continue to receive lower pay for doing essentially similar work to that done by men, but perhaps more importantly in the relatively low rates paid for 'women's work', such as certain types of semi-skilled factory work, a variety of service occupations, like shop work, secretarial work and cleaning, and also the professions of nursing, social work and teaching where women fail to climb organizational ladders (DES, 1982). There is also widespread use of married women in part-time work; 40 per cent of women now work part-time (Breugal, 1979). This may fit domestic responsibilities, but wages are low, insurance costs and fringe benefits can be minimized and employment can be expanded or contracted with little resistance. The most insecure and worst paid section of the female labour force consists of the home workers where women who are usually paid a pittance for piece-work simultaneously bear triple responsibilities as worker, housewife and mother.

It can be argued that to effect any real progress towards making opportunities for boys and girls equal, major changes in curriculum design would be required. For example, in Sweden's new comprehensive curriculum the traditional sex role pattern is being attacked in a deliberate way: home management, typing and technology are to be compulsory for both boys and girls at junior and senior level. Even so, it is arguable that without substantial changes affecting the socio-economic basis of the sexual division of labour such efforts on the part of schools are unlikely to achieve very much. As one teacher of family and child said on the issue of option choice:

I think on the whole boys are not going to be going in for careers where they see child care as relevant as a subject. Until you get to a point where child care or education for parenthood is seen as something that is relevant to everybody then you're never going to get everybody educated in it.

Given this, ironically, the introduction of a subject intended to improve familial relations within a progressive and liberal option choice system may actually have the consequence of reinforcing traditional gender stereotypes.

References

Ball, S., *Beachside Comprehensive*, Cambridge, Cambridge University Press, 1981.

Bardell, G., *Options for the Fourth*, London, Schools Council, 1982.

Bowlby, J., *Maternal Care and Mental Health*, Geneva World Health Organization, 1951.

Bowlby, J., *Child Care and the Growth of Love*, London, Pelican, 1953.

Breugel, I., 'Women as a reserve army of labour', *Feminist Review*, no 3, London, 1979.

Cox, M. H., *The Teaching of Child Development in Secondary Schools: A Preliminary Study*, unpublished master's thesis, University of Nottingham, 1976.

Deem, R., *Women and Schooling*, London, Routledge and Kegan Paul, 1978.

DES, *Education in Schools: A Consultative Document*, Cmnd. 6869, London, HMSO, 1977.

DES, *Aspects of Secondary Education in England: A Survey by HM Inspectors of Schools*, London, HMSO, 1979.

DES, 'The secondary school staffing survey: data on teachers' characteristics and deployment on average class sizes in England and Wales', *Statistical Bulletin*, **5** no. 82, March 1982.

DHSS, *The Family in Society: Dimensions of Parenthood*, London, HMSO, 1974.

DHSS, *The Family in Society: Preparation for Parenthood*, London, HMSO, 1974.

DHSS, *Prevention and Health: Reducing the Risk; Safer Pregnancy and Childbirth*, London, HMSO, 1977.

DHSS, *Violence to Children: A Response to the First Report from the Select Committee on Violence in the Family* (Session 1976–7), Cmnd. 7123, London, HMSO, 1978.

Pilling, D. and Kellmer Pringle, M., *Controversial Issues in Child Development*, London, Paul Elek, 1978.

Scott, M., 'Teach her a lesson – the sexist curriculum in patriarchal education', in Spender, D. and Sarah. E. (eds), *Learning to Lose*, London, The Women's Press, 1980.

Whitfield, R. C., *Education for Family Life: Some New Policies for Child Care*, London, Hodder and Stoughton, 1980.

Woods, P., *The Divided School*, London, Routledge and Kegan Paul, 1979.

8 Gender bias and test norms in educational selection

Harvey Goldstein

The Equal Opportunities Commission considers it discriminatory deliberately to balance the gender composition of schools or streams: 'any allocation made should be solely on the grounds of ability'. In particular, where tests are used, standardized scores should not be based on separate sex norms.

Some LEAs appear to have concurred readily with this view, while others have been more reluctant. A particular instance of the latter is where the existence of the same number of places for boys and girls in grammar schools has led LEAs to use separate sex norms for tests, leading to identical distributions of standardized scores for each sex, but also, because girls tend to have higher 11+ raw test scores, resulting in some girls being excluded from grammar schools who had higher scores than some boys who had been selected. The paper explores the arguments which have been used to justify this procedure, and the implications for assessment in general, including public examinations.

Background

According to Wilby (1983), a then current court case threatened the future of single-sex grammar schools because an LEA was operating separate sex norms for its 11+ selection tests. What was happening was that, because girls obtained higher average scores than boys but then had their scores adjusted downwards to equalize the sex distributions, some girls were being refused admission to grammar school despite having higher raw scores than some boys who had been selected. Wilby points out that: 'The case also has implications for councils with mixed grammar schools ... a single pass mark ... means that girls get a disproportionate number of places and many teachers feel the system is unfair to boys because their early development lags behind girls.'

The case was being brought by the parents of the girl, with the backing of the Equal Opportunities Commission (EOC). The commission, in its guidelines (1982) states that 'any allocation made (to schools or streams) should be solely on the grounds of *ability*' (my italics) and that separate sex norms should not be used. On the face of things, if the Commission's view is upheld in law, it would seem clear that this LEA and others with similar practices, would be obliged to alter them, resulting in a higher proportion of girls entering grammar schools. In the remainder of this paper I will examine the arguments which surround this issue and relate them to some issues basic to testing and selection.

Source: Extracted from Goldstein, H., 'Gender bias and test norms in educational selection', *Research Intelligence*, **23**, 1986, pp. 2–4.

Sex differences

Several studies using tests similar to those employed in 11+ selection (e.g. Douglas *et al.*, 1968, Yates and Pidgeon, 1957; Fogelman *et al.*, 1978) have found similar patterns of sex differences at the age of 11 years. Broadly speaking, for achievement in mathematics and reading the average differences are small, while for both verbal and non-verbal reasoning tests the girls have higher average scores than boys. By the age of 16 years the boys show distinctly higher mean scores for mathematics and reading but the girls retain their higher mean score on the reasoning tests.

Such findings, of course, are specific to the tests used and an immediate issue is whether, in some way, existing tests are 'biased'. Pidgeon (personal communication) reports an item analysis for two reading tests, one of which slightly favoured boys while the other slightly favoured girls. He concluded that these differences were due to a different balance of items favouring one or other sex and that appropriate selection of items could have yielded a test with any desired bias towards either sex; moreover that relative changes with age could also be manipulated.

It would be interesting to speculate on how existing tests have come to exhibit these differences, and whether test constructors have, in some way, built in particular sex biases as a result of their procedures. There is certainly evidence of how current cultural assumptions and expectations did influence test construction historically (Gould, 1981). Given the manner in which many new tests are validated by requiring them to correlate highly with existing tests, the persistence of historical biases is unsurprising. Nevertheless, the existence of the possibility of designing tests tailored to favour one sex raises a number of problems directly relevant to the EOC judgement. Indeed, we may apply the same arguments to any identifiable groups, such as black and white children or those from different social groups, and there have been attempts in the USA, for example, to devise tests which favour blacks over whites. It is worth noticing that this kind of manipulation of test items is quite different from procedures, as used at Educational Testing Services and elsewhere, aimed at producing sex and race-fair tests by eliminating negative stereotypes, derogatory references, etc. Even following such procedures, tests are still open to manipulation. I shall return to this issue after considering the principal arguments advanced in support of separate sex norms on the basis of existing testing using verbal or non-verbal reasoning tests.

Separate sex norms

Advocates of separate sex norms in selection argue that the relative superiority of girls over boys at the age of 11 diminishes or is reversed by 16, and is due to the earlier 'maturity' of girls. Thus, since this advantage is a temporary phenomenon, it should be allowed for and this is most conveniently done by selecting equal numbers of girls and boys. There are, however, a number of difficulties with this argument.

First, while the sex difference does change over time to favour boys in achievement tests, it appears not to do so for verbal and non-verbal reasoning tests. Since the latter are often the principal tests used in selection the maturity argument would seem to have little support. Second, there is no real educational justification given for selecting equal numbers of boys and girls. If we are to base an 'adjust-ment' on subsequent performance then, depending on the assessment used, this would not lead in general to equal proportions. Third, subsequent performance is an unreliable guide, influenced as it is by the selection process itself, or such factors as sex stereotyping and differential subject choice. Adams (1984), on the basis of a large scale study in Australia, concluded that 'direct sex differences were found to be slight. This indicated that biological differences might be of relatively little importance in comparison with the more powerful societal and attitudinal factors'. Fourth, the idea of 'maturity' is borrowed from physical maturity, where in terms of bone maturity and size, girls are ahead of boys at the age of 11. As Tanner (1963) points out, however, measures of intellectual maturity are not available so that the analogy with physical development is improper. The only practical operationalization of the term 'maturity' is with reference to changing performance differences over time, and there is no reason why these should be ascribed to some 'innate' difference between the sexes rather than, say, to factors operating within schools or society. In fact, the typical justification for the use of verbal and non-verbal selection tests is redolent of the old and largely discredited view that IQ and reasoning tests in general reflect innate and unchanging abilities; a view which accords with the lack of change in the sex difference during the secondary school period, but which then hardly allows such tests to be used as measures of relative maturity. Finally, if one does accept the maturity argument, it is pertinent to ask why one should be content with adjusting only for sex differences. Thus, for example, as the number of other children in a child's household increases there is a relative decrease in reading and mathematics test scores between 11 and 16 years (Fogelman *et al.*, 1978). It would seem quite plausible to argue that children from large households mature earlier and that this should be compensated for by using separate 'household size' norms. No-one seems seriously to have suggested this for 11+ selection although in the context of compensating for disadvantage, the issue may be very relevant.

In short, the major arguments in support of separate sex norms for 11+ selection have no sound rational justification and continued existence of the practice there-fore would have to be justified on political and social grounds.

Conclusions

The wording of the EOC guidelines quoted in the introduction assumes that 'ability' (or attainment, or achievement) is theoretically recognizable and empiri-cally measurable. Both these assumptions, however, are tenuous, but they raise the interesting question of whether it is legitimate to formulate a theoretical description of achievement which explicitly includes a sex difference or a difference between recognizable groups in general. Such a difference might involve the whole distribution of achievement scores or grades rather than simply a mean difference.

We can see that there may be a legitimacy if we try to imagine a formulation which requires no differences at all, for this would then be making the assumption of equivalence between all groups. It seems therefore that some notion of expected or desired group differences (even if these are zero) is a necessary component of any theoretical model. Given such a choice, the problem becomes one of deciding which value system should determine the choice and how to deal with arguments such as those concerning compensation for disadvantage in admission to schools, higher education, employment and so forth.

In the UK this debate has not been as obvious as in the USA, but the issues remain. For example, if an LEA wished to comply strictly with EOC guidelines it should have little difficulty in finding somebody to produce a test for it which resulted in equal mean scores for boys and girls, so having the same practical result as using separate sex norms but without falling foul of the law. Likewise, there seems to have been a movement in recent years by the public exam boards towards multiple choice questions. Yet there is evidence that such questions tend to favour boys as against girls (Murphy, 1982), so that this policy by the boards might be said to discriminate against girls, although the boards' motivations are, for example, financial rather than sexist.

If we accept that equality of outcome is both legitimate and desirable and so wished to have an exam which produced equal score or grade distributions for boys and girls, then we might well be able to achieve this by careful choice of question format, content, etc. There are, of course, considerable difficulties in the way of achieving such an end, one being that entry rates for different exams differ markedly. Nevertheless, the resulting examinations might do much to encourage the sexes to participate more equally in certain subjects and the resulting effects on teaching and curriculum would be a rather interesting example of an assessment led pedagogy. As suggested earlier, gender is not the only characteristic one might wish to treat in this way, although it may well be easier and more socially acceptable to promote equality of assessment for the sexes than, say, for different social or ethnic groups. Yet, even after carrying through a procedure to eliminate, say, ethnic differences in order to equalize achievement, and even if this were technically feasible, it is somewhat difficult to imagine a consensus of agreement on the desirability; of course, attempts of this kind are anyway predicated upon the 'equality of outcome' assumption and there is a great deal of ideological discussion to be had on that issue. Needless to say, these arguments are equally relevant to current developments in assessment such as graded testing, and given the early stage of development of these initiatives it might be appropriate for those concerned to give some thought to the problems.

If we relinquish the notion of verbal and non-verbal tests as measuring some kind of 'permanent' or 'innate' quality which achievement tests do not, there is no good reason why the latter alone should not be used for 11+ selection. In this case the girls would not in general surpass the boys. In fact, it would not be too difficult for an LEA which wanted to do so, to provide a coherent 'educational' rationale for using as selection instruments a collection of existing tests to produce any desired balance of the sexes. It would be an interesting point of law as to whether such a procedure would be considered inadmissible under the act. In reality, of course, there are no choices which are purely 'educational' set outside of a socio-cultural context. Cultural assumptions and expectations, organizational constraints and explicit ideologies all play a part in the measurement of achievement, and in inferring individual potential. Whenever selection occurs, such factors will influence the relative 'success' of certain groups over others, and there is still a great deal to be learnt about this.

As far as the 11+ is concerned, one resolution is to abolish selection at that age, and in so far as this would resolve some of the difficulties, it constitutes another argument in favour of comprehensive secondary schooling. The general issue, however, will not go away as easily so long as selection remains important elsewhere in the educational system, and the EOC might usefully turn its attention, for example, to the examination bodies. Thus, the apparent fairness and simplicity of the EOC guidelines advising against the use of separate sex norms for selection, hides a much more complicated and difficult problem. Mere paper compliance with the guidelines is no guarantee of effective change of practice at the age of 11 or at other stages of the educational system.

Notes and references

1 Adams, R. J., *Sex Bias in ASAT?*, ACER Research monograph no. 24, Australian Council for Educational Research, Hawthorn, Victoria, 1984.

2 Douglas, J., Ross, J. M. and Simpson, H. R., *All Our Future*, London, Peter Davies, 1968.

3 Equal Opportunities Commission, *Do You Provide Equal Opportunities?*, Manchester, EOC, 1982.

4 Fogelman, K., Goldstein, H., Essen, J. and Ghodsian, M., 'Patterns of Attainment', *Educational Studies*, **4**, 1978, pp. 121–30.

5 Gould, S. J., *The Mismeasure of Man*, New York, W. W. Norton, 1981.

6 Tanner, J. M., *Education and Physical Growth*, London, University of London Press, 1963.

7 Wilby, P., *Threat to Single Sex Schools*, London, Sunday Times, 20 November 1983.

8 Yates, F. and Pidgeon, D., *Admission to Grammar School*, Slough, NFER, 1957.

9 Murphy, R. J., 'Sex differences in objective test performance', *Brit. J. Ed. Psychol*, **52**, 1982, pp. 213–19.

9 The construction of masculine science

Alison Kelly

Introduction

Science is masculine. This is now a commonplace observation, and the masculinity of science is often considered the prime reason that girls tend to avoid the subject at school. But to say that science is masculine raises as many questions as it answers. In this paper I want to explore the various levels at which school science is masculine, and examine the ways in which this masculinity is constructed during the early years of secondary schooling. By so doing I hope to contribute to the debate about the cultural reproduction of gender in schools. I am also concerned with the ways in which this process may be interrupted.

There are at least [three] distinct senses in which it can be argued that science is masculine. The most obvious is in terms of numbers – who studies science at school, who teaches it, who is recognized as a scientist. Second, there is the packaging of science, the way it is presented, the examples and applications that are stressed. Third, there are the classroom behaviours and interactions whereby elements of masculinity and femininity developed in out-of-school contexts are transformed in such a way as to establish science as a male preserve.

A [fourth] argument – that science is masculine because of some biological sex difference – will not be explored. It has been thoroughly debated elsewhere (see, for example, the papers in Kelly, 1981) and is highly contentious. To me it seems fundamentally uninteresting. Schools and society can choose to either exaggerate (as in physical education) or minimize (as with remedial reading classes taken largely by boys) any sex differences which may be biologically based. This paper is concerned with the social factors which link science and masculinity, and I hope to demonstrate that these are sufficiently strong to render any discussion of biological links superfluous.

It is not difficult to show that science is perceived by schoolchildren as masculine – although any statement to this effect has to be immediately qualified to say that it applies more to physical science than to biology and more to physics than to chemistry. Weinreich-Haste (1981) has demonstrated this in a simple yet clear way. Thirteen- and 14-year-old children were asked to rate school subjects on a number of dimensions, including masculine–feminine. Woodwork and physics were rated most highly masculine, followed by maths and chemistry. History and biology were fairly neutral, with English, French, typing and cookery being seen as feminine subjects. Weinreich-Haste also demonstrated that science was

Source: Extracted from Kelly, A., 'The construction of masculine science', *British Journal of Sociology of Education*, **6** no. 2, 1985, pp. 133–46 and 151–4.

associated with factors such as difficulty, hard rather than soft, things rather than people, and thinking rather than feeling, all of which are part of the cultural stereotype of masculinity. She argued that the image of the scientist is similarly not only male but also masculine in the sense of being cold, unemotional and logical.

Other studies have reached similar conclusions. There is also some evidence that girls who see science as masculine achieve less well in the subject than other girls (Smail and Kelly, 1985). However, my main concern in this paper is not to document the existence of the masculine image of science, nor to explore its implications. Neither am I concerned with the totality of the image of science, or the extent to which this image is a valid representation. The much more modest task I have set myself is to examine how the masculinity of science is reproduced in schools.

Much of the paper consists of a review of previous work, but it also reports some empirical results. The new material used in the analysis was collected as part of the Girls Into Science and Technology (GIST) project. GIST was an action-research project concerned to explicate the reasons for girls' under-achievement in physical science and technical subjects at school and simultaneously to explore the feasibility and effectiveness of interventions aimed at improving the situation. The project has been fully described elsewhere (Kelly *et al.*, 1984; Smail *et al.*, 1982; Whyte, 1986) and the details will not be repeated here. Briefly, a cohort of 2000 children in 10 coeducational comprehensive schools in the Greater Manchester area were followed from the time they entered secondary school (aged 11) until they made their option choices at the end of third year. Both quantitative and qualitative methods of data collection were used; the pupils completed attitude tests at the beginning and end of the project and they were observed in science and craft lessons. The results – including the field notes reported here – were fed back to the teachers as the project progressed.

The numbers game

Perhaps the simplest way in which science – or to be more precise, physical science – acquires its aura of masculinity, is through the numerical dominance of boys in science classes. 70 to 80 per cent of all examination entries in physics are from males, who also form about 60 per cent of all candidates in chemistry, but only 30–40 per cent of candidates in biology. This implies that physics and chemistry classes in the senior part of the secondary school are predominantly male, a fact which is evident to junior children, and presumably influences their perception of the subjects. Also evident to pupils is the fact that men comprise about 80 per cent of physics and chemistry teachers, but only about 50 per cent of biology teachers. Irrespective of the content of the lessons, these simple statistics immediately convey to children the message that this area of the curriculum is mainly for boys.

Pupils' images of science are derived from their life experiences as well as from fiction. In the GIST study we asked 11-year-old children, 'Do you know anyone who works in a scientific or technical sort of job? If yes, please tell us who it is and what they do (e.g. my sister is a motor mechanic).' Despite the loose definition of a scientist and the deliberately countersexist example, only 4 per cent of the pupils said they knew a woman scientist compared to 26 per cent who knew a man. Boys and girls were similar in this respect. The point here is not to question whether this is a true reflection of the representation of males and females in technical work (census figures suggest that it is), but to suggest that these pupils' perceptions of their surroundings help to foster the association of masculinity with science.

The predominance of males in science text books has been well documented, not only in this country (Kelly, 1976a; Samuel, 1981; Smail, 1984; Taylor, 1979; Walford, 1980, 1981) but in places as diverse as the United States (Gaetana, 1966; Heikkenen, 1978), the Soviet Union (Kelly, 1982; Walford, 1983b), Norway (Hilmo, 1983) and Holland (Lensink, 1983). Typically there are between two and ten times as many illustrations of and references to men and boys as there are for women and girls. This applies not only to published materials but also to school-produced worksheets. Indeed in several years of working with teachers and asking them to count the illustrations and gendered references in the materials they use, I have not yet found an example containing equal numbers of males and females. However there are similar imbalances in many areas of the curriculum with a more feminine image (see Whyld, 1983), so the importance of this should not be overstated.

Packaging science

Many of the authors who have analysed science textbooks have commented not only on the numbers of males and females involved but also on the way they are represented. Taylor (1979) concludes that, 'references to females were few, references to active females even fewer and references to females in scientific activities were virtually non-existent'. Walford (1980) notes that textbook representations of women and girls include, 'women pushing prams, a woman floating on the Dead Sea, girls blowing bubbles, women cooking, women as radiographers, nurses or patients, women used as sex symbols, women looking amazed or frightened, or simply women doing "silly" things'. Other authors reach similar conclusions. Girls and women are seldom included in science textbooks; when they do appear they do so in sex-stereotyped roles which serve to emphasize their marginal position in science.

By the time they reach secondary school, girls and boys differ in many ways. They have different interests and hobbies, different background experiences and they envisage different futures for themselves. Girls' interests centre around people, boys' around control (Gilligan, 1982). Based on their toys and childhood hobbies boys have much greater experience than girls of tinkering activities. They are also more interested in traditional topics in physical science and more likely to aspire to a science-based job (Kelly *et al.*, 1984; Smail & Kelly, 1985). Science curricula and science books which take for granted the sorts of experiences and interests which are characteristic of boys but unusual in girls thereby help to create a science with masculine connotations.

The argument here is similar to Bourdieu's (1971) thesis that class-based advantage is perpetuated by the transference of cultural capital when schools behave as though all their pupils have access to resources of background know-ledge which are actually only possessed by the privileged group.

This sort of curriculum is not hard to find. Both Taylor (1979) and Heikkenen (1978) comment on the small number of representations of people of either sex in science textbooks. This reinforces the notion that science is about things, not people, and increases the alienation from science of girls whose socialization is primarily towards people. Topics which are presented in an abstract and theor-etical way have the same tendency – boys can often see the career relevence of studying science and persevere where girls will not. Examples which concentrate on guns, cars, football and the industrial uses of science are similarly biased towards boys.

Duxbury (1984) understands this point. He advises fellow physics teachers to 'never take an interest in old radios, broken tape recorders or any other trash that boys may bring in to show you; if girls see you taking an interest it will merely confirm their worst suspicions'. Yet a lesson observed during the GIST project was introduced with the question, 'has anyone ever smashed a transistor radio, and pulled one apart or looked at any electronics?'. This experience was in fact peripheral to the content of the lesson. But to the extent that smashing things is a boys' activity it enhances girls' feelings of inadequacy. Another lesson started with a discussion of the acceleration of a car. The boys could and did compare the performance of different makes of car while the girls sat silent. A bicycle would have been a far less sex-stereotyped example. Similarly a demon-stration of eclipses which used a football to represent the earth was preceeded by a discussion between the boys and the (male) teacher about whose football it was, why it had been confiscated and how Manchester United had performed the previous Saturday. Although brief, this served to establish a rapport between the boys and the teacher from which the girls were excluded; the same demon-stration using a netball or balloon would have set the scene rather differently. The implications of this incident were readily admitted by the teacher when they were pointed out to him, but he had never previously considered the point.

Re-contextualization of gender

The argument that science is packaged in a masculine way depends upon the assumption that girls and boys have different interests by the time they enter secondary school. However, adolescent girls and boys also differ in other ways which have less immediate relevance to science. These differences in behaviour and self-perceptions influence classroom interactions in science (and elsewhere). In this section I will examine the ways in which such behaviour contributes to the masculinity of science by forming an indirect link between pupils' gender identity and the school subject. This is an area which has not been widely discussed, and I will, therefore, explore this line of reasoning in rather more depth than the previous ones.

Drawing on the work of Bernstein and Bourdieu, MacDonald (1980) argues that gender is re-contextualized within school so that 'the notions of appropriate behaviour for each sex [are] converted into the appropriate academic disciplines'. In the familial environment, children develop gender-differentiated ideologies and behaviours. These do not necessarily have any direct relevance to school subjects such as French or physics. But new differentiations can be linked to existing ones, so that some school subjects come to be seen as masculine and others as feminine. This process is dialectical – there is a 'transference of femininity . . . from the student to the school subject and back again to the student' (MacDonald, 1980). Thus once a subject has acquired a masculine image, participation in it is seen to enhance a boy's masculinity and diminish a girl's femininity.

MacDonald's discussion is purely theoretical and she does not provide any examples of the ways in which gender is re-contextualized in schools. However, this idea can fruitfully be applied to the question of the masculinity of science and discussion in this area can illustrate the more general sociological point. The GIST project included a small amount of classroom observation. I certainly do not want to claim that we carried out a thorough-going ethnographic analysis of the way that gender is re-contextualized in science lessons; our observations were far too limited and sporadic for that. However, many of the incidents we observed do illuminate the processes involved.

One of the key components of adolescent masculinity is toughness. This takes many forms from physical rough and tumble to bravado and self-confidence and it is clearly evident in the science laboratory. Almost any piece of apparatus can be used or abused to demonstrate a boy's toughness, as these extracts from my field notes show:

One example of force was a very strong magnet. Handed to boy to pass rounded, he and another boy immediately started a tug of war with it, only passed on at teacher's insistence. Periodically throughout lesson boys would try with it, girls never.

Spring balance used as catapult (boys).

Boys try to give each other shocks (with 6V battery!).

One group [of boys] mimic an interrogation using ray box as a bright light.

This type of example could be multiplied endlessly. It happened in virtually every lesson where apparatus was used – which in the post-Nuffield era means virtually every science lesson.

Some apparatus really is potentially dangerous, and then boys' toughness may give them a real advantage. For example, in a chemistry lesson the pupils were heating a chemical and collecting the gas which was given off under water, there was a slight risk that the water could suck back into the test tube which might then crack and scatter its contents. The boys in the group commented 'great' when the teacher warned them of the danger, whereas the girls were obviously scared of the experiment. They approached it tentatively (which increased the danger) and panicked and squealed whenever a suck-back seemed imminent. The boys' greater confidence meant that their reaction to a potential suck-back was more positive – they heated the substance harder or took the tube out of the water. In the end several girls gave up their own experiments and joined the boys' groups as onlookers.

Boys' toughness can take a verbal form. When one class were asked what they had thought of a test, the boys chorused 'easy' while the girls said rather plaintively that 'the electricity was horrible'. In fact, the boys and girls had done equally well on the test, so the difference in response was more indicative of attitude than achievement. To admit that they had had difficulty might have been seen as a sign of weakness in the boys.

The boys' self-confidence is also shown in the way they answer questions:

... in class discussion round the front the boys were falling over themselves to give the answer and the girls were sitting back. . . . Boys know technical vocabulary. . . . Boys give lots of examples of light bending, mostly wrong (e.g. with magnet) but they don't care.

Here the boys are actively participating in the lesson, the girls are passively listening (or not listening). There is a considerable element of bravado in the boys' use of technical terms that they don't really understand, but if they don't mind taking the risk of being wrong there's always the chance that it will impress someone.

This enthusiastic participation by the boys left the girls at a considerable disadvantage, particularly over apparatus. The most striking instance of this was an incident observed by Barbara Smail, the Schools Liaison Officer in Science on the GIST project. Pupils were doing an experiment in groups which involved heating carbohydrates over a flame. There were insufficient goggles for everyone, so the teacher stressed that only the person actually doing the heating should have a pair. When it was time to start the experiment all the boys rushed for the apparatus and grabbed the goggles. Soon nearly every boy in the class had a pair, with none left for the girls. Since pupils of this age always work in single-sex groups by choice, the girls could not do the experiment. They had to go round the groups of boys begging for pairs of goggles – and generally getting short shrift until the teacher noticed what was happening and intervened. By the time the girls were properly equipped they were so behind with the experiment that they could not complete it before the end of the period, and so got very little out of that lesson – although they probably learned something about power relationships.

This is an extreme example, but similar situations are not uncommon. Boys frequently make a dash for the apparatus and end up with the lion's share, or at least the bits in better condition. Although this could be seen merely as an indication of boys' greater enthusiasm, it can also be interpreted in terms of male dominance. Whyte (1984) has described how boys push into queues ahead of girls, 'persuade' them to give up scarce pieces of apparatus and monopolize the classroom space. This is evident in science as elsewhere. For example:

Boys wanted to show teacher their completed table of results. Often pushed in on a demonstration to girls, twice taking the teacher away from that demonstration. When girls wanted help they waited till teacher had finished whatever she was doing.

At one point a boy donned the goggles that a girl had put down for a second . . . the teacher noticed this and reprimanded him. He gave the goggles back, assuming surprise that she had not finished.

Rush for apparatus at start of practical – a crush of boys with a few girls, most girls followed later.

The boys . . . moved freely around the room, chatting to each other. . . . The girls restricted themselves to their benches and the teacher's table.

Boys act as though they have automatic priority over the resources of the laboratory, whether they be the apparatus, the teacher's attention, or just the physical space. One of the general principles of a patriarchal society – that males are more important than females – is acted out in the science classroom in a way which limits girls' opportunities to learn.

Boys' assumption of their own superiority can also be seen in their interactions with girls in class. I have already remarked that boys are more willing to call out the answers to questions, and in the GIST project we advised teachers to minimize this behaviour by asking questions of specific individuals rather than the class as a whole. However, even when this was done, it was not uncommon for a boy to shout out the answer to a question directed at a girl before she had a chance to answer. Boys seemed to think they knew more about science than the girls and they tried to demonstrate their superiority. For example, I noted,

one boys cruises round inspecting girls' written work almost like a teacher.

boys outside look at girls work through window, make comments.

and sometimes the girls acquiesced:

several occasions on which girls watch boys doing experiments, as if to learn from them.

However, classroom interactions were not always as amicable as this. Adolescent boys are characteristically scornful of girls, and there were many instances of boys using ridicule to remind the girls of their inferior status.

when girls ask questions in class discussion, boys tend to groan (3 times). [Teacher] controls them, 'no it's a good question'.

quite a lot of put-down comments from boys to girls. Jane has already done today's work . . . and complains about doing it again. Boys call out, 'you're stupid though, aren't you, Jane'.

Girl: 'I got it wrong' (spelling).

Boy: 'You would do, wouldn't you?'.

There are no examples in the notes of this sort of comment directed at boys by girls.

Although there was some teasing of girls by boys (for example getting hold of and weighing a girl's shoe instead of their own) we recorded only one instance of anything that could be called sexual harassment. This was a poster on heat loss from a house which was up on the laboratory wall. It had been made by two girls, who had obviously put a lot of work into it, with text, pictures and beautiful lettering. Beside one of their names someone had written SLAG. The salience of this insult for girls has been discussed by Cowie and Lees (1981) and to run the risk of having it publically associated with your name must been seen as a strong sanction against a girl whose work is good enough to be displayed for all to see. Teenage schoolgirls often report sexual harassment, particularly when there are only a few girls in a class of boys (Kelly, 1981), but it may be that this is characteristic of an older age group than the 11 to 14-year-olds we observed in GIST.

On hearing these accounts, some people have commented on the terrible behaviour of the boys and asked whether they were drawn from a particularly anti-school sub-group. The answer is no. They were an ordinary cross-section of ordinary boys in ordinary schools. My argument is precisely that the ordinary, everyday, taken-for-granted ways that boys behave form a link between masculinity and dominance in science. These behaviours are commonplace – so commonplace that they are virtually invisible.

So far I have been concentrating on boys and the way their masculine behaviour, when imported into the laboratory, helps to establish science as a male domain. But boys' behaviour is only part of the picture. Girls' feminine traits also have a role to play. For example, girls' timidity may mean that they take less part in classroom discussions and avoid experiments which they consider dangerous. It also tends to make them fearful of venturing into new ground. This was illustrated in a lesson where the children were supposed to weigh a few things of their own when they had completed their worksheets: whereas the boys measured a great variety of objects, the girls tended to sit around doing nothing or repeated their previous measurements. In this and other experiments the girls checked with each other and with the boys that they had got the right answer.

Low self-confidence is linked to conscientiousness as pupils try to ensure that they are doing the correct thing. Teachers frequently remark that girls are more conscientious than boys and this was certainly evident in the science laboratories. Sometimes it stood the girls in good stead – they were more likely to be working than the boys who tended to play around with their apparatus the moment the teacher's back was turned (often to the annoyance of the girls). But sometimes it backfired. School science equipment is rough and ready and does not lend itself to precise measurement. For example, in a lesson, where pupils had to balance a ruler on a sharp edge by moving weights to different positions, the girls got worried if the ruler was not completely level and spent a long time trying to achieve perfect equilibrium. Because of this they did not experiment with many different positions of the weights; the boys' less precise approach meant that they quickly built up a table of results from which they could work out the general principles.

Of course some girls *are* good at science. But even they seem to realize that their success is not something to brag about. In a lesson on heat there were two girls, Jean and Helen, who obviously understood what was going on and handled the technical vocabulary with ease. Towards the end of the lesson the pupils had to write up the experiment, explaining the pattern they got on their graphs. A group of girls called out to Jean, asking her what to say. She replied, 'I don't know, I'll manage when I get home, I'll ask my Dad' and then went to give them the correct explanation. She was then called over by a group of boys and was explaining the work to them until the teacher sent her back to her seat. Although Jean's ability was clearly recognized by the rest of the class, she herself played it down and attributed her knowledge to her Dad (not, of course, to her Mum).

It could be argued that Jean was taking the teacher role here in the same way as the boys discussed earlier who inspected the girls' work. But the teacher in class acts both as helper and as judge of the pupils' work. In context it seemed that Jean was acting as a helper, called in where she was needed, whereas the boys were judging girls' work without being asked to do so. It was not unusual to see a group of girls being helped by a competent friend, but able boys were more likely to be working alone or competing with one other to see who could get through the worksheets fastest.

Another common sight was that of a girl acting as a helper to a boy. This again can be seen as a way in which familial gender roles are transformed at school. Girls are frequently socialized into a service role, providing for and tidying up after men, and they continue these tasks in the laboratory:

Boy (Nigel) on back bench has girls there working for him. They are getting on better with the experiment than he is, but he's definitely in charge. Pinches their light bulb, teases them with it. Girl helps him make his circuit work – he comments that hers (which is working) is wrong, and that he hasn't got the woman's touch. When they decide that his board is defective, Nigel sends girl to teacher with it. In cleaning up she again carries his board to put it away.

At one point a couple of boys moved their apparatus to a girls' table and girls helped them do it. After a short while the boys started using a ruler as a springboard to flip brass squares.

Four girls chosen . . . to give out workbooks.

At the end several girls were helping the teacher pack up the apparatus, count brass squares, etc. Other pupils were working on the arithmetical problems.

It does not take much insight to deduce that pupils who are working on arithmetical problems are learning a different lesson than those who are counting brass squares!

A strong component of femininity is concern with people. This can be difficult to manifest in science, where the brass squares, light bulbs and copper sulphate often seem to have nothing to do with people. Some girls solve this problem by focusing on the teacher rather than the subject matter. They manufacture opportunities for interaction with the teacher:

Teacher wanders round room. Whenever he approaches girls' bench they seem to find something to ask. . . . Boys more often ignore T's presence. Particularly noticeable with group of girls at front bench who chat to teacher whenever he sits to mark books, etc.

At start of practical work several girls seemed to go to [teacher] with trivial questions about what to do. [Teacher]: 'What does it *tell* you to do?' They prefer instructions in personal form, rather than impersonally from worksheets.

Some of the girls took a 'mothering' role, e.g. discussing boil on teacher's neck, advising him what to do about it. At other times he seemed to be almost flirting with them, discussing their English exam, their haircut, etc.

Although the freedom of movement and opportunities for conversation in the science lab do allow for interpersonal interaction this remains peripheral – or even antipathetic – to the science being taught. The masculine concern with things fits more easily with the dominant form of physical science than the feminine concern with people. This is much less true of biology and may be one of the reasons that biology has a feminine or neutral image.

Adolescent girls are generally greatly concerned about their looks. In every lesson I have observed one or more girls brushed or combed her hair. This is another aspect of femininity which can be at odds with science. For safety reasons hair is supposed to be tied back in laboratories and protective clothing sometimes has to be worn. None of this is glamorous and girls are often reluctant to comply:

Teacher tells kids to wear safety goggles during practical, when girl asks why he replies, 'you want to stay beautiful don't you?' I think this emphasis on beauty is counter-productive – safety goggles are anything but flattering and at later stages of the practical very few girls were actually wearing them – most propped up on their hair or lying on benches. No hair was tied back. Quite a lot of hairdressing (brushing, styling, etc.) during lesson.

In fact this reluctance to wear goggles seemed to be greatest in the class where the teacher (by his own admission) made a point of emphasizing the girls' femininity.

Many teachers, consciously or unconsciously, use gender stereotypes in their lessons. One head of science, reflecting on the experience of being observed in the GIST project, wrote that:

If no obvious interest in the subject or topic is displayed, the male teaching staff often flatter the girls or are mildly flirtatious towards them, finding that this is often a successful way of encouraging them. In the same circumstances male teachers will probably appeal to the boys' competitive instincts. We accept that treating the sexes differently in this way may well be encouraging them to see their roles in the world of science differently but are reluctant to abandon successful teaching techniques.

Here a 'successful teaching technique' seems to mean one that makes the lesson happen rather than one which develops in girls a lasting interest in science. One of the clearest cases occurred in a discussion between a male head of chemistry in a mixed school and a female head of chemistry from a girls' school. The man described how he conducted the common experiment in which coal dust is mixed with water and then filtered out so that clean water emerges from the black sludge. He commented that he always dared his class to drink the water; the boys usually did, but the girls hung back. He concluded from this that the girls were in some way inadequate in science – and presumably the girls reached a similar conclusion. However the woman teacher replied that when she did the same experiment she mixed some colouring with the water before filtering, so that a pretty pink liquid appeared at the end. By so doing she was appealing to the girls' aesthetic sense where the male teacher was utilizing the boys' bravado. The science was the same (except that the girls learned that only some impurities are removed by filtering – the colouring remained) but the context was masculine in one case and feminine in the other.

Another way in which teachers' preconceptions may influence their relationship with girls and boys is in their perception of who is competent and who needs help. Crossman (1981) has shown that science teachers (like teachers of other subjects (Spender, 1982)) generally interact more with boys than with girls in class. With the GIST teachers, who knew what we were interested in, we did not find any differences in the overall number of interactions with girls and with boys (Whyte, 1984). However there was a tendency for the interactions to be of a different nature. This was most obvious in a lesson taken by a probationary teacher where I noted that,

In the question and answer part of the lesson boys interacted with the teacher much more than girls. Boys were far more often picked to answer questions than girls, even when girls had their hands up. Girls were more tentative about volunteering, tended to put their hands up and down again. In the practical part of the lesson the teacher spent a lot more time helping the girls than the boys. In some cases he seemed to be setting the apparatus up for them rather than helping them do it themselves. At the end the boys were appealing, 'Sir, come and look at ours'. The distinct impression from this lesson was that the boys knew the answers and the girls couldn't do the practical.

This tendency for teachers to help the girls more than the boys was fairly common, but by no means universal.

Another common difference in the treatment of the sexes which does not show up in a simple count is that boys are often called on to give the correct answer that a girl has failed. For example:

Teacher: 'Does anybody except David know what that means? Do you know Linda or Tracey at the back? Sharon you've been quiet. Go on David, tell them.'

This emphasizes the fact that the boy, David, is more knowledgeable than the three girls. It would probably have been possible to find a girl in the class who *did* know, or to rephrase the question so that Linda, Tracey or Sharon could work it out.

Treating girls and boys in the *same* way in class sometimes means treating girls as though they were boys, so reinforcing girls' uneasiness in science lessons. This applies particularly in areas where there is potential danger. Many schools start their science courses with a safety lesson, emphasizing the need to take care with gas taps, acids, etc. While this may be necessary to quieten down the more exuberant boys it does nothing for the self-confidence of girls, whose worst fears about science may be confirmed. Similarly worksheets which are festooned with 'Do Not' instructions can inhibit girls so that they are reluctant to touch the apparatus at all (Smail, 1984).

However, I do not want to exaggerate the teacher's part in maintaining gender differentiation. On the contrary it is my contention that it is largely the behaviour of the children themselves which is crucial. Boys bring with them to science lessons a conception of masculinity which includes timidity, conscientiousness, deference, person orientation and a concern for appearance. These self-definitions lead girls and boys to behave in different ways, such that boys come to dominate the laboratory and establish it as their territory. Gender differentiated behaviour outside school leads to gender-differentiated behaviour in science lessons, which in turn leads to science acquiring a masculine image. The in-school and out-of-school behaviours are by no means identical, but they have a common source in children's gender identity.

There is also the question of the class structure of science and the way in which science changes from a predominantly practical subject in the lower part of the secondary school to an increasingly theoretical activity at higher levels. Willis (1977) discusses how manual work reinforces the masculinity of working-class boys and this is the version of masculinity fostered at school in technical crafts such as metalwork and car mechanics which are taken predominantly by working-class males. Physical science is somewhat different; it is considered a difficult subject, involving mental labour as well as manual, and leading to middle-class opportunities in research and teaching. The distinction must not be overdrawn;

47 per cent of all boys (compared to 12 per cent of girls) study physics in fourth and fifth year (DES, 1975) and working-class boys who get to university are more likely to study science and engineering than the arts subjects (Kelly, 1976b). Nevertheless there is a real sense in which the activity-based masculinity of science which is established in the early years of secondary school (largely by extending behaviour learned out-of-school into a new context) has to be transformed in later years into a version of masculinity where power is exerted through controlled thought and patient experiments. I would suggest that the few, almost exclusively middle-class, girls who persist with science are already seeing it in this way and utilizing their conscientiousness to construct a version of science consistent with their self-images. The larger, more socially mixed, group of boys have to restructure their notion of masculinity from physical power to mental power as they progress further in science. But my observations, confined as they are to the lower part of secondary school, cannot illuminate that process.

End piece

The gender stereotyping of science cannot be divorced from gender stereotyping generally and there are many communalities across the school curriculum. The images in science books of housewives delighting at how well their washing dries on a hot, windy day have their counterparts in the woman who dissolves into tears to get her way in a German text (Hingley, 1983). The GIST science teacher who introduced the behaviour of light by saying 'your Mum has just opened the curtains' is mirrored by the Technical Drawing teacher who used the example of how mother would cut a birthday cake to introduce the idea of degrees in a circle (Delamont, 1980). All are trying to make their lessons more relevant to their pupils' lives, but in so doing they are relying upon and reinforcing stereotypes of 'real life'.

My concern here has not been with these communalities, but with the specific features of physical science by which it acquires its masculinity. I have argued that there are two main mechanisms by which this masculinity is reproduced in schools. These are the curriculum packaging of science which, by its emphasis on controlling nature and its apparent irrelevance to people's lives, takes boys' orientations to life as normal. And the nature of classroom interactions in the laboratory which give scope for boys' bravado and disdain for girls to be transformed into superior competence at science.

References

Bourdieu, P., 'Cultural reproduction and social reproduction', in M. F. D. Young (ed.), *Knowledge and Control*, London, Collier Macmillan, 1971.

Cowie, C. and Lees, S., 'Slags or drags', *Feminist Review*, **9**, 1981, pp. 17–32.

Crossman, M., 'Sex differences and teacher/pupil interaction patterns in secondary school science', M. Ed. Dissertation, Manchester University, 1981.

Delamont, S., *Sex Roles and the School*, London, Methuen, 1980.

DES, *Curricular Differences for Boys and Girls*, Education Survey 21, London, HMSO, 1975.

DES, *Statistics of Education 1982*, London, HMSO, 1983.

Duxbury, J., 'Girls and physics – the role of a Head of Science', *School Science Review*, **65**, 1984, pp. 648–54.

Gaetana, M. A. K., 'A study to determine the distribution of male and female figures in elementary science text books', *Journal of Research in Science Teaching*, **4**, 1966, pp. 178–9.

Gilligan, C., *In a Different Voice*, Harvard University Press, 1982.

Heikkenen, H., 'Sex bias in chemistry texts: where is women's place?', *The Science Teacher*, **45**, 1978, pp. 16–21.

Hilmo, I., 'An analysis of Norwegian textbooks in science', paper prepared for 2nd GASAT Conference, Norway, September 1983.

Hingley, P., 'Modern languages', in J. Whyld (ed.), *Sexism in the Secondary Curriculum*, Harper & Row, 1983.

Kelly, A., 'Women in physics and physics education', in J. Lewis (ed.), *New Trends in Physics Teaching*, **III**, UNESCO, 1976, pp. 241–66.

Kelly, A., 'Family background, subject specialisations and occupational recruitment of Scottish university students', *Higher Education*, **5**, 1976, pp. 177–88.

Kelly, A. (ed.), *The Missing Half: girls and science education*, Manchester, Manchester University Press, 1981.

Kelly, A., 'Science in Soviet schools', *Women and Education Newsletter*, no. 24, 1982.

Kelly, A. *et al.*, 'Traditionalists and trendies: a study of teachers' attitudes to educational issues', *British Educational Research Journal*, **5**, 1985.

Kelly, A., Whyte, J. and Smith, B., *Final Report of the GIST Project*, Department of Sociology, University of Manchester, 1984.

Lensick, M., 'Girls, physics and technology in the Netherlands: the MENT project', paper prepared for 2nd GASAT Conference, Norway, September 1983.

MacDonald, M., 'Schooling and the reproduction of class and gender relations', in L. Barton, R. Meighan and S. Walker (eds), *Schooling, Ideology and the Curriculum*, London, Falmer, 1980.

Samuel., J., 'Experiences of teaching chemistry in a mixed comprehensive school', in A. Kelly (ed.), *The Missing Half*, Manchester, Manchester University Press, 1981.

Smail, B., *Girl-Friendly Science*, London, Schools Council/Longman, 1984.

Smail, B. and Kelly, A., 'Sex differences in science and technology among eleven year old schoolchildren: II attitudes', *Research in Science and Technology Education*, 1984.

Smail, B., Whyte, J. and Kelly, A., 'Girls Into Science and Technology: the first two years', *School Science Review*, **63**, 1982, pp. 620–30.

Spender, D., 'The role of teachers: what choices do they have?', in Council of Europe (ed.), *Sex Stereotyping in Schools*, Swets and Zeitlinger, 1982.

Taylor, J., 'Sexist bias in physics textbooks', *Physics Education*, **14**, 1979, pp. 227–80.

Walford, G., 'Sex bias in physics textbooks', *School Science Review*, 1980, pp. 220–7.

Walford, G., 'Do chemistry textbooks present a sex-biased image', *Education in Chemistry*, **18**, 1981, pp. 18–19.

Walford, G., 'Science education and sexism in the Soviet Union', *School Science Review*, **64**, 213–24.

Weinreich-Haste, H. E., 'The image of science', in A. Kelly (ed.), *The Missing Half*, Manchester, Manchester University Press, 1981.

Whyld, J. (ed.), *Sexism in the Secondary Curriculum*, Harper and Row, 1983.

Whyte, J., 'Observing sex stereotypes and interactions in the school lab. and workshop', *Educational Review*, **36**, 1981, pp. 75–86.

Whyte, J., *Getting the GIST*, Henley-on-Thames, Routledge and Kegan Paul, 1986.

Willis, P., *Learning to Labour*, Saxon House, 1977.

Part Three

Gender, Power and Schools

10 Education: the patriarchal paradigm and the response to feminism

Dale Spender

It can be established that feminism has made great gains within the field of education: the astounding growth of women's studies courses in many countries, the development of alternative and successful models of teaching and learning, the systematic and convincing critiques of the way in which knowledge is constructed and disseminated, and the establishment of diverse and far reaching research programmes are all testimony to the feminist achievement within the educational field. In the first part [of this chapter] I will be concerned with legitimated or mainstream education, which is male-controlled and which has remained almost impervious to feminism. In the second part I will document the achievements of feminist education and argue that it is more a case of what mainstream educationalists can learn from feminism than what feminism can learn from education.

It has been argued that it is difficult to talk about education in monolithic terms – even to call it a discipline – and to assume that it has a paradigm which informs and circumscribes its parameters. As D. R. McNamara (1979) has pointed out in reference to Thomas Kuhn's conceptualization, the existence of a paradigm would suggest that there is a single theory which provides educationalists with a means of explaining and understanding the world, and this is most certainly *not* the case. If education had a paradigm then we would expect to find a community of scholars who manifested a high degree of consensus working within a unified theoretical framework, whereas we find almost the reverse:

There is hardly ever (never?) a sustained endeavour by a community of researchers investigating a specific issue within the context of a dominant theoretical perspective. There is no group of researchers working in similar fields and ready to replicate each other's research – even if a replication were possible. There is no series of classic experiments or exercises which students must practice in laboratory-like settings (McNamara, 1979, p. 169).

While from McNamara's point of view it may be difficult to detect a 'dominant theoretical perspective' or a unifying framework, I do not find it a difficult task at all, for as a feminist it is possible to see that the diverse theories and practices – and the assumptions on which they rest – share common features which bring them together within a coherent framework. Whether it be educational theory *or* practice which is analysed it can generally be claimed that it is a product of male experience and remains firmly within male control. Patriarchy is the education paradigm.

Source: Extracted from Spender, D. (ed.), *Men's Studies Modified*, Oxford, Pergamon Press, 1981, pp. 155–73.

What I intend to do here is to (briefly) outline the nature and extent of male dominance in education and to comment on some of its implications. I want to show how that male dominance is used to perpetuate male dominance and to indicate the repercussions that would be the outcome of a successful feminist challenge to education.

In terms of the organization of education in Britain it is relatively easy to establish that education is male-defined and controlled with the result that women – and their particular experience of the world – are excluded. While it is indisputable that there are many women 'in' education, the crucial issue is when they arrived and what influence they possess, for women are to be found concentrated in a particular, and not always prestigious activity, that of teaching, and their entry even to this level is relatively recent.

Raymond Williams (1975) has claimed that the education model which we inherited in part and which we accept today (and which constitutes our notions of 'a good education' and how it can best be implemented) is in many respects one that 'was essentially created by the nineteenth century, following some eighteenth century models, and retaining elements of the medieval' (p. 172). Feminists do not need to be reminded that there were few – if any – women who were consulted or permitted to participate in the construction of that model in medieval times, in the eighteenth century or the nineteenth century. Indeed one of the features of that model was that it was most inappropriate for women; their brains would burst, their uteri atrophy, they would become unsuitable for motherhood if they were to receive what was considered 'a good education' for a man. Women were excluded then from conceptualizing education and they are still excluded today.

For while in the twentieth century there are women in education, they are not the policy-makers or decision-makers. They still do not participate in the process of deciding what education could/should be. The model of education which passes as the society's model is the model generated by men, based on men's experience of the world, and women are required to be educated in a manner devised by men as befitting men.

Statistics can sometimes expose the fallacies of our own perceptions. It is sometimes thought that there are quite a few women in influential positions in education in Britain (and other countries) but if we believe this we are forgetting just how 'visible' one woman in an influential position can be. To those who think that women have some say in the policy-making area of education Eileen Byrne's (1978) figures can come as a substantial shock for she states that 97 per cent of the 'government of education' is male. She also notes that girls get an 'inferior' education and draws a link between the two. Because the policy-making bodies are almost exclusively male, she says, women are given 'a different, often inferior education planned perhaps with no conscious ill-intent' (p. 15) but which nevertheless helps to maintain the asymmetry of the sexes.

While similar, Dorothy Smith's analysis is a more subtle one. She too notes that men are the predominant policy-makers in education in Canada but rather than seeing this as a means by which women are given an 'inferior' education, she sees this as a means of keeping women, and women's experience, out of education and out of the culture in general. 'Women's participation in the education process at all levels has increased this century' she says, and yet 'this participation remains within marked boundaries. Among the most important of these boundaries, I would argue, is that which reserves to men control of the policy making and decision making apparatus in the educational system' (Smith, 1978, p. 287).

This is a substantial source of power for it allows men to legislate on the substantive nature of education. As Smith says, it is men who are the 'gatekeepers', it is they who are setting the standards, producing the social knowledge, decreeing what is significant, appropriate, relevant, and what will and will not be admitted to the systems of distribution, determining what will count as innovation in thought, or values, ruling what is legitimate in the light of their own *male* experience (p. 287). As a result, the male experience becomes the norm, the yardstick against which any female experience that is different is found to be 'deviant'.

While men continue to consult only men, to validate educational theory and practice in the light of male experience (as they must almost inevitably do in Britain if males comprise 97 of the government of education) then it is almost *structurally* impossible for women to 'have a voice'. They have no access to the circles in which models of education are conceptualized, with the result that any models which they generate – and which may be different from men's – remain outside the educational process. Smith says, 'Let us be clear that we are not talking about prejudice or sexism as a particular bias against women or as a negative stereotype of women.' This is not just the provision of an 'inferior' education in which girls are in receipt of less educational resources and are channelled into humanities and typing (although as Eileen Byrne rightly points out, this is part of the pattern of precluding them from being the *future* members of the government of education). 'We are talking about the consequences of women's exclusion from a full share in the making of what becomes treated as *our* culture', says Smith (p. 283), their exclusion from a full share in the making of what becomes *our* education.

This is why it is difficult for feminism to enter the educational arena: it is also why many established educationalists consciously or unconsciously resist feminist influence and even discount or ignore the feminist voice.

In general, women depend upon men for promotion to influential positions. It is men who control who shall be admitted to their ranks (and in Britain, judging from the personal accounts I have access to, it seems, understandably, that they show little inclination to appoint feminists). When it is men who can decree what shall be recognised as 'proper qualifications' then women who seek to join their ranks must indicate their familiarity with and adherence to those male values which legitimate 'proper qualifications'. According to Dorothy Smith, such women have minimum 'voting power', they can endorse, but not veto. The women who do obtain influential positions, says Smith 'are those who have passed through this very rigorous filter. They are those whose work and style of work and conduct have met with the approval of judges who are largely men'. She adds, 'And, in any case, they are very few' (Smith, 1978, p. 289).

In these circles even if the few women who were permitted access were to propose models which were 'different' then they could find they were treated individually as women are collectively: their alternatives, by definition would be 'wrong'. The chances of alternatives which have their origin in women's experience being treated as a 'refinement', an 'improvement', an 'extension' are remote, in a society where women are 'deviants' and in a context where women are tolerated (provided they are 'well behaved'). It is more likely that women who suggested that education should incorporate features of women's experience (co-operation rather than competition, for example) would themselves be viewed as inadequate, rather than that the male norm should be exposed as inadequate: it would be the women who were perceived as 'incompetent' or 'unbalanced' and not necessarily education.

Because education as we know it today has always been controlled by men, the educational model(s) which they have devised have always assumed the status of the norm, and this has circumscribed (and still does circumscribe) the model(s) which women may generate. When women began to claim education as a right in Britain in the nineteenth century, men had already agreed the general nature of education and how it could best be brought to fruition, and women found themselves either obliged to adopt the norm, or to develop a 'deviant' model, for there was little or no opportunity to generate an autonomous model of their own. Frances Buss (the North London Collegiate School, Camden Girls' School) and Emily Davies (Girton College), for example, adopted the male model, and sought to have girls excel in its terms, while Dorothea Beale (Cheltenham Ladies' College), and Anne Clough (Newnham College, Cambridge) were concerned with protecting feminine accomplishments, with introducing academic work of a kind that was appropriate to girls, with special examinations for women, and they were among those who developed a subsidiary and subordinate form of education – for the subsidiary and subordinate sex (Jill Lavigueur, 1977, pp. 66–9). In either case it was the male version of education that was taken as the reference point. That any values which women may have been able to contribute have been excluded is a point which is made by Rita McWilliams-Tullberg in her book on women at Cambridge for while women have been admitted (though not to full membership until 1948) they have been submerged, and Cambridge remains '*A men's university – though of a mixed type*'.

And this does not just apply to Cambridge: Jenny Shaw (1976) has claimed that although it was initially believed that the collapse of a single-sex education would result in a 'mix' somewhere between an all-male and an all-female school, this has not happened. The identity of single-sex girls' schools has been lost, has been submerged, with mixed-sex schools actually more like boys' schools. Allowing females access but preserving the male ethos and definitions has been one way of 'accommodating' women without requiring modification from males.

Within any discipline there are agencies which help to promote, assess, legitimate and generally monitor the knowledge which is generated within that discipline. Professional associations, conferences and periodicals all help to 'make' the individuals (who in turn, 'make' their successors) by selecting who is to speak, who is to publish, who validates courses, acts as a referee or examiner, and therefore, who will 'shape' the direction in which the discipline proceeds. But these individuals are more than 'gatekeepers'; they do not simply check what passes through their hands, passing that which is acceptable and eliminating that which is not. They can play a much more active role. By having a say in what does and does not get funded as research they are also able to influence what knowledge gets generated.

There are two important issues here for feminists. The first is that what is perceived to be 'problematic', what requires explanation and research, is that which is problematic for men. The second is that because men fund their own research they are in a position to 'flood' the literature, to define the central foci as the problems of men and to perpetuate their own practices. At every level then, men are able to exclude women from the construction of knowledge: they can exclude them as subjects when they set up research which is problematic to men, they can exclude them as reseachers and theorists by not allocating funding to projects which are perceived as problematic to women and by 'disallowing' women's unfunded research (the bulk of feminist research in education).

Many of the women who are engaged in educational research outside educational institutions have stated that when they put forward their proposals *inside* the institutions, they were informed that they did not constitute a valid topic. Others have said that although their proposals were initially accepted so many attempts were made to 'neutralize' them, to shift them towards the central foci, the more 'important' issues, that they could see little point in continuing. Some women have been told that they must remove the feminist element from their research because it constituted bias: in a context in which masculism runs rife through research (but which is endorsed as the norm and therefore perceived as neutral) it is clear that the 'bias' resides in the established practitioners rather than the feminist research. Women engaged in research outside the official parameters seem to readily agree that if they wished to work inside they were obliged to fit their research to male standards, thereby directly or indirectly facilitating the perpetuation of male ends. Given the vast number of feminist projects underway in education, the fact that the 1978 *Index to Theses* reveals that there were only three degrees awarded on what could be called, broadly speaking, issues that were 'problematic' to women, it seems that most women are working outside the system. This of course is perfectly understandable, even predictable.

The scale on which women have been omitted from educational consideration is massive. Sandra Acker (1980) has surveyed the area of the sociology of education (in Britain) and from 184 articles published since 1960 she has been able to give some details of the absence of women. For example, the study of women has been minimal for while 58 per cent of the articles purported to be studying both sexes, 37 per cent had all male samples and only 5 per cent all female samples (and as she points out, these all-female groups were often *mothers* who were being studied in relation to their influence on children).

More knowledge is generated about males, more attention and signficance accorded to male experience, and if anthropologists were to use the literature of the sociology of education (and there is no reason to suspect that it is not representative of education as a whole) to 'crack the code' of our own culture in the way they do in other cultures, then, Acker says, they

would conclude that numerous boys but few girls go to secondary modern schools; that there are no girls' public schools; that there are almost no adult women influentials of any sort; that most students in higher education study science and engineering; that women rarely make a ritual transition called 'from school to work' and never go into further education colleges. Although some women go to university, most probably enter directly into motherhood where they are of some interest as transmitters of language codes to their children. And except for a small number of teachers, social workers and nurses, there are almost no adult women workers in the labour market (Acker, 1980, p. 5).

This enormous bias, however, generally goes unacknowledged: as Acker notes, most researchers do not even think it necessary to give reasons for excluding women. The fact that virtually no one in the research community (feminists excluded) has ever drawn attention to this bias would seem to indicate that the assumption that women were not data has been shared.

Even where women have been included as subjects for study, however, their presence can still be discounted – women can still be classified as non data. Having established their theories and formulated their hypotheses in terms of male experience, and having assumed that male experience constitutes human experience, many reseachers have expressed surprise and bewilderment when they have 'encountered' women in their research and found the behaviour of women inconsistent with or contrary to male predictions.

In the articles which she surveyed, Acker found that

Witkin is puzzled as 'the findings for girls in secondary modern schools were not anticipated'. For Synge, the high educational aspirations of rural girls were 'contrary to expectations'. Robinson and Rackstraw admit 'at present we have no supportable explanation to offer for these occasional sex differences in performance'. Liversidge is surprised that working class girls' occupational aspirations don't differ much between those in grammar schools and in modern schools, unlike those of boys. And Robertson and Kapur go so far as to say that their results for women students are bizarre (Acker, 1980, p. 9).

The surprise and bewilderment expressed by some researchers at the 'abormal' findings related to women has not always led them to question whether their theories apply to only half the human race. The 'deficiency' has been found in women and not the assumptions of male educationalists and by continuing to treat the different behaviour of women as 'deviancy' they have helped to reinforce the structural exclusion of women.

Research findings, however, are of little use if they go unreported. Part of the academic process is publication and here, again, we find that male control, and male interests, predominate. If it had been feasible Sandra Acker might have begun her survey of publications in the sociology of education, not with the material selected for publication, but with the material submitted for consideration. For if researchers are to be puzzled by the 'deviant' behaviour of females in their samples, is it not likely that articles which are concerned with women would surprise and bewilder editors who could well reject them?

In Britain, for example, there is a *British Research Index* which purports to 'list and analyse the subject content of all articles of permanent educational interest' and which through its operation provides a classic case of the structural exclusion of women. Criteria must be formulated and a selection must be made in determining which articles qualify for inclusion in the *Index* but from the outset there is little likelihood that feminist educational articles will ever get the stamp of approval for there are no feminist periodicals among the 195 used by the *British Research Index* to make their selection. Feminist material is by definition non-data despite the fact that in the two British-based feminist journals, *Feminist Review* has had an article on education (Naish, 1979) and *Women's Studies International Quarterly* devoted an entire issue to education (vol. I, no. 4, 1978). While the feminist contribution is structurally excluded in this manner what can be stated with some certainty is that feminist models of education will never become of 'permanent educational interest' through this channel. By not including material from feminist periodicals the *Index* helps to construct the invisibility of women. In 1978, for example, out of the 3384 listings in the *Index* there were only fourteen under the heading of sex differences and this helps to suggest that sex differences is an issue of minimal significance and attracts a minimal amount of research – a most misleading suggestion. Sexism and feminism were not entries in the *Index* and anyone who attempted to use the *Index* as a guide to research and publications could be forgiven for concluding that sexism and feminism were absent from the educational agenda.

Education is a classic case of *men's studies* but despite the apparent bleakness of the overall view, it does appear to be under threat and is, at least, in great danger of being modified. From being in a position where the patriarchal assumptions went unquestioned, the last ten years have seen those assumptions challenged, and some changes have been made. There is a growing demand that women be included as equals in educational theory and practice, as theorists and as subjects. So far the impact of feminism on education has been to insist that women have the right to participate in the creation of *our* education. It has been to 'put the case': this may even prove to be the most significant part of the struggle. For given the body of knowledge which feminists bring with them, getting our foot in the door might have been the hardest act of all.

The feminist model of education

There are difficulties associated with trying to conceptualize the feminist model of education in monolithic terms; this is partly because feminist education, unlike traditional education, has not been confined to narrow, institutionalized parameters, and partly because the feminist model is still evolving. Feminist education takes many forms, from consciousness-raising sessions to postgraduate courses in women's studies, and 'modifications' are constantly required in order to meet changing circumstances of time and place. But partly through necessity, all the many forms of feminist education share common assumptions and aims, common ways of organizing and distributing knowledge.

In the late 1960s when the modern women's liberation movement began to emerge and women started to ask questions about the condition of women, there was, as Joan Roberts (1976) has pointed out little or no readily available knowledge to help them in their quest. In terms of the criteria that women were using, there were no books, no courses, no 'experts' who could offer adequate explanations or data. It was in this context that the feminist model of education evolved, for women realized that if they wanted knowledge about women, authenticated by women, they would have to 'make it themselves'. If the knowledge produced by men was inadequate or false then there was no alternative but to set up a 'circle of women' to produce and validate knowledge about women.

Women believed (erroneously as we later discovered)[1] that there was no body of knowledge to transmit, no tradition, no heritage to impart; they believed that women had to become the authorities on women and that there was no better (or other) place to start than with themselves and their own lives. By placing this emphasis on personal experience and validation, they formed the basis of an educational model which constituted a radical departure from traditional education and which still distinguishes feminism from patriarchal education.

Women found themselves meeting with other women and talking about their personal experience (and validating it in the process); they were constructing a new reality without necessarily being able to state explicitly what it was they were doing. And because all those women who were involved were, to some extent, 'in the same boat', it was extremely difficult for any hierarchies to emerge. None of us (I recollect) had much more than our personal experience to go on. None of us was an expert who could rely on 'book learning'. We were all equal in the sense that we all felt that we had been 'misled' and we all wanted to come to understand how it had happened (and to make sure it didn't happen again). Under these circumstances it was not difficult for co-operative and collaborative activities to occur. The sharing of knowledge led to collective understandings which resulted in new knowledge; we 'recycled' the old and made the new together. And we called this 'learning process' consciousness-raising.

In attempting to describe feminist education there is a limit to the use which can be made of the customary terms in education. This was a learning experience, although qualitatively different from the learning which many of us had 'endured' in our own schooling.[2] It was part of living, not an activity which occurred in prescribed places and at prescribed times. That educationalists may not recognize this, says more about their restricted definition of learning than it does about feminism. The terms 'teacher' and 'learner' – as they have been defined by education – are also inadequate; while educationalists may wish to divide the world into these two polarized categories, they can become meaningless in a feminist context, where *all* are teaching and learning. Janet Robyns (1977) has described her experience of feminist education, which while it is much later and much more institutionalized than those first informal consciousness-raising groups, shares some of those same features; she too finds the conventional terms inadequate and says of feminist teachers that they

. . . were not set up as knowers among a group of non knowers. They were more like part time assistants. They helped as much as they could by giving information about their experiences. . . . Another thing became apparent. The 'teacher' did not remain the same person. In sharing our knowledge, our thoughts and experiences, the 'teacher' rotated among us. Each functioned as teacher at times because each had something to offer. There was no knower/non knower, judge/judged hierarchy (Robyns, 1977; p. 53).

This form of education, of course, stands in sharp contrast to traditional forms and suggests one of the reasons behind the 'dismissal' of feminist education. To conventional educationalists the failure to establish definite 'authority figures' no doubt resembles something approaching anarchy and the lack of a 'prescribed' curriculum (in conventional terms) would seem to pose a threat to standards. In one sense, educationalists are not mistaken, for feminists do seek an end to hierarchies and standards, as they have been constructed, on the grounds that they are *not* an inherent part of learning, but of a stratified society!

The success of feminism in developing an egalitarian and co-operative model of education (which appears to be more beneficial for students) would be difficult to dispute. Although currently this non-hierarchical structure is an explicit feminist goal, I do not think that the *aim* alone accounts for the achievement. It seems to me that equality and co-operation were almost the inevitable outcome of the circumstances in which feminists found themselves. However, in the current context where a body of knowledge is rapidly becoming available, and where the possibility of 'transmission' exists – with all its concomitant attributes of hier-archies and competition – it may be very important for feminism to focus on past achievements and to keep the co-operative model in mind, for it could begin to get 'lost' as feminism enters institutions. While this is a risk it is by no means inevitable, for even in institutionalized courses the feminist model of education still makes its presence felt (which is one of the reasons that it has met resistance).

By emphasizing the role that the personal plays in learning, feminists have developed an educational paradigm which is at times diametrically opposed to the patriarchal one (where the personal is seen as a source of contamination and the subjective, something to be avoided). If all were going well within the patriar-chal framework, if schooling could be seen as effective and successful, with students emerging from the process as literate, numerate, socially skilled, politi-cally aware and responsible for themselves then perhaps any comparison between the two models would be little more than an interesting exercise. But given that women are coming from the feminist experience testifying to (and exhibiting) its advantages, and students are coming from schooling and testifying to (and exhi-biting) its disadvantages, then this ceases to be just an interesting exercise and becomes a significant issue. One woman I interviewed helped to sum it up when she said

After institutionalised education you feel worse. After feminist education, you feel better. I left university convinced I was dim, I was always sure everyone around me was brighter than I was, and I was always frightened of being found out. I was frightened of the world. I felt incompetent. I had the mentality of a victim. All that changed after my women's studies course. I felt much more in charge of my own life, though I was more aware of the things that were against me. But I felt capable, I thought it was possible to do something about them.

Becoming a victim in educational institutions is not an uncommon experience; 'victims' are the predictable outcome given the way educational theory and prac-tice are organized. Fundamental to the patriarchal model of education are the concepts of 'compete and eliminate'. Students are isolated from one another, required to compete, frequently have their personal lives and experiences discounted (see Douglas Barnes, 1976) and are generally deprived of any autonomy or responsibility. Because the educational ladder has fewer places on each ascending rung, an arbitrary number of students must be designated as

'failers' at each stage, with the result that their educational experience is termin-
ated. Only within a patriarchal and hierarchical framework could it be seen as
logical that those who are classified as less able – determined by objective tests
of course – should be given the least educational experience. It is no wonder that
women leave feminist education feeling good (Freeman, 1975) and students leave
patriarchal education feeling devalued.

The difference between the feminist model and the patriarchal model is in
essence political. Feminism is a social and political movement, a revolutionary
movement, aimed at the redistribution of power. It has developed its own form
of organization and dissemination of knowledge which reflects its political nature
and aspirations. If feminism had remained outside educational institutions its
model could still constitute a threat, but the fact that it has moved inside as well,
(while still retaining many of its outside and informal bases) makes it an even
greater threat. Given the conservative nature of curriculum construction and the
usual methods by which knowledge becomes incorporated in the curriculum
(Williams, 1975), the establishment of so many women's studies courses in so
many institutions, at so many levels, and in so many countries in such a short
space of time, is little short of astonishing.

Ann Fitzgerald (1978) has said that 'women's studies confronts head-on the two
shibboleths of the traditional curriculum; disciplinary specialization and apolitical
objective knowledge' (p. 3).

Women's studies . . . is necessarily interdisciplinary and frankly political. It is problem
centered and challenges the ways in which social structures (the curriculum very much
included) create and foster ideas about ourselves and the world. In acknowledging the
male centeredness of the traditional curriculum, it points out the biases inherent in all
disciplines and thus the political nature of education itself. . . . Questioning the
underlying assumptions about the truth and supposedly objective knowledge of
academic fields is to recognize that the very chopping up and categorizing of knowledge
in the academy is itself a political act (Fitzgerald, 1978; p. 3).

From the feminist model where women have posed questions about women,
discipline boundary lines have blurred and even collapsed. The traditional
compartmentalization of knowledge has even been put forward as a possible
'divide and rule' strategy which has permitted the production and perpetuation
of false meanings about women; feminists have come to appreciate that many
divisions are arbitrary, often unnecessary, frequently misleading, and the product
of a male view of the world. The existence of multi/inter/predisciplinary feminist
knowledge is in itself a testimony to the dispensability of many discipline divisions
and this constitutes another threat to the patriarchal model of education.

It is becoming increasingly difficult to keep feminism out of education, particularly as it infiltrates educational institutions. What we have at the moment is a
complex situation in which there is a patriarchal paradigm of education where
men have not only decreed the boundaries, the rules, the definitions and methodologies, but where they have done it in such a way that females are excluded.
Alongside this, often in the same institutions, and sometimes in the same departments, is a feminist model of education which not only challenges those bound-

aries, rules, definitions and methodologies, but which also posits female experience as a viable alternative for organizing the theory and practice of education.

Thomas Kuhn (1972) has suggested that the history of scientific knowledge is the history of the shift from one paradigm which no longer adequately explains, which contains too many inaccuracies and contradictions to be tolerated, to a new paradigm which takes account of more evidence and which offers a more comprehensive explanation. It will be interesting to see whether this applies to education, for currently the feminist paradigm seems to take much more into account, provides a much more comprehensive explanation of human learning and a much more successful educational model.

Notes

1 Much feminist scholarship has been archivist in nature and has 'recovered' the work produced by women in the past; this excision of women from history, from the history of many of the disciplines, is itself an example of the exclusion of women from cultural institutions.
2 Perhaps the closest model is that of Freire; some work has been done indicating the parallels between Freire's version of education and that of feminism.

References

Acker, S., 'Feminist perspectives and the British Sociology of Education', paper presented at British Sociological Association, Annual Conference, Lancaster, 8 April 1980.
Barnes, D., *From Communication to Curriculum*, Penguin, Middlesex, 1976.
Byrne, E., *Women and Education*, Tavistock, London, 1978.
Carden, M., *The New Feminist Movement*, Russel Sage Foundation, New York, 1974.
Cassell, J., *A group called women: sisterhood and symbolism in the feminist movement*, David McKay, New York, 1977.
Fitzgerald, A., 'Teaching interdisciplinary women's studies', Great Lakes College Association *Faculty Newsletter*, 27 March 1978.
Freeman, J., *The politics of women's liberation*, David McKay, New York, 1975.
Freire, P., *Cultural Action for Freedom*, Penguin Education, Middlesex, 1972.
Freire, P., *Pedagogy of the Oppressed*, Penguin Education, Middlesex, 1973.
Kuhn, T., *The Structure of Scientific Revolutions* (2nd edn), University of Chicago Press, Chicago, 1972.
Lavigueur, J., 'Equality of educational opportunity for girls; and its relation to coeducation', unpublished M A Dissertation, University of Sheffield, 1977.
McNamara, D. R., 'Paradigm lost: Thomas Kuhn and educational research', *British Educational Research Journal*, **V**, no. 2, 1979 pp. 167–74.
McWilliams-Tullberg, *Women at Cambridge: a men's university – though of a mixed type*, Victor Gollancz, London, 1975.
Naish, J., 'The chance to say what they think: Teaching English as a second language', *Feminist Review*, **3**, 1979, pp. 1–11.
Roberts, J. I. (ed.), *Beyond Intellectual Sexism: a new woman, a new reality*, David McKay, New York, 1976.
Robyns, J., 'Reproductive versus Regenerative education; the extension of English education through reference to feminism', unpublished Associateship Report, University of London Institute of Education, 1977.

Shaw, J., 'Finishing schools; some implications of sex-segregated education', in Barker, D. and Allen S. (eds), *Sexual Divisions and Society; Process and Change*, Tavistock, London, 1976, pp. 150–73.

Smith, D., 'A peculiar eclipsing: women's exclusion from man's culture', *Women's Studies International Quarterly*, **I**, no. 4, 1978, pp. 281–96.

Williams, R., *The Long Revolution*, Penguin, Middlesex, 1975.

11   Dinosaurs in the classroom – the 'hidden' curriculum in primary schools

Katherine Clarricoates

The 'hidden' curriculum does what the official curriculum is presumably not supposed to do; it differentiates on the basis of sex. An analysis of some of the qualities of classroom life will reveal much of the social underpinnings of stereotyping. Classroom structure and organization is dependent upon the exercise of control by the teachers – this is their central focus.

In talking to teachers about their experiences in classrooms I found this to be very true. Consider some extracts from teachers' interviews, when asked, 'Have you noticed many changes, very few or none at all, in the way that children learn or in the way that they behave?':

Previously, in the first year you are always very nervous of losing the class . . . and you are constantly trying to keep a grip on it; so as soon as a kid laughs you think 'Ha' and jump on it (March 1978).

Obviously kids pick up a weakness and they'll play on it until they can get you . . . sort of to the stage you're running round almost rigid and saying 'stop that', 'stop that' all the time (February 1978).

Discipline, to them, is an important feature of their role as a teacher; indeed their very existence as teachers depends upon their 'skill' in keeping order in the class and in coping with the plethora of trivia that surrounds classroom life. This is a yardstick of 'ability' by which teachers and headpersons measure each other. Signs of chaos or disturbance in a classroom soon bring a teacher into disrepute amongst colleagues, and teachers were forever telling me why they thought the standard of discipline had gone down:

I think the discipline of the children is worse now than it was; they're not as well behaved . . . I think this is due to parents . . . discipline is not what it should be (July 1978).

In the way that they behave most definitely. They . . . the children rule the roost and won't be told . . . I don't think they have the respect of elders that we used to get in the old days (December 1977).

Teachers tended to reveal an obsessive concern with discipline and with the need for children to do just what they're told. Their replies highlighted an acceptance of educational standards as they are, in short the status quo:

Well the behaviour's worse. . . . A lot more answering back and having the last word. There's too much of it overall . . . and knowing better than you (December 1977).

Source: Extracted from Clarricoates, K., 'Dinosaurs in the classroom – a re-examination of some aspects of the "hidden curriculum" in primary schools', *Women's Studies International Quarterly*, **1**, 1978, pp. 353–64.

I want to turn round to parents and say 'before your child comes to school . . . discipline it first for us . . . socialize it for us'. That it will shut up when it's spoken to, and answer when it's spoken to . . . you know this easy-going atmosphere, lack of discipline at home . . . it's really bad (December 1977).

These replies tragically disclose the teachers' wish for children to be kept 'in their place', relying on a pattern of reward, reprisal and punishment to accomplish this. It is important however to point out that this tendency differed between the working-class schools and the middle-class schools, where teachers were not so rigid in the preservation of the social structure:

In some ways it's a good thing that children ask questions and answer back. But in other ways it can be very awkward (December 1977).

Children have much more to say for themselves . . . more interesting people, and they have more to offer in class-time (December 1977).

Years ago kids in a sense were much more biddable in that rather narrow sense . . . but now we're moving towards what is hopefully a more progressive society then clearly people have got to be encouraged to think for themselves (July 1978).

The interview excerpts would tend to support Ellis *et al.*'s view that middle-class children are encouraged to be autonomous, especially the boys, whereas working-class children need to be directed and led (Ellis *et al.*, 1976).

It is through their major concern with group control and discipline that teachers related to girls and boys in differing ways which were apparently in favour of the latter. Researchers have consistently noted the differences in behaviour between girls and boys in classrooms, with male pupils requiring more constant disciplinary censure from teachers than female pupils (Lobban, 1978; Jackson, 1968; Loo and Wenar, 1971) who are less difficult to control. Good *et al.* state that through their behaviour boys tend to receive more positive contacts with teachers than girls (Good *et al.*, 1973). My own observations and results obtained from teachers' interviews did reveal a marked difference in the way the two sexes behaved and the way teachers treated them. Teachers accept certain patterns of behaviour as given (though of course many approve), and assume they are features that they have to work with, rather than confronting or changing:

. . . the girls seem to be typically feminine whilst the boys seem to be typically male . . . you know more aggressive . . . the ideal of what males ought to be (July 1978).

I think the boys tend to be a little more aggressive and on thinking about it the male is the same in the animal world . . . we are animals basically (July 1978).

I try to treat them as near as I can without actually embarrassing the children. It would be very nice to think that you can just say 'they're children . . . two children . . . you and you'. I suppose in a way we kind of give way to pressure in our own way in order to be practical, for example, if I pick two people for a job I'll probably pick two boys or two girls knowing that if I choose one of each neither of them would be very happy with the job or choice, so I suppose in a way I'm being weak really (March 1978).

It would be very nice to treat them all alike on everything but I don't know if you'd be doing right because if you turn out a load of boys who are 'nice and considerate' and play netball I mean they're not going to get very far when they leave us. I mean they'll go off somewhere and it'll have no practical use for them . . . laughing and ridicule that's all (March 1978).

Within the primary school it is assumed that girls and boys learn the same subject. But within the classroom the teacher defines certain projects and activities which are presumed to be appropriate for girls and boys. We know from various studies that curricular materials have been found wanting in relation to sex, race and class (Lobban, 1975; Moon, 1974; Northern Women's Education Study Group, 1972; Children's Rights Workshop, 1976). The school-book world with its sexist implications reveals the implausible statistical ratio of twice as many boys than girls and seven times as many men than women, who are also predominantly white and middle class. Given the content, sexist materials could be used by teachers to question the implied assumptions and stereotypes, thus encouraging the children to question the sexist and racist world we actually live in. But this does not happen; indeed, I have found a situation even worse. Because of the problem teachers have in controlling boys and the fact that girls consistently score higher in intelligence (Douglas, 1964), it would seem that teachers are actually gearing the subject content of lessons in favour of boys. The education media[1] did an extensive television project on dinosaurs for top infant classes (6–7-year-olds). The teachers encouraged the children to participate fully in the venture by painting pictures and writing short essays on them, examples of which were hung around the walls of the classrooms. The impact of recognizing that a project is either boys' 'things' or girls' 'things' was apparent to pupils and teachers alike. During such a lesson a teacher (again in a top infant class) stated:

'Get your books out on dinosaurs please.'
'Oh no,' cried the girls. 'Not again, we're always doing boys' topics, Miss.'
'Well perhaps later on in the term we'll do something on houses and flowers', compromises the teacher.

Monosyllabic words and sounds of disgust are emitted from the boys. The children are, by this age, aware of the segregation by sex in all aspects of classroom life with boys – and anything connected with them – being looked upon as superior and exciting, while girls are treated as inferiors. Even if the teacher does turn his/her attention to something s/he has specifically referred to as girls' 'things' it can be guaranteed that the 'important' parts of the topics will be taken up by what men do: men build houses, women live and work in them (incarceration); men dig gardens, women pick flowers.

In an interview with this particular teacher I asked her 'Do you think boys and girls respond differently to your particular subjects?' She informed me:

Yes and this comes from home. We're doing dinosaurs at the moment and the boys are more enthusiastic about it. It tends to be a boys' 'thing' to do. If you had a topic about housing . . . houses . . . the girls would immediately begin to sit up and take notice (March 1978).

Like most teachers she is unaware she has actually acted out her beliefs that certain topics are appropriate for boys while others are appropriate for girls. It was only during long observations in the field, and listening and talking to, teachers, that the reasons for such behaviour became apparent. In the staffrooms of all the schools most teachers were in agreement:

'Boys are more difficult to control', said one teacher.

'Yes', said another, 'they're ever so lively and boisterous.'
'It's important to keep their attention for a certain length of time, otherwise they play you up something awful.'

Most of the teachers nod in agreement. Faced with the possibility of disruptive boys and the pressure by their colleagues to keep effective control over their classes, non-sexist teachers are in a dilemma, and it would seem on first sight that there is only an attenuative course of action open to them. We are all aware that children bring into school already preconceived ideas of sex roles (Maccoby and Jacklin, 1975; Oakley, 1972), and the main concern would be how to counteract them rather than to reinforce their already held notions. To make children aware of the similarities that exist between the sexes, rather than highlighting the so-called 'differences' is an all-important task – to bring them together on common ground would mean to annihilate the categorizing and labelling procedure that goes on in schools and is at the core of sexism. Teachers must come to terms with their worst failing, that of not challenging the categories and perception of what behaviour is appropriate for girls and boys.

The teachers' behaviour and reasons held for the sex-dichotomy became clear in interviews. Again on the question of different responses, on the basis of sex, to particular subjects:

Yes, I suppose so. I like doing subjects like geography and I do find that this is the area where the lads do come out . . . you know . . . they have got the scientific facts, they've got some geographical facts whereas the girls tend to be a bit more woollier in most of the things (March 1978).

They (girls) haven't got the imagination that most of the lads have got (March 1978).

I find you can spark the boys a bit easier than you can the girls. . . (February 1978).

Girls have got their own set ideas it's always '. . . and we went home for tea' and 'Mum and Dad were there' and 'we all lived happily ever after . . .'. Whereas you can get the boys to write something really interesting and there's nothing like '. . . and we all went home for tea . . .' you know this sort of thing (March 1978).

Boys seem to want more exciting projects to do than girls, whereas girls will fall in with most things . . . (October 1977).

You can choose a subject interesting to the boys, the girls would be interested just as well, something like transport. But the other way around you often find boys are not very interested if it's not directed at them . . . (October 1977).

If you are doing a transport type of thing boys will be into it whilst the girls are just tagging along and *vice versa* (December 1977).

What the teachers described as a boys' 'thing' or girls' 'thing' in class took on a set pattern with mostly boys' 'thing' (i.e. topics to interest boys) being discussed. The reasons for this:

The boys are more difficult to settle down to their work . . . they don't seem to have the same self-discipline as the girls do, so it's important to direct the subject at them (October 1977).

I'd tend to try and make the topic as interesting as possible so that the boys won't lose their concentration and start fidgeting . . . (July 1978).

It's a bit harder to keep the boys' attention during a lesson . . . at least that's what I've found so I gear the subject to them more than I do the girls who are good at paying attention in class (March 1978).

A pupil's sex is an important variable in determining teachers' behaviour or interaction, as the above examples go to show, with disruptive boys receiving more attention from teachers (similar findings being reported by Lobban, 1978; Weinreich, 1978; Good *et al.*, 1973). More time was spent listening, talking and helping the boys, not only because they needed more control but also because they were what teachers classed as 'behind' the girls in intellectual achievement:

The boys aren't as academic as girls . . . (December 1977).

In this primary school you find that girls tend to . . . there's simply more girls at the top of the class than boys (March 1978).

Girls tend to . . . I think in the past five years I've been here . . . they've always been my brightest pupils (March 1978).

It would seem a second reason for boys having subjects geared towards them, and having more attention paid to them, is that teachers feel they need to be pushed (this is as well as being restricted by the need to control the class). They see the boys as having the 'real imagination', in fact 'true creativity' while girls are good at 'tagging along', lacking reason and clear logic, which, as Pauline Marks points out, are qualities that are linked to maths and science (Marks, 1976). It could be that as early as the primary school girls are deterred from these subjects, long before the secondary school takes its toll. (For analyses of secondary schools see Wolpe's, Shaw's and Blackstones' published works.)

However, my own research corroborates evidence from previous studies that girls are more successful than boys at primary level on most subjects, particularly in reading, writing, English and spelling (Douglas, 1964; Sharpe, 1976). The assumed superiority in maths, geography and science is soon lost to boys because of the sex-bias in most subjects in secondary education rather than the maturational hypothesis. According to Sharpe, Douglas and Blackstone, the differences in performance of girls and boys can be explained both in terms of the differences in teacher expectations, and because girls can relate to an all-female staff. But although girls in primary schools are 'successful', they still lose out. What they really succeed in is conformity to institutional expectations and diligence in achieving them. This is seen as underlying their academic achievement; in short teachers do not perceive girls as being 'positively' intelligent:

On the whole you can generally say that the boys are far more capable of learning, more nicer to teach . . . (February 1978).

Boys are interested in everything and are prepared to take things seriously. They tend to ask the deeper questions while girls tend to be more superficial about subjects; they ask the 'right' questions simply because it's expected of them . . . (December 1977).

Although girls tend to be good at most things in the end you find it's a boy whose going to be your most brilliant pupil (March 1977).

So here is a further reason why teachers gear subject content to boys: they find them more interesting and rewarding to teach. The capacity of girls to be better behaved, more conscientious, cleaner and neater in all aspects of work and conduct, and the expectations of teachers in regard to this, leads to the wholesale theft of true intellectual development in favour of boys.

I'm always on at the boys to try a bit harder . . . (July 1978).

I find I have to be stricter with the boys and push them that little bit more . . . (April 1977).

You don't seem to be able to trust them to be sensible like you can the girls (December 1977).

I wouldn't sort of go off and leave them (boys) and expect them to stay in their places because I know most of them wouldn't (July 1978).

Because of their underlying beliefs about gender behaviour, teachers act out unconsciously a 'hidden' curriculum in favour of the boys and to the detriment of girls, and ultimately we see the unfolding of a self-fulfilling prophecy (Rosenthal and Jacobsen, 1968). Pivnick, in her dissertation on primary schools in America, states:

It is possible that by using a harsher tone for controlling the behaviour of boys than for girls, the teachers actually foster in boys the independent and defiant spirit which is considered 'masculine' in our culture but which in (extreme cases) may tend to inhibit learning. At the same time, the 'femininity' which the teachers reinforced in girls may foster the narcissism and passivity which results in lack of motivation and achievement in girls (Pivnick, 1974: p. 159).

The teachers' cultural expectations guided the behaviour of their pupils. There is no doubt in my mind that societal myths of stereotypes do influence teachers' beliefs about what girls are like and what boys are like. But what is most tragic of all is that girls' real ability is attributed to conformity to institutional expectations, and that the academic achievement of girls in schools is explained in terms of the feminine stereotype. The girls' conscientiousness and diligence makes them 'less bothersome' and 'less interesting' to the teachers who consequently turn all their energies and skills to the boys:

You look at your boys in a different way, you've got to push them . . . (March 1978).

It's always pushing the lads at the moment . . . I don't know why (March 1978).

Most of the boys are in the middle-bottom 'group'; they have greater difficulties. So if you are going to gear to the middle you are going to gear to the lads, so you try and find a topic that they are going to be interested in (March 1978).

It's easier to pull the girls in than it is to pull the boys in, so I try a topic that's usually got quite a lot for the lads (December 1977).

Faced with a restless 50 per cent of their class teachers will opt to 'entertain' that 50 per cent even though it is at the expense of the girls. Both sexes are required to work academically, but for different reasons, more emphasis is placed on achievement and success for boys (Weinreich, 1978) while girls are merely expected to accede to the teachers' desire for less disturbance so that the latter can concentrate their time and effort on the boys. In attempting to exercise control over the class, teachers operate a form of instruction aimed directly at the boys whom they find harder to control, lower in academic standards than girls, and more interesting and rewarding to teach, which contributes to the 'marginaliz-ation' of girls' education.

Linguistic sexism

Another aspect of the 'hidden' curriculum worth attention is that of linguistic sexism which is part and parcel of the interaction between teachers and pupils. During my observations in the field, teachers consistently and unconsciously used words and grammatical forms that denigrated women and emphasized the assumed superiority of men, not only in lesson content but in situations of disci-plinary procedure. As students of linguistic sexism have pointed out, language is not only a means of communication but also transmits shared assumptions (Spender, 1978; Miller and Swift, 1977). In primary school, children are taught that 'man' includes woman and child, besides being a male person, and with small children confusion easily arises when trying to get to grips with the foibles of the English language. During my observations a teacher of a class of 7-year-olds asked the children to write down an example of mammal and to give a particular feature that marked it off from other types, such as amphibians. Imagine the look on her face and the increased confusion of the child as she tried to explain why his wasn't exactly right when Peter had written: 'Man is a mammal. He breastfeeds his young.'

This small child was made to realize through his obvious mistake that males are central while women are peripheral. To gear subject content to boys is easy when one considers what men do and have done, and will continue to do; they 'create', 'invent' and carry out what are considered to be the most important jobs in our society. For a design project the teacher used as an example the designer Henry Ford: 'Henry Ford was quite a man; men worked for him and trained all their lives as engineers.' For boys, learning masculine pronouns is integrated into their view of themselves and the world; for girls this integration isn't possible. Secondary school children come to terms with the male pronoun 'he' as meaning both male and female but with younger children it is more confusing. The teachers, together with the TV presenters and characters, and the curricular materials all refer to dinosaurs, pandas, squirrels, mathematical characters (and even potatoes) as 'he' and children have no way of knowing that 'he' is not necessarily male. Only ladybirds, cows, hens, and mother animals are referred to as 'she'. Girls see through the school-book world and subject content that they do not create history, man does; thereby they assume that they cannot transform their world, whereas man can.

The use of the male pronoun is not the only area of discrimination in language. The various adjectives that teachers use when admonishing or rewarding their pupils (and consequently the children come to use them as well) have sex-related qualities. If boys get out of hand they are regarded as 'boisterous', 'rough', 'aggressive', 'assertive', 'rowdy', 'adventurous' etc.; for girls: the adjectives were 'fussy', 'bitchy', 'giggly', 'catty', 'silly'. It is obvious that the terms applied to boys imply positive masculine behaviour whereas the categories applied to girls are more derogatory:

I've noticed in particular that the girls tend to be sort of . . . more bitchy towards each other . . . (March 1977).

The boys are more rough, and they lean to boys' things (July 1978).

I think boys are more liable to be aggressive, more adventurous than girls (November 1977).

Girls are tidier and quieter . . . (July 1978).

Girls tend to congregate together gossiping in corners, whilst boys tend to get involved in more energetic play (October 1977).

Girls are fussy, boys are louder (July 1978).

Girls are very petty; this class in particular are very bitchy towards each other, I've noticed this over the past year (December 1977).

Girls can be very catty you know . . . (October 1977).

The common adjectives the teachers use contribute to social categorizing, a value-laden dichotomy, marking off males as superior and females as inferior. Teachers do not question what the words are communicating. Words like 'bitchy', 'catty' can be seen as words to 'serve the social function of isolating and discrediting a class of people who do not conform to the socially accepted patterns of behaviour' ('The Bitch Manifesto').[2] Certainly, as Miller and Swift point out in their book *Words and Women*, they are terms of abuse.

The way in which terms of derision are linked to gender categorization becomes apparent when noting certain words to define the different sexes' behaviour. The terms 'sissy', 'soppy', 'puffy' and 'bionic woman', used by both teachers and children to boys, carry connotations of 'effeminate' behaviour thereby threatening masculine identity: whereas the term 'tomboy' is temporarily acceptable and carries no such insult, due to its masculine implied behaviour:

Somehow, sissy is what tomboy isn't, a grave threat to the future of the child, and to the stability and social status of the entire family' (Pogrebin, 1972, p. 18 quoted in Pivnick, 1974, p. 158).[3]

Hence general categories are constructed from what are, in reality, limited aspects of the child's behaviour, and are interpreted by way of the teacher's gender expectations, following rules derived from the ideology of sex roles.

Teachers tend to censure girls more harshly than boys for the use of what they call improper language, thus creating a linguistic double standard which is another part of the 'hidden' curriculum. It is somehow seen as 'not fit' for girls to swear and use 'rough' speech, whereas for their male counterparts it is seen as part of the 'boys will be boys' syndrome, even though they also were admonished for such. Besides the teachers' expectations of physical restraint which the girls imposed upon themselves, the teachers also expected more verbal restraint from the girls than from the boys. In the schools that I observed there appeared a class divergence in such expectations of sex-role behaviour. Particularly in the middle-class suburban school, girls were expected to use more 'correct' grammar and pronunciation than boys.

Through their conditioning girls are more amenable to school and create fewer problems for the teachers. By being conscientious, neat and tidy, and able to 'get on' with their work without constant directives from the teachers, they are viewed as less problematic. For boys, the situation is different. In constant need of supervision, perceived as more forceful and concerned with the 'real' experience of masculine activities, boys are reassured of their superiority in their own immediate world. And just as teachers encourage and punish boys more often, so they find them more interesting. Most of the teachers I talked to regarded them as 'more teachable', the 'really bright ones' and having much more about them.

Intelligence for boys is seen by the teachers hand in hand with independence and confidence. Intelligence for girls seen as hand in hand with compliance and dependence (Lobban, 1978, p. 59).

Sex preference

The preferences and likes of teachers must also be equated to the type of school. Particularly in the working-class schools, high academic performance among boys was less of an achievement than being in the football team (especially if the team was doing particularly well that year). For girls it was expected, in all four schools that I observed, that they would achieve academically, though not in the 'real' sense but rather as part of the compliant and conforming behaviour which was expected of them. As Lobban states, girls were criticized for their academic failure while being ignored if they were academically successful (Lobban, 1978). For girls who were regarded as tomboys, I found that status among the peer group and the teachers varied according to catchment area, which is significantly related to the value structure of each individual school. In the urban traditional working-class area, the lively active girl was given more status than she was in the middle-class school, especially if she was a member of the school football team. Middle-class girls, though less segregated, were expected to comply more to 'ladylike' behaviour:

On my way through the main hall of the school two small girls ran past me shrieking with delight at hearing their voices echoing back at them. They were apprehended by the head of the school who sternly warned them against such 'unladylike' behaviour, and insisted they walk back to their class in a quiet and orderly manner which was more becoming of little girls. This they did with exaggerated gesture and the head returned to his study confident in his demand of their 'appropriate' behaviour.

Middle-class boys, like middle-class girls, were expected to achieve academically as the school and family environment tended to reinforce each other positively, which is not always the case in the working class community (Douglas, 1964).

Having highlighted the fact that classroom life is geared centrally to the boys and that it exercises discrimination towards girls, it seems plausible to draw the conclusion that girls who are regarded as a nuisance by teachers in classrooms do in fact become more of a 'problem' than the unruly boy. My contention rests mainly on the fact that, because the subject content of lessons and life in general is centrally directed towards boys, the 'troublesome' girl becomes more of a problem because her interests, far from being catered for, are virtually ignored, with teachers expecting her to 'tag along' with material which is mostly directed towards the boys. Therefore troublesome girls are not 'positively' stimulated within class because of the negative expectations teachers hold for them. The implications of this may support Martin's study,[4] where he found that girls with problems are neglected by the teachers in the class. I found that girls were expected to 'get on' with their work without needing as much of the teachers' attention as boys did.

The paradox

For girls, there is a 'Catch 22' in the 'hidden' curriculum. If the girl learns her lessons well, speaks appropriately, is considerate in all she does and is no bother to the teacher she is even then *not* accorded the full status due her appropriate behaviour, unlike her opposite number. Indeed she is scorned for having 'nothing about her', for being a 'goody-goody'. By conforming to institutional expectations she will invite ridicule and criticism as a lesser being than the boy; she will be perceived as weaker and less intelligent. She will learn submissiveness and self-deprecation, qualities which society does not hold in great esteem. Self-deprecation is derived from her internalization of the opinions her teachers hold of her. She becomes convinced of her own inadequacy and lacks confidence in herself as a true being, hence her capitulation to the feminine stereotype.

There has been much talk about the 'revolution' within the classroom – particularly within the primary school. But has there been any real change? The fossilized routine of the classroom has not really altered despite the new equipment, open classrooms and spacious surroundings. Children are still selected and treated differently on a gender and class basis. It is understandable that their responses should be different: it is, however, nothing short of a tragedy that this should be passed off as the 'natural order'.

Notes

1 BBC Television for Schools, March 1978, the programme 'Watch'.
2 From 'The Bitch Manifesto' quoted in Miller and Swift's *Words and Women*.
3 Pogrebin, Letty Cottin, 'Down with sexist upbringin', *MS*, spring 1972, quoted in Pivnick's Doctoral dissertation, 1974.
4 R. Martin's study quoted in Lobban (1978).

References

Berg, L., *Risinghill: Death of a Comprehensive*, Harmondsworth, Penguin Books, 1986.
Blackstone, T., 'The education of girls to-day', in Mitchell, J. and Oakley, A. (eds), *The Rights and Wrongs of Women*, Pelican, 1976.
Douglas, J. W. B., *Home and The School*, London, MacGibbon and Kee, 1964.
Ellis, T. *et al.*, *William Tyndale – The Teachers' Story*, Essex, Anchor Press, 1976.
Frazier, N. and Sadker, M., *Sexism in School and Society*, New York, Harper and Row, 1973.
Good, T. L. *et al*, 'Effects of teacher sex and pupil sex on classroom interaction', *J. Educ. Psychol.* **65**, no. 1, 1973, pp. 74–87.
Lobban, G., 'Sex-roles in reading schemes', *Educ. Rev.* **27**, no. 3, 1975, pp. 202–10.
Lobban, G., 'The influence of the school on sex-role stereotyping', in Chetwynd, J. and Hartnett, O. (eds), *The Sex Role System: Psychological and Sociological Perspectives*, London, Routledge and Kegan Paul, 1978.

Loo, C. and Wenar, C., 'Activity level and motor inhibition: their relation to intelligence performance in normal children', *Child Develop.*, **42**, 1971, pp. 967–71.

Marks, P., 'Femininity in the classroom: An account of changing attitudes', in Mitchell, J. and Oakley, A. (eds), *The Rights and Wrongs of Women*, Pelican, 1976.

Maccoby, E. E. and Jacklin, C. N., *The Psychology of Sex Differences*, London, Oxford University Press, 1975.

Martin, R., 'Student sex behaviour as determinants of the type and frequency of teacher–student contacts', *School Psychol*, **10**, no. 4, 1972, pp. 339–47, quoted in Lobban, 1978.

Miller, C. and Swift, K., *Words and Women*, London, Gollancz, 1977.

Moon, C., 'Sex role stereotyping in books for young children', unpublished Dip.Ed. thesis, Bristol University, 1974.

Northern Women's Education Study Group, 'Sex role learning: a study of infant readers', in Wandor, M. (ed.) *The Body Politic*, London, Stage One, 1972.

Oakley, A., *Sex, Gender and Society*, London, Temple Smith, 1972.

Pivnick, P., 'Sex role socialisation: observations in a first grade classroom (it's hard to change your image once you're typecast)', thesis of Doctorate of Education at the University of Rochester, USA, 1974.

Rosenthal, R. and Jacobsen, L., *Pygmalion in the Classroom*, London, Holt, Rinehart & Winston, 1968.

Sharpe, S., *Just Like A Girl: How Girls Learn to be Women*, Harmondsworth, Penguin Books, 1976.

Spender, D., *Educational Research and the Feminist Perspective*, paper given at the British Educational Research Association Conference on Women, Education and Research, University of Loughborough, April 1978.

Weinreich, H., 'Sex role socialisation', in Chetwynd, J. and Hartnett, O. (eds), *The Sex Role System: Psychological and Sociological Perspectives*, London, Routledge and Kegan Paul, 1978.

Children's Rights Workshop, *Sexism in Children's Books, Facts, Figures and Guidelines*, London, Writers and Readers Publishing Co-op, 1976.

12 Sex, power and pedagogy

Valerie Walkerdine

In this paper I want to address certain issues about the position of girls and women within the education system with reference to an examination of some observations collected in two nursery schools.[1] I shall draw out certain contradictions for traditional Marxist approaches to the relations of power within educational institutions. One such view is that education as a bourgeois institution places teachers in a position of power from which they can oppress children who are institutionally powerless. To somewhat overstate the case, the teacher, powerful in a bourgeois educational institution, is in a position to oppress children whose resistance to that power, like all resistance, is understood as ultimately progressive rather than contradictory. Children's movements have tended to understand resistance in terms of 'rights' or 'liberation'. Similarly, certain feminist accounts have used the psychological concepts of 'role' and 'stereotype' to understand women and girls as unitary subjects whose economic dependence, powerlessness and physical weakness is reflected in their production as 'passive', 'weak', and 'dependent' individuals. While such accounts have been extremely important in helping to develop marxist and feminist practices, I want to pinpoint some of the reasons why such analyses might not be as helpful as we might previously have supposed in understanding the phenomena presented in this paper. I want to show, using examples from classroom practice, that in both the case of female teachers and of small girls, they are not unitary subjects uniquely positioned, but produced as a nexus of subjectivities, in relations of power which are constantly shifting, rendering them at one moment powerful and at another powerless.

Additionally, I want to argue that while an understanding of resistance is clearly important, we cannot read every resistance as having revolutionary effects; sometimes resistances have 'reactionary' effects. I want to argue that resistance is not just struggle against the oppression of a static power (and therefore potentially revolutionary simply because it is struggle against the monolith) but that relations of power and resistance are continually reproduced, in continual struggle and constantly shifting.

An example of boys' resistance in a nursery school

The following interchange between teacher and children comes from a series of recordings which were made in a nursery school. The teacher who is a woman about 30 is seated with a group of children aged 3 and 4 around a table. The

Source: Extracted from Walkerdine, V., 'Sex, power and pedagogy', *Screen Education*, **38**, 1981, pp. 14–23.

children are making constructions from 'Lego'; we are concerned here with the actions of three children: a 3-year-old girl, Annie and two 4-year-old boys, Sean and Terry. The teacher's name is Miss Baxter.

The sequence begins when Annie takes a piece of Lego to add on to a construction that she is building. Terry tries to take it away from her to use himself and she resists. He says:

Terry: You're a stupid cunt, Annie.

The teacher tells him to stop and Sean tries to mess-up another child's construction. The teacher tells him to stop. Then Sean says:

Sean: Get out of it Miss Baxter paxter.

Terry: Get out of it knickers Miss Baxter.

Sean: Get out of it Miss Baxter paxter.

Terry: Get out of it Miss Baxter the knickers paxter knickers, bum.

Sean: Knickers, shit, bum.

Miss B: Sean, that's enough, you're being silly.

Sean: Miss Baxter, knickers, show your knickers.

Terry: Miss Baxter, show your bum off.

(they giggle)

Miss B: I think you're being very silly.

Terry: Shit Miss Baxter, shit Miss Baxter.

Sean: Miss Baxter, show your knickers your bum off.

Sean: Take all your clothes off, your bra off.

Terry: Yeah, and take your bum off, take your wee-wee off, take your clothes, your mouth off.
Sean: Take your teeth out, take your head off, take your hair off, take your bum off. Miss Baxter the paxter knickers taxter.

Miss B: Sean, go and find something else to do please.

Various people on reading this transcript have commented that they are surprised and shocked to find such young children not only making explicit sexual references, but having so much power over the teacher. What is this power and how is it produced? Here it is the case that, although the teacher has an institutional position, she is not uniquely a teacher, nor are the boys *just* small boys. Particular individuals are produced as subjects *differently* within a variety of discursive practices. A particular individual has the potential to be 'read' within a variety of discourses. We cannot say that the limit of the variety is determined in any direct or simple sense by the economic. However, the 'materiality' of the individual does have particular effects, though those effects are not solely determined by that materiality, but by the discourse in which it is 'read'. In this case the teacher is a woman and while that itself is crucial, it is only because of the ways in which 'woman' signifies that we can understand the specific nature of the struggle.[1] The resistance of the boys to her can be understood in terms both of their assertion of their difference from her and their seizing of power through constituting her as the powerless object of sexist discourse. Although they are not physically grown men they can take the positions of men through language and in doing so gain power which has material effects. Their power is gained by refusing to be constituted as the powerless objects in *her* discourse and recasting her as the powerless object of *theirs*. In their discourse she is constituted as 'woman as sex-object' and as that object she is rendered as the powerless object of their oppression. Of course, she has not in a sense ceased to be a teacher, but what is important is that she has ceased to *signify* as one: she has been made to signify as the powerless object of male sexual discourse. The boys' resistance takes the form of a seizure of power in discourse such that despite their institutional positions they achieve power in this instance.

It does not seem reasonable to assert a monolithic and ahistorical view of sexism and oppression in which the boys are *simply* either to be understood as powerless children oppressed by the control of an oppressive bourgeois educational institution or *simply* as the perpetrators of patriarchal social relations. The important word here is simply. For, indeed they have the potential to be produced as subjects/objects in *both* discourses, but inherent in the discursive positionings are different positions of power. Individuals, constituted as subjects and objects within a particular framework are produced by that process into relations of power. An individual can become powerful or powerless depending on the terms in which her/his subjectivity is constituted. The importance of this argument is in the way that we can assert that relations of power are not invested in unitary individuals in any way which is solely or essentially derived from their material and institutional position. This should not be taken as implying that the material or economic has no importance or force. However, the material and economic do not appear to be acting as unique and linear causes of the production of power relations in this example. The gender and the ages of the participants clearly have major effects which serve to displace other 'variables'. (The two boys are not yet capable of physically assaulting the teacher, but it may only be a matter of time.) Since the boys are both children and male, and the teacher is both teacher and female they can enter as subjects into a variety of discourses, some of which render them powerful and some of which render them powerless. It is important to note the way in which the boys refer to the teacher and to the 3-year-old girl, Annie, in the same terms. They call Annie a 'cunt'. In this way they bring the teacher down to size: she and a small girl are in discourse but the same thing – sex objects. The power of their discourse is one which renders all females typifications of the same qualities, in this case possessors of tits, bums and cunts. However, it is important that this argument is not just a concern for theoretical distinctions. The issue which I have raised would appear to have important consequences for practice. In this example we can understand the boys as both subjects in patriarchal discourse perpetrating patriarchal oppression upon their teacher and at the same time children oppressed/controlled by the authority of the teacher. Are we then to choose as our course of action one which wishes to potentially liberate them from their oppression or are they to be suppressed as sexist perpetrators of a patriarchal order?

The pedagogic discourse of the teacher

An important effect of this power struggle between the teacher and children is the way in which the teacher interprets the children's discourse so as to lessen its oppressive effect upon her, and to justify her failure to stop them as correct. To understand this we have to be aware of the psychological and pedagogic terms in which she understands herself as teacher and the children as learners. In particular, what concerns us here is the discourse on childhood sexuality. It was not by accident that the teacher waited so long to stop the children, nor that when she did so it was with a fairly gentle rebuke which did not take issue with the content of their talk.

When I discussed the incident with her later she explained what had happened in the following way:

The kind of expressions are quite normal for this age. . . . As long as they're not being too silly or bothering anybody, its just natural and should be left . . . coming out with that kind of expression is very natural.

How does she come to 'read' the children's actions as a harmless expression of a sexuality which is normal and natural? What are the main strands characterizing childhood sexuality? To understand that question it is necessary to examine the formation of those discourses and practices which inform and constitute 'progressive education'. We can understand the formation of the practices which make up progressive education in terms both of the necessity to reformulate a pedagogy which produced individuals who were controlled but not regimented. We can understand the insertion of psychoanalytic discourse as a way of understanding those concerns which were around at the time of the formation of the new education, that is in the second two decades of this century.

Take for example, the following remarks made by Margaret Lowenfeld in 1935 at the end of a book on the educational importance of play:[2]

Play is to a child, therefore, work, thought, art and relaxation, and cannot be pressed into any single formula. It expresses a child's relation to himself and his environment, and, without adequate opportunity for play, normal and satisfactory emotional development is not possible. . . . Emotional satisfactions, which the mind has missed at the period to which they properly belong, do not present themselves later in the same form. The forces of destruction, aggression and hostile emotion, which form so powerful an element for good or evil in the human character, can display themselves fully in the play of childhood, and become through this expression integrated into the controlled and conscious personality. Forces unrealised in childhood remain as an inner drive, for ever seeking outlets, and lead men to express them not any longer in play, since this is regarded as an activity in childhood, but in industrial competition, anarchy and war.

We can see in the end of this quotation the specific link made between the capitalist ethic, struggles and war, and the stifling of expression of emotion. The rise of totalitarianism (of the left and right) was attributed very clearly to the failure of current education and child-rearing to produce the right kind of individuals. It was felt that over-regimentation had produced the phenomenon described at the time as 'Prussianism'.[3] Psychoanalysis understood this failure as the result of repression. In relation to this a new discursive formation was produced, 'scientific pedagogy', based on a view of the production of control through self-control and self-regulation. The pedagogy took the form of the monitoring of the form and structure of development and of steering it along the right lines by provision of the right environment. Clearly, this is not the place to expand on the details of this pedagogy, but it is important here to understand the way in which it served to produce the terms and categories which provide the teacher's understanding of her experience. Central to the pedagogy was the unfolding of child development, understood as natural, and as a central part of this, the *expression* rather than *repression* of natural childhood sexuality. And, of course, according to the Freudian discourse this natural sexuality was essentially male.

The practice of the teacher here conforms to this 'scientific pedagogy'. While some activities are provided for the children, they are allowed to 'choose'. They are never coerced into doing something that they do not want to do, nor rarely taken away from activities in which they are engaged. They are natural normal children who should be left alone to develop at their own pace. This discursive formation, which constitutes the pedagogy and the experience of this teacher should be seen as neither 'knowledge' in her control, with which she can consciously oppress the children, nor a transparent 'experience' which will give the children access to knowledge which is liberating because they have produced it themselves. The knowledge is not inserted in the context of the school and set to work in the interests of the teachers to control the children. Conversely, its purpose is to produce better control through self-control and that ironically is what helps to produce the space in the practice for the children to be powerful. In this situation, the children have the power to define what they do within the limits of the pedagogy is that they can *choose* and they cannot be stopped in their choosing. The children recognize quickly that the uttering of the magic words 'I don't want to' quickly produces a situation in which they can control the flow of events. Thus the very discourse helps to produce the children as powerful. The space is already there for their resistance. Similarly, the discourse of the natural-ness of male sexuality to be expressed not repressed produces and facilitates in the teacher collusion in her own oppression. Since, if she reads actions as normal and natural, and suppression of those actions as harmful, she is forced into a no-choice situation. She cannot but allow them to continue, and she must render as harmless their power over her. The very practice which is supposed to liberate ('progressive education'), produces the possibility of this discursive power in the children. There is no counter discourse and the children know it . . . .

Girls and boys in the classroom

I want to extend this analysis to examine more interactions involving small boys, but this time in play with girls in the classroom. We can apply the kind of model that I have signalled above to understand the production of girls as subjects within pedagogic practices. Sex-role socialization accounts of the reproduction of girls understand them as produced as a reflection of traditional female sex roles. The economic dependence and oppression of women will produce girls whose personalities are passive and dependent, dominated and not dominant. Yet as I have asserted earlier, individuals are powerless or powerful depending upon which discursive practice they enter as subject. Recent work within the women's movement has pointed out that the oppression of women is not unitary, and that different discursive practices have different and often contradictory histories. This means that in some practices women are relatively powerful, for example, in those practices in which they signify as mothers (for example in custody cases). These practices are reproduced by the children in their play in the nursery classroom. This means that the girls are not always passive and dependent, just as their mothers are not, but are constantly struggling with the boys to define their play and to redefine it into discursive practices in which they can be powerful. To understand the power and resistance in the play of children we have to understand those practices that they are recreating in their play. These help to produce the children both as recreating the, often reactionary, discourses with which they are familiar, but also serve to constitute them as a multiplicity of contradictory positions of power and resistance.

Let us examine one small piece of play taken from the same classroom as before. This time, the children are playing hospitals. They have been given all the necessary equipment by a nursery nurse, and she has seen to it that the boys get the doctors' uniforms and the girls the nurses'. The nursery nurse constantly helps to maintain the power of the doctors over the nurses by constantly asking the nurses to 'help' the doctors. One girl, Jane, changes this into a situation where she is to make cups of tea for the patients. She goes into the Wendy House and has a domestic conversation with another girl and then the following sequence ensues:

One of the doctors arrives in the Wendy House and Jane says to him:

Jane: You gotta go quickly.

Derek: Why?

Jane: 'Cos you're going to work.

Derek: But I'm being a doctor.

Jane: Well, you've got to go to work doctor 'cos you've got to go to hospital and so do I. You don't like cabbage do you? (he shakes his head) . . . Well you haven't got cabbage then. I'm goin' to hospital. If you tidy up this room make sure and tell me.

Jane has managed to convert the play situation from one in which she is a powerless and subservient nurse to the only one in which she has power over the doctor, that of controlling his domestic life by becoming the controlling woman in the home. It is important that the other way in which she could have had power within that game, by, for example, playing a more senior doctor than Derek, is denied her by the nursery nurse's action and it is unlikely that she would be able to take that position by herself.

In another example of play between children in another nursery school we can examine another situation of struggle for power between girls and boys. This time the boy, Dean, is struggling for power to define and control the game. He comes to join Diane and Nancy, who are already playing mothers and daughters in the Wendy House. Diane is playing mother and controlling both the sequencing of the game and the actions of Nancy, who like any dutiful daughter goes along with mother's wishes. They are playing happily until Dean intervenes. Diane tries to tell him what to do as her son, but he tries to take over her commanding position. Diane says:

Diane: Well I'm playing mums and dads and girls. You're not. Or my, or my sister'll tell you off if you come in my house. She'll tell you off if you, if you come in my house. She will 'cos because I'm making 'er bed and if you get in 'er, in 'er bed she'll tell you off she will.
Let's go and get the baby, comeon then, you've got to go to bed now darling. You ain't been to bed yet have you?

Dean: (to Nancy) You don't like . . . you don't want to play with 'er do you?

Nancy: Yes, she won't let me go. . . .

Diane pushes Nancy a bit on the rocking horse and then tries to retrieve the domestic discourse:

Diane: Darling . . . I made the bed for you. Look what she's done. She's made it all dirty. All all new, I've made it all clean. Now I'll have to tidy up. Let's see my money, see if there's money. Here's your food. Meat, chicken and bacon and steak. Now d'you want the telly on? D'you want the telly on? I put it on for you. Here y'are I put the telly on for you. You can't turn it off.

Dean: What?

Diane: Can you?

Dean: I know you can't.

Nancy: She's our mum, she's our mum, yeah she's our mum.

Dean: (to Nancy)   If you're playing with 'er I'm not gonna be your friend any more . . . not ever play with you. So what you gonna do?

Nancy: (she looks first at one and then at the other, and 'turns tail')   I'll play with you.

Diane: Nancy, get off that horsey and go to bed now 'cos you're being naughty.

In both of these examples the struggle on behalf of the powerless child, the resistance of that child, takes the form of reading the individual as the subject/object of another discourse, just as in the Miss Baxter sequence. In both cases the girls' power is produced by their setting up the game as domestic, in which they, like their mothers, traditionally have power, though of course it is power produced through contradiction and paid for by their domestic labour: it is therefore severely limited and limiting, but not without effects. It is true that this is precisely what is asserted by sex-role stereotyping arguments, but there are several important points which, it seems to me, stereotyping arguments cannot explain. First, the girls are not always weak and dependent, but appear to be engaged in a *struggle* with the boys to read and to create the situations as ones in which they are powerful. The boys equally struggle to remove the play from the site of the domestic in which they are likely to be subservient. It is interesting to note that in the large number of play sequences recorded in these two nurseries, there were very few in which boys played powerful fathers *when girls were present* though they did do so when playing with other boys.

The position of girls in early education

. . . However, for these young children the domestic is not the only site of apparent female power. Their school lives are controlled by female teachers. There are many ways in which the discursive position adopted by the teachers is similar to that of mothers. Indeed, the nursery school provides a context in which good mothering and good pedagogy are seen as part of the same process – of aiding child development. I would argue that the very power of women in this transitory situation, between the domestic and the academic, is precisely what permits the early success of girls. It may be the similarity between these discursive practices, both sites of female power, that allows girls to take up positions of similarity with the powerful teachers. Indeed, the girls who are considered to be the 'brightest' by the teachers do indeed operate as subjects within the powerful pedagogic discourse. Within that discourse they take the position of the knower, they become sub-teachers.[4] For example, in one of the nurseries, Nancy, considered to be bright by the teacher, constantly asserts that she 'knows'. She continually finishes her work before the others to shrieks of 'Done it' and 'That's where it goes 'cos I know it does'. The boys in these exchanges are, by contrast, for the most part almost totally silent. They seem to be engaged in a resistance of silence, which is of course another way of resisting the discourse. Another example from an infant school will show just how the 'bright' girls act as sub-teachers. This is a typical conversation between Sally and a girl whom she had been helping with her work: 'Put your book away, come on. That's good work for today . . . slow to do everything. You take a minute to do it!' I would argue that it is the relation between the domestic and the pedagogic and the way in which women signify as mothers and teachers, taking positions of power within those practices, which provides the space for the early success of girls. This success is achieved precisely because successful school performance requires them to take up such positions in pedagogic discourses.[5] On the other hand, this is equally a site of struggle for the boys, a struggle in which they must work to redefine the situation as one in which the women and girls are powerless subjects of other discourses. It could well be this very resistance to that quasi-domestic power which results in the failure of the boys to do well in early education. . . .

Notes and references

1 The observations were made as part of the projects on developmental psychology and nursery education and girls and mathematics in the early years of schooling. The latter work was carried out jointly with Rosie Eynard and further details are contained in the project report: R. Eynard and V. Walkerdine, *The Practice of Reason: Investigations into the teaching and learning of mathematics*, vol 2: Girls and Mathematics, University of London, Institute of Education (mimeo).

2 Lowenfeld, M., *Play in Childhood*, London, Gollancz, 1935, pp. 324–5.

3 See, for example, Sellick, R. J. W., *English Primary Education and the Progressives 1914–1939*, London, Routledge & Kegan Paul.

4 See Eynard and Walkerdine, *The Practice of Reason*.

5 Madeleine MacDonald argues that accounts of education as reproduction are problematic in relation to the contradictory nature of women's education because of the

relations between the domestic and the academic: 'Socio-cultural reproduction and women's education', in Deem, R., *Schooling for Women's Work*, 1980; see also Carolyn Steedman's article, 'The tidy house', *Feminist Review*, **6**, 1980, in which she talks about girls' contradictory relations of power and powerlessness in relation to the home and childrearing and asserts the possibility of using an awareness of this to produce change.

13   The structure of sexual relations in school

Sue Lees

Visiting a comprehensive recently the first thing I heard on entering the gates was a girl discussing boys to her friends: 'All they do is call us slags.' It was statements such as this that led me to explore the way sexual insults function to control the social and autonomous behaviour of girls and steer them into marriage. My conclusions are based on a three year research project in three London comprehensive schools carried out in the early 1980s. A hundred 15- to 16-year-old girls from varied social class and ethnic groups were interviewed singly, in pairs or in group discussions. The first two schools were mixed: both had women headteachers who were attempting to put into force an equal opportunities programme. One school was predominantly white working class and the other had a high proportion of different ethnic groups. The third school was single-sex with a mainly middle-class intake – the fieldwork in this school was carried out a year later as the necessity to investigate the importance of social class differences became evident.

The research objective was to explore the subjective world of adolescent girls. I wanted to elicit the *terms* with which they describe and handle their world, to follow up the meanings through which they relate to that world, meanings both individually held and collectively shared. Such an objective required a qualitative method that allows the research to be sensitive to the girls' experience of the world. The need to examine the terms of their experience arises from the fact that language is generally deficient in expressing women's active experience – rather women are seen as the object of male experience. There is, for example, no word to describe the actively sexual woman – except derogatory abuse – which is why girls find it difficult to talk in terms of their own sexual desires. It is difficult for girls to conceptualize their feelings. Betty Friedan called the housewive's lack of self-identity 'the problem that has no name' (Friedan, 1976). In a similar way language is deficient at expressing the experience of adolescent girls.

I became convinced of the importance of analysing the experience of girls at the level of language and discourse as a form of power or material practice in itself – rather than as an ideological reflection of other practices. Language and discourse have material consequences (such as pushing girls into courtship and marriage and into forgoing their careers, or into only seeing themselves as the object of another's desire) which force girls to submit to the existing structure of patriarchal relations. Following Foucault (1980), the discussion of power does not relate to whether girls are concentrated in certain roles rather than others, but can be seen as a field of force in which boys and girls are equally trapped rather

Source: Commissioned.

than as something exercised by boys over girls. For example girls are as likely as boys to verbally sexually abuse other girls. The language of sexual abuse, where virtually all the terms of abuse available are ones which denigrate women and the only really abusive word for a man – a 'poof' – also denotes femininity, reflects the fundamental misogyny of our society.

Since the interviews raised very personal issues, it was particularly important that the girls should feel that the views they expressed were accepted. The interview technique was therefore non-directive, although it was semi-structured in that five main areas were explored: what the girls thought about school, friendship, boys, sexuality, and their expectations of the future. The aim was to understand the terms girls used to describe their lives and the various discourses through which they described their experiences. For example, it was more important to understand how girls talked about pre-marital sex than to establish how prevalent pre-marital sexual relations actually were.

Perhaps the first point to emphasize about the dynamics of sexism in the educational system is the need to look beyond the formal organization of the school as an institution to the cultural and social interaction that goes on in and around school life. The process of forming attitudes, cultural values, and group and individual identities is every bit as important as the formal educational process in the determination of girls' academic attainments. The system of social relations in the school – how boys treat girls and how girls respond in the playground and in the classroom – exercises an important influence on girls' academic lives. Furthermore, it is important to understand that the social and cultural life of the school is not insulated from that of the family and the neighbourhood which surrounds it. School life is an aspect of social life in general. This means that there is the strong pressure on girls, regardless of their social class membership, to regard marriage and domesticity as the main aim of life and their work in the labour market as secondary. This pressure is daily enforced in social and family life and will also be reflected in the social life of the school, exercising an influence far more powerful than the formal aspects of school organization or the structure of the curriculum. So when Sandy is asked how she sees herself in five years time, she replies

In five years time? Right, so I'm 21 right? I see myself pushing a pram. I don't see myself working.

What emerges from the transcripts is that girls' experience of school is contradictory, due to the ambiguity over what education is preparing them for. Is education, as the Newsom Report of 1963 argued, educating girls 'in terms of their main social function – which is to make for themselves, their children and their husbands a secure and comfortable home and to be mothers'? Sandy, a girl in our research, describes a teacher holding this view as follows:

He believes the woman is just there for the home and nothing else. We often have arguments with him. We say women should have equal rights to men and he says 'not really – you don't have to say yes when we ask you to marry us'. It's because girls have been brought up to think they should do lots of work (in the house) and the boys are expecting us girls to do all the work, they expect their mums to do it and when they marry they expect the girls to do it.

At the other extreme Annie describes teachers who emphasize that girls should put their career first and criticizes a teacher who argues that

We have got to fight against men. It puts you off. Like the Two Ronnies – Life of a Worm – have you seen it? It's like women do everything and men are absolute rubbish.

If girls opt out of school work and put their energies into attracting boys and getting married, it is too simple to categorize this as resistance to the school culture (see McRobbie, 1978). To see the rehearsal for entry into a major social institution such as marriage and the domestic sphere as a form of 'anti-school culture', or resistance, is in effect to deny the reality of the domestic sphere as a social institution akin, say, to economic life and social class relations and to see it purely as a cultural phenomenon. In this way the question of subculture and debate over sex and class relations are crucially linked. If the main structural forces or forms of stratification in our society are seen as economic class structures then, of course, rehearsal for domestic life will be viewed as a form of cultural behaviour unrelated to class. Alternatively it could be seen as a form of resistance to the consequences of class-determined life chances – in the way in which, for example, Willis describes the process whereby working-class boys reconcile themselves to working-class jobs (Willis, 1977). But if gender divisions are analysed as of equal significance to economic class in the constitution of social structure and social institutions then it is less easy to view girls' behaviour as 'subcultural'. Questions about sexual division cannot be inserted into a class analysis where the material base for that analysis lies in specific economic relations and their effects, unless gender relations are reducible to economic relations.

It is not just a question of girls receiving confusing messages but that these messages entail core dilemmas of sexual and social identity. The girl who opts for prioritizing a career has to face taunts over her lack of femininity. To explain why girls, who at 16 are academically surpassing boys, fail to go on to fulfil their potential, requires an understanding of the sexual relations in school.

Sexual reputation

I did not intend the research to focus on sexuality, but it gradually emerged that all girls – regardless of differences in social class and ethnic group – were concerned and anxious about their sexual reputation. While a boy's social identity is sustained through a wide range of activities, including, for example, sport, a girl's social identity seemed to depend much more crucially on her assumed sexual activity – whether she is a 'slag' (a girl who sleeps around) or a 'drag' (a 'nice' girl who does not and is considered by boys as marriageable rather than an easy lay) or perhaps worst of all if she is 'a lezzie' (or 'too tight'). For example, if a girl gained a reputation as a slag she would be ostracized by others, or if she ignored boys and concentrated on her studies then she would be in danger of being classed as 'a lezzie' or 'too tight'. Girls tread a very narrow line. They must not end up being called a slag, but equally they do not want to be thought of as unapproachable, sexually cold – 'a tight bitch'.

The constant concern that girls expressed about sexual reputation and the prevalence of sexual abuse led me to explore the way 'slag', the most common word of sexual abuse, is used. The term slag or its equivalents – 'slut', 'scrubber', 'old dog', 'easy lay' – is familiar in the literature on youth culture but has received little attention elsewhere. According to Paul Willis, 'certain reputations for "easiness" – deserved or not – spread very quickly. The "lads" are after the "easy lay" at dances, though they think twice about being seen to "go out" with them' (Willis, 1977). Here it seems that the term 'slag' or 'easy lay' simply applies to certain identifiable girls. But when you ask girls how it is applied and to whom, it is difficult to get a clear definition from those who use it. Take Sasha's description of what she calls a 'proper slag'

Sasha: I do know one or two slags. I must admit they're not proper slags.

Q: Can you describe what a proper slag is?

Sasha: Available aren't they? Just like Jenny, always on the look-out for boys, non-stop. You may not know her but you always see her and every time you see her she's got a different fella, every minute of the day.

Q: So is it just talking to different boys?

Sasha: You see them, some of them, they look as innocent as anything but I know what they're like.

The implication here is that the girl who is called a 'slag' sleeps around, but this is by no means clear and the insult often bears no relation at all to a girl's sexual behaviour. As Tania illustrates:

Tania: Like this girl that I know, this boy that she used to go with right, he started calling her names and so all his friends started calling her names.

Q: What sort of names?

Tania: Like slag, prostitute, whore all those things.

Q: While she was going out with him?

Tania: No after she had finished with him. He went round saying that she couldn't kiss, see, 'cos she sort of gets embarrassed, she's like that over the slightest thing. I admit that she only kissed him once but he knows that's why she wouldn't, because she was embarrassed.

Here a girl who is too shy and embarrassed even to kiss her boyfriend is nevertheless called a 'slag'. The lack of connection between sexual promiscuity and sexual abuse could hardly be greater.

Boys seem to be no better at agreeing who is or is not a slag than the girls. In their book about boys, *Knuckle Sandwich*, Dave Robbins and Phil Cohen write:

The boys classified all the girls into two categories: the *slags* who'd go with anyone and everyone (they were all right for a quick screw, but you'd never get serious about it) and the *drags* who didn't but whom you might one day think about going steady with. Different cliques of boys put different girls in each of the two categories (Robbins and Cohen, 1978, p. 58).

So, while everyone apparently knows a slag as someone who sleeps around, this stereotype bears no relation to the girls to whom the term is applied.

The function of 'slag'

What is striking is the sheer volume of denigratory terms for women. Julia Stanley estimated that there were 220 synonyns for the word 'whore'. The language of 'slag' forms part of a discourse on sexuality that is overwhelmingly characterized by a double standard. It is natural for boys to be after one thing in their relationships with girls – sex. A boy needs sex and it is quite acceptable for him to harass girls into bed – this is again 'natural' behaviour for a boy. After all sex is giving a girl what she really wants – although it would of course be 'unnatural' for her to openly initiate it – this would show she was really cheap and dirty. For a girl to want sex is for her to become an object of disdain. Yet there is a basic contradiction in this. To initiate sex is unfeminine behaviour, yet at the same time girls are seen in some respects as responsible for boys' sexual urges, which stem from a need for physical release. For example Maureen, when asked how she perceived 'old dogs', replied:

They've got their place haven't they? They're doing some job. They're stopping some people getting raped.

Similarly in Christine Griffin's research, when Treena is asked what she would do if a boy asks her for sex, she replies, 'I'd tell him to go off and have a wank' (Griffin, 1978). The implication here is that sex for men is a biological need that, if unreleased, would lead to rampant rape. It is a force of natural energy that seeks release and involves a progression from arousal to penetration to orgasm. It is a bit like a missile – once launched, there is no stopping it. Girls are also seen as 'asking for it' and a girl has only herself to blame ultimately if an encounter with a boy results in rape.

A further contradiction in discourses of sexuality is the idea that once a girl or a woman has had a sexual experience then it will not be possible to subdue her and she will become uncontrollable. As one of Willis's boys comments.

After you've been with one like, after you've done it like, well they're scrubbers afterwards, they'll go with anyone. I think it's that once they've had it, they want it all the time no matter who it's with (Willis, 1977, p. 44).

Is it perhaps, as Willis suggests, a fear that women will claim a right to their own sexual expression and be less controlled by men? Or as Anne Dickson proposes, a reflection of ideas rooted in the Christian tradition of Woman as Evil or as Chaste. Woman as Evil is derived from the story of Eve's seduction of an innocent man in the Garden of Eden by consorting with the devil and thereby bringing damnation to all humanity:

On the one hand, sex was envisaged as the devil's dynamite, a constant power in man's genitals, ready to be kindled in an instant by the tempting wiles of a woman. Or, on the other hand, the devil (and sexuality) was believed to reside in a woman's flesh; women's bodies were vehicles of evil, carriers of an evil force. Either way, women had to be avoided at all costs (Dickson, 1985, p. 6).

Sharon has picked up this male fear and disdain for adolescent girls. When asked whether there is anything she would like people to know about adolescent girls, she replies

Sharon: That they're not all cheap and easy to get.

Marion: 'Cos I think many girls once you're 16, 18 they think you're easy to get.

Sharon: Yes the girls put on a lot of make up and they go into the pub or something y'know nudge, nudge. She's all right. Force her to have sex and afterwards when she's pregnant abandon her and leave her alone. It's just like that.

Marion: Yeh a toy.

Sharon: Play with it and then chuck it away like it's broken.

To rebuff boys or take little interest in them is also regarded as unfeminine. So girls are faced with a contradiction. The girl is both blamed for exciting sex and for rejecting it. It is a 'no win' game.

Boys' reputations

A smaller pilot study is currently in progress in which boys of the same age at one of the same schools are being interviewed. A similar research design with group discussions and individual interviews was adopted. What emerges from these discussions is the way that every topic is laced with masculine or feminine connotations. It is 'cissy' to talk to girls unless you are chatting them up, or to be sensitive and gentle. To gain a 'black belt' or be on top, to boast about how many girls you have made or to put someone down is 'macho' and 'tough'. Boys have to act big in front of their friends. Their reputation is enhanced rather than damaged by sexual exploits, so the pressure is on them to 'mouth' – lie about how many conquests they have made. They do not, however, appear to suffer the kind of sexual abuse that girls experience. To call a boy a 'pooff' is derogatory, but this term, in denoting lack of guts, suggests femininity – weakness, softness and inferiority. Likewise boys describe how common ways to insult another boy include saying 'Your mum is a slag' or to 'slag' off their girlfriend. The insults have to be addressed at the women since the vocabulary for abusing men is so limited. A boy has to fight to defend his mum's reputation. One boy described to me how a long-standing friendship between two boys and their families had been broken by one of the boys calling the other's mother a 'slag'. The social life of the school and the community cannot be separated.

The power of discourse

An understanding of the power exercised over the girls by the language of sexuality lies in the hidden or unstated assumptions of the discourses in which they participate. These discourses are so taken for granted that few girls question their unfairness. What is of particular interest is the operation of an ideology that transforms the experience of unfair relations between the sexes into an acceptance of those relations as natural. It is somehow wrong and nasty for a girl to invite sexual activity but natural for the boy to be after it, to attempt to pester you into it, to tell if you do and to fabricate its occurrence if you don't. The taken-for-granted insolence of boys is evident in many accounts:

Like this boy was calling me a bitch. I don't know what he was calling me a bitch for, he was picking on me. 'You bitch' he goes, he knew my name. He just wanted to make fun or something because he was with his mates.

The other facet of 'slag' is its *uncontested* status as a category. Girls, when faced with sexual abuse, react by denying the accusation rather than by objecting to the use of the category. It is important to prove that you are not a slag. So Wendy, when asked what she would do if someone called her a slag replies: 'I'd turn round and say: "Why?' Tell me, why?" ' The term 'slag' therefore applies less to any clearly defined notion of sleeping around than to any form of social behaviour by girls that would define them as autonomous from the attachment to and domination by boys. This language is used by boys about girls and by girls of one another. Everyone is caught up in it. It determines how sexuality is talked about and displayed as a central feature of the social life of adolescents. It is reproduced as much by the social relations of the classroom as those of the disco.

Control over girls' autonomy

The language of sexual abuse enables boys to define the school and its resources as part of their public sphere to the exclusion of girls. At one school, for example, there was a table tennis craze and the boys wanted to push the girls off the tables. The girls who refused to be pushed were called 'show-offs', not just by the boys but by other girls. They were regarded as sexually forward in standing up to the boys. Girls' participation in the classroom is equally unwelcome and they are at best ignored, or at worst ridiculed or put down.

They don't take any notice of you when they're with their mates or they take the mickey out of you.

Much of a boys' group solidarity is based on collective denigration of girls who may even be their friends:

They talk about some of our mates horribly, the ones they know are really good friends. They say they know for a fact that she is a slag and has been passed around the five of them. They say awful things when it's not true. Even when you walk along the street they scream things at you.

Or as another girl put it:

When there's boys talking and you've been out with more than two, you're known as the crisp that they're passing around . . . the boy's alright but the girl's a bit of scum.

Putting down girls is a daily part of classroom life:

If he wants to borrow a ruler or something and we don't give it to him 'cos we borrowed him something before, and he like calls you a pratt. He says 'All right pratt. You're so damned tight you won't give us anything.' So we go 'That's right' then every time he comes to the lesson they call you 'pratt', 'pratt' . . . 'Pratt's sitting down on the chair', 'Pratt's got a ruler' and all the rest of it. You don't have a chance.

A constant sliding occurs between the use of the term 'slag' as a term of joking and of serious abuse. Any girl is always available to the designation in any number of ways. Appearance is crucial: by wearing too much make-up, by having your skirt too slit, by not combing your hair, wearing jeans to dances or high heels to school. Moreover, it is the girl who is unattached who is most likely to be called a slag, irrespective of her sexual activity – by acting independently, by going out with or merely talking to several boys rather than having a steady boyfriend, or by rebuffing a boy or being ditched. The term, therefore, functions as a form of control by boys over girls, a form of control which steers girls into 'acceptable' forms of sexual and social behaviour. The ambiguous way 'slag' is used means it is very difficult to contest its legitimacy. If a girl starts to get a reputation the only thing she can do to redeem herself is to 'get a steady boyfriend'. As one girl says: 'Then that way you seem to be more respectable like you're married or something.'

The threat of being regarded as a slag pushes girls to channel their sexuality into the 'legitimate' channels of courtship and marriage. This is illustrated by the girls' expectation that they will get married despite their holding realistic views about the subordinate position of women within marriage. Girls see marriage in terms of financial dependency, loss of freedom, being bossed around, loneliness and, at worst, being subject to violence in the home. Yet they see no alternative.

Sexism and racism

Sexist and racist stereotypes operate in ways which, although not identical, are in some respects similar. Both sets of stereotypes are difficult to pin down to any hard or specific content which could be shown to be untrue and thus lead to the withdrawal of the label. For 'slag', this is because of the ambiguous way in which it is used; in the case of racist stereotypes this results from a refusal to allow any exceptions (Allport, 1954, called this *re-fencing*). Karen elaborates on the sexual and racial prejudices of herself and her friends:

Like me . . . Pam and me and Susan. . . . And we were sat in these flats talking talking and I just said. . . . A Paki come along and Pam says 'Oh I hate Pakis' and I go 'Oh I hate the Jews' and Susan goes 'I hate black people'. And I goes 'How can you hate black people, Sybil's black?' And like Susan and Pamela and me were all white and she goes 'I don't really' . . . She goes 'I hate golliwogs'. That was it, she didn't say blacks. And I says 'What do you mean you hate golliwogs? My best friend's black' and she goes 'Yeah, so's mine'. So I goes 'Yeah? So how can you hate them' And Pamela goes, 'I hate all Pakis'.

The processes by which girls are labelled 'slags', irrespective of race, can become one component out of which racist views are elaborated. It is not just that 'slag' is a label that has a fluidity similar to racist stereotypes. Racism is able to absorb and work through sexist categories. Gerda Lerner argues that

Every black woman was, by definition, a slut according to racist mythology; therefore to assault her and exploit her sexually was not reprehensible and carried with it none of the normal sanctions against such behaviour (Lerner, 1981, quoted in Hooks, 1981, p. 59).

Black girls I interviewed did not mention racist insults from other boys and girls occurring in school, but referred to their experiences of racist and sexist taunts outside school. In school girls from different ethnic groups formed friendships and talked in similar terms about their experiences. Nor did I find any expression of strong personal racism on the part of white girls towards black girls:

The girls in school don't hang around in one group of coloureds, they sort of mix, they chip in. We've got one coloured girl and three white girls in my group and everyone gets on well together.

Some of the white girls will challenge racism when they come across it in their friends:

The other day it was a friend of ours got in an argument with a girl who had her cousin beaten up by coloured people and she said that she just can't stand coloured people and we said you should hate the people who did it but not just because of the colour of their skin or whatever. And she was really anti coloured from then on.

Outside school however, antagonism arose between groups of black and white girls. Jane, a white girl, is incensed about this.

Some white girls called some black girls outside of school bad names – how they can call them bad names I don't know. It's insane. Half of them don't even know what they're saying.

Though I was not able to differentiate between the transcripts of white and black (of West Indian origin) working-class girls, differences of experiences outside school were apparent between the Asian and Greek girls and the rest. Asian and Greek girls were more closely supervised at home and some were not allowed out. Meena explains:

Meena: 'Cos I'm Indian I'm not really supposed to go out with anyone. I don't think it's right.

Q: Your parents don't think it's right to go out with boys?

Meena: I suppose they taught me, but I'll go out with boys but I don't sleep around or anything. . . . My mum would tell me off 'cos she don't trust boys. It's not that she don't trust me, she don't trust other boys, she knows what they're like 'cos she has been through it all. She says it isn't not worth trusting them.

Meena went on to explain that she did not believe in sex before marriage since it would involve betraying her parents who did not believe in arranged marriages but insisted on her delaying sex until marriage. However, several girls mentioned the racism of their parents – particularly their dads. As Beryl says

My dad's quite a racialist. My mum and I have worked on him a bit. But I won't discuss it with him. I get very embarrassed. He sort of says all these things about all black people commit crimes and there was me and one other girl who were prepared to stand up to him in a group of eight. All the others were having a go. I really belittled him in front of everyone. He got me so angry that I couldn't help it.

Implications for education

There are three main implications for education where teacher intervention is important: first, the denigration of girls and pervasiveness of verbal sexual abuse needs to be challenged rather than 'swept under the table'. My research suggests that most teachers ignore verbal sexual abuse and show little understanding of the dynamics of the social life of the school. Take Myra's description of an incident which she describes as 'getting into trouble':

Myra: I got into trouble for my name being written on the wall. I went to the toilet and it was written about me in pencil so I rubbed it off. A few days later it was written in felt tip pen.

Q: What was written?

Myra: That I was a slag and so on. Then on Monday there it was again. The PE teacher got people scrubbing the toilet walls. Later I was looking for my little sister after school and the PE teacher says to me 'Myra come here'. I walked over to her and everyone's standing there thinking 'What's she want with her?' and she says to me 'I've just had people cleaning the walls and isn't it funny how your name comes up so many times.' She says 'You know what toilet I'm talking about'. I say 'Yeah'. She says 'Do you know who done it?' and I can't really tell her who done it especially with everyone looking on so I say 'No'. So she says 'If I see your name written up there again you and your friends are gonna get into trouble'. So I said 'Well it was nothing to do with me.' She says 'Well if that was my name written up there I'd have had it scrubbed off.' So I said 'It's in great big green felt pen.' She goes 'Let me see your name up there again and there'll be trouble.' She thinks I'm going to walk round all every toilet in the breaks scrubbing everything off the walls. I tell my dad. He said to tell her in future to find the idiots who wrote it and make them scrub it off. It really did annoy me.

This teacher, by focusing on Myra, is blaming her for having her name on the wall. Teachers are not encouraged to use such opportunities to challenge the use of verbal sexual abuse and denigration of girls. Instead Myra, a victim rather than a perpetrator of the abuse, is blamed and reprimanded for the incident. Teachers need to intervene by challenging the terms of the abuse, removing the focus from the individual, and allocating responsibility to the sexism within language and within the school culture.

Second, sex education should not be confined to special classes. It needs to be seen with reference to the powerful and taken-for-granted assumptions about sexuality which, rather than being natural and biologically given, are social and reflect and reinforce the subordinate position of girls and women. Whether or not romantic love is involved, the differential power of men and women is clearly expressed in sexual relations. It is only by approaching the question of sex education in this context, with a knowledge of how sexual relations are structured by the norms and constraints outlined in this article, that progress can be made. I would like to mention particularly two areas where a shift in standpoint is needed.

Although birth control is now free, in practice only a third of all sexually active teenagers regularly use contraception. This is usually put down to lack of information and reluctance to approach clinics, but what may be more relevant is the operation of the double standard which condemns a girl as irresponsible if she does not use contraception and as as a 'slag' if she does. Using birth control and contraceptives is particularly risky in relation to a girl's reputation. If she uses contraception on a casual date, this involves laying herself open to the charge that sex is premeditated and that she is therefore consciously choosing to anticipate that sex might occur with someone she is not 'in love' with or in a steady relationship with – she is therefore a 'slag'. On the other hand, if she has sex without contraception this can be explained as something that 'happens without previous intent'. Girls frequently describe their sexual activity (or perhaps one should say passivity) as something that happens to them rather than something they consciously choose. As Hannah said:

You might be at a party and someone just dragged you upstairs and the next thing you know you don't know what's happening to you. Even so the girl is blamed for laying herself open to attack. It happens a lot. But then it's the girl's fault for getting silly drunk in the first place that she can't, she doesn't, know what's going on or anything.

[You have to] watch yourself for things like that and you don't go to parties . . . like you know when you've had enough to drink, you know not to drink more.

Girls describe how boys refer to girls who are 'second-hand' and 'cheap' – a girl's status is lowered at the same time that a boy's is enhanced. Sexual experience makes her promiscuous where it proves him to be a man. The pervasiveness of gossip and the threat of ostracism is a more immediate problem than the possibility of pregnancy.

Sex education should therefore focus on the moral and social context in which relations between the sexes occur not only in the classroom but in the family, the neighbourhood and the entire arena of the social life of young people. 'My school work reflects how the rest of my life is going. If I'm being sworn at, at school, or have trouble at home, my work suffers.'

The need for sex education within the school must be reinforced, rather than negated, by current concerns. National media campaigns by central government on AIDS and heroin addiction, the growing number of young people on post-school government training schemes, intermediate treatment and community service, local authority funding of youth and community facilities: all these provide arenas within which explicitly sexist language and assumptions about behaviour can be challenged.

Third, the contradictory aims of education for girls must be recognized. Our educational institutions are male dominated and geared to the education of boys and the labour market rather than for both girls' and boys' dual role of work and the reproduction of children. As Gillian Pascall comments:

Educational institutions have frequently been analysed as middle class institutions bearing middle class culture. Less often is it noticed that they are male institutions bearing male culture. . . . From the most overt political mechanisms – democratically elected authorities – to the most covert – the assumptions written into the 'knowledge' which is taught – the same analysis can be made. From a history that is the history of men's wars to a literature that is dominated by men's books, to a social science that is constructed around men's position in the division of labour, the 'knowledge' purveyed is that women have no place in the world (Pascall, 1986, p. 131).

To change education is of course no easy task. It would involve a curriculum that prepares men and women for shared roles in domestic and work life and stops treating girls as second-class citizens; a curriculum that uses women's experience, knowledge and views of the world. The verbal denigration of girls and their sexual subordination will only be alleviated with such radical changes.

Notes

This article is based on research funded by the Inner London Education Authority and the Nuffield Foundation; Celia Cowie was funded by ILEA as research fellow. The research has provided the basis of my book *Losing Out; sexuality and adolescent girls*, London, Hutchinson, 1986.

References

Allport G., *The Nature of Prejudice*, London, Addison Wesley, 1954.
Dickson A., *The Mirror Within, A New look at Sexuality*, London, Quartet Books, 1985.
Foucault M., *The History of Sexuality*, vol. 1, London, Allen Lane, 1979.
Griffin C., *Typical Girls*, London, Routledge and Kegan Paul, 1978.
Friedan B., *The Feminine Mystique*, Harmondsworth, Penguin, 1976.
Lerner G., 'Black women in white America', quoted in Bell Hook's *Ain't I a Woman*, London, Pluto Press, 1981.
McRobbie A., 'Working class girls and the culture of femininity', in *Women Take Issue*, Women's Studies Group; London, Hutchinson, 1978.
Pascall G., *Social Policy, A Feminist Analysis*, London, Tavistock, 1986.
Robbins D. and Cohen, P., *Knuckle Sandwich*, Harmondsworth, Penguin, 1978.
Stanley J., 'Paradigmatic woman; the prostitute', paper presented to South Atlantic Modern Language Association, American Dialect Society, 1972.
Willis P., *Learning to Labour*, Farnborough, Saxon, 1977.

Part Four

Class, Race and Gender: Structures and Ideologies

14 'All the big bosses are men, all the secretaries are females': schooling women office workers

Linda Valli

Both traditional and radical versions of the role of school in the preparation of young people for the world of work emphasize the importance of students learning 'proper' dispositions and attitudes as well as necessary skills. A functionalist like Parsons would call this aspect of work preparation the moral dimension and would point out the necessity of students internalizing such qualities as responsibility, co-operativeness, respect for the teacher and good work-habits, qualities important for 'successful performance in their future adult roles' (Parsons, 1959).

[However], I [am unhappy with] the functionalist assumptions underlying the use of the concept 'moral' and would be more in agreement with Marxists like Althusser or Bowles and Gintis who would call this aspect of work preparation the ideological dimension. They would stress such qualities as 'respect for rules of the order established by class domination' (Althusser, 1971), or, as Bowles and Gintis (1976, p. 130) would phrase it: 'to reproduce the social relations of production, the system must try to teach people to be properly subordinate and render them sufficiently fragmented in consciousness to preclude them getting together to shape their own material existence'.

Yet, two other traditions within Marxist social science led me to be suspicious of the claim that the reproduction of the social relations in production was fundamentally and primarily the function of the education system inculcating students with the dispositions they would need to become good workers. These two traditions are cultural reproduction theory, best exemplified in Paul Willis's *Learning to Labour: How Working Class Boys Get Working Class Jobs* (1977); and labour process theory, best exemplified in Michael Burawoy's *Manufacturing Consent: Changes in the Labor Process under Monopoly Capitalism* (1979).

Cultural reproduction theory differs from what I will call ideological reproduction theory in that it identifies culture rather than ideology as the principal determinant of 'properly trained' labour power. In contrast to Althusser and Bowles and Gintis, Willis and Burawoy both argue that the school is not a privileged site of social reproduction. Burawoy claims that the labour process itself (and the practices, relations, ideologies and cultures produced in that process) is sufficient for the maintenance of capitalist relations. He claims there is no need for extra-productive conditions or ideological 'super-structures' to ensure their reproduction:

. . . consent is produced at the point of production – independent of schooling, family life, mass media, the state, and so forth (1979, p. xii).

Source: Extracted from Valli, Linda, *Becoming Clerical Workers*, Boston, Routledge and Kegan Paul, 1986, pp. 137–82.

While the organization of the labour process might indeed be sufficient to ensure the reproduction of specific aspects of the relations in production under certain conditions, I will argue that cultural and ideological processes outside the labour process do have a bearing on the way in which young workers participate in the labour process. Moreover, Burawoy himself admits the limitations of this work in testing for the possible differences between male and female orientations to work. My research suggests that the differences in male and female orientations are pervasive and are learned long before young people begin to participate in the labour process.

The analysis of female education presented here is based on an ethnographic study of a Cooperative Office Education Program (COOP), a vocational programme in which senior high school students went to school part time and work part time in an office. Students received help in finding career-related jobs and received on the job and classroom training. They were also paid wages for their office work. The data were collected during the 1980–1 school year at Wosdrow High School, Macomb, a mid west city in the United States. Three related techniques were used: participant observation in the school and at work (fourteen sites in all); formal and informal interviewing, throughout the year, of significant subjects (for example, teachers, students, alumnae and co-workers), and analysis of curriculum materials and other related documents.[1]

The analysis [of this data] proceeds by drawing upon and reconciling the best aspects of each of the three partially antagonistic theories [discussed above]. From the ideology perspective I utilize the notion that the school definitely is, and in many ways is consciously structured to be, an ideological training ground for workers. It is not and cannot be, as Entwistle (1979) for instance claims, an ideologically neutral institution. By analysing both the formal and informal aspects of the Cooperative Office Education curriculum I extract and analyse three sets of ideological configurations that represent essential aspects of current production relations (exchange relations, authority relations and gender relations).

From the cultural perspective, I utilize two notions. The first is that while ideological processes are real and pervasive, they are not necessarily internalized and do not themselves constitute working-class identities. They are negotiated, contested and reworked; they are transmitted through 'social and cultural dialectics, mediations, and struggle' (Willis, 1981, p. 57). The second notion I utilize is that while the school is an important site for cultural production and the constitution of various forms of consciousness and subjectivity, other sites must also be analysed, chief among them, the family and the labour process itself.

From the labour process perspective, I utilize the notion that there are times at which, or ways in which, the relations in production themselves are better at reproducing ideologically prepared workers than are the sites outside the wage labour process (e.g. the family and the school).

Extensive ethnographic accounts of exchange, authority and gender relations in educational ideology, in the organization of the labour process in the various offices, and in student/worker culture(s) form the basis of [this chapter].

Exchange relations

As the following account makes evident, ideological dimensions of the COOP programme generally supported employers' desires for highly productive and low-paid workers. The culture of the students and aspects of the labour process also formed them into hard workers with few demands, irrespective of a notion of a 'fair' exchange relation.

In the organizations I observed, employers seemed to use two tactics in directly controlling wage demands: discouraging workers from considering unionization and discouraging knowledge of and discussion about pay scales. Several of the workplaces had a 'no discussion' policy, which was commented on during the interviews. Donna, who worked at a Savings and Loan, said for instance: 'Employees can't cash their checks here. They don't want you to know how much each other makes, so nobody can say, "I do the same thing she does so I should be getting more money." ' When I asked how she knew that was the reason, she said her supervisor told her.

And although it is technically illegal for employers to retaliate against workers who organize, employees are often made to feel they would be jeopardizing their jobs if they talked union. As Mary, who had been working at the same bank for ten years said:

Union. That's a nasty word around here. So is asking for a cost of living increase. As far as I know there has been no serious union attempt; just a few of the girls talking about it among themselves. But that could be something that might get you fired if they ever heard about it. . . . It's probably not a bad idea though.

This perception of employer retaliation was corroborated by one of my union organizer informants who stated, in addition, that employers attempt to elicit information during interviews to determine whether or not the job applicant has a history of activism.

These were the most obvious attempts companies made to keep the cost of labour as low as possible. They constitute the employer's role in the wage side of the exchange relation between employer and employee, a role the students' school experience in many ways simulated.

Even though Mrs Lewis [the teacher] was herself a strong advocate of and participant in Macomb's teachers' union, she neither indicated to the students that clerical unions existed nor that they tended to play a part in determining exchange relations between employers and employees. Similarly, she actively discouraged students from discussing their hourly wage with anyone, saying it was a personal matter and no one else's business but their own.

This practice of not discussing pay, of treating it as a purely personal matter, [broke] down at the beginning of class one day, however, when Janie and her best friend, Dana, were speaking to Mrs Lewis in the privacy of her back office. When Dana and Janie came into the classroom Dana was obviously upset, complaining that she was still at minimum wage while Janie, who worked for the state and whose office workers were unionized, had received several raises (many of them automatic). Dana was saying things to Janie like, 'I hate you', and 'It's just not fair'.

Mrs Lewis later informed me that Janie had brought up her raises out of the blue and that (hyperbolically), she 'could have killed her'. She also informed me that she had taken Janie out into the hall and said to her

Don't you see how unhappy you've made your friend? You don't want to do that do you? Pay is a very personal matter. I don't know what any other teacher makes in the department and I don't want to know. That is something you really shouldn't discuss.

This incident happened only a few weeks before graduation. Janie and Dana were continually together during and after class and often planned after school activities together. If they did not know until May what each other was making, I doubt that many students did. In fact, I know of only one student who knew another's hourly wage.

I would suggest that the reason this 'pay is private' ideology is so acceptable to the students is because it converges with two basic aspects of their feminine culture: caring about others' feelings and identifying more with unpaid domestic labourers than with wage labourers. If this convergence were not present, if the 'wage packet' were as essential to their cultural identity as it is to masculine shop-floor culture, I would expect far more contestation or covert resistance to the idea that pay is a private concern.

Still, the tenuousness of this ideology is indicated by Dana's striking reaction to Janie's rate of pay. If workers *did* know what others made, their primary reaction probably would not be to feel bad about themselves, but to negotiate or struggle for more comparable rates of pay.

Lessons in productivity

Employers engage in numerous and varied practices to obtain the desired quantity and quality of work from their employees. Edwards (1979) classifies control mechanisms according to three types: simple, technical and bureaucratic. Simple control is embodied in personal authority relations, technical in the machinery itself, and bureaucratic in the organization and rules of the workplace.

Although the technical means to control and monitor both the pace and quality of office work has been marketed, I witnessed little of its implementation. So the two primary means of control brought to bear upon the students' production were simple and bureaucratic control. Since the relation of office workers to their floor supervisors will be analysed under authority relations, the remainder of this section will focus on the manner in which bureaucratic control can be used in offices to ensure production standards.

The fact that raises and promotions did not occur automatically, but were largely dependent on how hard they worked was no secret to the COOP students. Raises, Marion said, were

determined by things like 'workability,' how you can handle responsibility . . . it's measured by your attitude, how you apply yourself to the job. If you piss and moan all day long and give your supervisor nothing but baloney, well that's pretty obvious. But if you have a positive attitude you'll move up.

At least one employer started COOP students at the minimum wage for the explicit purpose of having a cash reserve with which to give merit pay increases during the course of the year. Adequate improvement would result in a 1–15 cent hourly raise. If improvement exceeded expectations, the increase would be in the 16–25 cent range.

The COOP students also knew that their jobs were not secure. They were informed at the beginning of the year that none of their employers had a commitment to them beyond their co-operative year, and that if they did not work out satisfactorily, they could be released. In fact, they knew that they could be fired during the year if all did not go well. Many of them had been employed in non-office jobs, prior to their senior year, in which being fired was a possibility. COOP students had also been dismissed from their workplaces in past years and Mrs Lewis made the students aware of this.

The most systematic attempt to procure a high rate of productivity was undertaken by United Group Insurance, one of the largest insurance companies in the area. Five of my interviewees had been employed there as COOP students in four different departments and each of them described the company's use of a 'time lapsing' system to measure productivity.

Time lapsing was an extremely rigid accountability system in which workers had to keep track of both time and quantity of work, sometimes every five minutes. The following statement describes how this system of bureaucratic control functioned:

Every night we have to fill out production sheets. These give the company an idea of how much work is actully being done. The supervisors then give percentages of how you are doing. Some jobs require writing down the amount of time you spend on the job. But most of them require the quantity of work. Everything we do must be counted so that it can go on your production sheet.

In addition to this time-study system, United Group had also instituted a rigid penalty system, with so many rule infractions leading to dismissal. As Joan explained it:

They have these things called freckles, like if you come in late or something. Six freckles lead to an occurrence and if you have so many occurrences you can be fired. It depends on your supervisor. . . . Like a phone call is a freckle. You get docked for it.

Although Mrs Lewis did not institute any bureaucratic policies that even remotely approximated United Group's time lapsing or 'freckle' system, she stressed the importance of the students improving their productivity, often using the maxim 'a fair day's work for a fair day's pay'. The issue of fair pay was never raised as a problem, however; the assertion was simply made that workers are being paid to be productive and that if they did not produce they should not be paid.

Quantity of work, for example, was one of the explicit areas in which students were evaluated in their jobs and the following remarks are characteristic of the comments Mrs Lewis made to the students' supervisors about the relation between productivity and pay:

The students need to learn that we are measuring their production. We, both of us, at school and work, need to emphasize that. We're watching to see how much they're getting done. They're getting paid for the hour's work they do, so they have to ask themselves 'What am I producing for that hour?' Many people go through their entire lives not even realizing that connection. That's especially a problem with state employees, particularly at the lower levels. . . . I had to tell one student in class today that she owed *me* money for the hour, that's how bad it was. She didn't get a thing done.

And although, in practice, Mrs Lewis seldom encouraged the COOP students to work diligently or to meet deadlines, she would direct the following types of comments to them:

Ladies, one reason people are fired is for standing around the door waiting for the bell to ring. Employers expect you to work until the last minute.

Okay, girls, we don't have any time to lose. We're not going to stand around here and take half pay today.

These remarks focus the problem of pay on the student/worker. The unspoken assumption in each of them is that a fair day's pay is offered, so the student/worker must live up to her part in the exchange relation and give the employer a fair day's work in return.

The ideological dimensions of the productivity/pay relationship presented to the COOP students are, then, twofold: fair work for fair pay is presented as a self-evident, natural relationship, and the fair pay element of that relationship is never questioned. Yet in reality, no objective or universal standards to measure 'fairness' exist; that concept has meaning only when embedded in concrete social and historical practices.

There were a few times, however, when Mrs Lewis presented curricular materials or made comments that suggested the possibility of workers being unfairly compensated for their labour. On the first day of class she told the students she used to feel sorry for COOP students hired by the city because it did not adhere to federal minimum wage regulations. She also told them later in the semester that women with the same skills and abilities made only 59 per cent of what men made in comparable jobs. On another occasion, when a student reported on a magazine article entitled 'Why secretaries are paid unfairly', Mrs Lewis commented that in private industry the secretary's salary is tied into the grade of her boss, while in government work there are generally set classifications.

Although in each of these situations Mrs Lewis was implicitly criticizing pay scales, the criticism was never made explicit. Nor was it presented to the students for reflection and discussion. And because the students' experience with and knowledge about wages and salaries was quite limited, they did not seem to have the conceptual sophistication needed to raise questions about exchange relations.

This does not mean, however, that the students never privately wondered about or discussed issues of pay, productivity and equity, especially as they gained insight from their work experiences. While most of the students believed that what others made at work was their personal affair, some resented being told what was or was not their business. As Dorothy said: 'I think that if you want to talk about pay and raises, that's your problem. I don't think they should tell you. I don't like the do's and don'ts of the whole thing.'

Moreover, the experience and bits of knowledge picked up from their workplaces led them to question whether pay was really based on productivity and whether it was or should be based on other factors. Eleanor, like a number of my interviewees, complained of salaried workers who took long lunch hours and coffee breaks, who stood around telling stories and jokes, and who sat at their desks with apparently little to do. Eleanor thought a solution to this problem would be to pay everyone on an hourly basis: 'I think it's better if people are paid on an hourly basis. That way, if they're not there, they're not paid for it. That's the way it should be. Everyone should be on that basis – even the big bosses upstairs.'

Other types of experiences also raised questions about whether or not pay was based on productivity. Connie, who compared her rate of pay to other employees within her own corporation rather than across sectors, thought there was a discrepancy. Referring to their work in the word processing department, she said: 'I think if you compared what we actually know, if you compared our knowledge to other workers, you would find we were terribly underpaid.'

Although Connie was implicitly drawing a connection between knowledge and productivity, the introduction of this concept is, of course, quite a different factor in the determination of pay than simply productivity. It was also a factor that a number of students referred to as a condition for higher levels of pay. More knowledge, skill, or responsibility were all considered to be good reasons for higher pay:

People should get paid more if what they're doing is harder and needs more thinking power. And supervisors should get more because they have a bigger responsibility.

I think you should get a raise every time you advance up.

Conversely, the students argued, if work was easy, if it did not require much thought or training, if it was a routine job anyone could do, then the level of pay should not be very high. During my week of observing her on the job, Katrina made an unsolicited remark about pay. She was stuffing a pile of envelopes and getting the day's mail ready to go out when she remarked, 'Isn't this work easy? Don't you think it's easy? It's so easy I probably shouldn't even be paid for doing it.'

This she contrasted with her normal typing duties which she considered to be real work: difficult and important. And although she did not follow her remark up with an implication about pay, Carolyn expressed a similar notion of what constitutes work, saying, 'the job I'm doing now I don't even consider work . . . I just purge files all the time, and it's not hard to do. I would like it better if it were harder and if it required more concentration'. If this attitude that easy or routine work is not real work is pervasive among office workers, processes which rationalize work tasks and deskill workers could definitely have the effect of lowering pay expectations. If workers see pay as the exchange they receive from the employer for what they produce and if they do not place a high value on either the product or the work process, they could quite conceivably feel as though they had no basis upon which to claim more pay. This tendency would be exacerbated by the fact, referred to earlier, that many of my interviewees had little knowledge of pay scales in general and often felt, and were taught, that they had no right to know. If workers have no basis of comparison for their own wage packet, they have more difficulty in claiming they are 'underpaid', as Connie was able to claim when a job study was done of the work in her department.

Lowering pay expectations is not, however, the only possible outcome of job fragmentation and rationalization. Not all the students thought easy or routine jobs should be low paying. Donna, who tried to make sense out of the fragmented information she had about wage scales, came up with a theory of compensatory pay. Reflecting on jobs that paid more than hers, Donna concluded that boring work brought higher pay. Carolyn, she said, was paid the relatively high wage of $4.00 an hour because she was filing all day, a job so boring she herself would refuse to do it for $10.00 an hour. When asked if she would be paid more by her company to file, Donna responded with an indirect yes:

I think the COOP student who works in the basement gets more than I do. And she does filing of records and record tapes. And it's the same way with Internal Revenue. A girl who was in the COOP class last year worked with Internal Revenue and she got $5 something an hour to sit there and file and sort papers. . . . She said it was the most boring job she's ever had in her life.

But even though the students did have some questions and criticisms about rates of pay, the most significant factor about their willingness to be productive was that they worked hard for reasons quite apart from believing they were engaged in a fair exchange relationship with their employers. These reasons were far more intrinsic to the student's culture and sense of identity and to the demands of the labour process itself.

First of all, the students derived a sense of personal pride from what they produced; they took great satisfaction in their accomplishments, often rendering close supervision unnecessary. One afternoon, for instance, while observing a COOP student's work at a photocopy machine, I inquired about a plastic object she was placing over the original copy. She offered the following comment by way of explanation:

I like myself to look good, so I make sure things are centered on a xerox machine, and I put a white plastic cover on the back so shadows don't show through, even though I don't have to.

Donna also said that she got 'a kick out of seeing letters I've typed actually mailed out to someone. I can say, "I typed this"!'

In explaining why she preferred clerical work to a job like waitressing, which she had also done, another student said it was because 'in a clerical position you can take more pride in your work and feel better about yourself. . . . I like to do things I do well. It makes me feel good about myself'. Jessica, a recent graduate of the COOP programme, described a similar sentiment regarding the increased responsibilities her new job entailed:

Just recently I had to take notes at a meeting. I had never done that before and I did really good. I got lots of compliments on them. . . . But it was hard to take minutes because they kept switching from one subject to another and I had to keep up and get everything.

The second reason why many students did not need to be taught productivity was because they saw their work as 'service' to the customer and wanted to deliver that service as well as they could. In explaining why she liked her job, for example, Marion stated: 'I feel as though I'm accomplishing something, as though I'm helping people who need help. If the insured aren't happy with what they have, it's important to me because they're paying my salary.' Other students extended this 'service' orientation to the nature of the company itself. [One] student wrote the following description of [her] workplace on [her] final examination:

Our bank is very important in today's society because it is a place where you can save your money and earn interest, but also get loans, a checking account and financial advice. . . . We have special events coming up like June Dairy Day where the bank gives away free ice cream cones and cheese.

This notion of serving or helping also extended to their co-workers and provides the third reason why 'teaching productivity' was not a critical task for the school or a critical problem for the employer. When I asked the students and graduates what they liked most about their jobs, one of the most frequent responses was, 'The people I work with'. They used expressions like 'they were very welcoming to me when I started working', or 'we're just like one big family'. Frequently, the women would shop together on their lunch hour or go drinking together after work. Nancy's description of her co-workers is typical: '. . . the people are really nice. They explain things well and don't just throw it in your face and say do it. . . . They treat you nice'. Because of these personal ties, the women wanted to get their work done and do it well. If they did not, friends and co-workers would have to share the burden.

Another way in which the labour process provided productivity incentive was that boredom was dreaded far more than hard work. In fact, as indicated earlier, hard work was often a very satisfying experience. Boredom, on the other hand, was one of the greatest sources of job dissatisfaction for these young workers. As Nancy said to me about her first COOP job:

At first I was bored, but now there's more stuff to do and I like it better. . . . Before when I was just in files I always felt like I was going to fall asleep. In filing it was the same stuff over and over. Now I do more exciting work; you have to use your mind more. It's more challenging and I like that.

Authority relations

Hierarchical structures are almost always used within work organizations not only to co-ordinate the flow of work, making production efficient, but to monitor the pace of it as well. In *Schooling in Capitalist America*, Bowles and Gintis argue that authority relations within a capitalist mode of production are always problematic: 'Wherever possible, workers demand control over the decision-making about working conditions toward the improvement of their conditions' (1976, p. 81). Attempts are therefore made to give hierarchical relations the appearance of legitimacy and inevitability, and to develop in workers those forms of consciousness necessary to 'facilitate their harmonious integration into the hierarchical order of the enterprise' (p. 95).

The legitimacy of authority relations, Bowles and Gintis continue, is achieved by fragmenting the labour force and work tasks so that workers are convinced they are incapable of controlling the labour process, and by ensuring that 'relationships among superiors, subordinates, and peers (do) not violate the norms of the larger society' (p. 82). In other words, authority figures should be members of the dominant sex and race, have the proper educational credentials, be the right age, and 'act, speak, and dress commensurate with their position' (p. 82).

The forms of consciousness and personality characteristics needed to integrate office workers into the right authority relations would include such qualities as perseverance, dependability and docility. These characteristics, Bowles and Gintis argue, are not primarily inculcated by the exhortations of teachers and the content of the formal curriculum, but by the very structure of educational relationships, which correspond to the structure of work relations. In this context, the key area of correspondence is that between teachers and bosses.

Legitimating authority relations

The Cooperative Office Education class at Woodrow High School attempted to convey two primary messages about authority relations to the students: that these relations were natural, right or inevitable, and that any problem with a workplace supervisor or manager was an individual matter and should be handled privately, if at all. As such, the messages bore a striking resemblance to those regarding exchange relations.

The first day of class can be seen as the students' initiation into proper respect for their supervisors. After speaking to a few students privately about their job interviews and spending a few minutes instructing students on public relations techniques, Mrs Lewis spent the rest of class time telling the students about the appreciation banquet they would have for their supervisors at the end of the year, as a thank you for all the supervisors would be doing for them.

The concept of authority relations also arose during a unit that taught students how to do a company's payroll. Mrs Lewis explained that there were three different types of employees who were paid in different ways: administrators, who were paid by the week and not paid overtime which was regarded as a normal part of their work; regular staff, like themselves, who were paid by the hour; and piece workers, who were paid according to the amount they produced. Piece work, Mrs Lewis said, was common in factories, but not in offices unless work had to be done at home where time could not be supervised as it could be at the workplace.

The payroll materials employed a system of penalizing workers 1/10 of an hour for every six minutes or fraction thereof that they punched in late for work. While Mrs Lewis was explaining to the class how to calculate this penalty and deduct it from the worker's pay-cheque, Dorothy asked what happened if someone punched in early: were they penalized for that? 'Or', Josie added, 'don't they get nothing?' To these questions Mrs Lewis responded that overtime had to be authorized, that they could not just 'work slow' every day and expect to receive overtime pay.

At this point, Mrs Lewis told the students that they were considered white-collar workers and were given more responsibilities and more respect than the type of factory workers they were dealing with in the payroll unit, who had to use a time clock to punch in and out of work (although Coleen and Pam immediately responded that they punched a time clock). Mrs Lewis concluded the discussion by telling the students they had to understand that a lot of people 'lived differently'.

Apparently, observations during their work times were more salient in determining the COOP students' attitudes about the productivity of bosses than were the lessons they were taught at school. Similarly, what they learned from their 'blue-collar' fathers and mothers sometimes contradicted the image conveyed in class of workers who needed to be under constant supervision because they were not the type of people who were responsible about doing their jobs.

Some of the students with parents who worked in blue-collar jobs learned about hard factory-like working conditions, about workplaces which pushed employees beyond the point of what was considered fair or tolerable. Rather than seeing blue-collar workers who would not put in a fair day's work unless coerced, students heard about employers who did not offer a fair day's pay or fair working conditions. Some of the students had parents go on strike, and they generally supported that activity. One alumna's father was on strike at the time of our interview. Her account of the conflict was that the employees were protesting working conditions, that the employer had attempted to speed up the pace of work, forcing workers literally to run when making deliveries. In addition, they worked in an unheated area and had to 'bundle up in coats' so that by the time they went outdoors into the cold they were 'overheated and ended up getting sick'. Her father was currently carrying a sign that said 'we're men, not machines'.

The students' work experiences also taught them that the designations administrators, white-collar workers, and blue-collar workers did not adequately describe the hierarchical division of labour they experienced. One quite salient division for many of them was that between upper managers and floor supervisors. As Erik Wright (1978, pp. 52–71) argues, this division is primarily the result of the expansion of the capitalist enterprise and the development of monopoly capitalism.

As would be expected, the top managers exerted little direct authority over the students' work process. None the less, more often than not, the women I interviewed were quite critical of these managers. As suggested by some of the women's reflections, these criticisms often focused on the perceived inactivity of this stratum of workers, a perception that seemed quite prevalent.

At the beginning of a COOP class one day in February, I overheard Katrina telling another student how angry she was about an incident that happened at work the day before. Because Katrina did not have time to eat lunch between the end of her morning classes and when she was scheduled to begin work, her supervisor had given her permission to eat at her desk for the first ten minutes of her pay period. Someone apparently objected, so Katrina was being docked for that time even though she continued to work and practically 'swallowed my lunch whole'. She went on:

It seems like the guys at work who are in charge just walk around and don't do much for most of the day. And they get paid so much money. I'd like to get their paycheck. And it's the people under them who end up doing all the work.

And although in the last sentence Donna attempts to rescind her statement, [in] her final examination, there is little doubt that a critical tone accompanies [her] description of her corporation's highest executives:

I don't know exactly what goes on up in Corporate. All I know is that the president of our Association, and all of his vice presidents have their offices up there. All I ever see them do is shuffle papers from one side of their desk to the other, sign their important John Hancock's on documents, smoke, drink coffee, and have never ending all day meetings. I don't mean to be critical or to make fun of them. I'm sure whatever they do is very important to the well-being of our Corporation.

Besides being critical of managers' apparent lack of productivity, the student-workers were also seldom taken by the trappings or symbols of status that so often accompany those positions.

These perceptions of managers, and the worker cynicism they seem to embody, probably undermine the very control a hierarchical division of labour supposedly ensures. Hierarchy comes to be seen not solely as an organizational necessity, but as a way in which individuals increase their status, power and wealth.

Somewhat contrary to the widely accepted position that complex hierarchies deflect class conflict by focusing worker aggression on foremen or immediate floor supervisors rather than higher level managers, who often come to be seen as workers' protectors (Rosenberg, 1953), I found that the student-workers had more favourable perceptions of their immediate bosses than they did of the managers.

This situation was, I believe, the result of two conditions that characterized the COOP students' work. First, as noted in the relationship between Mary Jo and her supervisor, the student was often in an apprentice relation to her supervisor, who functioned more as a teacher than a traditional floor supervisor. The COOP student primarily needed to learn the tasks and duties that were part of her work role in that particular office, seldom did she have to be disciplined to do that work.

This situation resulted in the COOP students being genuinely fond of and grateful to their supervisors, who often taught the students more 'useful knowledge' than they believed they were getting at school. Mary Jo's comment captures the sense of this relationship.

My evaluation of my supervisor is very high. She is always there to explain anything to me. Almost everything that I do is new to me, so she helps out a lot. My office situation is very casual; my supervisor makes everyone feel very comfortable. I think that we have developed a very good relationship. I feel that I learned a great deal from my supervisor, because she helped me learn so many things that I never knew before.

The second condition that evoked favourable perceptions of supervisors extended this role of helper. Not only did the supervisor teach new workers departmental tasks and assist even experienced workers with problems that inevitably cropped up, but she was also most often a worker herself and generally the most skilled worker in the department. Although she oversaw the work of the entire office (distributing, monitoring, collecting, and rerouting finished work), she was often engaged in doing much the same work as the office staff. She was, in many ways, one of them, not over them. In a few places, the COOP supervisor had a work role quite distinct from her supervisory capacity; sometimes she would be physically some distance from her supervisee, with walls or partitions separating them from one another. In these cases she would meet with the student at the beginning of the afternoon to explain the work that needed to be done, or would simply place self-evident work on the student's desk. In some instances the work flow carried on naturally from day to day so that daily direction was not even needed. If the student had a question, she would seek out her supervisor. The supervisor here carries the identity more of lead worker and helper than boss or watchdog, an identity that was invariably extolled by the students: 'The ideal boss would be understanding and would help out without griping.'

These teacher/helper roles played by the supervisors produced a community or family culture in many of the offices. In fact, the word 'family' was spontaneously used by a number of the students during interviews or on their examinations.

Our bank has approximately 100 employees. It may seem like a lot, but it really isn't. We are like one big family.

My company has grown from a one man development to one of the world's largest merchandising organizations. I am now considered part of the family of 400,000 employees.

This family culture that emerges in offices, and which seems in some instances to be consciously cultivated by the company, to a certain extent mystifies the authority and exchange relations at the heart of the capitalist enterprise. Just as United Group's time lapsing system was instituted to guarantee high rates of productivity, so too this family culture, whether consciously promoted or not, functions to guarantee a high level of worker loyalty. The supervisor's role in this culture, by relegating the authority aspect to the background, helps to affirm and create happy family members who produce without her supervision. These supervisors, so to speak, embody the concern of the company for the employee.

Privatizing authority relations

Because the syllabus for the COOP class was primarily skill-oriented, not many other occasions provided the opportunities for overt messages about authority relations to be conveyed to the class as a whole. Because I never intruded myself into private evaluation sessions Mrs Lewis had with the students, I do not know what they were told in that context, in which the topic of authority relations might well have been raised. I would assume, however, that those messages were consistent with responses Mrs Lewis gave when a student raised supervisor problems in front of the other students. At those times Mrs Lewis generally took the position that beginning workers did not know enough to evaluate their superiors, or that they needed to adjust to unpleasant situations.

When Katrina, for instance, elaborated on how the disorganization and carelessness of the men she typed for multiplied her own work, Mrs Lewis laughed, said 'that's life', and moved the discussion on to a different topic. The message seemed to be that even if bosses were not perfect, and order-giving not efficient, there was nothing to be done about it, so it was best to adjust to the situation.

This practice of diverting or cutting off discussions of conflictual relations with authority was particularly evident in the curriculum unit that directly addressed that area. One month, *Harper's Bazaar* magazine carried a special section called the 'New secretary's guide'. Mrs Lewis decided to utilize the articles in that section for instructional purposes and distributed them to the students to read. One of the articles was titled 'Office troublemakers: Ways to beat them at their own game!' The first sentence read:

No doubt you have run across them: hypercritical bosses who unerringly find flaws in your most creative work; overagreeable subordinates who cheerfully make promises they can't fulfill; indecisive associates forever fearful of upsetting the status quo

and went on to suggest strategies for handling all three types of problem situations: those with bosses, with subordinates, and with co-workers. The last example in the article dealt with know-it-all bosses, those who 'know the right way to do everything, and believe most people are inept and ill-informed'. None of the COOP students had subordinates. Most of them had associates, and all of them had bosses.

On the day Mrs Lewis handed this article out for the students to read she made the introductory remark: 'The reason I like these articles so much is that they don't just moan about the problem; they give you helpful hints on how to overcome some of them.' She then told the students that the word 'troublemaker' actually connoted peers, entry level workers, people who perhaps did not get their work done. When Mrs Lewis left [the room], Donna told Evelyn about this real 'snotty' lady at work who treated her as though she were her doormat and a guy who kept ordering her around. Although Mrs Lewis had clearly told the students to think of peer examples, troublemakers for Donna were obviously those who were in an authority relation to her.

Upon returning, Mrs Lewis distributed mimeographed sheets titled 'Petty larceny' and 'No personal calls'. Each was a brief scenario of an office situation followed by three questions asking students how they would respond to the two problems of seeing co-workers taking stationery and stamps, and of overhearing personal calls during work time on company phones.

After the students read the scenarios, Mrs Lewis asked what they would do if they observed something like that happening. They all said they would tell the boss. No one said why they would respond that way and Mrs Lewis did not ask them. She merely said that such peer behaviour could put them in a difficult situation since, on the one hand, they would not want to be implicated in the situation, but on the other, they would not want to gain a reputation of reporting co-workers. The class then discussed the different policies their offices had regarding personal calls. Once again students were assiduously kept from focusing on problems with supervisors; the only conflictual relations legitimate for discussion were those with peers.

Although Mrs Lewis was consistent, throughout the year, in her attempts to avoid group discussions of supervisor problems, she did alter her position regarding the students' ability, and therefore the students' right, to evaluate their supervisors by the end of the year. This change took the form of telling the students that as part of their final examination they were to evaluate their workplace as a training station, and if they wanted, they could also evaluate their supervisors. Two specific events influenced this change.

During a final student evaluation meeting, Mary Jo's supervisor, who always had the highest praise for Mary Jo's work and once called her 'a little bit of sunshine who comes in every afternoon', directly told Mrs Lewis that now that she was finished evaluating Mary Jo she would welcome Mary Jo's evaluation of the job she had done as a supervisor so she would know if there were any ways in which she could improve.

The other situation was Dorothy's criticism of her supervisor and her persistence in raising those issues in front of the class. During one such outburst, Mrs Lewis told Dorothy that the situation she was describing had nothing to do with her, that she should let those involved handle it and 'keep her nose clean'. Mrs Lewis did, however, emphathize with Dorothy's attitudes towards her supervisor and because she respected Dorothy's skill and work effort was influenced to let the students formally evaluate their supevisors if they wanted. Again, however, the form of the evaluation was totally private and individualized. It took place on the last day of school and was seen only by Mrs Lewis.

Gender relations

The organization of work within offices is characterized not only by a hierarchical division of labour but by a sexual division of labour as well – a division in which men and women both fill different positions and have different relations to wage and domestic labour. The ideological messages the students received were fairly congruent with the gender-specific patterns and relations they had become accustomed to both in their homes and at school. Their primary mode of behaviour, therefore, was to accept, almost naturally and spontaneously to fall into, a sexual division of labour and the subordinate roles for women it implies. In the process of elaborating their lives at work, the students utilized a fairly conventional culture of femininity which identified them not as 'raw labour power', but as sex objects, on the one hand, and as office wives and mothers, on the other. In so doing, they partially realized (in the dual sense of created and were aware of) their double subordination, in domestic labour and in wage labour. But because this awareness was only partial, and because they saw no alternative, they tended to fantasize an ideal future in which they worked part time and stayed home part time, regardless of the fact that this solution would only strengthen their subordination, keeping them dependent on a male provider and condemning them to low level positions in the job market.

The office worker as sex object

Messages about sexual appearance and sexual behaviour were integral elements of the students' office education training both at school and in the work-place. On the level of appearance and self-presentation, the young women were encouraged to emphasize and utilize their gender identities. But on the level of practice, when it came to actual behaviour, they were warned to control their sexuality. The subtle message was that they would be blamed if sexual improprieties occurred at work.

In terms of their mode of self-presentation, students were informed in numerous ways how important it was to cultivate a feminine, even provocative, appearance if they were serious about getting a job and being promoted once they had a job. Early in the school year, for instance, a woman from a job placement centre spoke to the students about interviewing, stressing the importance of their appearance:

Look professional. Your best source for that is GLAMOUR magazine. It regularly runs sections for the professional woman: her image, what to wear, how to get a job. Dress like you already have the job, like you would to find a boyfriend. That's a good parallel. You have to attract someone.

Later that week, Mrs Lewis re-emphasized how important it was for the students to sell themselves at an interview. In encouraging them to listen calmly and collect their thoughts before they answered a question in order to organize their ideas and speak intelligently she used the phrase, 'just like the finalists in the Miss America contest'.

The issue of appearance was also regularly discussed during Mrs Lewis's evaluation sessions with supervisors. Appearance was, in fact, one of the criteria on the formal student-trainee evaluation report, which included such items as quality and quantity of work, attitude, attendance, reliability. On the evaluation sheet, appearance was defined in a sex-neutral way as 'neatness and personal care, appropriateness to the job'. But in conversation Mrs Lewis often added a gender-specific element:

You might do her a favour. She's a pretty girl. She could do a lot with himself and I don't think she's doing it. A lot of women in businesses are making appearance an important part of their day. She could capitalize on that.

She puts herself together very nicely. She was wearing some very sexy shoes the other day.

One supervisor talked about how her student-trainee had a figure for skirts, not slacks, how slacks put 20 pounds on her, and how you could see the look of disgust on the older men's faces when young women came to work dressed casually. Appearance, she said, was a definite factor in promotability, even for a woman who was extremely capable.

The accuracy of this perception was born out in the students' experiences with job placement. Only the popular, attractive, cheerleader-type students obtained front-desk jobs. Other students often lost out to them in job interviews even though they were more qualified, and had to continue searching for jobs. If a student's appearance was unattractive, chances were she would be forced to take a position in a large routinized department with little public contact.

During a classroom discussion of a magazine article on the topic of sexual harassment [the] issue of 'contained sexuality' arose. Mrs Lewis stressed the importance of an appropriate degree and type of sexual conduct on the job. While on the other occasions she had been subtly encouraging the students to present themselves with a certain a amount of 'sexiness', on this particular day she highlighted the importance of knowing what the limits should be if they wanted to avoid detrimental consequences. She told them they would be asking for abuse if they were too timid to control the situation or if they wore attire that was too skimpy, giving signals that they wanted to be noticed. She cautioned them to be aware of what they were communicating through their dress and bodies, indicating an awareness that their sexuality was not only something they could use to gain job benefits but was also something that could be used against them.

In order to make the most of opportunities on the job, then, young workers apparently have to be skilled not only in running typewriters and photocopiers, but in monitoring their sexuality and sexual lives as well. But in case workers do not internalize the 'proper' sexual code, companies often have either formal or informal policies about social and sexual relations.

Needless to say, students and employees did not always appreciate or accept attempts to control their sexual identities and practices. One student, for instance, explicitly rejected the 'image of the secretary' that was conveyed to her. As she put it:

Mrs Lewis had this obsession with secretaries looking gorgeous. Getting up at 5:00 in the morning to do their hair and nails. She taught us a lot about appearance, eye contact, interviews, dressing up. I thought that was good, but you don't have to put on all that make-up. Cleanliness is the important thing.

Most students, however, did not verbalize any opposition to suggestions that were made about their appearances. But in their non-verbal behaviour, in the manner in which they actually dressed for work, there were indications that they, like many office workers, were not passively accepting imposed standards, but were negotiating and creating their own style. This style combined the popular men's cut slacks with open-toed, spiked, 'sexy' shoes. It was a definite blend of a unisex work look with a feminine social look, and appeared to be an attempt to control the issue of appearance while still emphasizing sexuality.

But all in all, most of the students seemed to internalize definitions of themselves as women workers that took into account traditional notions of what feminine appearance should be. Many of the jobs they could or could not imagine themselves doing hinged on physical criteria. As Jennifer said, 'I thought of being an airline stewardess, but I weighed too much. You have to only weigh 120 or something.' They could not envision doing work that caused them to get dirty or messy.

So, although there was some disagreement, resistance, and negotiation about the exact amount and type of 'femininity' women office workers should cultivate and display, there was basic agreement on a more fundamental level. In general, a gender-specific, feminine appearance that could be contrasted to a masculine appearance was accepted and adopted.

The office worker as wife and mother
The second way in which office work roles were linked to the students' gender identity was through an association of office work with domestic labour, either through the equation of the work with women's work in the home or through the subordination of their role in the office to their role in the home.

The observation has often been made that the role of women in the office parallels their role in the home: picking up after men; doing the daily, repetitive, tedious housekeeping tasks; and keeping men's lives organized and undisturbed, so they can concentrate on their important work. Quoting a 1935 *Fortune* magazine article, Margery Davies (1979, p. 257) claims that male bosses preferred women over 'pushy young men' as office workers because, as *Fortune* stated, women 'are capable of making the offices a more pleasant, peaceful, and homelike place'. Taking on this kind of work, which has changed little in half a century, deepens women's wage labour identity as secondary and peripheral, for it patterns a gendered subjectivity already deeply etched into their day-to-day existence.

The objective structuring of these asymmetrical roles, of male leading roles and female serving roles, was already so much taken for granted by the students that they were unable to even perceive it. One young graduate told me that during high school 'everyone wants to be a cheerleader'. She naturally presumed that in this context I would know 'everyone' meant 'every girl', so that she did not have to make it explicit.

In much the same way, the students took the sexual division of labour they found in their offices for granted. During an interview of a graduate who had worked in the same department of the same large corporation for almost two years, I asked her to mention the types of jobs that were filled by men, by women, or by both men and women. After reflecting for a few moments, she said,

All of the big bosses are men. I've never noticed that before, but that's the way it is. And all the secretaries are females . . . and all the key punch operators are ladies. I've never thought of that before.

The relation of the woman office worker's status to that of the male worker was objectified in the structure of the workplaces as well as in how the workers were addressed. Men often had offices that were private or closed off, in contrast to the public work areas of the women. Even if women had their own desks, they were generally grouped together in a large, open space. About eight or nine of the places at which students worked were fairly large bureaucracies housed on more than one building level. Inevitably, when this was the case, status differentials were structured into the floor on which one's office was located. So when referring to bosses, workers would naturally employ expressions like: 'I don't know if there are any ladies up there – up at the very top.' 'One of the big bosses who sits upstairs is over him.' These linguistic expressions reinforce notions of superiority and inferiority which are so naturally linked with the English language concepts of up/down, high/low, over/under, and top/bottom.

While the students often watched upper-level, male employees taking work home, having their work lives spill over into their home lives, so to speak, they usually saw the converse in the lives of the women with whom they worked. These women often worked only part time so they could see their children off to school in the mornings and be home before the school day ended. They often brought in candy or cookies to sell for their children's scout troop or hung home-made skeletons they had constructed in their role as den mother. Sometimes they had to take a temporary maternity leave or had to quit work altogether because they were no longer able to juggle working and child-care, even though the family needed the money. One of the students vividly recalled how her mother was fired from her clerical job years before because she and her siblings kept walking over to her office (located just blocks from their home) to visit, ask questions, or get permissions.

Mrs Lewis also underscored her own identity as mother by knitting baby clothes during class time and using traditional notions about sex-appropriate behaviour by advising the students not to express emotionalism if they wanted to rise up the corporate ladder, and not to shout since 'it's not ladylike'. One of their texts warned them not to 'chit-chat' during the workday since it wasted their employer's dollars.

Another teaching aid, a filmstrip, similarly reinforced traditional notions of the sexual division of labour. Titled 'Telephone impressions', the filmstrip was geared to teaching students good phone techniques: courtesy, clear speaking, and promptness. Mrs Lewis made a point of telling the class that although the filmstrip was excellent at demonstrating good phone usage, the school system could not purchase it because it was sexist. All the examples of the wrong way to answer the phone, she elaborated, were delivered by a male voice; all the correct examples were delivered by a female voice. Therefore, the filmstrip had an anti-male bias. It should have portrayed mistakes being made equally by the man and the woman.

There was, however, a deeper, more subtle sexism at play in the filmstrip. The incorrect phone manner was not just a male voice, it was an authoritative, busy, important-sounding male voice, one that was irritated that it had to be bothered by answering the phone. The female voice, on the other hand, sounded trained for the job: that was her proper work and the task for which she was perfectly suited. Far from being anti-male, the filmstrip reinforced that age-old notion that men have more important things to do than answer the phone. Since women are not doing anything of value, they are the ones who should be constantly interrupted to screen and direct messages.

At some of the work-places, however, women workers were beginning to resist this traditional telephone role, requesting the installation of a de-centralized phone system where each person would have to take his or her own messages. Mrs Carter was one supervisor who was adamant about this. Shortly after she was hired as an executive secretary she told her boss to take the phones away or she would leave the job. She resented the burden of answering her boss's phone, claiming that if women were relieved of that kind of task they would be freer to do 'the administrative work that men won't let women do'.

Office workers were also starting to resist the secretary's traditional task of serving coffee. Maureen, for example, was startled when a boss asked if she had offered coffee for the men who had arrived for a business meeting. She responded in surprise, 'No, was I supposed to?' Her boss replied, 'You bet you are, and do it with a smile, too!' Maureen characterized this attitude as chauvinistic, but when she checked with other office workers and was told the directive was appropriate she was reluctant to say anything because she feared it would turn people against her, and afffect the way she felt about working there. So even though she thought she would 'raise a ruckus' if she were an older worker, employed full time, and if the practice were habitual, because of her structural relationship to the job she ended up complying with the directive.

But, all in all, just as the students partially accept sexuality as a criterion of themselves as office workers, so do they tend to accept being defined as man's helper, as his office wife. Some students saw this as a natural division of labour, some as a social division, and some seemed unable to distinguish between the two.

Office work is mostly for women because it's typing and a lot of guys don't like to type. Filing and receptionist, that's more for girls too, because that's secretary work and girls are secretaries, you know.

Women shouldn't do construction work. Men are stronger and it's just the way it should be. Secretary jobs are probably for women mostly. That's just the way things are.

What 'is' often became equated with what 'should be' and, surprisingly enough, as late as 1981 many of these 18- to 20-year-olds had not seriously considered alternatives. In fact, the ideology of the sexual division of labour remained so strong that many of the students continued to advance arguments that their everyday experiences clearly contradicted (for example, seeing men who pushed pencils, having women as bosses).

When students elaborated on the reasons why men did not or should not do women's work and why women did not or should not do men's work, a striking contrast could be heard. Generally using euphemistic language, they explained that men who ventured into what was traditionally regarded as women's work would be considered homosexual.

I really can't picture a man doing a woman's job. My uncle is a nurse, but he's like this (she made a limp wrist). That's why it would be hard for guys to have a woman's job. Because it's considered delicate and people might think they're gay.

I guess guys don't take something like the cooperative office class because they don't think it's right for them. They think they'd be laughed at – wow, what a weirdo!

It's only in big cities that guys are secretaries; because they're able to get lost or hide more there.

On the other hand, the young women who thought that the sexual division of labour should be maintained explained that women who were after men's jobs were trying to be like men or trying to prove their (mistaken) equality.

According to these students, then, when men do women's work, they are denying or rejecting their masculinity, their natural claim to superiority. They are becoming effeminate. When women try to do men's work, they are not accepting their natural limitations and subordination, but are trying to be as good as men, when in fact they are not.

Just as most of these students had a hard time imagining men and women doing the same wage labour jobs, so too did they find it hard to imagine men and women filling the same domestic labour roles. For them, the notion of women's work automatically meant the primary role in domestic labour. In one way or another, they made it clear that men were the primary breadwinners and they, the women, the primary homemakers and child-carers.

If I were to marry, I would still want to work part time. Otherwise I'd get bored. But I wouldn't want to work full time if my husband were bringing in a good income. There's a lot to do already with housekeeping and kids.

If I had kids I would sit around the house with them. I wouldn't work. You can tell kids who have been raised by a baby sitter. I don't know if I would let John stay home with them or not. It's not what guys are supposed to do.

While they might have been able to imagine themselves having full-time, interesting or important careers when they were younger or if they were to stay single, the central force directing the students' sense of a work identity was the expectation of eventual marriage and family.

The kind of training the students received for office work served to further marginalize their work identities since this identity was presented as secondary to or synonymous with a sexual/home/family identity. While in some minimal ways the women may have rejected the ideology of male supremacy, at a more fundamental and persistent level, they affirmed it, granting superiority and legitimacy to the dominance of men in a way that appeared spontaneous and natural.

Conclusion

As the three [sections of this chapter] have demonstrated, labour process theory is not sufficient to explain the transformation of students into workers, because it disregards the potential effect cultural orientations and experiences outside the workplace can have on the way in which work identity is created. The only aspect of culture considered important is that which is created within the labour process itself. My data clearly reveal this is not the case.

Ideological reproduction theories (of which correspondence theory is one type) are inadequate to explain social process at two levels: at the level of actors and at the level of structures. In terms of actors, these theories fail because they do not analyse consciousness as an active, interacting medium of identity formation. For them, consciousness functions more like a mirror, passively receiving and reflecting the structures or messages around it. In terms of structures, these theories fail because they gloss over the many ways in which schools are 'semi-autonomous' organizations, having needs, rules, practices and structures that schooling brings about itself, without recourse to its relation to the economic sector.

[Nevertheless] even when [COOP students'] school experiences did not strongly promote their development as obedient, productive workers, elements within the labour process and their cultural backgrounds promoted the ongoing production of these orientations. In terms of the labour process, for instance, the students were encouraged to be productive by the need to overcome boredom, the desire to offer service to the customer, and by their relationships with their co-workers and supervisors. Their cultural orientation supported this inclination towards productivity since it stressed personal relationships and pride in personal achievements. These young female workers were quite prepared to transform and accept the transformation of what are essentially exchange relationships into personal relationships because family, community and service were highly salient to them. Immediate, surface, apparent relationships (which are none the less real relationships) serve to hide the structural relations that govern them. Workers willingly consent to work hard because they experience it as working for their supervisors (whom they like) or for the consumer (whom they identify with). They do not experience their productivity as co-operation in their own exploitation (except in the extreme instances I have noted).

But these strong pulls to be co-operative, loyal and productive workers do not mean that the social relations of labour are reproduced unproblematically. Tensions and conflicts are built into both capitalist and patriarchal relations, so that even over an issue like pay, for instance, where students' knowledge of pay scales (and the relations between worker pay and company profits) was highly constrained, room for questioning, insight and bargaining was definitely present.

The young women I observed and interviewed did not necessarily accept the legitimacy of company policies, demands or intrusions into their personal life. They rejected the right of bosses to demand coffee, for instance, or to tell them what they could do or talk about with co-workers outside of the office. At times, by teaching them how to be assertive with customers, bosses unwittingly taught the student-workers how to be assertive with them as well.

Yet, all in all, the structure of relationships in which the workers found themselves embedded interacted in such a way as to confirm a basically conformist and subordinate work identity. Partially because work identity was secondary to a home identity, quitting work or working part time was more natural for them than was engaging in struggles over the quality of work life. By denying wage labour primacy over domestic labour, they inadvertently consented to and confirmed their own subordination, preparing themselves 'for both unskilled, low paid work and unpaid domestic service' (MacDonald, 1979/80, p. 152).

Notes

1 Full details of the Cooperative Office Education Program and research methodology can be found in Valli, L., *Becoming Clerical Workers*, Boston, Routledge and Kegan Paul, 1986.

References

Althusser L., 'Ideology and ideological state apparatuses', in *Lenin and Philosophy and Other Essays*, trans. B. Brewster, London, New Left Books, 1971.

Bowles, S. and Gintis, H., *Schooling in Capitalist America*, New York, Basic Books, 1976.

Burawoy, M., *Manufacturing Consent: changes in the labour process under monopoly capital*, Chicago, The University of Chicago Press, 1979.

Davies, M., 'Women's place is at the typewriter; the feminization of the clerical labour force', in Z. R. Eisenstein (ed.), *Capitalist Patriarchy and the Case for Socialist Feminism*, New York, Monthly Review Press, 1979.

Edwards, R., *Contested Terrain: the transformation of the workplace in the twentieth century*, New York, Basic Books, 1979.

Entwistle, H., *Antonio Gramsci: Conservative schooling for radical politics*, London, Routledge and Kegan Paul, 1979.

MacDonald, M., 'Cultural reproduction: the pedagogy of sexuality', *Screen Education*, **32/33**, 1979/80, pp. 141–53.

Parsons, T., 'The school class as a social system; some of its functions in American Society', *Harvard Educational Review*, **29**, no. 4, 1959, pp. 297–318.

Rosenberg, M., 'Perceptual obstacles to class consciousness', *Social Forces*, **32**, no. 1, 1953, pp. 22–7.

Willis, P., *Learning to Labour: how working class kids get working class jobs*, Farnborough, Saxon House, Teakfield, 1977.

Willis, P., 'Cultural production is different from cultural reproduction is different from social reproduction is different from reproduction', *Interchange*, **12**, nos. 2–3, 1981, pp. 48–67.

Wright, E. O., *Class, Crisis and the State*, London, New Left Books, 1978.

15 Resistances and responses: the experiences of black girls in Britain

Valerie Amos and Pratibha Parmar

Afro-Asian unity

There are several reasons for writing jointly about the lives and experiences of Asian and Afro-Caribbean girls in Britain. First, most existing literature which seeks to articulate the experience of black girls begins from a racist standpoint, denying *the autonomy of black culture* and trying instead to integrate the experience of black people into more general discussions about life in Britain. On the other hand, token attempts have been made within feminist writing to include material on black girls but this serves only to add 'cross-cultural' spice to predominantly ethnocentric work. By this, we mean material written from and about the dominant culture, i.e. British culture, which ignores the existence of other cultures in the society. We feel strongly that there is a need for black women to write about their experience of living in Britain, but at the same time the particularity of a black woman's experience should be made visible not only in black writings, but within the context of more general writings on education, leisure, sexuality, family life *and other aspects of institutional racism* which impinge directly on the lives of black women. Thus we do not look into the black community for the answers to the problems we face as a result of racist practices in this country, we look to the structures and institutions which function in that racist manner.[1]

Second, we would like to explain what we mean when we talk about black girls and black women. We use the term black to refer to the two main groups of black people in this country, namely those people who came originally from India, Pakistan, Bangladesh, many via East Africa, and those people who have their origins in Africa or who as a result of slavery now have their immediate origins in a number of Caribbean countries. We are aware that many differences exist in the cultures, languages and religions not only between the Afro-Caribbean and Asian communities, but also within these two groups. We do not see our cultural differences as operating antagonistically because we recognize the autonomy of our separate cultures.

This is what the Organisation of Women of Asian and African Descent have to say:[2]

despite the ethnic and cultural differences between these two groups (Asian and Afro/ Caribbean), we do not distinguish between them unless it is necessary to refer specifically to one or other of the two groups, as it will be occasionally. This is because our joint historical experience as victims of colonialism, and our present experience as

Source: Extracted from McRobbie, A. and McCabe, T. (eds), *Feminism for Girls: An adventure story*, London, Routledge and Kegan Paul, 1981, pp. 129–48.

second class citizens in a racist society have created firm bonds between us which are more significant to us than any differences which may exist.

Our basic aim in this chapter is to challenge some of the myths and stereotypes that exist not only about black girls but about black people generally. We look at some of the existing attitudes to black people and through our criticisms of these approaches we outline our perspective which places a primary importance on an examination of racism, and the ways in which racism structures and determines black girls' life experiences. We then go on to examine some of the racist and sexist stereotypes that exist about black women. In our final section, 'Action and reaction' we look at the areas of employment and education and very briefly outline the struggles that black women have taken on in these spheres. In our conclusion also critically evaluate some of the reasons for black women's absence in the white women's movement.

Racism – our starting point

In the last few years there has been an increasing number of individuals and organizations which have been taking a keen interest in black youth in British society. The reasons behind this interest are as varied as the individuals and organizations who share it. Sociologists, journalists, social workers, teachers, community/youth workers, police, the schools and other institutions of the state have produced between them a vast amount of literature on black youth and their 'cultural conflicts', 'identity crises' and 'generational conflicts'.

Like other literature on the black community, material on black girls has started off from the premise that they are a problem for themselves, for their parents and for white society, more particularly for white teachers, social workers and the police force.

Our cultural norms and values have been seen as responsible for bad housing, overcrowded schools and unemployment, among other social ills. By adopting such a perspective, white academics and practitioners in the so-called 'helping and caring' professions have shifted the blame from the nature of the society we live in on to our religion, culture and communities.

The following quotes from some white social workers illustrate the above point quite clearly:[3]

Particularly with the West Indians, there are problems with teenage girls. Their *culture* is so different and the girls want more freedom.

I do a lot of work with adolescents – West Indians are particularly good at being caught by the police. It has a lot to do with police discretion, i.e. West Indian *culture* is to stand around the street corner and the police book them.

The problem then is us, our cultures, and the solution is seen as resting on the degree to which we are prepared to integrate, to accept white cultural values. By this they mean that if only Afro-Caribbean and Asian people would behave like whites, dress like them, eat like them, have the same family size as them, and speak like them, that is adopt white English cultural habits, then they would find it easier to ignore the fact that they are black and there would be no problem of race in Britain.

For example, some more telling quotes from white social workers:

I try to get minorities to understand the different values and parts of behaviour so that they fit in better.

They require more help with simple things like hygiene, child-care, health, more advice on family planning, more help for the women who are unhappy and isolated, more classes to learn English.

Our starting point, then, is that Britain is a racist society and it is racism which needs to be looked at, not multi-racialism, multi-culturalism, identity crises or other spurious notions which serve only to evade and/or deflect from the real issues.

Furthermore, any adequate account of the situation of black girls in Britain has to begin with the premise that their day-to-day experiences are determined by three crucial factors – race, class and sex/gender.

For instance, if we take the factor of race, then it has to be said that the situation of black girls cannot be isolated from that of the rest of the black community, as they are equally affected by bad housing conditions, unemployment, or employment in low-paid non-unionized sweat shops and factories, by a racist police force, by racist attacks on the streets and in schools, and racist immigration laws.

The area of racist immigration laws has a double disadvantage for black girls, particularly Asian girls.

On 14 November 1979 the Conservative government published their white paper proposals for revision of the immigration rules. These proposals, which are now law, are aimed at reducing immigration of Asian males. One of the ways in which they have attempted to do this is by taking away the right of Asian girls who either were not born in Britain or one of whose parents was not born here, to decide whom to marry. For example, if an Asian girl has lived in Britain most of her life, gone to school here and grown up here, then married a man in India and wanted to live with him in Britain, she could not do this.

Below are some views on this legislation of some Asian girls who have either lived in Britain most of their lives or who were born here.

On immigration
(16- to 18-year olds)

They are making too much out of arranged marriages and using it for their own purpose. We have to realise that (Abida).

It's for us, the girls and our families, to work out our problems and issues of marriage and it's not for the government to decide or to take a stand and say 'Oh, Asian marriages don't work out so we won't allow them' (Daxa).

The government doesn't really give a damn as long as there are no more black faces; they don't really mind who does what with their lives (Surjit).

The main point is really to stop black immigration and nought else. And the next thing they will say is 'go home, we have no more use for you' (Daxa).

You mean to tell me that once we come here, have our homes here and we work here and our life is here and everything else, and then they turn around and say 'go back to your jungle, we don't want you here' (Abida).

What we are saying is that we have the right to decide where we live, where we get married, who with and when and not have the government tell us (Surjit).

The girls are saying that they belong here. Britain is their home and they have every right to be here. But why is it that we came here in the first place and settled here?

We are here, because you were there

To understand the situation of Afro-Caribbean and Asian people in Britain today, we have to first look at the forces and motivations behind our migration here in the historical context of British imperialism. What has been termed the 'Third World' has always been a source of cheap labour to countries like Britain and the other western industrialized nations and in Britain's case this was a relationship based on the political and economic exploitation of her colonies. The West Indian islands and the Asian sub-continent present a classic example of this exploitation, which benefits the developed nation and hinders the development of the exploited nation.

Britain's relations with the peoples of the Caribbean and the Indian sub-continent did not begin in the 1940s [as is often believed]. For centuries, Britain ruled our countries and systematically perverted their economies for her own ends. The Indian sub-continent was used to produce the cotton, tea, jute, and other raw materials needed by Britain for her own industrial development. India's own textile industry was destroyed so that Britain could export her own cotton goods both to India and to other British colonies. Land policies destroyed many traditional agricultural and home craft industries such as weaving and spinning and this created widespread migration of peasants from the villages to the cities. Tremendous hardship and suffering was imposed on the Indian peoples as Britain continued to exploit and ignore their needs so that her own economic requirements could be fulfilled.

Britain's material prosperity and dominance was founded in the seventeenth century on the slave trade and the plantation system. After the abolition of slavery, no industrial development which would serve the needs of the people was allowed to take place in the Caribbean. The natural resources of the Caribbean – sugar, bananas, cocoa, bauxite, etc. – were sucked out for the requirements of British industry.

The inevitable result for the people both in the Indian sub-continent and the Caribbean was mass poverty and unemployment while the wealth acquired through conquest, colonization and trade continued to enrich the British nation.

Even after independence the situation in these less developed countries did not improve because the economic relationship remained the same. They were dependent on the colonial powers for the capital required to regenerate and redevelop their economies. There was little investment in these areas and widespread poverty and massive unemployment led to large-scale migration to the 'developed' nations in search of jobs. The period of the 1950s and 1960s was one of migration to Britain. The British economy was in a state of growth and there were a number of job vacancies which needed to be filled particularly in the non-growth sectors of industry. These jobs were characterized by low pay and bad working conditions and they were the jobs which white workers refused to do.

British people have been led to believe that we came here to take away their jobs, their homes, to overcrowd their schools and to 'swamp' their culture. What is conveniently forgotten and deliberately missed out from the teaching of British history is that we were, in fact, invited to come here and promised a better life in a country where the streets were apparently 'paved with gold'. This whole idea of the wealth and richness of Britain was not conjured up by us, but was deliberately perpetuated by particular British interests to encourage us to come to Britain and help rebuild its economy after the Second World War. For example, in the Caribbean, direct recruitment centres were set up by the National Health Service, by London Transport and the British Hotels and Restaurants Association. In India, Pakistan, and Bangladesh, managers for textile firms were sent out to recruit workers directly for their mills in the Midlands and in Yorkshire and in many cases they paid for the fares for workers to come here. The case of East African Asians is slightly different. The East African Asians were mostly small shop-owners, clerks in the government services and bankers. Most of them had migrated from the Indian states of Gujerat and Punjab to East Africa. A large section of them had originally gone as bonded labourers in the 1890s. They were the minority group which the British had brought in from India to serve as intermediaries between themselves, the white colonialists, and the indigenous, exploited African population. On the whole, the Indians did the smaller jobs which the Europeans could not be bothered with. For example, they became traders, merchants or petty officials.

This experience of migration from the Asian sub-continent to Africa is not dissimilar to the experience of African people during the slave period. Africans were brutalized, beaten and degraded before being herded together like cattle and shipped from the West African coast to America, the West Indian islands and Latin America. The slaves serviced the plantation economies of the American South and the Caribbean and the loss of human life was immeasurable. After the abolition of slavery *identured labourers* from India were transported to some parts of South America and the Caribbean and later to East Africa *to service the requirements of British capital*. Black people were treated as human cargo, their function was to secure a profit for British capitalist enterprise. Britain developed a particular relationship with her colonies, a relationship based on exploitation.

East African Asians came to Britain around 1966. In 1967 the Kenyatta government in Kenya, who had introduced the Africanization policies, granted only temporary residence to those British Asians who had not opted for Kenyan citizenship at the time of Kenyan independence in 1963.

The only viable alternative for the British Asians was to come to Britain. In 1965 and 1966, when they were not subject to any immigration control, 6000 Asians with British citizenship came to Britain.

But the British government at the time (which was Labour) was acutely aware of all those other British Asians and Africans all around the world, whom she had used to develop her imperial colonies. Therefore, keen to stop their mass entry into Britain, they moved very swiftly to try and control this new source of immigration to Britain. They did this by altering the legal rights of entry through the 1968 Immigration Act. The British Asians were redefined by this Act as Commonwealth Citizens and since the Commonwealth citizens were subject to *the voucher system*, the British Asians in Kenya would also be liable to this procedure for entry into the United Kingdom. The only distinction was that they would be allocated special vouchers as distinct from work vouchers.

A voucher system was first introduced through the Commonwealth Immigration Act of 1962. This act distinguished two kinds of citizens of the United Kingdom and colonies by dividing British passport-holders, whose passports had been issued by the British government, from those UK citizens whose passports had been, or could be, issued by a colonial government. The latter category were no longer free to enter the UK to take employment unless a voucher was obtained first. A limited number of these vouchers, which differentiated between skilled and unskilled work, were issued to Commonwealth countries each year, although after 1965 only 8500 in total were available and in that year vouchers for unskilled jobs were withdrawn completely.

This system established that immigration of heads of household from the black Commonwealth was geared to the requirements of the British economy. 'It was also a system which took discrimination out of the market place and gave it the sanction of the State. It made racism respectable and clinical by institutionalizing it.'[4]

Furthermore, vouchers for Kenyan Asians were only issued to heads of households, normally males, for themselves and certain categories of dependents. Here the dependent status of Asian women was made very clear. Women holding British passports had great difficulty in proving that they were heads of households. Widowed, divorced, deserted women and those women with British passports whose husbands were non-British citizens came into this group.

The problem of sexist discriminatory immigration laws is still continuing and further restrictions are being placed on black women's rights. A report was published in 1978 of the Parliamentary Select Committee on Race Relations and Immigration. This committee, which was composed of representatives from all the parties in the House of Commons, recommended that the government attack the right of our dependants in our countries of origin to join us here, and at the same time, allow the police to step up their harassment of our communities in the search for so-called illegal immigrants.

But one of the most serious threats posed by the report is to the future of black families and black culture. One of the recommendations of the report was that children over twelve years old born abroad to those settled here will not be allowed to join their parents. This kind of legislation has caused great bitterness because of the way in which it breaks up black families.[5]

Usha: I have two children in India. I can't see any reason for them not to be allowed to come and join their mother. They are being looked after by my mother. That's why I am working, to save enough money to bring them all over here. I have a wish to look after them ourselves. The government has to take notice of our customs. If I don't bring my mother here, she will be on her own with no one to look after her. Everyone should be able to bring their families and close relatives here.

Black female stereotypes

So what's it like for a black girl growing up in England today? There are many pressures, of course, to be this or to be that. In a sense black girls fall outside the stereotypical images which bombard white women every day of their lives. These images relate to all aspects of life, e.g. the family, where unreal images of family life are portrayed on television, particularly in advertisements. The most important area, however, is that of sexuality – the whole way in which girls and women are pressured to see themselves (especially) in relation to other people, particularly men. Girls are not expected to think for themselves – all this is supposed to be for the male to do. Women are not expected to think, to have ideas, to be creative. Girls have little or no opportunity to break out of this vicious circle because the only things open to them are marriage or work in a tedious monotonous job which is often described by career officers in glowing terms. Girls, then, don't have any *real choice* and for black girls the problems they face because of their colour worsens the situation.

Why is it that the images of the family presented in the media have so little relevance to the family situation of the majority of black women in this country? It all stems from the ways in which black people are perceived in this society. Black family life is seen as being in some way peculiar and different, and this difference means that the black family has no status, particularly in relation to the way in which the white, nuclear family structure is seen. Black family life cannot be described or explained in those terms so it has to be denigrated.

Black women are seen and represented in a particular way by white society. The stereotypes differ for the Afro-Caribbean and the Asian communities, but despite the difference in the stereotypes the racism underlying them is the same. Women of Asian origin range from being seen as sexually exotic creatures, full of 'Eastern promise', to being seen as completely dominated by their menfolk, oppressed wives and mothers who have little or nothing to say in relation to their families.

The images seem very far removed from the reality of life as lived by so many women in the Asian community. Working in sweat shops, as a number of them do, for low pay in overcrowded conditions. Facing constant harassment, not only on the street, physically, but also culturally, with attacks and abuse which attempt to degrade and denigrate their way of life. The criticisms of family life are again based on a number of 'common-sense' images of what family life in the Asian community is supposed to be all about. Asian people are said to live in over-crowded conditions, eat different food, wear different clothes and even speak a different language. All these things present a threat to what are seen as the dominant values of white society because Asians don't want to mesh in, they maintain their cultural traditions as far as that is possible, looking to each other for the strength and support they require to cope with living in a racist society.

In the Afro-Caribbean community stereotypes also exist but as mentioned before they are different. Women of Afro-Caribbean origin have long been outside western definitions of beauty. In sexual terms, they are perceived as 'prostitutes'. They have children outside the marriage relationship and in a number of cases do not even aspire to marriage. They are also seen as 'caring' women – personifying motherhood and domesticity. The image here is of the black Mamma or nurse ruling the kitchen or nursery with an 'iron glove'. But there is another, even more familiar, stereotype that we would like to examine and challenge. One which is often used as a means of demonstrating the so-called 'backwardness' of black culture; the myth of arranged marriages.

The myth of arranged marriages

The practice of arranged marriages is most frequently used as an explanation for the oppression of Asian girls. It is one area which has received frequent sensational news headlines in the papers and many television programmes have been made about it. Most of this coverage has given a distorted and false picture of the tradition and practice of arranged marriages. The overall stereotypical image is that of Asian girls caught between two cultures, their parents' culture and the culture of their white English peers. Asian girls are said to see their white friends at school or work going out to discos and films and 'choosing' their own boyfriends and potential husbands, while they (the poor Asian girls) are forced into a marriage with someone who is usually twice their age, someone who doesn't understand the English romantic etiquette like white men do and, of course, someone whom they have never seen until the actual wedding ceremony. Asian girls are said to have absolutely no 'freedom' to partake in the choosing of their husbands while white English girls have all the 'freedom' they want or need. If Asian girls had the same degree of so-called 'choice' about their marriage then it would help to create a more integrated society. Invariably, it is the parents with their archaic ideas who are seen as stopping this integration into white British society.

The stereotype that we have outlined might seem a little crude, but these are the ideas and attitudes which are dominant among most white people.

Nothing, however, could be further from the reality. This kind of gross generalization has led to many myths about the practice of arranged marriages. (We are not denying that arranged marriages are oppressive, but marriage as practised in white British culture is also oppressive.)

What we want to challenge is the illusion that white girls have a great deal of choice about whom they marry. The reality is that, in the majority of cases, if they marry they will marry boys from a similar class background, in the same region or geographical area.

For example, what chance does a white working-class girl who has left school at 16 with a few or no CSEs and is working in a factory or doing a typing course, have of meeting up with and marrying a white middle-class boy who has been to the local grammar school, then university, and is professionally employed? Not only is there not much chance of these two ever marrying, but there's not much chance of them ever even meeting.

So 'choice', 'arrangement' and 'freedom' are all relative concepts and often it is people's class which determines whom they meet, and whom they marry, more than any romantic or idealistic notions of falling in love with 'Mr Right' who happens to fatefully cross your path.

For Asian girls, the amount of choice they have over whom they marry varies from one Asian community to another, and from one Asian family to another. Some parents are more strict than others, just like some white English parents exercise more control over their children than others.

The following discussion between three 15-year-old Asian girls shows many similarities in their experiences of staying out late, etc., with that of their white peers. It also shows the closeness of some girls and their parents and destroys the myth of the Asian parents who keep their daughters locked up and chained in their rooms.

Kamaljit: I've known this boy for about two years now. We aren't thinking of getting married yet but if I was to tell my parents about it they would agree because he is my religion. Besides, all my sisters have married who they wanted to, so I don't see why they should refuse me. My mum knows this boy and she doesn't mind, but if he was English I think she would mind. I don't know how she would react. She wouldn't go angry, but she would tell me not to see him. Then it would be up to me to decide whether to see him or not. But I am the sort who can't leave a family but can leave a boy.

Yasmin: My brother is going out with an English girl and both my parents have seen them together and they don't say anything about it. But when they see me with a lad they always tell me off. My brother can stop out all night and they don't let me stop out even until midnight. Boys get more privileges than girls.

Rekha: My parents are all right because they let my sisters and I go anywhere we want to and come back when we like too. They are the same with my brother. It's all right as long as they know where we are going and who we are with.

Talking about going out in the evening:

Kamaljit: I love the discos and the parties. My friend and I go to a disco together. . . . We go about 8 and come back at 2 a.m. My mum says it's all right as long as I go with a friend.

Rekha: Since I have grown up in England I have been brought up to expect all these things. I like them, and if I went back to Africa I would like it but I would miss all the discos and fashions. My parents like the clothes I wear.

Yasmin: My parents don't like pop music and when I wear a dress which is a bit low they usually tell me off for wearing it.

Talking about who they can discuss boyfriends, etc., with at home:

Rekha: I can talk about a few things to my mum, about friends but I don't think I would talk about boyfriends. I can talk about boys generally to my sisters, but not saying I am going out with one.

Kamaljit: I am always telling my parents about my boyfriend. He is Indian and he comes to the house. My mother doesn't mind as long as I tell her everything. But I only tell my personal problems to my best friend. But my parents are broad-minded and they understand.

Rekha: My mother understands. I don't tell my father. There was this Indian boy going with me and she found out. I went on seeing him and she knew and didn't even tell my father.

One of the things the above discussion shows is that the problems Asian girls experience *vis-à-vis* their parents are often very similar to white English girls even though their difficulties are caused by different factors. The generalizations made about Asian parents forcing their daughters into arranged marriages gives a distorted picture of Asian cultural practices and ignores the positive and constructive relationship most girls have with their parents.

Action and reaction

The exploitation of black female labour is often overlooked because so many employment statistics and reports focus on the employment situation as it affects black men, especially as it is often assumed that black women have greater access to employment opportunities. What are these opportunities then?

Black women of Asian origin have had to come to terms with whole new spheres of experience, particularly in the area of employment, and they have had to redefine their many roles. Their economic situation makes it important for black women to work and they have to work in order to supplement the family wage. The Grunwick dispute was an example of the way in which black workers defied management and asserted their right to engage in trade union activity. The relationship of women, especially black women, to trade union activity has traditionally been one of indifference because unions have consistently ignored the needs of black female workers. Many women work because they have to, but the man in the family is still regarded by many as the main wage-earner. This situation is changing because so many black women are now the sole wage-earners in their families. Increasingly, black women have become active in trade union disputes and the militant position taken by them has helped to shatter a number of illusions held about women and work and has also gone some way to dispelling some of the stereo-typical images of black women mentioned earlier.[6]

Schools are another area where black girls have experienced racism not only from some white teachers and heads but also from their white peers. Asian girls are often picked on for the way they dress or for the food they eat.

Mumtaz: I have been called things like Paki and wog ever since I came to this school and ever since I moved into this area. I have got used to it now. People are a bit more friendly now.

Nisha: I think this school is better than most because at schools like E . . . or T . . . the Indians sit on one side and the English on the other. They call each other names and almost every day there's a fight. The girl next door goes to T . . . and she says I am different from other Indians, but I don't know how she means. She says that they smell. I think she's a bit stupid.

Rita: I get hurt by what they say, but I know they are just being stupid. They don't know what they are saying. They are only saying it because they are frightened of our culture and because they don't really understand it, I think if they know a bit more they might understand.

It's not only in schools that girls come under racist attacks, but also in their homes and on the streets.

Gulshan: It's worse where I live, because we are the only Indian family. Our next door neighbours are all right, but the people living further away call us names. 'Go back where you came from', 'wog', 'Paki', 'We are the National Front' and all the rest. I just ignore them.

Many girls fight back.

Nisha: If somebody calls me Paki I would go to them and kick them in the teeth. I don't often get called names, just about once a year, and then I get really angry and hit them. If somebody said that to me I would say 'Pink ice cream'. There are some English people in our country and we don't go around calling them names.

There are many racist practices in schools and in education generally that we have not mentioned. For example, bussing of black children into other areas, racist curriculum, the dumping of black children in educationally subnormal schools and biased intelligence tests. A more recent form of racist practice is the growing use of disruptive units or 'sin-bins' as they are commonly called. A high percentage of children in educationally subnormal schools or remedial units are West Indian. And if there is no room in these places then black children are suspended from schools on the quiet. All these are attempts by the authorities to try and control black children, make them passive and discipline them for the lowest paid and dirtiest jobs on the market.

As can be seen, no areas of black people's lives are untouched by the racism of British society. But despite these attempts to stereotype, control and demoralize them, black people have put up resistances and fought to gain control over their lives.

Conclusion

We would like to conclude by stating what we see as the importance of the growth and development of a black women's movement in Britain. We have tried to show a number of the ways in which racism limits and circumscribes the lives of black girls in Britain. We have tried to present that experience as it is lived. Racism, however, is not the only oppression a black woman faces. She is also oppressed in class terms, as part of the working class, and in gender terms, because she is a woman.

Most girls have a distorted image of what the women's liberation movement is all about and what organizing in a women's movement means. The only contact they may have with the ideas of women's liberation is through television or maybe through what men say about it. Black girls see the movement as dominated by white, middle-class women who in many cases fail to recognize the specific and complex nature of black women's oppression. For these reasons black girls feel they have nothing in common with a movement which does not even realize they exist.

It is all very well for white women to demand equal pay and abortion on demand but equal pay with whom, the other black women working in the over-crowded sweat shop or in the hot laundry or working as auxiliary nurses and cleaners? In asking for abortions on demand, white women are failing to recognize what contraception and abortion *mean* to black women. It may mean being sterilized without your knowledge or consent, it means black women being used as guinea pigs in experiments for new drugs, it means contraceptives like depo provera, which has numerous side effects, being used on black women, but not on white women. A number of women also fail to understand and recognize the importance placed by black women on having children. Having a child is sometimes the only way in which a black girl can show that she has some control over herself. It may be the only thing she *wants* that she can *have*.

The main issue here is the gap which exists between the experience of black women who face racism every day in addition to their oppression in class and gender terms and white women who are afraid to confront their own racism. White women fail to understand a number of the cultural traditions which exist in the black community and the important part they play in our growth and development as black women. They simply label practices they do not understand as oppressive and although there are some issues which we need to fight together as women, white women need to come to terms with the fact that they are part and parcel of a racist system, they are oppressors and as such are distanced from a number of the problems which black women confront every day.

Notes

1 Some of the issues touched on in this article are developed more fully in the Centre for Contemporary Cultural Studies, *The Empire Strikes Back: Race and Racism in 70s Britain*, London, Hutchinson, 1982.

2 *Black Women in Britain – Speak Out*, Organisation of Women of Asian and African Descent, 1979.

3 *The Views of Social Workers in Multi-Racial Areas*, Commission for Racial Equality, April 1977.

4 *Our Lives – Young People's Autobiographies*, Inner London Education Authority.

5 A. Sivanandan, 'Race, class and the state', *The Black Experience in Britain*, Institute of Race Relations, 1976.

6 See, for example, the Grunwick dispute (*Race Today*, 1977) and nursing disputes (*Race Today*, August 1974).

16   Gender relations in secondary schooling

Sandra Kessler, Dean Ashenden, Bob Connell and Gary Dowsett

Problem and approach

By and large, the discussion of gender and education has been guided by the concept of sex roles. The idea that boys and girls are socialized into different but complementary roles, which then shape their expectations of life and other people's expectations of them, is an appealing one. It fits much common-sense knowledge of how children are treated and provides a language for describing the pressures exerted by parents, peers, mass media, and schools. Perhaps most important, it provides a strategy for change: one must break down the stereotyped expectations and redefine the accepted boundaries of women's and men's respective roles. This, broadly, is the strategy pursued by liberal feminism. It can also be made to work for men, as shown by men's liberation publicists such as Nichols (1975) and Farrell (1974).

Yet there are problems. The sex-role concept is not as commonsensical as it often seems. It was introduced into mainstream social science in the 1930s and 1940s, and it displaced other concepts of gender relations, which had focused more sharply on questions of power and marginality. Talking about gender relations in terms of roles, internalized expectations, attitudes, and traits directs attention away from larger structures and focuses explanations of inequality on what is going on inside the heads of the subordinated group. It is a classic case of blaming the victim. As Franzway and Lowe (1978) point out in an excellent, brief critique, the idea of sex roles exaggerates the importance of individual attitudes and minimizes the importance of the economic and social forces to which those attitudes are a response. For instance, when a working-class family tries to ensure that the husband rather than the wife stays in full-time work, it is a question of rational judgement in the face of economic necessity rather than a matter of role expectations. Given a highly discriminatory labour market, men can generally get higher-paying jobs. If reformers focus just on attitudes and expectations in such situations, attempts at reform will misfire.

Furthermore, schools, operating in their traditional fashion, do not simply reproduce sex stereotypes or confirm girls in subordinate positions. Certainly they do that much of the time. But they have also long been a vehicle for women who reject conventional expectations and wish to construct their own intellectual lives and careers. There is, therefore, a need for a more sophisticated understanding of gender in its relations with education.

Source: Extracted from Kessler, S., Ashenden, D. J., Connell, R. W. and Dowsett, G. W., 'Gender relations in secondary schooling', *Sociology of Education*, **58**, 1985, pp. 34–45 and 47–8.

The theory of gender relations

Such an account has begun to appear in recent years from two main directions. First, authors such as Game and Pringle (1983) and O'Donnell (1984) have closely analysed social relations in the workplace and the segregation of the labour market. It has become clear that the sexual division of labour is not a superficial pattern of discrimination that might be cured by employers' change of heart. It is a fundamental structure that is constitutive of industrial and social authority, intricately interwoven with the design and application of technology, and crucial to profitability. Schooling not only reflects this but also helps constitute it. As O'Donnell argues, the development of the schooling system is part of the process that produces a sex-discriminatory labour market.

The second important development has been the attempt to combine the analysis of gender, as a psychological and interpersonal matter, with an understanding of how a social order as a whole reproduces itself. As Burton (1985) argues, this has been one of the key lines of development of feminist social theory in the last decade. Interesting examples of this work are Chodorow's (1978) psychoanalytic sociology of gender, which discusses how the sexual division of labour gets entrenched in the unconscious, and Willis's (1977) account of masculinity among British working-class youth. Arnot (1981, 1982) develops the line of thought in what is now the most sophisticated theoretical analysis of gender and education available.

This work has been important in bringing structures of power and large-scale social dynamics on to centre stage. It is clear that role theory underestimated what it was up against. The schools are an arena in which a complex, often contradictory, emotionally and sometimes physically violent politics of gender is worked out. The strength of the reaction against well-meaning minor reforms is understandable.

Yet there are problems with this theoretical framework too. There is a strong tendency towards functionalism in reproduction theory. It is difficult to incorporate the dynamics of historical change into social-reproduction analyses. There is a tendency to treat 'male' and 'female' as simple categories and to ignore their complexities and internal structuring. Homosexuality, once again, tends to get written out of the discussion of gender.

We argue, then, that the theoretical framework needs to be shifted further. First, we must find ways of talking about large-scale structures without reifying them and about personal practices without losing their large-scale contexts. To some extent this is a general problem of theoretical social science, which requires the development of an adequate theory of practice (see Giddens, 1979; Sartre, 1976; Connell, 1983). Second, we must find the right research techniques so that the issue can be worked out in relation to a particular problem.

Method

The project reported here was conducted in 1977–8 in twelve Australian secondary schools; the examples to be discussed in this article are drawn from four of them. A sample of 100 14- and 15-year-old students was drawn from two contrasting social-class milieux. Fifty came from working-class families, whose children were enrolled in large suburban co-educational comprehensive schools, which in the

Australian education systems are provided by the state governments. Fifty came from ruling-class families, who sent their children to high-fee private colleges, mostly single-sex institutions loosely connected with the major churches. Half came from the city of Adelaide, half from Sydney; regional differences turned out to be negligible. Half were girls and half were boys; sex differences were not negligible.

A cluster of interviews became the basis for a detailed case study of a particular pupil, in which the authors made a collective attempt to understand the person in terms of the whole network of social relations and socioeconomic circumstances in which the relevant family and school found themselves. This is a very time-consuming and labour-intensive process; but we argue that some such step is necessary if researchers are to understand the relation between individual practice and social structure in more than summary or schematic ways. As the file of completed case studies built up (two years of work produced forty-three case studies, at which point funds and time were exhausted), analyses of issues and themes across cases became possible. It also became possible to analyse particular schools as institutions and, finally, to analyse the dynamics of class and sex groupings on the larger scale. In a second round of analysis, the procedure was repeated with case studies of teachers (a total of thirty-seven were produced in three years). Material from the other interviews has also been used but in a less intensive way.

Extracts from fieldwork

The material available is very extensive. For this article we thought it more important to illustrate major dynamics than to present either representative cases or especially striking individuals. The first section illustrates an important pattern of interaction between activist teachers and non-academic kids in a working-class school. Next, we describe gender dynamics operating at the school level in the contrasting examples of two ruling-class schools. We then look at gender dynamics in families – first those in which the authority of men has been contested or eroded and then those in which it has been successfully asserted.

Interactions in a working-class school: resistance and promotion
Arlette Anderson is a young teacher at Rockwell High School, a state comprehensive school in a relatively new, working-class suburb. It was her first appointment after she finished teacher training. When she arrived, she was shocked by the hostility of her pupils. Within a day or two, one of the boys offered her a direct sexual insult: 'Why haven't you got a boyfriend? Is there something wrong with you?' This was but one instance of massive resistance by the kids; and in response, she formed an unflattering picture of them. She described the boys as 'ocker deluxes'* and the girls as 'loud-mouthed disco-maniacs'.

Arlette is nobody's doormat, and she bounced back, confronting the kids with

---

Ocker is an untranslatable term with overtones of macho masculinity, working-class slovenliness, aggressive Australian nationalism, and expertise in the national sport – beer drinking. The RSL (veterans' club), mentioned in the next paragraph, is by general repute the epitome of ockerdom.

their sexism. She tells them what she thinks the boys will be like in ten years: beer-bellied, boozing at the RSL club, totally lacking respect for women. They laugh. In a Year 8 class she organized a debate about the role of women; universal opinion among the boys was that women should stay home and have babies. The boys shy away from classes like domestic science: 'I'm not doing that; my Dad says sewing's sissy.' The girls, meanwhile, learn by the end of their first year in high school that having a boyfriend is a matter of status, and they jeer at those who have missed out. 'They don't seem to have any idea of sisterhood at all', Arlette concludes, depressed. The girls agree with the boys that the proper business of a woman is to be a mother. Arlette has pleaded with them. Aren't they interested in even a small career? 'Oh no, I want to be a mother.'

Bill Poulos, at first sight, might be thought of as a classic example of the 'ocker deluxes'. He has a contemptuous attitude towards women. He has begun to establish sexual relations with girls in the neighbourhood and treats his girlfriend in a decidedly exploitative way. He is in with the 'smoking crowd', as a teacher notes, and turned up drunk at a school dance. He is a tough proposition for his teachers – hard to control and very difficult to teach.

Bill is not just bored with school; he is actively angry with it. He feels that he was unjustly put in a bottom class when he came up to the high school, that he has been stigmatized as a result, and that most of the teachers do not give him credit when he does try with his work. However, he has a good relationship with one teacher, who gives him extra attention. He is resentful of the arbitrary authority and petty injustices of school life and has a rich fund of examples: a teacher who screamed at him – he walked out of the class and did not come back; inexplicable decisions by the school authorities, such as stopping competitive football; undeserved canings and detentions; and so forth. He wants to leave school and start an apprenticeship, against his father's advice.

There are some painful experiences, strong emotions, and more than a touch of self-doubt behind Bill's stroppiness towards his teachers. Yet there is also a logic to the combination of aggressive masculinity and resistance to school. Bill's claim to masculinity is reinforced by a touch, don't-push-me-around stance toward school authorities and by petty delinquencies like smoking and drinking. Conversely, his resistance to the school is stiffened by a need to protect a bruised sense of self and to assert his masculine claims to authority and personal space.

The situation is different for girls. Heather Arlott seems to be one of the 'disco-maniacs'. Though from a different ethnic group, she comes from an economic background similar to Bill Poulos's: her father is a contract labourer and her mother is a packer in a factory. Most of the time her teachers find her as difficult as Bill; maybe more difficult. When a teacher yelled at Bill, he walked out; when teachers yell at Heather, she yells right back. She will not do what she is told unless she wants to. She laughs out loud, stirs the class and, like Bill, has a fund of stories about teachers' injustices. 'Hell to teach' is the staffroom consensus about her. The exception is on the sports field. Heather is an excellent athlete and appreciates the coaching she gets from her teachers.

Heather's resistance to school is quite like the boys', but the situation in which she does it, and therefore its effect, is very different. While resistance among boys confirms and even exaggerates their masculinity, the same behaviour among girls violates conventional femininity. The convention is that proper girls should be controlled, polite, and biddable; swearing, smoking, yelling at teachers, and truanting are more like protests against femininity than confirmations of it. Heather is a strong person, not just in the physical sense. She is not going to be put down by the Arlette Andersons of this world, nor by the Bill Pouloses. The school resistance of young women like this is a genuine challenge to their subordination as women.

Yet Heather is by no means masculine in style or outlook. She is a keen dancer and often goes with her friends to the local disco. Though she has not thought much about getting married, she has no particular objection to the idea. Indeed it is very likely that she will have to. Working-class girls leaving school early because of conflict with the school are thrown into the least secure part of the labour market. Youth unemployment currently runs up to 35 per cent in areas like Rockwell. Within a few years, Heather's best chance of economic security will probably be to attach herself to a husband. Even then, given the decline in real wages, she will have to hold a job to keep a family much above the poverty line.

Much of this is not known very clearly in the Rockwell High staffrooms. The conditions of teachers work make it difficult for most of them to learn much about their pupils' personal backgrounds; and Heather's own responses inevitably antagonize the teachers, because she makes their work more difficult. Though Heather really needs help from teachers like Arlette Anderson in understanding this difficult and contradictory aspect of her life, and though Arlette really has something to give students like Heather by way of a new understanding, in practice they stand off from each other across a barrier of mistrust and incomprehension.

The girls who are different, in Arlette's eyes, are the 'bright' ones in the upper streams, those selected for academic success and headed – some of them at least – for matriculation. It is these girls who are finding something useful in Arlette's feminist ideas. We interviewed a number of girls in the 'A stream' at Rockwell High. While they express a good deal of tension and uncertainty about their futures, it is clear that they are contemplating patterns of work and marriage that are very different from those open to girls like Heather Arlott. For many of them, the sympathetic support of teachers like Arlette Anderson is the key to their project of constructing a career.

In two ruling-class schools: change and reaction

What is an uncertain prospect to the A stream at Rockwell High is a vivid reality to their counterparts at Auburn College, a prestigious and expensive private school for young ladies. While less than 30 per cent of Rockwell High's pupils go through to the Year 12 Matriculation exams, about 90 per cent of Auburn College's pupils do; and they do to some purpose. Auburn's pupils are consistently carrying off high honours in the hard sciences (maths, physics, and chemistry) and winning entry to the professional faculties at universities.

This school has, in fact, recently undergone a renovation of staff and curriculum, caused partly by changed ideas about careers for women among its clientele, augmented by feminist ideas among its staff. Formerly, the school's main concern was to produce young women properly fitted out for marriage, motherhood, and ruling-class social networks. Its main concern now is to equip the girls for academic competition and entry into the professions. The social set among the girls has lost its place in the sun to the academic high-flyers; and the consequences for relationships with the men of their class are already being registered, a little apprehensively, by their parents. Fathers contemplate their daughters' possible impact on the business world; mothers wonder if they will reject the traditional model of femininity-in-marriage.

We see here a shift towards a model of femininity in which marriage is expected to be integrated with professional careers, and the simple subordination of women's work to husbands' careers is challenged. No corresponding change has occurred in the ruling-class boys' schools.

Nevertheless, in boys' schools too, the school is an active maker of gender, in this case masculinity. A major focus is sport and the emotions surrounding it. This is very clear at Milton College, a boys' private school whose clientele is similar to Auburn's – i.e., mainly business and professional families. Every Saturday in the season, the boys play football against age-grade teams from similar schools under the eyes of their teachers (the coaches) and their parents, who come to shout encouragement, praise, and criticism. Winning the match matters to all three groups. Demotion to a lesser team can be deeply distressing to the boys. One boy we interviewed, small for his age, actually suffered concussion more than once before a teacher could persuade him and his father that he should play in a lighter grade.

Is this a cult of healthy bodies and school spirit slightly overdone? No, there is something much more systematic here. Football at Milton College is, above all, a medium for the construction of a particular kind of masculinity. It celebrates toughness and endurance, relentlessly promotes competitiveness and fear of losing, and connects a sense of maleness with a taste for violence and confrontation. Moreover, because the game has an honoured place in this school, the kind of masculinity it promotes, the tough and macho kind, subordinates other kinds of masculinity. The boys who for reasons of physique, capacity, or preference, have been relegated to study, non-violent games, debating, and the like, are condemned by the football heroes to be known as 'the Cyrils', a term indicating effeminacy.

Three families: patriarchy eroded

At the top end of the labour market, formal education has plainly been important as a route leading women into the professions. But this has not always worked smoothly, as is shown in the life of Dr Somerset, the mother of one of the girls at Auburn College. Sally Somerset, who is working very hard at school and doing well, is headed for the university and one of the professions; she is still undecided which. Dr Somerset went to a private girls' school herself and was its first graduate to become a doctor. But her promising career was cut short when its demands conflicted with her husband's. She was forced to give up the job and has not practiced for nearly twenty years. That was a bitter experience, and it shaped her view of women's place in the world in ways that have influenced her daughter's schooling. It is one important pressure behind Sally's trajectory towards the professions and a new model of marriage.

Of course theirs is a very privileged situation. But there is pressure for change in working-class families too; married women in these families have taken jobs as office cleaners, chicken packers, checkout operators, sandwich makers, label stickers, and so on. It was clear in many of our interviews with parents that wives who earned a wage did have an important resource in the internal politics of the marriage. Heather Arlott's mother, for example, works in a boring and low-paying job, but she is an equal partner in the family and vigorously resists any attempt to impose authority on her from any quarter, including the school.

In some cases the independence goes further. Mrs McArthur, who works as a clerk in a small firm, has no particular belief in solidarity among women. In fact she finds most women at her office small-minded and irritating and prefers dealing with men. Yet men's pretensions infuriate her. She is sharply conscious of managers' prejudice against women and of the limits therefore set to her own prospects; she is one of those women who run a business from behind the scenes while the men take most of the profits and all the prestige. She walked out of a first marriage, which she found unsatisfying. She is now without question the dominant partner in her second marriage, and the authority figure in her family as well as its main earner.

In situations like this, there is a real and conscious shift from earlier models of womanhood. This is often conveyed to daughters, just as Dr Somerset's views on independent womanhood have been. In Sally Somerset's case this led to an embrace of the academic curriculum, an enthusiastic endorsement of the educational goals of her school; but in working-class life it is very likely to lead to conflict with the school. That is true, for instance, of Mrs McArthur's daughter Kate. We have mentioned the state of war between Heather Arlott and Rockwell High. With Kate McArthur it is, if anything, worse. She is stubborn, opinionated, and regarded as a troublemaker. Like Bill Poulos, she is angry at the school for having shoved her into a low stream. She is fighting every authority in sight, her mother and the teachers equally. The teachers' picture of Kate is almost wholly negative. She is demanding to leave school so she can go on the dole – an ambition her mother is scathing about.

It is easy to see here that a strong and unconventional mother has conveyed some of those qualities to her eldest daughter. It is also understandable that the teachers, confronted with angry resistance, fail to see Kate's vulnerability and need. The education that working-class mothers got in their own childhood gave them no resources for understanding and working through the complex changes that are occurring in gender relations. It seems that the schools are proving no more useful to many of their daughters.

Yet conflict with the school is not the inevitable outcome of these changes. Elaine Markham is a member of the A stream at Rockwell High, in fact one of the school's academic stars. Her mother is a person quite like Mrs McArthur – equally the source of strength in the family and conscious of prejudice against women. Mrs Markham had wanted to become a journalist but was bitterly disappointed when forced to leave school early because *her* mother could see no point in education for women. Having fought free of a dominating mother, she is determined that her girls will not repeat her frustration and has pushed them hard at school. Elaine has taken over this project, internalized it, and become competitive at school. Like her mother, she is contemptuous of 'the little housewife' and of her schoolmates who are growing up in that image. Though she will not go as far as 'Women's Libbists', burning bras and demonstrating in the street, she firmly supports the overall idea of women being equal. But all this has not come easily. She sometimes comes home from school in tears, caused by tension and frustration. She talks of the school as a 'dead' place. She is thinking about leaving early despite her academic success.

The corollary of Mrs Markham's strength is Mr Markham's marginality. Elaine's father is a storeman and earns below average wages, which is why his wife had to take a job. He came from a very poor family, left school at age 15, and has held a range of jobs. He gets pushed around a good deal at work, and while he is antagonistic toward unions, he is angry at his bosses for not giving him recognition and a better wage. He finds that their pressure for profit erodes the service his unit can give and offends his pride in workmanship. The work situation, in short, constantly erodes his self-esteem. He tried to assert patriarchal rights in the family; for example, he refused to take on a share of the housework when his wife took a job. But the main consequence has been that he has become increasingly marginal in the household. The women have concluded that he has failed as a husband and father; and he too, rather wistfully, now accepts that opinion of himself.

Two families: patriarchy affirmed

Such situations of contested or eroded patriarchy are not found in the majority of families. The pressures experienced by Mr Markham are common, but the outcome is often different.

For example, Mr Poulos, Bill's father, has faced pressures at work possibly more severe than Mr Markham's, including a serious industrial accident, loss of his job, and a permanent loss of earning power. But he has successfully asserted patriarchal authority at home; his wife has accepted a subordinate place. Mr Poulos's male-supremacist attitudes – 'Thank heaven I haven't got a daughter,' 'I'm boss here' – go unchallenged. Bill's masculinity has been formed against this background, and it is plain that he has absorbed much of his father's outlook. Some hypermasculine interests, notably boxing, have been passed on. More importantly, Bill is beginning to reproduce the same pattern of relationships with women, treating his girlfriends the way he has seen his father treat his mother.

Because it is frequently assumed that the successful reproduction of such patterns in the younger generation is a smooth and easy process, it is worth dwelling for a moment on the difficulty and pain that is really involved. The economic and personal stresses on Mr Poulos have been severe. His masculinity, especially the way his sense of self is bound up with being a head of family and a good provider, has been sustained only at the cost of harsh struggle, which has left its mark in his attitudes toward women. Bill's relationship with his father is tense. He was severely beaten in childhood; after all, being beaten 'made a man of me', says Mr Poulos. Bill is resentful of his father now, especially over the issue of school leaving.

Bill's self-esteem is also under attack, not only from most of the teachers, who would be glad to see the back of him, but also from many of the other kids, who insult him because he is Greek. His family derides his enthusiasm for surfing. Another enthusiasm, music-making, is pursued entirely outside the school, since the music curriculum there is exotic and academic by turns. Bill is frustrated at the point where he really does want to make contact with the school. It is clear that his masculinity is being constructed in the context of a great deal of conflict, anxiety, and frustration. That he is in no sense an isolate – he has plenty of friends of both sexes and gets on well with his mother – perhaps makes this point even more significant.

The amount of effort that goes into apparently straightforward role modelling or social reproduction can also be seen in the Prince family. Here, things are a good deal more comfortable. The family revolves around the work and leisure of Mr Prince, who holds a steady job as a maintenance worker for a public authority and is a leading figure in the local junior football league. Mrs Prince is a nearly full-time secretary and a full-time mother. They have a comfortable and well-equipped home, which they built themselves in one of the older and more secluded streets of Rockwell.

Delia, their 15-year-old, is everyone's picture of a nice girl. She is quiet and pleasant, a shade diffident, and co-operative with her teachers. She would like to be a veterinarian, but if she does not get the necessary grades, she will take a clerical job, as her mother and older sister have. She then expects to marry at age 20 and have her children.

It all looks effortless. Not so. The central place that Mr Prince's work and interests hold in the family was achieved at the cost of Mrs Prince's ambition to become a nurse. He did not like the hours, so she gave it up. She got a job in a bank but, in accordance with its policy, was sacked when she married.

Mrs Prince did not stay at home when the kids were little, because she was working to pay off the block of land they built their house on. She now feels guilty about having neglected them and is running herself into the ground trying to be the perfect mother as well as a wage earner. Delia's peer relations are very carefully supervised; her parents even introduced her boyfriend to her! Her mother made her abandon a peer group who smoked and got drunk on weekends. In short, the production of Delia's conventional femininity has involved a lot of work and anxiety on all sides.

Rethinking gender and schooling

Most discussions of sexism in education have assumed that the school produces sex-role conformity in one way or another.

It is true that there are many ways in which schools mark out conventional gender differences. Girls' uniforms are skirts and dresses, boys' are slacks and suits. On sports days, girls are put in netball teams, boys in football. Timetables force choices between metalwork and cookery; because it is assumed that girls will become secretaries and boys draughtsmen, it is difficult for either to be the reverse.

The argument about stereotyped expectations is correct up to a point but does not catch the full force of this. The school is actively engaged in constructing gender. In this light we can see the cult of football at Milton College as a powerful masculinizing practice, quite consciously designed to that end. At Auburn College, the school is actively engaged in *re*constructing gender. Rockwell High, whose progressive headmaster has just abolished competitive sport, is trying, in a less systematic way, to do the same.

The stereotype argument is more seriously wrong in assuming that the school tends to impose just one sex-role pattern on its boys and one pattern on its girls. This is plainly not the case in either ruling-class or working-class schools. Even Milton College produces both the football heroes *and* 'the Cyrils'. Rockwell High produces Bill Poulos *and* the A-stream boys. Auburn College produces both the new professionals *and* the socialites, who have lost their pre-eminent position.

What the school is mainly doing here is arbitrating among different kinds of masculinity and femininity. Perhaps we should say that since much of this occurs outside the scope of any conscious policy, the school provides a setting in which one kind or another becomes hegemonic. The cult of football, for instance, does not and cannot obliterate all other kinds of masculinity. Indeed, Milton College needs boys whose character allows them to focus on academic work, because their high results in public examinations sustain the school's leading position in the market-place. Therefore, it produces other masculinities but marginalizes them, while giving most honour and admiration to a tough and dominant virility.

We may summarize these observations by saying that the school as an institution is characterized at any given time by a particular *gender regime*. This may be defined as the pattern of practices that constructs various kinds of masculinity and femininity among staff and students, orders them in terms of prestige and power, and constructs a sexual division of labour within the institution. The gender regime is a state of play rather than a permanent condition. It can be changed, deliberately or otherwise, but it is no less powerful in its effects on the pupils for that. It confronts them as a social fact, which they have to come to terms with somehow.

A great deal of what happens in schools is outside the immediate view of the school authorities. There is an unofficial school, constructed by the kids themselves, that exists in the gaps and crannies of the official institution. It is in this informal peer-group life that much of the politics of gender is worked out. It is here, for instance, that pressure to compete in sexual attractiveness to boys becomes a reality for the girls, a major source of the divisiveness that Arlette Anderson observed. The gender regime of the school includes the relationship between these processes and the policies of the authorities. Some teachers deliberately try to intervene in the kids' peer relationships. Other teachers do not intervene; and the contradictions between different teachers' strategies are fruitful sources of difficulty for the school.

A major reason the gender regimes of schools have proved difficult to analyse is that some of the most important effects are indirect, involving mechanisms that do not at first glance appear to be related to sex and gender. One such mechanism is the process of academic selection. In working-class high schools, selection in the form of 'streaming' or 'setting' and differential drop-out after the legal leaving age split off a relatively small group of boys and girls and define them as winners: the A-stream at Rockwell High, for example. The process encourages in this group a kind of masculinity oriented to competitive achievement and a kind of femininity directed towards careers. The difficulties encountered have already been discussed in the case of Elaine Markham. Most efficiently, the system of academic competition constructs a group of losers, such as Bill Poulos and Kate McArthur, and shapes sexual identities for them, as these cases suggest and as the research by Samuel (1983) and others on school resisters confirms.

At a deeper level, the academic curriculum itself, the core of the knowledge that the secondary school offers, is connected to the power relations of gender in the larger society. This issue is as yet poorly understood, but we can glimpse some of its main dimensions. First, the academic curriculum is constructed on a principle of authority: what is taught in schools is guaranteed by the authority of university disciplines. This authority is overwhelmingly in the hands of men, notably senior academics. Thus, the academic curriculum is based on knowledge that reflects practices and institutions controlled by men.

Second, the academic curriculum depends on clear-cut distinctions between right and wrong and between relevant and irrelevant. It has little room for ambiguity, for multiple layerings of truth and meaning, or for open-ended explorations. Some recent feminist research suggests that such a perspective on knowledge and such forms of expression are characteristic of masculine thinking. We qualify this and suggest that it is associated with a particular kind of masculinity that is currently hegemonic. Subordinated groups have a more decentered ego and a less single perspective on the world. Thus, the academic curriculum expresses the perspective of the dominant group in the dominant sex.

Third, the curriculum is divided into compartments, or subjects, that reflect the priorities of the dominant group. This organization of knowledge does not correspond to the needs of subordinate groups. For example, unemployed inner-city youth need survival science, not geography and chemistry.

Finally, the singleness of knowledge in each subject area finds expression in a technical language. 'Learning the subject' means mastering its technical terms and adopting its special style. A good deal of feminist research suggests that femininity does not find expression this way (Eisenstein and Jardine, 1980; Marks and de Courtivron, 1981). Rather, its expression is likely to be oblique and discontinuous – such as the kind of expression stigmatized by men as 'women's gossip' – and may even occur in the silences, rather than in what is explicitly said. Gay consciousness, too, has often found oblique and muted expression. The academic curriculum expresses a relation between knowledge and language that arises mainly from hegemonic masculinity.

The character of the curriculum in turn raises questions about the people who teach it. It is curious that much progressive writing on education has ignored teachers – their aspirations and ideas about what they are doing, their personal histories and emotional make-up, their work histories, industrial situations, and unions. The same is true of discussions of sexism in education, with some notable exceptions (e.g., Sexton, 1969). It is important to note that sexism in schools affects teachers as well as pupils. This is not just a matter of discrimination against women teachers, though that is real enough.

It is also important to examine the teachers' relations with their pupils. The whole system of gender relations is a major source of the tensions and difficulties teachers face in working-class schools. These range from drastic problems of discipline with rebellious kids like Heather Arlott and Bill Poulos, to the more subtle problems of student motivation or the hidden injuries of gender suffered by Elaine Markham and Delia Prince.

Teaching inevitably involves emotional relationships. How these issues are handled thus depends on the construction of masculinity and femininity in the teachers' own lives. The families sketched in this article produced the current generation of kids; families very much like them produced most of their teachers. The teachers have also been through a specific kind of training; many of the younger teachers in the schools encountered feminism in the universities and colleges and have reinterpreted their own lives in its light. Finally, as career teachers, their maculinities and femininities are worked out further as they deal with problems of authority and discipline, the curriculum, their own careers, and the complex emotions involved in caring for kids. To understand the gender regime of a school, one must understand the way gender relations impinge on different groups of teachers, the responses they make, and the strategies they try to follow.

It is clear that a patriarchal gender regime is embedded, at a number of levels, in virtually every recess of the Australian education system. There is every reason to think the same is true in other, comparable countries. This may appear to be a pessimistic conclusion, and in relation to the high hopes of liberal feminists and sex-role theorists it probably is. But if this conclusion forces us to see the whole structure as much more massive and intricate, that is not all on the debit side of the ledger. We can also see more of the tensions and incoherencies of the structure and hence the possibilities of structural change. It is the task of theory to try to make those clear.

Implications for theory

One aspect of the complexity of gender that is very clear in the material already presented is the diversity within masculinity and femininity. The biological processes producing male and female bodies interact with a whole range of different family patterns, courses of growth, institutional pressures, and personal choices. The dialectic issues in many kinds of emotional attachment, different personality traits, and different ways of participating in social life. Delia Prince, Elaine Markham and Heather Arlott illustrate the diversity within the one milieu; they all live within a few blocks of each other.

Yet this variation is not random. Particular kinds of behaviour, particular ways of being, are culturally dominant. These are the ones that come to be seen as the pattern of masculinity or femininity in general and are often assumed to be the natural characteristics of each sex. Other kinds of behaviour and character are defined as deviant or inferior and attract derision, hostility, and sometimes violence. We have come to refer to the dominant patterns as 'hegemonic maculinity' and 'emphasized femininity'. Their hegemony within particular institutions is defined by the gender regimes discussed above in relation to schools. It is clear that the pattern that is hegemonic in one institution is not automatically so in another.

To call them 'hegemonic' and 'emphasized' is to stress that they are not necessarily the *most common* patterns – the mistaken assumption made by most sex-role theorists. Not many men or boys really are the strong, cool, fit, competent, macho types who populate cigarette ads and other such daydreams, though most men's lives are still affected by the presence and potency of that image. What is hegemonic at any given time depends on how the relations among different kinds of masculinity and femininity have been worked out. That negotiation is one of the key roles of the school.

Negotiation is perhaps too mild a word for a process that involves unequal resources and a considerable amount of coercion. Part of this is a matter of direct control and force. We have referred to the bullying of 'the Cyrils' by the football heroes at Milton College, the muted violence that the school permits. Girls at ruling-class schools are mostly protected from such treatment, but working-class girls are much more exposed to it. Physical intimidation of women by young men in the streets of Rockwell was mentioned by several of the mothers we spoke to and is one of the reasons they place more restrictions on the movements of their daughters after dark than on their sons. Force is also a component of patriarchal authority within many families, as the case of Bill Poulos illustrates. Studies of domestic violence (Johnson, 1981; Craney and O'Donnell, 1982) demonstrate that this is far from an isolated case.

In other families, such as the Markhams, an internal struggle for power occurs and is resolved by other means. Who wins out in such circumstances largely depends on the resources that can be mobilized. A number of forces have caused women as a group to have less economic resources than men, often a great deal less. These include the way the labour market has generally assigned women to low-paying or part-time jobs; the way the education system has excluded women from most trade and professional training; and the way the relationship between jobs and families has made women rather than men leave jobs (like Mrs Prince) to take on childcare, thus losing seniority, skills, experience, and confidence.

To generalize, one of the key dimensions of gender relations is power. Analysis shows that the power dimension of gender regimes exists inside families as well as schools. The schools, in turn, connect to the larger structure of the state and are part of the sense in which we must understand the state as a patriarchal institution, constituted by sexual politics as well as by class dynamics.

In none of these cases is the pattern of power or the sexual division of labour completely fixed, as we have seen in working-class mothers' return to the labour market. The gender regimes of schools are capable of being changed, as Auburn College illustrates. The consciousness of groups of participants alters, as the emergence of feminism among teachers shows. The character of sexuality itself changes. The pattern of sexual relationships found among the kids in contemporary high schools has altered from what it was a generation ago; the students now are sexual beings in a much more open and obvious way, a change especially important for girls.

Gender relations, then, are historical. The pattern they assume in any society is produced by its particular history and is always in a process of transformation. Even when change is slow to the point of being invisible, the principle should be kept in mind, because it directs attention to the ways in which the patterns of gender are constantly being produced in everyday life. An awareness of the tensions and contradictions of that production process, the difficulties it encounters, and the resistance it arouses, is vital in understanding the way the structure changes as a whole.

It is a safe generalization that power is never exerted without arousing some kind of resistance. Women's liberation and gay liberation are the most organized and visible forms of resistance to patriarchal power at present, but they are not the only forms. Mrs McArthur, Mrs Markham, their daughters, and Heather Arlott embody a working-class feminism connected with the very large changes in women's employment and the power balance inside families. It is a feminism without banners, with a flavour and set of concerns different from those of the intellectuals' feminism, but none the less involving a real challenge to men's power and to the restriction of women's lives. The same is true among teachers.

Countersexist programmes in the schools, then, do not face a scene of total desolation. There is a widespread, though inchoate, concern with sexuality, sexism, and discrimination; and there is reason to think this grows out of some structural changes and can be mobilized to produce more. If the resources and ideas were widely available, a lot of people would use them. It is time to consider who and how. . . .

References

Arnot, M., *Class, Gender and Education*, Open University Press, 1981.

Arnot, M., 'Male hegemony, social class and women's education', Boston University, *Journal of Education* **164**, 1982, pp. 64–89.

Burton, C., *Feminism and Social Theory*, Sydney, Allen and Unwin, 1985.

Chodorow, N., *The Reproduction of Mothering*, Berkeley, University of California Press, 1978.

Connell, R. W., *Which Way Is Up? Essays on Sex, Class and Culture*, Sydney, Allen and Unwin, 1983.

Craney, J. and O'Donnell, C., *Family Violence in Australia*, Melbourne, Longman Cheshire, 1982.

Eisenstein, H. and Jardine, A., (eds.), *The Future of Difference*, Boston, Barnard College Women's Center and G. K. Hall, 1980.

Farrell, W., *The Liberated Man*, New York, Random House, 1974.

Franzway, S. and Lowe, J., 'Sex-role theory, Political cul-de-sac?', *Refractor Girl,* **16**, 1978, pp. 14–16.

Game, A. and Pringle, R., *Gender at Work*, Sydney, Allen and Unwin, 1983.

Giddens, A., *Central Problems in Social Theory*, London, Macmillan, 1979.

Johnson, V., *The Last Resort*, Melbourne, Penguin, 1981.

Marks, E. and de Courtivron, I., (eds), *New French Feminisms*, Brighton, Harvester, 1981.

Nichols, J., *Men's Liberation*, New York, Penguin, 1975.

O'Donnell, C., *The Basis of the Bargain*, Sydney, Allen and Unwin, 1984.

Samuel, L., 'The making of a school resister: a case study of Australian working-class secondary schoolgirls', in R. K. Brown and L. E. Foster (eds), *Sociology of Education*, 3rd edn, Melbourne, Macmillan, 1983.

Sartre, J. P., *Critique of Dialectical Reason*, London, New Left Books, 1976.

Sexton, P., *The Feminized Male*, New York, Random House, 1969.

Willis, P., *Learning to Labour*, Farnborough, Saxon, 1977.

17   From girls and boys to women and men: the social reproduction of gender

Claire Wallace

Yes, because I want, like everyone else, I want everything in life. I don't want to get married to a girl and 'ave nothing behind me. You know, I want something behind me before I get married. 'Cos it's no use getting married and you're on the dole, you ain't working or anything like that, I mean you've got nothing to look forward to. I'd sooner 'ave a job behind me, the money behind me, before I get married anyway (Unemployed man aged 18).

Q: What do you want to do?

Not just stay on this island and get married and have a husband and a baby and get out to work; dinner on the table and 'What did you do today?' That's terribly boring. I want to do something different. Do something with my life. Families are boring altogether. You know it's 'my family's better than yours, my baby's better 'n yours'. I live next door to a young family and it's all hassle all the time. The young girl up the road, she's got two children and she's worrying all the time about how she can pay the bills, because her husband's not living with her (Employed girl aged 17).

Until very recently it has been assumed that male school-leavers will become full-time workers for most of their active lives, and that female school-leavers will combine periods of employment with domestic labour. The process by which this takes place through schooling and after has been termed social and cultural reproduction.[1] Sociologists have shown how gender and class divisions in the labour market, the family and the education system have all been reproduced in parallel in the course of the transition to adulthood. But what happens to the growing numbers of young people in Britain whose only prospects are unemployment? We could hypothesize that an interruption on one plane of the process would have implications for transitions and transmissions on other planes.

With these considerations in mind, I conducted a longitudinal survey of young people on the Isle of Sheppey in Kent, where unemployment had always been around twice the national average. A cohort of 153 young people, 50 per cent males and 50 per cent females, were interviewed, firstly when they were 16 in 1979, then two-thirds were followed up in 1980. In 1984, eighty-four of these were interviewed for a third time when they were 21. This third survey constituted a 15 per cent sample of the population of that age. Respondents were asked about their experiences and expectations of work, unemployment and the transition to marriage and parenthood. In this way I was able to compare responses at 16 with those after five years in the labour market.[2] These three surveys were supplemented by participant observation and conversations with young people at

Source: Extracted from Walker S. and Barton, L. (eds), *Youth, Unemployment and Schooling*, Milton Keynes, Open University Press, 1986.

home, at school and in their places of recreation, so that both survey and more ethnographic forms of data collection could be combined.[3]

The surveys, tape-recorded interviews and detailed notes taken whilst 'in the field' form the basis of the material to be presented here. Firstly, however, it is necessary to consider social and cultural reproduction more generally and ways in which it might be reformulated. This has been based upon what I shall term a 'traditional' model of class and gender relations, one based upon an assumption of full employment.[4]

The traditional model of social reproduction

Rapidly rising youth unemployment is a relatively recent phenomenon. Having climbed throughout the 1970s, unemployment has more than doubled since 1979. Most accounts of youth are based upon their role in an era of expansion when unemployment of the levels we are presently experiencing was unforeseen and unexpected. Consequently, the traditional model of social reproduction focused attention upon the transition from school to *work* (Carter, 1966; Ashton and Field, 1976; Willis, 1977). In this model, groups of youth were reproduced through the education system so that they broadly fitted divisions between middle and working class, rough and respectable, short-term and long-term careers and so on. The 'problem' to be explained, then, was how young people came to accept these roles, or in the words of Paul Willis:

The difficult thing to explain about how middle class kids get middle class jobs is why others let them. The difficult thing to explain about how working class kids get working class jobs is why they let themselves (Willis, 1977, p. 1).

Willis also drew attention to the relationships between sexuality, employment and youth cultures. For example, he describes the functions of the wage packet and the valorization of low status manual labour as a way of demonstrating masculinity; and Brake (1980) describes youth cultures in terms of their representation of masculinity:

From the analysis of working class youth sub-cultures it can be seen that what emerges are several focal concerns which seem to be present in most of them. The most important is masculinity, and as I have suggested, these are predominantly masculinist cultures, offering forms of masculine identity (Brake, 1980, p. 82).

Thus, in the traditional literature, social relations were reproduced through different varieties of male labour. Although a number of different models were produced (Althusser, 1971; Bourdieu and Passeron, 1977; Bowles and Gintis, 1976), and several noted the complex and paradoxical nature of this reproduction, they were all either implicitly or explicitly androcentric (MacDonald, 1980).

Accounts of youth subcultures have been similarly gender-biased until recently, offering accounts of how male youth came to terms with their class position[5] (Hall and Jefferson, 1975; Mungham and Pearson, 1976). The neglect of the domestic dimension resulted in female youth being rendered 'invisible' (McRobbie, 1980; McRobbie and Garber, 1976).

The traditional models assumed that young women would be seeking employment immediately upon leaving school, but that their ultimate destiny is as wives and mothers, thus lowering their commitment to school and to employment. However, they also assumed that the economic and social subordination of women is based upon the fact that the persons to whom they are housewives will be male workers in full-time employment. Traditional assumptions about feminine roles therefore imply traditional assumptions about masculine roles and vice versa.

During the 1970s aspects of this traditional model were challenged by feminists. They attempted to compensate for androcentrism by concentrating upon the experience of girls in education and employment (McRobbie, 1978; Deem, 1980; Spender and Sarah, 1980). In doing so, they indicated the importance of the domestic sphere in determining the social and cultural reproduction of female school-leavers and its role in socialization into gender roles. Some argued that feminine youth cultures, the family and the labour market all reinforced one another to circumscribe the kinds of expectation that girls had:

Girls are still schooled with the marriage market in mind, although this may not be acknowledged consciously. This inevitability in their lives provinced as much excuse within the school, as for the girls themselves, for their ultimate under-achievement. The belief that girls find their deepest and truest satisfaction in a husband and children is ever prevalent (and many of the Ealing girls endorse this); despite discussions about sexual equality and women's increasing presence in the workforce. It shows the power of the market of romanticism portrayed in magazines, but also shows the investment in the care and needs of people that is perfectly understandable in the light of women's working history and their alternatives (Sharpe 1976, p. 130).

Because of this expectation, it is argued, teenage girls are heavily preoccupied with romantic love and catching the right man (McRobbie, 1978; Sarsby, 1983).

Others, however, have emphasized the contradictions inherent in the process of socially reproducing yong women as both wage-labourers and domestic workers. For example such pressures operate differently upon middle-class girls – who are educated for 'careers' – and working-class girls, who are given a more domestically oriented curriculum at school, despite the fact that they are likely to spend much of their lives in employment. This is reflected in women's own perception of their status. As Anna Pollert has observed in her study of women in a tobacco factory:

Working class women face a double, yet interconnecting of contradictions: those of class and those of sex . . . they both accepted and rejected their inferior position, they were both at once satisfied and dissatisfied, they lived in unresolved conflict (Pollert, 1981, p. 87).

Such contradictory pressures and the problematical nature of female social reproduction lead girls to use their femininity as a form of resistance at school (Anyon, 1983; Davies, 1983; Griffin, 1985), or even to resist feminine roles themselves (Gaskell, 1983). In general, however, accounts of male youth have emphasized their resistance to hegemonic ideologies, using masculinity as a weapon – as in Willis's study; while studies of female youth have tended to emphasize their subordination to patriarchal, as well as class, oppression. Thus, the 'problem' to be explained in the reproduction of femininity is the way in which future domestic roles come to dominate every other aspect of women's experience.

In general, then, accounts of male youth have concentrated upon their social reproduction in the 'public' sphere of school and the labour market, whilst accounts of female youth have shown how this is crucially related to the social reproduction of the 'private' sphere of the home. We do not know to what extent the private sphere affects masculine expectations. Thus concepts derived from feminist discourse could be usefully applied more widely.

In the context of rising unemployment research has indicated that there may be a growing *disjunction* between school and work, or a fracture in the 'traditional' process of social reproduction. Young people, it is argued, are unemployed because they are unemployable (OECD, 1977). Although some have dismissed this conclusion as a form of political scapegoating (Youthaid, 1981), others have argued perhaps young people are now less inclined to accept 'shit jobs' at 'slave wages' and that the mismatch therefore deserves some attention (Pryce, 1979; Roberts, Noble and Duggan, 1981, 1982a, 1982b, 1982c).

Discussion of *unemployment* has been likewise gender-biased. For males, it appears, unemployment is unambiguously disastrous, resulting in the loss of status, income and, identity; while for females, it is argued, there is the possibility of alternative domestic roles (Donovan and Oddy, 1982; Jahoda, 1982).[6] However, the discussion of young women's unemployment suffers from lack of theoretical clarity, since there is some uncertainty as to whether teenage female unemployment should be treated in any different way to male unemployment or to that of adult females.[7] On the one hand, the emphasis upon girls' domestic careers has obscured an appreciation of their position as workers, but on the other hand, the designation of youth as a general category has tended to obscure the differences between genders. Thus the conflation of female unemployment with domestic labour has tended to obscure our understanding of employment among women (Marshall, 1984).

I have indicated ways in which the traditional models of social reproduction are predicted upon full employment. The more recent rise in male unemployment means that traditional models may be becoming increasingly unrealizable for both genders. The 'problem' to be explained now is how traditional expectations based upon an era of full employment come to be readjusted to fit new circumstances.

An alternative conceptual framework

For analytical purposes I shall make distinction between three dimensions linking the public and private spheres. First, there is the *material* relationship between gender and employment roles. Young women generally have lower wages and fewer prospects than male youth. For these reasons, working-class girls can seldom afford to live away from the natal home, unless they move into the home of a spouse (Leonard, 1980). For young men, on the other hand, higher wages have reinforced their sexual dominance, ensuring a greater consumer capacity and greater access to adult life outside the home.

Second, there are *social* expectations transmitted through the school, the family and the ideology of romance and so on, which portray young men as masterful and financially advantaged and young women as dependent and subordinate (Sharpe, 1976; McRobbie, 1981; Sarsby, 1983). Finally, there are *symbolic* codes that define appropriate behaviour and provide the criteria for classifying the social world according to 'refined' and 'vulgar', 'rough' and 'respectable', 'good' and 'bad' and so on.[8] Girls who trespass across these symbolic boundaries become contaminated by being labelled as promiscuous or deviant (Shacklady Smith, 1978; Wilson, 1978). Conversely, young men who trespass across symbolic boundaries are labelled as effeminate or 'poofters' (Willis, 1977; Brake, 1980; Connell, 1983). Sexual labelling thus helps to maintain 'traditional' models of masculinity and femininity.

The material, social and symbolic relationships between gender and reproduction vary between social classes. Thus, for example, middle-class children are dependent upon their parents in a different way, and for a longer period, than working-class youth. Socially, middle-class young people expect to establish themselves in careers before reproducing families. Working- and middle-class youth also have different ways of defining desirable sexuality (Sarsby, 1983). Here I shall concentrate upon working-class youth, since they suffered more severely from unemployment, and constituted the majority of my sample.

These three dimensions are in practice intertwined and mutually reinforcing. Moreover, they can also be contradictory. The social expectations of women as dependent 'home-makers' can be at variance with their position as an important or even dominant wage-earner in the family (especially with rising male unemployment). However, as Porter (1983) has indicated, the ideology of male 'breadwinner' and female 'home-maker' remains intact. Similarly, young women working in factories risk being labelled as 'vulgar', for this undermines symbolic codes of femininity while it reinforces those of masculinity (Pollert, 1981). Thus in times of full employment these dimensions reinforce the position of young men, whilst creating tensions in women's position. The ways in which these dimensions operate during times of rising unemployment will be explored later in relation to my own empirical data.

Expectations and experiences of work

Most post-war studies of young people have emphasized the functional convergence between aspirations 'cooled out' or encouraged through the education system and experiences of employment. It is argued that the entry into employment is by no means a shock to working-class young people, because they have been schooled to accept their positions within a class society (Ashton and Field, 1976; Willis, 1977; Youthaid 1981). My research indicated that this traditional model may have changed. Many school-leavers in my sample rejected the work that they encountered on leaving school. This was not because they were inadequately prepared for working life, as recent government reports would suggest,[9] for all 153 school-leavers had had some work experience before leaving school; and, for a number, their first jobs were extensions of the part-time jobs performed while they were still at school. Rather, it was because many had had to accept jobs lower than their expectations due to a decline in the opportunities available in the local labour market.

On first leaving school, young people ranked local employment opportunities not just according to how much they paid, but according to the extent to which they fulfilled different gender-based identities. Hence, for boys, craftwork was the most popular aspiration (55 per cent) followed by outdoor labouring (29 per cent). These jobs conferred the most 'machismo'. Girls mostly preferred training in traditional feminine trades such as hairdressing and nursing (32 per cent), whilst 13 per cent preferred office work and others opted for retail work, these being the most 'feminine'. The least popular form of employment for both genders was factory work since it was heavily criticized by at least 80 per cent of the sample,[10] despite the fact that it was relatively higher paid and was indeed one of the main sources of juvenile employment. Thus, altogether one-third of the sample of 1979 school-leavers were downwardly mobile in relation to their original preferences. Adjustment to work had become a generational, rather than an individual, problem.

The aspirations of young people reflected traditional occupational roles and gender stereotypes. The fact that there were hardly any craft apprenticeships available did not prevent young males from wanting to become craftsmen; indeed the decline in opportunities seemed to reinforce aspirations offering a secure masculine status in circumstances where this was being eroded. Similarly, the absence of office work did not prevent young women from wanting to become secretaries. By the same token, the predominance of factory employment did not make it any more acceptable to school-leavers. This would suggest that aspirations were out of phase with labour market conditions. The 'reproduction' of such gender roles and expectations was inappropriate. One solution was to leave the local market altogether by joining the army, which around 10 per cent of the sample did, for it offered one of the only sources of secure employment.

Consequently, responses to unemployment should perhaps be seen in the context of these reactions to employment. These responses to unemployment were varied and depended upon the domestic circumstances of the individual and the number of friends or relatives who were simultaneously out of work. However, at the ages of 16 and 17 many presented a proud and defiant stance to the interviewer, claiming that they would not stoop to doing some of the 'shit jobs' available anyway:

There's Tesco's, the shirt factory and shit like that. Boring, repetitive jobs, sewing jeans and stacking shelves. I wouldn't do a lot of factory work unless I was really desperate because I would think it was a waste of my life. In a factory, doing the same thing all day. You need an awful lot of money to be able to stand that (Unemployed girl aged 19).

Well, I stayed six months but I was so pissed off with it I left. I'm just not cut out for factory work. It was terrible doing the same thing all day, and all those fiddling little bits you had to do [making fuses]. You couldn't stop for breath and I started to get headaches. It was just so boring – and the noise and the dirt and that. It is like a rabbit hutch in there: no windows, and it's so hot. I never thought it would be so awful (Unemployed girl aged 18).

When I left school I wanted a decent factory job, working. Get some decent wages. I thought, you don't need qualifications to do that, to get on. I was quite content with a factory job till I left school and realised what a factory job was: how tedious and boring it was (Unemployed boy aged 18).

Although there was a negative reaction to many of the jobs available and although aspirations were undoubtedly different to actualities, this form of presentation may also have been a *defensive* strategy, masking a more forlorn reality. Are such attitudes examples of defence or defiance?

Expectations of domestic roles

As might be expected, boys and girls viewed future domestic roles rather differently. At the point of leaving school in 1979, many girls were indeed subscribers to the ideology of romantic love and did see their lives as circumscribed by the inevitability of future domestic status. However, they did not necessarily cherish romantic illusions about the nature of this status. When I asked a group of girls in a coffee bar what qualities they sought in a husband, they chorused in unison: 'No drinking. No gambling. No violence.' The unromantic realism of these attitudes has also been confirmed in other studies of girls at this age (Gaskell, 1983). Indeed, even at 17 many girls still hoped to avoid or defer what they perceived as the unenviable fate of many of the women around them, as the girl quoted at the beginning of the chapter illustrates. These girls' expectations of domestic life could be chracterized as one of critical ambiguity. Thus during my first round of fieldwork in 1979 I concluded that traditional domestic roles were being challenged by young women.

Domestic activity had a low status in the eyes of many girls, and they hoped instead to escape and do something more exciting, or to postpone it. Employment offered a way out because it provided money to do what they wanted; many hoped that it would also provide an alternative short-term career of sorts. There was thus some friction in the reproduction of domestic roles for girls, although symbolically many of the jobs they aspired to were 'feminine' ones.

However, this proved to be short-lived. A year after leaving school, one-fifth of the sample had already adopted domestic roles, having got married, started cohabiting or had children. For some, this was a carefully planned strategy, but most had just drifted, or claimed that this had happened 'by accident'.[11] Thus it appears that domestic roles tended to catch up with young women, despite some initial antipathy.

One reason for this was that, despite being critical of traditional employment and domestic roles when they first left school, young people nevertheless held very conservative views of their *long-term* careers. Men were supposed to become 'breadwinners' and women were supposed to become the wives and mothers to male breadwinners. This appeared to be as important for young men as for young women, for in answer to my question, 'What do you think you will be doing in five years' time?', I received answers such as, 'Oh, usual thing, council house, wife and kids. Having a rest, sort of thing. Nice steady job'; or, 'Married, I suppose, by then. In my own house. I wouldn't get married unless I could afford to own me own house anyway' – from men and women alike. By the time they were 21, young people tended to regard their lives in terms of progressional careers, moving from one domestic status to another, and from one house to another. This ideal assumed that at least one partner would be in full-time employment. The transition to adulthood therefore required the assumption of new domestic roles, and this was equally important for male as for female youth.

Despite jibes about being 'trapped' or 'tied down' by women, a domestic status as head of the household was important for boys for them to assume their full status as adults in the community. While for girls there was some tension between work roles and domestic roles, for young men the two were mutually reinforcing. Symbolic, material and social dimensions were aligned, assuming they could find a permanent job. Indeed, the evidence suggests that, if anything, a future domestic status was more important for young men.

Because this ideal assumed the presence of a male 'breadwinner', unemployment would have a potentially disruptive influence upon life-cycle transitions. Despite the high rates of unemployment locally, young men were unable to conceive of getting married and settling down without full-time employment. The anxiety that such a prospect provoked is illustrated in such comments as:

I wouldn't get married if I didn't have a job. I'd feel cheap living off me wife's work. I'd want to get a job behind me (Unemployed man aged 18).

I wouldn't get married on the dole. Where could you live? How would you get food in? You couldn't build nothing up on the dole. You'd be stuck with what you've got (Unemployed man aged 18).

Young women were equally confident that they would marry a partner with a full-time job, and this was more important than having a job themselves in the long term.

Differences between 16 and 21

Had I finished my research in 1980, when my respondents were 17, I might have concluded that new attitudes were being developed as a response to mass unemployment. Young people were critical of traditional domestic roles and traditional employment roles, even if they rather wistfully hoped to assume traditional roles in the long term. However, I would have been mistaken. Attitudes to employment, to unemployment and to domestic roles had changed by the time they were 21, and this appeared to be related at least partly to life-cycle transitions.

At the age of 21 respondents were beginning to assume adult domestic roles. Getting married involved considerable financial commitment from both partners, as well as extended family, so that young people were no longer able to resist employment: the search for work became less discriminating and more desperate. They were now willing to contemplate doing jobs that they would not have considered when they first left school. It was at this point that they became more 'instrumental' in their outlook, prizing financial rewards above most others. The adoption of domestic roles seemed to make many young people more likely to conform in other respects. Rather than be unemployed as one young unemployed father of a family expressed it:

I'd do any job, anything. I've even been down the council to see if they want anyone to sweep the roads.

Q: Have your expectations gone down, then, do you think?

Yer, well, it's a real crusher, especially if you're two years out of work, like I was. In the end. You're hopeful at first. When I first got unemployed, I can remember, it was when Thatcher first got in and you could see the jobs disappearing then. Oh, it's a real killer being unemployed two years. See, it's not just me I get to think of now, it's them as well.

I asked another girl, who had left a series of factory jobs before having a baby, 'Have your ideas changed, do you think?' She replied: 'Yes, I would do machining work now, and I would stick at it.' 'Why?' 'Because I've got somebody to look after now.'

It appeared from my respondents that unemployment was far more serious in its effects at 21 than at 16. One young father, looking back upon his experience of unemployment when he first left school and comparing this with his experiences at the age of 21, stated:

Oh, I didn't mind then, it was just a laugh. Now, though, I've got a kid and family to keep, and you think of all the things which they should be having. Nah, it's worse now, it definitely is.

Women, too, saw the man's job as important for family-building, as a man was likely to earn more and to determine the standard of living of the household as a whole:

Q: Do you think you would have got married if Steve (husband) had been on the dole?

Well, no, I think it's silly. You start off on the wrong foot. You've got to have a good bank balance, I think, to get married, so you can get the things you want, get your house together. See we had nice furniture when we moved in here. It was all new. . . . We had a new kitchen and carpets and three-piece suite, and then we've just bought a new telly and video (Married women aged 21, two children).

Moreover, upon getting engaged or married, the dependence upon the extended family for donating items for the home meant that young people were forced to conform to their parents' expectations of good behaviour. This normally involved becoming a regularly employed 'respectable' worker, rather than, say, a punk or a skinhead.

The ideology of the home appeared to affect the behaviour of men and women as they grew up. The creation of a home ensured the reproduction of the work-force through *material* necessity; repaying a mortgage, renting a flat or taking on hire-purchase commitments required a regular income. *Socially*, the expectations of wider kin and community were more easily imposed at this stage, serving to reinforce internalized ideas of domesticity. Finally, *symbolically* the home represented security and adult status, which in turn had financial consequences for young people's behaviour. The ideology of the home required the acquisition of essential consumer items such as a three-piece suite, a television set, a bed. Together, these items symbolized the home and the status of the couple as a social unit. The acquisition of these items served to tie the youthful consumer into the capitalist economy more securely than work disciplines or training could ever do. In this way, the household as a consuming unit served to ensure the reproduction of the work-force.

The nature of this transition was class specific. It took place at an earlier age for working-class youth than for middle-class, and earlier for girls than for boys. By the time they were 17, 5 per cent of boys in the sample were married or cohabiting and one had a child, whereas 20 per cent of girls were married or cohabiting and 10 per cent had children. At the age of 21, half the girls and one-third of the boys had either entered, or were moving towards, a new family unit.

The most striking pattern to be observed amongst this sample was the increasing divergence between those who had been regularly employed, and were therefore able to accumulate possessions and purchase a home, and those who were excluded from this process through unemployment. Elsewhere we have termed this process *social polarization* (Pahl and Wallace, 1985). This contributes to a trend described by Ineichen (1977; 1981), who argues that the nature of family formation and housing careers interact to determine the life chances of the family thereafter. Unemployment during this stage of family formation could therefore contribute towards a cumulative disadvantage later in life.

Conclusions

The research described here would support the conclusions of those who argue that there is an increasing *disjunction* between school and work in the context of rising unemployment. As jobs become more scarce, and some teachers use qualifications as the 'carrot' to encourage commitment to education, this may serve further to artificially raise expectations of regular employment. Educators should perhaps be aware that the journey into work is no longer a one-way ride and may take many detours. Increasing numbers of school-leavers are likely to spend their first year in the labour market doing odd jobs or drifting in and out of employment and government schemes – a prospect that the increasing emphasis on certification and submission to formal schooling is unlikely to equip them for. The introduction of the Youth Training Scheme has served further to fragment these early careers of beginning workers. On the other hand, anticipation of these kinds of initial career could make young people more sceptical of the value of formal education, and likewise tends to undermine traditional models of careers education based upon a 'traditional' model of full employment for everyone.

It would appear that the 'stick' that finally serves to beat young people into submission to the labour process is the long-term reproduction of the domestic life cycle. This is more important at 21 that at 16.

The research has indicated the importance of the domestic and public sphere for both male and female school-leavers and has shown the essential interconnect-edness of both. Although male youth tend to be described in terms of their relationship to the public sphere of street corner and workplace, the private sphere, too – in terms of their expectations of becoming 'breadwinners' – was of crucial importance in the transition from school to work. Female youth, on the other hand, have tended to be described in terms of their relationship to the private sphere of home and family, thus confusing the discussion of female unemployment. I have indicated that girls' experience of work and unemployment should be situated in the context of their position within the life cycle for greater empirical and analytical clarity. Male and female youth may stand in different relations to the private and public spheres, but both should be taken into account in the case of both genders.

Social concern and social policy have tended to concentrate upon the initial entry of young people into work and the role that education and training play in this. My research would indicate that this is only one phase in a broader process of social reproduction. Viewed in this way gender identities and the role of the domestic sphere are an essential part of the process rather than something to be 'tacked on' when considering women. If education is to prepare young people for their broader roles as citizens in a changing society, it would seem that these wider issues need to be taken into account.

Notes

1 Reproduction is used in a number of confused and confusing senses (Edholm, Harris and Young, 1977). Here I am using it to mean the way in which one generation of children becomes the next generation of workers with values and attitudes appropriate to their position in the occupational hierarchy.

2 The original 153 young people were drawn from a cross-section of students within a single division of a local comprehensive school. Not all of these were minimum-age school-leavers, although 109 of them did leave at 16. A cross-section was followed up in 1980 and 1984, although in this chapter I have concentrated upon the minimum-age school-leavers who were predominantly working class.

3 These surveys were undertaken in an area that had already been extensively researched by a team at the University of Kent. This research was concerned with examining the relationship between work, the household and unemployment more generally. For the results of this research see Pahl (1978), Pahl and Wallace (1985), Wallace and Pahl (1985).

4 I recognize that 'full employment' is something of a misnomer, since there has been unemployment over the entire post-war period. However, it is a convenient term to describe the period before unemployment became widespread and endemic in Britain.

5 McRobbie (1978), McRobbie and Garber (1976) and Powell and Clarke (1975) have all criticized the literature on male youth sub-cultures. They posed the question: were girls not present in youth subcultures or had they been ignored by researchers?

6 Many of the classic studies of unemployment have concentrated explicitly upon men (Hill *et al.*, 1973; Marsden and Duff, 1975). Johoda (1982), for example, argues that unemployment is not so serious for women as they do have alternative domestic roles to turn to, but can the same be said about young unmarried women?

7 Some have assumed that the effects of unemployment upon young females would probably be the same as that upon young males (Bloxham, 1983). Others have argued that they should be regarded differently (Markall, 1980; Jahoda, 1982; Walsgrove, 1984; Griffin, 1985).

8 Symbolic codes that define acceptable and unacceptable behaviour have been described by Bourdieu and Passeron (1977) and Martin (1983). In the case of girls the distinction between 'slags' and 'drags' has been explored by Cowie and Lees (1981). My usage of this concept draws upon work by Wilson (1978).

9 The White Papers *A New Training Initiative* (1981), Cmnd 8455, and *Training for Jobs* (1984), Cmnd 9135, for example, emphasized the importance of training young people to prepare them for work, assuming that it was their ill-preparedness for work that prevented them from finding jobs. My own research indicates that this assumption is a complete fallacy.

10 These results refer to the 1979–80 sample.

11 These families happened 'by accident' because, despite extensive knowledge of contraception, many young people did not use effective methods of contraception, being

morally circumscribed by codes of sexual conduct described elsewhere (Rubin, 1976; Wilson, 1978). Those girls who tended to be most disadvantaged in the labour market also tended to be those most likely to fall pregnant 'by accident'. Those who had regular jobs and planned wedding ceremonies were also more likely to plan their families more single-mindedly. This association between irregular employment and drifting into pregnancy has been observed elsewhere (Jones *et al.*, 1981; Jenkins, 1983). However, the reasons for it are not clear.

Acknowledgements

I am grateful for the support of the Joseph Rowntree Memorial Trust in funding this research.

References

Althusser, L., 'Ideology and ideological state apparatuses', in *Lenin and Philosophy and other Essays*, London, New Left Books, 1971.

Anyon, J., 'Intersections of gender and class: accommodation and resistance by working-class and affluent females to contradictory sex-role ideologies', in L. Barton and S. Walker (eds), *Gender, Class and Education*, Lewes, Falmer Press, 1983.

Ashton, D. N. and Field, D., *Young Workers*, London, Hutchinson, 1976.

Bloxham, S., 'Social behaviour and the young unemployed', in R. Fiddy (ed.), *In Place of Work*, Lewes, Falmer Press, 1983.

Bourdieu, P. and Passeron, J. C., *Reproduction in Education, Society and Culture*, London and Beverley Hills, Sage 1977.

Bowles, S. and Gintis, H., *Schooling in Capitalist America: Educational Reform and the Contradictions of Economic Life*, London, Routledge & Kegan Paul, 1976.

Brake, M., *The Sociology of Youth Culture and Youth Sub-Cultures*, London, Routledge & Kegan Paul, 1980.

Carter, M. P., *Into Work*, Harmondsworth, Penguin, 1966.

Connell, R. W., *Which Way is Up? Essays on Sex, Class and Culture*, London, Allen & Unwin, 1983.

Corrigan, P., *Schooling and the Smash Street Kids*, London, Macmillan, 1979.

Cowie, L. and Lees, S., 'Slags or drags', *Feminist Review* **9**, 1981, pp. 17–31.

Davies, L., 'Gender, resistance and power', in L. Barton and S. Walker (eds), *Gender, Class and Education*, Lewes, Falmer Press, 1983.

Deem, R. (ed.), *Schooling for Women's Work*, London, Routledge & Kegan Paul, 1980.

Delamont, S., *The Sociology of Women*, London, Allen & Unwin, 1980.

Donovan, A. and Oddy, M., 'Psychological aspects of unemployment: an investigation into emotional and social adjustment of school-leavers', *Journal of Adolescence*, **5**, 1980 pp. 15–30.

Edholm, F., Harris, O. and Young, K., 'Conceptualizing women', *Critique of Anthropology*, **3** (9/10), 1977 pp. 101–29.

Finn, D., 'Leaving school and growing up: work experience in the juvenile labour market', in I. Bates *et al.*, *Schooling for the Dole?*, London, Macmillan, 1984.

Gaskell, J., 'The reproduction of family life: perspectives of male and female adolescents', *British Journal of Sociology of Education*, **4** (1), 1983, pp. 19–38.

Griffin, C., *Typical Girls?*, London, Routledge & Kegan Paul, 1985.

Hall, S. and Jefferson, T. (eds), *Resistance through Rituals*, London, Hutchinson, 1976.

Hill, M. J., Harrison, R. M., Sargeant A. V., and Talbot V., *Men Out of Work*, Cambridge, Cambridge University Press, 1973.

Ineichen, B., 'Youthful marriage: the vortex of disadvantage', in J. Peel and R. Chester (eds), *Equalities and Inequalities in Family Life*, London, Academic Press, 1977.

Ineichen, B., 'The housing decisions of young people', *British Journal of Sociology*, **32** (2), 1981, pp. 252–8.

Jahoda, M., *Employment and Unemployment: A Social Psychological Analysis*, Cambridge University Press, 1982.

Jenkins, R., *Lads, Citizens and Ordinary Kids: Working-Class Youth Life-Styles in Belfast*, London, Routledge & Kegan Paul, 1983.

Jones, P., Williamson, H., Payne, J. and Smith, G., *Out of School: A Case Study of the Role of Government Schemes at a Time of Growing Unemployment*, Special Programmes Occasional Paper no. 4, Sheffield, MSC, 1981.

Leonard, D., *Sex and Generation: A Study of Courtship and Weddings*, London, Tavistock, 1980.

MacDonald, M., 'Socio-cultural reproduction and women's education', in Deem (1980).

McRobbie, A., 'Working-class girls and the culture of femininity', in Women's Studies Group, Centre for Contemporary Cultural Studies (1978).

McRobbie, A., 'Settling accounts with subcultures', *Screen Education* **34**, 1980, pp. 37–50.

McRobbie, A., 'Just like a *Jackie* story', in McRobbie and McCabe (1981).

McRobbie, A. and Garber, J., 'Girls and subcultures: an exploration', in Hall and Jefferson (1976).

McRobbie, A. and McCabe, T. (eds), *Feminism for Girls: An Adventure Story*, London, Routledge & Kegan Paul, 1981.

Markall, G., *The Best Years of their Lives: Schooling, Work and Unemployment in Oldfield*, Occasional Paper No. 3, William Temple Foundation, 1980.

Marsden, D. and Duff, E., *Workless: Some Unemployed Men and their Families*, Harmondsworth, Penguin, 1975.

Marshall, G., 'On the sociology of women's unemployment, its neglect and significance', *Sociological Review* **32** (2), 1984, pp. 234–59.

Martin, B., *A Sociology of Contemporary Cultural Change*, Oxford, Blackwell, 1983.

Mungham, G. and Pearson, G. (eds), *Working Class Youth Culture*, London, Routledge & Kegan Paul, 1976.

OECD, *Entry of Young People into Working Life*, Paris, OECD, 1977.

Pahl, R. E., 'How school leavers see their future', *New Society*, **46** (839), November 1978, pp. 259–62.

Pahl, R. E. and Wallace, C. D., 'Household work strategies in an economic recession', in N. Redcliff and E. Mingione, (eds), *Beyond Employment: Household, Gender and Subsistence*, Oxford, Blackwell, 1984.

Pollert, A., *Girls, Wives, Factory Lives*, London, Macmillan, 1981.

Porter, M., *Home and Work*, London, Macmillan, 1983.

Powell, R. and Clarke, J., 'A note on marginality', in Hall and Jefferson (1975).

Pryce, K., *Endless Pressure*, Harmondsworth, Penguin, 1979.

Roberts, K., Noble, M. and Duggan, J., *Unregistered Youth Unemployment and Outreach Careers Work: Non-Registration*, Final Report Part 1. Research Paper no. 31. London, Department of Employment, 1981.

Roberts, K. *et al.*, 'Youth unemployment: an old problem or a new lifestyle?'. *Leisure Studies*, **1** (2), 1982a, pp. 71–182.

Roberts, K. *et al.*, 'Out-of-school youth in high unemployment areas: an empirical investigation', *British Journal of Guidance and Counselling*, **10** (1), 1982b, pp. 1–11.

Roberts, K. *et al.*, *Unregistered Youth Unemployment and Outreach Careers Work*, Final Report Part 2, Research Paper no. 32. London, Department of Employment, 1982c.

Rubin, L. B., *Worlds of Pain*, New York, Basic Books, 1976.

Sarsby, J., *Romantic Love and Society*, Harmondsworth, Penguin, 1983.

Seabrook, J., *Unemployment*, London, Quartet, 1982.

Shacklady Smith, L., *Sexist Assumptions and Female Delinquency*, in Smart and Smart, 1978.

Sharpe, S., *Just Like a Girl*, Harmondsworth, Penguin, 1976.

Sinfield, A., *What Unemployment Means*, Oxford, Martin Robertson, 1981.

Smart, C. and Smart, B. (eds), *Women, Sexuality and Social Control*, London, Routledge & Kegan Paul, 1978.

Spender, D. and Sarah, E. (eds), *Learning to Lose: Sexism and Education*, London, The Women's Press, 1980.

Walker, S. and Barton, L., *Gender, Class and Education*, Lewes, Falmer Press, 1983.

Wallace, C. D. and Pahl, R. E., 'Polarisation, unemployment, and all forms of work', 1985. BSA Conference paper.

Walsgrove, D., 'Policing yourself: youth unemployment, individualism and the amplification of normality', paper presented to the BSA Conference, University of Bradford, 1984.

White Paper, *A New Training Initiative*, London, HMSO, 1981; *Training for Jobs*, London, HMSO, 1981.

Willis, P., *Learning to Labour: How Working-Class Kids Get Working-Class Jobs*, Aldershot, Saxon House, 1977.

Wilson, D., 'Sexual codes and conduct', in Smart and Smart 1978.

Women's Studies Group Centre for Contemporary Cultural Studies, University of Birmingham, *Women Take Issue*, London, Hutchinson, 1978.

Youthaid, *Study of the Transition from School to Working Life*, vols. 1–3. London, Youthaid, 1981.

Part Five

Gender, Education Policy and Provision

18   Social class, education and ideals of femininity in the nineteenth century

June Purvis

The aim of this paper is to provide a general overview of the forms and content of education for both working-class and middle-class women. A major theme of my analysis is that the history of women's education in nineteenth-century Britain can only be understood in relation to wider economic, social, cultural and ideological factors outside the education field, and especially what has been called 'the domestic ideology'. I shall claim that within the domestic ideology we may identify ideals of femininity which helped to shape both the forms and content of education for nineteenth-century women and to pose contradictions for them.

The domestic ideology and the ideal of femininity: the contradictions that were posed for women

Catherine Hall (1978) has recently emphasized that the period from the late eighteenth to the mid nineteenth century in England was not only a time of transition from an aristocratic, mercantile, capitalist society to an industrial, capitalist society with a large and influential bourgeoisie, but also a period in which the domestic ideology became established within the dominant, bourgeois culture.[1] Certainly during this transition phase, we find a mass of publications, mainly written by the bourgeoisie, which uphold the notion of separate spheres for men and women. Thus the ideal location for women was represented as within the private sphere of the family as full-time wives and mothers while men were to be located within the public sphere of work whereby sufficient might be earned to support the economic dependents of wife, children and kin. However, though the bourgeoisie were prolific on this subject, this does not mean that other social groupings did not hold similar views nor that there was a dearth of ideologies competing to define the position of women. In particular, few records exist expressing the views of the working class on this matter. However there is evidence to suggest that especially in the latter decades of the century, working-class men came increasingly to take up the domestic ideology through the organization of the trade union movement.

Embedded in the domestic ideology were three major assumptions. First, the notion of separate spheres was frequently advocated in biological terms as being a 'natural' division between the sexes. Alexander Walker (1840), for example, claimed that the 'natural' pursuits for women were procreation, gestation, delivery, nursing, care of children, cooking and clothing while part of man's

Source: Extracted from Purvis J., 'Towards a history of women's education in nineteenth century Britain: a sociological analysis', *Westminster Studies in Education*, **4**, 1981, pp. 45–71.

existence was the advancement of knowledge.[2] Second, since women were to be primarily located within the home as wives and mothers, they were defined in relation to men and children rather than as individual beings with their own, independent, autonomous existence. This view is epitomized in the following statement by Mrs Ellis in *The Women of England* (1839):

Women, considered in their distinct and abstract nature, as isolated beings, must lose more than half their worth. They are, in fact, from their own constitution, and from the station they occupy in the world, strictly speaking, relative creatures.[3]

The relative nature of women's existence was given verbal support throughout the century. In 1799, Hannah More asserted that the main benefit of study for woman was that it would regulate her mind and make her 'useful to others', Mrs Taylor (1817) reminded Laura that every day would afford an opportunity of making an 'effort', 'sacrifice' or 'allowance' for the behaviour of others, Ruskin (1865) claimed that a woman should know a language or science only in so far as it enabled her to sympathize in her husband's pleasure and in those of his best friends.

Though the relative nature of women's existence was questioned by many feminists, particularly in the second decade of the century,[4] it was inevitably linked to the third assumption embedded in the domestic ideology – namely, that women were inferior to men. Mrs Ellis (1842), for example, claimed: 'As women, then, the first thing of importance is to be content to be inferior to men'.[5] Such an assumption was, of course, a reflection of the patriarchal nature of nineteenth-century society, and especially the patriarchal structure of the family.

The inferiority of the nineteenth-century woman and her subordination within the husband/wife relationship was advocated from a number of viewpoints. A particularly virulent attack on women was that which based itself on biological determinism. Thus one protagonist argued that since the head and brain size of women were, on average, much smaller than those of men, the reasoning power of women was small.[6] The general conclusion he reached, in regard to the relationship between husband and wife, was this:

It is evident that the man, possessing reasoning faculties, muscular power, and courage to employ it, is qualified for being a protector: the woman, being little capable of reasoning, feeble, and timid, requires protection. Under such circumstances, the man naturally governs: the woman as naturally obeys.[7]

Biological differences between the sexes and the supposed inferiority of woman's intellect were used too as arguments to oppose the entry of women into higher education in the 1860s and after. Thus the right wing newspaper, *The Saturday Review*, asserted in 1871 that these were 'bad times' for women and asked: 'what will be gained by further unsexing them, and encouraging their less muscular frames and smaller brains to a competition with men . . .?'[8]

Religion provided the base for the other main powerful viewpoint that advocated the inferiority of women and their subordination within the conjugal relationship: this time, of course, the arguments frequently refer to a divine order rather than to biological differences. Thus John Burgon, Dean of Chichester, in a sermon delivered in Oxford in 1884, preached:

Behold then, at the very outset, the reason of Women's creation distinctly assigned. She is intended to be Man's 'help' – Man's 'helper'. The expression 'meet for him' implies that she is to be something corresponding to him – a second self. Yet not a rival self, for, as the SPIRIT pointed out some 4000 years later, 'the Man was not created for the Woman, "but the Woman for the Man" ': and from this very consideration the SPIRIT deduces Woman's inferiority.[9]

To sum up so far then, we might say that despite the existence of a strong minority tradition that questioned the definition of women as relative creatures who were inferior and subordinate to men, the establishment of the domestic ideology within the dominant bourgeois culture was such that the social construction of the female gender came to be identified, in society at large, with domesticity. And this was something that both middle-class and working-class women, through the category of their common sex, held in common. But there the link between the women of these different social classes weakens since within the broad identification of femininity with domesticity we find that the bourgeoisie upheld ideals of femininity that were class specific – in other words, they upheld a double standard in that what was considered appropriate, relevant and attainable for middle-class women was inappropriate, irrelevant and unattainable for working-class women.

Within the domestic ideology, the ideal form of femininity that was held to be applicable to middle-class women was the ideal of the 'perfect wife and mother'.[10] This ideal was the cornerstone of the many contemporary writings about woman's position in society: the 'perfect wife and mother' was to provide a well-organized, stable, supportive environment for her husband and children though as Banks and Banks (1964) have stressed, this reflects what the middle classes believed their women ought to do and be, even if individual middle-class women did not always match precept with practice.[11] Nevertheless, the home was upheld as a sanctuary or, to quote Frances Power Cobbe (1869), the 'outermost garment of woman's soul',[12] since within the home, woman's moral power could find full expression.

In the performance of her duties, therefore, the 'perfect wife and mother' was expected to display certain Christian virtues such as self-denial, patience, resignation and silent suffering.[13] And, in addition, she was also expected to be ladylike. Being ladylike involved three fundamental assumptions. First of all, it was ladylike to be a manager of a household but not to engage in the routine, manual work involved: a 'lady' could afford to employ servants to perform such tasks. Second, it was ladylike to engage in unpaid, philanthropic work but never to engage in waged labour. As Mrs Ellis stated in 1869:

As society is at present constituted, a lady may do almost anything from motives of charity or zeal. . . . But so soon as a woman begins to receive money however great her need, or however glorious the escape from degrading dependence which she thus attains, so soon as she makes money by her own effort, and lays by a little store acquired by the work of her own hands, the heroine is transformed into a tradeswoman, and she must find her place in society as such.[14]

Third, being ladylike involved not only wearing appropriate apparel, but also learning a complex ritual of etiquette.[15] In particular, the 'perfect wife and mother' would, in bringing up her daughters, emphasize the importance of the system of chaperonage: it was considered a mark of gentility for young, unmarried middle-class women to be accompanied by a chaperon, often an older, married female, when they mixed in the world outside the private sphere of the home.[16]

In contrast to the prescriptive ideal of femininity for middle-class women, the ideal of femininity for working-class women, as evident in the contemporary writings, reveals quite different standards held by the middle classes for their 'social inferiors'. The ideal for working-class women was that of the 'good woman': like the 'perfect wife and mother', the 'good woman' was located within the home, but a much greater emphasis was placed upon her practical domestic skills as a housekeeper, wife and mother. The 'good woman' could have no pretensions to the ladylike behaviour of the 'perfect wife and mother' who employed domestic servants for the manual work within the home. Thus Sarah Austin (1857) quotes with approval a Mr Johnson who asserted:

We want good servants and good wives; women who know the value of a clean, well-regulated Christian home: for such alone can make 'men' sensible of the real merits of a home, the inestimable blessing of a good wife and tidy obedient children.[17]

while some two years later James Booth (1855) outlined even more clearly the importance of the practical domestic skills that were considered necessary for the 'good women' of the working classes:

how are the daughters of the working classes brought up to fit them for their lot in life, to be the wives and mothers of men in their own station? . . . Why should not 'young women' be taught a knowledge of those common things with which she will have to deal the whole residue of her life? Why should she not, for example, be taught to light a fire, to sweep a room, to wash crockery and glass without breaking the half of them, to wash clothes, to bake bread, to dress a dinner, to choose meat or fish or vegetables, and to know how to keep them when bought; what clothes are most economical – cheap, showy tawdry rags, to those which are perhaps more expensive but cheaper in the end? Why should she not be taught the use of savings banks and the results of thrift?[18]

The ideal for working-class women was seen as a solution to many of the problems of the working-class family. Middle-class commentators spoke of the 'slatternly habits' of the working-class women, their inability to make their 'husbands' homes comfortable' and their general 'miserable deficiencies'.[19] Thus working-class women were frequently blamed for a host of social problems such as alcoholism, crime, the spread of disease and a high infant mortality rate.

As Davin (1979) has recently commented, disharmony and malfunction in society was explained in relation to the failure of the working-class family,[20] and, we may add, especially the working-class wife. As Basch (1974) has noted, the working-class wife's ignorance of domestic matters was one of the most powerful arguments used by opponents of waged labour for women: the middle-class solution was to reaffirm the domestic ideology and insist that woman's sphere was in the home where she would be economically dependent.[21]

The ideal of the 'good woman' may be seen, therefore, as an attempt by the bourgeoisie to solve the various social problems associated with industrialization and urbanization. The 'good woman' was a dilution of the higher status ideal of the 'perfect wife and mother' and thus it may be interpreted as a form of 'intervention' into working-class family life, an attempt to convert and transmit that part of bourgeois family ideology that insisted that a woman's place was in the home, that she was responsible for the quality of family life and that her domestic skills were more important than say vocational skills that might be used in waged labour. The 'good woman' was, therefore, a form of class cultural control, an attack upon the patterns of working-class motherhood and parenthood as perceived by the middle classes.

The two bourgeois ideals of femininity formed part of the context within which educational institutions were founded and reformed: after all, most of the formalized educational provision offered in the nineteenth century was the result of middle-class voluntary effort. Even when the state became increasingly involved in educational provision in the later decades of the century, those who formulated educational policies were mainly drawn from the middle classes. Of course not all educational practice was homogeneous in assuming that women were primarily to be full-time wives and mothers, that they were 'relative' creatures who were inferior and subordinate to men and that they were biologically incapable of learning. But such assumptions would appear to be pervasive, though probably held in varying degrees. Within an educational context therefore, the bourgeois definitions of femininity posed a number of problems, contradictions and dilemmas for women of both social classes. For middle-class women, the linking of femininity with domesticity posed the contradiction that when they sought to improve the standard of their education, especially from the 1870s when they fought for access to the ancient universities of Cambridge and Oxford – universities that had been exclusively for men – they ran the risk of being labelled 'unfeminine' or 'unsexed'.[22] As Stephen (1927) commented, the popular idea of a well-educated women at this particular point in time was that she was a 'ridiculous monster'.[23] Middle-class women who fought for access to higher education had, therefore, to break away from the specifically male, bourgeois definitions of women and in demanding equal educational opportunities, they presented a new ideal of middle-class femininity – the 'new woman'. As Vicinus (1972) has noted, the 'new woman' struggled to enter higher education, engaged in waged labour and fought for improved legal and political rights.[24] It is likely that the challenge to the dominant ideal of the 'perfect wife and mother' came particularly from those daughters of the professional and business classes who saw education as a form of wealth, a passport to an élite occupation. The new ideal was, of course, partly a result of the demands of the bourgeois 'women's movement' for greater economic, political and social freedom[25] and partly a result of the demographic fact that there was a surplus of single, economically unsupported females. But other broader social and economic changes were occurring too that made the ideal feasible: for example, industrialization was creating new types of employment in which women might participate while the process of political democratization was placing greater emphasis upon the individual.[26] Within the context of higher education, therefore, the attempt to establish the 'new woman' ideal was essentially a gender struggle, but a struggle that was contained within the middle classes since few working-class women fought for the right to gain access to the universities. In demanding equal educational opportunities with men, the 'new women' were engaging them in a feminist struggle but not a class struggle.

The bourgeois definition of femininity as domesticity posed, however, rather different problems for those working-class women seeking an education since such women became involved in both class and feminist struggles. As suggested above, the bourgeoisie claimed that social stability and social order necessitated that working-class women should be full-time wives and mothers with practical, efficient domestic skills. In such a way, working-class women would service the capitalist economy by supporting and nurturing a healthy work-force through their care of menfolk within the family and through the rearing of strong children. The most fundamental tension that working-class women faced therefore was the friction between the demands of such an ideology and the realities of a capitalist economy which utilized and exploited them as a source of cheap, female labour. Most working-class women would, at some time in their lives, be forced to enagage in some form of waged labour in order to survive,[27] and the conditions of their work would be such as to hinder the fulfilment of their domestic duties as idealized by the bourgeoisie. In addition, since most of the formalized educational provision was organized by the middle classes, working-class women seeking education had to continually confront the rhetoric and content of education offered by their 'social superiors'. But such an attempt at class control is only one facet of patriarchy. As I have previously suggested, during the second half of the nineteenth century in particular working-class men, through their trade unions, began to take up certain aspects of bourgeois domestic ideology when they campaigned for a family wage. As Foreman (1977) comments, to be able to support a wife at home became a sign of working-class strength, of prosperity, of better days to come. And, of course, as Maria Gray (1879) has highlighted, the fact that women were regarded as an 'inferior caste' only intensified trade union opposition to the admission of women on equal terms to certain occupations.[28] Working-class women as women had, therefore, to struggle against the definitions imposed upon them by both sexes within the bourgeoisie and by their own menfolk. And those women who sought some form of education had to struggle against the exhaustive demands made upon their time for family responsibilities and endless childbearing in a patriarchal society which facilitated the entry of their husbands and brothers, rather than themselves, into a variety of forms of adult education.

Education for women of the middle classes

Educating middle-class girls and young women for the dominant ideal of middle-class femininity, that of the 'perfect wife and mother' who enjoyed a ladylike, leisured life style, usually involved, especially in the first half of the nineteenth century, a privatized education within a familial domestic setting. Thus most middle-class girls were educated at home and sometimes in a small, private school.

The principle of segregation between the sexes was not always adhered to when the children were young, but once the boys were old enough to be sent to school, the education of middle-class girls was usually contained within the home where teaching might be undertaken by the parents, or a governess, or both.[29] Yet as late as 1864, Emily Davies could still claim that 'sisters of public School boys' were probably mainly taught by governesses at home,[30] though she, as a child, had been taught mainly by her mother and elder sister Jane.[31] Whichever variant of the home education theme was followed, the basic principle remained the same – girls were to be educated in a cloistered environment for a separate and different life style from that of boys. Sometimes a girl might attend a small private school, usually managed by middle-class women. For example, Mary Marshall, born in 1850, the daughter of a country vicar, recollects that when about 13 years old, she and her sister went once a week to a 'select school' for young ladies: the school was managed by two maiden women who taught 'Mangnall's Question', the 'use of the globes' and 'deportment'. As she comments, after this experience, her education was considered 'finished'.[32] Such an experience was probably common for middle-and upper-class girls. Since they were defined as potential wives and mothers who would be economically supported rather than independent wage earners, the content of their education tended to stress ornamental knowledge that might attract a husband.

The emphasis upon social priorities in the education of middle-class girls necessarily meant a low standard of education in comparison with that offered to middle-class boys, and this was the general conclusion reached by the Schools Inquiry Commission in 1867–8. Thus after noting the 'general indifference' of parents to girls' education, both in itself and compared to that of boys,[33] the report went on to say that the deficiencies in girls' education included:

Want of thoroughness and foundation; want of system; slovenliness and showy superficiality; inattention to rudiments: undue time given to accomplishments, and those not taught intelligently or in any scientific manner; want of organization.[34]

Such a poor standard of education inevitably influenced both the forms and content of education for adult middle-class women. Women were largely denied access to higher education and were ill-prepared for it anyway. Male cultural hegemony maintained the universities as 'strongholds of masculine privilege'.[35] There were isolated examples where women were admitted access to various institutions of higher education though they were usually denied the right to take the same course and examination as men. In Scotland, for example, John Anderson, Professor of Natural Philosophy at Glasgow University, died in 1796 leaving an eccentric will that asked for the establishment of a rival university within which, at least once a year, a 'Ladies Course of Physical Lectures' should be given.[36] Anderson hoped that such courses would make the women the 'most accomplished Ladies in Europe'.[37] He was careful to add, however, that no women who were 'giddy or incorrect in their manners'[38] should be admitted. Such an experiment foreshadowed the development of the university extension movement in the late 1860s. In England, from 1828, women could attend the lectures at both King's and University College, London,[39] but as Alicia Percival was to comment in 1939, the standard of education was such that the colleges were inaccessible to all but exceptionally gifted or exceptionally placed women: even then, to share lectures with men students was considered too advanced and unladylike for most women.[40]

The first important attempt to provide some form of higher education for women was Queen's College, London, established in 1848 largely through the influence of the Rev. F. D. Maurice, a Professor at King's College.[41] Since it was founded to improve the education of governesses and was, in addition, a separate institution outside the university sector, it aroused little opposition and much support from male university academics.[42] As Emily Davies (1896) was to remark, even the name 'college', as associated with women, seemed to require apology.[43] Initially, 'young ladies over twelve years of age'[44] were admitted and one of the first tasks of the committee was to appoint 'Lady Visitors' who would chaperone the scholars to the various lectures and classes.[45] The dominant ideal of femininity for middle-class girls demanded that they should be supervised in this way: it would appear that, in this particular case, chaperonage offered some protection to these young scholars who came into contact with the men's sphere of learning and scholarship. In 1849, another separate college for women was founded in Bedford Square. Its establishment was largely due to the efforts of Mrs Reid who claimed that the new college was to 'provide for ladies, at a moderate expense, a curriculum of liberal education'.[46] Though both colleges really provided education of a secondary school standard, both were drawn into university work after 1878 when women were admitted to London University degrees.[47]

The struggle for women to enter higher education became mobilized particularly in the 1860s and subsequent decades. However, though an account of such a struggle is important in a history of women's education in nineteenth-century Britain, it is also important that our attention to that struggle does not obscure the fact that other major forms of education were available to middle-class women.

The first mechanics' institutes were established in the 1820s. It would appear that the aims of the institutes were both class and sex-specific, i.e. the diffusion of scientifically useful knowledge to working-class men.[48] Though there is some controversy about both the aims and the social class membership of the institutes,[49] the target audience was men, not women. Gradually, however, and often reluctantly, we begin to hear, from the 1830s onwards, of the admission of women.[50] It is highly probable that the female clientèle was largely of middle-class origins, especially in those institutes in southern England, though a much higher proportion of working-class women might be found in some of the northern institutes.[51] The entry of women into the institutes reinforced their subordinate status within the wider society since they were usually given junior membership status akin to that for youths and apprentices. At Plymouth Mechanics' Institute, for example, the membership rate in 1851 was 8s. per annum for 'Juniors' and 'Ladies' and 10s. for 'Seniors', i.e. adult males.[52] Such differential subscription rates were indeed common. In addition, men were often classified according to the achieved status of their occupation while women were always classified according to the ascribed status of their sex.[53] Though women were usually allowed to attend the lectures and use the libraries within the institutes,[54] it appears to have been common practice to exclude them from the more 'subversive' reading rooms and newsrooms. It is not until the 1860s, when various women's organizations begin to gather strength, that we hear of their admission to the newsroom at a large institute such as that at Manchester.[55] The subordinate status of women within the institutes is reflected too in the fact that they rarely enjoyed the right to vote, to participate in general decision making or hold an official position. At Thornton Mechanics' Institute, for example, as late as 1871, women were forbidden to use the refreshment rooms and to vote in the election of officers.[56]

In 1867, various associations of middle-class women invited James Stuart, a Cambridge don, to deliver a course of lectures, in Liverpool, Manchester, Sheffield and Leeds. Since a number of the women were involved with teaching and wished to improve the standard of women's education generally, they asked for lectures on the theory and methods of education. However, Stuart felt unable to talk about 'an abstract subject of that kind' and offered instead the history of astronomy. Thus the movement to offer part-time higher education to adults through university extension was initiated, and the women's movement, especially the North of England Council for Promoting the Higher Education of Women, was an important – though not the only – pressure group in bringing about such a scheme.

Middle-class women continued to be the main stalwart of the movement for the rest of the century. Sadler estimated that they formed two-thirds of the Oxford Extension classes in 1888–9,[57] and such a general pattern is confirmed by a number of accounts written by early extension lecturers. Roberts (1891) recollects that of the twenty-seven women who took an examination in connection with a course, held in Nottingham, on 'Political Economy', seven were daughters of manufacturers, two were daughters of a minister, twelve were daughters of tradesmen and six were milliners.[58] Middle-class women were particularly concentrated in the day courses where the fees could be as high as a guinea for a term of twelve weeks, but, as Roberts suggests, 'a large number of ladies' also attended evening classes.[59]

Within the women's movement, Emily Davies became concerned that part-time, university extension would become a substitute for full-time, university study: she wanted colleges for women that were fully integrated within the university structure rather than the separate, second best education that university extension might offer.[60] Her general position on such an issue is well stated in a letter she wrote dated 6 January 1869;

all separate schemes for women are objectionable . . . with Ladies' Committees, Ladies' Associations, Lectures to Ladies, and the rest, one does not quite see why we should not soon have also Ladies' Churches and Chapels, in which the duties of women as such should be specially inculcated . . . it is discouraging to see so many of the new things for women started on the basis of separation. It seems like getting more of a 'system' of separateness, and it makes one suspicious of anything like a step in that direction.[61]

This was a fundamental statement from which Miss Davies did not defer. She sought for equal educational opportunities for women within the universities and, as Stephen (1927) has noted, took a feminist rather than an educational view of the matter.[62] Thus the gender struggle against the prevailing bourgeois definition of middle-class women as domestic, 'relative' and 'inferior' beings began in earnest. A new ideal of middle-class femininity had to be fought for and established, that of the 'new woman' who could study the same subjects as men and enter paid, professional employment. The issue of whether women should follow the same or separate educational courses to men, and whether they should take the same or separate examinations, was, however, a dividing factor among those early pioneers who struggled to enter the universities, and especially the ancient universities of Cambridge and Oxford, as full-time students.

Largely due to the initiative and hard work of Miss Davies, the 'first genuine women's college'[63] was formally opened at Hitchin, Surrey, in October 1869.[64] The aim of the college was to prepare female students for the examinations of Cambridge University and in October 1873, the college moved to a site much closer to the university, at Girton. The scheme was experimental in that female students were to enter a domain of learning that had been preserved for men within the monastic, collegiate, university structure. But even though the women's college was outside, rather than integrated into, this structure, it was essential for the success of the scheme that the behaviour of the students should be above criticism. Miss Davies insisted therefore on ladylike behaviour and especially chaperonage.[65] This was essential in order to win the support of two groups necessary for the success of the venture – male, university scholars who would be willing to teach and examine the female students, and middle-class parents who were willing to pay the fees for the education of their daughters.[66] Yet despite the insistence upon ladylike manners, these students were advised to study such 'unfeminine' subjects as maths and classics, subjects that were part of the traditional male university curriculum.[67] As Delamont (1978) has argued, the students were caught in a snare of double conformity – conformity to certain rituals of behaviour and to the dominant, male, cultural system.[68] The social cost of Miss Davies' insistence on 'the same' educational opportunities for male and female students was, however, social isolation. Thus Louisa Lumsden, a tutor at Girton for 'two lonely and difficult years'[69] in the early 1870s, recollects that the differences of opinion held by Miss Davies and those of the creators of another Cambridge women's college – Newnham – separated her and Miss Davies from the social life of Cambridge.

Newnham was the outcome of principles different to those of Miss Davies since the antecedents to its foundation were largely based on the theme of 'separate and different' education for women. In the late 1860s, the North of England Council, of which Miss Clough was secretary, were of the view that identical examinations for women and men were not desirable and thus a memorial was sent to Cambridge University asking for an examination for women over 18 years of age: the request was granted and in 1869, thirty-six candidates sat the examination.[70] In 1870, mainly through the efforts of Henry Sedgwick, a Cambridge don, special lectures for women were established in order to prepare them for the Women's Examination.[71] The students needed a place of residence and in 1871, Miss Clough was asked to take charge of a house at 74 Regent Street[72] (Newnham Hall was not erected until 1876). From its very beginnings, therefore, Newnham was totally different in orientation to Girton. Whereas the latter wished to prove that women were capable of the 'same intellectual work as men', the former considered such a view 'undesirable' in the 'interest of the individual students' who were intellectually ill-prepared for such a hurdle.[73]

Such a compromising attitude towards women's education at Newnham, an attitude which did not fully challenge the dominant ideal of middle-class femininity but still upheld the notion of separate examinations for women, typically 'feminine' subjects such as history, English language and literature[74] and links with the typically 'feminine' occupation of school teaching[75] met with less fierce resistance than the Girton principles. The dominant middle-class ideal of femininity is evident too in the philanthropy that Miss Clough encouraged amongst her students. A 'noble enthusiasm' for social service flourished at Newnham and found concrete expression in ventures such as teaching working men.[76] Even so, Newnham students like their Girton sisters were encouraged to conform to ladylike behaviour, especially in the early days when Miss Clough was nervous lest any eccentricity in dress or conduct should attract attention.[77] Though many students resented such interference,[78] the 'new woman' in higher education often conceded to such restrictions. It was only gradually, during the next few decades, that such restrictions were slowly eroded.

Women's colleges were to be established too at Oxford University, though once again, not without a struggle.[79] In 1881, women students at Cambridge were formally admitted to degree examinations, though they could still not be awarded a degree: similar conditions prevailed at Oxford where examinations were gradually opened to women from 1884.[80] The first university to admit women to degree examinations on equal terms with men was London University, in 1878. During the next two decades, a number of other universities also allowed women to be awarded degrees, e.g. Victoria University in 1880, the Scottish universities in 1892 and the University of Durham in 1895.[81] But the ancient universities of Cambridge and Oxford refused to yield. Thus, as Holcombe (1973) notes, despite repeated attempts by the feminists, the struggle for women to be awarded degrees at Oxford and Cambridge did not end until 1919 and 1947 respectively.[82]

The experience of higher education for women facilitated their entry into certain forms of waged labour, and paid work became a legitimate area of activity for middle- and upper-class women, a goal to be aimed for, if desired. The entry of women into higher education had, therefore, profound implications for their subsequent social placement within the economic structure. By the beginning of the twentieth century, we find a new, female educated élite who were concentrated in certain kinds of employment. Among the students who took the Hygiene Course at Bedford College, for example, was Miss Maud Hartland, who became, in 1913, one of the first women Inspectors under the National Insurance Act and Miss Hilda Martindale who became Deputy Chief Inspector of Factories in 1921 and then Director of Women's Establishment, HM Treasury, from 1933–7.[83] But this new female élite was especially concentrated in teaching posts in the expanding, fee-paying, middle-class girls' schools established by the Girls' Public Day School Trust.[84] Thus ex-Newnham students such as Edith Creak and Miss F. R. Gray became headmistresses – the former at a GPDST school in Brighton and the latter at St Paul's Girls' School.[85] The presence of such well-educated teachers within the GPDST schools helped, of course, to increase the pool of recruits for the women's colleges and thus a cyclical relationship was established between the two kinds of educational institutions. Generally, college educated women avoided teaching in the state financed, elementary sector that catered almost exclusively for working-class children: there was in fact much debate about whether it was 'genteel' for middle-class women to enter elementary school teaching.[86] Some of the women students eventually became college or university lecturers themselves. Miss Welsh, a Girton student, became a mistress at that college from 1885–1904,[87] while Margaret Murray, a student, in the 1890s, of Egyptology at University College, London, became a member of the academic staff there.[88] However, the number of college educated women entering occupations in industry and business was very small.[89]

Education for women of the working classes

Before the advent of the 1870 Education Act which made full-time elementary education for working-class children a possibility, working-class girls might experience co-education in a variety of forms e.g. dame schools, charity schools, day schools of the British and Foreign School Society (largely supported by religious dissenters) and of the National Society for Promoting the Education of the Poor in the Principles of the Established Church, Sunday schools and industrial schools. In contrast to the accomplishments curriculum for middle-class girls, with its emphasis upon social priorities, working-class girls were offered a basic curriculum that might comprise reading, writing and practical, utilitarian skills such as plain sewing and knitting. Such subjects might teach working-class girls not only literacy but also certain skills, such as mending or the making of clothes, which could be used in both the domestic situation and in various forms of waged labour, especially domestic service and dressmaking.[90] Though the quality of education obviously varied greatly, it is highly probable that the overall standard was very low. For example, Mary Smith (1892) the daughter of a shoemaker, attended a succession of schools and recollects that when she was about 7-years-old, she was sent to another dame school where the knowledge of the dame was: 'very small. The girls had a lesson once a day in the New Testament, and the little ones read out of the "Reading Made Easy". But knitting and sewing occupied nearly the whole time of the girls'.[91]

It is not surprising to find, therefore, that for most of the century, the literacy rate of women, especially working-class women, was lower than that for men.[92] In the eyes of the bourgeoisie, therefore, the femininity of working-class girls and women lacked that 'finesse' that was expected amongst middle-class females: in particular, the experience of waged labour, both before and after marriage, cast a blemish on their femininity. Working-class females were defined by the bourgeoisie as ignorant and incapable of learning anything but the most basic knowledge. In addition, the bourgeoisie upheld the domestic ideology as particularly important for such women since it was believed that their inadequacies as wives and mothers accounted for many of the social problems associated with the working classes. Since most of the formalized educational provision was organized by the middle classes, the ideal of the 'good woman' necessarily involved therefore, an emphasis upon the 3 Rs (reading, writing and arithmetic) and practical domestic skills. These are indeed common themes, as we shall now see, in the rhetoric that justifies the forms and content of adult education for working-class women in nineteenth-century Britain.

In the early nineteenth century, adult Sunday schools for working-class men and women began to flourish. The movement developed particularly from the Bristol area where from February 1812 to March 1813, nine schools for men and nine schools for women were established.[93] Middle-class, male Quakers, such as Stephen Prust – 'a very respectable merchant' and 'a member of the Auxiliary Bible Society's Committee' – were influential in shaping the provision.

As I have argued elsewhere,[94] though the manifest function of adult Sunday schools was teaching people to read the Bible, the latent functions may have related to class cultural control. In middle-class eyes, the working classes were culturally deficient: one way to improve them was to use adult education as an agency for socialization into a different group of values. For working-class females, the ideal of the 'good woman' involved the hope that they should become 'better wives'.[95] But in addition to such an attempt to change their way of life, working-class women also had frequently to face a gender struggle within their own immediate family. Thus a woman who had diligently attended one of the Bath Adult Schools was, on that account:

roughly treated by her husband, who had been a seafaring man, and much addicted to drunkenness and swearing; this obdurate man threatened his wife, that if she continued to go to the school or to meeting, he would break her bones.[96]

Though not all working-class women experienced such opposition to their attempts to gain access to education, we do find, as we shall see, many recorded instances of such a gender struggle.

The adult schools declined in importance as alternative forms of adult education offering subjects other than basic literacy began to develop. One such alternative form were the mechanics' institutes. But as we have already seen, the aims of the institutes were both class and sex-specific. Since the institutes generally failed to attract the mass of unskilled, male workers[97] it is hardly surprising to find that they failed to attract large numbers of working-class women too.[98] Working-class women were most likely to be found in the smaller, northern mixed-sex institutes and in the two large single-sex institutes at Huddersfield and Bradford. At the small, mixed-sex institute at Northowram, for example, the membership in 1861 was seventy-nine males and forty-two females:[99] weekly subscriptions are usually a reliable indication of working-class background and at this institute, the number of males paying 2d. and the number of females paying 1½d. weekly was twenty-nine and thirty-four respectively. Within the mixed-sex institutes that particularly attracted working-class scholars, we tend to find that education was organized along principles similar to those forms of education attended by the bourgeoisie, i.e. segregation on the basis of sex. Thus in regard to the instruction provided within the classes, we tend to find a female section and a male section, based on the separation between the domestic sphere and waged labour. Thus at Gomersal Mechanics' Institute, in Yorkshire, the committee regret, in their annual report for 1859, that the female class which meets on Tuesday and Thursday evenings has not succeeded to the extent:

commensurate with the necessity and importance which the proper education and improvement of the minds of the 'gentler sex' demands for qualifying them, in some respects, for more efficiently discharging the important duty incumbent upon all who have the training of the rising generation.[100]

But while adult education for working-class women within the institutes is justified in relation to domesticity, the education for working-class men is justified in terms of its vocational value. For example, the new class in mechanical and freehand drawing introduced at Northowram Mechanics' Institute in 1857 is justified as being 'useful' and 'serviceable' to the young male members such as 'joiners, masons, mechanics, and designers' in their respective trades.[101] The emphasis upon the domestic sphere for working-class women is continually reiterated in the rhetoric that justifies their presence within the institutes, and the implications of this rhetoric for the kinds of curricula that working-class women might be offered relate to the ideal of the 'good woman'. Thus an educational diet of the 3 Rs and selected, practical skills such as sewing is all that is considered necessary since such a curriculum might improve the quality of domestic work, the standard of family life and solve generally the social problems associated with the working classes.

Working-class male supporters of the mechanics' institutes movement frequently upheld the rhetoric of the domestic ideology too. For example, Rowland Detrosier, the working-class radical, when addressing fellow institute members in 1829, asks them whether it was not essential to 'the comfort of man' that young women of the working classes should be taught 'the duties of housewifery'.[102] And bourgeois female supporters, such as Fanny Hertz, who was on the committee of the Bradford Female Education Institute, though complaining that the education of women within the institutes should not be considered from the viewpoint of the duties of wives, mothers, mistresses and servants, nevertheless argued that the education of female factory operatives within the institutes would help them to become a 'suitable and worthy helpmates for the educated and intelligent working men, who are the glory of England'.[103]

Working-class women were thus bombarded on all sides with the basic assumptions of the domestic ideology – reaffirming their 'relative', 'subordinate' and 'inferior' status. Within this bombardment, bourgeois women participated in the imposition of class ideology upon their sisters in the lower social orders as well as bourgeois men. But, as the above quotation from Detroisier illustrates, the struggle of working-class women to obtain an education within the institutes may be interpreted as not only a class struggle but also a gender struggle within their own social grouping. As Elizabeth Wilson (1977) has commented, the reactionary attitude to women adopted by many male, working-class radicals has been one of the saddest and most persistent themes in the history of socialism.[104]

Another major attempt by the middle classes to educate their social inferiors was through the working-men's college movement. A number of influential middle-class men, such as the Rev. F. D. Maurice, a prominent Christian socialist, felt that the mechanics' institutes had failed to attract a large number of the working class and that democratic control within the institutes had been frustrated by middle-class control amongst the boards of directors.[105] In particular, Maurice felt that the curriculum of the institutes had aimed at popularity and did nothing more than 'graze the surface of men's minds than penetrate into them'.[106] The aim of the colleges was to provide, therefore, an 'enrichment of personal life'.[107] However, as the name implies, the working men's colleges were, in their original conceptions, both class and sex specific. The first college, the People's College, Sheffield, established by the Rev. R. S. Bayley in 1842, did in fact admit women, but it was regarded by even the most 'ardent' supporters of popular education as a great 'novelty'.[108] Maurice, who had held several meetings with other interested parties drew up, in 1854, an outline for a London 'College for Working Men' and point 3 of this plan illustrates how marginal women were to the whole enterprise:

3 It was agreed that adult males (that is to say, at all events, not younger than 16) should be contemplated first and chiefly in our education; though it was thought desirable that provision should in due time be made for the teaching of boys and of females.[109]

Once again it would appear that working-class women would have to struggle to survive within such male-oriented colleges.

Maurice, in the 1854 plan, upheld the principle of sex segregation for certain classes, especially the more abstract and controversial subjects such as ethics and politics while the low status, recreational subjects such as languages, drawing and music might be shared: he also stated that women ought to have lessons in 'social life and order' and 'health' since the 'domestic life' was their prime location.[110] Once again, a differential curriculum for working-class women was justified in terms of their domesticity. As Sadler was to comment in 1907, the co-educational plan that had been adopted at the Sheffield People's College did not commend itself to Maurice.[111] The question of the admission of women was in fact an important dividing issue between the opinions of Maurice and another bourgeois supporter of the new college – the philologist Frederick James Furnivall, son of a physician.[112] The issue of whether women should be educated in separate or co-educational classes had profound social implications. Once women were offered separate rather than integrated education with men, there was always the risk that women's education would develop into an inferior, second best system outside and distinct from the dominant, male, cultural world: a double educational standard could then be more easily created and maintained. If, on the other hand, women at least shared the same educational facilities – if not the same curricula – as men, then there was always a chance that sex segregation and sex-based inequalities could break down. The London Working Men's College, founded in 1854, and the dozen or so other Colleges established between 1855 and 1868, illustrate only too well some of the problems associated with this issue.

In 1865, the Working Women's College was founded in Queen Square, Bloomsbury with the intention of being a counterpart to the London Working Men's College. Arthur J. Munby, the poet and barrister, who was actively involved in the initial discussions about the college, notes that they hoped to attract 'teachers, shopgirls, and even servant maids' as members and pupils: the college was largely successful in this aim since by 1866 the majority of the students were milliners, shopgirls or young women living at home.[113] However, the issue of co-educational classes eventually divided the College in two. The Working Women's College became 'The College for Men and Women' and remained at the original site while a new institution, 'The College for Working Women' established itself in Fitzroy Street in 1874.[114] The curriculum at the new college included not only the 3 Rs but also bookkeeping, drawing, French, German, geography, English history, English literature, physics, hygiene and singing[115] – as well as 'cheap cookery' classes.[116] But even though the range of subjects was much wider than that previously offered by many middle-class individuals, it did not embrace a number of subjects taught at the London Working Men's College, e.g. public health, algebra, geometry, natural philosophy, astronomy, machinery, and law.[117] As these examples illustrate, by the 1870s, the wider stratification of knowledge had a well-established sexual base.

Throughout the century, a number of other attempts were made by the middle classes to educate working-class women through various forms of part-time evening schools. For example, some middle-class 'ladies' opened an evening school for working-class women in Birmingham, in September 1847: they offered instruction in reading, writing, arithmetic, sewing and Biblical knowledge and hoped eventually to teach also subjects such as cookery and vocal music. The scholars, most of whom were married, are described as 'Poor things' who are ignorant of 'household business'.[118] It is particularly in the advocacy of arithmetic, sewing and cookery that we can see the way such middle-class women tried to impose the domestic ideology and the ideal of the 'good woman' upon their working-class sisters:

They (the scholars) have a good deal of reckoning to do every day – most of them. . . . They do learn arithmetic to some purpose: and they learn something else by means of it: – nothing less than that it answers better to some of them to stay at home and keep house, than to earn wages in the manufactory. . . . With great satisfaction, a wife . . . now finds herself able to check . . . mistakes. When, added to this, she has become a reasonable thinker and planner, can understand her business – can make and mend, and buy and economise, and suit her ways to her means; she may easily find that it answers better, as regards mere money, to stay at home, than to work at the factory. The great truth will be more evident still when the kitchen is opened, and the world of economy and comfort belonging to that department is revealed to minds at present wholly dark in regard to it. The young women think they can cook, as before they thought they could reckon and could sew. They will soon see.[119]

It is difficult to estimate how many such evening schools, organized privately by the middle classes, were established: at the above school in Birmingham, for example, the scholars had to pay thirteen pence plus an extra penny for the copybook in which they practised their exercises.[120] The 1851 Census tells us that the vast majority of evening schools taught only the 3 Rs and that of the 1545 schools from which information was obtained, more than half the total number of scholars are male – thus 27,829 male but only 11,954 female scholars are recorded.[121] As the state began to increase the extent of grant aid for evening schools, the number of scholars expanded. By 1902–3, 657,594 scholars are recorded of whom 403,629 are male and 253,965 are female.[122] Working-class women were increasingly drawn into such state financed classes where they were concentrated particularly in 'Division V' type subjects – 'Home Occupation and Industries'. Under this broad heading came subjects such as needlework, dressmaking, domestic tailoring, millinery, embroidery, lace making, domestic economy and cookery.[123] The link between femininity and domesticity became further institutionalized. But before state aided evening classes expanded in the latter decades of the nineteenth century, a new challenge to the dominant middle-class ideal of the 'good woman' came from among working-class women themselves, through the organizational structure of the Women's Co-operative Guild.

Particularly in the early years of the Guild, educational activities revolved around domestic subjects. For example, the annual report for 1889 notes that five branches had lecture courses on dressmaking and two had lecture courses on sick nursing, though classes were also held in basic skills such as reading the writing; single lectures during the year covered topics such as 'Political Economy', 'Money', 'The Air we Breathe', 'The Industrial Revolution' as well as the more predictable 'Domestic Economy', 'Food', 'Clear-starching' and 'Ironing'.[124] It would appear that working-class women were still primarily defined as domestic beings. However, when Margaret Llewelyn Davies became Secretary of the Guild, from 1889–1921, a clear change of direction in guild policy becomes evident.

Miss Davies was one of that élite of educated women who had attended both Queen's College, London and Girton College, Cambridge.[125] For Miss Davies, the chief aim of the Guild was to educate women and to give them 'a wider life',[126] i.e. to extend interest from outside the sphere of the home to broader social and political issues. Under her guidance, and presumably with the support of the majority of Guildswomen who were organized in democratic, self-governing branches, a new ideal of working-class femininity was upheld – that of woman as 'homemaker and peaceful reformer'. Miss Davies hoped that the democratic structure of the Guild, whereby all who joined enjoyed equal voting rights, would ensure against middle-class domination.[127] It does appear that at long last, working-class women were in an organizational structure where they had the power to decide, through the vote, on various policy matters, including the content of their own education. The ideal of the 'homemaker and peaceful reformer' reflected both the reality of their own lives, as full-time wives and mothers, and also an increasing self and social awareness. The double edge of 'homemaker' and 'reformer' is well reflected in the curricular provision of the 1890s. Thus for the year 1893–4, ninety-three Guild branches held classes in domestic subjects while discussions included the topics of free education, old age pensions, sick benefit societies and socialism.[128] With the home as the base, many Guildswomen began to engage in activities as diverse as pensions for widows, divorce law reform, the ending of half-time education for children, trade unionism for women and the campaign for women's suffrage.[129] Other Guildswomen prepared and read papers at conferences. At the Autumn Conference of 1907, for example, Mrs Gasson read a paper on 'Wives' Savings' in which she argued that a wife should have a legal claim to a part of the family income.[130] Through the solidarity of a single-sex organization, working-class women were 'finding a voice'.[131] The consciousness raising that Guild activities developed is evident in accounts such as that of Mrs Scott, a felt hat worker, who notes that the Guild taught working-class women to become articulate and ask for the things they needed.[132]

By the end of the century then, the education of working-class women was such that their social placement within the economic structure would reflect their low level of educational attainment. Though a variety of forms of education had been offered to working-class women throughout the century, the content of their education tended to reflect the same basic curriculum of the 3 Rs, some limited general knowledge and certain domestic skills such as sewing and cookery. The standard of education of working-class women was directly related to the standard of education they received as girls: as late as 1899, MacNamara could still claim that as the present law stood, a child might leave school at 11-years-old to work 'half time' in a factory or workshop or 'full time' outside a factory, workshop or mine, provided a certain educational standard had been attained.[133] As Sterns (1972) has noted, at the turn of the century, most working-class women still lived in a 'culture of poverty'[134] – a poverty that is reflected in their poor material conditions and in their standard of education. For working-class women, therefore, the part-time education offered through state aided evening classes or Guild meetings could be an invaluable means of retaining and improving that basic education already received. Even so, for most working-class women, marriage was still the ideal end state and before marriage most engaged in forms of waged labour that were shunned by their middle-class sisters – domestic service and various kinds of factory work such as manufacturing, food processing, clothing.[135] Generally their lives were lives of toil in which not only the demands of waged labour had to be met but also the demands considered appropriate for their sex – the demands of home and family responsibilities.

Conclusion

In conclusion I would like to make four main points. First, I have tried to illustrate how the domestic ideology, which located women within the home as full-time wives and mothers, helped to shape both the forms and content of education for nineteenth-century women. The domestic ideology which defined women as relative, inferior and subordinate beings whose femininity was linked with domesticity, became a part of the dominant, male, bourgeois culture but it was also increasingly taken up by working-class men, especially in the second half of the century. However, since the bourgeoisie were the main providers of formalized education their class-specific ideals of femininity – that of the middle-class 'perfect wife and mother' and that of the working-class 'good woman' – tended to be the dominant ideals which provided part of the context within which educational institutions were founded and reformed. Second, both middle-class and working-class women used education as a form of struggle against male, bourgeois definitions of women. For middle-class women the struggle was essentially a feminist struggle which particularly gathered force when they attempted to enter the most prestigious, male, bourgeois institutions – the universities. Their attempt to establish the ideal of the 'new woman' who could enjoy equal opportunities in higher education and engage in various forms of professional work was an attempt, therefore, to break free from the bonds of domesticity and to create a definition of woman as a careerist, someone who could be dedicated to her work, professionally trained, financially independent and therefore not in need of the economic support that a husband might provide. However, for working-class women, for much of the century, the struggle was both a class and feminist struggle that was contained within low status educational institutions. Their attempt to establish the ideal of the 'homemaker and peaceful reformer' never broke with the bond of domesticity – though such a bond was redefined, it was also re-affirmed. Third, by the 1900s, the educational changes that had occurred during the course of the nineteenth century served only to reinforce and polarize the differences between middle-class and working-class women.

Notes and references

1 Hall, C., 'The early formation of Victorian domestic ideology', in Burman. S. (ed.), *Fit Work for Women*, Croom Helm, 1979, pp. 18–19.

2 Walker, A., *Woman Physiologically Considered as to Mind, Morals, Marriage, Matrimonial Slavery, Infidelity and Divorce* (2nd edn), London, A. H. Bailey, 1840, pp. 43 and 47.

3 Walker, A., *Woman Physiologically Considered*, p. 149.

4 Such a questioning did not necessarily mean that marriage and the family were regarded as unnecessary for women. See Bryant, M., *The Unexpected Revolution: a study in the education of Women and Girls in the Nineteenth Century*, University of London Institute of Education (1979), pp. 118–19, where she argues that the family could provide a secure economic and emotional centre, a supportive rather than restrictive base from which women could articulate new demands.

5 Ellis, Mrs, *Education of the Heart: Woman's Best Work*, London, Hodder and Stoughton, 1869, p. 3.

6 Walker, A., *Woman Physiologically Considered*, p. 13.

7 Walker, A., *Woman Physiologically Considered*, p. 129.

8 'The probable retrogression of women'. *The Saturday Review*, 11 July 1871, pp. 10–11. For a general discussion of the biological arguments regarding brain size and the intellect of women see Burstyn, J., 'Brain and intellect: science applied to a social issue 1860–1875', *Actes du XII Congress International d' Historie des Sciences, 1971*, pp. 13–16 and Burstyn. J. *Victorian Education and the Ideal of Womanhood*, London, Croom Helm, 1980, chapter 4.

9 Burgon, J. W., *To Educate Young Women like Young Men, and with Young Men – a Thing Inexpedient and Immodest*, London, Parker & Co., 1884, p. 15. For a general discussion of the religious arguments advanced to oppose higher education for women see Burstyn, J., 'Religious arguments against higher education for women in England, 1840–1890' *Women's Studies*, **1**, no. 1, 1972, pp. 111–31, and *Victorian Education*, chapter 6.

10 See the useful discussion offered in chapter 5 of J. A. and O. Banks, *Feminism and Family Planning in Victorian England*, Liverpool University Press, 1964.

11 Banks, J. A. and Banks, O., *Feminism and Family Planning*, p. 58.

12 Cobbe, F. P., 'The final cause of woman' in Butler, J. (ed.), *Woman's Work and Woman's Culture*, London, Macmillan and Co, 1869, p. 10.

13 Dyhouse. C., 'The role of women: from self-sacrifice to self-awareness', in Lerner, L. (ed.), *The Victorians*, London Methuen, 1978, p. 175.

14 Ellis, Mrs, *Education of the Heart*, p. 14.

15 See Davidoff, L., *The Best Circles: Society, Etiquette and the Season* (2nd edn), London, The Cresset Library, especially chapter 3, 1986.

16 Davidoff, L., *The Best Circles*, p. 50.

17 Austin, Mrs, *Two Letters on Girl's Schools, and on the Training of Working Women*, London, Chapman & Hall, 1857, p. 11.

18 Booth, J., *On the Female Education of the Industrial Classes*, 1855, London, Bell and Daldy, pp. 12–15.

19 Ingestre, Lord Viscount, *Social Evils: their Causes and Their Cure*, London, William Parker, 1853, p. 12; Greg, W. R., 'Why are women redundant?', in Greg, W. R., *Literary and Social Judgements*, London, N. Truber & Co., 1868, p. 373, and Austin, Mrs, *Two Letters*, 1857, p. 34.

20 Davin, A., ' "Mind that you do as you are told": reading books for Board School Girls', *Feminist Review*, **3**, 1979, p. 90.

21 Basch. F., *Relative Creatures: Victorian Women in Society and the Novel 1837–67*, London, Allen Lane, 1974, p. 50.

22 See, for example, Maudsley, H., 'Sex in mind and in education', *Fortnightly Review*, 1874, pp. 166–83.

23 Stephen, B., *Emily Davies and Girton College*, London, Constable & Co., 1927, p. 13.

24 Vicinus, M., 'Introduction: the perfect Victorian lady', in Vicinus, M. (ed.) *Suffer and Be Still: Women in the Victorian Age*, Indiana University Press, 1972, p. ix.

25 Perhaps the best known history is Strachey. R., *The Cause: a Short History of the Women's Movement in Great Britain*, London, G. Bell, 1928. For an account of the part that working-class women played in the suffrage movement see Liddington, J. and Norris, J., *One Hand Tied Behind Us: the Rise of the Women's Suffrage Movement*, London, Virago 1978.

26 See, for example, Williams, R., *The Long Revolution*, London, Pelican Books, 1965, chapter 3.

27 Alexander, S., 'Women's work in nineteenth-century London: a study of the years 1820–50', in Mitchell, J. and Oakley, A. (eds), *The Rights and Wrongs of Women*, Harmondsworth, Penguin Books, 1976, pp. 59–111 provides a recent account of some aspects of this issue. See also Pinchbeck, I., *Women Workers and the Industrial Revolution 1750–1850*, London, George Routledge & Sons, 1930, and Margaret Hewitt, *Wives and Mothers in Victorian Industry*, Rockliff, 1958.

28 Gray, M. H., 'Men and women', *The Fortnightly Review*, **26**, New Series, 1 July to 1 December 1879, p. 681.

29 Bryant, M., *The Unexpected Revolution*, pp. 30–2.

30 Davies, E., *On Secondary Education as Relating to Girls*, London, William Ridgway, 1864, p. 4.

31 Stephen, B., *Emily Davies*, p. 21.

32 Marshall, M. P., *What I Remember*, at the Cambridge University Press, 1947, p. 7.

33 *Reports from Commissioners: Schools Inquiry Vol. 1*, Session 19 November 1867–31 July 1868 p. 546.

34 *Reports from Commissioners*, pp. 548–9.

35 Kelly, T., *A History of Adult Education in Great Britain*, Liverpool University Press, 1962, p. 228.

36 Muir, Professor J., *John Anderson: Pioneer of Technical Education and The College he Founded*, edited by Macaulay, J. M., Glasgow, John Smith & Son, 1950, p. 147.

37 Muir, Professor J., *John Anderson*, p. 147.

38 Muir, Professor J., *John Anderson*, p. 148.

39 Kamm, J., *Hope Deferred: Girls' Education in English History*, London Methuen, 1965, p. 175.

40 Percival, A. C., *The English Miss To-Day and Yesterday*, George Harrap, 1939, p. 124.

41 See, for example, Kamm, J., *Hope Deferred*, p. 173.

42 Burstyn, J., *Higher Education for Women: the Opposition in England during the Nineteenth Century*, PhD thesis, May 1968, University of London, p. 25.

43 Davies, E., *Women in the Universities of England and Scotland*, Cambridge, Macmillan and Bowes, 1896, p. 4.

44 Stanley, Lady H. M., of Alderley, 'Personal recollections of women's education', *The Nineteenth Century*, August 1879, p. 309.

45 Percival, A. C., *The English Miss*, p. 126.

46 Quoted in Tuke, M. J., *A History of Bedford College for Women*, Oxford University Press, 1939, p. 21.

47 Kamm, J., *Hope Deferred*, p. 176 makes the point, however, that unlike Bedford, Queen's College was not destined for university status.

48 Purvis, J., 'Working-class women and adult education in nineteenth century Britain', *History of Education*, **9**, no. 3, 1980, p. 198.

49 Inkster, I., 'The social context of an educational movement: a revisionist approach

to the English mechanics' institutes, 1820–1850', *Oxford Review of Education*, **2**, no. 3, 1976, p. 280 suggests that the origins, motivations, provisions and social class membership of the institutes were marked by variety rather than uniformity.

50 For example, at the London Mechanics' Institution, a decision was made in 1830 to admit female relations and friends of members to the lectures and circulating library on the same terms as sons and apprentices – Kelly, T., *George Birkbeck: Pioneer of Adult Education*, Liverpool University Press, 1957, p. 126.

51 Purvis, J., 'Working-class women and adult education', p. 200.

52 *Census, 1851: Education Section: List of Literary and Scientific Institutions from which Returns were Procured at the Census of 1851*, p. 457.

53 Most of the women are listed as 'Ladies' in the various reports of the institutes.

54 See note 50 above.

55 Manchester Mechanics' Institution, *Annual Report*, 1862, p. 13.

56 Dyer, J., 'Nineteenth century community centres Part 1 Thornton Mechanics' Institute', *Adult Education*, **21**, p. 19.

57 Quoted in Jepson, N. A., *The Beginnings of English University Adult Education: Policy and Problems*, London, Michael Joseph, 1973, pp. 44–5, p. 104.

58 Roberts, R. D., *Eighteen Years of University Extension*, Cambridge, The University Press, 1891, p. 14.

59 Roberts, R. D., *Eighteen Years*, p. 13.

60 Jepson, N., *The Beginnings*, p. 41.

61 Stephen, B., *Emily Davies*, p. 195.

62 Stephen, B., *Emily Davies*, p. 194.

63 Kamm, J., *Hope Deferred*, p. 174.

64 Stephen, B., *Emily Davies*, p. 218.

65 Burstall, S., *Retrospect and Prospect*, London, Longmans, 1933, p. 86 recollects that the social rules for women students were very strict in her student days at Girton (1878–81). Women students could be chaperoned to men's college parties only by some lady known at home, independently of Cambridge.

66 Pascoe, C. E., *Schools for Girls and Colleges for Women: a Handbook of Female Education*, London, Hardwick & Bogue, 1879, p. 144 notes that the charge for board, lodging and instruction at Girton was £35 per term, paid in advance.

67 Stephen, B., *Emily Davies*, p. 232. Miss Davies allowed no extra time for the ignorance of her students but 'scorned' all compromises and insisted that if men prepared for the Tripos in three years and one term, then female students must conform to the same rule (p. 231).

68 Delamont, S., 'The contradictions in ladies' education' in Delamont, S. and Duffin, L. (eds), *The Nineteenth Century Woman: Her Cultural and Physical World*, London, Croom Helm, 1978, p. 160.

69 Lumsden, L., *Yellow Leaves: Memories of a Long Life*, London, William Blackwood, 1933, p. 58.

70 Clough, B. A., *A Memoir of Anne Jemima Clough*, London, Edward Arnold, 1897, pp. 129–30.

71 Clough, B. A., *A Memoir*, p. 130.

72 Clough, B. A., *A Memoir*, p. 197.

73 Clough, B. A., *A Memoir*, p. 175.

74 Clough, B. A., *A Memoir*, p. 169 notes that Miss Clough encouraged the students to begin with familiar subjects, such as arithmetic, history, English language and literature, and then to study whatever was of most interest.

75 Clough, B. A., *A Memoir*, p. 177.

76 Glendinning, V., *A Suppressed Cry*, London, Routledge & Kegan Paul, 1929, p. 52.

77 Clough, B. A., *A Memoir*, p. 232.

78 Clough, B. A., *A Memoir*, p. 196 – most of the students 'were old enough to have already tasted some amount of liberty'.

79 See, for example, Rogers, A., *Degrees by Degrees*, Oxford, OUP 1938; and Brittain, V., *The Women at Oxford*, George Harrap, 1960.

80 Sedgwick, Mrs H., 'The higher education of women', in Roberts, R. D. (ed.), *Education in the Nineteenth Century*, Cambridge, CUP, 1901, p. 203.

81 Sedgwick, Mrs H., 'The higher education of women', p. 203.

82 Holcombe, L., *Victorian Ladies at Work: Middle-Class Working Women in England and Wales 1850–1914*, Newton Abbot David & Charles, 1973, p. 49.

83 Tuke, M., *A History of Bedford College for Women*, pp. 159–60.

84 The Girls' Public Day School Company was founded in 1872 with the aim of providing, at a moderate cost, sound, secondary education for middle-class girls. See Kamm, J., *Indicative Past, a Hundred Years of the Girls Public Day School Trust*, London, Allen and Unwin, 1971, for a detailed account.

85 Hamilton, M. A., *Newnham: an Informal Biography*, London, Faber & Faber, 1936, p. 114.

86 Purvis, J., 'Women and Teaching in the nineteenth century' in Dale, R., Esland, G., Fergusson, R. and MacDonald, M. (eds), *Education and the State*, vol. 2, *Politics, Patriarchy and Practice*, Falmer Press 1981, p. 371. For a recent study that explores this issue see Widdowson, F., *Going Up Into The Next Class: Women and Elementary Teacher Training, 1840–1914* (2nd edn), London, Hutchinson, 1983.

87 Stephen, B., *Emily Davies*, p. 314.

88 Murray, M., *My First Hundred Years*, William Kimber, 1963, pp. 93–6.

89 Sanderson, M., *The Universities and British Industry 1850–1970*, London, Routledge & Kegan Paul, 1972, pp. 328–9.

90 For further discussion of this issue see Purvis, J. 'The double burden of class and gender in the schooling of working-class girls in nineteenth century England, 1800–1870', in Barton, L. and Walker. S. (eds), *Schools, Teachers and Teaching*, Falmer Press, 1981.

91 Smith, M., *The Autobiography of Mary Smith, Schoolmistress and Nonconformist, a Fragment of a Life*, Bemrose & Sons, 1892, pp. 24–5.

92 The issues of defining and measuring literacy in the nineteenth century are, of course, highly problematic.

93 Hudson, J. W., *The History of Adult Education*, London, Longman, 1851, pp. 3–5.

94 Purvis, J., 'Working-class women and adult education', p. 198.

95 Pole, T., *A History of the Origins and Progress of Adult Schools* (2nd edn), Bristol, C. McDowall, 1816 p. 19.

96 Pole, T., *A History of the Origins*, p. 29.

97 Kelly, T., *A History*, p. 128.

98 Telecote, M., *The Mechanics' Institutes of Lancashire and Yorkshire Before 1851* Manchester, Manchester University Press, 1957, p. 265, suggests that this was even so in those institutes in Lancashire and Cheshire.

99 *Report of the Yorkshire Union of Mechanics' Institutes held in Scarborough, 22nd May, 1861*, 1861, p. 103.

100 *Report of the Yorkshire Union of Mechanics' Institutes held in Rotherham, 15 June, 1859*, p. 79.

101 *Report of the Yorkshire Union of Mechanics' Institutes held in Huddersfield, 29th July, 1857*, p. 102.

102 Detrosier, R., *An Address* delivered at the New Mechanic's Institution, Pool Street, Manchester, on Wednesday evening 30 December 1829, T. Forest, Manchester, (n.d), p. 12.

103 Hertz, F., 'Mechanics' institutes for working women, with special reference to the manufacturing districts of Yorkshire', *Transactions of the National Association for the Promotion of Social Science 1859*, p. 354.

104 Wilson, E., *Women and the Welfare State*, London, Tavistock Publications, 1977, p. 26.

105 Harrison, J. F. C., *A History of the Working Men's College 1854–1954*, London, Routledge & Kegan Paul, 1954, p. xvi.

106 Harrison, J. F. C., *A History*, p. xvii.

107 Harrison, J. F. C., *A History*, p. 26.

108 Rowbotham, T., 'Account of the origin and progress of the People's College at Sheffield', *The Working Men's College Magazine 1859*, no. 1, p. 71.

109 Furnivall, F. J., 'History of the London Working Men's College', *The Working Men's College Magazine 1860*, p. 146.

110 Furnivall, F. J., 'History of the London Working Men's College', pp. 147–8.

111 Sadler, M. E. (ed.), *Continuation Schools in England and Elsewhere* (2nd edn) Manchester, Manchester University Press, 1908, p. 41.

112 Harrison, J. F. C., *A History*, p. 39.

113 Munby, A. J., *Man of Two Worlds*, London, John Murray, 1972, pp. 177, 215.

114 Harrison, J. F. C., *A History*, p. 109.

115 Martin, F., 'A college for working women', *Macmillans Magazine*, 1879, p. 487.

116 Harris, R. M., 'Frances Martin College', *Further Education*, **1**, 1947–8, p. 225.

117 Sadler, M. E. (ed.), *Continuation Schools*, p. 44.

118 'The new school for wives', *Household Words*, 1852, pp. 85–6.

119 *Household Words*, p. 88.

120 *Household Words*, p. 88.

121 *Census, 1851: Education Section: Evening Schools for Adults*, pp. 80–1.

122 Sadler, M. E. (ed.), *Continuation Schools*, p. 111.

123 Sadler, M. E. (ed.), *Continuation Schools*, p. 108.

124 Webb, C., *The Woman with the Basket*, Manchester, Co-operative Wholesale Society's Printing Works, 1927, p. 52.

125 Dallas, G., 'New introduction', to the Virago reprint of 1978 of Margaret Llewelyn Davies, *Maternity: Letters from Working Women*, 1915.

126 Davies, M. L., *The Women's Co-operative Guild 1883–1904*, Kirby Lonsdale, the Women's Co-operative Guild, 1904, p. 73.

127 Davies, M. L., *The Women's Co-operative Guild*, p. 150.

128 Webb, C., *The Woman*, pp. 55–6.

129 Webb, C., *The Woman*, pp. 98–9, 100, 101, 107.

130 Webb, C., *The Woman*, p. 100.

131 Davies, M. L., *The Women's Co-operative Guild*, p. 103.

132 Scott, Mrs, 'A felt hat worker' in Davies, M. L. (ed.), *Life as We Have Known it* by Co-operative Working Women (1931) reprint by Virago, 1977, p. 38.

133 MacNamara, T. J., 'Joints in our educational armour', *Fortnightly Review*, June 1899, p. 921.

134 Sterns, P., Working-class women in Britain, 1890–1914' in Vicinus, M. (ed.), *Suffer and Be Still*, Indiana University Press, 1972, p. 106.

135 Sterns, P., 'Working-class Women', pp. 109–10.

19 'Sex antagonism' in the teaching profession: equal pay and the marriage bar, 1910–39

Alison Oram

The period 1910 to 1939 was one of bitter debate and crucial policy decisions concerning the pay and position of women elementary school teachers. Two major issues were equal pay and the marriage bar.[1] The equal pay argument split the National Union of Teachers (the main teachers' union) and immediately after the First World War, some teachers broke away from it to form the feminist National Union of Women Teachers and the anti-feminist National Association of Schoolmasters. During the early 1920s, the majority of local education authorities (LEAs) brought in regulations compelling women teachers to resign their posts on marriage; a policy which continued until the Second World War. This article will critically assess the arguments used to justify equal pay and the marriage bar and then examine the response of teachers through their unions.

Education policy was made in the context of a short-lived post-war boom followed by the economic crisis of 1921 and major cuts in public expenditure. Financial restraint continued during the period and cuts in education spending were repeated in 1931. Like other women workers, women teachers made important political and economic gains during and just after the First World War, such as the vote and wider job opportunities, only to suffer attacks on their newly won status during the 1920s and 1930s. This backlash was not only the result of the economic situation but was also caused by the changing dynamics of power between the sexes, a change illustrated by events in the teaching profession.

Equal pay for equal work

'Equal Pay for Equal Work' was a live issue for many women workers during and just after the First World War, both in industry and white-collar sectors, and one linked to women's new political and social emancipation. Several government committees considered the question, most of them giving only qualified support to the principle. There was also increasing parliamentary discussion of equal pay, encouraged by the political pressure of newly-enfranchised women. Soon after the end of the war, however, the tide turned for women in employment. They were forced to leave many of the occupations they had entered, there was growing female unemployment and women were accused of taking the jobs of ex-servicemen.[2]

Women teachers' pay followed this pattern of high hopes, soon dashed. Prior to 1920 teachers' salaries were decided locally. Women teachers' salaries were approximately 75 per cent of those of men with the same qualifications and status,

Source: Commissioned.

but the extent of the differentiation varied between local authorities. In a few areas where women teachers were strongly organized they had gained a near approximation to equal pay.[3] Concern over low morale, the supply of teachers and rapid inflation during the war led to the setting up of the Burnham Committee in 1919 to negotiate national salary scales between representatives of the local authorities and the teachers. The teachers' representatives came from the National Union of Teachers (NUT), and included only five women out of the twenty-five, while on the local authorities' panel there were no women at all. Despite the positive atmosphere and pressure for equal pay, it was never really considered by the Burnham Committee, and from the outset the ratio of women to men teachers' pay was established at a ratio of 4:5. This represented an improvement in most women teachers' salaries relative to those of men, and the average salaries received by women teachers rose from about 75 per cent to about 80 per cent of their male colleagues'. But women teachers' gains did not go unchallenged for long.

The economic crisis of 1921 forced savage cuts in educational expenditure. From 1922 teachers' salaries were subject to a 5 per cent deduction as a contribution towards superannuation and in 1923 the Burnham Committee and the teachers accepted a 'voluntary abatement' of 5 per cent of their salaries for one year. When the Burnham salary agreement expired in 1925 there was pressure to reduce salaries further, particularly those of women teachers. The new scales reduced the yearly increment from £12,10s for both sexes to £12 for men and £9 for women certificated assistant teachers. In this way the 7½ per cent saving made in salary expenditure was achieved mainly at the expense of women teachers. Again in 1931 teachers' salaries were in the forefront of spending cuts and a 10 per cent reduction was imposed which was restored in two stages, in 1934 and 1935. Despite these cuts teachers as a group made real gains since the cost of living fell during the interwar period. However although the 4:5 ratio established by the Burnham agreement represented a general improvement in women teachers' salaries, it also locked them into a position of inequality which remained generally unchanged for many years. It was only after 1936, when equal pay had been raised in the Commons by Ellen Wilkinson and the need for economy had eased, that it became possible for the issue to be seriously discussed again. Equal pay for teachers was finally agreed to in 1955 and introduced during the years 1955–61.

The politics of the marriage bar

The implementation of a marriage bar in teaching paralleled the 'ups and downs' of women teachers' pay. Before the First World War it was unusual for women of any class to be employed outside the home after marriage. Despite this, a significant minority of women elementary school teachers were married – 12 per cent – and married women were encouraged to return to teaching during and just after the war, so that by 1921 almost 19 per cent of women teachers were married.

Some local authorities operated a marriage bar before the First World War, but it was only in the years 1921–3 that the vast majority of education committees clamped down on the employment of married women, as 'the most obvious and natural way' of mitigating teacher unemployment and education cuts. The regulations which were introduced differed slightly from one area to another, but they generally combined a ban on appointing married women to teaching posts with a rule requiring the resignation of women teachers on marriage. One third of local authorities also dismissed married women teachers who were already employed in permanent posts – a conservative estimate suggested that 3000 women teachers were dismissed by 1923.[4] The marriage bar is a concrete example of the postwar backlash against women. By the 1930s, the proportion of women teachers who were married had dropped to about 10 per cent, although this figure conceals great local variations. In most areas however, married women continued to be employed as supply or temporary teachers when needed, without having the security or benefits of a permanent post.

In 1929 the new Labour government proposed to raise the school leaving age, and efforts were made to expand training facilities to meet the need for extra teachers. In a 1929 circular, the Board of Education suggested that LEAs should, 'temporarily at any rate', suspend their marriage bars and that married women teachers who had been forced to resign should be invited back into teaching.[5] But in 1931 the idea of re-employing married women teachers was hastily dropped, with the failure to raise the school leaving age, the cuts in the education budget and the revival of the problem of unemployed young teachers. Some LEAs reaffirmed their marriage bars or reviewed the cases of married women still in employment and in some areas a few more married women were dismissed, but on the whole there was little change.

LEAs had considerable freedom to organize the staffing of the schools as they wished, and did not need the approval of the Board of Education to introduce a marriage bar. In any case there is evidence to show that the Board privately agreed with the policy in the early 1920s.[6]

The Sex Disqualification (Removal) Act of 1919 should have protected married women teachers from dismissal. This stated:

A person shall not be disqualified by sex or marriage from the exercise of any public function or from being appointed or holding any civil office or post or from entering or assuming or carrying on any civil profession or vocation.

However in a series of court cases brought in the 1920s by married women teachers claiming unfair dismissal, this act was almost totally disregarded. After a case brought in 1922 by a group of married women teachers in the Rhondda, it was established that married women teachers could be dismissed if the reason was to promote the efficiency of education in the area. Further test cases in 1925 confirmed that LEAs were quite free to dismiss married women employed in their schools.[7] So local authorities had almost complete powers to bring in a marriage bar, if they wanted to. It was not until the Second World War that the marriage bar was suspended in most areas and finally outlawed by the 1944 Education Act.

Women teachers' position by the late 1920s and in the 1930s had certainly worsened since 1919–20, and had deteriorated in comparison with the prewar period as far as the marriage bar was concerned, although not as regards relative salaries. During and just after the First World War, it had seemed possible for women teachers to improve their position in the profession, but during the early 1920s nationally agreed salaries and the introduction of the marriage bar meant that inequality was more firmly entrenched and thus more difficult to challenge.

Economic factors and policy-making

There were two main economic causes for these changes in women teachers' position at work, the erratic supply and demand of teachers and the financial context of educational policy-making. First, since there were still severe limitations on the number of comparable occupations for women, during much of the period there was a greater supply of women teachers than of men. This did not favour women's position within the profession. In the early 1920s excess supply, particularly of women teachers, stimulated the introduction of marriage bars and the attempts by LEAs to depress women teachers' salaries.

Local authorities used the argument of 'market values' regarding teachers' pay. Teachers' salaries should be sufficiently high to attract able men and women, but since women would work for a lower salary there was no need to pay them at the men's rate. The 4:5 ratio set by the Burnham Committee reflected this argument, and it was widely accepted in this period of restraint on government expenditure. It is easy to see how it operated in practice. Women teachers' pay was raised when they were in short supply at the end of the First World War, but in 1925 the existence of unemployment among newly trained women teachers favoured the efforts of local authorities to depress their salaries.

The unemployment of young teachers fresh from training college also led to demands that married women should be sacked because they were in jobs which other people 'deserved' more. The oversupply of new teachers was first felt in the summer of 1922 and continued in the following years. It was alleged that in London alone there were 800 teachers without work, and letters and articles in the national press such as this one to the *Daily Mail* suggested: 'If there are 800 certificated teachers unemployed it is time that all married women whose husbands have employment should be forced to resign.'[8] Similar letters were sent directly to LEAs. 'The married woman teacher with husband in good position is common knowledge and a crying shame on the Council. Clear your conscience, dispose of these and help solve the unemployment problem.'[9] These views were taken very seriously by local education officials who were considerably embarrassed by the problem of a large number of unemployed teachers who originally had been encouraged to enter the profession.

The attempt to eliminate one group of teachers in order to create jobs for the unemployed disguised the lack of long-term planning for the supply of teachers. It was a short-sighted policy, a once-and-for-all measure to cope with the crisis. The debate was really about whether one group of teachers had a greater right to employment than another group. Married women who were already employed, sometimes for a considerable time, were still more vulnerable than the group of inexperienced young teachers.

The poor regulation of teacher supply resulted from sudden changes in the funding of elementary education. The need for economy in expenditure was the dominant and recurring factor in education policy-making for much of the interwar period. The teachers' position was favoured during the postwar reconstruction years but their salaries became the first line of attack during the economic crises of the early 1920s and 1930s, both in terms of the actual level of salaries and the number of teachers employed. The LEAs gained financially by employing women teachers at lower salaries than men and also hoped to save money by dismissing married women teachers, who were older and therefore more expensive.

The main argument against equal pay used by the government throughout the period was that the country could not afford the extra expenditure involved. The LEAs were not prepared to finance it out of the rates alone, particularly since the Board had drawn attention to the expense of equal pay long before the economy cuts began, and in later years the argument gained more force. The potential cost of equal pay for teachers ensured that it never received serious consideration during the interwar period. There was heavy pressure on the Burnham Committee from central government to reduce teachers' salaries and by 1925 women's salaries were considered by the LEAs to be 'the crux of the matter' in the drive for economy and some reduction of them was achieved.[10] This was a period when it was publicly acceptable not only to cut women's pay more than men's but also to reduce their health insurance and unemployment benefits.[11] The government and the local authorities benefited financially by employing women teachers at lower salaries and blatantly brushed aside demands for fair play.

. . . the Government accepts the principles of equal opportunity for women and of fair
wages for persons in its employment of either sex. It does not consider however that
the fair wages principle justifies the great expenditure which would be involved by
applying 'equal pay' in the sense of levelling up the pay of women generally to that of
men.[12]

The marriage bar likewise offered LEAs a means of reducing staffing costs. Public criticism of the cost of employing married women centred on absenteeism caused by pregnancy and looking after sick children and husbands. Critics argued that the cost of supply teachers and sick pay was excessive. Linked to this were allegations that married women were less efficient teachers than single women, an argument for dismissal that was legally and morally more acceptable, though unsubstantiated. Education officials were also conscious of the higher salaries paid to married women, who formed a group of older, more experienced and senior teachers.

Most local authorities did not attempt to estimate the financial costs and benefits of a marriage bar, but when they did, their reports showed that the savings to be made were negligible. For instance, if senior married women teachers were sacked, other teachers would have to be promoted to take their place – it was inevitable that some teachers should be older and more highly paid. Savings, if any, would be very short-term. In London, the average service of women who resigned on marriage was 8 years and of those who carried on, 17 years. If women were required to retire on marriage the value of their training and extra years of service would be lost, and to compensate for this, more teachers would have to be trained every year. The cost of these factors generally outweighed the cost of the absenteeism of married women teachers.[13]

Married women teachers were clearly used as a 'reserve pool of labour' at the convenience of the authorities. As the London Teachers' Association (NUT) complained in a letter to *The Times* in 1929:

It has become the custom of LEAs to regard married women teachers as the means whereby they can solve staffing difficulties, dismissing them when there is a surplus of available teachers and re-engaging them when there is an insufficiency of supply.[14]

However while these economic factors were vital features of women teachers' continuing inequality and weak position, their vulnerability was underpinned by the widespread assumption that women's 'natural' place was in the home, subordinate to men.

Ideology and policy-making: the family wage

The most constantly used argument against equal pay was that men should get more because they were the breadwinners: they had wives and children to keep and so they should receive a family wage. This argument was used throughout industry and commerce to obtain and justify higher rates of pay for men, and was a main demand of the trade union movement in the nineteenth and, indeed, in the twentieth century. The argument was well ventilated in the educational press and put forward strongly by the National Association of Schoolmasters (NAS): 'What was an adequate wage for the spinster teacher was entirely inadequate for the family man.'[15] The family wage principle certainly influenced the differentiation in teachers' pay, the Burnham 4:5 ratio being taken to imply some recognition of dependency.

The family wage ideology assumed a dependent wife at home, not out at work. This was argued as a self-evident truth, providing a context in which the abrupt dismissal of long-serving teachers through the marriage bar could be presented as natural, justified and even praiseworthy. It was assumed that for women, marriage was a job in itself. As one letter from the public put it: 'If marriage as a profession does not appeal to a woman she should remain single.'[16] The housewife's position was supposed to entail financial dependence on her husband. 'No injustice will be done, because the men who married them should be made to do their duty as "men" and "citizens" and maintain their wives in their proper sphere – the home.'[17] The idea that a wife could earn a salary undermined the husband's ability to claim a higher 'family wage', and also eroded the advantages which this gave him in the home.

The family wage was normally taken to cover the maintenance of both wife and children, but provision for the latter was particularly emphasized. It was suggested that it was desirable for men teachers to be able to marry at a young age and to have larger families. The eugenic argument that this was the man's national duty and that it should be made economically possible for him to do it was increasingly emphasized as the birth-rate fell. For example a letter to the *Times Educational Supplement* in 1919 stated:

It is just about time that the malignant, avaricious, and anti-racial activities of the 'equal pay' people were firmly opposed. In a few years there will be no children to teach if we lavish large salaries on persons without family responsibilities.[18]

In the marriage bar debate too there was considerable emphasis on the married woman teacher's role as actual or potential mother, especially as teachers were said to be physically and mentally 'the cream of British womanhood'. Doubts were cast upon the character of married women teachers unless they became full-time mothers.

After the birth of her child, the woman teacher, if she resumes her duties, must forgo the happiness of looking after her baby and entrust it to another – either this or the couple must agree not to have children. A woman who is content to adopt either of these alternatives cannot be said to have a real love of children.[19]

Concern and hostility were also generated about the relative standard of living enjoyed by men and women teachers. It was alleged, again most often by the NAS, that even with unequal salaries women teachers could afford to take holidays abroad, while men had to take on additional work, such as teaching evening classes, in order to fulfil their family responsibilities. The family wage argument was also stretched by the NAS to justify paying single men more than single women teachers. They were seen as potential husbands who had to be in a financial position to prepare for marriage in the future.[20]

This argument, which some men continued to press, was not easily sustained. Counter-arguments, however, revealed that the NAS and some local education officials thought that women teachers should get less money on the grounds of their sex alone. They were paying

too much money to bachelor women. . . . It must be obvious to anyone that in starting a young man at £172,10s, scale 2 and a girl of the same age and same scale with £160 was grossly unfair in the social system of the country. It was productive of late marriages instead of early marriages, and was inclined to elevate the bachelor girl to a position in this country that she should not attain.[21]

There was widespread anxiety throughout the period, and particularly after the First World War, that greater opportunities and higher wages for women would mean they could avoid marriage. They would have less incentive to provide domestic services in the home, for their husbands as well as for their children.[22] Indeed only the single woman was seen to have the right to work at all; in marriage she was compelled to depend on a man. This attack on women's financial independence from men was particularly significant in the case of teachers, since they earned relatively high salaries.

In practice there was, of course, a gap between the ideology of the family wage and the reality of teachers' household organization which did not necessarily follow the pattern of either the nuclear family or the self-supporting spinster. A higher family wage for all men was clearly unjust because it made no distinction between the bachelor, the married man without children and the married man with children. Also, many women had dependents, generally elderly or ailing parents.

An intolerably large number of women turn up who have dependents, and it is not really easy to explain exactly why a man should have his dependents taken into account and a woman not.[23]

Furthermore, the notion of dependence is itself problematic. The 'dependent' wife provided cooking, housework and laundry services for her husband's benefit, or as the National Union of Women Teachers put it: 'A man who marries obtains an unsalaried housekeeper for life.'[24] The single woman teacher on the other hand, could not usually afford to employ a housekeeper. Rather than a dependent, a wife was a financial asset to the man teacher. Children, on the other hand, were more obviously dependents while still at school but in the long term might provide support and care to their parents in old age, as indeed many spinster teachers found to their cost.

The 1921 Census showed that fewer than 20 per cent of all men teachers had one child and a further 17 per cent had two or more children under sixteen. Thus over 60 per cent of men teachers had no responsibility for dependent children (including those who were not married), and this proportion probably increased as the birth rate fell. During the same period as many as 30 per cent of women teachers partially or wholly supported other family members.[25]

In sum, the local authorities and the government gained financial benefits from employing women teachers at lower salaries than men and hoped to save money by bringing in a marriage bar, although in the latter case, few if any savings were achieved. They were however able to justify these policies at the time by pointing to the difficult economic situation and the over-supply of women teachers. But their argument was only acceptable because it was widely assumed that men should be paid extra because of their family responsibilities, and that married women should not work outside the home. Not only was this justification based on a familial ideology which benefited men while narrowly prescribing women's role as dependent wife and mother, but it also clearly did not accord with reality in this period.

The response of the teachers' unions

The positions taken by the teachers' unions towards equal pay and the marriage bar show the degree of 'sex antagonism' which was aroused by these issues. About 80 per cent of elementary school teachers were members of the NUT. Although two-thirds of NUT members were women during this period, the executive of the union and its annual conference were dominated by men. The advantages which men derived from higher pay created an ambivalence in the tactics used by the NUT to demand higher salaries for teachers. There was a degree of underlying conflict over whether teachers, as professionals, should receive 'the rate for the job' or whether they could more profitably ally themselves with a trade union demand for a 'family wage' which implied salaries fixed in relation to social need, with the corollary that there should be lower pay for women. The division between these ideas was frequently, although not necessarily, a sex-based one, most clearly seen in the support of the National Union of Women Teachers (NUWT) for equal pay and in the opposition of the NAS. The trade union movement had traditionally taken an ambivalent and contradictory attitude towards equal pay, preferring to press for a family wage partly because of the benefits it gave to male workers, but sometimes supporting equal pay to protect men's jobs from being undercut.

In 1919 equal pay became the official policy of the NUT after fifteen years of pressure from within the union by women teachers, following a referendum of members which approved equal pay by 35,004 votes to 15,039. It was disagreement with this policy change which led the NAS to formally break from the NUT in 1919. The NUWT broke away in 1920 because it believed (rightly as it turned out) that the NUT would not fight for the principle.

Throughout the interwar period the NUT sought a professional level of salaries for teachers. It emphasized the qualifications, skill and long training of teachers and the service they provided to the community as well as their material needs. Different rates of pay not based on professionalism were a threat to the level of salaries of all teachers. But it was not until the late 1930s that the equal pay policy was explicitly linked with the fight for professional salaries.

During the Burnham negotiations of 1919 the question of equal pay was raised briefly by the NUT but not pressed. The union was prepared to compromise in order to come to an agreement quickly over salary scales; but once a ratio had been established it was difficult to effect any change later. The issue of equal pay was not raised by the teachers' panel in the Burnham negotiations after 1923, but it accepted the 1925 changes (discussed earlier) only under protest.

After the intense activity and debate of 1918 and 1919, equal pay was rarely discussed by the NUT, and the policy was shelved. A 1921 recruitment leaflet for women teachers set out the NUT's policy of equal pay and emphasized that this could only be achieved through unity in the profession. But subsequent leaflets issued between 1923 and 1930 failed to mention equal pay as a way of attracting women members; in fact throughout the 1920s the union appeared to be more concerned with preventing a decrease in male membership over the issue.[26] By the 1930s the subject was so dormant that at the women's conference meeting in 1933, there was an inquiry as to whether equal pay was still union policy.

Indeed there is plenty of evidence to show how divided the NUT was on equal pay during this period. In 1920 Miss Conway, the union's second woman president, stated that all the NUT women on the Burnham Committee were in favour of equal pay, and that all the men were against it.[27] There were unsuccessful attempts to force the annual conferences between 1922 and 1924 to debate motions dropping the equal pay policy in favour of supporting the 4:5 ratio instead, but in practice the NUT had already adopted this course. During the period of attacks on teachers' salaries the NUT continually argued in its public propaganda for the need to raise teachers' salaries to a level befitting their status. The union was particularly concerned to argue in favour of raising men teachers' pay in order to maintain its male membership, and did so in terms of supporting professional rates of pay without ever mentioning equal pay. The union was on the defensive during the 1920s and 1930s. It argued along the lines of the NAS terms of reference to men teachers, rather than positively supporting its own policy of equal pay.

This defensiveness was due partly to the interwar depressions and the consequent cuts in education and other public spending. The unemployment of teachers reduced their bargaining power, and the union was concerned to hold on to existing salaries and reduce cuts to the minimum. As the NUT journal put it in 1921: 'These are not times in which "equal pay" can be either protagonised or antagonised with any advantage to anybody.'[28] As a party to the Burnham agreements itself, the NUT had to persuade its members that they were acceptable under the circumstances. The union's adherence to the equal pay principle also cooled as the breakaway unions gained strength.

The NUT was similarly ambivalent over the marriage bar, and for the same reasons. Although the union condemned the marriage bar and took action to help married women teachers, it was unable to wholeheartedly challenge the policy, because it did not want to alienate its male members. The national machinery of the NUT enabled local associations to exert pressure on behalf of individuals threatened with dismissal. The NUT felt there was a greater chance of success, however, if they intervened either on moral grounds where a teacher had given long service and had only a short time to go before being entitled to her pension, or on compassionate grounds where the husband was unable to support the family. Action was taken in many districts, but there were also cases of the local NUT official actually supporting the marriage bar.

The union was prepared to bring a test case in defence of married women teachers only if this was likely to be successful. It investigated the case of the 64 Rhondda married women teachers but refused to help them because they were advised by their lawyers that there was little chance of success. The Rhondda women were angered by this lack of support. They pointed out that the union normally used all its legal resources in tenure cases, but despite the fact that they had been union members for many years and their posts and pensions were in danger, protection had been withheld.[29] The women themselves thought their jobs were important enough to take the case to court at their own expense but they lost. The NUT supported the Poole married women teachers in 1925 as a test case, but although initially the teachers won, the case was lost on appeal.

Despite these legal defeats, the NUT was reluctant to push for fresh legislation. It took part in a deputation to the Board of Education in 1927, but only after considerable pressure from its London members, a high proportion of whom were married women.

The general status of women teachers as professionals was diminished by the marriage bar – they were seen as having a 'fill-in' job rather than a life-long career like men. Although security of tenure was one of the main aims of the NUT, the union never fought the marriage bar as a matter of principle, and it was seen as a peripheral problem affecting only a few members. While some action was taken to defend married women teachers' jobs, the leadership crucially failed to challenge the view that married women had less right to employment. The union executive (80 per cent men) said they were afraid that any wholesale commitment or intervention might arouse divided opinion among the membership. However resolutions were passed at conferences every year between 1924 and 1927 condemning the dismissal of women teachers on marriage, so it seems that the rank and file (two-thirds of whom were women) were firmly against the marriage bar.

Women teachers' attempts through the NUT to obtain equal pay and resist restrictions on their right to work, were thus thwarted by the male-orientated structure and aims of the union. Equal pay had been adopted as policy in the first place as a result of pressure from feminist teachers in the Equal Pay League, which became the National Federation of Women Teachers. After 1919 the most active of these women broke away from the NUT to establish a separate union, the National Union of Women Teachers (NUWT). The NUWT also campaigned for professional salaries for teachers, emphasizing that salaries should be paid according to work done, not the sex of the teacher. It was a strongly feminist union. Many of its members had formerly been involved in the suffrage struggle and it worked closely with other feminist organizations such as the National Union of Societies for Equal Citizenship (NUSEC), the Six Point Group and later the Open Door Council to press the demand for equal pay. However unlike NUSEC, the NUWT did not advocate family allowances in order to facilitate equal pay. The NUWT was particularly strong in some parts of the country, and it was successful in achieving equal pay in a few localities before 1920, especially in the outer London areas, but this ground was lost by the introduction of Burnham Standard Scales. After the NUWT had broken from the NUT, it changed its tactics to publicizing the arguments for equal pay through its journal *The Woman Teacher*, in meetings and demonstrations, and by bringing pressure to bear on the government. In this way the union effectively kept equal pay on the agenda, especially prior to general elections and when the Burnham Committee was meeting, during a period when the NUT virtually ignored the issue.

The NUWT campaigned in the same way on the marriage bar, working with other feminist organizations to publicize the arguments in favour of married women teachers' employment and trying to influence central and local government. In 1925 it sponsored the election of one member, Agnes Dawson, to the London County Council in order to work for the removal of the marriage bar and generally watch over the interests of women teachers. She became prominent in the Labour Party and her efforts eventually helped to get the bar abolished in London in 1935.

The NUWT argued against the bar from both a feminist and professional point of view, emphasizing the fact that it was an encroachment on individual liberty. 'It is a woman's right to decide for herself, in view of all her circumstances, whether she wishes to work outside her home or not.'[30] The union also argued that the dismissal of women on marriage was a waste of their work experience, as well as the expense of their training. By getting the marriage bar raised as an issue in the House of Commons and by changing the policy of the London County Council, and one or two other LEAs, the energetic campaign of the NUWT made an impression out of all proportion to its size.

The National Association of Men Teachers, later the National Association of Schoolmasters, on the other hand, was formed within the NUT in 1919 solely in response to the referendum in favour of equal pay and a feeling that the women were gaining power in the union to the detriment of their male colleagues. The decision to secede from the NUT was taken in 1922, although only a minority of NAS members were prepared to do this. The NAS probably spoke for many men in the NUT who disagreed with its equal pay policy, but who were not prepared to relinquish the benefits of belonging to the larger union. The NAS actively attacked women's position in teaching throughout the interwar period, campaigning not only against equal pay but also against women heads of mixed schools and against women teaching boys over seven.[31]

It called for 'Separate Consideration' for men teachers' salaries, maintaining that the Burnham settlement favoured the women teachers, giving them a better standard of living compared to family men. Its emphasis on the family wage for the purpose of salary bargaining can be compared to the strategy of industrial trades unions, but since it was based on the needs of the worker rather than the nature of the work, it conflicted with the drive to professionalize teaching. However in conjunction with the demand for 'separate consideration' the NAS also focused on their policy of 'men teachers for boys'. This justified their demand that men should get more on the grounds that they were doing a different, and by implication, a more important job than women; at the same time it avoided the possibility of being undercut by women.

The NAS constantly attacked the NUT for its commitment to equal pay, accusing it of being dominated by 'purse-proud feminists', even when it was patently avoiding any discussion of this policy. Like the NUWT, the NAS adopted the tactic of having questions raised in the House of Commons, drawing attention to its claims. It pressed the Burnham Committee for separate representation, claiming that in some areas such as Liverpool and Leeds the NAS represented the majority of schoolmasters. The NAS succeeded to a large extent in getting its ideas discussed, and thus contributed to the muffling of the NUT on the equal pay issue.

While some men teachers supported equal pay and opposed the marriage bar, there were undoubtably many, especially NAS members, who were not sorry to see women teachers' professional sphere restricted since it meant less competition for them. The exclusion of married women teachers would not directly benefit men by providing more jobs, as there were fewer unemployed male teachers. But the higher posts, for instance the headships of mixed schools, were likely to be filled less often by women if they had to resign halfway through their careers.

Conclusion

The employment position of women teachers was restricted compared to that of men, not on the basis of their worth as employees, but upon what was perceived as women's role. This gave material and financial advantages to men both as husbands and other teachers, and to women teachers' employers. Women teachers' worsening position in the interwar period can only be explained by considering the economic recessions and men's fears in conjunction with each other. The real gains women had made during the First World War gave some men cause to fear that their privileges might be eroded. These gains had been in employment and the public sphere in general, through the franchise and the Sex Disqualification (Removal) Act for example, as well as in the teaching profession itself. In teaching, the NAS was the prime example of men's antagonism to the perceived advance of women, which some men in the NUT also shared.

The re-establishment and deepening of unequal gender relations was given greater emphasis as a result of the economic recession when it was in employers' interests to bow to a climate of public opinion which emphasized women's 'true domestic duties'. Restrictions such as unequal pay and the marriage bar enforced the family wage idea and its consequence of women's economic dependence in marriage. The recession also made the debate more desperate and hostile, since men and women teachers were fighting over real material benefits: financial rewards for work, access to work and men's expectation of services from women in the home. During the 1920s and 1930s other issues of social concern helped reinforce this backlash such as eugenic theories and anxiety over the falling birthrate.

Women teachers then were not just passive victims of government policy. They also acted to amend it. The action taken was mainly defensive because of the strong forces of reaction they were up against, but small successes were achieved both through the NUT and the NUWT. These included a slight advance in women teachers' salaries compared with men's at the end of the war and the removal of the marriage bar in London and elsewhere in the 1930s. However the main teaching union, the NUT, did not give priority to issues affecting women teachers and at times effectively obscured them, for fear of further splitting the union along sex lines. In my view, it is clear that the NUT acted in men's interests rather than for the professional good of teachers as a whole. Although some male unionists supported the women's cause, others acted in accordance with the feminist Eleanor Rathbone's description of male dominance as 'the Turk complex': 'an impersonal instinct, which creates between those who share it a kind of common sex bias which is often stronger even than self-interest or the interests of class'.[32] Women's voice within the union was thus limited by the same structural factors which served male dominance in the wider world.

Notes

1 A third area of conflict was equal opportunities for promotion. See Oram, A., 'Inequalities in the teaching profession: the effects on teachers and pupils', in *Lessons for Life: The Schooling of Girls and Women 1850–1950*, Oxford, Basil Blackwell, 1987.

2 Braybon, G., *Women Workers in the First World War*, London, Croom Helm, 1981.

3 East Ham, Tottenham, Hendon, Finchley, Wood Green, Swansea and Mountain Ash paid equal minima and increments (except Swansea) although higher maxima for men.

4 Public Records Office: (PRO) Ed 24/1744, minute, 1 February 1923.

5 Board of Education, Circular 1404, 1929.

6 PRO, Ed 24/1744. Minute to President from Selby-Bigge, 31 January 1923.

7 *Price v. Rhondda UDC 1923*, see *Daily Telegraph*, 4 May 1923. *Short v. Borough of Poole 1925*, *The Times*, Law Report, 1 August 1935, also *Fennel v. East Ham 1925*.

8 *Daily Mail*, 2 October 1922.

9 London County Council, Greater London Record Office (LCC Records). EO/STA/2, 12. Letter to LCC, 20 June 1922.

10 PRO, Ed 108/11. Burnham Committee minutes, 16 November 1923 and subsequent meetings.

11 Thane, P., *The Foundations of the Welfare State*, London, Longman, 1982, pp. 177, 192. N. Branson and M. Heinemann, *Britain in the Nineteen Thirties*, Panther, 1973, p. 32.

12 PRO, CAB 27/590, EBC (35)10, 20 November 1935.

13 The London County Council was one authority which did work out the costs of a

bar. See LCC Records, EO/STA/2, 13. Reports and papers, 29 July 1922 and 15 November 1922.

14 *The Times*, 5 November 1929.

15 *Times Educational Supplement*, 3 April 1937, p. 112 (report of NAS conference).

16 LCC EO/STA/2, 13, letter to LCC, 28 October 1922.

17 LCC EO/STA/2, 13, letter to LCC, 27 September 1922.

18 *TES*, 16 October 1919, p. 525 (letter).

19 Letter to *New Statesman*, 3 March 1923, pp. 628–9.

20 *TES*, 5 June 1919, p. 276; 23 October 1919, p. 536.

21 *Education*, 22 June 1923, pp. 401–2. Annual meeting of Education Committees. Several speakers expressed similar views.

22 Land, H., 'The family wage', *Feminist Review*, **6**, 1980, pp. 58–62; Braybon, *Women Workers*, pp. 220–1; Cole, M., *Marriage: Past and Present*, London, Dent, 1938, p. 150.

23 *TES*, 27 November 1919, p. 600.

24 Board of Education, *Report of the Departmental Committee for Enquiring into the Principles which should determine the construction of scales of salary for teachers in Elementary Schools*, 1918, vol 2, Evidence, Cd. 8999, p. 69.

25 Smith, E., *Wage-Earning Women and their Dependents*, The Fabian Society, 1915, pp. 10, 13, 34; *Report of the Royal Commission on Equal Pay 1944–1946*, 1946, Cmd 6937, pp. 126–30.

26 NUT, *What the Union Does for Women Teachers*, Leaflet no. 10, 1921; *Why Women Should be Members*, leaflet no. 47, 1923–30.

27 *TES*, 8 January 1920, p. 21.

28 *Schoolmaster*, 18 June 1921, p. 1115.

29 NUT Law Committee Minutes, 1 December 1922, letter from the Rhondda women.

30 *TES*, 19 May 1921, p. 227.

31 For a detailed discussion of this see A. Oram, 'Inequalities in the Teaching Profession'.

32 Rathbone, E., *Family Allowances*, 1949, p. 217.

The antagonism between women and men teachers over equal pay and the marriage bar has been discussed in more detail in my articles 'Serving two masters? The introduction of a marriage bar in teaching in the 1920s', in London Feminist History Group, *The Sexual Dynamics of History*, London, Pluto Press, 1983, and ' "Sex antagonism" in the teaching profession: the equal pay issue 1914–1929', *History of Education Review*, Australia, **14**, 1985, pp. 36–48, as well as in my MSc thesis, Bristol University, 1983, *'Sex Antagonism' in the Teaching Professions: Employment Issues and the Women Teacher in Elementary Education; 1910–1939*. 'A new comradeship between men and women: family, marriage and London's women teachers, 1870–1914' by Dina Copelman in Jane Lewis (ed.), *Labour and Love: Women's Experience of Home and Family 1850–1940*, Oxford, Basil Blackwell, 1986, is an interesting discussion of a slightly earlier period. Useful background material on women teachers can be found in Geoffrey Partington's *Women Teachers in the Twentieth Century*, Slough, NFER Publishing Company, 1976, and Gosden, P. H. J. H., *The Evolution of a Profession*, Oxford, Basil Blackwell, 1972.

20 Gender divisions, training and the state

Ann Wickham

Introduction

In the last ten years training, particularly training for young people, has become a central political issue. There can be very few people in Britain today who have not heard of the Manpower Services Commission (MSC), the institution that oversees training provision of all kinds. Yet the MSC itself was only set up by the Employment and Training Act of 1973. Today it heads a programme that not only attempts to develop training opportunities for adults but which also, through the Youth Training Scheme (YTS), aims to promote a permanent bridge between school and work for all young people. Alongside the efforts of the MSC lie the training programmes and opportunities opened up by the voluntary sector, often drawing on financial assistance from local councils and the ESF (European Social Fund). From being an area of little concern in the immediate post war years of economic boom, training is now a focus for wide ranging activities and massive financial outlay. Even 'The Archers' now features a YTS trainee as part of its storyline. Yet if the range of training activities on offer has expanded and if a greater number and greater diversity of opportunities are available, does this mean that everyone now has an equal opportunity to take advantage of these increased resources, particularly when race and gender are taken into account?

A quick look through any report on what is actually happening in training clearly shows that this is not so. To anyone accustomed to debates about the effects of education and educational institutions upon opportunities and social mobility over the last thirty years, such conclusions will hardly be surprising. Studies have consistently shown that children from working-class backgrounds fare less well than their middle- and upper-class peers. Such results led to substantial research on both home and school in an effort to identify the reasons for under-achievement. Only more recently has this exclusive focus on class been abandoned for a more wide-ranging assessment of the forms of inequality in our society and the interlinkages with education. Increasingly, it is being realized that gender and race are equally important elements in the structure of inequality in society and research is now trying to deal with the delicate interaction between these three. Therefore if we come to examine the development of training and training opportunities in Britain it should not be surprising to find the same elements at work there also.

I think it can be argued that training provision of the kind offered so far in

Source: Revised version of 'Gender divisions, training and the state', in Dale, R. (ed.), *Education, Training and Employment: towards a new vocationalism*, Oxford, Pergamon Press, 1985.

Britain has consistently been biased against the interests of women in general. This chapter, will, I hope, show some of the ways in which this has happened. However, if women as a group are not properly catered for in our training facilities, it is also necessary to recognize that women are not an homogeneous category. The kind of opportunities open to a middle-class woman are likely to be substantially different to those offered to a working-class women, and within all ethnic groups there are likely to be such differences. Yet the differences between ethnic groups will also add to the problems many women face. Many black women find they are doubly discriminated against in our society, first because they are women and second because they are black. Whether those concerned are immigrants themselves or the children of immigrants, all members of ethnic groups tend to be harder hit by unemployment. For instance, it is estimated that two young West Indians are unemployed for every one 'indigenous' white youngster. For women the unemployment situation is likely to be far worse. In 1975, for instance, the rate of increase in unemployment for black male workers was twice as large as the increase in unemployment, but for black women workers the increase was three times as large (see Wickham, 1986 for a fuller discussion). If employment opportunities for Afro-Caribbean or Asian women, for example, are generally worse than those for white women this makes the provision of effective training opportunities for these groups of particular importance.

What form these opportunities should take and what occupations should be opened up to women through training will vary a great deal according to local labour markets. Britain is going through a rapid form of industrial restructuring in the present decade and this, together with the impact of new technology, is both closing down many occupations and establishing new ones, often along strong regional lines; the south of England, for example, being seen as the main site of the new microelectronics firms. However, there are comments that can be made about the overall forms of provision.

What we are faced with is a labour market situation where women in general have far fewer opportunities than comparable male members of the same class or ethnic group. Women, themselves, then have a diverse educational employment pattern according to ethnic groups, class, age, marital status etc. Training in its various forms, whether offered in the educational system, for example at Further Education Colleges, within special programmes and centres, such as those run by the Manpower Services Commission, or within employment, such as training schemes run by employers or professional bodies associated with specific occupations, therefore has an important role to play for women. It cannot alone atone for the problems of the labour market. Training cannot in itself create jobs or ensure that women get them. What it can do, however, is enable women to get the qualifications that will open up existing jobs to them or ensure that they can take advantage of career opportunities. In examining the training opportunities open to women today we then have to ask how far women have been admitted to training programmes and therefore to job and career opportunities, and also question how far these existing opportunities fully meet the needs of women. I would argue that training opportunities to the present day have consistently failed women in both respects.

This chapter will concentrate on state activities in the area of training. In the immediate post-war period there has been a staggering transformation in the attitude towards training expressed by successive governments. We have moved from a situation where little if any government intervention took place, to a situation where some form of provision is being made for every school leaver who does not go on to some sort of higher education. Today the Manpower Services Commission has a major role to play in the life of every British teenager, as well as being a major source of opportunities for many older workers. If there are inadequacies in the provisions of such schemes, especially in relation to women, this does not mean that they are the only institutions at fault. Training schemes within occupations can be just as, if not more, inadequate at meeting women's needs and offering them proper career opportunities, even within female-dominated occupations. It has been left to the voluntary sector to provide many of the more innovative and radical schemes which go some way towards a truly women-oriented policy.

The exclusion of women from many training opportunities is not just an oversight or explainable by reference to a lack of interest by women whose central concerns are thought to be the home and family. Instead many feminists now argue that it is in male interests to continue to exclude women from 'masculinized' jobs and confine them to the female ghettoes of low-level, low-paid, jobs in feminized work sectors, thus producing the sex-segregated patterns of employment with which we are all familiar.

A recent paper recognizes that men organize to exclude women from certain jobs, struggle with women over entry to certain occupations, and that the presence of women in some jobs has materially damaged men's chances. Such conflict could be put down to 'false consciousness' and to not seeing that capital is the real enemy. But in fact material advantages accrue to men from women's disadvantaged position at work.[1]

The authors also comment on men's control over technology and the question of skill. In both cases these are elements which are the outcome of class struggle but also of gender struggle. Work skills, especially in relation to industry, have traditionally been seen in terms of craft skills and craft workers have almost overwhelmingly been male workers. While the concept of skill can refer to technical competences, it can also cover more subjective judgements, elements that workers or unions can use to defend themselves against other employers or workers.[2] In this context the assets which women bring to their work have been persistently devalued. As Phillips and Taylor[3] note, skilled work has become almost by definition that work which women do not do. This definition of skill is seldom challenged although, as Pollert emphasizes in a study of female tobacco workers:

The irony comes when a system of co-called non-discriminatory 'objective' job 'measurement', aimed at getting rid of the awkward 'interference' of ideological judgements, succeeds in rooting them more deeply. . . . One might legitimately inquire why such a job as hand stemming (in practice, female) in Group A should be rated lower than security patrols (in practice, male) in Group D. One job might hold more responsibility and danger but the other involves more patience and physical discomfort.[4]

In other words, the definition of a skill is socially constructed and whilst the concept of 'skilled work' may be used by working-class men for their own benefit in maintaining privileges in relation to employers, it can also be used against women whose work, once defined as low skilled, is also low paid. These practices help reinforce subjective perceptions of women's marginal place in the labour market and their dependence in the home.

Training is traditionally seen as the means through which skills can be acquired and the apprenticeship system is at the basis of this approach. In the post-war period more and more training schemes have been introduced at different levels and for different periods of time, culminating in the present youth training programmes of the Manpower Services Commission. Such schemes are presumed to pass on those technical skills which the economy requires. However, in many cases it seems clear that training involves the acquisition of social attributes required in the labour process – work discipline, for instance – just as much as technical skills. When women have no access to training it effectively excludes them from many occupations, whether it is technical or social skills that are required, or even if training qualifications are being used solely as a form of entry requirement without reference to their content. Undoubtedly the absence of schemes for women is important when women want to enter what have been male-dominated occupations. However, it is essential not to overemphasize the impact of training. One must realize that even if women replicated the training available to men it is unlikely that they would gain an equal place on the labour market given the existence of competition from males, and when they are faced by male-dominated unions, male employers and a capitalist system that has profited from the use of women as a marginal, low-paid labour force.

Despite this, the extension of training opportunities to women could be of benefit to some and their entrance into less marginal areas of economic activity could help weaken the dominance of the belief that the place of women is in the home.

Early developments

For much of the post-war period little attention was paid to the training of women workers. In the pre-war period, state involvement in training in general was minimal. After the First World War instructional factories were set up for ex-servicemen. In the 1920s training centres were used to deal with unemployment and in the Second World War they were used to provide rapid training for hurriedly mobilized workers. In the 1950s, however, there was even a decline in the number of such training places and the main concern expressed in government circles was for apprentices, that is mainly male workers.[5] However, labour shortages, technological changes and a 'baby boom' prompted more wide-ranging considerations which were embodied in the assumption that 'upskilling' (the need to increase the skills of the workforce) was essential for economic growth.

In 1956 a sub-committee was set up under the Ministry of Labour which produced the Carr Report, *Training for Skill*,[6] in 1958. In this report, which was concerned with the adequacy of the training of young workers for industry, only one short section dealt with opportunities for girls. It was assumed in the report that girls would marry and therefore would not need training. The main concern expressed was for the above average female grammar school pupil who might be expected to make a sustained contribution to the labour force. In this the report both reflected much of the current thinking about women in other areas of social policy and anticipated the relative neglect of women's training over the next decade.

In terms of school education, for instance, the Crowther Report[7] published in 1959 (the year after the Carr Report) also assumed that the main interest of girls was in their future role of wives and mothers. Similarly, the Newsom Report[8] in 1963 concentrated upon marriage as the more important vocational concern of girls, despite mounting evidence of the importance of women workers within the economy.

The emphasis upon marriage and the notion of the dependence of the woman upon the male wage-earner which was implicit in so many areas of British welfare state policy[9] reduced the pressure for any further training provision for women even when, as in the Crowther Report, the paucity of women's day release opportunities was specifically commented upon. Curricular differentiation in the schools both taught girls that their main interests were in the home and closed them off from many of those training opportunities which existed. The clustering of girls in arts subjects is well known,[10] yet various apprenticeships and forms of training often require a maths or science qualification. Thus even when girls did enter further education and training, it was likely to be in areas defined as 'female', such as secretarial work or nursery nursing.

While many government reports and the whole thrust of the welfare system emphasized the place of women in the home, the development of training opportunities for women would remain a rhetorical commitment. When changes were initiated in the 1960s and the government started to introduce training legislation, the issue of provision for women was still not regarded as one of importance. In 1964 an Industrial Training Bill[11] was brought into parliament which marked a revolution in state thinking in relation to training. Until then, training had mainly been left to the efforts of individual firms. However, this *ad hoc* process was now considered inadequate, especially in the face of overseas industrial competition. Industrial Training Boards were to be set up which would help establish an overall training policy and oversee its implementation. A levy system was to spread the cost across industry. Yet in the debate around this bill, the problem was conceptualized in almost exclusively male terms and the absence of reference to the numbers of women entering employment was publicly noted.[12] The dominance of human capital theory in this period reinforced this emphasis on men. Education and training were regarded as an investment which would later produce calculable returns. However, only men were regarded as producing economic returns. The benefit of any investment in women was regarded as social and not economic.[13] This approach both legitimated and reinforced women's perceived marginality in the world of work and their role in the home.

State policy towards the training of women in the 1970s

The Industrial Training Bill, which set up training boards, reflected a commitment by the state to positive intervention in the field of training and the levy system gave a financial leverage on firms. However, as the training boards were mainly concentrated in those industries which had few women workers, their establishment did not help many women.[14] Furthermore, it was apparent to observers that the boards did not consider it their role to encourage the training of women and girls.[15] Commercial and clerical training which might have suited women were resisted by employers.[16]

In their failure to identify and come to terms with the specific training needs of women, the training boards reflected the opposition of employers and unions to women's training as well as social constraints. The TUC had issued a charter of aims for women workers as early as 1963 in which the need for the development of training for women was emphasized. In 1972 the TUC was still pressing for the development of training, on the grounds that the impact of the Industrial Training Bill had been negligible. Representatives of the TUC argued that when levy grants were made to firms the boards should insist that a proportion of the training places went to women and that special grants should be made for 'non-traditional' training and for training for those returning to work.[17] Yet at the same time many of the prevailing assumptions about the training of women were also evident in statements of the TUC representatives. These statements, in fact, often contradicted stated TUC goals. For instance, the Expenditure Committee on the Employment of Women noted that:

The unconscious acceptance of traditional roles and occupations is well illustrated by the TUC evidence which, while favouring equal training opportunities for women, describes 'the vast majority of courses' at Government Training Centres as 'clearly appropriate only for men'.[18]

However, it was not that the courses were only suitable for men but that only men were admitted to them. The fact that the majority of places were for the engineering and construction industries was seen as the 'natural' reason for the bias towards male students. However, the unions were not the only ones to show some ambivalence towards the employment and training of women. The National Council of Women gave evidence to the Expenditure Committee that:

. . . a spokesman from the Department of Employment has recently suggested to one of our members that (a) many girls do not want training, (b) the overall employment position should be considered before training more married women; and that (c) it may not be good for the community that married women should be trained, and that the only circumstances in which more women will be trained is when there is economic need.[19]

Women were doing badly in many areas of training. In 1970 only 110 females were apprenticed to the skilled craft occupations compared to 112,000 males and less than one-fifth of those on day-release courses were female. Where girls were in apprenticeships the majority of these were in hairdressing. This situation is clearly related to the kinds of attitudes displayed by the unions and the Department of Employment.

However, further changes in training policy were introduced at the beginning of the 1970s which appeared to offer some means of altering this situation. Whilst no specific mention of women's needs was made in either the Green Paper[20] of

1972 or the White Paper[21] of 1973, the Employment and Training Act (1973) initiated developments which were to have relevance for women.

The act provided for the setting up of the Manpower Services Commission which was to manage public employment and training services through two executive arms, the Employment Services Division and the Training Services Division. The Training Services Division was to be responsible for the Training Opportunities Scheme (TOPS) which was replacing the old vocational training schemes in government training centres. Furthermore, Section 2 of the Act which enumerated the functions of the commission made special mention of arrangements that could be made to encourage increases in the opportunities available to women and girls.

The Training Services Division made the first important gesture towards a consideration of the special needs for women in the training process. The government had already argued that the introduction of legislation on equal opportunities for women could be expected to be beneficial in this area. In connection with the Equal Pay Act, it had agreed to remove male–female differences in training allowances. The government did not, however, propose to deal with other issues such as the distance of training centres or the absence of childcare facilities which might well have hindered the training of women. Yet the government was prepared to consider some experimental part-time training courses, even if these were only in the female-dominated commercial and clerical fields.[22]

In 1976 the Training Services Division brought out a report on 'Training Opportunities for Women'.[23] This was a result of a decision by the commission in 1975, the year of the Equal Pay and Sex Discrimination Acts, that women were one of the groups whose training needs should be treated as a priority of special national importance. The Sex Discrimination Act[24] in fact, had gone a long way towards encouraging more and wider training facilities for women by specifically exempting certain forms of training provision from the terms of the act. Section 47 allowed for positive discrimination in the provision of training courses for men or for women where the number of persons of that sex in the jobs that the training scheme provided for had been extremely small in the previous year. It also allowed for schemes in particular areas. Section 47 also dealt with the needs of those returning to work after a period of domestic responsibility and permitted both special training schemes and discrimination in selection for training programmes.

The report of the Training Services Division, issued against this background, recognized the inadequacy of existing training provision for women in every aspect, from day-release and apprenticeship to government training schemes.[25] It also admitted that there was an unsatisfied demand for training, and argued that there were legislative, economic and social justifications for the provision of training for women. However, while the report must be welcomed as the first major initiative by the state in the post-war period to consider the specific training needs of women, it gives the impression of a lack of dynamism and of a failure to develop a commitment to positive intervention. The emphasis in the report is on research into ways of assisting women and the exploration of possible ways of extending training.

The lack of dynamism in training policy is understandable in terms of the deepening economic crisis in Britain. Training provision had made no great progress in the late 1960s even though there had been open encouragement to women to enter the labour market. In the 1970s policy statements had been made in favour of women's opportunities but these were seldom put into practice as economic problems grew.

The provision of training opportunities for women

The full impact of this lack of commitment is evident in the provisions the MSC made for women. When set up, the Training Services Division was made responsible for the Training Opportunties Scheme (TOPS). The programmes in this scheme were not aimed at school-leavers but at those who had been out of permanent education for more than two years, and were aged at least 19. The TOPS programmes offered a wide variety of courses from higher level programmes in management, science and technology to craft courses and provision for the commercial and clerical sectors. Both men and women were eligible for TOPS courses and the number of women on the programme gradually increased. In 1972, before the Manpower Services Commission took over, only 6000 women trained on the TOPS programme.[26] By 1975 the numbers had increased to 27,000; in 1977 the figure reached 40,8881 and the figure was the same in 1978. By then women made up around 43 per cent of those completing TOPS courses and the percentage in 1980 was around 45 per cent.[27] In terms of encouraging numbers of women to train, it is clear that MSC programmes had considerable success. Unfortunately whilst the numbers of women involved increased, the schemes did not represent a change in the range or level of opportunities open to women.[28]

Women on TOPS schemes were found mainly in 'female' occupations. Most of them took courses in clerical work, shorthand and typing and they made up the majority on courses concerned with education, office machines, food preparation, hairdressing, cleaning, etc. Very few women were to be found in the higher level courses or in the government skill centres where subjects such as engineering, vehicle repair, carpentry and joinery, capstan setting machining and bricklaying were taught. (In 1978 only 658 women were on such courses in skill centres compared to 23,357 men, and women on these courses made up only 1.5 per cent of the women taking TOPS courses that year.)[29]

Although the actual numbers in these courses may have increased slightly over the years, the overall expansion of TOPS courses meant that women represented no greater proportion of the overall student number.

Even though the numbers of women on TOPS schemes appear to have grown so rapidly, albeit in female-dominated occupations, there were still many other drawbacks associated with the schemes. The failure to provide childcare facilities and the fact that there were virtually no part-time training opportunities was a major hindrance. The small training allowance paid to women who also had to pay for childcare was another limitation. The small numbers of women entering courses for areas of work dominated by men has been partly blamed on the limited guidance offered by those administering the schemes[30] and the need for effective occupational guidance was continually stressed by those examining this area of work preparation.[31]

A special development in the TOPS programme has been the introduction of Wider Opportunities for Women (WOW) courses in colleges. These courses are designed, administered and financed by the Training Services Division, and aimed at women who are likely to enter manual or skilled employment. Even though participants can be 19 on entry, the courses have tended to attract older women. The courses are short and are meant to help women formulate realistic re-entry plans for work, as well as providing the information and self-confidence that will help them carry these out. Welcome as such courses are because of their particular concern for the older woman worker, it is clear that the numbers at present attending them are infinitesimal. Even more important, so far as discrimination faced by women on the labour market is concerned, is the fact that an evaluation of pilot courses found that the courses were not leading women to enter into a wider range of jobs.[32]

There is some provision of similar courses for women outside the MSC. New Opportunities for Women (NOW) courses or similar 'return to work' courses are to be found in many further education colleges. These too are mainly concerned with women returning to work after a break and they do not demand any entry qualifications. The courses vary a great deal in content, emphasis and duration. Indeed there is no clear information on how many such courses are available in Britain.

The Industrial Training Boards were also empowered by the Sex Discrimination Act to run positive discrimination and return to work schemes. However, many of these twenty-four training boards have now been closed down by the Conservative Government, leaving only seven training boards in existence. MSC scrutiny and control has increased and finance has been changed. Some of the boards, like the Engineering Industry Training Board, have set up initiatives to try and improve the position of women in their sector but such initiatives tend to focus on school-leavers rather than older women and deal with very small numbers.[33] It is clear that, despite verbal commitment to the training needs of women, a commitment fuelled by government equality legislation, very little has so far been achieved in practice by state training bodies. This situation would be bad enough in a period of rising employment for all groups. In the current context it presents a gloomy picture. As current unemployment figures rise, many women are being thrown out of work and there has been a more rapid rise in their rate of unemployment than there has been for men.[34] Men's and women's jobs are segregated both vertically and horizontally in such a way that women are found primarily in the lower paid, lower level jobs and in female-dominated sectors of the economy.

Further opportunities for training at least offer some women the chance to move into male-dominated occupations where there are still employment opportunities or open paths to promotion. Training for women could also help prevent the further 'masculinization' of new occupations that are opening up. This is an important issue when it is expected that current female occupations will be hardest hit by new technology.[35] It seems clear, however, that many of the training programmes that recognize women's problems are being set up outside the MSC, although often drawing on sources of state financial assistance. Finance through the Inner City Partnership scheme can be used, for instance, to help establish training courses for women that are part-time and provide nursery facilities, both of which are essential for women with children. Such schemes are most often the ones that aim to open up opportunities in previously male-dominated areas of work.[36]

The opening up of training opportunities to women in this way merely juggles numbers within an existing work pattern where the majority of women workers provide a cheap source of labour. If women were to enter male-dominated occupations in large numbers, it seems likely that these could become 'feminized occupations' with associated problems of low pay and status. Women would not necessarily make any major gains in the long term.

The possibility of more radical gains for women comes from an area of state training policy that is highly controversial and which is not aimed solely at women. It is the area of youth policy.

The development of youth programmes

The youth programmes of the MSC developed from the Holland Report, *Young People and Work*, which was published in 1977.[37] This report marked the start of new developments inside the MSC which have had a major impact on the forms and sites of training offered to young people in Britain. The report was particularly concerned with the phenomenon of rising youth unemployment[38] and led to the establishment of a third agency inside the MSC, the Special Programmes Division which was set up in 1978. The Holland Report described previous efforts to deal with the unemployed in the 16–18-year-old age group as 'piecemeal and *ad hoc*', involving a variety of unco-ordinated agencies.[39] The view of the committee responsible for the report was that youth unemployment could be expected to rise as a result of demographic trends until at least 1981. The numbers of young unemployed were expanding rapidly, especially among girls, and as well the duration of unemployment was increasing. The report proposed a new and coherent programme to help this group find permanent jobs.

Two kinds of opportunities were to be offered to young trainees, work experience schemes and preparation for work courses. Many of the latter were to be offered in further education colleges and consisted of assessment, short industrial and remedial courses. This marked the intervention of the Department of Employment into the specifically educational area since the MSC bought its courses in the colleges. At the same time the development of the courses marked a revolution in the concept of training itself and in what constituted the skills which training courses were to pass on.

The courses were seen by the MSC as a bridge between school and work, a period of transition which had to be situated outside of a school system which so many pupils rejected by leaving as early as possible.[40] The courses were meant to provide those 'skills' which many school-leavers were felt to lack and which employers were assumed to require. In the past the notion of skill had been associated with craft work, with a combination of mental and physical dexterity in a particular area of work. Under the aegis of the Special Programmes Division a much wider definition of skill came into use. Skill was regarded more as a way of organizing activity and involved a combination of what are now regarded as individual skills and general skills, that is numeracy, communication and practical skills, together with social and life skills, attitudes to work and a knowledge of working life.[41] Training was, in this respect, given a new meaning which was removed from that traditionally used and evoked in the earlier MSC reports.

The development of MSC programmes dealing with youth unemployment came against a more general background of political concern with the process of transition from school to work that was part of a redefinition of educational objectives under the Labour government. This in turn was part of wider concern for economic and social problems. James Callaghan's speech[42] at Oxford in October 1976 had expressed concern about the links between education and the economy. The new political priority expressed there generated a number of consultative papers[43] and initiatives which are still continuing in the 1980s. This concern was not merely British but found expression throughout the European Community at this period.[44]

The focus on the problems created by 'youth' meant that schemes concentrating on this issue made provision for females as well as males. Widespread action in this area of training could not be seen entirely in male terms, especially as in many areas it was the young women who were suffering most from the effects of unemployment.

In 1979 a report was published on the opportunities for women and girls in the special programmes in the MSC. This report's special concern was with the ways in which women could be introduced into 'non-traditional' areas of work. The report started from the assumption that 'there are practically no jobs which cannot be done by girls, given the opportunity and appropriate training'.[45] It also recognized the specific form of disadvantages suffered by the female work-force. These included a lack of confidence to enter new areas and the problem of having different educational experiences. The report thought that girls' lack of technical and mathematical skills could be directly compensated for. Stress was placed on the need to avoid reinforcing female patterns of work in the courses, work experience and temporary schemes by making use of the exemptions allowed by the Sex Discrimination Act. The problems of older women with domestic responsibilities were also acknowledged. However, once again practice failed to match up to stated policy. The Youth Opportunities Programme (YOP) offered work experience schemes and work preparation courses. In the first year there were 162,000 participants in the scheme.[46] In 1981 around 500,000 took part. This represented a rise from one in ten school-leavers to one in two. Female school-leavers made up 50 per cent of those participating in YOPs and maintained this percentage despite the rise in the absolute numbers involved. However, within the programmes the same dispiriting pattern of work opportunities for women was to be found. Far more girls for instance, went into community work experience schemes, a continuation of women's role in 'caring' areas,[47] while more boys entered the training workshops. Work experience places in employers' premises made up the majority of opportunities in the YOPs programme and here the tendency was for further reinforcement of occupational segregation. To some extent the MSC could claim that this was out of their control, for the commission had to rely on the voluntary co-operation of employers. Employers, particularly in small firms, were notorious for their maintenance of segregated work-roles.

Sponsors could only be encouraged, not forced, to make provision for women in 'non-traditional' areas.[48]

Yet the problem was not just one of employers. Action research funded by the MSC found that MSC employees were also at fault. Staff would not accept, for instance, that girls could handle heavy weights in the building industry and thought that therefore to recruit them was to waste opportunities boys could profit from. A tutor only involved girls in a motor bike maintenance class by suggesting they upholstered the seat.[49]

The YOP scheme has now been replaced by the YTS, the Youth Training Scheme which became fully operational in September 1983. While YOP was always seen as a programme to solve what was presented as a temporary problem, the new scheme is regarded by policy-makers as a step towards a permanent scheme for young people in general.

The scheme offers twelve months' work experience with occupationally relevant education through one of two Modes, Mode A and Mode B. In Mode A financial support is given to employers to train employed and unemployed young people. In Mode B there are schemes for unemployed young people through Training Workshops, Community Projects, Information Technology Centres (B1) and small employers (B2). Mode A schemes take by far larger numbers and girls made up about 44 per cent of those on the scheme at the end of 1983, and around 35 per cent of those in Mode B schemes at the same time. The acceptance by the MSC of many of the inadequacies of the YOP programme, including the recognition of the sex stereotyping that the programme mainly reinforced, led many to hope that the new scheme would be able to offer women[50] the opportunities YOP had denied them. However, all the signs suggest that exactly the same patterns are repeating themselves and that exactly the same excuses are being used. The use of Occupational Training Families (OTFs), for instance, to help structure the curriculum is thought to reinforce gender segregation. Career advisors, YTS managers and employers are thought not to encourage, and even on occasions discourage, any preferences by girls for 'non-traditional' areas of experience. The reliance of Mode A upon employers obviously raises the question again of how far it would be possible to impose changes on employers who cling to existing sex stereotyping in their attitudes to employees.

The MSC continues to stress the importance of opening up new opportunities to women but there is little evidence to suggest that, as yet, the YTS is doing other than to perpetuate pre-existing stereotypes and divisions. There is even evidence of occasions when the MSC has appeared to be deliberately unwilling to countenance any expenditure on facilities like childcare that are a necessity for many women attempting to take first steps outside the home and into the labour market.[51]

The issue of racism and racial stereotypes has also to be faced. Assumptions about the cultural features of various ethnic groups can intertwine with other assumptions about the 'true' role of women in our society to produce a double burden on some women. One commentator looking at the earlier YOP schemes of the MSC stated:

The prevalence of sex-role stereotyping existing in the wider context of society is reflected in YOP schemes through gender appropriate training schemes such as community service, sewing and typing for the young female trainees and building maintenance, carpentry and painting and decorating for the young male trainees. This gender-ascribed job training is compounded by specific cultural and racial features in the case of Asian girls. One YOP scheme in Yorkshire trained the predominantly Muslim female trainees by taking them out to the park for walks and their work placement consisted of them watching male trainees dig up old people's gardens.[52]

The effective provision of training opportunities for women has to be seen as involving more than formal access to courses. Effective provision has to counter sexism within the courses and the paths into certain occupations but, as importantly, it has also to involve the provision of certain elements which recognize the demands placed on women by their existing dual role in the home. Flexibility of starting dates, compensatory pre-programmes in technical areas, childcare provision, advertising in the kinds of areas women frequent such as playgroups, health centres and supermarkets, all such elements should be seen as part of effective state training provision for women especially in the light of calls for on-going and recurrent training in the context of a changing labour market. Training is not just a matter for youth, but even where attention is focused on the school-leaver substantial changes need to be effected to cope with the present patterns in training provision. These changes will require both internal re-education within the MSC and careful negotiation with employers. Such changes are not impossible if commitment rather than rhetoric is the keystone for MSC policy.

The importance of such a commitment in both policy *and* practice by the MSC is further illustrated by recent developments. In the not too distant past, training and education were regarded as separate entities. In practice the distinction was not always so clear cut, but education was, in general, regarded as a more general preparation for life while training was felt to involve the provision of more explicitly technical skills that certain occupations required. Over the last decade and a half, in a context of rising youth unemployment, an economic recession and a tight labour market, a new vocationalism has developed in schools, a sense that schooling should prepare more directly for the labour market. One recent development has been the TVEI, the Technical and Vocational Education Initiative launched in 1983. In this initiative the MSC has poured funds into pilot projects in schools with the aim of producing more skilled youngsters, and equal opportunities was one of the main criteria the MSC expected LEAs (Local Education Authorities) to meet. Despite this, the structure of the pilot programmes appears to have been blatantly sex stereotyped in most cases.[53] Eagerness to get programmes set up combined with lack of effective equal opportunities criteria and efficient monitoring has resulted in a continuing gap between policy programmes and actual practice.

Conclusion

Women are faced with patterns of representation which are male and therefore express male interests. There are few women in positions of authority in the government, in the MSC, amongst employers' federations or in the unions, yet these are precisely the groups mostly involved in policy decision-making in the area of training. When this situation changes then so will the prospects for women in general. Increasingly, analyses indict the way in which unions fail to represent their women members and conceptualize demands in terms of the interests of male members.[54] At the other extreme very few women have made it into high level managerial positions and their lack of promotion reflects very clearly a refusal by male managers to value women's work or open up opportunities.[55] If women did get into positions of authority a more general recognition of the abilities of women is likely to follow. However, to achieve this a programme of positive action and education appears necessary inside unions, inside the civil service, and inside business organizations. A similar problem exists in relation to racism in our social, educational and training institutions and at the moment there are very few studies to even indicate the extent of the problem.

Currently women of all ethnic groups are meeting obstacles at all levels and in a wide variety of sites. Without such changes it seems only too likely that the present pattern of limited opportunities for women and continued sex stereotyping will continue to exist. Organizations such as the MSC do not have the resources for evaluation and monitoring of their schemes even where a commitment to do better for women does exist at the top. It seems therefore that the focus of attention should be on the transformation of the practice of those on the ground in state training programmes so that they open up and welcome all women in every area of work.

Notes and references

1 CSE Sex and Class Group, Mimeograph, 1981.

2 Cockburn, C., *Brothers*, London, Pluto Press, 1983, p. 113.

3 Phillips, A. and Taylor, B., 'Sex and skill: notes towards a feminist economics', *Feminist Review*, no. 6, 1980.

4 Pollert, A., *Girls, Wives, Factory Lives*, London, Macmillan, 1981, p. 65.

5 The number of centres fell from twenty-three in 1951 to thirteen in 1962. However, by 1971 the numbers had increased to 1952. House of Commons Expenditure Committee, Seventh Report, London, HMSO, 1973.

6 Ministry of Labour, *Training for Skill: Recruitment and Training of Young Workers in Industry* (Carr Report), London, HMSO, 1958.

7 Ministry of Education, *15–18* (Crowther Report), London, HMSO, 1959.

8 Ministry of Education, *Half Our Future* (Newsom Report), London, HMSO, 1963.

9 Land, H., 'Sex role stereotyping in the social security and income tax systems', in J. Chetwynd and O. Hartnett (eds), *The Sex Role System*, London, RKP, 1978; Land, H., 'Who cares for the family?', *The Journal of Social Policy*, July 1978; Land, H. 'The family wage', *Feminist Review*, no. 6, 1980. The male breadwinner family makes up 5 per cent of the present workforce. See Coussins, J. and Coote, A., *The Family in the Firing Line*, London, CPAG, 1981.

10 For example, in 1974 in CSE examinations 191,275 girls compared with 185,562 boys passed English; 59,482 girls passed in French compared with 37,127 boys. However, when it came to maths 142,801 girls passed compared to 152,672 boys; in physics the difference was even more notable – 10,221 girls passed compared to 76,074 boys. The GCE results showed similar differences. See Deem, R., *Women and Schooling*, London, RKP, 1978, tables 3.2 and 3.3, pp. 67–8.

11 The Industrial Training Bill, 1964.

12 Frank Cousins of the Transport and General Workers Union is quoted to this effect in Perry, P., *The Evolution of British Manpower Policy*, London, Bacie, 1976, p. 106.

13 Woodhall, M., 'Investment in women: a reappraisal of the concept of human capital', *International Review of Education*, **19**, 1, 1973.

14 House of Commons Expenditure Committee, *The Employment of Women*, Sixth Report, London, HMSO, 1973. Evidence of the National Joint Committee of Working Women's Organizations, p. 84.

15 HCEC, *The Employment of Women*, Memorandum of the National Council of Women of Great Britain.

16 Dept of Employment, *Government Observations on Three Reports on Youth Employment Services, the Employment of Women, and Employment Services and Training*, Cmnd. 5536, London, HMSO, 1974.

17 House of Commons Expenditure Committee, *The Employment of Women*, Sixth Report, London, HMSO, 1973, p. 2106.

18 HCEC, *The Employment of Women*.

19 HCEC, *The Employment of Women*, Memorandum of the National Council of Women of Great Britain, p. 97.

20 Dept of Employment, *Training for the Future – A Plan for Discussion*, London, HMSO, 1972.

21 Dept of Employment, *Employment and Training: Government Proposals*, Cmnd. 5250, London, HMSO, 1973.

22 Dept of Employment, *Government Observations on Three Reports on Youth Employment Services, the Employment of Women and Employment Services and Training*, Cmnd. 5536, London, HMSO, 1974.

23 MSC, 'Training Opportunities for women', Training Services Agency, London, MSC, 1976.

24 Sex Discrimination Act, 1975.

25 Type of employment entered by school leavers in 1974:

Class of employment	Boys (per cent)	Girls (per cent)
Apprenticeship to a skilled occupation	43.0	6.5
Employment leading to recognized professional qualifications	1.3	1.7
Clerical employment	7.0	40.5
Employment with planned training	17.1	17.3
Other	31.6	34.0

Source: Figure 4, *Training Opportunities for Women*.

26 Alexander, M., *Equal Opportunities and Vocational Training*, Berlin, European Centre for the Development of Vocational Training, 1980, p. 9.

27 These statistics can be found in Fonda, N., 'Current entitlements and provisions: a critical review', in Fonda, N. and Moss, P. (eds,), *Mothers in Employments*, Middlesex, Brunel University, 1976, p. 43; Rothwell, S., 'United Kingdom', in Yohalem, A. (ed.), *Women Returning to Work*, London, Frances Pinter, 1980, p. 197; Alexander, *Equal Opportunities*, p. 9; Robarts, S., *Positive Action for Women*, London, NCCL, 1981, p. 87.

28 These have been the elements the EOC is most concerned about. See EOC, *Review of the Training Opportunities Scheme*, Manchester, EOC, 1978.

29 Alexander, *Equal Opportunities*, p. 9.

30 Fonda, *Mothers in Employments*.

31 Rothwell, *Women Returning to Work*.

32 Stoney, S., and Reid, M., *Further Opportunities in Focus*, report of a project commissioned by the FEU from the National Foundation for Educational Research, 1980.

33 Keil, T., and Newton, P., 'Into work – continuity and change', in Deem, R. (ed.), *Schooling for Women's Work*, London, RKP, 1980; Cook, A., 'Vocational training, the labour market and the unions', in Steinberg Ratner, R. (ed.), *Equal Employment Policy for Women*, Philadelphia, Temple University Press, 1980.

34 *Registered Unemployment*

	1975	1980
Female	141,600	457,400
Male	650,200	1031,500

that is a 59 per cent rise for men, a 223 per cent rise for women.
EOC, *Submission of Written Evidence to the House of Lords Select Committee on Long-Term Remedies for Unemployment*, Manchester, EOC, 1980.

35 Some take a minimizing view of the possible impact of new technology, Sinfield, A., *What Unemployment Means*, London, Martin Robertson, 1981, p. 137. Others anticipate catastrophic effects. There appears to be no exact way of calculating the possible effects of technological change, Hesselman, L. and Spellman, R., 'Responses to the employment consequences of technological change', paper given to the Production Studies Group Conference on the Employment Consequences of Technological Change, September 1980. However, there is a consensus that it is areas of female employment that will be worst hit. Gershuny, J., 'Technical innovation and women's work in the EEC: a medium-term perspective', mimeograph, EEC Seminar on Women's Employment Prospects, Manchester, May 1980; Bird, E., *Information Technology in the Office: the impact on women's jobs*, Manchester, Equal Opportunities Commission, 1980.

36 Fawkes, J., 'Breaking the mould', *The Guardian*, 16 December 1981.

37 MSC, *Young People and Work* (Holland Report), London, MSC, 1977.

38 Between 1972 and 1977, the year of the report, the number of unemployed 16–17-year-olds had risen 120 per cent compared to an overall rise of 45 per cent in unemployment.

39 MSC, *Young People and Work*, London, MSC, 1977, p. 7.

40 Holland, G., 'The Youth Opportunities Programme', *Trends in Education*, summer 1979.

41 A typology of this new definition of skills is available in Schools Council Discussion Document, *Skills for Employment 1980*.

42 *TES*, 22 October 1976, 'What the PM said'.

43 After that three clear directions for future development emerged. The first dealt with vocational preparation for the employed. See DES, *A Better Start in Working Life*, Consultative Paper, London, HMSO, 1979. The second dealt with schools and work. See *Education in Schools: a Consultative Document*, Cmnd. 6869, London, HMSO, 1977. The third dealt with the area of training. An overview of the latter two was provided in DES, *16–18, Education and Training for the 16–18 year olds: a Consultative Paper*, London, HMSO, 1978.

44 A major European Communities Action Programme was launched in 1976 by a resolution of Council and the Ministers of Education meeting in Council. It included pilot projects, reports on common themes, study visits and workshops, statistical guidelines and information arrangements. The European Social Fund has also been changed to provide assistance in this area.

45 MSC, *Opportunities for Girls and Women in the MSC Special Programmes for the Unemployed*, London, MSC, 1979.

46 MSC, *Annual report 1978–9*, London, MSC, 1980.

47 MSC, *Review of the Second Year of Special Programmes*, London, MSC, 1980, p. 7.
48 Green, S., 'The employer's attitude to working mothers', in Fonda, N. and Moss, P. (eds), *Mothers in Employment*, Middlesex, Brunel University, 1976; MSC, *Opportunities for Girls and Women in the MSC Special Programmes for the Unemployed*, London, MSC, 1979.
49 Brelsford, P. *et al.*, *Give Us a Break*, MSC Research and Development Series no. 11.
50 Davies, S., *Women and Training News*, no. 13, 1983.
51 Greenwich Employment Resource Unit, Skill Centre Report, 1984.
52 Quoted in Carby, H., 'Schooling in Babylon', in Centre for Contemporary Cultural Studies, *The Empire Strikes Back*, London, Hutchinson, 1982.
53 Millman, V., 'The new vocationalism', in Whyte, J. *et al.* (eds), *Girl Friendly Schooling*, London, Methuen 1984.
54 Phillips, A., *Hidden Hands*, London, Pluto Press, 1983.
55 Crompton, R. and Jones, G., *White Collar Proletariat*, London, Macmillan, 1984.

Part Six

Sex Equality and Education Policy

21   Political lip-service or radical reform? Central government responses to sex equality as a policy issue

Madeleine Arnot

Between the late 1960s and the mid 1980s, equality between the sexes became a major focus of debate within the education service. Attention focused primarily, although not exclusively on the problem of female education. In the past, the criterion used for educational planning had been one of maintaining gender differentiation – of educating male and female pupils for different, complementary roles in adult life. By the early 1970s, however, such criteria were challenged by a new set of principles concerning social equality. In the new economic and ideological climate, such principles appeared conservative, if not unjust.

The primary aim of this chapter is to investigate how equality between the sexes became an educational issue and why anti-discrimination legislation was passed in 1975. I will consider what implications such legislation had for education and how the law has been implemented. I shall also consider the responses of three major policy-making bodies – the Equal Opportunities Commission (EOC), the Department of Education and Science (DES) and the Manpower Services Commission (MSC) – to the issue of sex equality in education, and suggest ways in which their responses can be interpreted.

Sex discrimination and the policy agenda

Since the Second World War, a number of major changes had taken place which were key factors in reshaping education policy. Some of the most noticeable of these were changes in the economic position of women, economic expansion and the construction of new political debates and ideologies around concepts of equality and civil rights.

One of the major changes in employment patterns in the twentieth century was clearly evident by the 1960s – namely the increased proportion of married women workers. Between 1911 and 1961 the proportion of married women who were economically active had risen from 10 to 30 per cent (EOC, 1981a).[1] This increase in married women workers had repercussions for the patterns of female employment. For example, lack of adequate childcare facilities and the domestic responsibilities of women with families led a large proportion of women to take part-time employment. By 1978, 84 per cent of all part-time workers were women: women part-time workers represented 40 per cent of the female work-force (DES, 1981).

Large numbers of women were clustered in a very small range of occupations,

Source: Commissioned. This is an adapted and expanded version of Open University *Race, Gender and Education Policy-Making*, Module 4, E333, *Policy-Making in Education*, Milton Keynes, Open University Press, 1986.

usually described as 'women's work'. For example, by the early 1970s over two-thirds of women workers were employed in service industries (e.g., financial, professional and scientific services, distributive trades and miscellaneous services such as catering and laundry work). Men and women worked essentially in different sets of occupations, in what has been called a *segregated* labour market (see, for example, MacDonald, 1981; Beechey, 1986).

Other aspects of female employment which also became significant in debates about women's work and their education were unequal pay and restricted access to higher status employment. Between 1970 and 1978 women's average earnings were below 65 per cent of men's average earnings. Even where women achieved equivalent educational qualifications to men their pay was substantially less (Reid, 1981, p. 211).[2] Also, women were not often employed in the higher levels of skilled work or in supervisory or managerial/professional positions. Skilled work had become defined as work which men did (Phillips and Taylor, 1980). This became even more evident in the early 1970s when only 14 per cent of skilled manual workers were women, and the proportion of female unskilled workers reached 37 per cent (Hakim, 1978, p. 1267).[3]

Evidence of such patterns of female employment collected by various campaigning groups (see Rendel, 1985) in the late 1960s helped gather support among politicians and policy-makers who, if not convinced of the injustice of such sexual divisions, saw their implications for manufacturing industry. Post-war reports on education and training were concerned with shortages of skilled labour and scientists and technologists needed for economic expansion. The Robbins Report (Committee on Higher Education, 1963), for example, pointed to the 'reserves of untapped ability' among girls and women, but mostly it was the career interests of grammar school or 'academically able' girls that had captured policy-makers' attention (Deem, 1981; Wolpe, 1976). Ironically, little attention was paid to the need to draw girls into apprenticeships for skilled work or non-traditional courses (Wickham, 1986).

The political and social climate of the 1960s also provided a conducive environment for those concerned with social inequality in post-war prosperity. In this decade, political movements campaigned for civil rights – for a less hierarchical society and for a more equal distribution of wealth and power. In the United States the black civil rights movement and the women's movement fought for policies to tackle race and sex discrimination.

Although few accounts are available of the politics surrounding the passage of the Sex Discrimination Act, 1975, it is clear that the impetus for reform came largely from the developing women's movement and from individuals active in political parties and trades unions (see Bryne and Lovenduski, 1978; Rendel, 1985). By the late 1960s only a limited number of strategies to combat social inequality were available to reformers, particularly those concerned with education. Important precedents had been set by experiments to reduce social class inequalities (e.g., Educational Priority Areas, comprehensive school reorganization, the removal of the 11-plus examination, the expansion of higher education). However, none of these strategies had proved to be particularly effective in eradicating class differences. Attempts to tackle the 'problem' of 'immigrant' education and race relations had also yielded few results – race discrimination and conflict apparently becoming more widespread.

Anti-discrimination legislation had also been developed. The Race Relations Acts, 1965 and 1968, paved the way through opposition to the use of legislation to tackle social disadvantage and prejudicial attitudes, even if these were weak in their formulation and powers of enforcement (McCrudden, 1982). Such legislation was an important means of changing the climate of opinion by legitimating the concept of 'discrimination' in policy debates and giving credibility to attempts at social reform. However, as yet, no-one had attempted to use anti-discrimination legislation for the education system.

Experience from the United States suggested that a centralized enforcement agency in addition to the courts would be useful in co-ordinating policy on discrimination. Where the power lay to enforce change in the education system in the UK was a matter of interpretation. The assumed 'partnership' between the DES, LEAs and teachers was not one which could easily embrace coercion on such issues as sex or race discrimination.

The education system is essentially conservative. If discrimination exists within it, considerable pressure would be required to produce any major change. Women's access to power within the education service has been, therefore, a critical determinant of the choice of political strategy. The fact that women constituted the majority of teachers, in Scale 1 and 2 posts in primary and secondary schools, but that only a small proportion of deputy heads or heads were women has been significant. Also relevant, perhaps, has been the fact that the proportion of women in leadership roles in primary and secondary schools in the period between 1965 and 1974 actually declined, particularly in headships in secondary schools. In further and higher education the picture has been similar (see Byrne, 1978).

Where women have been given higher scale or special responsibility posts, these tended to be typically 'female' – for example, as senior mistresses in mixed schools responsible for the pastoral needs of girls, social functions, pregnant schoolgirls, 'difficult' parents, or school attendance. The mainstream responsibilities of school organization, curriculum arrangements, administration, examinations and resource allocation have been primarily given to men (Byrne, 1978, p. 233). School ancilliary staff also reflected this sexual division of labour – office staff, 'dinner ladies' and librarians were usually female, and caretakers invariably male (Marland, 1983, pp. 52–3).

Few women have been able to use the channels of access to policy-making available to HM Inspectors, Chief Education Officers, local authority inspectors or even advisers, since these positions were generally filled by men. The under-representation of women was such that there were often no women at all in the most senior positions in educational management. Women could have gained access to policy-making as teacher governors or parent governors, especially when explicit attempts were made to improve their representation: 'Note III of the Model Instrument of Government for County Secondary Schools (1945) proposed that "adequate representation" should be given to women in the constitution of Governing Bodies' (Johnson, 1983, pp. 6–7). A recent survey (Johnson 1983) revealed a low female participation level, the average being around 35 per cent.

However it is not clear whether the Sex Discrimination Act actually reduced the proportion of female governors by ruling out the possibility of any positive discrimination in their favour.

Women have not fared much better in the world of local and national politics. Seven years after the Sex Discrimination Act, women constituted only 18 per cent of local councillors, and between 1945 and 1985 there were never more than twenty-eight female MPs in parliament (EOC, 1983). Of the few women who reached Cabinet level, they have been more likely to be given the post of Secretary of State for Education and Science than to be made Chancellor or Home Secretary, and of the forty-one Presidents of the Board of Education, Ministers of Education and Secretaries of State for Education and Science so far this century, only four were women: Ellen Wilkinson (1945–7), Florence Horsburgh (1951–4), Margaret Thatcher (1970–4) and Shirley Williams (1976–9).

Given such a distribution of women in policy-making, it was likely that those campaigning for education reform and for equal opportunities for girls and women would seek new legislation, especially if (as was the case in the US: see Fishel and Pottker, 1977) policy-makers in local authorities and in schools and colleges were unsympathetic to the view that education might be sex-biased. Using the courts as agents of change also had the advantage of offering a stronger mechanism for enforcing policy intentions than could be gained through the usual channels of policy-making.

Education and the Sex Discrimination Act

By the end of the 1960s, the Labour government had responded to political and economic pressures by setting up the Women's National Commission (WNC) in the Cabinet Office to represent at the highest level 'the informed opinion' of women in the country; by sponsoring a number of private members' bills on abortion reform and divorce reform; and by formulating its first major intervention in the shape of the Equal Pay Act 1970. However members of the Labour Party, trade unions and other political organizations mobilized to gather support for a more comprehensive measure, to tackle, at national level, the major obstacles to equality between the sexes.

There was some debate about whether such a measure should be part of the policies designed to deal with racial inequality. The Labour government considered how the procedures, coverage and enforcement provisions of the Sex Discrimination Act (1975) and Race Relations Act (1976) could be 'harmonized', and whether a single agency could deal with both issues. Working against the idea of a single agency was, perhaps, the view that women in the UK were unlikely to be happy with such close association with the 'problem' of racial groups, and would expect more serious attention to be given to women's issues. In the end the government moved in favour of

adopting, almost entirely, similar coverage and enforcement details for the eradication of race and sex discrimination.

Not only should this have the practical advantages of increasing public understanding of how the two Acts operated and of enabling both enforcement agencies to work on similar lines, there also appeared to be political advantage in easing the passage of any race relations legislation since Parliament would already have approved virtually identical enforcement provisions in the Sex Discrimination Act, 1975 (McCrudden, 1982).

Although the wording of the two acts was often identical, the legislation differed in several crucial aspects. For example, certain practices were to be exempt from the provisions of the Sex Discrimination Act: it was felt justifiable to allow some separate and different facilities for each sex but not for each racial group (Home Office, 1974).

A number of features distinguished the Sex Discrimination Act from previous anti-discrimination legislation. Clearly it represented a victory for campaigners for sex equality: 'An ideal which had been thought unimportant had become a matter of government policy' (Rendel, 1978, p. 900). However another distinguishing feature was the inclusion of education for the first time despite opposition from the DES. The surprise with which campaigners greeted such success is conveyed in Byrne's recollections:

Late in the evening, late in November 1975, the telephone rang in the study. The voice of a colleague from Westminster came over the line, succinct, tired, but satisfied. 'It's through'. 'With education and training still in?'. 'Yes'. The Sex Discrimination Act 1975 had finally received the Royal Assent, with, as Huxley would have said, 'all its parts of equal strength and in smooth working order' – or nearly. We had won the first hurdle in legislative terms, in the race to convince government that it is useless to attempt to tackle inequality in employment, in pay and salary, or social discrimination, without simultaneously attacking their causes and counter-remedies – the formative years of education and training (Byrne, 1978, pp. 245–6).

In 1973, while considering its own Sex Discrimination Bill, the Conservative government concluded that there was adequate provision for the Secretaries of State for Education and Science to make sure that the education system was not discriminating on grounds of sex. In contrast the Labour government's *Equality for Women* (Home Office, 1974, p. 13) took the view that these powers of the Secretaries of State for Education and Science did 'not relate expressly to sex discrimination', and did not 'apply to private educational institutions which receive no financial assistance and do not provide education for children of compulsory school age'. Further there were no specific powers in Scottish legislation.

The new legislation, therefore, contained the provision that it was the duty of LEAs, governing bodies and proprietors of schools, colleges and other educational institutions, universities and private educational institutions to provide, for both sexes, facilities of *like quality*, in *like manner* and on *like terms*.

The education sections of the Sex Discrimination Act were contested (see Rendel, 1986, for a full account). The price paid for allowing education to remain in the legislation involved the exemption of single-sex schools and sport from the act. 'Positive action' (i.e. positive discrimination which could take the form of quotas, special access routes or courses) was only permitted within training programmes in the post-compulsory sector (not in general education). Also 'contract compliance' (i.e. funding criteria) was omitted as a strategy. Further the powers of the EOC in implementing the law were curtailed as far as education was concerned. The EOC was unable to issue non-discrimination notices in relation to investigations into education and complaints about education had to be referred to the Secretary of State in the first instance (Rendel, 1985).

Further the legislation did not deal with sex-stereotyping in school curricula and textbooks either 'because of the administrative opposition it would have aroused' or 'because the content of education was not at that time a subject open to direct ministerial intervention, still less to statutory intervention' (Rendel, 1985, p. 91).

Like the 1976 Race Relations Act, the Sex Discrimination Act, as a policy, can be evaluated in several different ways. Lester and Bindman (1972), for example, see the legislation as representing 'a radical departure from the traditional neutrality and passivity of our legal system'. Britain is unique in western Europe in not having any Bill of Rights or formal constitution. The Race Relations Act (and by implication the Sex Discrimination Act) could therefore be seen as a major step towards attempting to guarantee that every person was treated on the basis of individual merit and towards providing an effective legal remedy for the most unfair or 'degrading' type of discrimination (Lester and Bindman, 1972, p. 15).

Other positive views of the anti-discrimination legislation have been put forward by McCrudden (1982) and Dorn (1985). They point in particular to the new definitions of *indirect discrimination* contained in the Sex Discrimination and Race Relations Acts which were substantially different from earlier versions. The new definition of discrimination took into account some prior existing disadvantages, and encouraged employers not just to refrain from certain actions but to promote equality. The old principle of 'non-discrimination', with its emphasis on removing prejudice, was replaced by a concept of 'fair equality of opportunity' which recognized 'the structural sources of unequal opportunity', in particular 'institutional discrimination'. 'Fair equality of opportunity . . . requires questions to be asked not only about the precise basis on which the good being distributed is deserved but also about the nature of the good being distributed' (McCrudden, 1982, p. 343). The shift in policy represented by the Sex Discrimination Act and the Race Relations Act could be interpreted as a move towards 'stronger' versions of equal opportunity. Dorn called this new policy stance a 'fair-shares approach' because of its concern with 'consequences, effects and outcomes', with promoting equality and justice rather than merely with removing acts of discrimination. Such an approach has considerable potential if adequately used.

A more sceptical view of the legislation saw its failure to tackle equality and to opt yet again for the safer concepts of equality of opportunity (e.g. Byrne, 1985). However even here such legislation was inadequate since it did not require equal opportunities policies to be formulated. The only *duty* expected of a person was not to discriminate against others. Such a limited duty, Bindman (1980) argued, does not encourage a redistribution of the benefits of society. A genuine equal opportunities policy would require at least one of three following methods:

a vigorously enforced law against discrimination which creates a strong motivation to take steps to avoid the risk of legal action; . . . making the adoption of suitable policies itself a legal requirement; and the government using its commercial and other executive powers to stimulate equal opportunity policies (Bindman, 1980, p. 255).

Other criticisms of the Sex Discrimination Act came from feminists who pointed to the failure of the legislation to challenge the covert social mores and the structure of the private sphere particularly of the family.[4] With no attempt to design complementary social policy that could tackle the inequalities between men and women in family life, politicians had ensured that women would retain their traditional roles – the effects of the legislation could at best be marginal. Policies – for example, on school hours, school meals and transport, school dress, and the timing of extra-mural classes – would still be premised upon the work of housewife mothers; as would health care, care of the aged, early childrearing, etc. (see David, 1984).

Such criticisms questioned whether the Sex Discrimination Act could ever be effective in promoting sex equality or even equal opportunity. Was it ever intended to be effective? Rendel has argued that 'equality is a principle to which lip-service is paid but was not (and is not) regarded as one of the great principles which should have priority in implementation' (Rendel, 1985, p. 89). The impact of the Sex Discrimination Act on education was dependent initially on the Equal Opportunities Commission and the courts and it is to these we now turn.

The Equal Opportunities Commission

The implementation of the Sex Discrimination Act is the responsibility of the EOC, a quasi-autonomous non-governmental organization (or quango) set up, like the Commission for Racial Equality (CRE), to have a 'strategic' role. The EOC's role was 'to eliminate discrimination; promote equality of opportunity between men and women; help individuals seek redress under the law and keep under review the working of the Sex Discrimination Act and the Equal Pay Act 1970' (EOC, 1976, p. 4).

EOC commissioners (unlike those of the CRE) were selected to represent the wider political and industrial constituencies in society; for example, the Trades Union Congress (TUC) and Confederation of British Industry (CBI) were each given three seats. Appointees have not been selected on the basis of their involvement in the women's movement nor their 'feminist' stance. Indeed commissioners and officers were apparently encouraged to 'leave their feminist hats' at home (Meehan, 1982, p. 15).

The initial approach of the EOC towards its role was excessively cautious. In its first annual report it was at pains to stress the difficulty of its task and the need to tread carefully.

Sex discrimination is rooted deep in the soil of attitudes, expectations and institutional practices. Many of its manifestations are obvious; the remedies, frequently, are not. Sometimes there is more than one option available; they all have to be weighed carefully. Nor would it serve the public interest to convey the impression that this most ancient form of inequality can be remedied overnight with a few, spectacular strokes. There is much undramatic, patient, humdrum work necessary; the results will not be visible instantly. It is especially important that the credibility of this powerful law should not be weakened on account of lack of forethought or deliberation. Neither the public interest nor the cause of equality for women would be served by precipitate action or the indiscriminate use of powers because these powers exist. The Commission is under no illusion that the road ahead is long, that the challenge of equality is a hard one, and it believes that it has been important to take stock of its priorities, so that in the years ahead its powers of enforcement can be deployed with the full force which Parliament intended (EOC, 1976, pp. 4–5).

The extent to which such caution determined policy was nowhere more clear than in the case of education. The EOC first concentrated upon removing sex discrimination as defined by the letter of the law. Such discrimination, it argued, occurred more *by default* than by intent. Given that its legal powers were limited in terms of enforcing change in the education system and that education planning was largely decentralized, the EOC faced a number of dilemmas. How could a quango promote fast policy change in education, given its location outside the education system and the belief in local autonomy which then existed? How could it produce change in education without using the law unless really necessary, or unless legal procedures could produce more significant reform of behaviour than gaining the consent of the individuals or the agency involved?

The line which the EOC adopted towards education has been one of operating within the structure of education policy-making, rather than insisting on new strategies of centralized direction. It has concentrated its efforts on opening negotiation channels with LEAs, schools and colleges and with the DES, MSC, teacher unions, etc. The policy approach has been largely proscriptive rather than prescriptive, reactive rather than proactive (see Arnot, 1986). The impetus for its work has been a belief that sex discrimination can be removed from the education system by increased knowledge of the issues, rational discussion and limited coercion mainly using the threat of the law. The option of using the courts to enforce change appeared unattractive. Judges, after all, were not trained to deal with such legislation (Rendel, 1985; Kant, 1985); discrimination in education was hard to prove; the curriculum courses to which pupils might be denied access were likely to have already finished by the time the courts had ruled; parents would be reluctant to put their child through the courts only to be criticized by the judge for so doing; and compensation, if awarded, was difficult to collect.[5] Further some of the most contentious educational issues, such as sexual harassment, were not challengeable in law.

Teacher employment appears to be the only educational issue which could be effectively tackled through the courts. The EOC has taken a number of cases of discrimination in teacher employment to court and has won some important victories. The principle of equal pay for work of equal value enshrined in the Equal Pay Act (1984) is also likely to produce an increase in such cases being taken to court.[6]

The central policy goals of the EOC's education department have been to gain *equal access* and *treatment* for all pupils and students to educational facilities and benefits. Equal opportunities has been framed within liberal concerns of promoting equality of educational opportunity, maintaining an individual's freedom of choice by removing 'obstacles', increasing student motivation and re-educating the teaching profession and its managers. The primary source of sex discrimination has been defined as that of *curriculum differentiation*. The patterns of male and female subject choice and specialisms in school, college or university or within the teaching profession, different teaching and assessment styles, and classroom practice, have been the main focus of attention. The ideal has been to encourage boys and girls into 'non-traditional' courses, and to encourage more female teachers into senior posts, into education management and into scientific and technical subjects. Attention has focused on providing examples of good practice for teachers at all levels of the educational system and codes for employment practice.

The goals of the EOC are essentially liberal, in so far as they aim for improvement in the distribution of education, compensation for individuals for past disadvantage and changes in social attitudes. Its approach emphasizes the impact of traditional sex-role socialization and attempts to replace it with a fairer system of preparation for family and work lives.

The strategy adopted by the EOC to obtain these objectives has much in common with the 'softly softly approach' initially adopted by the CRE (Arnot, 1986). By negotiating with chief education officers, inspectors and the advisory services in LEAs, the EOC has tried to settle complaints without going to court. One of the priorities has been to promote good practice through the distribution of booklets such as *Do You Provide Equal Educational Opportunities?* (EOC 1980) to every educational institution and LEA. (Other more specialized booklets on, for instance, caring for the under-fives, careers guidance, home economics, craft, design and technology, post-compulsory school, and school governors have also been produced.) Heads of schools and colleges have been requested to place sex discrimination on the agenda at staff meetings and to encourage teachers and lecturers to help change institutional practices.

Such a strategy has been fraught with difficulties. For example, there were few guarantees that teachers would receive or even read the material (booklets were distributed on the basis of one per school). Further, such material was often interpreted in a way that confirmed existing attitudes. Borley (1982) evaluated the impact of *Do You Provide Equal Educational Opportunities?* on a sample of coeducational secondary schools and found that the material was 'preaching to the converted', or it reaffirmed the view that schools could continue as they were and still be within the law, or it confirmed change already in progress. She concluded that publication and dissemination was not likely to be an adequate way to change the status quo, particularly if too much discretion was left to LEAs and schools. Indeed the evidence suggests that teachers are still conservative in their attitudes towards sex equality issues, and display little commitment to change (Pratt, 1985).

The EOC, however, has seemed reasonably happy with the impact of its policy. In 1983 it came to the conclusion that:

The Commission has played a major part in bringing equal opportunities into the mainstream of educational debate. The evidence is visible in many ways. Some local education authorities have now appointed Equal Opportunity Advisers; most HM Inspectorate reports include comments on aspects of the curriculum and staffing relating to equal opportunities; and the educational press regularly features articles on issues central to the Commission's concerns. It may be some years before this increased awareness is translated into quantifiable results, but the reality of the process is evident to all those familiar with the educational world (EOC, 1983, p. 2).

It is certainly to the EOC's credit and to the force of the Sex Discrimination Act that, when complaints are made, LEAs apparently '. . . almost without exception have demonstrated a willingness to comply with the legislation and to improve the education facilities for the pupils concerned' (Carr, 1984). However, many would challenge the EOC's view that '. . . although ten years ago the educational establishment regarded the Sex Discrimination Act as at best marginal to its concerns. Today equality of opportunity in education between boys and girls is regarded *as a central part of a school's business*' (EOC, 1985, p. 2) (my emphasis).

The EOC's policy on education has been much criticized, not least for its failure to use civil litigation to settle complaints and its failure to use what has been called the most powerful tool of the legislation – formal investigations (e.g. Byrne and Lovenduski, 1978; Applebey and Ellis, 1984). By 1985 only four formal investigations had been conducted – none of which appears to have any major impact. No sizeable body of case law has been established and the law remains largely untested.

However by the mid 1980s, the EOC has taken a more active interest in proposing reforms of the Sex Discrimination Act. EOC education officers have argued for the better use of this legislation and have allowed that the reluctance of some LEAs and schools to change their practice is attributable to indifference or hostility rather than ignorance of the law or of good practice (Carr 1985). Recent successful cases are likely to encourage further the use of courts and the investigative powers of the EOC to initiate its own agenda.[7]

Other criticisms of the EOC are, however, harder to meet. Feminist influence appears to have had little impact on the EOC as an organization. Meehan (1982) pointed to the failure of the EOC to orchestrate and use a policy network of women's groups and to organize a political constituency to keep women's issues on politicians' agendas. In the educational world, teachers' anti-sexist and anti-racist projects are not publicized and there is little support for them, other than occasional project or conference grants (despite a commitment by the EOC to fund networking especially after the demise of the Schools Council). The impact of the legislation and the EOC are also disappointing for those who wish to see greater evidence of sex equality in schooling – i.e., improvements in the quality of schooling for girls and in the experience of women teachers.

The EOC appears to be trapped within the structure of the legislation and its legal procedures. It is also limited by the political and administrative structure of government in the UK. The EOC's role as a quango has meant maintaining a stance of political neutrality (even though appointing EOC commissioners and allocating funds are the responsibility of the Home Office) and coping with a lack of security about its future. Although set up by a Labour government, the EOC has been maintained through a long period by a Conservative government. It is perhaps the liberalism of its stance and also its lack of threat to the tenets of conservatism which paradoxically has ensured its survival at times of government cuts in expenditure.

Central government policy and gender differentiation

Under the terms of the 1944 Education Act, the responsibility of ensuring that LEAs were not acting *unreasonably* lay with the DES. These responsibilities would, however, be irrelevant to the issue of sex equality unless sex discrimination in education was defined as unreasonable behaviour (Bloomfield and Pratt, 1980). But in fact this has not occurred and neither has the DES interpreted its 'powers' under the Education Act as those of defining and implementing an equal opportunities policy. The Sex Discrimination Act, it seems, also allowed the DES the opportunity to choose how far it would involve itself in promoting equal opportunities or implementing the legislation. The main responsibility for ensuring that unlawful behaviour did not occur within the maintained sector of education lay with LEAs, and this delegation, as we shall see, appears to have met with DES approval.

Clearly the extent to which the DES involves itself in gender issues is determined by the extent of the political will of the government in power, not merely its own interpretation of its 'powers'. If the political will is there, the DES has a variety of policy options available to it. Theoretically it could offer grants to encourage the development of curriculum initiatives, establish in-service courses and improve initial teacher education. It could use its approval mechanisms and its involvement in school/college building programmes and school reorganization to encourage particular policies (e.g. co-education or single-sex schools, science laboratories for girls' schools, adequate craft workshops for mixed schools etc.).

Assessing the DES stance towards sex equality in education is not a simple task. One could, for example, try and identify a policy within DES reports and publications, or one could assess the record of DES interventions. The latter activity would yield few results. The only projects with which the DES appears to have been directly involved are small numbers of DES/regional in-service training courses on aspects of sex-stereotyping in education, and short courses promoting equal opportunities in schools (Orr, 1985). Theoretically, the establishment of the Council for the Accreditation of Teacher Education (CATE) responsible for validating courses according to new DES criteria for initial teacher education contains the possibility of creating more substantial change.[8] One of these criteria is that students need to learn how 'to guard against preconceptions based on the race or sex of the pupils' (Circular 3/84, para 11). Wormald (1985), however, questions whether members of CATE (three women and fifteen men) are 'sensitized' sufficiently to the issues. For example, will they inquire if a course alerts students to the implications of such 'preconceptions' for resource allocation, for school and classroom organization or for the structure of the teaching profession, etc? Further, 'It will be important to know what questions CATE . . . is going to ask in its visits. . . . Will [it], for instance, report on sexist language and attributes in the training institutions?' (Wormald, 1985, p. 115).

Some scepticism about the impact of this initiative will no doubt remain. For example, the recent failure of the DES to use the opportunity provided by the Education (Grant and New Awards) Act 1985 to allocate funds to curriculum projects on gender gives grounds for suspicion that the sentiments expressed about equal opportunities in recent initiatives are indeed only lip-service.

It is significant that no explicit policy statement has been issued by the DES concerning equal opportunities for girls/women. A policy statement on sex equality would be even less likely, given the current political climate. Further, there has been no committee of inquiry to examine sex inequality comparable to the Rampton/Swann Committee investigating racial disadvantage in education. No central funds have been allocated to cater for the needs of girls along the lines of Section 11 grants for schools with a high proportion of ethnic minority pupils, nor has the DES prioritized gender as a concern for in-service funding. The DES has selected a role which one could argue is minimal and non-interventionist. A generous interpretation might argue that, as in the case of race (Kirp, 1985), the DES has developed a 'gender inexplicit policy' in order to 'do good by stealth'.

The central premise of the DES approach has been to maintain publicly that the prime responsibility for implementing the Sex Discrimination Act lies with local authorities and that the DES only has an 'advisory' role. The autonomy of local authorities and schools/colleges was reinforced clearly in Circular 2/76 (DES 1976) when the DES informed local authorities of their obligations under the Act:

9. . . Responsibility for evaluating curriculum to provide equal access to experience, information and guidance rests with local education authorities, managers and governors, and, most important of all, the teachers. While the Secretary of State will not hesitate to use his powers to stop any particular act of discrimination, he does not control the curriculum and it is important for teachers, with the support of local education authorities, to take a hard look at the organization of the curriculum and to consider whether the materials and techniques they use, and the guidance they give, especially in the early years, inhibit free choice later.

23 The Secretary of State expects that most local education authorities will be able to comply with the requirements of the Act by making appropriate administrative arrangements without incurring significant extra expenditure. If, however, any authorities find that their existing arrangements imply some unlawful discrimination within the terms of the Act and that in consequence some extra expenditure is unavoidable, they will be expected to contain that expenditure within budgets which are consistent with the Government's general advice on local authority expenditure. It will be the responsibility of local education authorities and other responsible bodies to ensure that their existing facilities and resources are so used as to ensure that there shall be no discrimination on grounds of sex (DES, 1976, pp. 3–4, 5 and 8).

Complying with the sex discrimination legislation was, it seems, a 'cheap option', to be catered for by existing budgets. The particular interpretation of sex discrimination in education as a *curriculum* matter allowed the DES to maintain such a stance. The only form of pressure it seems to have exerted on LEAs was to ask for information on what steps were being taken 'so far as the curriculum is concerned with the provisions and intentions of the Sex Discrimination Act 1975' (DES, 1977a). The use to which such information was put is unclear – it was never published. Whatever the response, in the same year the Green Paper *Education in Schools* firmly declared that 'distinctions between what boys study and what girls study are disappearing, and in many schools both are now educated for shared domestic responsibilities, including the responsibility of future parenthood' (quoted in Hannon, 1979, p. 105).

Various interpretations of DES policy on equal opportunities are available.

Some attempt has been made to glean a policy stance in the few sentences which appear on the subject in various official reports and policy documents. Arguably the absence of reference to gender issues (or 'gender blindness' – see Wormald, 1985) is more significant then the limited number of references to be found. Byrne (1985) takes such neglect of the issues as a sign that the DES has had no clear or coherent policy other than a series of initiatives which are addressed more towards equal opportunities than sex equality. Hannon (1979), on the other hand, identified DES policy as being one of 'negative exhortation' seen, for example, in such statements as 'care must be taken to see that girls do not, by subject choice, limit their career opportunities'. Schools should not, according to the DES 'by their assumptions, decisions or choice of teaching materials, limit the educational opportunities offered to girls' (DES, quoted in Hannon, 1979, p. 105).

However by 1985, Orr (an HMI with a strong concern for equal opportunities) saw, 'a clear commitment in government policy statements to the need to promote equal opportunities in schools and to encourage girls, in particular, in those areas of the curriculum where there is evidence of sex-related separation or under-achievement' (Orr, 1985). In contrast with Hannon's observation six years earlier that government policy lacked any 'serious intention to change matters', Orr identified a policy shift in, for example, *The School Curriculum* (DES, 1981), *Science Education in Schools* (DES, 1982) and the Cockcroft Report (Committee of Inquiry into the Teaching of Mathematics in Schools, 1982) which dealt specifically, although briefly, with girls' education or equal opportunities between the sexes. Other education policies, Orr argued, which focused, for example, on the importance of science for *all* pupils in primary schools or the development of new curricula in secondary schools, had significant implications for girls' education (e.g. DES, 1978, 1979).

Such positive views of recent trends in DES thinking are not supported by commentators such as Acker (1986) who points to the 'vague support' – indeed lip-service – given to equal opportunities' issues. In *Better Schools* (DES, 1985), a publication heralded as 'the blueprint for the next century', sex equality was referred to only twice in a chapter on the curriculum; the first reference indicated a need to remove 'preconceptions based on pupils' sex or ethnic origins' in determining curriculum objectives and the second reference states that the curriculum for all pupils should be broad, 'leaving no room for sex discrimination'. These were the only references to equal opportunities in ninety-one pages of text (quoted in Acker, 1986, p. 70).

Further Acker argues that general education policies, rather than benefit women as Orr suggested, have had damaging effects on women (e.g. the cuts in teacher training and adult education, the 'swing to science' and cuts in the arts).[9]

In 1973 the DES was criticized for its 'complacent' reaction to criticisms of the education system in terms of gender differences (House of Commons Select Committee, quoted in Rendel, 1985). Ten years later the Women's National Commission's working group on secondary education also challenged the DES's reluctance to commit itself to firm policies and extra funds. Representatives from the DES giving evidence to this working group argued there was a need for

gradual reform of the curriculum and a move towards greater conformity between schools.

They stressed that the secretary of state had no powers to enforce changes in the curriculum countrywide. There were at present enormous divergences between schools, especially in the third and fourth years when an infinite variety of option choices could be found. DES said that the majority of LEAs were now taking a close interest in the curriculum in their schools, and DES would encourage remaining LEAs to do so. But at present individual schools determine their own curriculum, and progress had to be mainly through persuasion (reported in WNC, 1983, p. 11).

The working group did not entirely accept such arguments for local autonomy or DES 'powerlessness'. They felt that the

DES had the means to give a strong lead through HMIs and through making *extra* resources for particular ends available in a judicious way. They should aim to create the conditions (which might mean more teachers and more facilities) for all girls and boys to experience the main areas of the curriculum (including CDT) before fourteen (WNC, 1983, p. 11).

The belief of the WNC in the possibilities of producing change in education through HM Inspectors would have been strengthened by the unexpected, although not excessive, amount of interest in gender issues they had already displayed. Such interest, particularly in curriculum differentiation, was perhaps initiated by the Inspectorate's involvement in two surveys on curricular differences between boys and girls in preparation for the Sex Discrimination Act 1975. These two reports (DES, 1975 and SED, 1975) represented landmarks in that, for the first time since the 1944 Education Act, an official survey examined the extent of sex differentiation in schools and raised questions about the benefits of co-education for girls. The two surveys provided an important basis for the inclusion of education in the legislation. Feminists such as Dale Spender (Spender and Sarah, 1980) drew on the findings which, although not conclusive nor indeed directly relevant for comprehensive schools, nevertheless played a part in opening a debate about co-education policy – a debate which had not taken place when comprehensive reorganization was introduced in the 1960s.[10]

The initial concern for curriculum differentiation developed into a commitment to encourage girls into science (*Girls and Science*, DES, 1980). However other strands were also visible in HMI reports. The HMI took the unusual step of arguing that schools should recognize that 'the role of women continues to change and with it, inevitably, the role of men. Both contribute to the care and upbringing of children' (DES 1977b, p. 10). Providing equal opportunities in education, they argued, must 'lead to some redistribution of responsibilities within the home as well as in the world of work' (DES, 1977b, p. 10). Rather more radical than equal opportunities statements concerning the need to encourage girls into science, these opinions, although brief, suggested a more active role for schools in changing rather than merely reproducing family relations.

Given the unique relation of the Inspectorate to the DES, it is hard to assess how far these views were actively encouraged, tolerated or largely ignored by DES officials. Interestingly a more limited and pragmatic version of the HMI view was expressed by Sir Keith Joseph, who argued that 'girls'' education must reflect the fact that most women will be working for much of their lives and that many may be the sole or principal breadwinner for a family' (quoted in Orr, 1985).

The possibilies of producing change using the Inspectorate, however, have been severely limited. Orr himself was quoted as saying in 1981 that there were limits to how far the Inspectorate could keep an eye on discrimination. The Inspectorate had been reduced to 400 and could inspect each secondary school only every twenty-five years. The goal was therefore to encourage each school to monitor the progress of its pupils according to sex, develop a curriculum policy that reflected the spirit and not just the letter of the Sex Discrimination Act 1975, and aim for a broader curriculum for all pupils (quoted in *Education* **6**, November 1981, p. 349).

Increased pressure has been put on the DES by the EOC, WNC and teacher unions, among others, to formulate a more committed response to equal opportunities. Some would argue it is difficult to see how much further the DES could go without treading on the toes of local authorities. Also local authorities themselves now appear to be taking up the challenge. Orr (1985) confirmed that although many might desire 'bold curriculum reform' and 'direct interventionist' strategies on a national scale, the decentralized nature of the English education system, whatever its strengths, was a major constraint on government action and increased the difficulty of 'achieving any ambitious and co-ordinated intervention'. Quoted in an earlier statement (1981), however, Orr had pointed to the fact that 'the whole business of equal opportunities just does not have enough political clout': a view that would probably be shared by many.

The MSC and positive action

In contrast to the DES, the Manpower Services Commission has taken up the challenge of equal opportunities far more directly and apparently with more political will. The reason for this is unclear since there is, as yet, no insider's account of how gender was placed on the MSC agenda in the early 1980s. Probably such a policy shift was brought about by committed individuals within the MSC, by pressure from trade unions, the EOC and also critically the European Economic Community (EEC). The fact that the MSC receives a large proportion of its funding for education projects from the EEC meant that the MSC had to be seen to be at least responsive to EEC equal opportunities initiatives.

In the early 1970s pressure from the EEC alone was not sufficient to press the UK government to respond positively to the Equal Treatment Directive (ETD). Initially the UK was reluctant to act, perhaps because of resentment to EEC interference in national educational systems rather than explicit opposition to dealing with girl's education (ROWE, 1983).

By the late 1970s a variety of EEC programmes of action had been set up which related to girl's education, including the promotion of textbook reform and in-service training. Although smaller than other EEC programmes, some believed that these projects 'went further towards the promotion of equal opportunities for girls than the provisions of the Sex Discrimination Act 1975' (ROWE, 1983, p. 102). The DES response was to consult a number of groups including teachers' unions, the Schools Council and LEAs. It came to the view that the proposals were 'so tiny as to be insignificant' (ROWE, p.102). In the event, the programme was dropped because of Denmark's opposition.

EEC proposals on equal opportunities were again dismissed in 1985 by the DES when Education Ministers pledged to tackle a range of issues in a ten-point programme designed to reform sex-stereotyping in teaching materials, subject/career choices, teacher training and the employment of teachers. Sir Keith Joseph, the Education Secretary, was quoted as saying such strategies had 'long been our practice' and that Britain had achieved 'considerable success in this field' (*Times Education Supplement*, 7 June 1985).

However, the Sex Discrimination Act had changed the terms of the debate in the training sphere by allowing the possibility of positive action programmes. The MSC was identified as a designated 'training body' in the legislation (the others were industrial training boards, the Training Services Division, and the Employment Service Division). These training bodies had the right to take 'positive action' to overcome the 'effects of past discrimination, as well as the effects of broader cultural and educational influences on people's choice of work' (EOC, 1981b). Such positive action could take the form of 'training' and 'encouragement' for one sex only. Training could include: **a** specific training or education in skills or subject matter; **b** development programmes for women in management; **c** career counselling; **d** integrated programmes comprising a number of these or similar steps (EOC, 1981b, p. 2). The incentive and the possibilities of action on equal opportunities were therefore more positive for the MSC than the DES.

The MSC made its first tentative steps towards providing new opportunities for women through the Training Opportunities Scheme (TOPS) and Wider Opportunities for Women (WOW) courses. However these new courses did little to break down stereotypes – if anything they aggravated the divisions between men's and women's choices. The Youth Training Schemes (YTS) faced similar problems of sex-stereotyping. Little emphasis was placed on training careers' advisers or YTS managers or on pressuring employers to encourage students into non-traditional areas. Although verbal commitment to increasing women's opportunities became more public, state training programmes were still primarily concerned with the needs of men (see Wickham, this volume for more detail; also Arnot, 1986).

The Technical and Vocational Educational Initiative (TVEI) provided those already concerned with gender with the opportunity to push harder for equal opportunities in general education, not only training. The MSC announcement of the first criterion for funding schools for TVEI was, however, somewhat unexpected: 'Equal opportunities should be available to young people of both sexes and they should normally be educated together on courses within each project. Care should be taken to avoid sex-stereotyping' (quoted in WNC, 1984, p. 51).

The MSC required that those receiving TVEI funds show some 'measurable response' to this criterion, and it put pressure on recipients to find solutions to the problem of sex differentiation in curriculum choice, even if the MSC itself had few answers. It was, in effect, the first time that some form of 'contract compliance' was used to promote equal opportunities in education in the UK. Arguably this placed the MSC in a far stronger position than the DES or even the EOC to bring about change in the school system.

The difficulties faced by schools with TVEI funding trying to reduce gender differentiation in curriculum choice were considerable. The MSC provided little help in terms of guidance or information about existing experiments and their effects. Co-ordinators for TVEI schemes were eventually offered some workshops on how to promote equal opportunities – curiously the grants for in-service provision (Grant Related In-service Training (GRIST)) did not specify equal opportunities as one of its priorities for funding. Nevertheless Millman and Weiner (1987) found the following positive effects:

TVEI's equal opportunities criterion had obliged many LEAs who had not previously addressed gender issues to at least look as if they were doing so. Though most TVEI personnel were initially ill-prepared, persistent requests from the MSC for 'hard evidence' of progress on equal opportunities prevented LEAs from backing away from the undeniably complex issues. Some projects maintained a superficial concern but others . . . moved towards a deeper personal and professional understanding of the underlying issues, accompanied by a stronger commitment to tackle them. These are likely to continue asking questions beyond the lifetime of TVEI . . . (Millman and Weiner, 1987).

The possibilities for change 'engendered' by the TVEI approach (such as the collection of data required by the MSC and the availability of resources), indicated the advantages of the MSC approach compared with the advisory role assumed by the DES, or the negotiating role of the EOC. On the other hand, as Millman and Weiner point out, there seems to have been little discussion of the contradictions underlying this new initiative. For example, conflicts between the different strategies adopted by LEA projects, especially the tension between strategies which use compulsion and those supporting freedom of choice, have not been discussed. Also, the MSC TVEI Unit and individual projects have 'disregarded the importance of equal representation of women and men at senior and management levels of TVEI' – TVEI projects are largely run by men. Further, no attempt has been made by the MSC to draw on earlier experiences of the DES, HM Inspectorate, LEA or teacher initiatives.

The MSC has extended this concern for equal opportunities into youth training although criticism is still being expressed about the MSC's lack of policy on such issues as sexual harassment on training courses (e.g. Women in the Manual Trades). The approach of the MSC is still essentially similar to that of the DES and EOC. It maintains the *equal-access* approach, which is dominant in official thinking about equal opportunities, even if some lip-service is paid to the need to ensure equal outcomes. The result is, according to the WNC, 'a training policy for men and a dead end for women' (WNC, 1984, p. 5).

Conclusion

Interpreting central government responses to sex equality in education is complex. Clearly there has been a policy shift in that the conventional approach of differentiating pupils by gender (an approach which Wolpe (1976) described as the 'common code' of government planning) has been challenged by the Sex Discrimination Act, as well as by the EOC and the MSC. Three different strategies may have been developed by the EOC, DES and the MSC but all three appear to have adopted an equal opportunities approach (even if only in rhetoric in some instances) rather than a concern for sex equality. For the optimistic, the policies developed by the EOC, the MSC and the support of HM Inspectors indicate positive moves in the direction of change.

Yet there are also signs that such policy shifts and initiatives might affect education only superficially, particularly since no major funding has been available to develop broad programmes of action in nursery, primary, further and higher education. Indeed it seems that only one part of the secondary school curriculum is being developed in terms of equal opportunities (TVEI). The main curriculum initiative on sex-differentiation supported by the Schools Council ended with the demise of that body, and it is not clear how far the new School Curriculum Development Committee (SCDC) will go in providing sufficient resources or the commitment to expand its work on equal opportunities.[11]

Eleven years after the Sex Discrimination Act was passed, belief in the potential of anti-discrimination legislation appears to be waning. In employment, it is unclear whether the legislation made any 'fundamental impact on the low status, low paid and marginal position of women in the labour market' (Jackson, 1984, p. 194), though the initial impact on women's employment was dramatic. However, some or all of these gains were reversed in the latter part of the 1970s (Hakim, 1981). By the early 1980s, the economic recession and increased unemployment, which affected women even more than men, had left their mark. Employers, too, had begun to find new ways of maintaining current patterns of male and female employment and differentiating pay scales.

In education, although the performance of girls and young women had improved greatly, with far more obtaining examination certificates and university degrees than previously, patterns of gender segregation in education remain. The 'hidden curriculum' of schooling (gender dynamics in the classroom, sexual harassment, gendered youth cultures and 'traditional' teacher attitudes) have not proved amenable to reform through persuasion or legislation, especially since the Sex Discrimination Act required little action from schools. Many of the conditions in educational institutions did not need to change in order to fulfil the criteria outlined in the education sections of the act. Further, the argument that inadequate resources have prevented the extension of the curriculum to provide equal opportunities, together with the administrative consequences of falling school rolls, has allowed institutions and local authorities to delay their response.

A number of issues have been raised in this analysis of equal opportunities initiatives and policy. It is becoming increasingly clear that if reform in individual schools and colleges is hard to establish, it is even harder to extend reform to other institutions without some central support and intervention. Equal opportunities policies have revealed the difficulty of resolving the tension between demands for local autonomy and centralization, between calls for *laissez-faire* and interventionist policies, between grassroots or 'top down' initiatives. Until the 1980s, the approach of central government has been to stress the value of teachers as agents of change, the importance of local autonomy and diversity of provision and experiment. The strengthening and widening of the powers of the MSC under a Conservative government signified a move towards greater centralized control and direction, with more attempt to enforce policy goals than previously allowed under a social democratic consensus. The effects of this shift towards centralized planning for gender issues still need to be assessed.

In the 1980s major contradictions can also be found between the liberal approach to equal opportunities taken by central government and its economic/social policies. On the one hand the close association between liberal ideology and policy on equal opportunities and the requirements of an inequitable economic system must concern those who wish to support concepts of justice and social equality. One could argue that the development of education policy has more to do with the needs of the state than concepts of justice (Finch 1984). Clearly such equal opportunities initiatives in education are also part of an economic strategy in which greater, though limited, investment in women is thought useful as a source of skilled labour, particularly as scientists and engineers.

On the other hand, the philosophy underlying equal opportunities policies sits uneasily under the umbrella of New Rights politics. Although it has hardly challenged social policies which support the maintenance of traditional patriarchal family structures and the role of the housewife mother (David 1984), some equal opportunities initiatives have indicated a need for social reform through educational change and the need to reduce, or at least temper, existing inequalities between men and women.

In the educational sphere, the choice of strategy for equal opportunity policies is undeniably complex. Central government strategies have tended to utilize concepts of individual freedom of choice and action, existing institutional frameworks, and professional understandings about the role and value of education as currently defined. However there is also increasing evidence that the greater the amount of discretion and freedom of choice left to LEAs, educational institutions, teachers and pupils, the more likely it is that traditional patterns will be reproduced, and the less likely it is that change will occur. Will compulsion at national level, through legislation or contract compliance, and at institutional level, through, for example, a compulsory curriculum, be the next stage of development? For some, such increased central control and 'intervention' has disturbing consequences (see Kirp, Yudof and Strong Franks, in this volume).

Other major contradictions have emerged between central government approaches to equal opportunities and their relationship to the grassroots women's movement. Feminist teachers have made a number of demands of education and of educational reform. Major transformations within education are needed, it is claimed, to challenge the hierarchies of the teaching profession, the structure of educational knowledge, conventional teaching styles, etc., particularly in so far as they privilege male interests. Such 'radical' perspectives and the activism they generate among teachers *in combination* with 'top down' liberal initiatives', according to Acker (1986), give the movement for sex equality 'a power unmatched by other reform movements'.

Others, however, take a critical view of such 'combinations', arguing that liberal policies of equality of opportunity are incompatible with feminist principles. O'Brien points out that

as feminism is committed to equality of condition rather than to equality of opportunity with its radically unequal reward system, many feminists ... believe that liberalism is not ultimately consistent with feminism. Despite the lip-service to women's rights and the quite concrete gains . . . which liberalism has grudgingly given to women, it remains fundamentally patriarchal in theory and practice (O'Brien, 1986, p. 95).

The fundamental conservatism of the education system will be hard to shift. Whether the impetus for change generated in the last two decades will be sufficient to encourage new, more committed, responses to sex equality among educational professionals, managers and politicians remains to be seen. The type of strategy needed for the reform of education, however, is still not clear, neither has the political will been evident.

Acknowledgements

A good deal of the content of this chapter was developed for *Race, Gender and Education Policy-Making*, Module 4, E333, *Policy-Making in Education*, Milton Keynes Open University Press, 1986.

I would like to thank Sandra Acker, Laurily Neale, Jenny Ozga, John Pettit, Margherita Rendel and Gaby Weiner for their considerable help and support.

Notes

1 By 1981, 49 per cent of married women were economically active (EOC, 1981a).

2 In 1978, for example, women with degrees or equivalent earned, on average, only 76 per cent of the income earned by men with similar qualifications (Reid, 1981, p. 211).

3 Between 1911 and 1971, there had been a decline of 11 per cent in women skilled workers and an increase of 22 per cent of female unskilled workers (Hakim, 1978).

4 See, for example, Rossi (1972) and Hewitt (1980).

5 The Helen Whitfield case, discussed in Rendel (1985), provides a good example of these problems.

6 The Equal Pay Act 1984 amended the Equal Pay Act 1970 to include the principle of equal pay for work of equal value, as a result of pressure from the EEC to bring UK legislation in line with Community law.

7 In 1984, Bromley Education Authority had to pay compensation to three female pupils who were made to remain in the same class for two years because the school wished to avoid a sexual imbalance in the year above. This represented illegal sex discrimination.

8 Wormald (1985) provides an interesting and detailed analysis of the implications for women teachers of DES policy on teacher education. She discusses DES, *Teaching Quality* (a White paper, Cmnd 8836, London, HMSO, 1983), Circular 3/83, *Initial Teacher Training: Approval of Courses* and *New Teacher in School* London, HMSO, DES, 1982. She argues that little attention is paid to the specific career patterns of women, their subordinate position in the school hierarchy, and the sex composition of the teaching force.

9 For another discussion of the effect of 'cuts' in education on women see Deem (1981).

10 Weinberg (1979) offers an interesting discussion of coeducation as an example of the 'politics of non-decision making'.

11 The SCDC recently published (together with the EOC) *Genderwatch: self-assessment schedules for use in schools*, devised by K. Myers, 1987 as its first major initiative on gender issues.

References

Acker, S., 'What feminists want from education', in Hartnett and Naish, M. (eds), *Education and Society Today*, Lewes, Falmer, 1986.

Applebey, C. and Ellis, E., 'Formal investigations: the Commission for Racial Equality and the Equal Opportunities Commission as law enforcement agencies', *Public Law*, summer 1984, pp. 236–76.

Arnot, M., *Race, Gender and Education Policy-Making*, Module 4, E333, *Policy-Making in Education*, Milton Keynes, Open University, 1986a.

Arnot, M., 'State education policy and girls' educational experiences' in Beechey, V. and Whitelegg, E. (eds), *Women in Britain Today*, Milton Keynes, Open University Press, 1986b.

Beechey, V., 'Women's employment in contemporary Britain', in Beechey, V. and Whitelegg, E. (eds), *Women in Britain Today*, Milton Keynes, Open University Press, 1986.

Bindman, G., 'The law, equal opportunity and affirmative action', *New Community*, **VIII** 3, 1980 pp. 248–60.

Bloomfield, J. and Pratt, J., *Guidelines on secondary school reorganization: a report for the Equal Opportunities Commission*, Centre for Institutional Studies at North East London Polytechnic/Essex County Council (Commentary no. 13; unpublished), 1980.

Borley, J., *Equal Opportunities in Education*, unpublished thesis submitted to Faculty of Economics and Social Studies, Manchester University, 1982.

Byrne, E. M., *Women and Education*, London, Tavistock Publications, 1978.

Byrne, E., 'Equality or equity?: a European overview', in Arnot, M. (ed.), *Race and Gender: equal opportunities policies in education*, Oxford, Pergamon Press/Open University, 1985.

Byrne, P. and Lovenduski, J., 'The Equal Opportunities Commission', *Women's Studies International Quarterly*, **1**, 1978. pp. 131–67.

Carr, L., 'Legislation and mediation: to what extent has the Sex Discrimination Act changed girls' schooling?', in Whyte, J. *et al.* (eds), *Girl Friendly Schooling*, London, Methuen, 1985.

Committee of Enquiry into the teaching of Mathematics in Schools, *Mathematics Counts* (the Cockroft Report), London, HMSO, 1982.

Committee on Higher Education, *Higher Education* (the Robbins Report), Cmnd. 2154, London, HMSO, 1963.

David, M., 'Women, family and education', in Acker, S., Megarry, J., Nisbet, S. and Hoyle, E. (eds), *Women and Education*, London, Kogan Page, 1984.

Deem, R., 'State policy and ideology in the education of women, 1944–80', *British Journal of Sociology of Education*, **2** no. 2, 1981, pp. 131–44.

Department of Education and Science, *Curricular Differences for Boys and Girls*, London, HMSO (Education Survey 21), 1975.

Department of Education and Science, *Sex Discrimination Act 1975*, London, HMSO (Circular 2/76), 1976.

Department of Education and Science, *Local Education Authority Arrangements for the School Curriculum*, London, HMSO (Circular 14/77), 1977a.

Department of Education and Science, *Curriculum 11–16*, London, HMSO (HMI Working Paper), 1977b.

Department of Education and Science, *Primary Education in England*, London, HMSO, 1978.

Department of Education and Science, *Aspects of Secondary Education in England*, London, HMSO, 1979.

Department of Education and Science, *Girls and Science*, London, HMSO, 1980.

Department of Education and Science, *The School Curriculum*, London, HMSO, 1981.

Department of Education and Science, *Science Education in Schools: a consultative document*, London, HMSO, 1982.

Department of Education and Science, *Better Schools* (Cmnd 9469), London, HMSO, 1985.

Dorn, A., 'Education and the Race Relations Act', in Arnot, M. (ed.), *Race and Gender: equal opportunities policies in education*, Oxford, Pergamon Press/Open University, 1985.

Equal Opportunities Commission, *First Annual Report*, Manchester, EOC, 1976.

Equal Opportunities Commission, *Do You Provide Equal Educational Opportunities?*, Manchester, EOC, 1980.

Equal Opportunities Commission, *Sixth Annual Report*, Manchester, EOC, 1981a.

Equal Opportunities Commission, *Positive Discrimination in Training Schemes*, Manchester, EOC, 1981b.

Equal Opportunities Commission, *Eighth Annual Report*, Manchester, EOC, 1983.

Equal Opportunities Commission, *Tenth Annual Report*, Manchester, EOC, 1985.

Finch, J., *Education and Social Policy*, London, Longman, 1984.

Fishel, A. and Pottker, J., *National Politics and Sex Discrimination in Education*, Lexington, Massachusetts, D. C. Heath, 1977.

Hakim, K., 'Sexual division within the labour force: occupational segregation', *Department of Employment Gazette*, November 1978, pp. 1264–8.

Hakim, K., 'Job segregation: trends in the 1970s', *Department of Employment Gazette*, December 1981, pp. 521–9.

Hannon, V., 'Education for sex equality: what's the problem?', in Rubenstein, D. (ed.), *Education for Equality*, London, Harper and Row, 1979.

Hewitt, P., 'Sex equality', in Bosanquet, N. and Townsend, P. (eds), *Labour and Equality*, London, Heinemann, 1980.

Home Office, *Equality for Women*, Cmnd 5724, London, HMSO, 1974.

Jackson, C., 'Policies and implementation of anti-discrimination strategies', in Schmid, G. and Weitzel, R. (eds), *Sex Discrimination and Equal Opportunity: the labour market and employment policy*, Hampshire, Gower, 1984.

Johnson, D., *School Governing Bodies Project, 1980–83: final report*, Uxbridge, Educational Studies Unit, Brunel University, 1983, unpublished.

Kant, L., 'A question of judgment', in Whyte, J. *et al.* (eds), *Girl Friendly Schooling*, London, Methuen, 1985.

Kirp, D. L., 'Racial inexplicitness and education policy', in Arnot, M. (ed.), *Race and Gender: equal opportunities policies in education*, Oxford, Pergamon Press/Open University, 1985.

Lester, A. and Bindman, G., *Race and Law*, Harmondsworth, Penguin, 1972.

MacDonald, M., *Class, Gender and Education*, Units 10/11, E353, *Society, Education and the State*, Milton Keynes, Open University Press, 1981.

Marland, M., 'Staffing for sexism: educational leadership and role models', in Marland, M. (ed.), *Sex Differentiation and Schooling*, London, Heinemann Educational, 1983.

McCrudden, C., 'Institutional discrimination', *Oxford Journal of Legal Studies*, **2** no. 3, 1982 pp. 303–67.

Meehan, E., 'Implementing equal opportunities policies: some British-American comparisons', *Politics: journal of the Politics Studies Association of the UK*, **2** no. 1, 1982, pp. 14–20.

Millman, V. and Weiner, G., 'Engineering equal opportunities: the case of TVEI', in Gleeson, D. (ed.), *A Critical Appraisal of TVEI* (provisional), London, Routledge and Kegan Paul, 1987 (forthcoming).

O'Brien, M., 'Feminism and the politics of education', *Interchange*, **17** no. 2, summer 1986, pp. 91–105.

Orr, P., 'Sex bias *in schools*: national perspectives', in Whyte, J., Deem, R., Kant, L. and Cruickshank, M. (eds), *Girl-Friendly Schooling*, London, Methuen, 1985.

Phillips, A. and Taylor, B., 'Sex and skill: notes towards a feminist economics', *Feminist Review*, no. 6, 1980.

Pratt, J., 'The attitudes of teachers', in Whyte, J. *et al.* (eds), *Girl Friendly Schooling*, London, Methuen, 1985.

Reid, I., *Social Class Differences in Britain* (2nd edn), London, Grant McIntyre, 1981.

Rendel, M., 'Legislating for equal pay and opportunity for women in Britain', *Signs: journal of women in culture and society*, **3** no. 4, 1978, pp. 897–908.

Rendel, M., 'The winning of the Sex Discrimination Act', in Arnot, M. (ed.), *Race and Gender: equal opportunities policies in education*, Oxford, Pergamon Press/Open University, 1985.

Rights of Women in Europe, *Women's Rights and the EEC: a guide for women in the UK*, London, ROWE, 1983.

Rossi, A. S., 'Sex equality: the beginnings of ideology', in Safilios Rothschild, C. (ed.), *Toward a Sociology of Women*, Lexington, Massachusetts, Xerox College Publishing, 1972.

Scottish Education Department, *Differences of Provision for Boys and Girls in Scottish Secondary Schools*, Edinburgh, HMSO, 1975.

Spender, D. and Sarah, E. (eds), *Learning to Lose; sexism and education*, London, The Women's Press, 1980.

Weinberg, A., *Non-decision-making in English Education: the case of single-sex secondary schooling*, paper to the BSA Annual Conference, Aberystwyth, University College of Wales, 1979.

Wickham, A., *Women and Training*, Milton Keynes, Open University, 1986.

Wolpe, A. M., 'The official ideology of education for girls', in Flude, M. and Ahier, J. (eds), *Educability, Schools and Ideology*, London, Halsted Press, 1976.

Women's National Commission, *Report on Secondary Education*, London, Cabinet Office, 1983.

Women's National Commission, *The Other Half of Our Future: report of the WNC's ad hoc working group on training opportunities for women*, London, Cabinet Office, 1984.

Wormald, E., 'Teacher training and gender blindness', *British Journal of Sociology of Education*, **6**, no. 1, 1985 pp. 112–16.

22 The construction of women and black students as educational problems: re-evaluating policy on gender and 'race'

Jenny Williams

Introduction

Are women and black students defined as educational problems? The emergence of 'race' and gender policies in a significant minority of Local Education Authorities suggests that they are. *Ad hoc* responses by LEAs and the Department of Education and Science to the arrival of black New Commonwealth migrants from the 1950s onwards were numerous and varied. These have already been well documented and analysed (see, for example, Mullard 1982; Carby 1982; Troyna 1982). During the 1980s more formal policy statements have been developed which are labelled by themselves and their critics as multicultural or anti-racist in their orientation (see Arnot, 1986b, pp. 26–30, for an outline of the differences between these two approaches). Also during the 1980s a minority of LEAs have established working parties, produced discussion documents and, occasionally, formal policy statements, which define the educational problems of girls and women and propose solutions to them.

This chapter focuses on the underlying assumptions of such policies and the ways in which educational problems are defined as issues needing attention. My purpose is to look closely at educational policies concerned with issues of race and gender, at what they regard as problematic, at what they take for granted. In doing so I shall demonstrate the ways in which such policies show similarities and the ways in which they frequently mirror each other in rhetoric and analysis. At the same time they contain both obvious and hidden differences which also need exploring. A number of themes and questions are raised by such a comparison. For example:

'Race' and sex as categories
In what ways are the categories of 'race' and sex constructed in educational policies? What are the links between this process and wider structural inequalities?

'Race' and gender as educational problems
How are female and black students defined as problems?

Explanations of educational problems
How are the educational problems of black and female students formulated and understood?
What different theoretical approaches underpin the development of particular policies?

'Race' and gender policies
What differing solutions stem from the alternative explanatory frameworks?
What similarities and differences are there between anti-sexist and anti-racist policies?

Source: Commissioned.

The goals of educational reform
What do policies hope to achieve?

Policy rhetoric and structural realities
Why do anti-racist and anti-sexist policies which appear so similar in their rhetoric, surface concerns and policy goals reveal deep conflicts and contradictions when analysed more closely?

'Race' and sex as categories

The emergence of educational policies which focus on the school and college experiences of black and female students necessitates the use of 'race' and sex as significant categories, labelling students in such a way as to highlight both specific aspects of their identity and group membership and particular educational problems. Girls and boys, women and men, black and white students, are differentiated and polarized. Girls' educational experiences are shown to compare unfavourably with those of boys; similarly black students' experiences are contrasted with those of white students, or West Indian and Asian students are contrasted with white students. These are taken-for-granted groupings which assume some form of unity within each category without ever clearly identifying the source of this unity. Is it biological, cultural or material, or is it the result of some aspect of personal and social experiences?

It may appear obvious to teachers that male and female students are polarized on the basis of biology. But the emergence of the term *gender* to signify social arrangements consequent upon, but not determined by, biological differences, highlights the complex relationship between biology and culture. The first task in scrutinizing educational policies, therefore, must be to examine their implicit categorization and labelling. We must question whether the concepts of 'race' and gender are based on some notion of 'inherent' differences. Do educational policies assume that biological or cultural categories are unproblematic? Do they posit a neat and straightforward relationship between biology, culture and differential educational needs? Why and how are these categories used?

Most educationalists, teachers and politicians, probably accept that there is no biological basis for the notion of 'race'. Nineteenth-century 'scientific racism', with its discrete, hierarchical and inherited categories has been significantly challenged, even if not eliminated, from popular consciousness. The significance of ancestral origins from different geographical regions, however, has been retained in academic and popular discussion as an important discriminating variable. 'Asians' and 'West Indians', for example, are labelled by their country of origin, even those third or fourth generation resident in this country. They are commonly referred to as belonging to different 'races', and the relations between Asian and West Indian communities and the white British population are referred to as 'race relations'. (See, for example, the Race Relations Acts.) There is, however, little recognition of the cultural origins of such terminology. We conveniently forget that these divisions, and the classification of people as 'races', have been historically and politically created. Indeed in post-1945 Britain, it is the political creation and solidification of such categories, enshrined in legislation for immigration control, which provides one crucial context within which educational policies emerge (see Sivanandan, 1982; Carby, 1982; Troyna and Williams, 1986).

How then has the acceptance and understanding of racial differences been perpetuated and built into policy discussions during the past forty years? The most obvious way, clearly demonstrated in educational literature, has been to associate the label 'race' with some notion of cultural unity, encapsulated in the term *ethnic group*. It has become commonplace in educational debates to assert that schools should reflect cultural differences, that the divisions within the school population are cultural ones, represented in different ethnic identities. One form of 'inherent' characteristic appears to have been replaced by another, as manifested, for example, in the Swann Report (1985). In chapter 1 of this report the discussion of ethnicity and culture prioritizes cultural differences as *the* fundamental division within contemporary Britain. It talks about an *indigenous* ethnic group, as though the white majority shared a homogeneous and cohesive culture until the arrival of new immigrants. The consensus and stability of this indigenous group is threatened by these new cultures and so the task of education is to forge an acceptable pluralism (see Troyna, 1986 and Carter and Williams, 1987, for a more detailed analysis of the underlying assumptions of the Swann Report).

The recommendations of the Swann Report spell out one version of this new plurality, in which the privileged position of Christianity is abandoned and some cultural elements from the language, literature, religion and history of the 'new' groups incorporated into the curriculum (even though most have been intimately linked to Britain for four centuries!). In the process of recommending such policies to change the educational experiences of pupils, a particular view of culture emerges. It is as though it was somehow 'out there', existing in a pure form, waiting to be understood by teachers and incorporated into the curriculum. Each ethnic group appears as homogeneous and as possessing a culture that is fixed, static and unrelated to the changing material conditions and political practices experienced by the group. In other words, even from this approach, the divisions between groups are defined as inherent; white and black children are different because of the cultures to which they inevitably belong. Equality is achieved by developing an understanding of minority cultures and incorporating some aspects of these cultures into that of the majority.

A very similar discussion concerning the need for educational reform takes place round the notion of *gender*, though frequently in a less explicit and straightforward form. Again we can ask whether the special needs of girls are attributed to their biology or to a notion of femaleness which implies some form of cultural unity. Gender has been used historically as a basis of the organization of educational provision, whether in terms of separate schools or of separate curricula (David, 1980). It was seen as the most 'natural' division given the separate roles of men and women in society. Biological differences were seen to give rise to different needs, interests and abilities. Cultural differences resulting from the division of labour into productive and domestic forms provided a common-sense justification for separate educational provision, focusing for girls on childcare and domestic science. Gender divisions were an obvious and convenient division for teachers to use and one that was not seen as contentious by policy-makers during most of the twentieth century. During the 1970s and 1980s the problem became redefined. For some feminists the 'problem' was the masculine culture of mixed schools, which made them problematic for girls (Spender and Sarah, 1980). Within this framework, one solution is to incorporate some aspects of the less valued 'female' culture into the curricula. 'Femaleness' has been used by radical feminists as a justification for more co-operative, less competitive forms of learning, as if these were inherent in all female cultures.

One justification, therefore, for using 'race' and sex as significant divisions is that these designate important cultural differences as educationally relevant. Unfortunately it also encourages the use of a concept of culture which is highly problematic, particularly when used in policy discussions.

An alternative classification to one which focuses on the culture of designated groups is an analysis of students' social and educational experiences as the key variable. The way women and black citizens are treated in society and in schools provides for a unity among female students on the one hand and black students on the other; such experiences are summarized in the terms racism and sexism. The ILEA documents (1983; 1985) provide a clear example of this alternative approach. New educational policies take their justification from the experiences of racism suffered by black citizens. 'There are certain routine practices, customs and procedures in our society whose consequence is that black people have poorer jobs, health, housing, education and life chances than do the white majority' (1983, p. 6). Similarly girls and women suffer from living in a society in which sexism

is based on and perpetuates a notion of male superiority. Greater value and status is more often given to traditional male pursuits and occupations than female ones. This places men generally in a position of power over women, whether at home, at work or through the political, social and economic systems and institutions which govern our lives (1985, p. 4).

ILEA also brings the issue of race and gender together by stating that 'sex and race inequalities are linked through the experience of discrimination, prejudice, stereotyping and powerlessness' (1985, p. 5). A whole range of examples of sexism within education are given, including textbook biases, differential teacher expectations concerning pupil abilities, differential teacher behaviour with regard to discipline and attention, sexual harassment, assumptions concerning the leadership qualities of males and the monopolization of power by males. This list is mirrored very clearly in discussions concerning racism in schools, where equivalent differential experiences can be found. All aspects of education are included and the relationship of black and female students to schooling is seen to be very different to that of white male students. Thus the implication is that this polarization of sex and 'racial' categories is based on fundamental educational experiences rather than inherent cultures or biological attributes.

Educational problems, within this interpretive framework, stem from the failure of the educational system to treat black and female students equally with other groups. However, the way the experiences of schooling are outlined, as in the examples given above, rests on the assumption that, in almost every respect, the experiences of white male students are qualitatively different from females and blacks. That males and whites are not homogeneous groups, and many school experiences are similar for all students tends to be ignored. As Lynn Davies (1978) graphically puts it: 'it is rather like highlighting the lion's view of captivity, it implies that this is demonstrably different from the tiger's view, and this draws attention away from the significant fact of captivity' (p. 103).

In both the dominant and alternative classifications of 'race' and gender, certain aspects of school experiences are highlighted and others are ignored; certain aspects of group unity are emphasized and others rejected. This arbitrary selection becomes more evident when we consider what is excluded from most policy discussions when 'race' and sex are on the agenda. As Ira Katznelson has recently argued (1986) both the silences within policy discussions and the limits of permissible agendas illustrate and illuminate the framing of social policy issues. The relationship of 'race' and gender to class and regional/urban inequalities are two such 'silences'.

During the 1950s and 1960s social class inequalities in terms of access to different forms of education, in educational experiences and in educational achievements, were documented in sociological studies and government reports. By the 1980s ethnic and gender research studies appear to have replaced social class studies as explorations in educational inequalities. Though often replicating the earlier studies (in terms of research methods and explanatory frameworks) such research has tended to remain separate. Thus educational research initiated, or selected as deserving attention, by policy-makers rarely allows for ethnic or gender issues to be placed within a social class context. The presentation of educational data, which form the justification for most policies, is documented in discrete and unrelated forms. In ILEA (1983a), for example, social class, sex and 'racial' achievements in education are documented in separate sections. The relationships between the three sets of data are hardly explored. Few references are made to the social class distribution of West Indian and Asian parents found in other studies, and no supporting evidence is offered for the following statement: 'our ILEA studies suggest that only about half the difference between reading scores of children from West Indian homes and their white counterparts may be accounted for by socio-economic factors' (p. 17). However there are suggestions that the differences *within* the group labelled Asian are large but here again no details are provided.

The Rampton Report (1981) had used the same processes of data collection and presentation, comparing only overarching ethnic categories such as West Indian, Asian and White (with no discussion of sex differences within each). In spite of sharp criticism of this practice from researchers such as Reeves and Chevannes (1981), the Swann Committee repeated this model of data collection. Research by Craft and Craft (1983) which includes a division between middle- and working-class black groups is reported in the Swann Report (p. 60) but little interpretive use is made of these data.

Regional/urban inequalities in educational achievement were also identified as significant in educational research in the 1960s and 1970s. The 'inner city' emerged as a descriptive concept linked to a spatial interpretation of educational problems and to particular ameliorative policies such as Educational Priority Areas (Plowden Report, 1967). Although the problems of black youth have been associated by the media and politicians with inner city residence in the last decade, particularly in connection with crime, drugs and unemployment, little analytical (as opposed to ideological) use of this association can be found in educational policy debates. Yet research evidence has suggested that the spatial distribution of particular groups within urban areas is important in any comparative analysis of educational achievement (see Roberts, *et al.* 1983; Troyna and Smith, 1983). Byrne (1978) refers specifically to the position of working-class girls in *rural* areas as particularly underprivileged. Brah and Deem suggest that the occupational distribution and inner city residence of most black citizens has meant that their children attend schools that historically produced a white 'gendered working class' (1986, p. 73). In other words the comparatively low educational achievements and the occupational destinations of pupils from such schools reinforced and continued working-class membership, but through processes that were different for boys and girls. To unravel the social process through which this continues to occur is a project of considerable complexity.

However, such research is beginning to surface. It is becoming clear that very different forms of racism and sexism are experienced by different groups in different educational settings. Detailed exposition is now required of the relationships of inferiority or disadvantage between males and females, immigrants and indigenous, black and white students and teachers. In an early example of such research, Clarricoates (1980) illustrates the relationship between different constructions of masculinity and femininity within the classroom and the social class composition of the school catchment areas. Lynn Davies (1984) describes the ways in which, within one largely working-class comprehensive school, differing versions of femininity interrelate with differing levels of academic achievement.

Racism, similarly, is a complex phenomenon. Not only does the level of racist abuse or harassment vary in different schools and localities, but teacher stereotypes and the labelling of black children vary according to pupil, age, social class, and the demographic distribution of ethnic minority groups. The responses of black students to these different forms of racism has been shown to result in a range of black male and female identities in different settings (see, for example, Fuller, 1982; Riley, 1985; Brah and Minhas, 1985). Initial research suggests, for example, that black students in further education colleges may view education in a utilitarian manner, placing more emphasis upon the credentials available within FE than upon their culturally specific or anti-racist provision (FEU, 1985a; Reeves, 1986). Such research emphasizes the importance of defining the experiences of black and female students as multifaceted, of documenting how they perceive and respond to racism and sexism within society and education in many different ways. Clearly the way forward is to interpret gender and colour inequalities within wider forms of inequality; within the structural processes which reproduce a hierarchical society. I would argue that it is only within these contexts that the categorizations of 'race' and gender provide a basis for educational policies.

The power relations between white and black people and between men and women can then be understood not as 'inherent' and hence natural relations, but as variable elements within different political and economic structures. From this point of view we can then understand why the categorization of male and female (sex) or black and white (i.e. 'race') was politically necessary and why such classifications have shaped educational experiences and policy debates.

'Race' and gender as educational problems

Three themes have dominated political and professional debates on social class, 'racial' or gender aspects of education over the past four decades. These are the under-achievement of particular groups, the harmony/integration of youth and mainstream society and the relationship between employability and education. Each of these themes can be found in 'race' and gender debates illustrating very clearly both the similarities and differences in the framing of educational problems. The 'problem' of under-achievement illustrates this particularly well.

As far as female students are concerned,

Statistics show that girl's academic achievement is at least as good as boy's and that more girls than boys are entered for all levels of public examinations. The relative position of girls and boys becomes sharply divided only when we look at two factors behind the generalised statistics: (1) subject choices; (2) post-school experiences (ILEA, 1985f, p. 5).

These two aspects of gender differences provide the context within which policy-makers frame the discussion of female educational experience and achievement. In particular attention is focused on girls' differential engagement with and performance in certain scientific and technical subjects (see, for example, The Further Education Unit, 1985b; The Schools Council Project on Reducing Sex Differentiation in Schools, 1983; Brent LEA, 1982). The Girls into Science and Technology and Girls into Craft, Design and Technology projects and the DES (Orr, 1985) all focused their attention on female subject choice and career aspirations. The MSC in both the YTS and TVEI programmes takes the view that the perpetuation of sex-differentiated subject and skill areas is a major problem, at least in those areas where there is a shortage of skilled male labour. At the level of rhetoric much concern has been expressed about female under-achievement even if the reference is generally to the experiences of white girls.

Under-achievement, however, means something rather different when the focus of educational concern is black pupils. Here the issue is one of general educational failure, as measured, for example, by reading age, CSE and 'O' level passes, entrance to higher education, etc. (see, for example, Little, 1975; Tomlinson, 1986; Rampton, 1979; ILEA, 1983; Swann, 1985). The research which underpins current understanding of black under-achievement, and the political and professional reinterpretation of it, rests upon ethnic categorizations. 'West Indians' are grouped together and contrasted with 'Asians' and 'whites'. Avoiding a black/white categorization which might have revealed the impact of racism, this oversimplified ethnic categorization results in an association between black educational underachievement and a notion of 'West Indianness'.

The two frames of reference within which the problems of female and black under-achievement are located, therefore, are quite different. The central issue for girls is one of employability within a changing job market where there are specific skill shortages and taken-for-granted assumptions concerning future labour demands. 'Science' and 'technology' cover a very wide range of occupations, and in practice policy-makers may have little idea of either the extent of skill shortages or how to redirect girls' energies towards these.

Nevertheless arguments about the current failure of schools are put forward, for example, 'by still preparing many school girls for a sheltered life with the emphasis upon "suitable" female skills we may "educate for incapability" – that is, for frustration, unemployment and second-class citizenship in a technological society' (FEU, 1985b, p. 16). Here the imagery of traditional female occupations contrasted with high status technology is representative of most of the policy documents of gender inequality in education.

The passivity and conformity of girls, their lack of assertiveness and ambition, their refusal to study 'hard', rational subjects are defined as the problem. From such a perspective, girls frequently appear as innocent victims of the sexism in education apparent to others (Brah and Deem, 1986). On the other hand girls' lack of femininity or their 'masculinity' may be seen as a more of a problem than that of under-achievement. Girls' subject choices, their lack of competition with boys, their restricted career choices, etc., can be interpreted as self-chosen, rational (even if misguided) responses to the position of women in society.

In contrast, the problem of black under-achievement is almost never interpreted in this manner. The relationship of under-achievement with employability is constructed through an assumption that it is the lack of academic achievement which renders black students unemployable (Scarman, 1981). Black pupils apparently need to achieve academically in order to enter the labour market even at the lowest level, in spite of evidence that qualifications do not necessarily lead to jobs. The concept of black under-achievement provides an even greater contrast when it is associated with 'trouble', defined as indiscipline and truanting, and results in suspensions and local 'law and order' problems. Teacher assumptions concerning the classroom problems exhibited by 'West Indian' students have been documented for the past twenty years (Brittain, 1976; Rampton Report, 1981). Key statements in many LEA policy documents show a concern for 'harmony' and 'stability', which is never the case in sex equality policies or statements on girls' education. It is significant that most formal policies on 'race' and multicultural education have been formulated after 1981 when the 'riots' forced the issue of inner city youth on the political agenda (Troyna and Williams, 1986; Solomos, 1986a).

Since the 1950s an association between low school attainment, the problems of classroom discipline and delinquency was accepted by academics and practitioners as a male, white and predominantly working-class phenomenon. Now the 'problems of black male youths in schools' have adapted and adopted the 'law and order' discourse, and its associated imagery of violence, discontent and public concern (Fisher and Joshua, 1982). One consequence of this scenario is that black under-achievement is portrayed as meaningless, destructive and irrational (Solomos, 1986b). Alternatively there is a tendency to present blacks-as-victims even in studies which focus upon the racism in education, such as the CRE investigation into suspensions in Birmingham schools (1985). In contrast with the analysis of female under-achievement, there appears to be a refusal to even consider that black under-achievement (and disruption) could be a collective, rational, response to a discriminatory social system (Gus John, 1981, is an exception).

It is quite clear from these contrasting analyses of under-achievement, employability and disruption, that the differential experiences of black girls are given minimal attention. Stereotypes associated with black girls have been constructed along ethnic lines, and cut across the more general male/female, black/white images (see Allen, 1982; Carby, 1982; Brah and Minhas, 1986; Riley, 1986). As Brah and Deem (1986, p. 73) point out, Afro-Caribbean young women are stereotyped as 'pushy', but achieve better in schools than their male counterparts. Asian young women are seen as passive, meek, ruthlessly oppressed by their families, not being allowed to take courses and jobs commensurate with their abilities and achievement. Thus Afro-Caribbean young women disrupt the supposed association between femaleness and passivity, and between achievement and the acceptance of school norms (Fuller, 1982). Asian young women disrupt the supposed association between educational achievements, employability and individual social mobility, leading to integration. 'The experiences of black women can only be adequately understood from a perspective which recognises that black women are subject to the simultaneous oppression of race, sex and class' (Brah and Minhas, 1985, p. 23). Such an analysis would try to pinpoint the different relationships between these three factors in different educational situations and encourage more research on how the problems of black girls are defined and so responded to.

Explanations of educational problems

'Race' and gender problems within education can be interpreted from numerous theoretical and political standpoints. Educational professionals and politicians, however, are likely to favour explanations which point the way clearly towards possible and pragmatic policies. I have argued elsewhere (Williams, 1986) that the theoretical frameworks that were developed to understand social class disparities in educational achievements in the 1950s and 1960s are continuing to be used to interpret 'racial' and ethnic problems. I now want to extend this analysis to include the construction of gender as a problem. Four differing explanatory frameworks were summarized and labelled by Flude (1974) as first, cultural deficit, second, cultural difference, third, teacher labelling and stereotyping, and fourth, discrimination. I shall briefly consider each set of explanations in terms of 'race' and gender.

Cultural deficit theories
Many multicultural analyses of the nature and function of school curricula rest on a compensatory model of education. Schools are places where new learning occurs which will remedy deficiencies in home cultures. Black pupils can be seen as having 'special needs', because their cultural background is inadequate. Interestingly however, anti-racist proposals very often assume whites suffer from a cultural deficit, i.e. from racist attitudes which are simply a legacy from imperialism and colonialism (Swann Report, 1985). Lyn Yates (1985) suggests that this type of deficit approach, which in effect blames the victim, is also the most

common approach to girls' schooling. Teachers are asked to develop an alternative female culture of achievement and independence which will compensate for the romanticism, dependency and passivity found among women in society.

Theories of compensatory education rest on certain important assumptions. First, deficit cultures are portrayed as irrational. There is little if any analysis of why particular attitudes and behaviours have developed, of the ways in which cultures are related to and continuously reinforced by the wider structural position of particular groups. Second, a change in the overt and hidden curriculum is presented as a solution which will lead to changed attitudes and behaviours, irrespective of other changes outside the control of the school.

Cultural difference theories
Notions of cultural deficits frequently have been replaced by an emphasis upon differences with apparently no pejorative connotations. It is argued that cultural discontinuities between homes and schools do exist, are inevitable and are to be celebrated. This results in an explanation of gender and 'race' problems in schools in terms of teachers' inability to use these cultural differences. Teachers lack the skills necessary to incorporate and transform ethnic or gender cultures into a form which is educationally relevant. The solution, again, is to retrain teachers, to enable them to understand, interpret and incorporate cultural differences which do exist into their teaching and to reflect these back to pupils in a way which leads to high achievement and satisfaction within schooling.

Again the relationship between curriculum and culture is oversimplified. The slow but crucial institutionalization of a particular class culture in the form of received notions of academic standards is ignored. The question which is not addressed is which aspects of black or female cultures are or could be incorporated into high status knowledge. Some black and female writers can be brought into English literature classes, or 'O' or 'A' level Punjabi can be developed, but other aspects can just as easily reinforce low academic status and perpetuate differences and segregation. Classes on childcare, personal health and beauty, or African music are currently only likely to be options for those with few alternative examination subjects. We must therefore question very carefully indeed why schools should and how they could reflect the different cultures of the local community.

Teacher labelling and stereotyping
In the third explanatory framework, teachers' attitudes rather than their knowledge are described as crucial. Teachers' expectations, stereotyping and labelling are seen as the mechanisms by means of which membership of an ethnic or gender group results in ethnic or sex disparities in achievements or in particular types of classroom behaviour. It is a salutary exercise to compare research from the 1970s on teachers' perceptions of students from different social classes with more recent research concerning their expectations of female and black students. For example:

Teachers tend to have stereotyped views about children from different social classes. Because of this, they tend to expect less of working class pupils, to assess their abilities as lower than they are and to have less ambitious goals for them (Morrison and McIntyre, 1971, p. 74).

Similarly the Rampton Report argued 'that teachers had stereotyped or patronising attitudes towards West Indian children which, when combined with negative views of their academic ability and potential, may prove a self-fulfilling prophecy' (1981, p. 70). Stanworth documented very cleary the differential assumptions which teachers held about male and female pupils including 'the implicit assumption that girls' capacities for effciency and initiative will be channelled into nurturant or subordinate occupations, rather than into other, less traditional, spheres' (1981, pp. 30–1). The solution, again, focuses upon re-educating teachers to reduce if not remove racial and sex stereotypes. Course materials and texts would be scrutinized for bias.

Discrimination

The final explanatory framework is quite different. It pinpoints direct and indirect discrimination both within and outside education, consequent upon the unequal distribution of economic, political and ideological power and resources (Wright, 1984; Spender, 1982). The labels racism and sexism are used as summary terms for a very wide range of attitudes, behaviours and institutional processes which result in unequal access to material resources and personal dignity and choices.

Remedial policies again tend to focus upon the school, upon unintentional and institutional discrimination within education. But there are attempts to link educational examples with key political and economic processes in the wider society, such as the institutionalization of racism within the Nationality Acts, with the differential occupational recruitment of women and black students, or the lack of childcare provision which limits the realistic achievement of female career options. Thus the remodelling of teachers and schools is linked to wider social and political changes.

It is clear that a wide range of recommendations will stem from these alternative understandings. In different circumstances and for different audiences LEA policies may use several justifications, moving from deficit approaches to those which focus on teacher's attitudes and practices or 'outside forces'. It is to these policy consequences that we now turn.

'Race' and gender policies

Although the effect of different forms of categorizations and different explanatory models of 'race' and gender issues leads to very different policy recommendations, it is important to analyse their complexity. It is not possible to cover all four approaches. I shall focus therefore on the range of policies which attempts to tackle *discrimination*, often subsumed under the labels of race equality or sex equality initiatives. I wish to concentrate upon this 'radical' end of the educational policy spectrum (see Arnot, 1986b, pp. 26–32, Weiner, 1985, pp. 5–10 for policy typologies) because most academic and professional discussion has concentrated on the more mainstream multicultural and equal opportunity policies. It is also the case that LEAs trying to develop coherent and linked policies on 'race' and gender, tend to do this through an anti-racist and anti-sexist focus.

On the surface anti-racist and anti-sexist educational policies are in tune with each other. The early anti-racist initiatives of the 1960s and 1970s were school-based and developed by teachers drawing their strength and legitimacy from both their professionalism and their identification with local community issues (e.g. ALTARF, 1980; 1984). Anti-sexist initiatives initially were also likely to be 'bottom-up' developments (Taylor, 1985). However, by the early 1980s some LEAs began to adopt more prescriptive and proscriptive approaches, insisting on school policies fostering racial equality within given time limits (e.g. ILEA, Brent), prescribing aspects of headteacher behaviour to ethnic minority parents (e.g. Bradford), making certain forms of racist behaviour a disciplinary offence (e.g. Manchester), or establishing central mechanisms to decide upon school suspensions and so removing power from head and governors (e.g. Birmingham). Similarly a few LEAs stepped up pressure on schools to implement anti-sexist policies, asking for school policies within a particular time limit (e.g. Brent, ILEA) pressuring heads to implement change; organizing in-service courses (Humberside, Brent) replacing textbooks and appointing Advisers/Inspectors.

There are, however, quite important differences of emphasis. There appears to be far more concern in anti-racist policies to alter the behaviour and attitudes of white personnel compared with the attention devoted to altering male behaviour in schools. The issue of separate provision is suggested by anti-sexist policies, which might prioritize the creation of girls-only classes, women-run support groups, assertiveness training, etc. (Weiner, 1985). It is not a usual part of anti-racist strategies to create black-only classes within ordinary schools to prevent unfair competition with white pupils who get more than their share of teacher attention. Black pupils are given more attention by teachers only in terms of discipline and punishment. Black teacher groups are becoming more common,[1] and supplementary schools exist in many cities, but support groups for black students within schools are not usually on the list of policy priorities. Also while women's studies, particularly in higher education, appears to have achieved a certain respectability and is flourishing, black studies in on the decline and receives little public support from those concerned about racism. In short, there is no clear anti-racist equivalent of girl-centred schooling, or indeed girl-friendly schooling (see Weiner, 1986, or Weiner and Arnot in this volume for the distinction between these two approaches).

The creation of specialist hierarchies of teacher advisers, curriculum centres and school working parties are common to both policy arenas. But again certain differences are clear. Sex equality policies are not widespread, yet they do relate to mainstream education practice and funding: for example policies concerned to alter ordinary timetabling processes, counselling systems and resource allocation. The Technical and Vocational Educational Initiative, a nationally funded, vocationally oriented programme, has been able to incorporate some anti-sexist aspects as part of its normal aims and activities, even if the implementation of these aims is limited. In contrast, Section 11 grants available since 1966 to some authorities to provide funding for the special needs of ethnic minority pupils, have tended to marginalize spending on ethnic minorities. The existence of this funding has been the key factor in LEAs development of specialist appointments and experimental initiatives. The effect on mainstream education and ordinary professional practice has been minimal (Troyna and Ball, 1985).

Single-sex schooling is clearly an issue within the state sector of education. Although the numbers of single-sex schools have declined dramatically during the past three decades, girls' schools have been supported as a desirable alternative to co-education in some LEAs. Political campaigns have been organized to preserve existing single-sex schools when under the threat of closure. In contrast, most debates concerning black schools have centred upon voluntary supplementary schools or private religious provision (with one or two exceptions). As far as official policies are concerned, assumptions concerning integration have been based on the acceptance of white majority schools as both normal and desirable. Demands for some form of separatism on grounds of religion, for example, has been perceived as a threat to mainstream education (see Ball, 1986; Swann Report, 1985). When particular ethnic groups have campaigned to preserve single-sex schools, because of the compatability with cultural norms, this have been perceived as a form of cultural imposition and indoctrination and even sexism. Thus separate schooling for white girls, while not generally accepted, is seen as a legitimate demand, linked with high academic achievements, and mainstream educational issues. When such demands become part of a debate concerning black issues, they are marginalized and perceived as a threat to harmony and integration.

When we turn to the overall political context within which 'race' and gender policies develop, race equality policies appear to be far more politically contentious, more likely to be linked with political campaigns and disciplinary disputes, than are sex equality policies. Local disputes between authorities and particular teachers have become much publicized national issues.[2] They have been used to challenge the legitimacy of multicultural and anti-racist policies and the right of an LEA to discipline teachers within that policy. Troyna and Williams (1986), when analysing anti-racist policy developments, suggested a link between ethnic minority voting strength and mobilization and policy developments initiated by local white politicans representing particular inner city wards. Other writers (e.g. Bourne, 1983) stress the importance of community-based struggles and campaigns, particularly around education and harassment.

In contrast, anti-sexist policies do not appear to have become a party political or an electoral issue in the same way. Though they have often developed in the same local authorities as anti-racist polices and are similarly linked with a particular form of local Labour Party politics, sex equality policies are much less likely to be used by opposition parties in electioneering.[3] The reasons for these are perhaps that there is a stronger possibility of activists working from within existing institutions; e.g., party politics, teaching professions, council members. This helps to legitimize the issue, channel complaints in certain directions and mobilize support. There is a strong possibility that personal, professional and political campaigns are combined. Indeed this has been the case among groups of radical teachers and womens' groups. It is often feminist teachers and politicans who have led these campaigns, and though they have faced strong opposition, even ridicule, they can still operate within existing institutional forms.

The contexts within which 'race' policies have developed nationally and locally are quite different. 'Riots', 'law and order' campaigns, school suspensions and classroom discipline problems may define the form of local educational issues for professionals and politicians but the Nationality Acts, restrictions specifically on black immigration, the pervasiveness of racial harassment and discrimination in employment also contribute to the politicization of 'blackness' and black political struggles. The organization of local pressure groups along ethnic lines is both a response to and a reinforcement of this form of political identity. Such black individuals and groups are much less likely however to have access to or support from existing power bases within the system.

Thus although the political rhetoric and bureaucratic instigation of 'race' and gender policies are increasingly being brought together in particular LEAs, I would argue that the framing of educational problems and the political and professional contexts within which they have to be implemented are quite different.

The goals of educational reform

The analysis of individual and group inequalities raises questions about the goals of educational reforms. There are a number of possible outcomes which might be defined as achieving anti-racist and anti-sexist goals. For example:

a Where the behaviour and attitudes of all members of an educational institution are not based on factors such as colour or sex, where these are irrelevant to the relationship.
b When institutional processes were not found to discriminate on such grounds.
c When a 'fair' distribution of educational rewards was achieved; i.e., when different groups achieved similar standards and levels.
d Where a 'fair' representation of different groups was maintained in the power hierarchy of the education system.

Clearly these goals are not unambiguous and there is considerable room for dispute about their interpretation. Furthermore such goals raise fundamental questions about whether the purpose of reform is to give different groups of pupils a fair share within existing education processes or to change the nature of educational forms and occupational hierarchies. Most LEA policies argue for a 'fair shares' approach. Berkshire's anti-racist policy probably presents this type of goal most explicitly.

There will be perfect racial equality in Britain if and when Asian and Afro-Caribbean people participate fully in society and the economy and are therefore proportionately involved in management and government at all levels, and are not disproportionately involved in manual work or in unemployment or under-employment.

There will be racial equality in education, it follows, if and when Asian and Afro-Caribbean people are proportionately involved in teaching and administration at all levels, in higher and further education, and in streams sets, classes and schools leading to higher and further education (Berkshire (1), p. 5).

A Brent LEA Report (1982) states

It must be made manifest that it is the right of women to be equal with men, economically independent and able to make choices about their lives. The loss to society at present of the contribution that could be made by the able women who do not reach senior positions is incalculable (p. 2).

Two points can be made here. First it is clear that the traditional educational goal of *equality of opportunity* provides yet again the acceptable ideological framework for tackling inequality. The continuities in the framing of educational policies are remarkable, particularly in an era when a number of radical new initiatives have been put forward challenging meritocratic goals as inadequate. Cosin (1986) has outlined over a century of educational policy making aimed at increasing equality of opportunity, a goal which has widely differing interpretations and practical consequences. Equality of opportunity has remained a potent 'condensation symbol' in Edelman's terms (1971) capable of uniting diverse political and educational campaigners precisely because of its vagueness. Still, in educational policies, there is a refusal to define what is meant by equality or tackle issues of equity (Byrne, 1985).

Second, such policy goals aim to change practices within education but presuppose that the mechanism for doing so is through educational reforms. As Dale suggests

a great deal of the failure of education policy to come up with effective responses to the problems with which it is presented is due to the fact that many of these problems are not and are never going to be, amenable to solution by education policy (Dale, 1986, p. 64).

This belief in educational reform is again being continued in the context of 'race' and gender. Let us look briefly at each goal in the light of the above points.

Evidence demonstrates the pervasiveness of racist and sexist attitudes and behaviours within education (see, for example, Wright, 1984; Jones, 1985; Suleiman and Suleiman, 1985; Brah and Minhas, 1985). Attempts to change these attitudes and alter behaviour are clearly necessary. Arguably what is at issue here is not just individual prejudice, ignorance and misunderstandings, but socially supported and patterned ways of preserving individual dignity and of gaining access to scarce resources and power. Power in this context might mean straightforward physical power, or the control over the allocation of a range of resources within a classroom or access to a particular range of occupations or promotion possibilities. Only rarely can social attitudes and behaviours be 'educated' away. The institutions and ideologies which provide the context within which attitudes make sense are usually outside the control of education. For example, Kant argues, 'until boys are educated to participate fully in parenthood and running the home, girls will not be in a position to achieve equality in employment' (1985, p. 8). At what point in this process will the conditions of employment for the majority of workers change to allow for the expression of their newly acquired skills and attitudes?

The second goal, changing institutional processes to remove discrimination, needs to be scrutinized in a similar manner. Forms of discrimination are not incidental and accidental to the operation of institutions. Curricular change of any significant nature is a political, not just educational process. The introduction of core curricula, for example, has been defined as in the interests of girls, as they would no longer be able to opt out of scientific and technological knowledge. Alternatively Lyn Yates interprets the move as a mechanism for persuading girls to do what boys do, where 'the criteria of success and the norms of teaching and curriculum are still defined in terms of the already dominant group' (Yates, 1985, p. 212). It is naïve to argue that racism/sexism damages whites/boys, so *all* students will benefit from policy changes. The existing allocation of status, resources, etc., *advantages* certain groups.

The third goal, an equitable distribution of educational rewards, illustrates this problem precisely. Equality of outcome for sexual, colour or ethnic groups remains an educational goal alongside increasing cynicism concerning the possibility of altering class disparities in achievement. ILEA (1983a) reflects these contradictions. The document acknowledges the near impossibility of improving the position of working-class students 'because whatever innovations are introduced the pupils most able to benefit will be those coming from the most advantaged backgrounds' (p. 10). But then several pages later suggests that it is possible to ensure that the bottom 40 per cent of pupils does not contain an over-representation of black and female or working-class students. Who will it contain then?

Lastly, the fourth goal concerns the representation of groups in the occupational structure, particularly within the education system. The development of local authority equal opportunity policies is directly concerned with this issue; strategies are designed to intervene in their *own* recruitment. The labour market as a whole does not operate in this manner. In spite of government rhetoric, there is little evidence of any clear and direct link between educational achievements, occupational status and life chances. Indeed there is growing evidence that colour, rather than qualifications or motivation, persistence and commitment, is a prime determinant of occupational status (see Troyna and Smith, 1985; Lee and Wrench, 1985; Roberts *et al.*, 1983). A survey in Sheffield (quoted in Newnham) demonstrated that 'while higher qualifications were found to increase young black peoples' chance of finding a job, the level of discrimination faced by the highly qualified black youth was greater than that faced by the less qualified blacks' (1986, p. 18). A study in Nottingham (Nottingham CRC, 1980) revealed the gender elements within this colour discrimination process at different levels within the job market.

The relationship between white female educational achievements and occupational success is similarly complex. The labour market is sex-segregated and the same educational qualifications provide different openings and promotion chances for men and women (see Arnot, 1986). Cynthia Cockburn (1985) has detailed the history of the appropriation of particular occupational skills as an element in a gender struggle around job opportunities. Girls, as stated earlier, have now achieved at least overall parity with boys in the gaining of school level qualifications. This has not produced so far any overall improvement in occupational positions. Indeed the evidence from YTS studies shows a sharpening of sex-segregated channelling into traditional female occupations (Cockburn, 1987).

It is clear, therefore, that the goals of anti-racist and anti-sexist policies, though focused on educational change, cannot be easily achieved by strategies which are confined to education. Schools cannot be isolated from the wider structural inequalities through which colour and sexual divisions are continually being created and recreated.

Conclusions: policy rhetoric and structural realities

In this article I have tried to tease out the underlying assumptions of educational policies concerned with 'race' and gender. Two particular themes have guided the analysis. The first is an exploration of the language of explanation and the language of reform and policy change through which particular educational issues come to be debated and understood. The second theme concerns the similarities and differences in these understandings when focused upon 'race' and upon gender.

I have tried to show where explanations and policies are similar and where the rhetoric of analysis reflects similar concerns; but also where there are deep and crucial differences. I have suggested that official LEA policies on 'race' and gender reflect each other and contain similar kinds of rhetoric; significantly policies in both areas have ignored social class inequalities,[4] and both have tended to isolate education from wider structural issues. Policies on 'race' and gender often work within a compensatory model of education. Both also work with polarized categories, black/white, male/female, which by implication if not design make other forms of inequality acceptable. As Solomos (1986b) suggests a symbolic political and educational language is generated which explains problems and constructs acceptable reforms but the tension between the legitimacy of the explanation and the promise of reform remains. At this level of problem analysis, of political and administrative policy formation, anti-sexist and anti-racist initiatives appear to mirror each other.

However, behind this surface similarity lie the deeper conflicts and contradictions which have been illustrated earlier. These differences are inevitable given the distinct economic, political and professional contexts of such policy formation.

Both black and female labour has been defined as part of the 'reserve army' of labour, as a secondary source to be used for low paid, temporary, unskilled or semi-skilled jobs when needed by upturns in economic activity. Black or female workers in economic crises/recessions are redefined as surplus labour, and suffer high levels of unemployment. Clearly there is considerable evidence to support this interpretation, and as an overall theoretical perspective it is useful. But the different position of women and black workers must also be considered. For example there is a higher chance of a white woman attaining a professional or executive position (even if on the lower rungs and with less promotion than white men) than a black person of either sex. The sex segregation of the labour market and its accompanying ideologies are such that most women are channelled into the 'appropriate' areas. But these appropriate areas cover the social class range of occupations, so that socially and educationally ambitious girls can be accommodated, at least initially. 'There is ample literature to demonstrate that qualified women have not attained full equality with men, but nonetheless they do have considerable economic and occupational advantages compared with less qualified women' (Bonney, 1986, p. 17). Individual mobility as a solvent for group discontent is at least a partial reality. It is later in their careers, when seeking promotion, that direct and indirect discrimination becomes more visible, when women's domestic position impinges most directly on occupational participation, and the monopolization of power by men is starkly evident.

In contrast, discrimination against black students occurs at the initial entry stage into the labour market. The concentration of black workers within manual occupations is being consolidated rather than eroded (Newnham, 1986). The association of colour with particular low status, low paid occupations continues with generations born in this country (see, for example, the Swann Report, 1985, ch. 15 on Liverpool's blacks). The quite different nature of the female labour market means that it is easier to introduce measures in schools and colleges which will improve the initial occupational choices of some female students, particularly middle-class or 'academically able' girls. The changing labour market and economic structures therefore allow a certain 'space' for gender reforms even within an overall operation which reinforces existing patterns. The nature of this 'space' is much more limited for black students. Attempts to improve occupational mobility for them may concentrate on a few professional openings where their colour is defined as an occupational advantage (e.g. race relations advisers) or on employers (e.g. local authorities) with positive action policies, or self-employment (small businesses).

Another major factor we need to consider for black citizens in the UK is the way in which black groups have been defined politically over the past four decades. Their presence in this country and the meaning of their citizenship is continually questioned. The Nationality Acts and the revision of entry rules and procedures for example perpetuates the association between blackness and 'alien invaders', bringing unnecessary social problems with them. The changing and complex political definitions of race (see Miles and Phizacklea, 1984; Solomos, 1986b) probably help to account for the fraught and conflictual nature of most anti-racist politics.

Finally and briefly the professional contexts within which policies are generated and implemented differ. There are clearly far more women teachers than black teachers, some in influential positions; yet promotion remains limited and the working environment is controlled by men. Therefore it is in women teachers' own interests, as well as those of their female pupils, to initiate or support anti-sexist reforms. In a recent study of all higher education institutions it has become quite clear that the main impetus towards equal opportunity policies has come from female members of staff or particular unions representing female members (CRE, unpublished). This is certainly not to argue that all female professionals are active in anti-sexist developments, or that implementation of policy is easy. Rather the professional context again provides limited space where reforms can be articulated, particularly if their aim is to change one particular institution.

With so few black professionals in post, most pressure for anti-racist reforms has to come from a variety of sources, from white politicians or administrators or black pressure groups working in particular localities in conjunction with anti-racist teachers. It is interesting to note the changing nature of anti-racist reforms and opposition to them when black professionals and politicians gain more influence in particular localities (Brent LEA, for example). Over most of the country, anti-racist reforms within schools have had to rely on the political commitment of white teachers. It is less likely that any significant number of such staff will be persuaded that it is in their own interests to initiate sweeping reforms.

I am not arguing that either form of struggle is more important than the other, or minimizing the difficulties of policy generation and implementation in both areas. But, these differing economic, political and professional contexts provide quite distinct settings for the translation of the language of problem construction and policy generation into reforms that can be implemented. Detailed local case studies would highlight the interplay between national and local factors, and the specific issues, alliances, conflicts and compromises which are part of struggle for anti-racist and anti-sexist policies. Detailed comparative evidence from such studies is not yet available. The building of successful alliances necessitates careful consideration of the differing positions of the partners. It is towards this reflective goal that this comparison between 'race' and gender policy formulation in education has been explored.

Notes

1 The National Anti-Racist Movement in Education, for example, has a black caucus.
2 For example, disputes between Bradford LEA and Ray Honeyford, Bristol and John Savery, and Brent and Ms McGoldrick.
3 There is some limited evidence of this now happening – see Headlam Wells (1985) and Taylor (1985). The incorporation of discussions of gay rights within the curriculum is being used as an aspect of party politics but this particular issue is not discussed in this paper.
 4 Except when they use the meaningless term 'classism'.

Acknowledgements

Madeleine Arnot, Gaby Weiner, Barry Troyna, Lynn Davies and Wendy Ball for reading earlier drafts of this paper and for providing many helpful comments and suggestions.

References

Acker, S., 'What Feminists want from Education', in Hartnett, A. and Naish, M. (eds), *Education and Society Today*, Lewes, Falmer Press, 1986.

Allen, S., 'Perhaps a seventh person', in Husband, C. (ed.), *Race in Britain*, London, Hutchinson, 1982.

ALTARF, *Teaching and Racism*, London, All London Teachers against Racism and Fascism, 1980.

ALTARF, *Challenging Racism*, London, All London Teachers against Racism and Fascism, 1984.

Arnot, M., 'State education policy and girls' educational experiences', in Beechey, V. and Whitelegg, E. (eds), *Women in Britain Today*, Milton Keynes, Open University Press, 1986a.

Arnot, M., *Race, Gender and Educational Policy-Making*, E333 Module 4, Milton Keynes Open University Press, 1986b.

Arnot, M. (ed.), *Race and Gender: Equal Opportunity Policies in Education*, Oxford, Pergamon, 1985.

Ball, W., *Policy innovation on multicultural education in 'Eastshire' Local Education Authority*, Policy Papers in Ethnic Relations no. 4, Centre for Research in Ethnic Relations, Warwick University, 1986.

Berkshire LEA, *Education for Racial Equality: Policy Paper 1: General Policy. Policy Paper 2: Implications. Policy Paper 3: Support, 1983.*

Bonney, M., 'More equal than others', *Times Higher Education Supplement*, 31.10.86.

Bourne, J., 'Towards an anti-racist feminism', *Race and Class*, **XXV** no. 1, 1983, pp. 1–22.

Brah, A. and Deem, R., 'Towards anti-sexist and anti-racist schooling', *Critical Social Policy*, **16**, 1986, pp. 66–79.

Brah, A. and Minhas, R., 'Structural racism or cultural difference: schooling for Asian girls', in Weiner, G. (ed.), *Just a Bunch of Girls*, Milton Keynes, Open University Press, 1985.

Brent LEA, *Equal Opportunities for Pupils of Both Sexes*, Report no. 114/82 of the Director of Education, 1982.

Brittan, E., 'Teacher opinion on aspects of school life', *Educational Research*, **18**, 1975/6, pp. 96–107 and 182–91.

Byrne, E., 'Equality or equity', in Arnot, M. (ed.), *Race and Gender*, Oxford, Pergamon, 1985.

Byrne, E., *Women and Education*, London, Tavistock, 1978.

Carby, H., 'Schooling in Babylon', in CCCS, *The Empire Strikes Back*, London, Hutchinson, 1982.

Carter, B. and Williams, J., 'Attacking racism in education', in Troyna, B. (ed.), *Racial Inequality in Education*, London, Tavistock, 1987.

Clarricoates, K., 'The importance of being Ernest . . . Emma . . . Tom . . . Jane', in Deem, R. (ed.), *Schooling for Women's Work*, London, Routledge and Kegan Paul, 1980.

Cockburn, C., *Machinery of dominance: women, men and technical know-how*, London, Pluto, 1985.

Cockburn, C., *Two-track Training – Sex Inequality in YTS*, London, Macmillan, 1987.

Commission for Racial Equality (CRE), *Youth in Multiracial Society*, London, Commission for Racial Equality, 1980.

Commission for Racial Equality (CRE), *Birmingham Local Education Authority and Schools Referral and Suspension of Pupils. Report of a Formal Investigation*, London, Commission for Racial Equality, 1985.

Commission for Racial Equality (CRE), *Equal Opportunity Policies in Higher Education*, unpublished.

Cosin, B., *Equality of Opportunity and Educational Policy*, E333 Module 1, Milton Keynes, Open University, 1986.

Craft, M. and Craft, A., 'The participation of ethnic minority pupils in further and higher education', *Education Research*, 25.1.83, pp. 10–19.

Dale, R., *Introducing Education Policy: principles and perspectives*, E333 Module 1, Milton Keynes, Open University, 1986.

David, M., *The State, the Family and Education*, London, Routledge and Kegan Paul, 1980.

Davies, L., 'The girls' view of schooling', *Educational Review*, 30.2.78, pp. 103–9.

Davies, L., *Pupil Power: deviance and gender in school*, Barcombe, Falmer Press, 1984.

Edelman, M., *Politics as Symbolic Action: Mass Arousal and Quiescence*, Chicago, Markham, 1971.

Fisher, G. and Joshua, H., 'Social policy and black youth', in Cashmore, E. and Troyna, B. (eds), *Black Youth in Crisis*, London, George Allen and Unwin, 1982.

Flude, M., 'Sociological accounts of differential educational attainment', in Flude, M. and Ahier, J., *Educability, Schools and Ideology*, London, Croom Helm, 1974.

Fuller, M., 'Young, female and black', in Cashmore, E. and Troyna, B., (eds), *Black Youth in Crisis*, London, George Allen and Unwin, 1982.

Further Education Unit, *Black Perspectives of FE Provision*, London, FEU, 1985a.

Further Education Unit, *Changing the Focus: Women and FE*, London, FEU, 1985b.

Headlam-Wells, J., 'Humberside goes neuter: an example of LEA intervention for equal, opportunities', in Whyte, J. *et al.* (eds), *Girl Friendly Schooling*, London, Methuen, 1985.

Inner London Education Authority (ILEA), *Achievement in Schools*, 1983a.

ILEA, *Multi Ethnic Education in Schools*, 1983b.

ILEA, *A Policy for Equality – Race*, 1983c.

ILEA, *Anti-racist Statement and Guidelines*, 1983d.

ILEA, *Multi Ethnic Education in Further and Higher Community Education*, 1983e.

ILEA, *A Policy for Equality: Sex*, 1983f.

John, G., *In the Service of Black Youth*, Leicester, National Association of Youth Clubs, 1981.

Jones, C., 'Sexual tyranny: male violence in a mixed secondary school', in Weiner, G. (ed.), *Just a Bunch of Girls*, Milton Keynes, Open University Press, 1985.

Kant, L., 'Secondary schooling: the constrained curriculum', *School Organisation*, **5** no. 1, 1985, pp. 7–16.

Katznelson, I., 'Rethinking the silences of social and economic policy', *Political Science Quarterly*, no. 2, 1986, pp. 307–25.

Lee, G. and Wrench, J., 'A subtle hammering – young black people and the labour market', in Troyna, B. and Smith, D. (eds), *Racism, School and the Labour Market*, Leicester, National Youth Bureau, 1983.

Little, A. N., 'The educational achievement of ethnic minority children in London schools', in Verma, G. and Bagley, C. (eds), *Race and Education across Cultures*, London, Heinemann, 1975.

Miles, R. and Phizacklea, A., *White Man's Country*, London, Pluto, 1984.

Millman, V. and Weiner, G., *Reducing Sex Differentiation in Schools*, Harlow, Longmans, for the Schools Council, 1983.

Morrison, A. and McIntyre, D., *Schools and Socialisation*, Middlesex, Penguin, 1971.

Mullard, C., 'From assimilation to cultural pluralism', in Tierney, J. (ed.), *Race, Migration and Schooling*, London, Holt Education, 1982.

Murphy, L. and Livingstone, J., 'Racism and the limits of radical feminism', *Race and Class*, **XXVI**, 1985, pp. 61–70.

Newnham, A., *Employment, Unemployment and Black People*, London, Runnymede Trust, 1986.

Nottingham CRC and Commission for Racial Equality, *Half a chance*, CRE, 1980.

Orr, P., 'Sex bias in schools: national perspectives', in White, J. *et al.* (eds), *Girl Friendly Schooling*, London, Methuen, 1985.

Plowden Report, *Children and their Primary Schools*, Central Advisory Council for Education (England), London, HMSO, 1967.

Rampton Report, *West Indian Children in our Schools*, Committee of Inquiry into the Education of Children from Ethnic Minority Groups, Cmnd 8723, London, HMSO, 1981.

Reeves, F. and Chevannes, M., 'The underachievement of Rampton', *Multiracial Education*, **10**, no. 1, 1981, pp. 35–45.

Reeves, F. and Chevannes, M., 'The ideological construction of black underachievement', *Multiracial Education*, **12**, no. 1, 1983, pp. 22–41.

Reeves, F., *Culture, Race and Education*, Bilston Community College Occasional Paper, 1986.

Riley, K., 'Black girls speak for themselves', in Weiner, G. (ed.), *Just a Bunch of Girls*, Milton Keynes, Open University Press, 1985.

Roberts, K., Noble, M. and Dugan, J., 'Young, black and out of work', in Troyna, B.

and Smith, D. (eds), *Racism, School and the Labour Market*, Leicester, National Youth Bureau, 1983.

Scarman Report, *The Brixton Disorder 10–12 April 1981*, Cmnd 8427, London, HMSO, 1981.

Sivanandan, R., *A Different Hunger*, London, Pluto, 1982.

Solomos, J., 'Political language and violent protest: ideological and policy responses to the 1981 and 1985 riots', *Youth and Policy*, no. 18, 1986a, pp. 12–24.

Solomos, J., 'Riots, urban protest and social policy: The interplay of reform and social control', *Policy Papers in Ethnic Relations*, no. 7, RUER, University of Warwick, 1986b.

Spender, D., *Invisible Women*, London, Writers and Readers Publishing Cooperative, 1982.

Spender, D. and Sarah, E. (eds), *Learning to Lose: Sexism and Education*, London, The Women's Press, 1980.

Stanworth, M., *Gender and Schooling*, London, Hutchinson, 1981.

Suleiman, L. and Suleiman, S., 'Mixed blood – that explains a lot of things', in Weiner, G. (ed.), *Just a Bunch of Girls*, Milton Keynes, Open University Press, 1985.

Swann Report, *Education for All*, Committee of Inquiry into the Education of Children from Ethnic Minority Groups, Cmnd 9453, London, HMSO, 1985.

Taylor, H., 'A local authority initative on equal opportunities', in Arnot, M. (ed.), *Race and Gender*, Oxford, Pergamon, 1985.

Tomlinson, S., 'Ethnicity and educational achievements', in Modgil, S. *et al.* (eds), *Multicultural Education: the interminable debate*, Barcombe, Falmer Press, 1986.

Troyna, B., 'The ideological and policy responses to black pupils in British schools', in Hartnett, A. (ed.), *The Social Sciences in Educational Studies*, Heinemann, 1982.

Troyna, B. and Smith, D. (eds), *Racism, School and the Labour Market*, Leicester, National Youth Bureau, 1983.

Troyna, B. and Williams, J., *Racism, Education and the State*, London, Croom Helm, 1986.

Verma, G. *et al.*, *Ethnicity and Educational Achievement in British Schools*, Basingstoke, Macmillan, 1986.

Weiner, G. (ed.), *Just a Bunch of Girls*, Milton Keynes, Open University Press, 1985.

Weiner, G., 'Feminist education and equal opportunity: unity or discord?', *British Journal of Sociology of Education*, **7**.3.86, pp. 265–74.

Whyte, J. *et al.* (eds), *Girl Friendly Schooling*, London, Methuen, 1985.

Williams, J., 'Education and race: the racialisation of class inequalities', *British Journal of Sociology of Education*, **7**, no. 2, 1986, pp. 135–54.

Wright, C., 'School processes – an ethnographic study', in Eggleston, J. *et al.*, *The educational and vocational experiences of 15–18 year old young people of ethnic minority groups*, 1984. Report submitted to the Department of Education and Science, University of Keele, Department of Education, pp. 201–78.

Yates, L., 'The theory and practice of counter-sexist education in schools', *Discourse*, **3**, no. 2, 1983, pp. 35–44.

Yates, L., 'Is girl friendly schooling really what girls need?', in Whyte, J. *et al.* (eds), *Girl Friendly Schooling*, London, Methuen, 1985.

23   Teachers and gender politics

Gaby Weiner and Madeleine Arnot

Introduction

Teachers have played a central role in challenges to the traditional sexual divisions of schooling. Yet there has been no national survey of the extent of teacher involvement in gender issues and no evaluation of their achievements. This paper, though exploratory, attempts to set the record straight first by identifying the differences in teachers' approaches to the problem of sex inequality in schooling, and then by evaluating the range of experiments and implementation strategies devised.

We shall show how reform initiated by teachers represents the hidden level of gender policy formation, only becoming visible when part of national or LEA policy development. Academic researchers, the HMI, local authority advisers and inspectors, the Equal Opportunities Commission (EOC), etc., all *rely* on teachers to see that desired changes in the education system are carried out. Teachers are often explicitly referred to as agents of change, though they are also frequently condemned for their perceived inability to move with the times (Wickham, 1986). Teachers' potential to initiate change and the long history of teacher-inspired innovation are rarely referred to or acknowledged.

Further, little attention has been paid to the personal and professional implications for teachers as change agents. Involvement in gender politics has had major repercussions for their experiences within classrooms and schools. Good relations with colleagues may be sacrificed when there are disagreements about the goals or strategies of school reform, or when colleagues display hostility to work on gender. Further, promotion prospects inside the school (as well as outside), for instance, in the allocation of special responsibility posts other than for 'equal opportunities', may also be affected. The political atmosphere of a school will also determine how far individual teachers become the 'token' equal opportunities specialists, or part of a general plan of working within the school.

Similarly, teachers' understandings about the nature of teaching or the most appropriate teaching styles have been challenged by their involvement in feminism or gender politics. No matter how committed teachers are to sex equality in education, they will find themselves questioning their own preconceived notions of what constitutes good classroom practice and good pupil relations. Trying to be 'fair' to both girls and boys in mixed classrooms, for instance, raises difficulties not only for indifferent or hostile teachers but also for committed teachers trained in certain 'progressive' pedagogical styles (Walkerdine, 1983).

Source: Commissioned.

Despite such difficulties, teachers have become more interested in gender issues at all educational levels, especially in secondary schools. The demand for information about work on gender reveals the extent of that interest (for example, the mailing list for the *Sex Differentiation Project* was the largest of all the Schools Council projects). What are the reasons for all this activity? For some teachers, their contact with the woman's movement has led them to ask questions about their workplace. Others volunteering for the first time for in-service courses on gender are not so 'politicized', but have become concerned about gender inequalities either because of their own experiences or through encouragement from colleagues and/or local authority policy initiatives. Many teachers retain a general interest in social inequality and the way it is shaped by schooling experiences.

Despite criticisms in the late 1970s of liberal beliefs in educational reform, and despite the lack of interest in social inequality (particularly in class inequality) shown by governments of recent times, teachers still appear to believe that education is an important 'site' and 'stake' of political struggle – that what happens in the school system *is* important. Teachers, if anything, appear to be now more aware of the contradictions of their positions especially when acting as reformers within, what some see as, an 'oppressive' system. Gender (and race) politics offer them chances to liberate not merely their pupils but also themselves.

The teaching profession in the late 1960s and early 1970s, was affected by the change of ideological climate brought about by the women's liberation movement in the United States and Europe, and the development of feminist ideas. In the UK, during this period, work with girls was carried out by individual feminist teachers; however, there was no real evidence of concerted teacher or government interest in combating gender inequalities in education until the Sex Discrimination Act (1975). The response to the letter and spirit of the law by teachers, particularly from those working in the metropolitan authorities, provided the basis for a teacher movement. This movement has constituted a major challenge to mainstream educational ideas and practice.

While, in the main, feminist teachers had relatively little power in the hierarchies of the education system, they were sufficiently organized to make their views known at a number of levels; for instance, by writing reports on the male bias of curriculum content and school organization, and by formulating school policy for presentation at school staff meetings; or by lobbying advisers or inspectors for resources to prepare non-sexist teaching materials (Myers, 1982; Cornbleet and Libovitch, 1983). Also, particularly in the days before local education authorities (LEAs) sanctioned work on gender, feminists working in different schools and educational institutions within the same or neighbouring authorities established *Women in Education* groups to provide forums for discussion, action and support.

The main focus of action for these teachers was on *practical* change; how could they help reduce inequalities between the sexes by changing their own perceptions and practice? They therefore focused on projects dealing with these issues within their own schools and classrooms. The considerable diversity of these projects, however, did not stem merely from the variety of locations and individuals involved; it was also based on critical differences in the perspectives of teachers.

Teacher perspectives on gender and equal opportunities

A number of attempts have been made to classify these different teacher perspectives – for instance, Acker (1986) identified three major approaches, those of socialist-feminism, radical-feminism and liberal-feminism. In contrast Weiner (1985a) suggested a polarization between what she called 'equal opportunities' and 'girl-centred' education.

By the early 1980s the concept of girl-friendly schooling (i.e. making schools more responsive to the needs of their female pupils) was being developed by those concerned with equal opportunities (see Whyte *et al.*, 1985), while teachers committed to girl-centred schooling were developing 'anti-sexist' approaches (see, for example, Cornbleet and Libovitch, 1983). A number of differences between the goals, topics and implementation strategies of educational initiatives on gender could now be discerned:

Equal opportunities/girl friendly	Anti-sexist/girl-centred
Persuading girls into science and technology	Recognizing the importance of girl-centred study; for example, what is 'herstory', or girl- and woman-centred science or technology?
Providing a compulsory common core of subjects, to include 'hard' sciences for girls and humanities for boys	Providing girls with skills and knowledge to challenge the male system in the workplace and the home
Rearranging option blocks to reduce stereotyped choices	Giving girls a sense of solidarity with other members of their sex, and hence greater confidence and motivation
Analysing sexism in textbooks, readers and resources	Widening girls' horizons while not denigrating the lives and work of their mothers, female friends and women in the community
Reviewing school organization – for example, registers, assemblies, uniform, discipline	Changing the nature of schooling: replacing hierarchy, competitiveness, authoritarianism and selection with co-operation, democracy, egalitarianism and community
Producing in-service courses and policy guidelines	Exploring the relationship between sexuality, women's oppression and sexual harassment in school and the workplace
Establishing mixed-sex working parties to develop and monitor school policy	Establishing schoolgirls' and women's support groups
Creating posts for equal opportunities	Decision-making through wide consultation and collective working

Source: Adapted from Weiner (1985a), quoted in Arnot (1986).

Criticisms of this typology (e.g. Acker, 1986; Arnot, 1985) pointed to the difficulty, in practice, of identifying such clear differences in perspective or strategy. Teachers' initiatives often crossed over such boundaries and there were alliances between individuals and groups holding different views. For example, schools, colleges and LEAs often used 'equal opportunities' rhetoric to develop girl-centred or anti-sexist projects.

Moreover the anti-sexist approach to education was adopted by feminists with different political affiliations. Consequently, there were also disagreements about focus and strategy *within* the approach. Black feminists were critical of equal opportunities and radical feminist initiatives which appeared to focus exclusively on the needs of white female pupils and teachers. Lesbian feminists were concerned about the heterosexual bias of most initiatives on gender. Socialist feminists, on the other hand, wanted to place more emphasis on the relationship between anti-sexist initiatives and the policies and pedagogies needed to challenge capitalism; and were ambivalent about the need for the development of separate strategies to deal with gender, especially if not linked to changes in social class inequalities.

Yet a common understanding united these groups, and provided a fundamental challenge to the 'egalitarians' – those advocating equal opportunities. This latter group, described by Weiner (1986) as drawing on the ideas of liberal feminism and equal rights campaigners, wanted to redistribute the rewards of education. In contrast the 'radicals' (i.e. radical, socialist, lesbian and black feminists), each in their own way, wished for no less than the transformation of the education system. They had no wish to ameliorate the existing inadequate education system: they wanted to transform its power base.

While central government has never been entirely enthusiastic about educational reforms concerned with gender (see Arnot in this volume), it was clearly much more tolerant of egalitarian strategies for change. The principal aim of egalitarian teachers was to improve the life chances of girls and women by equipping them, through improved schooling and counselling, to move into more highly paid jobs, hitherto dominated by men, and into senior management posts in education and other government or industrial institutions. The emphasis, within schools, focused on both pupils and teachers.

At pupil level initiatives concentrated on improving motivation (e.g. for girls to take up technology, and boys, home economics), encouraging wider subject choice at 13+, and attempting to diminish the perceived 'wastage of talent' in the case of 'academically able' girls who choose domesticity in preference to a career or paid employment. Emphasis was also placed on the improvement of teaching methods and the raising of awareness of issues of inequality through dissemination of research findings on gender inequalities and in-service work. While consideration of the needs of girls has been uppermost, it was argued that achieving equality in schools would provide benefits for *all* pupils. Such concerns are reflected in the HMI report on *Girls and Science* (1980):

If formal education is concerned, as it ought to be, with the identification of talents and skills of pupils across the broad range of the curriculum, then, in order to achieve their goals, all pupils – whatever their difficulties in a particular area, and irrespective of the origin of these difficulties – must be given adequate help and support . . . especially in science subjects where girls might experience greater learning difficulties than boys (*Girls and Science*, 1980, p. 2).

Whereas girls were encouraged to move into male-dominated areas of the curriculum, e.g. science and technology, so that their job prospects could be enhanced, boys were encouraged to take up traditionally female subjects such as the humanities or childcare courses, so that they would become more sensitive and caring parents.

> ... just as girls do not grow 'naturally' into members of a dominated group, boys do not 'naturally' grow up to be oppressors. The whole process is learnt and much of this learning takes place in school where teachers must take some of the responsibility for the situation.
> Growing up to be 'a man' – to feel superior, independent and self-reliant, to be the big boy who doesn't cry, places boys on the end of a sex-role bias as strong as that experienced by girls but which has different effects (Schools Council/ILEA 1983).

The 'anti-sexist' approach adopted by radical teachers was harder to incorporate in mainstream educational developments. It was too radical and 'confrontational' for some teacher activists, who argued that such a stance was more likely to alienate than persuade. Its influence was therefore only discernible in some LEAs (e.g. Brent, ILEA) where it received support from education officers and elected members.

The main concern of the anti-sexist approach was to uncover the extent of female oppression, generally and in schools in particular, in order to explore ways of *empowering* girls and women. Doubts were expressed about the value of policies of equal opportunities which deny or ignore competing educational (and economic) interests, and criticisms were made of policies of educational change which fail to acknowledge existing power relations; between men and women, black people and white, between heterosexuals and homosexuals/lesbians and between different social classes. Radical feminist teachers, in particular, aimed at placing girls and women at the centre rather than at the periphery of classroom life, and so challenged the dominance of male experience (Beecham, 1983; Cornbleet and Sanders, 1982). They emphasized the importance of transforming 'male' school knowledge and curriculum content, as well as changing school structures and organization.

Socialist feminist teachers also attempted to uncover the hidden sources and processes of gender differentiation and power within schooling, and supported the development of a critical feminist pedagogy to challenge dominant ideological assumptions.

> If we aim to transform the consciousness of our pupils so they can recognise the divisions ideology has created between race, class and sex then we will frequently find ourselves in conflict with the wider function of the school as a state institution serving the needs of our society – which means the needs of a capitalist and patriarchal society. We are faced with the problem of how to change consciousness within such a framework (Payne, 1980, p. 34).

Many socialist teachers chose, however, to devote their energies to developing policy within the teacher unions, rather than developing school-based initiatives; yet here too there were tensions in defining the 'problem' of gender (as we show later in this chapter).

Pressure from black feminists (see for instance Amos and Parmar, 1981, Brah and Minhas, 1985) led to an increased awareness among some teachers (particularly in the metropolitan authorities) about the need to relate anti-sexist work to anti-racist policies. Parallels were drawn and alliances forged between anti-sexist and anti-racist work in defining sexism as a 'male' problem and racism as a 'white' problem. Black feminists urged teachers, particularly white teachers, to tackle the problem of racism, to gain an understanding of the experiences of the Asian and Afro-Caribbean girls in their schools, and to become aware of the different ways in which race, class and gender affect black communities. For example:

The accounts of physical and verbal abuse experienced by the community is endless and horrifying. Schools cannot ignore this overt racism in society, just because there appears to be no overt racism in the school. Schools still expect British Sylheti-speaking girls to adopt the culture and values of the indigenous population, despite the fact that both the curriculum and the hidden curriculum perpetrate racism. So if teachers are to develop and implement anti-sexist, anti-racist policies, they should listen first to what girls, like these British Sylheti-speakers, have to say about their own experiences of school and society (Patel, 1986, p. 54).

Sexuality, as a theme of educational debate, also became more important to feminist teachers in the mid 1980s. In taking up issues of sexuality within schooling teachers have initiated discussion about the relationship between heterosexuality, homosexuality, lesbianism and homophobia and were particularly successful in highlighting the incidence of sexual and verbal harassment in schools. By 1986, however, more sophisticated attempts to deal with prejudice – for example, courses in heterosexism awareness – attracted the hostility of some local parents and the DES (see *Times Educational Supplement*, 1986a and b).

Raising such highly contentious issues presented, not unexpectedly, problems of strategy as well as principle.

Do we concentrate on formulating whole school policies or focus on small, sometimes trivial issues? When do we take on the more contentious issues, for example, sexual harassment or male disciplinary procedures, and when do we opt for 'safer issues', for example registers in alphabetical order or girls wearing trousers all year (although having said that, we are aware that in some schools all anti-sexist issues are 'hot')? (Ord and Quigley 1985, p. 105).

Uniting the different groups using anti-sexist approaches was the recognition of 'struggle' as an inevitable by-product of attempts at social change. Emphasis on the value of collective action, support groups and networks highlighted the need for the development of strategies to deal with the opposition and hostility that feminist ideas are bound to attract. Frankie Ord and Jane Quigley reflect on this theme:

It is frightening how quickly we run into hostility or dismissive amusement when even quite small changes are suggested, and facing such reactions alone can be a daunting prospect . . . power is not given away . . . there will always be conflict and . . . we need to be prepared for it. Opposition takes various forms: aggressive personal attacks, the raised eyebrows of 'oh no, not this again', the stereotyping of one or two members of staff as 'the equal opportunities people'. In this situation a support group is both a retreat and a base from which to launch further initiatives (Ord and Quigley, 1985, p. 106).

Whatever the origins and ideologies of these different anti-sexist perspectives, a recognition of the significance of the unequal power relations between the sexes marked the critical difference between the 'radical' and 'egalitarian' traditions. Further, this difference dictated the choice of strategy. Teachers, like Ord and Quigley above, have had to make choices; between, for example, establishing senior posts of responsibility to organize and co-ordinate activities within school, setting up working parties to investigate issues and make recommendations to the staff and governors, or working at classroom level. The choice of strategy has also, to some extent, been dependent on the policy and commitment of teaching staff and LEA, and on availability of resources, though clearly these are linked. The *Developing Anti-Sexist Initiatives Project*, for example, took a strong 'radical' stand against setting up special responsibility posts, since these allowed individuals to advance their careers as a result of their work on gender, with potentially contradictory outcomes:

Within the hierarchy of a school structure, a senior teacher cannot fail to be divided in her loyalties between the interests of management and those colleagues who are trying to initiate change. The fundamental changes that are brought about by a feminist perspective on education, are in direct conflict with the power structure of the school. To appoint an individual to a position of power tends to contradict the nature of the work and necessarily subsumes it. So during the year 1981–2 it was agreed by the staff to discontinue the senior teacher post and for the women's group collectively to take on the responsibility (Cornbleet and Libovitch, 1983, p. 146).

Nevertheless, alliances between 'radicals' and 'egalitarians' have been forged because teachers needed support in the struggles they were facing, and needed to be optimistic that change was possible.

Radical and socialist feminists *do* work within education to improve the quality of girls' experiences, whatever their theories say about structures. And some liberals advance strategies of 'positive action', by which they mean giving special attention to girls . . . (Acker, 1986, pp. 67–8)

Teachers attempted to put gender inequalities on the school or college agenda using a variety of methods, often cutting across the equal opportunities and anti-sexist divisions mentioned earlier. So, for example, projects aimed at encouraging girls in science and mathematics used single-sex classes to provide a remedial 'catch-up' environment (see Smith, 1984); yet single-sex groups were also used to encourage more open discussion about sex-stereotyping and gender relations in school. Further, most of the projects focused on girls, although there was some interest in boys, particularly in boy-only environments (see, for instance, Mahony, 1985; Askew and Ross, 1985).

Clearly teachers wanted to be agents of change rather than instruments of an oppressive system. Also work on gender provided them with an opportunity to reassess educational values and practice, even at times of low teacher morale, cuts in resources and attacks on their own competence. In considering race and gender as the equality issues of the 1980s, they were reclaiming the equality debates of earlier decades, in order to initiate major educational reforms from within.

Providing the evidence

For many, the choice of strategy depended less on principles than on the availability (or absence) of information about *how* to tackle the issues. The task of collecting information on the extent of gender inequalities in schooling and what people were trying to do about them was made considerably easier by academic research and official investigations sponsored by organizations such as the Equal Opportunities Commission (EOC), the Schools Council, the Women's National Commission (WNC) and individual *Women in Education* groups. Not only were these useful in providing the basis for informed approaches to change, but the networks and support systems established, for example, by the Manchester Women and Education Group's or Schools Council's newsletters (1981–3), helped to rescue beleaguered individual teachers or groups from isolation and sometimes, even, despair. Also useful for teachers were guidelines and suggestions for observation and data collection, so that teachers could conduct their own 'institutional evaluation', and provide local 'evidence' for the need for change (Hannon, 1981; ILEA, 1985; Millman and Weiner, 1985; Adams and Walkerdine, 1986; Adams and Arnot, 1986).

The desire of teachers for more information provided its own dynamic for change in schools and colleges. As Millman noted (1984), the more sophisticated school-based research became, the more schools required some form of co-ordination and contact with other local schools; to compare findings and to discuss strategies for reform. And increasingly, teachers and schools looked towards LEAs for political support and advice, or financial assistance.

By the mid 1980s a number of different strands of activity emerged within the teacher movement (see Arnot, 1986), although these activities overlapped. The most active teachers were likely to be involved in more than one. They were:

a teacher-initiated changes;
b action research involving collaboration between external researchers and practitioners;
c teacher contact and communication networks;
d initiatives undertaken by teacher unions.

Teacher-initiated changes

Most projects, initiated by individuals or groups of teachers, were small-scale, and short-lived due to lack of 'official' support or commitment, with consequent problems of under-financing and resourcing. Moreover, the majority of the teachers involved were at the lower end of the school hierarchy, and from the secondary rather than the primary sector (though Brent, 1984, provided an indication of the potential for change at primary level). Yet these projects were important in that they provided the main challenge to traditional educational assumptions about gender; and they also offered insights into how teachers could develop their own educational goals and implementation styles.

Teachers committed to change faced a number of difficult questions. First, how could they impress on others the importance of gender as an educational issue, and convince the unconvinced? Second, what was the best way to promote change within an educational institution? Given the 'political' nature of the work, how far could teachers go in challenging gender differences in school and in society?

Should they set up projects to deal specifically with gender inequality and stereo-typing, or would it be more fruitful to 'sensitize' the school as a whole?

The projects generally focused on the curriculum, on pupils' attitudes, on teachers' attitudes – or some combination of the three. Few dealt with the sex structure of the school management and teaching profession, since this was not seen as within the scope of teacher influence. Some chose to experiment with single-sex groups, some developed core curricula or altered the timetable to provide 'non-traditional' options; yet others provided career advice for girls or ran courses on gender relations in society. The choice of potential strategy was considerable (e.g. Adams, 1986a and b).

The Spring 1982 *Schools Council Newsletter* reported activities as varied as promoting girls' football (Havering), developing an anti-sexist core curriclum course for years one to three of a boys' secondary school (ILEA), and a 'Young Women's Activity Day' for the young unemployed in Coventry which demon-strated alternative possibilities for girls, 'that women can become skilled and successful at a wide range of activities from acupuncture to karate, from motor-cycling to popmobility'. Another newsletter produced later in the same year reported on experiments with single-sex grouping for mathematics and science in a Doncaster comprehensive, developing a 'sexually undifferentiated' core curriculum in a Northern Ireland high school, and Introduction to Industry and Girls into Engineering courses for Trafford girl pupils. The 'Equal Opportunities Activities Week' in a Leeds secondary school was fairly typical of many early initiatives:

Parkland organized a week of activities during October aimed at raising awareness of sexism at different levels through a variety of media. Photographic exhibitions of 'Women at Work and Leisure' were hired, together with films and videos for use on the Careers Day. Discussions included a Sixth Form Seminar, meetings with parents and a dramatic presentation to illustrate sex-role stereotyping. A 'multi-cultural day' focused on the special problems and experiences of women and girls from minority ethnic groups. Materials contributed by members of staff and pupils were on display throughout the week (Schools Council, 1982b, pp. 17–18).

One of the most common responses to the requirements of the Sex Discrimi-nation Act was the establishment of 'rotating' craft courses ('craft circuses'), whereby all pupils received 'tasters' of the whole range of craft activities. Despite this, the patterns of subject choice among girls and boys appeared to have changed little since the 1973 HMI survey (Pratt *et al.*, 1984). Even the establishment of a core curriculum, adopted by some schools, only 'delayed the problem' (Orr, 1985) since girls and boys still opted for 'traditional' subjects as soon as they were allowed some degree of choice. A rather more contentious experiment, as we mentioned earlier, was that of establishing single-sex groups in mixed schools. For example:

The working party has produced a paper . . . which recommends that Maths, Physics and Chemistry are taught to single sex groups in the third year. Thus, the first major area of change has taken place and plans are in hand for videoing classroom interaction in Maths lessons and for testing boys' and girls' attitudes towards Maths and Physical Science subjects (Northcliffe Comprehensive School, Doncaster, quoted in Schools Council, 1982b, p. 16).

Claims were made that girls do much better academically when taught away from boys, though critics suggested that this may be due more to the extra attention that the girls receive than to the single-sex grouping itself (Harding, 1982).

Other initiatives concerned with supporting adolescent girls were established outside the school system, in youth clubs and girls' projects. Involving youth workers and teachers, these projects were avowedly feminist and united in their commitment to show that 'young women are alive and kicking . . . can achieve something in their lives, and play a more active part in controlling their lives' (Manchester Education for Women Project, 1984).

Attached in the main to the Youth Service, rather than to the schools or colleges, project organizers sought to redress the traditional male dominance of youth work by offering special provision for young women.

Girls' nights, groups or clubs aim to meet the needs of young women in ways in which mixed provision does not, through:

* offering facilities to girls and young women either not served, or inadequately served by existing provision,
* offering to girls and young women the chance to develop and value skills they already have and to try activities not usually available to them in a safe, unthreatening and non-competitive atmosphere,
* improving young women's self esteem, self sufficiency and self confidence through creating a facility where they can enjoy and value each other's company, and therefore themselves,
* offering young women the chance to explore and question the range of options and choices open to them (Foster, Carpenter and Rowley, 1984).

Such initiatives on gender, however, were often pushed out of the educational mainstream and many teachers remained unsupportive. In a study of teacher attitudes towards equal opportunities, Pratt found a large number of teachers (and more men than women) unsympathetic to the issue (Pratt, 1984). The main response of teachers was to stress that pupils or students should be treated according to their individual needs, not according to their skin colour, their country of origin or their sex. Teaching should be 'gender-blind', and schools and teachers should not be expected either to discriminate in favour of girls or to assume responsibility for social change. Stanworth (1983) called this belief the 'politics of non-intervention'.

Action research projects
Other projects drew on the experiences of educationists working in different institutions to help initiate change. Researchers, usually from higher education, worked with teachers to intervene in pupil subject choice or to develop curriculum materials. Challenging inequalities in education also led them to attempt to narrow the traditional distance between educational researchers and teachers. The best known projects of this kind focused on the curriculum choices of girls, and in particular, their level of interest in science and technology. The Girls and Technology Education Project (GATE) investigated ways of improving the curriculum and assessment of CDT, and developing 'good practice'. The Girls into Science and Technology Project (GIST) on the other hand, worked directly

with teachers, attempting to reduce sex-stereotyping on the part of pupils and teachers, and promoting 'gender-fair' interaction in classrooms, so that girls would feel encouraged to study scientific subjects.

The main difficulty for the GIST team was that of trying to work with teachers who were not already sympathetic to the goals and methods of the project.

The main drawback . . . was that, by and large, the teachers did not see girls' underrepresentation in science as a problem. Nor were they willing to re-examine their own values. Most teachers readily agreed that equality was important, but thought that it already existed, and that any residual differences between girls and boys were genetic. Since they did not accept that there was any sex stereotyping in their classrooms, many teachers did not see the problem as theirs, and did not feel motivated to search for solutions (Kelly, 1985, p. 139).

An unexpected spin-off for the GIST team, however, was the success of the dissemination of project ideas and strategies, and the impact of this on the project schools:

Publicity about the research project brings the problem into the public eye, and leads other teachers to define it as their problem. This reflects back to the original school, where teachers now feel they are receiving recognition for something that was previously considered an imposition. . . . Rather than being a nuisance, which distracts one from the important business of work in the schools, publicity becomes an essential element of action research (Kelly, 1985, p. 145).

Other research projects focused on working with, and supporting teachers already convinced of the need for change – in the hope of a 'ripple' effect spreading to others working in the school (see for instance, Millman, 1987). Equality of project participation was stressed by the *Girls And Occupational Choice Project* (GAOC) which chose to:

go for small-scale seeding in fertile soil; a small number of participating schools, with volunteer teachers and intensive research attention. We wanted to establish our role as facilitative only, in equal partnership with the teachers who together would be devising and implementing a curriculum unit. This, together with a hopefully shared political commitment, would ease the potential tensions typically found in the relations between researchers and teachers . . . (Chisholm and Holland, 1984).

The project therefore chose a 'participatory democratic' style in relation to teachers and researchers, and also identified itself as feminist in orientation, i.e. girl-centred, collaborative and non-hierarchical.

An alternative approach was to help teachers become independent researchers. May and Rudduck (1983) conducted a project in first and middle schools in Norfolk. The goal was to raise awareness about sex-stereotyping in the early years of schooling by encouraging teachers to explore the dynamics of their schools and to enable them 'to understand better their own practice as a basis for informing future curricular decisions'. Teachers volunteered for the project, and with the help of a skilled researcher designed and carried out investigations. The effects of such investigations, however, are difficult to assess. Would they have any long-term effect? Would the teachers continue with such research or put their skills to further use in the development of school policy? Could the data generated be useful for other schools?

Similar concerns confronted the *Schools Council Sex Differentiation Project* which adopted the teacher-researcher approach and did much to legitimize both the area and the method of producing innovation in schools (see Weiner, 1985b; Millman, 1987, for a more detailed discussion of teachers as researchers). The model of innovation and curriculum developed by the Schools Council was that of self-education and then collective re-education. Teachers first developed small research studies of their own, which replicated as far as possible social scientific methods of research and data collection. The findings from these projects provided the basis for changes of practice, within schools or individual classrooms. An account of the studies and evaluation of the changes made were then brought to the attention of school colleagues, usually through presentation of a report at a staff meeting. At this stage it was important to convince colleagues of the validity of the studies if the 'ripples' were to spread more widely. Millman noted:

When the research findings are presented to other staff and disseminated more widely throughout the school, data will be necessary to convince staff of the validity of the teacher's findings. Classroom research, particularly in the area of sex differentiation, is likely to raise some very sensitive questions and often teachers will find it hard to accept that their methods and interactions are sexist. In view of this, research findings will need to be presented in a full, thoughtful and objective manner so that teacher consciousness is raised as widely as possible. The 'success' of a teacher's research in raising consciousness is impossible to measure and often she will feel dispirited at the apathetic or hostile reactions within her school. At this stage it is important not to be impatient – attitudinal and behavioural change is a slow process (Millman, 1983, p. 31).

Building on this tradition, LEAs such as Brent and ILEA designed their in-service courses around the concept of teacher-researcher (see, for example, Brent Education Department, 1984; Adams and Walkerdine, 1986; Adams and Arnot, 1986).

Teacher contact and communication networks

The development of action research and teacher-initiated projects relied on access to information and advice about how to proceed. The existence of a network of teacher organizations was therefore critical in encouraging innovation and reform. Though it was evident that the EOC did not see its role as the initiator of a UK gender network (Meehan, 1982), the *Schools Council Sex Differentiation Project* attempted to construct such a network among teachers. Throughout the two-year project, it produced a series of newsletters for participant and other interested teachers, and also established an information centre with resources and materials produced by the range of gender initiatives of the time. The *Working with Girls Newsletter*, a similar newsletter series for youth workers, aimed at keeping workers throughout the country in touch with each other. This newsletter had several functions:

* to keep people aware of what is happening now, with new developments, and with debates and current thinking in the whole area;
* to inform workers about projects, conferences, seminars, training, resources and jobs, and provide general information relating to work with girls;
* to function as an arena for debate, opening up a dialogue around the 'whys' and 'hows' of girls' work;

* to carry funding news and ideas, and practical suggestions for working with girls (reported in Schools Council, 1982a, p. 17).

One of the Schools Council's final publications was a directory (1983) of equal opportunities projects set up by local authorities, schools and individuals, which itself constituted a sizeable research effort.

However, for teachers distant from its London offices, such a centre had limited appeal. Instead, by the end of the 1970s, a number of regional teachers' organizations and groups had been established. They included:

a *Teacher/subject groups*: Women in History, Women in Geography, Girls and Mathematics (GAMMA), Women in Computing, Women in Economics, etc.;
b *Women in Education groups*: organized locally – in Hull, Oxford, Manchester, Cambridge, London, etc.:
c *Resource centres and newsletters*: for example, the Women's Educational Resource Centre, the Campaign Against Sexism and Sexual Oppression in Education (CASSOE) and the Women's Education Group (GEN);
d *Publishing ventures*: Schools Council/Longmans, Pandora Press, the Explorations in Feminism Collective/Hutchinson, the Open University Gender and Education series, etc.,
e *Learning materials*: for example non-sexist books, films, exhibitions, teaching and in-service packs on different subjects produced by such groups as GAMMA, and the Campaign to Impede Sex-stereotyping in the Young (CISSY).

Teacher union initiatives

Teachers committed to change also came together in the teacher unions. Given the context of union work, they focused on different topics compared to the school-based initiatives, yet they faced similar obstacles – male-dominated union hierarchies, low status, inability to influence the union agenda, etc.

Since the sex discrimination legislation in 1975, union interest in equal opportunities has been patchy, though there has been some activity, particularly in the National Union of Teachers (NUT), National Association of Teachers in Further and Higher Education (NATFHE) and Association of University Teachers (AUT), and also in the Educational Institute of Scotland (EIS) and the Assistant Masters and Mistresses Association (AMMA).

NATFHE has established a national women's rights study panel, a structure of regional panels and produced, in 1986, guidelines on how to establish a joint union and LEA equal opportunities policy; the AUT set up a women's committee and distributes a regular and popular newsletter; AMMA sponsored a survey on women teachers' career prospects in 1985; and the EIS established, in 1980, an *ad hoc* Committee on Sex Discrimination in Education. Despite its blemished history on equal opportunities (see Oram in this volume) the NUT has set the pace for such work in the 1980s. Through its equal opportunities advisory committee and department at union headquarters, it sponsored a survey, *Promotion and the Woman Teacher*, with the EOC in 1981, and has run training courses for its women members.

These courses aim to promote women's self-development, particularly in relation to their careers, their more active involvement in the Union and their role in establishing equal opportunities within their individual schools (National Union of Teachers, 1986, p. 4).

It has also encouraged local equal opportunities initiatives, drawn up 'model' job descriptions, provided advice on maternity provision and developed a formal policy on gender equality in the teaching profession.

However, despite the large numbers of women members in the teacher unions, most of the top union jobs continue to be filled by men. This has lead to the establishment of campaigning groups within unions to challenge male dominance. For example, in the NUT, a Women in the NUT group was set up in 1978, as a response to the low priority given to women's rights issues in the union, the 'ghettoization' of women in the lowest paid and poorly financed sectors of teaching, and the general domination of the union and its policy-making by men (*Women in the NUT Newsletter*, 1981). Such 'gender-blindness' was identified by Jones (1985) as a major structural problem of the union, a consequence of its unwillingness to respond to the needs of the majority of its membership. The 1984 NUT Memorandum was therefore significant in its attempts to deal with not just women's careers in teaching (for example, part-time work, maternity leave, job sharing, fixed term contracts and promotion) but also with the position of women in the union itself and with girls' and boys' education (NUT, 1984). Additionally union representatives on the Schools Council Secondary Committee and its sub-committee, the Schools Council Sex Differentiation in School Working Party (acronym SIDESWIPE) played a major part in promoting initiatives on gender within the Schools Council (Weiner, 1985b).

Summary and conclusions

The strategies chosen by, and the obstacles facing, school-based projects on gender were determined by the level of support they received from teachers of different subjects, from heads and senior school management, and from LEAs and other educational bodies. The topics and methods adopted by the teacher projects were also shaped by the ideological perspectives of the teachers involved, whether 'equal opportunities' or 'anti-sexist'. Clearly, all such projects were also dependent on the enthusiasm of committed teachers, predominantly female and often in the lowest status and lowest paid teaching jobs. For these reasons, the long-term outcomes of many of these projects have been unpredictable. Nevertheless the commitment to a just future for their pupils, daughters and colleagues, the struggle and the optimism often hard to sustain in times of retrenchment, and an educational vision, marks this teacher movement out as a worthy successor to the campaigns for equal pay and the removal of the marriage bar in the first half of the twentieth century. Acker continues to be optimistic about future possibilities:

Whatever the difficulties encountered in introducing and sustaining feminist activities in education, the efforts of committed teachers and parents are likely to continue and spread as long as feminism survives. It is a paradox that although education provides the conditions under which people are channelled into limited futures, it is also the primary means for liberation and transformation. Feminists will continue to use it in a liberating spirit, in and out of school. The efforts of each feminist teacher and parent will be reflected in the generations to follow (Acker, 1986, pp. 72–3).

Important though this movement was, and still is, in the struggle for equal educational opportunities, it is yet to be seen whether, given the short-term existence of the initiatives, the low status of the teachers involved, and its marginality to the main concerns of policy-makers, it is able to continue to apply pressure at local and national levels.

References

Acker, S., 'What feminists want from education', in Hartnett, A. and Naish, M. (eds), *Education and Society Today*, Lewes, Falmer, 1986.

Adams, C. (ed.), *Primary Matters*, London, ILEA, 1986a.

Adams, C. (ed.), *Secondary Issues*, London, ILEA, 1986b.

Adams, C. and Arnot, M., *Investigating Gender in Secondary Schools*, London, ILEA, 1986.

Adams, C. and Walkerdine, V., *Investigating Gender in Primary Schools*, London, ILEA, 1986.

Amos, V. and Parmar, P., 'Resistances and responses; the experiences of Black girls in Britain', in McRobbie, A. and McCabe, T. (eds), *Feminism for Girls: An Adventure Story*, London, Routledge and Kegan Paul, 1981.

Arnot, M., 'Current developments in the sociology of women's education', *British Journal of Sociology of Education*, **6**, no. 1, 1985 pp. 123–30.

Arnot, M., *Race, Gender and Education Policy-making*, Open University Course E333, *Policy-making in Education*, Module 4, Open University Press, 1986.

Askew, S. and Ross, C., 'Sexism in boys' schools: a tentative appraisal', *GEN* **4**, winter 1984–5.

Beecham, Y., 'Women's studies and beyond – the feminisation of education', *GEN*, **1**, autumn 1983.

Brah, A. and Minhas, R., 'Structural racism or cultural difference: schooling for Asian girls', in Weiner, G. (ed.), *Just a Bunch of Girls*, Milton Keynes, Open University Press, 1985.

Brent Education Department, *Seeing is Believing: teacher investigations into gender differences in the classroom*, Brent Curriculum Support Unit, Brent LEA, 1984.

Chisholm, L. and Holland, J., *Sinking and swimming: the experience of developing affirmative-action collaborative research in schools*, paper to the Girl Friendly Conference, Manchester Polytechnic, 1984.

Cornbleet, A. and Sanders, S., *Developing Anti-Sexist Initiatives (DASI); Project Report*, ILEA, 1982.

Cornbleet, A. and Libovitch, S., 'Anti-sexist initiatives in a mixed comprehensive school: a case study', in Wolpe, A. M. and Donald, J. (eds), *Is there anyone here from education?*, London, Pluto Press, 1983.

Department of Education and Science, *Girls and Science*, London, HMSO, 1980.

Education for Women Project, Manchester Polytechnic, 1984.

Foster, S., Carpenter, V. and Rowley, L., 'Setting up a girls' night: a check list', *GEN*, **3**, summer 1984.

Hannon, V., *Ending Sex-Stereotyping in Schools*, Manchester EOC, 1981.

Harding, J., 'Bring on the girls', *Times Educational Supplement*, London, Times Newspapers, 31.12.82.

Inner London Education Authority (ILEA), *Race, Sex and Class: A Policy for Equality: Sex*, London, ILEA, 1985.

Kelly, A., 'Changing schools and changing society; some reflections on the Girls into Science and Technology Project', in Arnot, M. (ed.), *Race and Gender; Equal Opportunities Policies in Education*, Oxford, Pergamon, 1985.

Mahony, P., *Schools for the Boys? Coeducation Reassessed*, London, Hutchinson in association with the Explorations in Feminism Collective, 1985.

Millman, V., 'Teacher research', in Elm Bank Teachers' Centre (ed.), *Equal Opportunities in Secondary Schools; what does it mean for girls?*, Coventry, Elm Bank Centre, 1983.

Millman, V., 'Teacher as researcher: a new tradition for research on gender', in Weiner, G. and Arnot, M. (eds), *Gender Under Scrutiny: New inquiries in education*, London, Hutchinson, 1987.

Millman, V. and Weiner, G., *Sex Differentiation in Schools: is there really a problem?* York, Longman for the Schools Council, 1985.

May, N. and Rudduck, J., *Sex Stereotyping and the Early Years of Schooling*, Norwich, Centre for Applied Research in Education, UEA, 1983.

Meehan, E., 'Implementing equal opportunities policies: some British-American comparisons', *Politics: journal of the Politics Studies Association of the UK*, **2** no. 1, pp. 14–20.

Myers, K., 'Equal opportunities in Haverstock School', in EOC (ed.), *Gender and the Secondary Curriculum; EOC Research Bulletin* **6**, Manchester, EOC, spring 1982.

National Union of Teachers (NUT), *Promotion and the Woman Teacher*, Manchester, EOC/NUT, 1981.

NUT, *Four memoranda to be presented to the 1984 NUT conference by the executive: equal opportunities in education*, London, NUT, 1984.

NUT, *Briefing*, **2**, London, NUT, autumn 1986.

Ord, F. and Quigley, J., 'Anti-sexism as good educational practice; what feminists can realistically achieve?', in Weiner G. (ed.), *Just A Bunch of Girls*, Milton Keynes, Open University Press, 1985.

Patel, L., 'Girls' experiences of racism in schools', in Adams, C. (ed.), *Secondary Issues*, London, ILEA, 1986.

Payne, I., 'Sexist ideology and education', in Spender, D. and Sarah, E. (eds), *Learning to Lose*, London, The Women's Press, 1980.

Pratt, J., Bloomfield, J. and Seale, C. (eds), *Option Choice; a question of equal opportunity*, Berkshire, NFER/Nelson, 1984.

Schools Council, *Sex Differentiation Newsletter*, **2**, London, Schools Council, April 1982a.

Schools Council, *Sex Differentiation Newsletter*, **3**, London, Schools Council, November 1982b.

Schools Council, *Equal Opportunities in Education: Contact Directory*, London, Schools Council, 1983.

Schools Council/ILEA, *Equal Opportunities; what's in it for boys?; Conference Report*, London, Schools Council, 1983.

Smith, S., 'Single-sex setting', in Deem, R. (ed.), *Coeducation Reconsidered*, Milton Keynes, Open University Press, 1984.

Stanworth, M., *Gender and Schooling: study of social divisions in the classroom*, London, Hutchinson in association with the Explorations in Feminism Collective, 1983.

Times Educational Supplement, 'Marginally liberal Angela; interview with Angela Rumbold Minister of State for Education', 14.11.86a, p. 8.

Times Educational Supplement, 'Being ernest about homosexuality', 26.12.86b, p. 3.

Walkerdine, V., 'It's only natural: rethinking child-centred pedagogy', in Wolpe, A. M. and Donald, J. (eds), *Is there anyone here from education?*, London, Pluto, 1983.

Weiner, G., 'Equal opportunities, feminism and girls' education: introduction', in Weiner, G. (ed.), *Just A Bunch Of Girls*, Milton Keynes, Open University Press, 1985a.

Weiner, G., 'The Schools Council and gender: a case study in the legitimation of curriculum policy', in Arnot, M. (ed.), *Race and Gender; Equal Opportunities Policies in Education*, Oxford, Pergamon, 1985b.

Weiner, G., 'Equal opportunities and feminist education; unity or discord', *British Journal of Sociology of Education*, **7**, no. 3, 1986, pp. 265–74.

Whyte, J., Deem, R., Kant, L. and Cruickshank, M. (eds), *Girl Friendly Schooling*, London, Methuen, 1985.

Wickham, A., *Women and Training*, Milton Keynes, Open University Press, 1986.

Women in the NUT, *Newsletter*, 1981.

24 Gender in the house of policy

David L. Kirp, Mark G. Yudof, and Marlene Strong Franks

I

What should be the substance of gender policy? Is is one thing to advocate autonomy in the domain of gender, quite another to specify what the political branches of government can do to aid autonomous decision-making. That is the task of this chapter, which offers a structure for analysing policy.

Some caveats are in order. The issues summed in the phrase 'gender policy' are legion, the political environments that nurture them disorderly, the competing claimants many and vociferous. To deal fittingly with topics ranging from the protection of pregnant women in the toxic workplace[1] to the awarding of custody to gay would-be parents,[2] would require an encyclopedia; we mean to be illustrative and not exhaustive. We also stint on detail, leaving fine points to be elaborated within the framework. Although we are not timid about urging particular policy outcomes in the name of choice, we recognize that in many instances there is no clearly best approach, for the evidence is too unclear, the results of intervention too uncertain, or the play of preference too substantial.[3] Our larger intention is not to insist upon some pet scheme but to show by example that thinking about policy issues in principled terms, as properly aimed at enhancing personal choice, is both useful and potentially consequential.

From both ends of the political spectrum, much of what passes for gender policy discussion is disappointing in its content and form. The expectation that government can decree gender justice, ushering in the future or reinstating a sanitized version of the past, is strongly held, even in the face of evidence that most Americans question the usefulness of new government interventions and doubt that officialdom will usually do what is right.[4] And conflict among the partisans over gender policy resembles less the familiar jockeying for attention among interest groups than a death-struggle to validate one or another conception of the right and true.

The platform of the 1978 National Women's Conference offers a useful introduction to the policy aspirations of politically active leftist feminists. Delegates declared that government should eliminate violence in the home and develop shelters for battered women, support women's businesses, eradicate child abuse, provide federal funding of non-sexist daycare, assure full employment in order

Source: Extracted from Kirp, D. L., Yudof, M. G. and Strong Franks, M., *Gender Justice*, Chicago, University of Chicago Press, 1986, pp. 124–39 and 227–30.

that all women who wish to work may do so, protect home-makers who would make their marriages into partnerships, end the sexist portrayal of women in the media, establish reproductive freedom and end involuntary sterilization, revise the criminal codes dealing with rape, eliminate discrimination on the basis of sexual preference, establish non-sexist education, review all welfare proposals for their specific impact on women, and so forth.

What is remarkable about this litany is the implicit expectation that anyone, let alone government, might accomplish all those things – that government might, for instance, actually end child abuse. The conference recommendations ignore priorities – everything is important – and acknowledge no limits to collective action or resources in the public and private spheres, thus linking the plausible and significant with the petty and unachievable. Naïvely enough, they reflect the belief that a Big Sister government which policed daycare programmes and the media to root out sexism would be less coercive than Big Brother, that thought control in the pursuit of benign outcomes is acceptable. It is the kind of public document that gives gender policy a bad name.[5]

Beginning in 1963 with the passage of the Equal Pay Act, a great deal of federal legislation aimed at undoing one or another form of unfairness has been adopted. That roll-call includes the provisions of the 1964 Civil Rights Act dealing with sex discrimination, the 1972 legislation proscribing sex discrimination in schools and universities, the 1974 law mandating equal credit opportunity, the 1978 bill assuring that employers treat pregnancy as a normal disability in calculating benefits, and the pension equity and child support enforcement measures of 1984.

These bills did not pass because of the sheer good will of legislators. Although there were some fluke victories – the 1964 Civil Rights Act included sex as one of the prohibited bases of discrimination only because southern legislators thought that was a good joke, a way of pointing out the absurdity of the larger civil rights enterprise – these measures were, for the most part, energetically promoted by a coalition of activists who played conventional politics like maestroes. They effectively mustered pressure in aid of goals that could be depicted as unthreatening to the general scheme of things – as extending to women the rights enjoyed by men, for instance, without disturbing women's role as home-maker.[6]

There are, for instance, treatments of childcare that reckon frankly with the tension between the interest of women in freedom and the interest of children in nurturance,[7] and discussions of the need for a federal housing policy that would respond to changing family demographics by increasing options, both in the siting and character of publicly supported housing.[8] But these analyses remain the exception; even among mainstream gender policy analysts, there is a stubborn persisting preference for the costly, the centralized, and the uniform, an unwillingness to learn from the demise of the Great Society mode of governing.

Judged by the criterion of political success, feminists have fallen far short of the mark, as the possibility for action on behalf of women's causes has remained greater than the performance. The failure of the Equal Rights Amendment, a failure above all of political acumen, is the best example of this; but in Congress and the statehouses too, stamina has sometimes been in short supply.

This mixed track record is partly attributable to the view, held by some leftist feminists, that only transformational politics is worth struggling for, that meliorist politics, which is what legislatures routinely traffic in, is useless. There is also a tendency among radical feminists to emphasize the psychological at the expense of the political, 'a preoccupation with internal processes' of personal or small group dynamics that has taken 'precedence over program or effectiveness'.[9] Furthermore, supporters of feminist causes, like activists in other social movements, have often confused formal victories – the passage of a bill – with real change, ignoring the grubby but vital business of policing the implementation of new laws. There have been great difficulties in enforcing the new credit restrictions, for instance, but little demand for strengthened enforcement.

This decade has been a difficult time for feminists of whatever ideological stripe. Although the attention paid to the gender gap by both parties has enabled women to preserve past gains, there have been few new triumphs to shout about, and certainly none that cost Washington any money. Meanwhile, beginning in 1980, the right has had its chance to rewrite the rules of the game, and its proposals are more unnerving than even the woolliest fantasies of the left.

One might imagine that conservatives would be more chary of government intervention or more respectful of past practice, but this turns out not to be the case – or, more accurately, these new activists turn out to be, not conservatives, but radical reactionaries. Radicals of the right and left appear equally willing to be prescriptive, differing only in the substance of the government policy being commended. For instance, in turning conventional liberal thinking on its ear, the indefatigable Phyllis Schlafly proposes to define as 'discrimination' any policy concerning work that does not favour 'the traditional family, and the one-paycheck family, where the father is the primary provider and the mother the primary homemaker'.[10]

There is more, but not better, in this vein. Legislation designed to teach teenagers 'self-discipline and chastity' has been introduced into Congress. A Family Protection Act, which has also been before Congress, urges everything from 'an expansive interpretation' of the role of parents in the moral and religious upbringing of their children and a relaxation of restrictions on parental administration of the strap to a requirement that educational materials purchased with federal dollars 'reflect different ways in which men and women live' and 'contribute to the American way of life as it has been historically understood'. It would deny federal funding, including social security and welfare benefits, to anyone who 'promoted' a life-style that the New Right finds distressing. Advocates on the far left would lead us into the Brave New World, complete with BioLib. Their radical right antagonists would return us to the imaginary world of yesteryear, when men wore the pants, gays stayed in the closet, and children were seen but not heard.

In style as well as substance, gender politics has often been the politics of Armageddon, characterized by clashes between social movements that do not know the language of compromise. When President Nixon expressed fears for the demise of the American family and the rise of 'communal approaches to childrearing', as he did in vetoing daycare legislation in 1971, he set the ideological tone of debate.[11] The issues have since evolved but the element of moral crusade has only grown stronger. If the participants believe that each has a monopoly on virtue, if opponents are labelled as wrong or unvirtuous, as regularly occurs in disputes over such bitterly contested questions as homosexual rights, childcare, and abortion, political civility is hard to sustain. Here the moral dilemmas are truly vexing, the stakes high, the strain in the social and constitutional fabric considerable, the winners of public debate harder to determine than the losers.

Ideological donnybrooks are not unique to gender. But the ferocity of the clashes masks a complicating truth: on a great many subjects of policy debate, the right answer is not really ascertainable, either by recourse to theory or by reliance on data. There is, for instance, no unassailable argument for the proposition that the traditional household is best – for what has been functional isn't necessarily right – or, conversely, for the view that an imposed egalitarianism in the household would be preferable. A political system that insisted on greater female participation might produce a more humane government or just more Margaret Thatchers. The increasing reliance on daycare for children whose parents both work may yield more neurotic progeny, deprived of a nurturing figure – or healthier offspring, freed from ever-obsessing Mom. There is no way to know these things.

Present societal norms reflect this relativism, and mark a change from the apparently greater certainties of the past. A thousand flowers bloom in the American social garden, and the extent of variability has been increasing rapidly. Survey data reveal a growing tolerance for life choices that once would have seemed wholly out of bounds, a diminished willingness to condemn the aberrational, whether that person be a househusband, a lesbian, or an unmarried mother. This is new: a 1984 Harris survey finds that 70 per cent of men and 64 per cent of women report that women are regarded with greater respect as individual human beings, compared to a decade earlier.[12] Moreover, the aberrational has increasingly become the norm, with respect to the proportion of working mothers, unmarried couples living together, abortions performed, and the like. These developments have taken us ever farther from a normative societal consensus on which a detailed and prescriptive gender policy might conceivably be based.

II

Some gender policy is an inevitability, because government actions necessarily affect individual choices. In its arrangements for childcare, job training, taxation, abortion, military service, education, and in myriad other instances, government broadens or narrows the sphere of individual volition. Offer subsidized state-run daycare and fewer children will be raised by stay-at-home mothers; make marriage a tax haven and more individuals may be tempted to tie the knot; turn homosexuality into a crime and gay men and women will lead furtive private lives; choose a different approach and the outcome will change. As long as the government is to have some responsibility for raising and spending taxpayers' dollars and regulating the economy, it cannot avoid affecting men's and women's choices.[13]

Policy is not only inevitable; deliberate polities also make considerable sense for a great many gender issues. 'End government intrusion' may be a catchy slogan, but it offers small comfort to the battered spouse or the victim of job discrimination. 'Getting government off our backs' has little meaning to the poor family that hopes to raise its children decently and maintain an adequate standard of living. Government involvement becomes especially appropriate when traditional institutions such as churches, families, and local communities can no longer do their jobs, when once-private shames become public dilemmas. Although the market-place is in many instances a valuable safeguard of individual choice, the unregulated market will not respond to many legitimate grievances of men and women, nor will it routinely furnish individuals with the information they need to make choices for themselves. In short, a 'night watchman' state is not what justice entails.[14]

The question remains: is it possible to harness policy shaped by the political branches to a useful set of principles?[15] This is not a question that one poses about the judiciary, since what makes courts distinctive, what gives this unelected 'least dangerous' branch[16] of government its legitimacy, is the principle-driven character of judicial decision-making.[17] Judges do not just act but also explain themselves. They elaborate reasons for a decision; search for consistency with earlier cases to justify the opinion at hand; appeal variously to historical evidence, constitutional text, and inferences from the structure of the Constitution.[18] Courts deprecate short-run considerations, and treat bargaining and vote-swapping as unacceptable behaviour. Most important, perhaps, they assign rights, which are absolute in nature, rather than trafficking in interests that can more readily be 'satisfied'.[19] Appeals to principle come naturally to such an institution.

This distinction between courts and the co-ordinate branches of government cannot be pushed too far, of course, for the day is long past when informed commentators believed that law awaited discovery by the diligent application of logic and the scientific method, free of value judgments. Particularly in settling disputes to which the law offers no straightforward answer, judges take note of the political as well as the legal ramifications of their decisions. Accommodation and uncertainty in law are dictated by the vagueness of legal principles, the difficulty of applying principles to concrete cases, and conflicts among principles. None the less, judging differs in salient ways from overtly political decision-making, and those differences consistently point to the far greater status of principle in judicial argument.

Some who disparage the pragmatic nature of politics would turn elsewhere – to experts, for instance – or recast the political process in a more rationalistic mould. Such alternatives are theoretically possible, but far less attractive than more familiar incrementalist politics in their implications for gender justice. Although experts play a dominant role in many policy arenas, especially where technical knowledge is crucial, gender policy seems an unlikely domain for the ministrations of specialists.[20] Indeterminacy concerning what works and what doesn't, what policy initiatives succeed and why, is no pathological condition but appears imbedded in the subject of gender itself; because disagreements about values dominate many of the central issues, expertise offers little guidance.[21] Under such circumstances, everyone becomes an expert; what feels right may well *be* right. Expertise can, of course, be useful at the margin of decision, as in long-term evaluations of childcare programmes, and expertise can better inform individual decisions. But much too little is – or is likely to be – known, for a Bureau of Gender Policy or gender impact statements to be helpful.

Nor would we be better off with a system of decision that aimed at remodelling 'the whole of society in accordance with a definite plan or blueprint',[22] as rationalist politics envisions. Rationalism of this stripe quests after perfection.[23] It aims at defining and controlling the future, since 'from any department of social life which is not so controlled there may lurk the dangerous forces that make for unforeseen changes'.[24] But 'unforeseen changes', popular subversions, give gender policy its dynamic quality; it is those changes, those acts of *private* policy, that should be encouraged, and not tamed by regulation. The prevailing political order, incrementalist in character, is preferable to rationalist government in good part because it attempts to calibrate and respond to such preferences rather than imposing policy.[25]

Incrementalism embraces, a politics of limits, not of enormous official appetite, relying on 'diversity, conflict, openness and improvisation', rather than expertise, as 'society's main assets in problem solving'.[26] Moreover, by searching for compromise rather than all-or-nothing judgements, incrementalist politics tends to diffuse the ideological passions that, unchecked, can split a society into interests that cannot be accommodated. Simply put, incrementalist politics obliges people to talk with one another.

Even in the tug and haul of incrementalist politics, where advocates shamelessly plead for special treatment and the accolade 'statesman' is reserved for someone who cobbles together a serviceable compromise, principle is not irrelevant. The 'conscientious legislator' or executive sometimes acts in ways reminiscent of a judge;[27] and, other things equal, politicians generally prefer to do what is right. If politics puts the claims of principle in their place, principles none the less can have a place in politics.

III

The basic principles of sound gender policy are readily specified. If liberty is to have meaning, individuals must have the *opportunity* to choose, the *capacity* to make choices, *information* on which to base preferences, and a climate of *tolerance* in which to explore alternatives. These elements, taken together, form the core of a choice-enhancing approach to gender policy.

Opportunity
Discrimination offends the idea of gender justice precisely because it robs individuals of the chance to make important life determinations for themselves. Rules that restrict opportunities to one or another sex – for example, by preferring mothers over fathers in child custody disputes or barring women from ostensibly hazardous work – subordinate the person to the group. They favour categories over persons, and for that reason are the enemy of claims based on personal merit, desert, or preference, the kinds of claims that a concern for liberty makes centrally important. Discrimination may in fact appear efficient from the viewpoint of the discriminating organization, because in certain situations it is cheaper

to apply rules than to make case-by-case determinations; where members of a group share a prejudice, honouring that view may be the least costly course.[28] But what is efficient is not necessarily right, and the very fact that discrimination *does* sometimes pay makes government policing essential.

Opportunities must also be made widely known, especially where they are new opportunities, the result of abandoning a past pattern of discrimination. A school that opens its home-making class to boys or its auto mechanics class to girls, for instance, should couple that action with a clear message that the new option is not mere window dressing. So too for the craft union that admits women or the airline that hires male flight attendants after years of doing otherwise; wide publicity, coupled with attempts to make the jobs appealing, are critical to creating real opportunities in the aftermath of discrimination. Promoting the opportunity for choice thus requires taking positive initiatives as well as abandoning old practices.

Government may go further, providing a range of opportunities as well as requiring that private opportunities be made well known, without skewing choice. Just as options are overly constricted if marriage is the only legally permissible relationship, so too choices are impoverished if there are no opportunities for taking care of children outside the home. As long as government does not press its alternatives over those privately generated, it may expand the market-place of options, for 'people will have more freedom if the society in which they live restructures its institutions so as to provide more and more attractive alternatives among which to choose'.[29]

Markets of one form or another, not government, routinely offer these choices.[30] Communes spring up as living arrangements for those dissatisfied with marriage, employers offer daycare services to satisfy the demands of workers. Yet markets are subject to failure. The cost of introducing some new service may be too great, would-be suppliers may not accurately forecast demand, or would-be demanders may ask for too little because they do not take into account the full social benefits of their actions. In such circumstances, government-managed alternatives make sense. It was on this premise that John Stuart Mill contemplated state-run schools to compete with private education,[31] and it explains why government subsidizes solar energy. In the gender realm, daycare centres might need direct government aid for start-up costs, and subsidies such as scholarships to increase opportunities in fields that have historically catered to only one sex may be appropriate.

The risk of subsidizing choices is that such assistance makes the government-aided opportunity very much more attractive than its non-favoured alternatives. The line is indeed thin between expanding the range of opportunity by offering options that the market will not provide, which seems appropriate, and specifying a particular outcome that is attractive to policy-makers, which we reject. An autonomy-promoting approach to gender policy will emphasize the power of government to enhance the capacity of all individuals to choose, not promote a particular end. For that reason, it will favour providing money without strings attached rather than in-kind support. Thus, for instance, children's allowances that can be used as a family wishes resolve the childcare problem in a more liberty-enhancing manner than does government provision of daycare.

Capacity

Removing barriers to choice frees people to make their own life plans. While such freedom is essential to the exercise of volition, it is not sufficient if individuals lack the capacity to make choices. For that reason, liberty-expanding gender policy should also incorporate assurances that the basic social and economic wants of persons have been satisfied. As a political matter, this is hardly controversial. Even as the Reagan administration was busily trimming social programmes, it insisted that a 'safety net' be maintained; indeed, talk of this 'safety net' may have been the conscience-easing rhetoric that made the cuts possible. The limits of basic state support need to be clearly delineated, however, since arguments for social minima may be all too easily transformed into demands for equal distribution of goods, a very different proposition. What constitutes one person's safety net is another's ceiling; an acceptable minimum is necessarily a function of the resources available to the society.

The concern about a policy of satisfying wants is that it so expands the scope of the state's authority that it may subsume choice in the name of a rational collective will, but it is too late in the day to argue that meeting the minimum needs of persons courts this danger. Democratic nations have long been able to couple redistribution with personal liberty; as long as government support takes the form of an assured social minimum, most likely the form of a guaranteed income, and not a more wholesale redistribution of resources, the threat to classic understandings of liberty seems insubstantial. Indeed, the two forms of liberty are intertwined. Negative liberty, freedom from arbitrary government controls over persons, constrains the state from distributing goods according to favouritism or whim. Without the positive liberty offered by a decent social minimum, choice is as illusory as Anatole France's quip about the theoretically equal right of the rich and poor to sleep under the bridges of Paris. Basic support offers individuals the wherewithal to pursue their own ends.

One trap is easy to fall into, and that is to ask of liberty what it cannot deliver. 'Everything is what it is,' philosopher Isaiah Berlin writes. 'Liberty is liberty, not equality or fairness or justice or culture, or human happiness or a quiet conscience.'[32] Guaranteeing the prerequisites of choice does not mean that people will have the identical capacity to choose, that they will automatically make agreeable choices, that they will not often regret their choices, or that they will not often be irrational. Liberty is concerned with the process of choice, not its outcomes, and those who would influence outcomes directly must look to some other tool. We believe that government's role is to ensure that the process is comparable for all, not that the outcomes conform to some predetermined plan.

Information

A choice-promoting policy requires that information be disseminated, so that individuals may learn of the opportunities that are available. Much of that knowledge will doubtless be transmitted informally, from old boys' – and, increasingly, old girls' – networks, and some will be offered by the market.[33] But government too has a place here, for society as a whole is better off if individuals can choose from the full range of alternatives available to them. Because that range is vast and potentially overwhelming, government might sensibly concentrate its attention on publicizing unconventional, option-expanding possibilities, for by definition those are least familiar. Men are likely to know, without government telling them, that they can be telephone linesmen but they need to be told that they can be telephone operators; women will be more aware of secretarial than trucking jobs.

If government is to emphasize the unfamiliar, its stance is not neutral with respect to the availability of choice, since an individual who knows of new opportunities may well decide to do something previously unimagined, such as suing her employer or raising his children at home. This suggested policy of publicizing the new makes knowledge of opportunities as widespread as possible, but still leaves government neutral with respect to the ends of choice. In the name of furthering volition, government cannot force people to act against their wills or bring about a social order, a 'people's dictatorship' that the people do not want. It can only give men and women knowledge of possibilities that they might not otherwise acquire.

Some of that knowledge may derive from government-sponsored research on questions of gender policy. It makes sense for the state to take some part in filling the knowledge gaps concerning policy-relevant gender issues. This activity might not only lead to better informed choices by individuals; in so far as data affect value preferences, it could also bring us closer to the consensus that may be the warrant for future substantive gender policy.[34]

Tolerance
Finally, government should do what it can to promote tolerance of diversity, both by enforcing liberty-enhancing standards and through education, since the quest for self-definition 'will be distorted if it occurs under manipulative, coercive, or silencing conditions'.[35] Although one might wish for a world in which differentness was regarded as a good thing, differentness must, at the least, be accepted as necessary if personal liberty is to flourish. A liberty-enhancing policy can succeed only if there is suffused throughout the republic an acceptance of the choices that others make, even – perhaps especially – when these seem 'wrong' choices. Such toleration, as philosopher R. M. Hare notes, implies 'a readiness to respect other people's ideals as if they were his own'. Advocates of particular alternatives are, of course, free to persuade others of the rightness of their vision, so long as persuasion does not become coercion, fanaticism about the *'content* of the ideal'.[36] The ideal of tolerance does not require accepting intolerance.

Protecting against discrimination, intervening in instances of market failure, providing minimum economic support, disseminating information, promoting tolerance – these are the essential affirmative elements of a choice-enhancing policy. What government should *not* be doing deserves equal attention. Most significantly, the state should not be 'fostering . . . good lives' by imposing a particular conception of virtue on the minority.[37]

Sticking to means is a hard rule to follow. For one thing, the distinction between creating the circumstances of choice and imposing particular prefererences on individuals may fade in practice. For another, public officials are often tempted to believe that they know, if not best, at least better than the rest of us. Precisely because resources are scarce, law-makers would have them spent wisely. Since wrong choices also seem to inflict unnecessary pain, legislators, like the monkeys in Thurber's fable, are inclined to liberate the bears from freedom and the dangers of choice. In the face of such temptations, it is vital to maintain the proposition that individuals, not the state, best know their own interests, and that in almost all instances where gender-based preferences are involved, collective well-being requires empowering people to follow their own inclinations.

Because this stress on choice inveighs against governmentally set policy outcomes, it is hostile to quotas of any sort, for quotas withhold from individuals the right of self-determination that is critical for self-respect. Quota schemes impose plans on individuals, robbing them of the dignity that stems from defining themselves as persons. Moreover, quotas specify a necessarily arbitrary conception of the good life. In a world that celebrates volition, who can predict how many pilots, poets, houseparents, and presidents will be female, or how many teachers, tennis players, and TV repair-persons will be male? There is no answer to such questions, and attempts to supply one have had the unfortunate side effect of obliging men and women to embrace the unconventional. In this way, quotas embody a tyranny of the new.

The choice model also resists limiting options, whether by offering child support exclusively in the form of daycare, thus discouraging parents from raising their own children, or using veterans' preferences for government jobs, thus effectively restricting those jobs to men. It resists coercion, whether by the yahoos or the enlightened. Choice-promoting policy does not aim to demonstrate how well government can solve problems, but to extricate individuals from circumstances that hinder them in making their own life commitments. The care of children, the allocation of household responsibilities, opportunities for political involvement, the distribution of the work-force by sex – all are matters best left to individual preference, once non-discrimination, basic economic support, and the provision of useful information are assured. The aspiration is for 'a dialectic of choice, variability, and possibility grounded in a conviction which disallows absolute certitude and the destruction it brings in its wake'.[38]

IV

Will such a policy work? Were choice chimerical, we might be tempted to define the problem as one calling for a group-focused, not an individual-focused remedy, despite the high price that such an approach exacts.[39] Because group-based solutions disregard a person's individuality in favour of categories – sex, race, and the like – over which he or she lacks any control, only where reliance on volition has failed are such costs worth paying. The most persuasive argument for a racial preference policy is that native will not work, at least for now, and hence more directly and overtly redistributive measures are needed in the short term.[40]

With gender, though, the facts are otherwise. The evidence of the past decade gives cause to believe that, offered the opportunity, men and women will take more control over their own lives. New life-styles and forms of communion have emerged. The family, though remarkably durable, looks very different than it did even ten years ago. Nearly one household in seven is now headed by a woman.[41]

Women are postponing decisions to bear children well beyond what used to be customary. Even as proportionately fewer men are employed, over half of all women are working or looking for work – a change described by economist Eli Ginzberg as the 'single most outstanding phenomenon of our century'.[42]

Attitudes as well as behaviours have changed. Americans sense 'that, unlike their parents, they have the freedom to choose'. While in 1957, 80 per cent felt that an unmarried woman was sick, neurotic, or immoral, two decades later only 25 per cent held that opinion. More than half the populace believes that husbands as well as wives should care for small children; as recently as 1970, just one-third thought so.[43] There is now overwhelming support for women who opt to work, whether out of economic necessity or for personal satisfaction.[44]

A considerable number of men and women are designing their working and personal lives in new ways.[45] As the rules and customs that once limited the options available to men and women have been overturned or discarded, changes in behaviour have followed. The extent of this transformation in both private and public life seems remarkable. For an individual contemplating his or her life prospects, the stakes are high, the costs that accompany what proves to be a wrong decision sizable; none the less, many are deciding not to play it safe. An increasing proportion of men and women are embarked on lives that would be unimaginable to their elders.

Choice does lead to change, but what of the *pace* of change? Although we readily understand the impatience of the activists, particularly in the more benighted corners of the social universe, we do not share that impatience. Had we in mind some goal of tender parity, an ideal state in which men and women were indistinguishable in their wants and needs, we might well be displeased with the world in flux, but that is not how we comprehend social justice. Our benchmark is the reality of choice, which is generally apparent if far from perfected, and not any particular pattern of behaviour.

Available evidence suggests that many people can and will alter their own lives to suit their needs and desires. Although this evolution has something to do with such government initiatives as childcare benefits, anti-discrimination efforts in the workplace, and expanded opportunities for women in the sciences and the military, it is not primarily attributable to public policy. Shifts in feelings and beliefs came first. These gave force and meaning to the new rules, for without individuals willing to challenge the old norms, government permission to do so would have meant little. Such individuals have fuelled a movement, not merely a politically motivated interest group, which shows no signs of vanishing even with the failure of its most potent symbol, the Equal Rights Amendment.[46] There is every reason to believe that the movement has done its most valuable work already, that the forms of gender will continue to evolve, implacably, over time.

The idea of choice promises fairness in theory and appears to work in practice. But empowering individuals cannot settle all the problems of gender justice. Some fear the very idea of choosing, for it risks uncertainty and insecurity; hence the worry of some women that liberation may have set them adrift without the commitment of their one-time male protectors, or the concerns of some husbands that they have 'lost' their wives.[47] Betty Friedan reminds us that 'it is precisely the consciousness of "choice" and of "equal rights" and opportunities that is resisted by women, or men, whose identity rests on passivity toward authority, inequality and hierarchy, no matter the resentments and human potential suppressed'.[48] For others, circumstances make choice implausible: what are the options of the Appalachian coal-miner with a ninth grade education or the 20-year-old unskilled black woman with three children to raise? Moreover, discrimination – subtle and hard to detect, but present none the less – will persist despite government policies. And the ties of family may be felt as constraints, particularly in the black community, where women bear enormous responsibilities.

These facts of life are a reminder that a choice-enhancing policy cannot completely realize its aim. But what policy will? Reliance on fixed quotas, it is said, forcibly overcomes recalcitrance, yet quotas tend to acquire their own justification, becoming ends in themselves rather than means. Acting in another's best interest by taking that person out of the rut of circumstance has all the appeal of a rescue mission, but who can confidently assert that the person in question would act in the same way, if truly free to choose?

Public policy designed to spark choice will leave many unreached. And although the private policies that spring up around choice-promoting government action will affect far more individuals, some will remain untouched. It seems preferable to acknowledge the remarkable if incomplete success that such an approach promises than to insist that government favour only the new orthodoxy, or the old. In judging between approaches to governance, the relevant comparison is not between an imperfect choice-enhancing policy and an idealized alternative, but between the real cost of imposition on the one side and inattention on the other.

Notes and references

1 See, e.g., Hill, Anne Corinne, 'Protection of woman workers and the courts: a legal case history', *Feminist Studies*, **5**, 1979, p. 249; Samuelson, Joan, 'Employment rights of women in the toxic workplace', *California Law Review*, **65**, 1977, p. 1113.

2 See, e.g., Armanno, Benna F., 'The lesbian mother: her right to child custody', *Golden Gate Law Review*, **4**, 1973, p. 1; Hunter Nan, and Polikoff, Nancy, 'Custody rights of lesbian mothers: legal theory and litigation strategy', *Buffalo Law Review*, **25**, 1976, p. 691.

3 'The choice is not always between some selfish temptation and some obvious responsible course [but] among values that one can be responsible to.' Schelling, Thomas, 'Command and control', in McKie, James, (ed.), *Social Responsibility and the Business Predicament*, Washington, DC; Brookings, 1974, p. 79.

4 See, e.g., Yankelovich Danie, and Kaagan, Larry, 'Proposition 13 one year later: what it is and what it isn't', *Social Policy*, **10**, May/June 1979, p. 19; Kuttner, Robert, *Revolt of the Haves: Tax Rebellions and Hard Times*, New York; Simon & Schuster, 1980; Schelling, Thomas, 'Economic reasoning and the ethics of policy', *Public Interest*, **63**, spring 1981, p. 37.

5 See generally Eisenstein, Zillah, *The Radical Future of Liberal Feminism*, New York, Longman, 1981.

6 See Gelb, Joyce, and Lief Palley, Marian, *Women and Public Policies*, Princeton, Princeton University Press, 1982; Costain, Anne, 'Representing women: the transition from social movement to interest group', in Boneparth, Ellen, (ed.), *Women, Power and Policy*, New York, Pergamon, 1982, p. 19.

7 See Jaffe, Carol, 'Why the United States has no child-care policy', in Diamond, Irene

(ed.), *Families, Politics and Public Policy*, New York, Longman, 1983, p. 168; Steiner, Gilbert, *The Futility of Family Policy*, Washington, DC, Brookings, 1981.

8 See Simms, Margaret C., 'Women and housing: the impact of government housing policy', in Diamond, *Families*, p. 123; Diamond, Irene, 'Women and housing: the limitations of liberal reform', in Boneparth, *Women, Power and Policy*, p. 109.

9 See Evans, Sara, *Personal Politics*, New York, Viking, 1980, p. 203.

10 *Eagle Forum*, December 1980, quoted in Friedan, Betty, *The Second Stage*, New York, Summit, 1981, pp. 232–3.

11 Nixon, Richard, 'The President's message to the Senate returning S. 2007 without his approval', 9 December 1971, *Weekly Compilation of Presidential Documents VII*, 1971, p. 1634.

12 'Public opinion is catching up with the women's movement', *Washington Post National Weekly Edition*, 25 June 1984, p. 37.

13 See, e.g., Berger, Brigette, 'The helping hand strikes again', *Public Interest*, **65**, fall 1981, p. 3; Uink, Michael, 'Abortion and birth control in Canton, China', *Wall Street Journal*, 30 November 1981, p. 14.

14 Compare von Hayek, Friedrich August, *The Road to Serfdom*, Chicago, University of Chicago Press, 1944; Nozick, Robert, *Anarchy, State, and Utopia*, New York, Basic Books, 1974.

15 See Yudof, Mark G., 'Plato's ideal and the perversity of politics', *Michigan Law Review*, **81**, 1983, p. 730.

16 Hamilton, Alexander, *Federalist Papers*, no. 78.

17 See, e.g., Wechsler, Herbert, *Principles, Politics, and Fundamental Law*, Cambridge, Harvard University Press, 1961. Compare Bickel, Alexander, *The Supreme Court and the Idea of Progress*, New York, Harper & Row, 1970; Cox, Archibald, *The Role of the Supreme Court in American Government*, London, Oxford University Press, 1976; Hart Ely, John, *Democracy and Distrust: A Theory of Judicial Review*, Cambridge, Harvard University Press, 1980.

18 See, e.g., Bobbitt, Philip C., *Constitutional Fate*, New York, Oxford University Press, 1982; Carter, Lief H., *Reason in Law*, Boston, Little, Brown, 1979; Levi, Edward, *An Introduction to Legal Reasoning*, Chicago, University of Chicago Press, 1949. But see Unger, Roberto, 'The critical legal Studies Movement', *Harvard Law Review*, **96**, 1983, p. 561.

19 See generally Simon, Herbert A., *Models of Man: Social and Rational*, New York, Wiley, 1957.

20 Kirp, David, 'Professionalization as a policy choice: British special education in comparative perspective', *World Politics*, **34**, 1982, p. 137.

21 See, e.g., Szasz, Thomas, *Sex by Prescription*, Garden City, New York, Doubleday, 1981; Ehrenreich, Barbara, and English, Deirdre, *For Her Own Good*, Garden City, New York, Doubleday-Anchor, 1978.

22 Popper, Karl, *The Poverty of Historicism*, Boston, Beacon Press, 1957, p. 67.

23 See Oakeshott, Michael, *Rationalism in Politics*, New York, Basic Books, 1962.

24 Popper, *Poverty of Historicism*, p. 74.

25 Braybrooke, David, and Lindblom, Charles E., *A Strategy of Decision*, New York, Free Press, 1963; Wildavsky, Aaron, *Speaking Truth to Power*, Boston, Little, Brown, 1979.

26 Lindblom, Charles E., *The Policy-Making Process*, Englewood Cliffs, New Jersey, Prentice-Hall, 1980, p. 36. See also Lindblom, Charles E., 'The politics of "muddling through" ', *Public Administration Review*, **19**, 1959, p. 79.

27 Brest, Paul, 'The conscientious legislator's guide to constitutional interpretation', *Stanford Law Review*, **27**, 1975, p. 585.

28 See, e.g., Akerlof, George, 'The market for "lemons": quality, uncertainty, and the

market mechanism', *Quarterly Journal of Economics*, **84**, 1970, p. 488. Compare Becker, Gary, *The Economics of Discrimination*, Chicago, University of Chicago Press, 1957.

29 Gutmann, Amy, *Liberal Equality*, Cambridge, Cambridge University Press, 1980, p. 11.

30 See, e.g., Lindblom, Charles, *Politics and Markets*, New York, Basic Books, 1977.

31 Mill, John Stuart, *On Liberty*, 1859: reprint, Indianapolis, Hackett, 1978.

32 Berlin, Isaiah, *Four Essays On Liberty*, Oxford, Oxford University Press, 1969, p. 125.

33 See Granovetter, Mark S., *Getting A Job: A Study of Contacts and Careers*, Cambridge, Harvard University Press, 1974.

34 Research may also lead to greater disagreement by heightening uncertainty. See Lindblom, Charles, and Cohen, David, *Usable Knowledge*, New Haven, Yale University Press, 1979.

35 Elstain, Jean Bethke, *Public Man, Private Woman*, Princeton, Princeton University Press, 1981, p. 311.

36 Hare, R. M., *Freedom and Reason*, New York, Oxford University Press, 1965, p. 177. The coercive tenor of the abortion debate is instructively examined in this light.

37 Dworkin, Ronald, 'Liberalism', in Hampshire, Stuart (ed.), *Public and Private Morality*, Cambridge, Cambridge University Press, 1978, pp. 113, 117. See also Selznick, Philip, *Law, Society, and Industrial Justice*, New York, Russell Sage, 1964.

38 Elshtain, *Public Man, Private Woman*, p. 353.

39 See Fiss, Owen, 'Groups and the equal protection clause', *Philosophy and Public Affairs*, **2**, 1976, p. 107.

40 See, e.g., Fullinwider, Robert, *The Reverse Discrimination Controversy*, Totowa, New Jersey, Roman and Littlefield, 1980. Compare Glazer, Nathan, *Affirmative Discrimination*, New York, Basic Books, 1975, who would treat evidence that preferential treatment actually reduced the black-white gap as reason to abandon principled opposition to such a policy.

41 US Bureau of the Census, *Statistical Abstract of the United States: 1982–83*, Washington, DC, Government Printing Office, 1982, table 73.

42 Quoted in Ginsburg, Ruth Bader, 'Sexual equality under the Fourteenth and Equal Rights Amendments', *Washington University Law Quarterly*, 1979, pp. 161, 168.

43 Yankelovich, Daniel, *New Rules*, New York, Random House, 1981, pp. 58, 93, 94.

44 Degler, Carl, *At Odds*, New York, Oxford University Press, 1980, pp. 418–35.

45 On the changes in men's lives, see Friedan, *The Second Stage*, pp. 125–62.

46 Carden, Maren, *The New Feminist Movement*, New York, Russell Sage, 1974.

47 See FitzGerald, Frances Ford, 'The triumphs of the new right', *New York Review of Books*, **28**, 19 November 1981, p. 19.

48 Friedan, *The Second Stage*, p. 315.

Index

The index is in two parts. Part 1 is an index of subjects and Part 2 is an index of names. Authors of chapters in this volume are not indexed except where another of their publications is referred to.

Part 1   Subject index

Part 2   Name Index